FRIARS' GUIDE
To
NEW ZEALAND
ACCOMMODATION
FOR THE
DISCERNING TRAVELLER
2006

11TH EDITION

DISCLAIMER: The contents of this Guide were believed to be correct at the time of printing.

Prices are subject to change and should be confirmed at time of booking.

All wording in these editorials is based on information provided by the hosts, who approved proofs before publication.

However, the publishers and authors can accept no responsibility for errors, or omissions, or changes to details herein. Nor are they responsible for any guest dissatisfaction with any accommodation included in this Guide.

We would like to thank those who helped us with all the work on this 11th edition, and to all those relatives, friends and hosts who supported us by kindly offering hospitality on our busy itinerary around New Zealand.

ISBN 1-86971-018-5

© 2006 – original text, Jillian Friar, and original photographs, Denis Friar, FRIARS
The moral rights of the authors have been asserted
© 2006 – concept, Jillian & Denis Friar and Hachette Livre NZ Ltd
© 2006 – design and formatting, Hachette Livre NZ Ltd

A Hodder Moa book
Published in 2006 by Hachette Livre NZ Limited
4 Whetu Place, Mairangi Bay, Auckland, New Zealand

Typeset by FRIARS, Wanganui, New Zealand
Colour separations by Microdot, Auckland, New Zealand
Printed by Everbest Printing Co Ltd, China

FRIARS' GUIDE

TO

—— NEW ZEALAND ——

ACCOMMODATION

FOR THE

DISCERNING TRAVELLER

◆ LODGES ◆ FARMS ◆ PRIVATE HOMES ◆ BOUTIQUE HOTELS ◆

◆ B&BS ◆ SELF-CONTAINED COTTAGES ◆ APARTMENTS ◆ INNS ◆

—— 2006 ——

11ᵀᴴ EDITION

Text and typesetting by
Jillian Friar

Photography by
Denis Friar

Hodder Moa

This cast bronze plaque graces many accommodation venues recommended by Friars' Guide

EVALUATION

We appreciate comments from guests who stay at the accommodation included in this 11th edition of *Friars' Guide*.

If you would like us to consider any other accommodation for our next annual edition of *Friars' Guide*, please forward the details to us. We begin our next evaluative and photographic trip in spring 2005.

Please send any feedback and suggestions, positive or critical, on any aspect of the accommodation, to the new owners:

John and Lois Allen
P O Box 125 135
St Heliers
Auckland 1130
NEW ZEALAND

Phone +6-4-9-974 2146
Fax +6-4-9-974 2321
Email feedback@friars.co.nz
Website friars.co.nz

PERSONAL INTRODUCTION

WELCOME to our 11th edition of *Friars' Guide*. This book marks the end of an era and the beginning of another. After over a decade of successfully producing this annual publication, Jillian and Denis Friar are moving on to other projects. They are leaving *Friars' Guide* in the capable hands of Lois and John Allen. The Allens will uphold the high standards of the publication and will take it to even greater heights. They will travel throughout the length and breadth of New Zealand to meet as many of the hosts as possible, and to inspect, evaluate and select superior and special venues for the next edition. The Friars are personally training the Allens in every aspect of their work, so that they will be able to continue the process of recommending suitable accommodation for the discerning traveller to New Zealand. They will continue declining places that are not up to the standard set in the book, while maintaining the features for which *Friars' Guide* is renowned – reliability, accuracy, attention to detail and comprehensiveness.

AFTER A DECADE of *Friars' Guides*, 25 percent of the original 100 properties are still featured in the book, more than half of them still run by the original owners, who have been given a commemorative hand-made glass piece. The current edition showcases a total of over 450 venues that have been found to meet the selection criteria and provide accommodation with a level of personal service and quality to put them in a class of their own.

Diverse features make each place unique. Sometimes it is the distinctive architecture, interior design, or quality furnishings, from historical to contemporary, that is special. Fine cuisine may be the outstanding point of difference. Some properties are located in magnificent settings commanding sweeping views over pristine lakes or lush green countryside, to snow-capped mountain ranges beyond. But it is the intangible qualities that make the guest's stay at each place so memorable. It is the personal touches, little surprises and unexpected extras that contribute to the indefinable ambience that sets the places in this directory apart.

THE FRIARS personally endorse the top-class accommodation in this edition. Exterior and interior shots by professional photographer Denis Friar highlight the special features of each establishment. The accompanying editorials have been written by Jillian Friar to provide all the information the traveller needs to know. Jillian uses a descriptive, objective and informative style of writing to detail the characteristics of each property clearly, without overstatement, exaggeration, florid prose or mood writing. The Allens will photograph and write *Friars' Guide* in the same style in order to produce a book of equal quality, as well as the new *Friars' Guide* website.

A WIDE DIVERSTIY of accommodation is featured in this edition of *Friars' Guide*, as well as three exclusive tours, by land, sea or air. We also include a specialist real estate broker who buys and sells lodges. Each venue is individual, not conforming to any prescribed pattern. Tariffs range from over $NZ100 to more than $NZ1,000 per couple per night. Guestrooms range from one-bedroom cottages to multi-bedroom boutique hotels. Luxury lodges, bed and breakfast inns, self-contained apartments, homestays, farmstays, resorts, health spas and retreats also feature. Each place specifies whether breakfast, lunch or dinner are offered and if they are included in the tariff or optional. See pages 6 and 7 for a detailed explanation of how to use this Guide.

FRIARS' GUIDE is published annually, to keep the information up-to-date and reliable. Guests who stay at any of the accommodation included in this guide are invited to send feedback to the new owners of the business (*see details on page 4*). New hosts can apply to be included in the next edition by contacting the Allens. (As with most accommodation guides, there is a charge for appearing in this full-colour book which assists in offsetting the retail price.) Any property is eligible for inspection and evaluation if it incorporates private bathroom facilities for guests and is of sufficient standard to rate in the class of accommodation included in this book.

STRETCHING from the Far North down to Stewart Island, there are venues within this 11th edition to satisfy every discerning traveller's itinerary. Over the past decade *Friars' Guide* has gained a reputation with travel professionals and independent travellers of providing access to the best of accommodation in New Zealand. Many loyal users refer to it as their "bible". The current edition upholds this high accolade. We can assure our hosts and readers alike that the Allens will continue this tradition. And we would like to take this opportunity to thank all those who have helped us along the way – hosts, guests, publishers, staff, family and friends. We have learnt a lot and it has been a pleasure meeting or working with you all.

Jillian and Denis Friar

HOW TO USE THIS GUIDE

The editorials on each page aim to cover all the relevant details the discerning traveller needs to know. Because conventions vary and overseas terminology is not always consistent with that used in New Zealand, we have compiled and updated the following explanations for clarity.

- MAP NUMBERS
  These correspond to the numbers on the large North and South Island maps inside the front and back covers of the book, respectively. These maps show the geographical relation of each location, to help travellers plan their itineraries.

- PHONE NUMBERS
  The international code for NZ is 64, then drop the 0. Eg 64-9- for Auckland, 64-3- for the South Island. Freephones and freefaxes are for reservations within New Zealand only.

- INTERNET
  Most pages in this book are on the website
  http://friars.co.nz
  Some include Virtual Tours (indicated by our VT symbol). The accommodation properties often have additional websites, usually linked from the Friars' site. Bookings can be made via the Internet enquiry form to all hosts.

- TARIFFS
  Tariffs are calculated in New Zealand dollars and cents. All tariffs include GST (Goods & Services Tax of 12.5%). Each tariff indicates a nightly rate, unless otherwise stated.
  Double indicates the tariff for two people sharing one double or one twin room.
  Single indicates the tariff for one person occupying a room.
  Room rate indicates the tariff for one room, single or double.
  A **deposit** is often required on booking.
  Cancellation fees usually apply, although these vary.
  All tariffs are subject to change – confirm with your hosts. Tariffs are correct at time of printing in 2005. Tariffs include breakfast or provisions unless otherwise stated.
  Sometimes dinner is offered which is either included within the tariff, or is charged for separately as indicated.

- BOOKING
  All accommodation must be booked in advance unless otherwise stated. Cancellation policies usually apply. These vary from place to place, so please check at time of booking. Most hosts take credit cards for deposits, which also vary. These are only refundable if the booking is cancelled within the specified time.
  If hosts also offer lunch or dinner, they usually need prior notice.
  Single, private, exclusive, or one-party bookings mean that only one group of people is booked at a time. If there is a shared bathroom, this means it is shared only within that same party.

- BEDROOMS AND BATHROOMS
  The following abbreviations are used:
  bdrm = bedroom
  enst = ensuite bathroom
  prbth = private bathroom
  shbth = guest-share bathroom
  pdrm = powder room (extra guest toilet near the dining room)

  Ensuite: An ensuite means a bathroom directly adjoining a bedroom. An ensuite can include just a shower and toilet, or else it can be a spacious bathroom incorporating a bath or even spa bath. "Ensuite" does not indicate size, only position.

  Private bathroom: A private bathroom, including a shower and toilet and maybe a bath, is separated from the bedroom, perhaps across the hallway, but is dedicated for that bedroom's sole use. If single-party bookings are indicated, then the bathroom is private to that one party. Bathrobes are usually supplied for guests' use.

  Guest-share bathroom: This bathroom is usually shared between two guest bedrooms, occasionally more, within the same party. It is rarely shared with the hosts. If only one bedroom is occupied, it becomes that room's private bathroom. It contains shower, toilet and maybe a bath.

  Powder room: This means an extra separate toilet serving the general living areas, dining room/restaurant or lounge.

  King/twin: This is either a king zipper bed or two singles that can be configured as one king-size or two single beds.

  Super-king: This bed is 15cm longer than king-size.

  Californian-king: This is 15cm wider than super-king.

  Queen: This is 15cm narrower than a king-size bed. A **queen/twin** means either that the bed can be configured as two singles, or that an extra bed is available, as a triple.

  Double: This means one double bed. An additional single bed may be available, sometimes indicated as **double/twin**. This can also be referred to as a triple.

  Twin: This means two separate beds. Often both are single beds, and occasionally one or both twin beds may be double beds. If the twin room can sleep three guests, it is sometimes known as triple.

  King-single: This means a single bed, an extra 15cm long.

  Suite: This means a bedroom and an ensuite bathroom, as well as an additional room, usually a separate lounge that belongs exclusively to that guest's bedroom.

- METRICS
  Measurements in this book are calculated in metrics. Eg:
  1 foot = 30cm (centimetres)
  3.28 feet = 1m (metre)
  6 miles = 10km (kilometres)
  5 acres = 2ha (hectares)

- MEALS
  Breakfast or a breakfast basket or provisions is included in the tariff unless a separate charge is stated.
  A **continental** breakfast can be buffet style or quite elaborate, but excludes cooked dishes.
  A **cooked** breakfast may also be offered, either included in the tariff or charged in addition to a continental breakfast, as indicated.

  Occasionally tariffs include dinner or **all** meals as stated.

  Sometimes **lunch** is available, by prior request, at an extra charge. This may be either a light luncheon, a full lunch with wine, or picnic hampers may be offered.

  Self-catering means that there is a fully equipped kitchen where guests can make their own meals. If full cooking facilities are not provided, it is referred to as a kitchenette. Tea, coffee and maybe provisions or a pantry are supplied.

  Dinner may be available, usually by prior arrangement. A courtesy car may be provided for nearby restaurants.

  Booking is usually necessary for lunch or dinner, unless included in tariff. Hosts need at least a few hours' notice, unless there is an in-house restaurant. Most hosts cater for **vegetarian** or other dietary requirements if notified in time.

  Lunch and dinner **charges** are per person.

  Drinks are complimentary if indicated, or charged separately.

  À la carte means there is a menu choice.

  Table d'hôte indicates a fixed menu.

  BYO means you can Bring Your Own alcohol.

  Licensed means all the alcohol is sold on the premises. Even without a licence, alcohol or wine with meals can be charged for as long as the number of guests does not exceed 11.

- TOURS
  Exclusive tours can be booked in specific regions or throughout New Zealand. Land, sea and air tours are all available – see pages 12, 13 and 252–255.

- ROAD TRAVEL

  The directions given beneath each map are intended to guide self-driving guests to their destinations. Vehicles drive on the left-hand side of the roads in New Zealand. Overseas travellers should keep this in mind when starting off after a roadside rest stop, as research has shown that this is the time when many accidents involving tourists happen. The left-hand road rule means that, when turning left, drivers must give way to right-turning traffic. When booking for the winter months, it pays to check road conditions with South Island hosts, in case of icy conditions or snow.
  Off-street or on-site parking is usually indicated, and sometimes garaging is available.

- PETS
  Pets are not welcome, unless specified, by prior arrangement.

- AIR TRAVEL
  A shuttle service delivers passengers to destinations in most major cities. Some hosts operate a courtesy passenger transfer service. Sometimes a helipad is available for helicopters. Air tours can be arranged – see Tours.

- BUSH WALKS
  This activity indicates formed walkways through native New Zealand forest.

- Weather Forecasts
  Because New Zealand's weather can be unpredictable, it is advisable to listen to a weather forecast before travelling. For the most up-to-date weather information, ring Metphone for the location you will be visiting. There is a charge for these calls:
  0900 99 909 for Northland and Auckland regions
  0900 99 907 for Waikato and Bay of Plenty regions
  0900 99 906 for Gisborne, Hawke's Bay, Taranaki, Wanganui, Manawatu and Wairarapa regions
  0900 99 904 for Kapiti Coast and Wellington region
  0900 99 903 for the South Island

- RADIO FREQUENCIES
  The traveller may wish to tune into the national public non-commercial network. These are the AM and FM National programme (current affairs and light entertainment) and FM Concert programme (mainly classical music, with jazz reviews and composer profiles).

- LOCATION GUIDE
  On page 10 is a location guide, showing the traveller the salient features of each region throughout New Zealand. The accommodation properties in each region are indicated by the relevant page numbers.

- EXPLODED PAGE
  On page 8 there is a sample page from this book, with the layout and all the logos, symbols, icons and tabs explained. Each page is designed in a standardised way for ease of reference. The individual logos used are further identified on page 9.

- INDEXES
  At the end of the book, on pages 482–484, is the Accommodation Index. This provides an alphabetical listing of each property featured in this book, including a yacht. Three exclusive tour operators are listed under **Tours**. Then on pages 485–488 is the Hosts Index. This enables the traveller to locate the accommodation by looking up the host's name, again alphabetically listed.

- EVALUATION
  Each place showcased in this book is personally evaluated and recommended by Denis and Jillian Friar who have stayed at most of them. The success of this book depends on its reliability and accuracy. They therefore welcome evaluative comments from guests who stay at the accommodation included in this book. To send your feedback to the authors, please refer to the address, phone, fax and email details on page 4. They always follow up all feedback, both complimentary and critical, although they are not responsible for any guest dissatisfaction.

SAMPLE PAGE KEY

hosts' names, usually also the owners

accommodation name

postal address, if different from physical address

physical/geographical address

location name indicates local area

logos indicate smoking restrictions, children accepted, wheelchair access, or chef

phone, freephone, mobile phone, fax, email and website address

local map, with accommodation at red dot

numeral corresponds to numerals on the maps inside the covers of book

regional map, red dot shows location in either North or South Island

directions to accommodation

green tab indicates B&B option is available

burgundy tab indicates dinner is available

credit cards accepted

blue tab indicates self-catering is available

total number of bedrooms available

total number of ensuites

logos for virtual tour on web, affiliations, Historic Places Trust category, etc

number of private bathrooms

tariff in New Zealand dollars includes 12.5% tax

meals available for extra charge

meals included in tariff

description of accommodation

in-house facilities offered

activities on site and nearby

host supplied photo credit

copyright and Friars' credit

page number

Sample Page

WAIHI

Woodland Park Lodge

Hosts Barbara and Ken Hogg

418B Woodland Road, R D 2, Waihi
Phone 0-7-863 8168   *Email* barbara@woodlandpark.co.nz
Fax 0-7-863 8596   *Website* www.woodlandpark.co.nz

DIRECTIONS: From Waihi or Tauranga, take SH 2 & turn south into Woodlands Rd. Travel 4km & turn right into 418B driveway. Travel 1km & take left-hand fork. Travel uphill & take middle fork to Lodge.

4 bdrm	2 enst	2 prbth

Lodge room rate $425–$475
Punga House rate $475–$795

Includes breakfast
Minimum 2-night stay

Lunch & dinner extra
Includes breakfast or provisions

The philosophy of Woodland Park Lodge is to provide for guests' every need, from fine cuisine to health treatments in a relaxing environment. Set in a restful rural location, with views down the valley to the ocean beyond, Woodland Park is a 112-hectare farm with extensive native bush walks designed for rejuvenation. Guest are offered hosted accommodation in the Lodge, or self-contained privacy in the separate Punga House, both with quality furnishings and attention to detail. Breakfast provisions can be supplied in the Punga House if preferred, or breakfast is served in the dining room upstairs in the Lodge, with choices from a comprehensive breakfast menu the evening before. Lunch, gourmet picnic hampers and dinner can also be requested.

FACILITIES

- Lodge: 2 super-king bedrooms, 1 with ensuite & spa bath, 1 with private bathroom
- Punga House: 1 super-king bedroom with double bath & double shower in ensuite; & 1 queen bedroom with bathroom; self-catering kitchen; lounge; single-party bookings only
- hair dryer, bathrobes, toiletries, demist mirror & heated towel rails & floors in all 4 bathrooms

- full breakfast or provisions
- lunch, $20–$40 pp; dinner, $80–$95 pp; wine extra
- complimentary apéritifs; special diets catered for
- Lodge guest lounge & Punga lounge both with Sky TV, DVD, videos, music, games, books, artwork, bar & nibbles
- phone jacks; helipad

ACTIVITIES AVAILABLE

- in-house aromatherapy massage, extra
- personalised health & rejuvenation retreats
- gourmet picnicking; birdlife
- garden & bush walks on site
- seasonal farm activities on site
- beaches; watersports, 15 mins
- golf course adjacent
- Karangahake walkway, 20 mins

- guided beach & bush walks
- Coromandel Peninsula & Bay of Plenty nearby
- heritage sites & steam train
- gardens open to visit
- open-cast working goldmine; historic Waihi, 10 min drive
- wineries, collectables, antiques, art & craft trails
- murals at Katikati, 25 mins

118

© Friars' Guide to New Zealand Accommodation for the Discerning Traveller

---

KEY TO LOGOS, SYMBOLS AND TABS

- **AFFILIATION LOGOS**

  Accommodation establishments are members of the following affiliations wherever the relevant logos are displayed:

   Heritage & Character Inns of New Zealand

   @ Home

   Small Luxury Hotels of the World

   New Zealand Lodge Association

   Select Hotels & Resorts International

   The Charming Hotels

   New Zealand Historic Places Trust (category 1 or 2)

   NZ Beef & Lamb Hallmark of Excellence

   New Zealand Tourism Awards winner/finalist (only awards from 2003 awards displayed)

   Qualmark 5-star plus – defined by Qualmark as a new "Exclusive" category. Only six "Exclusive" ratings have been given to those applying to be assessed so far

   Qualmark 5-star – defined by Qualmark as "Exceptional. Among the best available in New Zealand"

   Qualmark 4-star plus and Qualmark 4-star – defined by Qualmark as "Excellent. Consistently achieves high quality levels with a wide range of facilities and services"

   Qualmark 3-star plus – defined by Qualmark as "Very good. Provides a range of facilities and services and achieves good to very good quality standards"

   Qualmark without any stars indicates that the establishment has applied for Qualmark rating and is awaiting grading

  Qualmark category "guest & hosted" corresponds to the *Friars' Guide* green or burgundy tabs

  Qualmark category "self-contained & serviced" corresponds to the *Friars' Guide* blue tab

  NOTE: All Qualmark gradings are assessed and rated by Qualmark, **not** Friars. *Friars' Guide* has its own criteria for accepting or declining applicants.

- **COLOURED TABS**

  The coloured tabs at the side of each page indicate categories of accommodation. **Green** means that a full bed and breakfast option is offered – continental and/or cooked breakfast is served; if breakfast provisions are supplied for self-catering a green tab is **not** used. **Burgundy** means dinner is offered – either within the tariff, or at an extra charge. **Blue** means that a full kitchen is provided for self-catering. A kitchenette does **not** qualify for a blue tab. Provisions are supplied if indicated.

  > Green tab – indicates B&B option available

  > Burgundy tab – indicates dinner available

  > Blue tab – indicates self-catering available

- **SYMBOLS**

  The following apply wherever the symbol is used:

   this means that smoking restrictions are to be observed – these vary, but often limit smoking to outdoors. Some establishments do not permit smoking at all. Please enquire. If there is no smoking restriction symbol, then smoking is permitted.

   this means there is wheelchair access to at least one bedroom, and there are wheelchair facilities available in at least one ensuite or private bathroom.

   this indicates child-friendly accommodation and it means children are accepted by arrangement. Children are the responsibility of their parents or guardians unless otherwise arranged with the hosts. Reduced tariffs may apply. Age restrictions often apply. Some places are unsuitable for children and for pets.

   this means that there is a professionally qualified chef. Dinner may be offered, ranging from home cooking to gourmet cuisine, and vegetarians may be catered for. Meals are usually available only by prior arrangement.

   this means there is a Virtual Tour available on the host's website, usually on http://friars.co.nz

- **CREDIT CARDS**

  The following are accepted wherever displayed:

   Visa

   Mastercard

   Amex (American Express)

   JCB (Japanese)

   Diners

   Eftpos

- **FRIARS' PLAQUE**

  The solid cast bronze plaque depicted on page 4 graces many of the establishments in this book. It reassures guests that the accommodation has been recommended by Friars, and is relinquished if hosts are no longer in the *Friars' Guide*.

NEW ZEALAND LOCATION GUIDE

NORTH ISLAND FEATURES

Far North: subtropical beaches, Cape Reinga, Ninety Mile Beach, sparsely populated

Bay of Islands: "winterless north" climate, big-game fishing, watersports, historic sites, Waitangi Treaty House, walking tracks

Northland: warm climate, kauri forests & museums, watersports, northernmost city Whangarei, Poor Knights Islands Marine Reserve, Whangarei Harbour Basin

Auckland: largest city in NZ, "City of Sails", beaches, watersports, Devonport ferry, 48 dormant volcanoes, Kelly Tarlton's Antarctic Encounter & Underwater World, MOTAT Technological Museum, War Memorial Museum, Maritime Museum, zoo, art galleries, parks & reserves, walking tracks, public & private gardens to visit, Muriwai mainland gannet colony, offshore islands

Coromandel: historic gold trails, golden beaches, Hot Water Beach, surfing, fishing, wading and shorebirds, native forest, kauri groves, tramping, crafts, sparsely populated

Bay of Plenty: sunny east coast, orchards, Rotorua with boiling mud pools, geysers & steaming lakes, Maori culture, redwood forest, crafts, surf beaches, big-game fishing, Mayor Island, active White Island volcano

Waikato: longest NZ river, biggest inland city Hamilton, crafts, river sports, mineral pools, rich dairy farmland, horse studs, gardens

King Country: Waitomo Caves, glow-worms, gardens, sheep farming

Central Plateau: Taupo – NZ's biggest lake, trout fishing, watersports, Mt Ruapehu, skiing, Tongariro National Park, walks

Gisborne: sunny, "First City of the Sun", surf beaches, isolated, Lake Waikaremoana, Te Urewera National Park, wineries

Hawke's Bay: sunshine, wineries, Wine Festival (Feb), Blossom Festival (Sept), Art Deco Napier, Cape Kidnappers gannet colony, beaches, fishing, National Aquarium

Taranaki: mountain, skiing, climbing, tramping, gardens, Rhododendron Festival (late Oct), Egmont National Park, New Plymouth city, cheese-making

Rangitikei & Wanganui: river sports, gardens to visit, historic homes, tramping

Manawatu: Palmerston North inland city, farming, agricultural university, wind farms

Wairarapa: wineries, gardens, historic museums, Cape Palliser seal colony, historic Maori sites, farming, wind farms

Kapiti Coast: Kapiti Island wildlife sanctuary, gardens to visit, car museum

CONTENTS

Wellington: capital city, parliament, museum, theatre, arts, political centre, history, Cook Strait ferries, only NZ cable car, Botanic & Native Gardens

SOUTH ISLAND FEATURES

Marlborough: "Gourmet Province", interisland ferries, temperate climate, wineries, Marlborough Sounds, fishing, whale, seal & dolphin watching, boating, tramping, skiing, gardens, history

Nelson: sunny climate, arts & crafts, pottery, limestone caves, river, lakes, golden beaches, city, early colonial buildings, wineries, native forest, walks, deer hunting, watersports, trout/salmon fishing, shellfish, horse trekking, gold trails, gardens, three National Parks, northernmost tip of Island

Westland: gold trails, lakes, trout fishing, rainforest, walks, glaciers, rivers, greenstone, underground coalmine, heron sanctuary

North Canterbury: Southern Alps, glacier lakes, trout fishing, skiing, climbing, hot springs, hunting, river sports, gardens to visit, scenic flights, tramping, plains, farming

Christchurch: largest South Island city, English stone buildings, history, parks & gardens, cycling, arts, River Avon, Antarctic Centre, beaches, Lyttelton Harbour

Banks Peninsula: old French town of Akaroa, bays, seabirds, salmon, shellfish, boating, gardens

Mid & South Canterbury: highest NZ mountain Mt Cook/Aoraki, Southern Alps, glacier lakes, salmon & trout fishing, skiing, climbing, hunting, river sports, gardens to visit, scenic flights, tramping, plains, farming

North Otago: Oamaru historic limestone buildings, quarry, blue penguins, heritage trail

Dunedin: stone buildings, gardens, history, arts, albatross colony, yellow-eyed penguins, Carisbrook sports park

Central Otago: glacial lakes, Clutha River – NZ's largest, gold trails, gold panning, river sports, skiing, climbing, bobsledding, walks, gardens to visit, April Arrowtown Autumn Festival, museums, historic steamer, fishing, golf, bungy jumping, jet boating, stonefruit orchards

Fiordland: glacial lakes, fiords, walking tracks, rainforest, National Park, Doubtful Sounds, Milford Track, fishing, isolation

Southland: trout fishing, hunting, sheep farming, alpine lakes, rainforests, Catlins, southernmost city – Invercargill, gardens

Stewart Island: rainforest, native birds, brown kiwi, penguins, walks, boat charters

CONTENTS

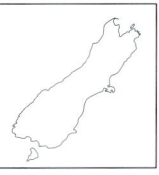

CHRISTOPHER BROWN & ASSOCIATES LTD, MREINZ
LODGES – HOTELS – BUSINESS BROKERS

Broker Alison Marks, AREINZ

Level 9, 17 Albert Street, Auckland Central
Postal P O Box 106 019, Downtown, Auckland
Phone 0-9-377 7741   *Mobile* 021 974 203   *Fax* 0-9-377 7742
Email alison@businessbrokers.co.nz   *Website* www.businessbrokers.co.nz

Selling a Lodge is a complex procedure that requires a thorough knowledge of the New Zealand lodge and tourism industries, of business sales and of the relevant real estate market. It is a specialist field that Alison has made her own. By being a specialist broker in the buying and selling of lodges and new development projects throughout New Zealand, Alison is familiar with the requirements of the lodge market. As a business broker with 23 years' experience in all aspects of real estate sales and leasing, she is mindful of the level of confidentiality expected by both vendors and purchasers. Advertising widely in the overseas market and consistently in the domestic market, Alison has a significant database of qualified buyers, with an ever-increasing number of transactions completed outside the public gaze. Alison travels extensively throughout New Zealand, wherever possible meeting with the current owners of lodges and introducing well-qualified buyers. Acknowledged as a professional in her field, Alison places considerable value on the relationships built with both vendors and purchasers. Alison has an excellent support team assisting her with her busy workload. She is only a phone call away.

ALISON'S SPECIALITIES:

- has 23 years' experience in the selling of commercial investments in NZ
- has a high level of industry knowledge & strong industry networking skills

- understands the needs of vendors & purchasers
- is backed by a support team within the company
- constantly travels throughout NZ

- has a large database of purchasers for the industry
- undertakes to maintain confidentiality
- www.friars.co.nz

- has access to overseas purchasers through media representation worldwide
- is a skilled negotiator
- is only a phone call away

© Friars' Guide to New Zealand Accommodation for the Discerning Traveller

NEW ZEALAND
DREAM PLACES

Host Tony Lilleby

P O Box 1504, Nelson
Phone 0-3-548 1081   *Email* enquiries@dreamplacesnewzealand.com
Fax 0-3-548 1691   *Website* www.dreamplacesnewzealand.com

DIRECTIONS: Guests are collected & dropped off at selected airports & towns by arrangement. Driver is Nelson-based & charges will reflect distances incurred.

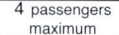

4 passengers maximum

Motorhome rate $415–$655 for 2 persons	Extra persons, $125 each	*Includes all meals*
Motorhome rate $370–$550 for 2 persons	Extra persons, $75 each	*Self-catering*

Dream Places

Dream Places features flexible guided travel in a motorhome that provides customised touring for guests according to their interests. The 10.5-metre motorhome is fully self-contained, with spacious interiors for comfortable accommodation in back country locations. Guests can either cater for themselves, or have all meals provided. Menus are arranged with guests prior to travel. Dream Places offers a range of tours, personalised to suit individual interests, or guests may choose to travel with no pre-arranged or set timetable at all. Tony, your host, driver and guide, has a background of working in New Zealand's National Parks and back country, and uses a network of special and secluded places for overnight stops.

FACILITIES

- single-party bookings only in 10.5m motorhome
- 1 king bedroom & vanity
- lounge/dining area with extra fold-down king/twin bed
- driver sleeps in cab or tent
- large, high-pressure hot shower
- separate full-size flush toilet
- quality linen & towels
- air-conditioning & heating

- meals catered, optional; local food & menus arranged with guests
- full kitchen with fridge/ freezer & gas cooker
- BBQ & outdoor furniture
- sound system
- phone, computer & email
- collection & drop-off at selected airports & cities of guests' choice, extra

ACTIVITIES AVAILABLE

Guided or individual:
- 3 quality serviced road & mountain bikes, extra
- kayaks, paddles & life jackets, extra
- personalised itineraries
- walking; hiking
- road cycling; mountain biking
- sea & lake kayaking
- photography & film making

- *The Lord of the Rings* tours
- fly fishing
- watersports
- rural golf
- national parks
- back country travel
- garden tours
- horse trekking
- customised sightseeing & tours throughout NZ

Dream Places

Dream Places

New Zealand
Platinum Tours

Operator Dolphin Travel

Postal P O Box 15 358, Tauranga
Phone 0-7-578 8950   *Email* luxury@platinumtours.co.nz
Fax 0-7-578 3299   *Website* www.platinumtours.co.nz

North Island tour $5,625 per person in double room
South Island tour $5,690 per person in double room

Includes accommodation & meals
Includes accommodation & meals

Platinum Tours

Platinum Tours

Platinum Tours design fully tailor-made itineraries for travelling the length and breadth of New Zealand, covering any duration of time required. Considering guests' special interests and requests, all arrangements are carefully planned and arranged by Dolphin Travel, New Zealand's leading boutique inbound tour operator. Established in 1997 and specialising in the discerning traveller's needs, their friendly, flexible and multi-lingual team offer a vast array of options. Top service, quality accommodation and personalised travel documentation are the hallmarks of Dolphin Travel's Platinum Tours brand. As well as their range of private chauffeur-driven and self-drive tours, they approach tailor-made itineraries in an enthusiastic and positive way, and provide creative suggestions to even the most challenging requests. Their extensive knowledge and broad network of connections in the tourism industry ensures that guests will experience New Zealand's very best. Tour rates vary according to the itinerary.

FACILITIES	NORTH ISLAND TOUR SAMPLE	SOUTH ISLAND TOUR SAMPLE	TOUR PRICE INCLUDES
• team of experienced & creative travel professionals • chauffeur-driven tours • fly/drive tours arranged • group tours with general or special interest • 24-hour emergency multi-lingual guest assistance • personalised daily itineraries, travel documents & driving directions provided • welcome information pack • English, German & French spoken proficiently; basic Spanish & Italian spoken • 24-hour turn-around for guest bookings & inquiries • 100% NZ owned & operated • variety of tour options available: general sightseeing tours, nature tours, golfing, fishing, arts & crafts, gardens, bird-watching, Maori culture, food & wine tours	• Day 1: Arrive at Auckland Airport; stay in Auckland • Day 2: Auckland City; visit museum, Sky Tower & Auckland attractions • Day 3: scenic drive to Coromandel Peninsula & Mt Maunganui to stay • Day 4: drive to Rotorua; Maori culture & geothermal activity; stay in Rotorua • Day 5: drive to Taupo, visit Wai-O-Tapu & Huka Falls; drive to Napier to stay • Day 6: Napier; visit gannet colony, vineyards, Art Deco buildings & other attractions • Day 7: scenic drive to Wellington; visit Te Papa Museum & other attractions; farewell dinner • Day 8: depart Wellington Airport	• Day 1: Arrive Christchurch Airport, stay in Christchurch • Day 2: visit parks & gardens; leave Christchurch & travel to Lake Tekapo to stay • Day 3: drive through Twizel, Omarama & Oamaru; arrive in Dunedin & visit heritage buildings; stay in Dunedin • Day 4: travel to Otago Peninsula to view wildlife & Larnach Castle; stay in Dunedin • Day 5: drive to Manapouri, Fiordland National Park, Wilmot Pass & board vessel for overnight cruise in Doubtful Sound • Day 6: disembark vessel, travel back through Wilmot Pass & Manapouri to Arrowtown, Lake Wakatipu; stay in Queenstown • Day 7: travel by limousine to Glenorchy for Dart River Safari; stay in Queenstown • Day 8: Depart Queenstown Airport	• limousine driven by experienced English-speaking driver for entire journey; other languages, extra • pre-dinner drinks & nibbles at some accommodation, where offered • luxury accommodation: 7 nights' in North Island; 6 nights' in South Island, plus overnight cruise in Doubtful Sound • daily cooked breakfast at accommodation & on cruise • 3 lunches (North Island) or 4 lunches (South Island); both include 3 dinners • all travel arrangements • admission to activities in North Island tours in Auckland, Rotorua & Napier • admission to activities in South Island tours in Dunedin & Queenstown

13

North Island

Waioeka Gorge, between Opotiki and Gisborne – see accommodation page 180.

Taharangi Marie Lodge

Hosts Ron and Connie Adams

700 Sandhills Road, Ninety Mile Beach, Far North   *Postal* P O Box 59, Kaitaia
Phone 0-9-406 7462   *Mobile* 021 926 949   *Fax* 0-9-408 3085
Email taharangi@xtra.co.nz   *Website* friars.co.nz/hosts/taharangi.html

2 bdrm	2 enst

Room rate $400   *Includes continental breakfast*
Winter rates available   *Dinner extra*

DIRECTIONS: From Awanui, take Gill Rd west. Turn right before end of tarseal into Sandhills Rd. Travel 7km to gate on right. Take driveway approx. 0.75km to Taharangi Marie. From Ahipara, take Sandhills Rd for 8.8km.

Built among the sand-dunes bordering Ninety Mile Beach, Taharangi Marie is aptly named "peaceful horizon". The relative isolation of the accommodation, with the ocean only 50 metres away, makes it a tranquil get-away for relaxation and rejuvenation. Guests find the constant sound of the waves soothing, complemented by activities for the energetic. Opened in 1998, the house features stone pillars, timber ceilings, a mezzanine floor separating the two ensuite guestrooms, extensive decking and uninterrupted sea views. Guests enjoy breakfast indoors, or alfresco, and in season, freshly gathered seafood is a highlight of the dinner menu. The hosts are willing to share knowledge and experience of their Maori culture and tradition.

FACILITIES

- 1 king & 1 queen ensuite bedrooms upstairs
- 2 ensuite bathrooms with toiletries & hair dryers
- cotton bed linen
- tea/coffee facilities in both bedrooms
- lounge with open fire
- Sky TV & video in lounge
- panoramic ocean views
- continental breakfast
- dinner with wine, by prior arrangement, with fresh local seafood gathered from adjacent beach
- extensive decking
- laundry available
- courtesy passenger transfer
- garaging for guests
- beach access

ACTIVITIES AVAILABLE

- hiking over sand-dunes
- beach, 50-metre walk
- swimming; surfing
- tuatua shellfish gathering
- beach walks
- historic kauri log site
- fishing; diving
- sand-dune adventures
- Ninety Mile Beach drive
- quad bike hire
- personalised tours in Far North
- restaurants, 15-min drive
- horse treks
- gum fields; glow-worms
- golf
- Ancient Kauri Kingdom
- Maori arts & crafts
- Cape Reinga, 1-hour drive

NINETY MILE BEACH
Siesta Guest Lodge & Villa Apartment

Hosts Carole and Alan Harding

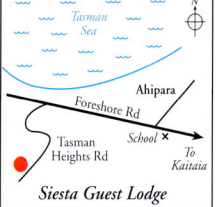

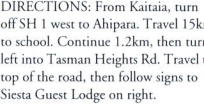

Tasman Heights Road, Ahipara   *Postal* P O Box 30, Ahipara, Northland
Phone 0-9-409 2011   *Mobile* 021 260 6732   *Fax* 0-9-409 2011
Email ninetymile@xtra.co.nz   *Website* www.ahipara.co.nz/siesta

5 bdrm	3 enst	1 prbth	1 pdrm

Room rate $150–$195
Apartment rate $150–$250

Includes breakfast, or extra in apartment
Long-stay rates available   *Self-catering*

DIRECTIONS: From Kaitaia, turn off SH 1 west to Ahipara. Travel 15km to school. Continue 1.2km, then turn left into Tasman Heights Rd. Travel to top of the road, then follow signs to Siesta Guest Lodge on right.

Alan and Carole's Mediterranean-style house overlooks Ninety Mile Beach. Facing north, the upstairs guest wing is warmed by all-day sun, the guest balconies overlook the secluded subtropical gardens and sheltered bay below. The guest dining and lounge areas are quiet and spacious, with native rimu wood panelling and terracotta tiles. Guests enjoy sleeping to the sound of the sea, and relaxing in the privacy and tranquillity. Carole and Alan have lived locally since 1974 and know all the sunny local white-sand beaches and hidden treasures. Long-stay guests have the option of adjacent Siesta Villas with two self-contained apartments, where guests can self-cater and stay in spacious comfort with panoramic ocean views, even from their bed.

FACILITIES

Main house:
- 2 ensuite queen bedrooms with tea/coffee & ocean views
- continental breakfast, or cooked on request
- private guest balconies
- guest lounge & reading room
- courtesy transfer from Kaitaia airport or bus depot

2 Villa apartments:
- 1 upstairs apartment with king bedroom & ensuite
- 1 studio downstairs with 1 queen & 1 twin bedroom, 1 bathroom
- Sky TV, video & stereo with CDs
- full kitchen with dishwasher
- breakfast available, extra
- indoor/outdoor living & BBQ
- panoramic seaviews, east & west

ACTIVITIES AVAILABLE

- licensed restaurant 400m away
- beach, 5-min walk
- safe swimming; surfing; diving
- fishing, on or off-shore
- sand-dune wilderness, close by
- guided hikes
- personalised luxury 4WD tours
- bush, coastal & wilderness walks
- horse riding on beaches & sandhills

- local award-winning winery
- Cape coach tours
- Ninety Mile Beach
- links golf course, 5 mins
- Glow-worm Grotto & Kiwi House, 30 mins
- quad bike hire
- local kauri forests, 1 hour
- Bay of Islands, 1¼-hr drive
- Kauri Coast, 2-hour drive

AHIPARA
Beachfront

Hosts Jenny and Paul Steele

14 Kotare Street, Ahipara, Ninety Mile Beach, Far North
Postal P O Box 174, Ahipara   *Phone* 0-9-409 4007   *Fax* 0-9-409 4007
Email pauljenny@beachfront.net.nz   *Website* www.beachfront.net.nz

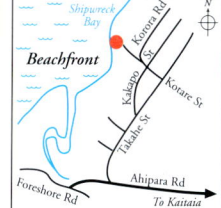

DIRECTIONS: From Kaitaia, turn off SH 1 west to Ahipara. Travel 15km to school. Turn right into Takahe Rd & left into Kakapo St. Turn left again into Kotare St & travel to Beachfront at seaward end of street.

4 bdrm	4 enst

Apartment rate $120–$270
Extra persons $20 each

Breakfast & dinner extra
Self-catering

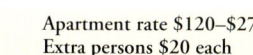

Set right on the water's edge at Ahipara, at the beginning of Ninety Mile Beach in the Far North, Beachfront offers two fully self-contained apartments. With sea views from each bed, Beachfront provides two ensuite bedrooms in each apartment with extra beds available. The downstairs apartment opens to a private deck with pathway leading directly to the beach, and the other apartment is upstairs with a private balcony overlooking the ocean. Both apartments have full kitchens for self-catering if desired, and a guest barbecue. Breakfast is available by arrangement, and dinner can also be served in the apartments or at the hosts' table. Alternatively, restaurants are just a short drive away. There is a marmalade cat called Sunshine on site.

FACILITIES

- upstairs apartment: 2 super-king ensuite bedrooms
- downstairs apartment: 2 super-king ensuite bedrooms
- extra divan bed in each lounge
- cotton bed linen
- hair dryers, heated towel rails & toiletries in all ensuites
- private guest lounge in each apartment with Sky TV, video, DVD, CD-player & tea/coffee
- full kitchen for self-catering in each apartment
- cooked or continental breakfast, $10–$20 pp
- 3-course dinner, $45 pp, wine extra
- fresh flowers; 2 BBQs
- laundry, $5 per load
- courtesy passenger transfer
- on-site parking; garaging

ACTIVITIES AVAILABLE

- direct access to beach from site for swimming, walking & watersports
- surfing
- 18-hole golf course
- horse riding
- Ahipara village nearby
- ATV tours, guided & self-drive
- sand boarding & sand yachting
- beach & deep-sea fishing
- restaurants, 8-min drive
- tours to Cape Reinga
- shellfish gathering
- gardens tours
- wineries
- walks
- Ninety Mile Beach
- bird-watching
- 4WD tours

Beachfront

Beachfront

© Friars' Guide to New Zealand Accommodation for the Discerning Traveller

CABLE BAY
Carneval Ocean View

Hosts Martha and Roly Fasnacht

360 State Highway 10, Cable Bay, Mangonui
Phone 0-9-406 1012   *Mobile* 021 214 6524   *Fax* 0-9-406 1012
Email holiday@carneval.co.nz   *Website* friars.co.nz/hosts/carneval.html

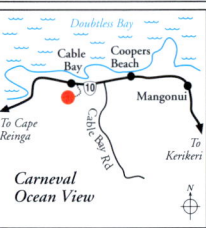

DIRECTIONS: From the turn-off to Mangonui, follow SH 10 to Coopers Beach. Continue to Cable Bay. Cross bridge & opposite rest area turn left up driveway 500m to top of hill, to Carneval Ocean View at end.

2 bdrm	2 enst

Room rate $150–$190

Includes breakfast
Picnic baskets & dinner extra

Located 80 metres above sea level, Carneval Ocean View provides panoramic vistas of Doubtless Bay. Carneval is Swiss for the hosts' surname. Martha and Roly speak Swiss-German and French, and Roly is a qualified chef. Swiss-style cooked breakfast is served in the dining room or alfresco on the terrace. Swiss-French style or Kiwi cuisine is also available for dinner using fresh local fish and produce. Built in Mediterrean style, Carneval overlooks the pink sand beach at Cable Bay where guests enjoy swimming and diving or fishing trips can be arranged. European-style accommodation comprises two king-size ensuite bedrooms with Finnish Tulikivi wall heating and a Tulikivi fire warms the lounge in winter.

FACILITIES

- one-party booking; sea views
- 2 ensuite king bedrooms
- dressing room, TV, tea/coffee, soda water, mini-fridge & Finnish Tulikivi wall heater in bedrooms
- hair dryers, toiletries, bathrobes, heated towel rails in ensuites
- guest lounge with Tulikivi fire, tea/coffee, cable TV, video, books, CD-player & writing desk
- email, fax & phone available

- Swiss-style cooked breakfast
- 3–5-course Swiss/French-style dinner, $45–$65 pp
- Swiss-German & French spoken by hosts
- beach towels supplied
- laundry, $10
- wheelchair access
- on-site parking
- courtesy passenger transfer

ACTIVITIES AVAILABLE

- sauna room on site
- dartboard & darts available
- windsurfer & snorkelling gear
- large landscaped gardens on site
- kayak available
- pink-sand beach, 3–5-min walk
- Coopers Beach village, 3 mins
- Mangonui township, 8 mins
- diving & fishing trips arranged

- restaurants & cafés, Coopers Beach & Mangonui
- safe swimming
- golf, 15-min drive
- gardens & potteries to visit
- Butler Point historic visit
- Glow-worm Grotto & Kiwi House, 45-min drive away
- day trips & tours arranged
- www.carneval.co.nz

Coopers Beachfront Suites

Hosts George Van Valkenburg and Janet Brennan

18 Bayside Drive, Coopers Beach   *Postal* P O Box 385, Mangonui
Phone 0-9-406 1018   *Freephone* 0800 169 020   *Fax* 0-9-406 1018
Email stay@coopersbeach.net   *Website* www.coopersbeach.net

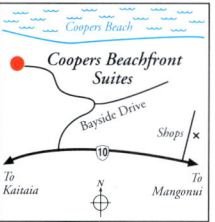

DIRECTIONS: From the turn-off to Mangonui, follow SH 10 to Coopers Beach. Past the shopping centre, turn right into Bayside Drive to Coopers Beachfront Estate. Bear left to Coopers Beachfront Suites at end of private road.

2 bdrm	2 enst

Suite rate $175–$290
Weekly rates available

Includes continental breakfast provisions for 1st morning
Winter rates available   *Self-catering*

Coopers Beachfront Suites were purpose-built in 1997 beside the ocean, with only native pohutukawa trees separating them from the seashore. Adjacent is George and Janet's home, ensuring total guest privacy, yet accessibility if desired. Guests have exclusive use of either the upstairs suite with balcony overlooking the beach, or the similar downstairs suite with larger verandah providing direct access to the beach. Each totally smoke-free suite comprises a queen-size bedroom with ensuite bathroom, kitchenette, lounge and dining area, all facing the ocean. The peace and quietness of the setting is broken only by the soothing sound of the waves breaking on the shore. There is no traffic noise, yet the shops are only two minutes' walk away.

FACILITIES

- 1 upstairs & 1 downstairs suite
- 1 queen bedroom per suite
- sea views from both beds
- quality bed linen, bathrobes, reclining chair & insect screens
- hair dryer, heated towel rails & toiletries in both ensuites
- ceiling fan, TV, music in suites
- teas & plunger coffee in suites
- global cable television
- unsuitable for pets or children
- fridge/freezer, microwave, water filter & frypan in kitchenettes
- guest phone in both lounges
- laptop computer with free internet access available
- email, fax & laundry available
- gas barbecue available
- private guest entrances to suites
- off-street parking

ACTIVITIES AVAILABLE

- direct access to beach
- sea kayaks for hire
- walking; swimming
- scuba diving; jogging
- deep-sea fishing
- historic sites; hiking
- Whaling Museum
- cinema with latest releases, 15-min drive
- ATM; Medical Centre
- restaurants & cafés, 5-min drive
- historic Mangonui, 2.5 km away
- 3 golf courses, range of difficulty
- arts & crafts; gardens to visit
- day trips to Cape Reinga
- Ninety Mile Beach, sand-dune buggies
- Ancient Kauri Kingdom, 20-min drive
- Maitai Bay, 30-min drive, for picnics, swimming, snorkelling
- northernmost award-winning winery

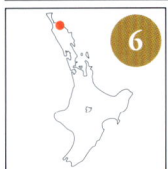

COOPERS BEACH
35 Bayside

Hosts Jenny and John Baird

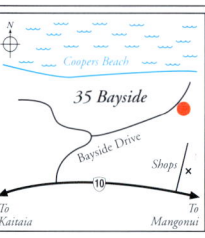

35 Bayside Drive, Coopers Beach   *Phone* 0-3-332 5996
Postal P O Box 28–118, Beckenham, Christchurch 8030   *Fax* 0-3-332 8947
Email jenny@35bayside.co.nz   *Website* www.35bayside.co.nz

| 4 bdrm | 1 enst | 1 shbth | House rate $250–$380
Minimum 4-night stay | *Self-catering, no meals available*
Long-term rates available |

DIRECTIONS: From the turn-off to Mangonui, follow SH 10 to Coopers Beach. Travel past shops, then turn right into Bayside Drive, to Coopers Beachfront Estate. Continue to 35 Bayside on right at end.

Located on the Coopers Beachfront Estate is 35 Bayside, a self-contained holiday home built in 2001 to sleep 10 persons, including children. Set in fully landscaped gardens, with tropical plantings, this contemporary house provides extensive views of the pohutukawa-lined beach and Doubtless Bay. Four bedrooms are provided on two levels, with the full kitchen and two bathrooms by a multi-award-winning kitchen designer. Quality fittings and furnishings feature throughout and there are ceiling fans to enhance comfort. Guests can relax to the sound of the waves from the beach only 30 metres away via a private accessway, and the large paved patio area with gas barbecue is well sited for alfresco dining in the "winterless north" climate.

FACILITIES

- private-party bookings only
- self-contained house for 10
- 1 queen ensuite bedroom downstairs with bath
- 1 queen bedroom & 2 rooms with 1 bunk & 1 single upstairs share 1 bathroom
- cotton bed linen
- heated towel rails
- extra toilet; outdoor shower

- full kitchen for self-catering
- lounge with TV, video, CD-player, games & books
- children's TV area upstairs
- 2 phones; ceiling fans
- fully equipped laundry
- stair-guards, highchair & cot
- children welcome; no pets
- double garage
- on-site parking for boats

ACTIVITIES AVAILABLE

- paved gas BBQ area on site
- 30m private accessway to Coopers Beach
- safe swimming
- shops & restaurant, 100m walk away
- historic Mangonui, 2km
- scuba diving
- deep-sea fishing
- 4 wineries within 45 mins

- restaurants & cafés, 5 mins
- boat launching ramps, 5 mins
- golf courses – Carrington Estate 15 mins, Kauri Cliffs 30 mins
- kauri forest, 30 mins
- Kauri Kingdom, 30 mins
- historic Bay of Islands, 45-min drive south
- Ninety Mile Beach, 35 mins
- day trips to Cape Reinga

COOPERS BEACH
Beach Lodge

Host Margaret Morrison

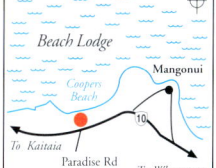

DIRECTIONS: From the turn-off to Mangonui Village, follow SH 10 for 2km. Beach Lodge is the last dwelling on the beach side of the road (45 minutes north of Kerikeri, or 25 minutes east of Kaitaia).

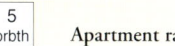

121 State Highway 10, Coopers Beach *Postal* P O Box 190, Mangonui
Phone 0-9-406 0068 *Email* margaret@beachlodge.co.nz
Fax 0-9-406 0068 *Website* www.beachlodge.co.nz

| 10 bdrm | 5 prbth | Apartment rate $250–$400 | *Self-catering, no meals available* |

Overlooking the Pacific Ocean, Beach Lodge comprises a series of separate self-contained apartments sited directly above Coopers Beach. The waves breaking on the shore create a constant soothing sound and beachcombing is a relaxing pursuit. Native pohutukawa trees edge the beach, their red blossoms in December giving them the name "New Zealand Christmas Trees". The two-storey apartments are architecturally designed using native timbers, with each kitchen and bathroom built in solid rimu. Double-doored showers are a feature of the bathrooms. Total privacy is ensured with double French doors opening to private decking surrounded by an attractive garden. Shops are within walking distance along the beach and cafés are nearby.

FACILITIES

- 5 self-contained **apartments**
- single-party bookings
- 1 queen downstairs & 1 twin upstairs bedroom & 1 bathroom per **apartment**
- 50-channel cable TV in each **apartment's** lounge
- direct-dial phones
- ocean views from every room
- children over 8 years welcome
- 1 fully equipped kitchen for self-catering per **apartment**
- fax, email & BBQ available
- sundecks overlooking ocean
- Margaret speaks German
- gym facilities on site
- self-serve guest laundry
- "winterless" North climate
- off-street parking
- courtesy passenger transfer

ACTIVITIES AVAILABLE

- private access to beach
- boogie boards & kayaks
- safe swimming
- shellfish gathering
- restaurants & cafés nearby
- shops easy walk; golf courses
- historic Mangonui, 2km away
- fishing trips; dolphin swims
- Glow-worm Grotto & Kiwi House, 24km away
- sailing trips to Cavalli Islands
- Maori pa sites, Butler Point
- Karikari Peninsula beaches, golf course & restaurant
- door-to-door tour service to: Cape Reinga, gum fields, kauri forests, Ninety Mile Beach, sand-hills with Paradise Connections
- arts & crafts – paintings, Maori weaving, fabric design, carving, pottery & swamp kauri turning

MANGONUI
Mill Bay Haven

Hosts Anette and Anthony Norman

19 Silver Egg Drive, Mangonui   *Postal* P O Box 295, Mangonui
Phone 0-9-406 1113   *Mobile* 021 346 118   *Fax* 0-9-406 1130
Email anthonynorman@xtra.co.nz   *Website* www.millbayhaven.co.nz

DIRECTIONS: Take SH 10 north & turn right to Mangonui. Travel thru village, turn right into Mabel Thorburn Dr & continue into Mill Bay Rd. Turn right into Silver Egg Dr & travel thru boat ramp area to end.

| 5 bdrm | 5 enst | **Double $200–$400**
Single $90–$140 | *Self-catering*
No meals available | |

Mill Bay Haven is sited on the waterfront of Mangonui Harbour and backs onto a nature reserve. This historic kauri mill site now offers three self-contained options. Mill Lodge (*behind trees to left above*) still retains original rimu and kauri panelling, and provides three ensuite guestrooms, all with harbour views through mature pohutukawa trees at the lawn edge on the sea wall, from where guests can fish. A spa pool is located on a large deck backed by subtropical gardens. Rose Cottage (*also behind trees*) is set in a private garden and Seaview Studio (*to right of hosts' house above*) looks onto Mill Bay Haven's private beach. Moored in front of Mill Lodge are boats available for fishing or sailing charters. Anthony enjoys hosting guests on his yacht *Hinemoana*.

FACILITIES

- Mill Lodge: 1 twin & 2 queen ensuite bedrooms with bathrobes; 1 double basin, powder room, mezzanine & self-serve laundry
- Rose Cottage: 1 queen bedroom, ensuite & living room
- Seaview Studio: 1 queen ensuite bedroom with harbour views
- heated towel rails, hair dryers & toiletries in all 5 ensuites
- cotton bed linen; fresh flowers

- 3 kitchens for self-catering, or caterer by arrangement
- fruit baskets on arrival
- Sky TV in all 3 venues
- lounge in Lodge with open fire, phone, video & CDs
- children welcome
- spaniel dog & cat on site
- French & Swedish spoken
- parking; courtesy transfer

ACTIVITIES AVAILABLE

- spa pool on Lodge deck
- BBQ on site
- fishing from front lawn or jetty
- private beach access
- safe swimming nearby
- 13.5m (44 ft) yacht *Hinemoana* on site, for hosted sailing charters with Anthony to Cavalli Islands, Karikari Peninsula, or Whangaroa
- golf courses

- Maori pa site & walks in nature reserve adjacent
- cafés & restaurants within walking distance
- Mangonui township 1km
- Coopers Beach, 2km
- Cable Bay pink sand, 5 mins
- door to door Cape Reinga day trips via 90 Mile Beach & sandhill tobogganing

WHANGAROA
Kingfish Lodge

Hosts Bernice and Roger Cairns

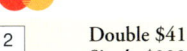

Kingfish Cove, Whangaroa Harbour, R D 1, Kaeo, Northland
Freephone 0800 100 546   *Phone* 0-9-405 0164   *Fax* 0-9-405 0163
Email fish@kingfishlodge.co.nz   *Website* www.kingfishlodge.co.nz

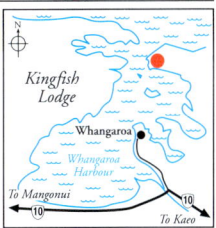

DIRECTIONS: Take SH 1 north from Whangarei, through Kawakawa, to Pakaraka. Turn right into SH 10. Travel to Kaeo then turn right & continue 10 mins to Whangaroa. Boat for Kingfish Lodge leaves from wharf.

12 bdrm	12 enst	Double $415 Single $330	*All meals extra* **Packages available**

Built in 1947, Kingfish Lodge is the oldest coastal fishing lodge in New Zealand. It now provides 12 waterside guest bedrooms, including two family suites. Guests need no fishing experience, as total tuition is provided. Under new management, this family-owned historic lodge is set in Kingfish Cove at the headland of Whangaroa Harbour. Surrounded by water and native bush, it provides tranquil isolation, accessible by helicopter or by boat from Whangaroa Wharf. After the courtesy 10-minute scenic cruise, guests land at the jetty adjacent to the lodge set in a subtropical garden. All dietary needs are catered for, including Japanese cuisine. Meals are served in the dining room or alfresco with harbour views.

FACILITIES

- 10 guest bedrooms with ensuite bathrooms
- 2 family suites each including 1 double/twin bedroom & 1 ensuite bathroom
- hair dryers, toiletries & heated towel rails in each ensuite
- TV, tea/coffee, iron & board, & phone in each bedroom
- weddings, functions, business groups, conferences catered for

- English breakfast, extra
- picnic or lunch, extra
- 4-course fine dining, extra
- fully licensed
- private guest entrances
- laundry available
- courtesy boat transfer
- 2 helipads
- full business facilities

ACTIVITIES AVAILABLE

- full sauna & gym on site
- conferences catered
- complimentary fishing tuition
- kayaking
- clay-bird shooting
- lawn games eg croquet, volley ball, beach pétanque
- board games
- yachting
- hiking in 220ha native bush

- swimming & snorkelling
- salt fly-fishing & all light tackle fishing options
- big-game fishing – marlin, tuna & shark
- scuba diving by arrangement
- small power fishing boats, extra charge
- off-site: golfing; horse trekking; & sea kayaking

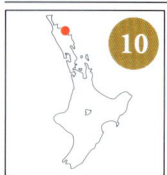

Mahinepua/Cavalli
Waiwurrie

Hosts Vickie and Rodger Corbin

Mahinepua Road, R D 1, Kaeo, Whangaroa, Northland
Phone 0-9-405 0840   *Email* wai.wurrie@xtra.co.nz
Fax 0-9-405 0854   *Website* www.coastalfarm-lodge.co.nz

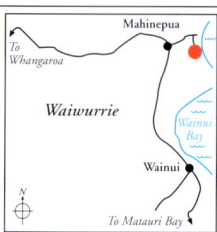

DIRECTIONS: Take SH 10 north & turn right into Matauri Bay Rd for 15 km. Turn left into Wainui Rd for 10km & right into Mahinepua Rd. Turn right thru gates to Ronaki, then 2nd drive right uphill to Waiwurrie.

| 2 bdrm | 1 enst | 1 prbth | Double $300–$400 Single $200 | *Includes breakfast & dinner* *Lunch extra* |

The new Kauri Cliffs golf course is less than15 minutes' drive away from Waiwurrie. Located on the sunny east coast, surrounded by private farmland and forestry, Waiwurrie provides two large bedrooms and bathrooms, and a guest balcony featuring panoramic sea views. Situated near the Cavalli Islands, Whangaroa, Waiwurrie offers game fishing in the deep-sea fishing ground which is renowned marlin territory. Alternatively, guests may enjoy the Bay of Islands, sightseeing to Cape Reinga, diving to see the *Rainbow Warrior*, fishing, swimming, or just relaxing on the beach. Dinner is New Zealand cuisine and included in the tariff. It is served with a complimentary bottle of wine, overlooking Mahinepua Bay to Cavalli Islands.

FACILITIES

- 1 king ensuite bedroom upstairs
- 1 queen bedroom with bathroom & bathrobes downstairs
- heated towel rails & toiletries
- private guest balcony opens from upstairs bedroom with sea views
- fresh flowers in bedrooms
- guest lounge with open fire, tea/coffee, TV, video & music
- phone, fax & email available
- home-made bread & cooked breakfast available
- lunch by arrangement, extra
- dinner served with bottle of complimentary wine
- complimentary laundry
- black labrador & cat on site
- garaging available
- on-site parking
- boating access

ACTIVITIES AVAILABLE

- walks on site
- swimming & fishing from site
- golf at Kauri Cliffs, Kerikeri, Whangaroa & Waitangi
- fishing for marlin at Cavalli Islands, Whangaroa
- sightseeing; watersports
- Cavalli Islands trips
- Bay of Islands boat trips
- friars.co.nz/hosts/waiwurrie.html
- restaurants, 10km
- deep-sea fishing at Whangaroa, 20-min drive
- diving to *Rainbow Warrior* & Cavalli Islands
- Kerikeri township, 45km
- Paihia township, 60km
- ferry trip to Russell from Paihia or Opua, 1 hr drive
- Cape Reinga day trips

Waiwurrie

MAHINEPUA/CAVALLI
Cavalli Beach House Retreat

Hosts Carrie and Richard Barron

Mahinepua Road, Whangaroa   *Phone* 0-9-405 1049
Postal Mahinepua Road, R D 1, Kaeo 0471   *Fax* 0-9-405 1043
Email carrie@cavallibeachhouse.com   *Website* www.cavallibeachhouse.com

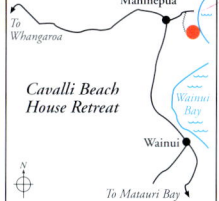

DIRECTIONS: Take SH 10 north towards Kaeo. Turn right at Matauri Bay. At "T" junction, turn left to Wainui & travel 10km. Turn right into Mahinepua Rd, then right into Ronaki. Drive over hill to Cavalli on right.

3 bdrm   3 enst   Room rate $650–$775   *Includes breakfast*   *Dinner extra*   qualmark ★★★★

Cavalli Beach House is an exclusive private beachfront retreat, only 20 metres from a secluded bay. Featuring wide, unimpeded ocean views from all rooms towards the Cavalli Islands, this sail house concept was architecturally designed by Martyn Evans and Chris Howe, and purpose-built in 1999 to cater for six guests. The three king-size guestrooms all include generous ensuites. The interior design reflects the tones of the sand and the atmosphere of the Pacific enhanced by Island tapa cloth. Meals are served in the dining room or alfresco on the balcony in summer. The cuisine emphasises ocean fresh and Pacific tastes, accompanied by home-grown organic produce. Table d'hôte dinner is available by prior arrangement.

FACILITIES

- 3 king ensuite bedrooms opening to balcony decks
- 3 large ensuites with double basins, hair dryers, bathrobes, heated towel rails & toiletries
- cotton bed linen
- guest lounge with open fire, tea/coffee, TV & video
- private guest entrance
- email facilities available
- breakfast with local fruits, Greek yoghurt & full cooked options, served in dining room
- 3-course table d'hôte dinner, $90 pp
- NZ wine list
- dietary requirements catered
- laundry, by arrangement
- on-site parking
- airport transfers arranged

ACTIVITIES AVAILABLE

- hillside spa pool on site
- kayaks available
- swimming in private bay
- snorkelling gear available
- dinghy available
- fishing gear available
- star gazing, star charts available
- gardens to visit
- sketching easel & pastels available for guest use
- Kauri Cliffs Golf Course, 10–15-min drive away
- Wildlife Reserve coastal walks; big-game fishing
- Cavalli Islands
- deep-sea diving & *Rainbow Warrior*
- wine & cheese tasting tours
- art & design stores tour
- historical day trips

Te Ngaere Bay
Huntaway Lodge Northland

Host Greg Hunt

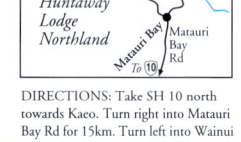

Wainui Road, Te Ngaere Bay   *Postal* Te Ngaere Bay, R D 1, Kaeo
Phone 0-9-405 1611   *Mobile* 021 405 161   *Fax* 0-9-405 1612
Email greg@huntawaylodge.com   *Website* www.huntawaylodge.com

3 bdrm	3 enst

Room rate $375–$440
House rates available

Includes breakfast
Lunch & dinner extra

DIRECTIONS: Take SH 10 north towards Kaeo. Turn right into Matauri Bay Rd for 15km. Turn left into Wainui Rd for 5km. Continue past Te Ngaere Bay to black gates on left. Take private road & turn right at top to Huntaway.

At Huntaway Lodge Northland, Greg specialises in personalised accommodation. The contemporary cedar beach house was built in 2000 high above Te Ngaere Bay to capture the sea views, and located just 10 minutes from the Kauri Cliffs Golf Course. Guests are offered a choice of three queen ensuite bedrooms, all opening to the expansive deck with 180-degree ocean views. Each bedroom is furnished in classical style with all the facilities for guests' comfort in mind. Meals are tailored to the guests' needs, with an emphasis on using locally sourced produce and seafood. Breakfast is served alfresco on the deck year round, weather permitting, and special picnic lunches and dinners are also available by arrangement.

FACILITIES

- 3 queen ensuite bedrooms opening to deck, each with fan, TV, CD-player, CDs & tea/coffee
- cotton bed linen; beach towels
- hair dryer, toiletries, heated floor, heated towel rails & bathrobes
- guest lounge with teas/coffee, nibbles, bar, Sky TV, CD-player, games, books & magazines
- children welcome in single parties or house bookings only
- breakfast served in dining room or alfresco on balcony
- lunch, $30 pp
- 3-course table d'hôte dinner with wine list, $80 pp
- dietary needs catered for
- fax & email in office
- honeymoons catered for
- 1 labrador & 1 cat on site
- on-site parking; helipad

ACTIVITIES AVAILABLE

- therapeutic massage
- pétanque court on site
- kayaks, snorkelling gear & surf-casting fishing gear available
- swimming at white sand beaches
- coastal walkways; native bush
- big-game fishing; sailing
- deep-sea diving, *Rainbow Warrior*
- private gardens to visit
- wineries; arts & crafts trail
- restaurants, 30-min drive
- golf courses, Kauri Cliffs
- Cavalli Islands
- Far North day tours
- Kerikeri, 30-min drive
- Paihia, 45-min drive
- Waitangi, 45-min drive
- Auckland, 3½ hours south
- Auckland airport, 50 mins by air

CAVALLI/TAKOU BAY
Cavalli View Cottage

Hosts Sharon Burges and Rick Harris

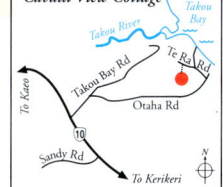

Phone 0-9-407 9019   Te Ra Road, Takou Bay, R D 2, Kerikeri
Mobile 021 118 5047   *Email* takoubay@acute.co.nz
Fax 0-9-407 9018   *Website* friars.co.nz/hosts/cavallicottage.html

DIRECTIONS: From SH 10 turn east into Takou Bay Rd. Travel 1km, then take right fork into Otaha Rd. Travel 4km & turn left into Te Ra Rd. Travel 0.5km & veer left at fork. Take 3rd drive on left to Cavalli Cottage.

1 bdrm	1 prbth

Cottage rate $150–$165   *Self-catering, no meals available*

Cavalli View Cottage is set in a large rural property with peaceful views over Takou Bay beach to the Cavalli Islands beyond. This north-facing cottage is separate from the hosts' home, completely self-contained and features natural timber throughout. A fully equipped kitchen allows guests to self-cater, and they can enjoy the barbecue on the deck where they can dine alfresco. The queen-size bedroom opens onto a spacious sundeck with its claw-foot bath for relaxing in private under the stars. There are two extra single pull-out beds in the lounge and a porta-cot is also available. Cavalli View is close to many beaches, Kerikeri attractions, and the Kauri Cliffs golf course. A friendly border collie, Kimo, two cats and chickens are on site.

FACILITIES

- 1 self-contained cottage
- single-party bookings
- 1 queen bedroom opening onto private deck
- 1 private bathroom
- heated towel rail
- children welcome
- porta-cot available
- panoramic sea views from inside cottage & sundeck
- fully equipped kitchen for self-catering
- lounge with TV, video, stereo & CD-player
- laundry facilities available
- gas BBQ
- outdoor furniture
- claw-foot bath on deck
- private guest entrance
- under-cover parking

ACTIVITIES AVAILABLE

- small orchard on 4ha (10-acre) property on site
- 2 cats, border collie & chickens on site
- beaches nearby
- kauri forest, 30 mins
- scenic coastal drives
- historic buildings at Kerikeri
- golf courses including world-class Kauri Cliffs
- restaurants, wineries & cinema in Kerikeri, 15 mins
- arts & crafts
- gardens to visit
- Kerikeri, 15 mins south
- Whangaroa Harbour, game fishing & boat trips, 20 mins
- Paihia, 40 mins south
- Mangonui, 40 mins north
- Cape Reinga day trips

TAKOU BAY, KERIKERI
Magic Cottage & Takou River Lodge

Hosts Ian and Anna Sizer

Takou Bay Road, Takou Bay   *Phone* 0-9-407 8065   *Mobile* 027 545 7633
Postal P O Box 55, Waipapa, Northland 0470   *Fax* 0-9-407 8403
Email takouriver@xtra.co.nz   *Website* www.takouriver.com

DIRECTIONS: Take SH 10 north to Waipapa. Continue for 8km. Turn right into Takou Bay Rd. Travel 1km & take left fork. Continue 5.5km to end of unsealed road. Magic Cottage & Takou River Lodge at end.

| 5 bdrm | 5 enst | **Cottage rate $170–$300** | *Self-catering* | *No meals available* | |

Magic Cottage and Takou River Lodge offer a tranquil riverside retreat, featuring three self-contained cottages set in subtropical gardens. Located on the banks of the Takou River, just upstream from Takou Bay, Magic Cottage provides total privacy. Perched beside the river, this stand-alone cottage features an antique claw-foot bath on the deck, super-king-size bed, ensuite, kitchen and gas power only. The Garden and River Cottages are semi-detached, spacious and contemporary in style, adjoining the hosts' house. Each includes a small garden barbecue area, two ensuite bedrooms, a living area and fully equipped kitchen opening to an upper sundeck. River frontage, a floating jetty, summer house, extensive gardens, kayaks and access to Takou Bay are available.

FACILITIES

- one-party bookings per cottage
- Magic Cottage: 1 private self-contained studio cottage with 1 super-king bed, ensuite, claw-foot bath on sundeck, estuary views, BBQ, all gas heating & lighting, no electricity available
- Garden & River Cottages: 2 self-contained cottages adjoining hosts' house, 1 king & 1 queen ensuite bedroom per cottage, CD-player, sundeck & small garden area
- full self-catering kitchen & BBQ per cottage
- cotton bed linen, feather duvets, bathrobes, quality toiletries & fresh flowers
- magazines & local books
- laundry, email & fax available
- Dutch, German, Polish, Spanish & French spoken
- 2ha subtropical gardens, summer house; boathouse

ACTIVITIES AVAILABLE

- beach access at Takou Bay, a short boatride downstream
- private river frontage for swimming, boating & fishing
- private jetty & boat ramp
- kayaks, canoes & mountain bikes available for guest use
- diving, sailing & big-game fishing nearby
- 60ha (150-acre) organic farm, including historic Maori site
- Kerikeri historic sites, wineries & restaurants
- Kauri Cliffs golf course
- Cavalli Islands
- Bay of Islands tours
- Waitangi Treaty House & grounds
- historic Russell & Paihia
- kauri forest
- Cape Reinga day trips

Above: Like Garden Cottage, River Cottage includes an open-plan living area upstairs, with two ensuite bedrooms below.
Below: The Garden Cottage living area opens to a balcony overlooking the garden, with an outdoor seating area on the grass.
Opposite top: Magic Cottage opens to a private sundeck, now featuring an antique claw-foot bath, beside the Takou River.
Opposite bottom left: The interior of Magic Cottage includes a super-king-size bed, ensuite and fully equipped kitchen.
Opposite bottom right: Magic Cottage features total seclusion and privacy for guests on the riverside with extensive estuarine views.

15

The Summer House

Hosts Christine and Rod Brown

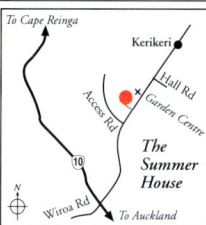

To Cape Reinga · Kerikeri · Hall Rd · Garden Centre · **The Summer House** · Access Rd · 10 · Wiroa Rd · *To Auckland*

424 Kerikeri Road, Kerikeri, Bay of Islands   *Mobile* 027 409 288
Phone 0-9-407 4294   *Email* summerhouse@xtra.co.nz
Fax 0-9-407 4297   *Website* www.thesummerhouse.co.nz

DIRECTIONS: From Whangarei, take SH 1 north to Pakaraka. Turn right into SH 10 & travel 18km. Then turn right into Kerikeri Rd & travel 1.7km to The Summer House on left, 1.5km from Kerikeri village.

| 3 bdrm | 2 enst | 1 prbth | 1 pdrm | **Double $215–$285** **Single $195** | *Includes breakfast* |

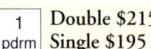

Summer House

The Summer House is an architecturally designed French Provincial-style home, built using energy conservation principles. Set in a hectare of citrus orchard with a subtropical garden and pond, The Summer House offers a peaceful retreat close to Kerikeri village. Upstairs are two ensuite guest bedrooms, one with a queen-size Victorian brass bed and the other a queen antique French bed. A comfortable guest lounge provides tea and coffee-making facilities. Downstairs is the self-contained Pacific Pavilion with super-king/twin bed, dressing room, private bathroom, kitchenette for self-catering, and a private guest entrance and deck. Christine serves gourmet breakfasts in the dining room or patio overlooking the water feature.

FACILITIES

- 1 super-king/twin suite with kitchenette, decking & private entrance
- 2 queen bedrooms upstairs, both with ensuite bathrooms
- hair dryer, toiletries & heated towel rails in all bathrooms
- cotton bed linen; fresh flowers
- guest lounge with bar & tea/coffee-making facilities
- broadband, fax & TV available
- gourmet breakfast served in dining room, with organic coffee/tea & free-range eggs
- German & French spoken
- off-street parking
- courtesy transfer to/from Kerikeri airport
- Birman cat, Panda, on site
- world's 1st B&B environmentally benchmarked by Green Globe 21

ACTIVITIES AVAILABLE

- picking citrus fruit; subtropical garden, pond & native forest walk
- cafés/restaurants/shops, 1.5km
- diving, fishing, sailing, kayaking
- Kerikeri Golf Course, nearby
- Waitangi Golf Course & Treaty House, 20-min drive
- Kauri Cliffs Golf Course, 30 mins
- pre-European Maori fishing village
- kiwi viewing by night, in season
- vineyards & wineries
- craft shops & galleries trail
- boat charters arranged
- historic buildings & sites
- Puketi forest giant kauri trees, 20-min drive
- beaches, swimming
- dolphin watching, 20 mins
- day trips to Cape Reinga, Doubtless Bay, etc

KERIKERI
Sommerfields Lodge

Hosts Sandra and Bob Murphy

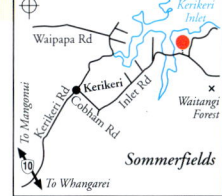

405A Inlet Road, Kerikeri   *Postal* P O Box 726, Kerikeri
Phone 0-9-407 9889   *Mobile* 027 441 1689   *Fax* 0-9-407 1648
Email hosts@sommerfields.co.nz   *Website* www.sommerfields.co.nz

DIRECTIONS: From SH 10 turn east to Kerikeri. At roundabout turn right into Hobson Ave, then right again into Cobham Rd. Turn left into Inlet Rd. Travel 4km & cross one-way bridge to Sommerfields on left.

| 3 bdrm | 3 enst | Room rate $335–$435 | Includes breakfast | Dinner extra |

Sommerfields provides uninterrupted views from every room over pastureland to the historic Kerikeri Inlet waterway. Architecturally designed to capture the all-day sun, Sommerfields offers three super-king or twin guestrooms, each with an ensuite bathroom and private deck. An exclusive-use guest entrance and guest lounge ensure privacy and comfort. Personalised service in a relaxing environment is enhanced by the tranquil surroundings. Evening dining is by prior arrangement and features the freshest of local produce. Sommerfields is only minutes from Kerikeri's cafés, restaurants, shops and historic buildings. Guests enjoy the Kauri Cliffs Golf Course, award-winning wineries, watersports and other Bay of Islands attractions.

FACILITIES

- 3 super-king/twin bedrooms
- 3 ensuites with hair dryers, heated floors, heated towel rails, bathrobes & toiletries
- spa bath, dual basins & double shower in Premium ensuite
- cotton bed linen, writing desk, internet jack, TV, coffee/tea, ceiling fan, fridge, iron & board in all 3 bedrooms
- phone, fax, email, photocopying

- full cooked breakfast
- 3-course dinner, $60 pp, wine list available
- laundry by arrangement
- private guest lounge with open fire
- private decks from bedrooms
- Japanese spoken
- courtesy B of I airport transfer; on-site parking

ACTIVITIES AVAILABLE

- 18-hole golf courses inluding Kauri Cliffs
- award-winning wineries, 5 mins
- Historic Stone Store
- Kemp Mission House
- historic Treaty House at Waitangi, 20-min drive
- walk into Waitangi Forest
- steam sawmill, 5-min drive
- Kerikeri centre, 5.1km

- restaurants, 7-min drive
- arts & crafts trails
- private boat charters
- Rainbow Falls; Rewa's Village
- Kerikeri Inlet steamboat rides
- all-weather tennis club
- numerous beach excursions
- deep-sea fishing
- Cape Reinga trips & Bay of Islands boat tours

RANGITANE, KERIKERI
Fernbrook

Hosts Margaret and Robert Cooper

Kurapari Road, Rangitane, R D 1, Kerikeri
Phone 0-9-407 8570   *Email* tfc@igrin.co.nz
Fax 0-9-407 8572   *Website* friars.co.nz/hosts/fernbrook.html

5 bdrm	5 enst

Room rate in house $200–$220
Apartment rate $230

Includes breakfast
Cottage rate $300–$400

Dinner extra
Self-catering

Meals extra

DIRECTIONS: Take SH 10 north & bypass Kerikeri turn-off. Turn right into Kapiro Rd & travel 4km. Turn left into Redcliffs Rd. Continue to T junction, turn right & travel 1km. Take Kurapari Rd to Fernbrook, 2nd drive on right.

Fernbrook covers 27 hectares (65 acres) reaching from the Kerikeri Inlet uphill to the homestead, through native bush with tree ferns, a stream and waterfall. Set in an extensive garden including olive, macadamia nut and citrus trees, the large cedar homestead offers two ensuite guestrooms (*see below, left*). The library and sitting room are furnished with antiques, oriental rugs and original artworks. Self-catering accommodation is also provided in a semi-detached one-bedroom apartment, and a restored two-bedroom beachfront cottage originally built in 1917. Meals are served in the homestead dining room or on the terrace overlooking the bay, and guests can listen to the evening call of the kiwi, and walk through the bush to the secluded beach.

FACILITIES

- homestead:
  2 queen ensuite bedrooms
- self-contained apartment:
  1 queen ensuite bedroom upstairs
- self-contained cottage:
  1 king, 1 queen, ensuite bedrooms
- hair dryers, toiletries & heated towel rails in bathrooms
- cotton bed linen, fresh flowers, TV
- open fire, Sky TV, video, CD-player, & piano in sitting room in house

- gourmet breakfast served in house or alfresco on terrace; $15 pp for cottage/apartment guests
- picnic lunch on request
- 3-course dinner in house with wine, $55 pp
- 2 self-catering kitchens
- French spoken; laundry available
- on-site parking

ACTIVITIES AVAILABLE

- BBQ on site
- pétanque & croquet on site
- brown kiwi sanctuary on site
- fishing; painting & sketching
- secluded beach & bush walks
- golf at Kauri Cliffs & Waitangi
- swimming; scuba diving
- charter sailing by arrangement
- boat tours in bay; watersports

- Kerikeri restaurants, 12km
- horse riding; hiking
- Kerikeri gardens & orchards open to visit
- Kerikeri Stone Store & Kemp House, 10-min drive
- historic sites; kauri forest
- scenic flights; paragliding
- arts & crafts trail
- day trips to Cape Reinga

KERIKERI
Ora Ora Eco-Wellness Resort

Hosts Inge Bremer and Rolf Mueller-Glodde

28 Landing Road, Kerikeri, Bay of Islands
Phone 0-9-407 3598   *Email* inge@oraoraresort.co.nz
Fax 0-9-407 8712   *Website* www.oraoraresort.co.nz

DIRECTIONS: From Auckland, take SH 1 north to Pakaraka. Turn right into SH 10. Turn right to Kerikeri. Continue on Landing Rd past the Stone Store & cross bridge. Ora Ora Eco-Wellness Resort is 200m on left.

7 bdrm	5 enst	1 prbth	1 pdrm

Villa rate $210–$570

Includes breakfast
Lunch, dinner & treatments extra

Ora Ora Eco-Wellness Resort is set in subtropical permaculture gardens surrounded by the Kerikeri River Basin Reserve where New Zealand's oldest buildings are located. "Ora" means "zest, health and contentment" in Maori. The Resort provides six private villas featuring Asian arts. Organic gourmet food, juices and wines are served at Makai Restaurant, which caters for all diets, and rejuvenating spa-treatments are offered at the private Maora Wellness Centre. Ecology and permaculture are combined with comfort, health and personal service. The herb garden, orchard and wildflower meadows provide a holistic experience for guests. There is direct access to the well-known Rainbow Waterfall walk and the Kerikeri Basin with its numerous activities.

FACILITIES

- 6 villas: 1 super-king/twin with kitchenette, 3 king/twin, 1 single, & 1 with 2 bedrooms: king/twin & queen & kitchen
- all villas include ensuite, lounge area, private deck, mineral water, tea/coffee, nibbles, fruit, radio, TV & direct-dial phone/internet
- hair dryers, toiletries, bathrobes, slippers & 1 double spa bath
- hosts speak German, Spanish & French
- in-house organic restaurant
- Wellness Centre for massage, bodywork, reflexology, yoga, Kneipp hydrotherapy, Finnish sauna & plunge pool
- reunions, meetings, seminars & health programmes
- piano lounge with Sky TV
- guest laundry on site
- 12 parking spaces on-site; courtesy passenger transfer

ACTIVITIES AVAILABLE

- Wellness Centre treatments, extra
- star gazing; meditation pond
- historic Stone Store & Mission House, Rewa's Maori Village, Kororipo Pa, 200m
- steamboat rides, 200m
- steam sawmill, 3km
- Kerikeri township, 3km
- art galleries & shops
- Puketi Kauri Forest, 15km
- Matauri Beach, 35km
- Ngawha hot springs, 35km
- Rainbow Falls walk, nearby
- native kiwi watching, 12km
- sailing on 17m (51-ft) yacht
- cruises in Doves Bay, 13km
- swimming with dolphins; fishing; scuba diving, 35km
- 4 golf courses, 4–30km
- air/bus trips to Cape Reinga

Ora Ora Resort

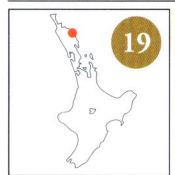
Paihia/Kerikeri, Bay of Islands
Appledore Lodge

Hosts Janet and Jim Pugh

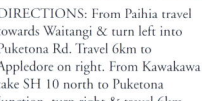

624 Puketona Road, Paihia/Kerikeri   *Phone* 0-9-402 8007
Mobile 021 179 5839   *Email* appledorelodge@xtra.co.nz
Fax 0-9-402 8007   *Website* www.appledorelodge.co.nz

<VT>

DIRECTIONS: From Paihia travel towards Waitangi & turn left into Puketona Rd. Travel 6km to Appledore on right. From Kawakawa take SH 10 north to Puketona Junction, turn right & travel 6km.

| 4 bdrm | 4 enst | Apartment rate $160–$230 Room rate $150 | Includes breakfast basket Includes breakfast | Self-catering | | | | | |

Set in a large garden on Waitangi River, Appledore Lodge features private river frontage with uninterrupted rural views over farmland to the forest beyond. A full home-made breakfast is served to house guests from the Victoria Room on the ancient kauri table in the dining room or alfresco on the grand deck overlooking the river. The Victoria Room features Queen Anne-style furniture including a draped four-poster double bed. The Riverside Suite is furnished in native rimu, and an adjacent cottage purpose-built in 2002 accommodates four guests and has a spacious lounge with river views. Adjoining is a self-contained studio with wheelchair access. Home-made continental breakfast baskets are supplied to the suite, cottage and studio.

FACILITIES

- main house: Riverside Suite with 1 super-king/twin ensuite bedroom, dressing room & TV; Victoria Room with 1 double ensuite & bath
- cottage: 1 super-king/twin ensuite bedroom, 1 double sofa bed, writing desk & TV in lounge, kitchen & laundry
- studio: 1 queen ensuite bedroom with wheelchair access & kitchen

- full breakfast, or continental breakfast basket for suite, cottage & studio guests
- hair dryer, toiletries & heated towel rails in all 4 ensuites
- email, fax & phone available
- children over 12 years
- in-house laundry service, $10
- courtesy passenger transfer
- on-site parking; helipad

ACTIVITIES AVAILABLE

- golden retriever, Misty, on site
- outdoor spa pool on site
- 2 mountain bikes for guest use
- reserve walk on site
- jet ski hire; kayaks, parasailing
- sailing/motorised yacht trips
- deep-sea fishing for marlin
- scenic flights; microlite flying
- watersports; skydiving; Zorb ride

- restaurants in Paihia, 6km
- horse or quad bike treks
- Waitangi Treaty House & Golf Course, 6 mins
- Paihia beach, 6km
- Kerikeri, 15-min drive
- gardens open to visit
- swimming with dolphins
- day trips to Cape Reinga
- Auckland, 3½ hours

PAIHIA, BAY OF ISLANDS
Abri Apartments

Hosts Terrie and Bill Wood

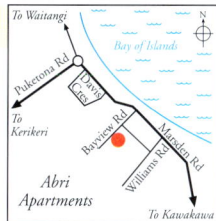

10/12 Bayview Road, Paihia, Bay of Islands   *Postal* P O Box 509, Paihia
Phone 0-9-402 8003   *Email* abriaccom@xtra.co.nz
Fax 0-9-402 8035   *Website* www.abri-accom.co.nz

DIRECTIONS: From Kawakawa, travel for about 20 mins towards Paihia. Continue down Seaview Rd, into Marsden Rd. Turn left into Bayview Rd. Abri Apartments on left.

| 3 bdrm | 3 prbth | Apartment/suite rate $130–$250 | *Includes breakfast basket for 1st morning Self-catering in apartments* | |

Located in the heart of the Bay of Islands, in the small coastal town of Paihia, Abri Apartments comprise two stand-alone studios and one suite, all with sea views. Each is spacious and individually styled, incorporating native timbers, in contemporary design, with accommodation for one couple per studio or suite. Nestled in gardens, Abri Apartments are north facing to benefit from all-day sun, with private decks providing panoramic views of the Bay of Islands to Russell and beyond. Guests enjoy the short stroll to the beach and to Paihia's shops, cafés and restaurants, or they can self-cater in the full kitchens of Abri's two self-contained apartments if preferred. A breakfast basket is supplied for the first morning and a barbecue is available on request.

FACILITIES

- 2 self-contained studios each with 1 queen bedroom & 1 private bathroom with double spa bath in each
- 1 suite with queen bedroom & private bathroom
- hair dryer, heated towel rails, demist mirror, bathrobes & toiletries in all 3 bathrooms
- 3 lounges with tea/coffee, TV, video & music
- complimentary breakfast basket on 1st morning
- full cooking facilities for self-catering & filtered water in 2 studio apartments
- fresh flowers in rooms
- air-conditioning
- private decks with BBQ
- private guest entrances
- off-street parking

ACTIVITIES AVAILABLE

- boat & bird-watching on site
- beach, 2-min walk
- restaurants in walking distance
- marlin & line fishing
- watersports; scuba diving
- Cape Reinga bus tour
- vehicular & passenger ferries
- Hole-in-the-Rock cruise
- historic Waitangi
- golf course; tennis courts
- sailing & parasailing
- swimming with dolphins
- bush walking
- horse riding
- sea kayaking & canoeing
- kauri forest, 1-hour drive
- Russell, by ferry or car
- Kerikeri, 20-min drive

PAIHIA, BAY OF ISLANDS
Paihia Beach Resort and Spa

Hosts Helen and Ray Arnesen

116 Marsden Road, Paihia   *Postal* P O Box 180, Paihia
Freephone 0800 870 111   *Phone* 0-9-402 6140   *Fax* 0-9-402 6026
Email pbr@xtra.co.nz   *Website* www.paihiabeach.co.nz

23 bdrm	23 enst

Room rate $450–$670   *Includes breakfast & steam/sauna session*
Lunch & dinner extra   *Self-catering*

DIRECTIONS: From Auckland, take SH 1 to Kawakawa turn-off. Continue straight ahead for 17km to Paihia. Travel on Marsden Rd along waterfront to Paihia Beach Resort on the left.

Paihia Beach Resort

Paihia Beach Resort and Spa is part of La Spa Naturale Day Spa (*see opposite page 37*). Offering an international spa experience, this five-star waterfront property features unobstructed sea views from every studio and suite, and is located on Ti Bay – one of the premier beaches in Paihia. All apartments are spaciously furnished, with air-conditioning, DVD-players and hi-fi systems. Each ensuite includes a spa bath with candles and bath gel, bathrobes, slippers and chocolates. Guests enjoy the resort facilities such as the 20-metre salt-water heated swimming pool and large jacuzzi, licensed poolside restaurant, and the new Day Spa, offering a full range of body and water treatments and Corporate Wellness programmes, from 30 minutes to five-day packages.

FACILITIES

- 2 family 2-bedroom suites, each with 2 ensuites & 2 baths
- 10 king suites each with ensuite & full kitchen
- 9 queen/twin studios, each with ensuite & kitchenette
- bathrobes, hair dryers & toiletries in all bathrooms, 18 with whirlpool spa baths
- direct-dial phone per bedroom
- 1 wheelchair access bathroom

- full à la carte gourmet breakfast
- The Black Rocks in-house poolside restaurant open for breakfast, Spa lunch, cocktail hour & dinner, extra
- La Spa Naturale Day Spa, extra
- mini-bar; email & fax service; guest laundry
- air-conditioning, TV, DVD & hi-fi equipment in rooms
- under-cover parking

ACTIVITIES AVAILABLE

- in-house conferences & Corporate Spa Wellness programmes
- panoramic heated 20m swimming pool & jacuzzi
- private sauna & steam-rooms
- massages, facials, body treatments, manicures, pedicures by qualified therapists, extra
- Day Spa packages for couples
- sailing, fishing & dolphin watching trips

- Paihia shops & wharf, easy walk away
- Waitangi & Kauri Cliffs golf courses
- Waitangi Treaty House
- bush & coastal walks
- boutique vineyard nearby
- Bay of Islands cruises
- day trips to Cape Reinga
- Auckland, 3-hr drive south

Paihia Beach Resort

Paihia Beach Resort

Paihia, Bay of Islands
La Spa Naturale Day Spa

Hosts Helen and Ray Arnesen

116 Marsden Road, Paihia   *Postal* P O Box 180, Paihia
Freephone 0800 870 111   *Phone* 0-9-402 6140   *Fax* 0-9-402 6026
Email pbr@xtra.co.nz   *Website* www.paihiabeach.co.nz

21 trtmnt rm	6 day-spa rm

Treatment rate $25–$415   *Day packages include Spa lunch*

DIRECTIONS: From Auckland, take SH 1 to Kawakawa turn-off. Continue for 17km to Paihia. Travel on Marsden Rd along waterfront to Paihia Beach Resort. Turn left into Davis Cres. La Spa Naturale immediately on left.

Voted by Condé Nast (UK), as one of the top 10 spas in the South Pacific, La Spa Naturale is the Day Spa located at Paihia Beach Resort (*see opposite page 36*) on the waterfront at Paihia. Opened in 2003, this five-star facility offers an international health spa experience. Located in a private garden setting, La Spa Naturale features cascading waterfalls and candlelit treatment rooms with tranquil music throughout. Fully qualified beauty and massage therapists offer a range of day treatments from half an hour to five-day packages. La Spa Naturale provides relaxing, nourishing and revitalising treatments for in-house guests and day visitors.

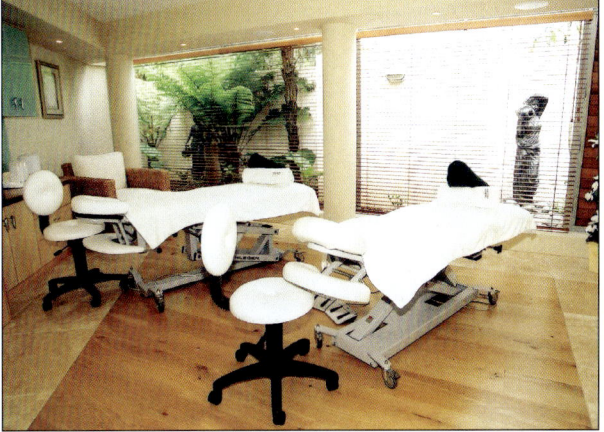

Facilities

- 21 in-house treatment rooms
- 6 day-spa treatment areas
- selection of herbal teas
- quality spa products for sale
- pedicure chair with heat & massage controls & foot spa
- manicure & make-up areas
- double massage room
- Vichy shower room with 8-head shower roses
- fusion shower room for wet treatments & mud wraps
- changing room with private lockers & toilet facilities
- private sauna with double shower & changing area
- private steam-room with shower & changing area
- 20m saltwater heated pool & jacuzzi spa pool
- licensed poolside restaurant with panoramic sea views

Activities available

- Corporate Wellness Programme: for health & well-being
- packages for her: "Girls Day In", "Bride-to-be-Day", "Aromarine Bliss", "Delightful Indulgence"
- packages for him: "Relaxation Day for Men", "Executive Break", "Groom's Day"
- facial treatents for him & her: deep cleansing & Darphin signature treatments
- massage: Swedish, deep tissue, aromatherapy, reflexology, shiatsu, Indian head massage
- body treatments: "Darphin Signature", "Absolute Heaven", "Marine Magic", "Vichy Shower", "Jet Lag Solution"
- manicure & pedicure
- waxing for him & her
- Darphin make-up: weddings & bridal parties, special occasions
- gift vouchers for Mother's Day, Valentine's Day, special occasions

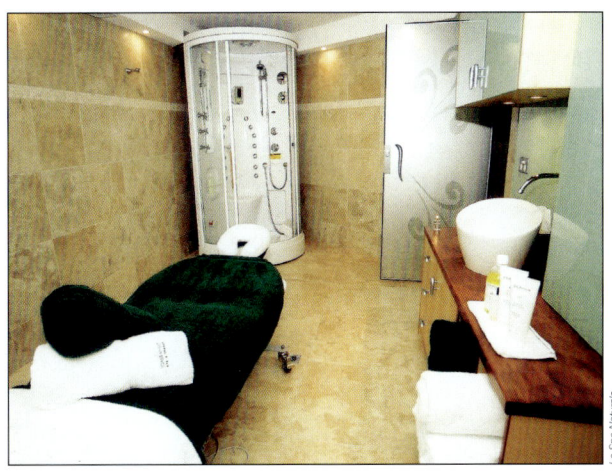

PAIHIA, BAY OF ISLANDS
Chalet Romantica

Hosts Inge and Ed Amsler

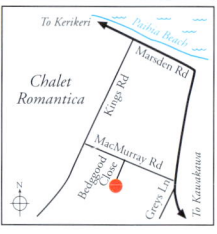

6 Bedggood Close, Paihia, Bay of Islands   *Phone* 0-9-402 8270
Freephone 0800 124 253   *Email* chalet-romantica@xtra.co.nz
Fax 0-9-402 8278   *Website* chaletromantica.homestead.com/accom1.html

DIRECTIONS: From Auckland, take SH 1 to Kawakawa turn-off. Continue straight ahead for 17km to Paihia. Turn left into MacMurray Rd, then left again up Bedggood Close. Chalet Romantica at top of road.

| 3 bdrm | 2 enst | 1 prbth | **Room/suite rate $135–$225** Off-season rates available | *Includes breakfast* *Self-catering in suites or breakfast extra* | |

Nestled on a hillside with expansive views over the village and bay, yet only a short stroll from the beach and town centre of Paihia, Chalet Romantica is a spacious Swiss chalet-style complex. Accommodation comprises three options, each featuring private balconies overlooking the sea. Guests in the queen-size bedroom, with a separate private bathroom, are served a gourmet breakfast with fresh fruit, muesli, freshly baked breads, croissants and eggs. Two king-size suites include ensuites and kitchen facilities for self-catering, with breakfast optional. Edi skippers day and overnight charters on his 14-metre Catalina yacht, while Inge runs the Chalet, popular for special occasions. Guests enjoy the indoor exerjet swimming pool, spa pool and mini-gym.

FACILITIES

- 2 super-king/twin suites each with ensuite, kitchen facilities, private lounge & balcony
- 1 queen bedroom with private bathroom & bathrobes, tea/coffee, fridge & balcony
- hair dryers, heated towel rails
- full-length mirror, sewing kit & fresh flowers in each guestroom
- sea views, phone, TV, video & CD-player in each guestroom
- gourmet breakfast served in conservatory for queen room, or $15 pp extra for suites
- hosts' Swiss Café & Grill for meals in Paihia, 5-min walk
- fax & email available
- German & French spoken
- self-service laundry, $3
- local courtesy transfer
- ample secure parking

ACTIVITIES AVAILABLE

- in-house gym equipment
- indoor spa pool & heated swimming pool with exerjets
- skippered private yacht charter, www.yachtcharter.homestead.com/nz1.html
- safe, sandy swimming beaches
- Waitangi Treaty House, 2 mins
- historic Russell, 15-min car ferry
- marlin & light tackle fishing
- restaurants & Paihia township, 5-min walk
- tennis court, short walk
- sailing; kayaking
- dolphin/whale watching
- Bay of Islands cruises
- golfing, 2-min drive
- gardens to visit; hiking
- day trips to Cape Reinga & Ninety Mile Beach

Chalet Romantica

OPUA, BAY OF ISLANDS
Crows Nest Holiday Homes

Manager Marj Browning

20 Sir George Back Street, Opua, Bay of Islands   *Postal* P O Box 176, Paihia
Phone 0-9-402 7783   *Mobile* 027 210 5242   *Fax* 0-9-402 7783
Email marj@vivid.net.nz   *Website* www.crowsnest.co.nz

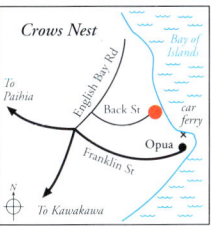

DIRECTIONS: 3-hour drive from Auckland. From Kawakawa, turn right & travel towards Opua. At intersection, continue into English Bay Rd. Turn 1st right into Back St. Crows Nest at end of cul-de-sac. Yacht moorings.

4 bdrm	4 enst	Room rate $280–$550 Low-season rates available	*Includes continental breakfast for 1st morning* *Self-catering*

Crows Nest Holiday Homes are perched on a cliff above the sea at Opua, where the port activities and yacht haven provide endless interest below. Two individually designed and crafted villas offer exclusive accommodation for up to four guests each. A nautical theme unifying the villas includes porthole windows. The "Bridge Deck" offers two queen ensuite bedrooms, separated by the living area featuring swing couches, kwila flooring and canopied deck beyond overlooking Opua Bay. "Sails", with queen and twin ensuite bedrooms, features large bi-fold doors and windows opening to the sea views. The queen bedroom opens to a private sundeck for relaxing above the bay. Guests need to phone, in order to be met on arrival.

FACILITIES

- single-party bookings
- 2 separate self-contained villas
- Bridge Deck: 2 queen bedrooms with ensuite bathrooms
- Sails: 1 queen & 1 twin ensuite bedroom
- host off-site ensuring guest privacy
- servicing by arrangement
- hair dryers, heated towel rails
- sea views
- continental breakfast supplied for 1st morning
- 2 fully equipped kitchens for self-catering
- 1 lounge with TV & music per villa
- laundry in each villa
- 1 villa with sundeck
- children welcome
- secure off-street parking

ACTIVITIES AVAILABLE

- yacht moorings adjacent
- yacht charter from Opua Wharf
- restaurant at Opua Wharf
- historic Waitangi Treaty House
- boat tours around the bay
- golf at Waitangi, 10-min drive
- car ferry to Russell from Opua
- dolphin watching from Paihia
- historic Kerikeri, 30-min drive
- cafés & restaurants at Paihia & Russell
- watersports
- swimming & diving
- Hole-in-the-Rock cruise
- Fullers cruises
- deep-sea fishing charters
- private gardens to visit
- Ninety Mile Beach
- Cape Reinga day tour

OPUA, BAY OF ISLANDS

Harbour House Villa

Hosts Robert and Masae Serge

7 English Bay Road, Opua, Bay of Islands
Phone 0-9-402 8087   *Email* stay@harbourhousevilla.com
Fax 0-9-402 8688   *Website* www.harbourhousevilla.com

DIRECTIONS: From Auckland, take SH 1 past Whangarei to Kawakawa. Take SH 11 for 12km towards Opua. At intersection, cross into English Bay Rd. Travel 500m to Harbour House Villa on right.

3 bdrm	3 enst	2 pdrm	Room rate $200–$295	*Includes breakfast*	*Lunch & dinner extra*
			Apartment rate $260–$590	*Includes breakfast provisions*	*Self-catering*

Featuring panoramic sea views of the Bay of Islands, Harbour House Villa is located on a promontory overlooking the scenic Opua recreational marina. All guestrooms have water views. The Villa has been designed to include aspects of Masae's Japanese culture. The upstairs living room opens to a large viewing deck where guests can watch sailing races, boating activities and some of the 500 yachts from around the world that enter the harbour each summer to escape the northern winter. If notified the night before, Masae serves Japanese breakfast, in the dining room or alfresco on the deck. Bob prepares the western cuisine. Lunch and dinner are available by arrangement, or guests can use the barbecue and self-cater if preferred.

FACILITIES

- 1 king & 1 queen/twin ensuite bedroom, can be 2-bedroom apartment with lounge, TV & kitchen
- 1 super-king/twin bedroom apartment with ensuite, lounge, TV & kitchen
- hair dryers, toiletries, heated towel rails, demist mirrors & bath or spa bath in ensuites
- 2 powder rooms; laundry; children welcome

- full breakfast or supplies
- lunch & à la carte dinner by request; complimentary wine
- 2 full self-catering kitchens
- upstairs lounge with Sky & World TV, DVD, CDs, books, grand piano, artwork, desk, phone, fax & computer station
- Japanese spoken
- on-site parking; courtesy passenger transfer

ACTIVITIES AVAILABLE

- tours & itinerary assistance
- playing & listening to acoustic/digital grand piano
- small spa pool
- access via on-site garden & bush to coastal walking path & beach for swimming, fishing or shellfish collecting
- Opua wharf, boat charters & sea fishing, 15-min walk
- rainforest, 20-min walk

- Paihia restaurants, 3-hour scenic walk or 7-min drive
- sea kayaking, scuba diving, scenic flights, golf & horse riding at Paihia
- swimming with dolphins
- historic Russell by Opua ferry
- Waitangi Treaty grounds, Maori culture, golf course
- Cape Reinga day trips
- Auckland, 3½ hours south

Opua, Bay of Islands
The Boathouse Opua

Manager Wendy Younger

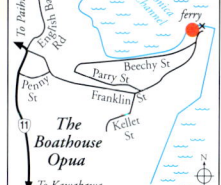
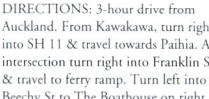

Beechy Street, Opua   *Postal* c/- 5 Richardson Street, Opua
Freephone 0800 683 722   *Email* info@theboathouseopua.com
Phone 0-9-402 6800   *Website* www.theboathouseopua.com

3 bdrm	1 enst	1 prbth

Apartment rate $500
Winter & weekly rates available

Self-catering

No meals available
High-season surcharge

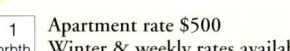

DIRECTIONS: 3-hour drive from Auckland. From Kawakawa, turn right into SH 11 & travel towards Paihia. At intersection turn right into Franklin St & travel to ferry ramp. Turn left into Beechy St to The Boathouse on right.

The Boathouse provides over-water accommodation in two contemporary self-contained apartments, designed with a nautical theme. Upstairs is The Bridge apartment and downstairs is The Landing, both with spacious decks over the water, reminiscent of the prow of a boat. Opened in 2002, both apartments feature a large, fully equipped kitchen, each including dishwasher drawer, fridge/freezer with ice-maker, full oven, coffee machine and floating floor. The Bridge offers a king-size bedroom with dressing room and office, and The Landing has two bedrooms. Located adjacent to the Opua car ferry, the Boathouse offers endless 270-degree views of boating activities from the deck, where guests can also enjoy fishing and barbecues.

FACILITIES

- The Bridge upstairs apartment: 1 king ensuite bedroom with dressing room, 1 queen sofa-bed in office, dining/lounge & writing desk
- The Landing downstairs apartment: 1 king/twin & 1 twin bedroom, 1 bathroom & dining/lounge
- hair dryer, toiletries, heated towel rails, heated floor, bidet in bathrooms
- Sky TV, video, DVD, music & CDs in both apartments
- full kitchen for self-catering per apartment
- central heating
- phone, fax & jacks
- guest laundry
- children welcome
- spacious decking
- monitored security system
- 270° sea views
- off-street parking

ACTIVITIES AVAILABLE

- gas BBQ on decks on site
- on-site fishing from lower deck
- Opua marina; beach; diving
- sailing charters; kayaks
- coastal walkway; golf courses
- swimming with dolphins
- bus tours; boat tours
- vineyards & wine trails
- car rental; scenic flights
- restaurants in Paihia, 10 mins
- superette & bakery adjacent
- car ferry, 4-min crossing every 20 mins, 5-min drive to Russell
- arts & crafts in Kerikeri, 30 mins
- Hole-in-Rock trips
- gardens open to visit in Kerikeri
- Waitangi Treaty House; Kemp House; Stone Store; Pompallier
- Auckland City, 3½ hours south

The Boathouse

27

Orongo Bay Homestead

Hosts Michael Hooper and Chris Wharehinga Swannell

Orongo Bay Homestead

Aucks Road, R D 1, Russell, Bay of Islands
Freephone 0800 242 627   Phone 0-9-403 7527   Fax 0-9-403 7675
Email bookings@thehomestead.co.nz   *Website* www.thehomestead.co.nz

DIRECTIONS: Take Twin Coast Discovery Route 1 hour north of Whangarei. Travel via Kawakawa to Opua. Take car ferry to Russell. Travel 2 mins towards Russell township. At Orongo Bay, Homestead is on right.

4 bdrm	4 enst	Double $650 Single $400	*Includes breakfast* Weekend & off-season rates available	*Dinner extra*

Orongo Bay

This fully restored historic homestead was built in the 1860s for the first American Consular Agent in New Zealand. Now set in organic gardens with sweeping views of Orongo Bay, this country home features original native timbers including the kauri ceilings, large open fire and 1000-bottle underground wine cellar. Peacefully sited on seven spring-fed hectares (17 acres), the two-bedroom homestead is complemented by the separate garden Retreat, with the Pacific Suite upstairs overlooking the duck pond. There are sea, bush or meadow views from each bedroom. The resident hosts serve gourmet dinners by prior arrangement, matching each course with wine from the cellar. Healthy organic luxury food is the keynote at Orongo Bay Homestead.

FACILITIES

- 4 super-king/twin bedrooms
- 4 ensuites; 1 with spa bath & 1 with double basin
- hair dryers, heated towel rails, bathrobes & toiletries
- wheelchair access to Retreat
- DVD/CD systems in rooms
- broadband internet available
- fine art collection
- laundry available, $30

- "Bubbly Bakehouse Breakfast" with à la carte options, served until midday in dining room
- 4-course gourmet table d'hôte dinner, served in dining room, fireside, or on verandah, $120 pp
- complimentary coffee, teas & cookies available
- turn-down service
- open fire & grand piano in lounge
- helicopter landing area

ACTIVITIES AVAILABLE

- dry Finnish lakeside sauna
- massage by appointment
- native bush walk on 7ha (17 acres) of private coastal land, including wildlife pond on site
- swimming at nearby beaches
- boating
- kayaking
- organic culinary garden tours
- aquatic activities

- several golf courses nearby, including Kauri Cliffs
- Russell township, 5-min drive
- world record big-game fishing
- restaurants nearby
- vineyard visits & tastings
- swimming with dolphins
- Bay of Islands sightseeing
- flightseeing, including fly/ 4WD to tip of North Island

Orongo Bay

Orongo Bay

ORONGO BAY, RUSSELL

Hardings' – Aotearoa Lodge

Hosts Barbara and Trevor Harding

Orongo Bay Farm, Aucks Road, R D 1, Russell, Bay of Islands
Phone 0-9-403 7277   *Mobile* 021 184 2023   *Fax* 0-9-403 7277
Email info@the-lodge.co.nz   *Website* www.the-lodge.co.nz

DIRECTIONS: From Auckland take SH 1 north to Kawakawa. Turn right to SH 11 & travel to Opua. Take car ferry for Russell. Drive 2 mins towards Russell township. At Orongo Bay, Hardings' – Aotearoa is on right.

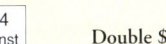

4 bdrm	4 enst	**Double $200–$285**	**Single $185–$250**	*Includes breakfast*

Overlooking Orongo Bay and a scenic reserve, midway between the car ferry and Russell, is Hardings' – Aotearoa Lodge. Set in two and a half hectares (seven acres) of rolling countryside, the Lodge provides two ensuite guestrooms upstairs, with adjoining lounge and balcony, and two further ensuite super-king rooms in Brook Barn down the driveway. Originally built in the late 1970s, the Lodge has been extensively refurbished to provide quality accommodation. A full breakfast of fresh fruit and home-made muesli, as well as a special cooked dish daily using free-range eggs from the property, is served in the breakfast room or alfresco on the deck. The sauna and spa pool are popular on the separate secluded deck, and guests enjoy dining at historic Russell nearby.

FACILITIES

- 2 super-king/twin ensuite bedrooms in Brook Barn, each with lounge & deck
- 2 queen ensuite bedrooms upstairs in house
- cotton bed linen
- hair dryers, heated towel rails, bathrobes & toiletries
- fans, tea/coffee & mineral water in bedrooms
- laundry available, $15
- breakfast served in breakfast room or alfresco on deck
- lounge downstairs with open fire, Sky TV, CD-player & games
- guest lounge upstairs with phone jack & balcony; phone available
- decks & patios from lounges & barn; large spa pool decking
- on-site parking
- outdoor pets on site

ACTIVITIES AVAILABLE

- sauna & spa pool on site
- bicycles for guest use
- snorkelling; scuba diving
- fishing; swimming; sailing
- swimming with dolphins
- canoes & kayaks for hire
- Waitangi Treaty House
- historic buildings & locations
- Russell township, 5-min drive
- restaurants, 5-min drive
- scenic flights & cruises
- vineyards & wine tasting
- golf courses; gardens to visit
- 4WD day trips to Cape Reinga & 90 Mile Beach
- car ferry, 3-min drive
- Kerikeri, 25-min drive
- Auckland 3½ hours south

RUSSELL
Kimberley Lodge

Hosts Jenny Wilson and Chris North

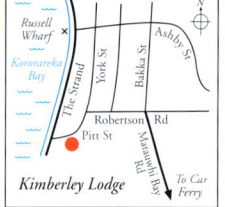

2 Pitt Street, Russell, Bay of Islands   *Postal* P O Box 166, Russell
Phone 0-9-403 7090   *Email* kimlodge@ihug.co.nz
Fax 0-9-403 7239   *Website* www.lodges.co.nz

DIRECTIONS: Take car ferry from Opua. Travel 8km to Russell township. Turn left into Robertson Rd, left again at intersection with York St. Turn bend to Kimberley Lodge's white gates on left. Use intercom to notify hosts.

5 bdrm	5 enst	**Double** $695–$845	*Includes continental breakfast & cocktail hour*
		Single $660–$805	**Honeymoon package & low-season rates available**

Built in 1989 in colonial style, Kimberley Lodge features classic symmetrical architecture with native timber panelling and hand-crafted furniture. Overlooking the Bay of Islands and the historic township of Russell, most rooms have panoramic views. Each bedroom has a spacious ensuite including bath, double basins and bidet. The Kimberley Room ensuite features a double spa bath with television, stereo and phone. Continental breakfast is served alfresco, or in the dining room with its sea views. Guests can easily walk to the many restaurants and cafés in Russell. The swimming beach is also within walking distance and visiting the historic buildings is popular. There is a heated swimming pool on site, with exer-jets for the energetic.

FACILITIES

- 5 super-king/twin bedrooms
- 5 ensuites each with bidet, double basins, bath, bathrobes, toiletries, hair dryer & heated towel rails
- spa bath in Kimberley Room
- TV & phone in each bedroom
- fax, photocopier & internet access
- air-conditioning & heating
- private guest verandahs
- children 15 yrs & over welcome

- continental breakfast, served in dining room or alfresco
- fully licensed
- guest laundry facilities
- luggage lift
- security gate
- burglar alarms
- private on-site parking
- guest transfer arranged
- outdoor furniture

ACTIVITIES AVAILABLE

- heated swimming pool with exer-jets, on site
- swimming at beach
- sailing; diving; sea kayaking
- historic Pompallier
- swimming with dolphins
- Ngaiotonga forest
- fishing – game, in-shore & trips
- golf; museums
- arts & crafts

- restaurants, 2-min walk
- Maori cultural experiences
- historical sites & buildings
- guided Cape Brett walks
- scenic flights
- Waitangi Treaty House
- Cape Reinga day trip
- heritage trail
- Hole-in-the-Rock, speed boat & Cream trips

RUSSELL
Flagstaff Lodge

Hosts Beth Strickland and Darryl Smith   *Mobile* 021 586 190

17 Wellington Street, Russell, Bay of Islands   *Phone* 0-9-403 7117
Postal P O Box 40, Russell, Bay of Islands   *Fax* 0-9-403 7817
Email info@flagstafflodge.co.nz   *Website* www.flagstafflodge.co.nz

DIRECTIONS: From car ferry, take main road to Russell. Take York St & turn right into Wellington St. Flagstaff Lodge on left on corner Queen St. From passenger ferry, turn left into The Strand & right into Wellington St.

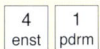

4 bdrm	4 enst	1 pdrm

Room rate $350–$600
Low-season rates available

Includes breakfast & apéritifs
Massage & beauty treatments extra

At the foot of Flagstaff Hill, just one minute's walk from the township of Russell, is Flagstaff Lodge. Originally built in 1912, this historic villa has been extensively renovated to provide four spacious ensuite guestrooms, each themed in an individual style. A qualified therapist offers relaxation massage to guests in the purpose-built massage room where beauty treatments are also available. A verandah wraps around the villa, opening to the garden and large lawn with sea views beyond. Breakfast is served alfresco in the courtyard, on the verandah or in the guest dining area. There is a choice of cooked options on the menu, and complimentary apéritifs and hors d'oeuvres are offered in the evening. Restaurants and cafés are a short walk away.

FACILITIES

- 2 super-king/twin ensuite bedrooms with double showers
- 2 king ensuite bedrooms
- hair dryer, toiletries, demist mirror, bathrobes, heated floor & heated towel rails in all 4 bathrooms
- cotton bed linen, phone, tea/coffee & internet access in all bedrooms
- lounge with gas fire, tea/coffee, nibbles, bar, Sky TV, DVD, music, CD-player, artwork & books

- full cooked or continental breakfast served
- complimentary pre-dinner drinks & platters
- fresh flowers
- air-conditioning/heat pump
- email & fax available
- laundry service, $10
- children over 12 yrs
- on-site parking

ACTIVITIES AVAILABLE

- massage room & shower
- beauty treatments on site
- 2 outdoor baths on site
- game fishing; sailing
- swim with dolphins
- historic sites & heritage trail
- museums; art galleries
- diving; kayaking
- "Hole-in-the-Rock Experienz"

- restaurants & cafés, 1-min walk; vineyard restaurant, 5-min drive away
- golf courses
- self-drive rent-a-boat
- parasailing; sky-diving
- charter fishing trips
- tall ship sailing
- cruises; bus tours
- flights to Cape Reinga

RUSSELL
Pukematu Lodge

Hosts Kay and Colwyn Shortland   *Mobile* 027 245 7640

Top Flagstaff Hill, Russell   *Postal* P O Box 145, Russell
Phone 0-9-403 8500   *Email* pukematu.lodge@clear.net.nz
Fax 0-9-403 8501   *Website* www.pukematulodge.co.nz

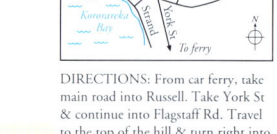

DIRECTIONS: From car ferry, take main road into Russell. Take York St & continue into Flagstaff Rd. Travel to the top of the hill & turn right into private road. Travel approx. 200m to Pukematu Lodge on right.

2 bdrm	2 enst	Double $395 Single $330	*Includes breakfast*	*Picnic hampers extra*	‹VT›

Pukematu, the name of the hill on which the Lodge is sited, means "hill of hospitality", echoed by their byword: "Haere mai ki to tatou kainga i roto i nga kapua" meaning "Welcome to your home within the clouds". Overlooking almost five hectares (12 acres) of native bush with panoramic views of the Bay of Islands and Russell, Pukematu was built in 1992, and offers two guestrooms with private entrances. Breakfast is often served alfresco on the spacious decking where small weddings are held. Colwyn is a marriage celebrant and fluent Maori speaker, and Kay's floral expertise enhances such occasions. Pukematu is a specialist location for both weddings and honeymoons. Home baking is provided and organic produce is used in season.

FACILITIES

- 2 ensuite queen bedrooms
- seating area, TV, fridge & coffee/tea in both guestrooms
- hair dryers & toiletries
- cotton bed linen & bathrobes
- both bedrooms open to balcony
- chocolates & fresh flowers
- phone & fax available
- complimentary laundry
- continental and full cooked breakfast, alfresco or indoors
- picnic hampers by request
- large deck overlooks bay
- Colwyn, marriage celebrant, speaks fluent Maori
- wedding consultant, Kay
- private guest entrance
- small functions venue
- on-site parking

ACTIVITIES AVAILABLE

- ceremonies, celebrations, small conferences, small weddings & honeymoons catered
- outdoor spa pool on site
- almost 5ha (12 acres) native bush on site with pheasants, quails, tui, kingfishers, kiwi & morepork at night
- Flagstaff Hill walk to Hone Heke's flagpole
- picnicking on islands
- 8 restaurants & shopping in Russell township, 3-min drive
- boat trips & fishing arranged
- swimming with dolphins
- historic buildings – hotel, police station & church
- kiwi eco tours; oyster farm visits
- Waitangi Treaty House & golf
- Ninety Mile Beach tours
- day trips to Cape Reinga

RUSSELL
Titore Lodge Retreat

Host Carolyn Mills

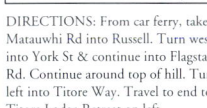

32 Titore Way, Russell, Bay of Islands
Phone 0-9-403 7335   *Mobile* 021 138 8337   *Fax* 0-9-403 7335
Email titorelodge@xtra.co.nz   *Website* attitorelodge.com

DIRECTIONS: From car ferry, take Matauwhi Rd into Russell. Turn west into York St & continue into Flagstaff Rd. Continue around top of hill. Turn left into Titore Way. Travel to end to Titore Lodge Retreat on left.

| 3 bdrm | 3 enst | Suite rate $200–$500   *Includes breakfast*   *Dinner & retreats extra* |
| | | Lodge rate $4,000–$10,000 per week   **Low-season rates available**   **2-night minimum stay** |

Perched on a hill overlooking the harbour of historic Russell, the oldest whaling station in New Zealand, Titore Lodge Retreat is surrounded by forested reserve land. Pathways take guests down to a private sandy beach cove and the village with its restaurants, cafés, galleries, shops and museums. Titore Lodge features fine furnishings, original art and offers three guest suites, each opening to its private patio where breakfast can be served, or guests can breakfast in the enclosed glass dining room. Popular activities include walking, watersports, history tours, relaxing in the hammock, reading and bird-watching. For the benefit of the environmentally sensitive, Titore is chemical free. Retreats can be designed for guests by Carolyn.

FACILITIES

- 1 super-king/twin & 2 queen suites each with ensuite, lounge, patio & pathway
- hair dryer, toiletries, heated towel rails & bathrobes
- fine bed linen; beach towels; torches; fresh flowers & fruit
- some heated floors in suites
- CD-player in each bedroom
- TV, phone, & fax available

- full breakfast in dining room; continental on patio, or in suite
- dinner arranged with chef, extra
- bar service
- extensive library
- kitchenette in each suite
- original artwork throughout
- private guest entrances
- courtesy transfer from wharf
- off-street parking

ACTIVITIES AVAILABLE

- walk to private sandy beach cove from site
- watersports – scuba diving, snorkelling, sea kayaking, swimming, parasailing, sailing, fishing & deep sea
- bird-watching from site
- organisational/clinical psychologist designed retreats for individuals, couples, or businesses, extra

- wine tasting at vineyards
- restaurants, cafés, museums & shops in Russell village, short walk
- beach, coastal, mangrove, forest & Flagstaff Hill walks
- Hole-in-the-Rock trip to watch dolphins & whales
- golf; tennis; lawn bowling; croquet
- horse riding; mountain biking
- day trips to Ninety Mile Beach

TAPEKA POINT, RUSSELL
Anchorage of Russell

Hosts Anna and John Boulter

43 Tapeka Road, Russell   *Postal* P O Box 170, Russell, Bay of Islands
Phone 0-9-403 8410   *Mobile* 021 293 0360   *Email* anchorage.boi@xtra.co.nz
Fax 0-9-403 8410   *Website* www.bay-of-islands.co.nz/accomm/anchorage.html

DIRECTIONS: Take car ferry from Opua to Okiato. Drive to Russell. Continue on Tapeka Rd, over Flagstaff Hill towards Tapeka Point. Turn left into continuation of Tapeka Rd. Anchorage of Russell on left.

| 3 bdrm | 3 enst | Double $150–$195 | Single $120–$150 | *Includes breakfast* | |

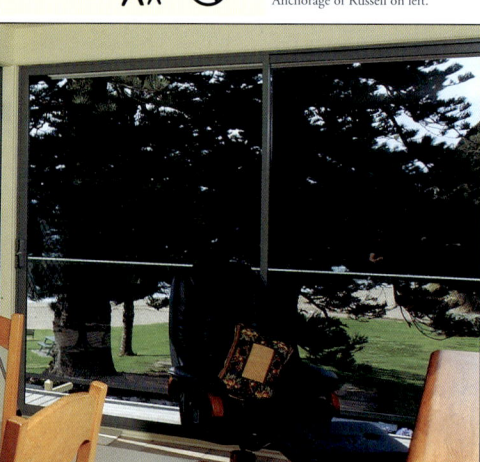

Built opposite Tapeka Beach, which is framed by two historic Norfolk Island pines, The Anchorage offers three guestrooms on the ground level, each opening towards the beach. The Endeavour Suite is named after Captain Cook's ship that landed in 1769 at the Bay of Islands, the Hazard Suite after the ship which was involved in the "sacking" of Russell by local Maori in 1845, and the Charlotte Jane, a migrant ship from England. The beachside guestrooms are contemporary and tiled, with private guest entrances. Breakfast can be served in the suites or the upstairs dining room if preferred. Guests are welcome to use the barbecue and the mountain bikes, dinghy and kayaks. Swimming, fishing and other watersports are popular activities around Tapeka Point.

FACILITIES

- 3 queen ensuite bedrooms
- hair dryers & toiletries
- all 3 guestrooms open to private verandah
- fresh flowers
- seating area with tea/coffee, herbal teas, nibbles, mineral water, Sky TV, CD-player & writing desk in all 3 guestrooms
- 3 private guest entrances

- gourmet continental breakfast; cooked on request
- cordless phone, fax & email available on request
- sea views from all rooms
- children by arrangement
- courtesy passenger transfer
- off-street parking
- mooring available
- closed June to August

ACTIVITIES AVAILABLE

- 2 mountain bikes, 2 kayaks & dinghy for guest use
- BBQ on site
- safe swimming – towels & beachchairs supplied
- snorkelling, diving, fishing & rock pools across road
- boating; kayaking; sailing
- boat tours & Cape Reinga tours
- Waitangi Treaty House & golf

- 6 restaurants nearby
- paragliding; heritage trail
- sport & big-game fishing
- dolphin watching
- historic Russell buildings
- gardens to visit; tramping
- Christ Church in township
- historic Pompallier & garden
- Kerikeri crafts; wine tours
- scenic coastal & bush walks

TAPEKA POINT, RUSSELL
Villa du Fresne

Hosts Maureen and Ron Redwood

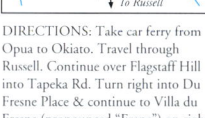

23 Du Fresne Place, Tapeka Point, Russell   *Phone* 0-9-403 7651
Postal P O Box 208, Russell   *Mobile* 021 636 121   *Fax* 0-9-403 7651
Email m.redwood@xtra.co.nz   *Website* friars.co.nz/hosts/dufresne.html

DIRECTIONS: Take car ferry from Opua to Okiato. Travel through Russell. Continue over Flagstaff Hill into Tapeka Rd. Turn right into Du Fresne Place & continue to Villa du Fresne (pronounced "Frane") on right.

2 bdrm	2 enst	Villa suite rate $240–$295	Minimum 2-night stay	*Includes breakfast provisions*	*Self-catering*
		Roberton Room rate $150–$180	Low-season rates available	*Includes continental breakfast*	

Located on Tapeka Point, just two kilometres from Russell, is Villa du Fresne. This Mediterranean-style villa offers a spacious self-contained guest suite with one or two ensuite bedrooms. A full kitchen, with stocked pantry, fridge and breakfast supplies for self-catering, is complemented by a vege garden and grapevine in season. The Roberton Room, king/twin with ensuite, is available for the bed and continental breakfast option. The bedrooms and lounge lead into a conservatory opening to the lawn overlooking the beach. The uninterrupted sea views and sound of waves provide a relaxing atmosphere where guests can escape from day-to-day stress beside the ocean. The hosts live in a separate wing of the villa, which ensures guest privacy.

FACILITIES

- 1 super-king/twin ensuite & 1 queen ensuite bedroom
- hair dryers, toiletries, bathrobes & beach towels
- fresh fruit, flowers, TV, video, CD-player, fridge & tea/coffee facilities in all bedrooms
- laundry available
- private guest lounge with log fire, TV & piano in villa suite
- guest conservatory
- continental or self-serve breakfast in conservatory; or self-catering breakfast provisions for suite
- full kitchen with provisions for self-contained option
- phone & fax available
- honeymooners welcome
- private guest entrance; off-street parking
- courtesy passenger transfer

ACTIVITIES AVAILABLE

- unimpeded sea views from site
- direct access to 2 beaches
- gas barbecue on site
- swimming; snorkelling
- fishing off rocks
- walk up hill to Tapeka Reserve
- boat trips
- swimming with dolphins
- chartered sailing
- deep-sea fishing
- "Hole in the Rock" trips
- high-speed scenic boat
- restaurants, 2km away
- historic buildings & gardens
- forest walks
- historic Pompallier, 2km
- Cape Reinga Day Trip
- heritage trails
- Waitangi Treaty House
- ferry services

Tio Bay Lodge

Hosts Dawn and Richard Wall

Waikino Road, Opua   *Postal* P O Box 19, Opua Post Office, Bay of Islands
Phone 0-9-403 7963   *Mobile* 027 496 2885   *Fax* 0-9-403 7963
Email stay@tiobay.com   *Website* www.tiobay.com

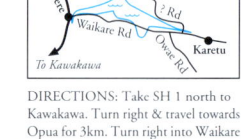

DIRECTIONS: Take SH 1 north to Kawakawa. Turn right & travel towards Opua for 3km. Turn right into Waikare Rd. Travel 5km & turn left into Waikino Rd. Travel 8km on gravel to end. Take left gate & follow drive down to Lodge.

| 3 bdrm | 3 enst | Double $600 | Single $300 | *Includes breakfast & dinner* | *Lunch extra* | |

Set on the water's edge in over eight hectares (20 acres) of private land, Tio Bay Lodge offers privacy and tranquillity. Separate from the main house, each of the three ensuite guestrooms is individually styled with wide sea views and sunny decks. Extra touches include the fresh fruit, freshly roasted home-grown macadamia nuts and the bottle of wine in the bedrooms upon arrival. Tio Bay Lodge operates its own 10-metre high-speed launch and with a qualified skipper, available for sightseeing and fishing, by arrangement. Trips to the Hole-in-the-Rock are always popular. Included in the tariff is a three-course dinner with wine, featuring innovative dishes using fresh local produce and seafood. Richard is happy to cook guests' own catches of fish.

FACILITIES

- 3 queen ensuite bedrooms with private decks & sea views
- hair dryers, toiletries & bathrobes
- CD-player, tea/coffee & mineral water in all 3 rooms
- cotton bed linen; fresh flowers
- private guest entrance
- lounge with open fire, Sky TV, video, CDs, bar & tea/coffee
- laundry facilities extra

- breakfast served in dining room or alfresco on deck
- lunch, $25 pp
- 3-course dinner with wine
- powder room
- phone, fax & internet access
- transfer by boat from Opua
- on-site parking; helipad
- closed June, July, August

ACTIVITIES AVAILABLE

- BBQ & spa pool on site
- Tio Bay's 10m (30-ft) launch with skipper for sightseeing & fishing trips, extra charge
- walking on 8ha (20-acre) site
- oyster collecting at Tio Bay
- Hole-in-the-Rock boat trips
- sailing; boating
- sea kayaking
- diving; snorkelling

- dolphin watching
- fishing; swimming
- golf; walks
- saltwater fly fishing
- kauri forest
- Ninety Mile Beach tours
- Waitangi Treaty House
- ferries from Paihia to historic Russell

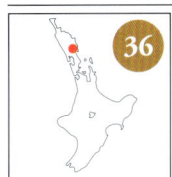

WHANGARURU NORTH, BAY OF ISLANDS
Pawhaoa Bay Lodge

Hosts Bill and Claire Hurst   *Fax* 0-9-433 6563

946 Whangaruru North Road, Bland Bay, R D 4, Hikurangi, Northland
Phone 0-9-433 6566   *Mobiles* 025 399 440 *and* 021 714 243
Email cbhurst@ihug.co.nz   *Website* www.pawhaoabaylodge.co.nz

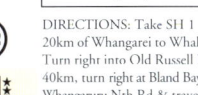

 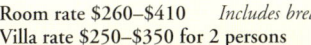

4 bdrm	4 enst	1 pdrm

Room rate $260–$410   *Includes breakfast* $450–$600   *Includes breakfast & dinner*
Villa rate $250–$350 for 2 persons   Extra persons $40 each   *Self-catering*

DIRECTIONS: Take SH 1 north for 20km of Whangarei to Whakapara BP. Turn right into Old Russell Rd. Travel 40km, turn right at Bland Bay sign into Whangaruru Nth Rd & travel 1km past camping ground to Pawhaoa on right.

Located on the water's edge, in established subtropical gardens, Pawhaoa Bay Lodge has panoramic views from all rooms over the harbour to the bush-clad hills beyond. Purpose-built and opened in 2003, Pawhaoa Bay Lodge provides two spacious guest-rooms in the Lodge and two self-contained Villas, all with French doors opening onto decks, lawn and beach. The Villas offer self-catering, and dinner is available at the Lodge, the cuisine emphasising fresh produce from the extensive vegetable garden, fruit trees and the sea, complemented by a small select list of fine New Zealand wines. Pawhaoa adjoins conservation land, with easy access to walking tracks, safe all-tide swimming and snorkelling beaches, kayaking, boating and fishing charters.

FACILITIES

- 2 Villas, each with 1 super-king/twin bedroom, with ensuite & extra rollaway bed
- 2 super-king ensuite bedrooms in Lodge
- cotton bed linen
- hair dryer, toiletries, heated towel rails, heater & bathrobes per ensuite; 3 include baths
- lounge area with tea/coffee, herbal teas, DVDs & CDs
- full kitchen for self-catering in each villa, plus BBQ
- dinner, $70–$90 pp
- powder room
- laundry facilities in Villas & Lodge
- balcony overlooking harbour & garden from all bedrooms & living rooms
- on-site parking

ACTIVITIES AVAILABLE

- BBQ & pétanque on site
- large subtropical garden for relaxing
- small boat mooring available on request
- direct beach access; swimming
- kayaks available to guests
- holistic health massage available by appointment
- bush & beach walks; fishing
- snorkelling & equipment
- Oakura store, 30-min drive
- charter fishing from local company available
- bird-watching
- beaches, wide selection
- surfing & diving
- Whangarei, 1 hr south
- Paihia or Russell, both 45-min drive away

TUTUKAKA, WHANGAREI
Poor Knights Lodge

Hosts Yvonne Clark and Jim Mason

 eftpos

 VISA MasterCard

Tutukaka Block Road, Tutukaka   *Postal* P O Box 1526, Tutukaka, Whangarei
Phone 0-9-434 4405   *Email* jamesandyvonne@poorknightslodge.co.nz
Fax 0-9-434 4401   *Website* www.poorknightslodge.co.nz

2 bdrm	2 enst

Room rate $240   *Includes breakfast*   *Picnic lunch & wine extra*

DIRECTIONS: From Whangarei bypass, turn right before Advocat Stadium & left at 2nd lights into Mill Rd. Travel 24km to Ngunguru, then 2km & turn right into Tutukaka Block Rd. Lodge is 0.5km on left.

Named after the Poor Knights Islands, 20 kilometres off-shore, Poor Knights Lodge offers an exclusive guest floor downstairs. Two separate super-king-size ensuite bedrooms open to a spacious guest deck for relaxing and appreciating the views over the Marina and Oturu Bay. Privacy is ensured and a full breakfast is served in the guestrooms or alfresco on the guests' decking in the warm Northland weather. Picnic lunches and wine are available, there is a barbecue for guest use and restaurants are a short drive away at Tutukaka Marina. The secluded setting is landscaped with native plants and overlooks the harbour out to the ocean. Nearby activities are popular with guests, including swimming, diving, fishing, the surf beaches and coastal walks.

FACILITIES

- 2 super-king/twin ensuite bedrooms downstairs
- hair dryers, bathrobes, heated towel rails & toiletries
- cotton bed linen, writing desk, phone jack, fruit, tea/coffee & fridge in bedrooms
- TV & stereo in bedrooms
- fresh flowers
- phone, fax & email available

- continental or cooked breakfast served in guestrooms or alfesco on guests' decking
- picnic lunch, $25 pp
- large, sunny guest deck with views over Oturu Bay & Marina
- private guest entrance for each bedroom downstairs
- off-street parking

ACTIVITIES AVAILABLE

- BBQ available; wine extra
- honeymoons catered for
- diving around Poor Knights, shipwrecks, *Tui* & *Waikato*
- game & line fishing
- snorkelling
- swimming at local beaches
- surfing
- beach & coastal walks

- restaurants at Tutukaka Marina, 5-min drive away
- horse trekking
- gardens open to visit
- bush walks
- golf, 5-min drive, or 20-min drive for Whangarei golf
- Whangarei City, 20-min drive
- Bay of Islands, 1 hour north
- Auckland City, 2⅓ hours south

Poor Knights

Poor Knights

Sail Inn

Host Jan Malcolm

148 Beach Road, Onerahi, Whangarei
Phone 0-9-436 2356   *Email* sailinn@xtra.co.nz
Fax 0-9-436 2356   *Website* friars.co.nz/hosts/sailinn.html

DIRECTIONS: From Auckland, take SH 1 to Whangarei. From Whangarei township, travel through Onerahi towards Whangarei Heads. Turn right into Beach Rd. Continue about 1km to Sail Inn on right.

| 1 bdrm | 1 enst | Room rate $195 | *Includes breakfast* | *Lunch & dinner extra* | ⊲VT⊳ | 🚭 |

Jan designed Sail Inn in 1990 to be spacious and airy with expansive harbour views. Sited directly across the road from the harbour inlet, Sail Inn is strategically positioned for viewing craft of all shapes and sizes, for swimming, fishing and boating. This peaceful retreat offers an ensuite bedroom with private decks, walk-in dressing room and sunken sitting room. Tea, coffee and fresh baking are provided for guests on arrival and flexi-time breakfast is served alfresco on the deck or indoors overlooking the harbour. Picnic hampers can be arranged for hosted day trips to the Bay of Islands. A barbecue or dinner can also be provided, with apéritifs, wine and port, and guest are welcome to cook in collaboration with Jan who operates on relaxed "island time".

FACILITIES

- 1 queen ensuite bedroom with walk-in dressing room, fridge, & sitting room
- sitting room with tea/coffee, TV, extensive CD collection & decks
- toiletries, hair dryers, heated towel rail in ensuite
- phone & fax available
- French & Japanese spoken
- complimentary laundry
- fresh flowers

- full breakfast served alfresco on deck or at dining table
- 3-course dinner or BBQ, with wine, $50 pp
- picnic hampers on request
- on-site parking
- courtesy airport transfer
- Scottish terrier, Mac, in residence
- massage & facials on request

ACTIVITIES AVAILABLE

- pétanque court, spa pool & BBQ area
- feeding doves on site
- restaurant, 5-min walk
- swimming beach across road
- viewing yachts to tankers passing by window up harbour
- spearing flounder across road
- fishing for snapper & tarakihi
- tennis court, 2-min walk

- hosted day trips within Bay of Islands
- Town Basin for shopping & restaurants, 10-min drive
- golf course, 10-min drive
- gardens open to visit
- deep-sea game fishing
- chartered scenic flights
- airport, 5-min drive
- Auckland City, 2 hours south

PARUA BAY, WHANGAREI HEADS
Parua Bay Cottage

Hosts Marian and Greg Innes   *Phone* 0-9-436 5626

Parua Bay Cemetery Road, Parua Bay, Whangarei Heads
Postal P O Box 1370, Whangarei   *Website* friars.co.nz/hosts/parua.html
Freephone 0800 116 626   *Email* paruabaycottage@innes-strategy.com

2 bdrm	1 prbth

Cottage rate $150 for 2 persons
Extra persons $30 each

Self-catering, no meals available
5-day minimum stay in peak season

DIRECTIONS: Take Whangarei Heads Rd to Onerahi. Fork left & travel 10 mins to Parua Bay. Continue past tavern, then turn right into Parua Bay Cemetery Rd. Travel 1km to end of road to Parua Bay Cottage.

Set beside a secluded private beach, on eight hectares of bush including ecologically significant kauri forest, this historic cottage is fully self-contained for one-party bookings. Originally built with three rooms circa 1860, Parua Bay Cottage was carefully restored in 1995 to sleep seven, and kitchen, bathroom and laundry were added. The kitchen is fully equipped for self-catering and the verandahs are popular for alfresco dining. Fishing, diving and sightseeing trips can be arranged and mooring is available for large yachts and other boats. There is direct access from the cottage to Parua Bay with its safe swimming and an extra shower on the beach. Children are welcome to view the farm animals on site and the mature kauri forest attracts native songbirds.

FACILITIES

- one-party bookings only
- 1 twin & 1 double bedroom with private bathroom
- cotton bed linen
- hair dyer, toiletries & heated towel rail in bathroom
- extra double fold-out beds in lounge and in dining area
- lounge with open fire, TV, music, CD-player, games, magazines & writing desk

- full kitchen for self-catering
- self-serve laundry
- children welcome
- phone jack for email
- fax available
- fresh flowers
- Marian speaks basic German
- pets welcome if supervised
- on-site parking; helipad

ACTIVITIES AVAILABLE

- private beach access from site
- sheep, ducks & hens on site
- safe swimming beach from site, with extra beach shower
- mature kauri forest on 8-ha (20-acre) property
- bush & beach walks on site
- native bird-watching on site
- kayaking; boating
- mooring available in bay, extra

- restaurants, 2km drive
- fishing in bay; diving trips
- golf, 3km drive
- surf beaches, 15-min drive
- boat charters for fishing, diving & sightseeing
- walkways at Bream Head reserve, 15-min drive
- tramping, 15-min drive
- Whangarei Basin, 20 mins

TAIHARURU, WHANGAREI
Ara Roa

Hosts Paul and Susanne Olsen

Harambee Road, Taiharuru   *Postal* R D 1, Onerahi, Whangarei
Phone 0-9-436 5028   *Mobile* 021 293 5981   *Fax* 0-9-436 5028
Email pvista@xtra.co.nz   *Website* www.araroa.co.nz

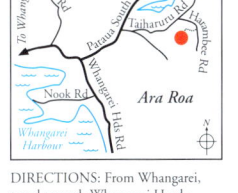

DIRECTIONS: From Whangarei, travel towards Whangarei Heads. Continue into Pataua Sth Rd & turn right into Taiharuru Rd. Travel 6km & turn right into Harambee Rd. Take 1st drive on right for 1km up to Ara Roa.

2 bdrm	1 prbth	House rate $190–$220 for 2 persons Extra persons $45 each	Multiple-night rates available	*Self-catering* *Dinner extra*

Ara Roa is set on an elevated site with views over 36 hectares of native bush and pastureland to the Pacific Ocean beyond. Meaning "long road", Ara Roa is a self-contained retreat which is just five minutes' drive from surf beaches. Purpose-built in 2001, the contemporary retreat includes two bedrooms, a bathroom with a full double bath and fully equipped kitchen for self-catering. If guests prefer, dinner can be provided for them, or there is a restaurant nearby. The city of Whangarei is 30 kilometres west and the Bay of Islands is accessible to the north. But there are many attractions in the surrounding locality and on site, as well as the native flora and fauna including resident kiwi. Ocean views enhance the rural ambience.

FACILITIES

- single-party bookings only
- 1 super-king/twin & 1 king bedroom with cotton bed linen
- 1 bathroom with double bath, hair dryer, demist mirror, heated towel rails & heated floor; separate toilet
- lounge/dining area with TV, video & CD-player
- laundry available, $20
- email & phone available
- dinner available, served in retreat, $30–$60 pp
- full kitchen for self-catering
- both bedrooms open onto separate decks
- fluent Danish spoken
- children welcome
- on-site parking; helipad
- courtesy passenger transfer
- private guest entrance

ACTIVITIES AVAILABLE

- bush walks on site
- honeymoons catered for
- 36 hectares (95 acres) of native bush & pasture on site
- bird-watching on site
- hiking
- golf courses
- fishing; kayaking
- boating
- surf beaches
- restaurant, 10-min drive
- swimming; diving
- biking tours
- scenic flights
- Poor Knights Marine Reserve, diving & tours
- horse trekking
- local arts & crafts
- private gardens to visit
- Whangarei, 30-min drive

© Friars' Guide to New Zealand Accommodation for the Discerning Traveller

WAIPOUA FOREST, KAURI COAST

Waipoua Lodge

Hosts Nicole and Chris Donahoe

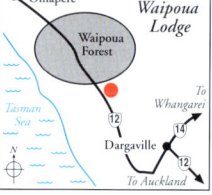

State Highway 12, Katui, Waipoua Forest   *Phone* 0-9-439 0422
Postal Waipoua Lodge, R D 6, Dargaville   *Fax* 0-9-523 8081
Email nicole@waipoualodge.co.nz   *Website* www.waipoualodge.co.nz

DIRECTIONS: Take SH 12 north to Dargaville. Turn left through township & continue on SH 12 for 48km. Waipoua Lodge on right of highway, 2km before forest.

5 bdrm	3 enst	1 prbth	1 pdrm

Apartment rate $420–$560 for 2 persons
Rate available including breakfast & dinner

Includes breakfast

Located on the southern boundary of the Waipoua Forest, Waipoua Lodge was built over a century ago as a private residence, and has housed guests to the forest over these years. The fully restored Lodge features native kauri timber construction and rimu ceilings in the dining room, bar and guest lounge. Guests can enjoy notable New Zealand wines while relaxing on the leather couches in front of the original fireplace. Historical antique farm and kauri milling implements hang in the lounge, and the sunroom/library overlooks the gardens and forest beyond. Adjacent to the lodge, the original working sheds have been transformed into four pupose-built apartments, each opening to private balconies with views to the forest beyond.

FACILITIES

- Stables: 1 king bedroom, ensuite with bath, lounge, kitchenette, balcony
- Calf Pen: 1 king bedroom, ensuite, lounge, kitchenette & balcony
- Woolshed: 1 king bedroom, ensuite with bath, kitchen, lounge, twin mezzanine over lounge (suitable for children), wrap-around balcony
- Tack Rooms: 1 super-king & 1 king bedroom opening to balcony, 1 bathroom, lounge, kitchenette

- full breakfast
- organic local produce prepared by chef
- guest lounge, bar, library & dining room
- fine linen & toiletries, bathrobes, hair dryer, TV, stereo/CDs per apartment
- laundry, extra; hi-speed internet access
- on-site parking

ACTIVITIES AVAILABLE

- helipad available on site
- bush walk on site – native birds
- guided night walk in kauri park to view NZ's rare & endangered kiwi
- Kai Iwi Lakes for swimming, water skiing, kayaking & fishing, 20 mins
- guided trout fishing & farm tours
- longest beach in NZ, golden sand, unpopulated, beach fishing, 15km
- biggest kauri tree in NZ, 16km

- forest headquarters adjacent
- waterfall, 15-min drive
- Waipoua Forest walks
- swimming in river waterhole
- horse trekking
- 4WD beach tours
- Hokianga Harbour views, 30-min drive
- Matakohe Museum, 1 hour
- Dargaville, 30-min drive

DARGAVILLE
Kauri House Lodge

Host Doug Blaxall   *Mobile* 025 547 769

Bowen Street, Dargaville   *Postal* P O Box 382, Dargaville
Phone 0-9-439 8082   *Email* kaurihouse@xtra.co.nz
Fax 0-9-439 8082   *Website* friars.co.nz/hosts/kaurihouse.html

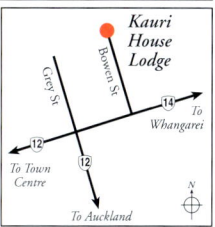

DIRECTIONS: Take SH 12 north to Dargaville. At cross-road junction, turn right into SH 14. Turn first left into Bowen St. Continue to end of road, to driveway entrance to Kauri House Lodge.

| 3 bdrm | 3 enst | Double $200–$275 Single $200 | *Includes breakfast* Weekend & off-season rates available |

Kauri House Lodge is set among mature trees, three kilometres from the township of Dargaville. The historic style and ambience of this 1880s villa has been retained, with the original kauri panelling and period antiques in all rooms. Surrounded by extensive landscaped grounds, the quiet at Kauri House Lodge is broken only by native birds. In summer guests enjoy the large swimming pool. In winter, the billiards room is popular with its log fire and library for relaxing in the evening. The hosts also invite guests to explore the mature native bush on their nearby farm overlooking the Wairoa River and Kaipara Harbour. Some of the activities available in the area include the deserted beaches, lakes, river tours, horse treks, walks and restaurants.

FACILITIES

- 1 super-king, 1 king & 1 twin bedroom, each with ensuite
- hair dryers & toiletries
- wheelchair access to 1 bedroom
- children over 9 years welcome
- piano & open fire in billiards room
- verandah overlooks 3ha garden
- TV lounge & library
- satellite Sky TV & VCR
- fresh flowers

- continental or cooked breakfast, served in dining room
- teas & coffee available
- night-store heating
- self-serve laundry
- Spud, the dog, & Spook, the black cat, in residence
- courtesy passenger transfer
- on-site parking

ACTIVITIES AVAILABLE

- in-house billiards & piano
- cattle farm tour on site
- large swimming pool on site, available in summer season only
- surfing, swimming & cliff views from 100km beach, 10km away
- 16ha (40 acres) native bush, steers & donkeys, 5km away
- horse rides/treks on beach
- walking tracks; garden visits

- licensed restaurants, 3km
- trout fishing in Kai Iwi lakes, guides available
- river cruises & boat trips
- Waipoua kauri forest treks
- Matakohe Kauri Museum
- wood turning & crafts
- Dargaville shops, 3km
- Whangarei, 40-min drive
- Auckland, 2½ hrs south

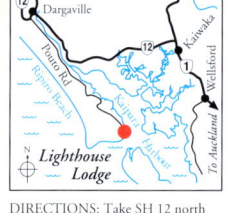

POUTO POINT, DARGAVILLE
Lighthouse Lodge

Hosts Christine Findley and Bob Benseman

6577 Pouto Road, Pouto Point, Dargaville   *Phone* 0-9-439 5150
Postal 6577 Pouto Road, R D 1, Te Kopuru   *Fax* 0-9-439 5150
Email email@lighthouse-lodge.co.nz   *Website* www.lighthouse-lodge.co.nz

DIRECTIONS: Take SH 12 north to Dargaville. Turn left into Pouto Rd & travel south for 1 hr to Lighthouse Lodge. Alternatively 4WD along Ripiro Beach at low tide, or access Lodge via boat, or helicopter.

6 bdrm	3 enst	1 prbth	1 pdrm

Room rate $210–$420

Includes breakfast
Lunch & dinner extra

With uninterrupted ocean vistas, Lighthouse Lodge is sited at the tip of Pouto Point, on the secluded headland of Kaipara Harbour, one hour south of Dargaville. Set in a subtropical garden, this contemporary cedar-clad Lodge has been designed on a nautical theme incorporating local historical artefacts. The spacious interiors open to the balcony, with sea views from every room. Accommodation comprises three guest suites, which can be configured as six bedrooms. Full breakfast is served in the dining room, or alfresco on the deck, with special diets catered and seafood a speciality. A three-course table d' hôte dinner is also offered. Lighthouse Lodge has direct access to the longest drivable beach in New Zealand, 101 kilometres in length.

FACILITIES

- 1 king/twin suite with private access
- 2 queen suites open to balcony & patio
- TV, writing desk, fridge & tea/coffee in suites
- hair dyers, toiletries, heated towel rails & bathrobes
- wood burner, bar, Sky TV & books in lounge
- cotton bed linen
- continental & cooked breakfast
- lunch & picnic baskets, extra
- dinner, $40–$60 pp; seafood speciality; special diets catered
- email, fax & phone available
- fresh flowers
- laundry available
- conferences & weddings
- on-site parking
- helipad

ACTIVITIES AVAILABLE

- private jacuzzi under stars
- bird-watching on site
- picnicking on beach
- golf, 45-min drive via beach
- wilderness coastal walks
- 1884 wooden lighthouse, 7km
- 4WD truck tours
- Pouto sand dune tours; quad bike safaris
- gannets & seals
- restaurants, 1 hour north
- beach & boat fishing; fishing gear & charters
- swimming & surfing
- pétanque & clay bird shooting
- scenic Kaipara boat cruises
- Dargaville, 1 hour north
- Auckland, 3-hour drive or 20-min heliflight

44

LANG COVE, WAIPU
Royal Palm Lodge

Hosts Jan and John Allen   *Mobile* 025 948 863

19 Highland Lass Place, Lang Cove, Northland   *Phone* 0-9-432 0120
Postal P O Box 88, Thistle Post Office, Waipu, Northland   *Fax* 0-9-432 0368
Email hosts@royalpalmlodge.co.nz   *Website* www.royalpalmlodge.co.nz

DIRECTIONS: From SH 1, turn right at Wellsford into coastal road & travel towards Mangawhai. Continue towards Waipu. At Langs Beach turn right into Hector Lang Drive & left into Highland Lass Pl. Royal Palm Lodge on left.

7 bdrm	3 enst	2 prbth	1 shbth

Room rate $250–$400
Off-season rates available

Includes breakfast
Self-catering available downstairs

Lunch & dinner extra

Royal Palm Lodge is set right on the beachfront at Lang Cove. Constructed in 1997, in a classical style with spacious covered balconies overlooking the sea, the Lodge provides a variety of accommodation options. An exclusive guest floor is situated at beach level, which offers self-catering with a full kitchen. On the main level of the Lodge are another three bedrooms and the dining facilities. Meals are served upstairs in the spacious dining room with ocean views, or alfresco on the extensive sundeck. Restaurants are ten minutes' drive. There is a relaxed beach-house ambience at Royal Palm Lodge. Popular on-site activities include an exercise gym, spa pool, billiards table, pétanque, swimming, walking, jet skiing and kayaking at the beach.

FACILITIES

- Royal Palm & King Palm Rooms: king/twin bed in each & ensuite
- Queen Palm Room: queen/twin bed with private bathroom
- Phoenix Palm Room: super-king/ twin with private bathroom & bath
- Music Room: king bed & ensuite
- Arabian Room: queen bed & Tulip Room: queen/twin bed share 1 bathroom
- hair dryers, toiletries & bathrobes

- continental or cooked breakfast served upstairs or alfresco on sundeck
- light lunch by request, extra
- 3-course dinner by arrangement, extra
- full kitchen & lounge downstairs with Sky digital TV, stereo & tea/coffee
- guest laundry, email, fax & phone facilities

ACTIVITIES AVAILABLE

- direct access to safe swimming beach from site
- ocean kayaks, wave ski & jet ski, all available on site
- spa pool & BBQ on site
- pool table; pétanque on site
- massage & facials by arrangement
- honeymoons/conferences catered
- 2 golf courses; tennis courts
- fishing charters; coastal walks

- Mangawhai & Waipu restaurants, 10-min drive
- horse riding; fishing
- glow-worm caves
- gardens open to visit
- Scottish Heritage Museum
- Mangawhai & Waipu, 10-min drive
- Whangarei City, 30 mins
- Auckland City, 1½ hours

Royal Palm

MANGAWHAI HEADS
Milestone Cottages

Host Gael McConachy

27 Moir Point Road, Mangawhai Heads
Phone 0-9-431 4018   *Email* gael@milestonecottages.co.nz
Fax 0-9-431 4018   *Website* www.milestonecottages.co.nz

VISA MasterCard

DIRECTIONS: From Te Hana, turn right on to coastal road & travel to Mangawhai. Turn right into Moir Rd, then left into Molesworth Drive. Cross causeway & turn right into Moir Point Rd. Travel 200m to Cottages on left.

| 5 bdrm | 5 prbth | Cottage rate $140–$250
Extra persons $35 each | *Self-catering, no meals available*
2-night minimum on weekends |  |

Milestone Cottages are individually designed by Gael's architect sister, Philippa Johnson, to complement the natural setting of the private estuary with sandy beach and coastal bush at Mangawhai Heads. Gael's husband, Ian, built and hand-crafted the cottages in an environmentally sensitive way. The Schooner and Gumdiggers Cottages overlook the estuary, while the Puka (with sea views) and Palm Cottages are nestled in the hectare of subtropical gardens around the swimming pool. A second earth-brick cottage, The Gardners Cottage, is adjacent to the thatched adobe and manuka wharekai where guests enjoy barbecues. Palm trees fringe the croquet lawn and steps lead from a tree-framed viewing platform down to the private beach below.

FACILITIES

- private-party bookings per cottage
- 5 fully equipped self-contained cottages – individually named
- 1 queen or twin bedroom & bathroom in each cottage
- lounge area with TV & fully equipped kitchen in each cottage
- private decking overlooking garden
- barbecue/wharekai area available
- conference facilities
- self-catering for all meals
- videos in all cottages
- wheelchair access to Palm Cottage
- extensive subtropical garden with fish pond
- BBQ per cottage
- total privacy
- ocean views
- native bush setting

ACTIVITIES AVAILABLE

On site:
- swimming pool
- croquet lawn
- pétanque court
- gazebo in garden
- kayaks available
- safe sandy swimming beach
- sheltered estuary & sand-dunes
- garden & beach walks

Off site:
- coastal walkways
- café serving breakfast, restaurant & hot bread shop, 150m walk
- white sandy surf beaches
- bird sanctuary; gardens to visit
- 18-hole golf links nearby
- tennis courts; bowls
- Matakohe Museum
- Goat Island Marine Park

MANGAWHAI HEADS
Mangawhai Lodge

Host Jeannette Forde

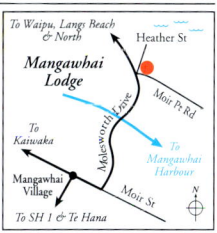

4 Heather Street, Mangawhai Heads
Phone 0-9-431 5311   *Email* mlodge@xtra.co.nz
Fax 0-9-431 5312   *Website* www.seaviewlodge.co.nz

DIRECTIONS: From Te Hana, turn right into Twin Coast Discovery Route to Mangawhai. Turn right into Moir St, then left into Molesworth Drive. Cross causeway & turn right into Heather St. Lodge on right corner.

5 bdrm	3 enst	2 prbth	1 pdrm

Double $150–$165
Single $120–$140

Includes breakfast
House rate & seasonal rates available

This two-storey colonial-inspired house features wrap-around verandahs which provide panoramic ocean views. Vistas extend to the sheltered harbour and sand-dunes, upper reaches of the Hauraki Gulf, and the Hen and Chickens Islands. Mangawhai Lodge is sited adjacent to an 18-hole championship all-weather golf course and a licensed café. The Lodge caters for couples, small conferences, and social and golfing groups of up to 10 guests. The five guestrooms open to verandahs with tables and chairs. Continental or cooked breakfast is served upstairs or alfresco on the adjacent verandah. The guest kitchenette downstairs provides tea and coffee facilities and the upstairs reading lounge includes a television. A barbecue is also available.

FACILITIES

- 2 queen ensuite bedrooms
- 1 super-king/twin ensuite bedroom & 2 super-king/twin bedrooms with private bathrooms
- hair dryers & toiletries
- high quality bed linen
- verandahs opening from all bedrooms, with table & chairs
- TV in all 5 guestrooms
- groups catered for

- full breakfast served in upstairs dining room, or alfresco on verandah
- tea/coffee facilities in guest kitchenette
- guest lounge with TV, video, CDs & books
- sea views
- email, fax & phone & barbecue available
- on-site parking

ACTIVITIES AVAILABLE

- beach, 2-min walk away
- licensed café opposite
- 18-hole golf course adjacent
- safe swimming beach, 300m
- kayaking; boogie boarding
- bird sanctuary
- coastal walkway; gardens to visit
- sand-dunes; surfing; watersports
- mountain bike tracks, 10 mins

- 5 restaurants nearby
- white sandy surf beaches
- tennis; bowls; horse riding
- quality crafts
- Matakohe Kauri Museum
- boat charters – fishing/diving
- Goat Island reserve, 35 mins
- midway between Auckland Airport & Bay of Islands, 2 hours drive north or south

© Friars' Guide to New Zealand Accommodation for the Discerning Traveller

TE ARAI POINT, MANGAWHAI
Lake View Chalets

Host Arnim Pierau

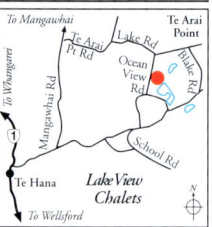

662 Ocean View Road, R D 5, Mangawhai/Te Arai   *Freephone* 0800 LAKEVIEW
Postal 662 Ocean View Road, R D 5, Wellsford   *Phone* 0-9-431 4086
Email info@chalets.co.nz   *Website* www.chalets.co.nz

DIRECTIONS: From Auckland take SH 1 north to Te Hana. Travel 13km & turn right into Mangawhai Rd. Turn right into Te Arai Pt Rd. Take Lake Rd to right, & turn right into Ocean View Rd. Chalets on left.

| 12 bdrm | 6 prbth | Chalet rate $130–$200 for 2 persons
Extra adults $45 each   Extra children $25 each | *Self-catering*
Breakfast extra |

Purpose built to capture individual lake views, all six Lake View Chalets are positioned in established gardens to create privacy and peace. Set on 80 hectares (200 acres) of farmland, Lake View Chalets provide direct access to the Slipper and Spectacle Lakes where guests can enjoy kayaking or rowing. Biking through the adjacent Mangawhai pine forest to 14 kilometres of unspoiled white-sand Pakiri Beach is also popular. Each Chalet is self-contained with a full kitchen for self-catering, and breakfast is available on request. Guests are welcome to pick citrus from the on-site orchard in season. There are two bedrooms per Chalet, and a private sundeck with outdoor furniture and barbecue for alfresco dining, relaxing and taking in the lake views.

FACILITIES

- 6 Chalets, each with private-party bookings only
- each Chalet includes 1 twin & 1 super-king/twin bedroom with 1 private bathroom
- cotton bed linen
- hair dryer & toiletries
- dining lounge in each Chalet, with Sky TV & phone jack
- video, games, books available
- breakfast available, $20 pp
- full kitchen for self-catering in each Chalet
- guest deck from each Chalet
- lake views from all Chalets
- phone & email available
- complimentary laundry
- German spoken
- on-site parking
- children welcome

ACTIVITIES AVAILABLE

On site complimentary:
- access to Slipper, Spectacle & Tomarata Lakes
- 14km beach access via forest
- row-boat & kayaks available
- walks around lakes
- citrus for guests to pick
- mountain bikes available
- pétanque/boules
- swimming in lakes

Off site:
- restaurants, 15-min drive
- golfing; walking; horse riding
- gardens open to visit
- boat charters
- big-game fishing
- Wellsford shops, 20km south
- Whangarei, 30km north
- Warkworth village, 50km south
- Auckland City, 1 hour south

48

Tera del Mar Country B & B

Hosts Teresa Gibson and Marshall Lefferts

140 Rodney Road, Leigh, R D 5, Warkworth
Phone 0-9-422 6090   *Mobile* 027 478 8202   *Fax* 0-9-422 6090
Email be@teradelmar.co.nz   *Website* www.teradelmar.co.nz

DIRECTIONS: From Auckland take SH 1 north to Warkworth. At 2nd lights turn right & veer left to Matakana & Leigh. Continue on Pakiri Rd past Goat Island. Turn left into Rodney Rd. Travel 1.4km to Tera del Mar on right.

4 bdrm	3 enst	1 prbth

Double $255–$320
Single $210–$280

Includes breakfast
packages available

Tera del Mar

Set in a peaceful and secluded country location, just over an hour north of Auckland, Tera del Mar was opened in 2003 on Teresa and Marshall's 32-hectare (90-acre) property. Guests enjoy expansive rural and ocean views to Pakiri Beach and beyond. Designed in Victorian style, Tera del Mar features four open fireplaces in the upstairs guestrooms, and all bedrooms open to the extensive wrap-around verandahs overlooking the landscaped garden. The two-course gourmet breakfast or brunch is served downstairs in the lounge or library, alfresco on the verandah, or room service is offered. Teresa and Marshall's two young sons and Misty, their friendly Samoyed dog, complete the family. Cafés and restaurants are a short drive away in Leigh and Matakana.

FACILITIES

- 3 queen bedrooms with ensuites
- 1 super-king/twin or 1 queen bedroom with 1 private bathroom & double spa bath
- hair dryer, toiletries & bathrobes
- sea views, phone jacks, tables & 4 open fireplaces in bedrooms
- guest lounge with open fire, complimentary beverages, wines & liqueurs, wide-screen DVD, surround-sound & CD-player
- 2-course gourmet breakfast
- panoramic ocean views
- library with open fire, games, magazines & writing desk; fax & email in office
- children by arrangement
- private guest entrance
- special occasion & group bookings welcome
- on-site parking; helipad

ACTIVITIES AVAILABLE

- outdoor spa pool/jacuzzi, sauna & changing room
- gazebo, landscaped gardens & scenic ridge walk on site
- children's sandpit, tree house & trampoline on site
- Goat Island Marine Reserve & glass-bottom boat, 5 mins
- safe swimming beach & playground, 7-min drive
- Matakana wine trails, 20 mins
- restaurants & cafés, 5–25 mins
- scenic & fishing charter tours
- coastal & bush walks, 5–8 mins
- snorkelling & diving
- kayaking nearby
- Pakiri Beach surfing & horse riding
- art & craft galleries, 5–30 mins
- pottery & café, 20-min drive
- Tawharanui Regional Park, 40 mins
- Auckland airport, 2 hours south

Tera del Mar

Tera del Mar

MATAKANA, WARKWORTH
Sandpiper Lodge

Hosts Robin and Louise Fischer

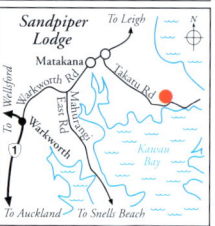

Takatu Road, R D 6, Warkworth
Phone 0-9-422 7256   *Mobile* 025 283 6853   *Fax* 0-9-422 7816
Email sandpiper.lodge@xtra.co.nz   *Website* www.sandpiperlodge.co.nz

DIRECTIONS: From Auckland, take SH 1 north to Warkworth. At lights turn right & veer left to Matakana. Continue through Matakana & take 2nd right into Takatu Rd. Travel 10km & turn right 150m to Sandpiper Lodge.

| 9 bdrm | 9 enst | 1 prbth | Room rate $250–$450 | *Includes breakfast Lunch & dinner extra* |

Overlooking a tidal estuary with views to Kawau Island, Sandpiper Lodge is located in over two hectares (6.5 acres) of subtropical and native gardens at Christian Bay on the Takatu Peninsula. This boutique hotel includes an à la carte restaurant and is also suitable for hosting conferences. Accommodation comprises nine ensuite super-king/twin bedrooms each with direct dial phone, television and tea/coffee facilities. Meals prepared by an award-winning chef are offered alfresco on the pool deck, or in the fully licensed restaurant, featuring wine from local vineyards. Picnics are available for trips to Tawharanui Regional Park and the beach. Sandpiper Lodge is a tranquil country hotel, 15 minutes from the colonial township of Warkworth.

FACILITIES

- 9 super-king/twin ensuite bedrooms with dressing rooms
- cotton bed linen, writing desk, phone, tea/coffee, mineral water & TV in all 9 bedrooms
- bathrobes, hair dryers, toiletries, demist mirrors, heated towel rails
- guest lounge with open fire, tea/coffee, mineral water, bar, TV, CD-player & games
- fax & email available

- à la carte breakfast
- à la carte lunch, $40 pp
- à la carte dinner with wine at licensed restaurant, $60 pp
- picnics on request, $25 pp
- laundry services, $10
- German & French spoken
- guest entrances & balconies
- courtesy passenger transfer
- on-site parking; helipad

ACTIVITIES AVAILABLE

- croquet & pétanque on site
- 2ha landscaped gardens on site
- swimming pool on site
- rowboat on estuary
- kayaking, diving, fishing & sailing access from site
- 2 golf courses; quad bikes
- clay pigeon shooting
- walks; horse riding
- tennis court

- vineyards; wine tours
- antiques shops at Warkworth
- Matakohe Kauri Museum
- marine farm; surf beaches
- local crafts, artwork & pottery
- historic Mansion House on Kawau Island
- Tawharanui Regional Park
- helicopter sightseeing
- Goat Island; nature trails

MATAKANA, WARKWORTH
Takatu Lodge

Hosts Heather and John Forsman   *Phone* 0-9-423 0299

518 Whitmore Road, Matakana, Warkworth   *Fax* 0-9-423 0299
Postal P O Box 129, Matakana, Auckland 1241   *Mobile* 021 825 285
Email heather@takatulodge.co.nz   *Website* www.takatulodge.co.nz

DIRECTIONS: At Warkworth, turn right into Matakana/Leigh Rd. Travel 1km past Matakana & turn right at Omaha sign. Turn right into Takatu Rd, travel 2km, turn right into Whitmore Rd & travel 1.2km to Lodge on left.

| 4 bdrm | 4 enst | Room rate $390–$490 | *Includes breakfast, apéritifs & hors d'oeuvres* | *Dinner extra* | |

Takatu Lodge is contemporary in style, using natural timber, stone and marble to reflect its environment. Architectural features include open log fires inside and out, a guest library, and landscaped courtyards. Four spacious guest bedrooms, each with ensuite bathroom, open to individual terraces, capturing views over the surrounding vineyard to the ranges and sea beyond. Attention to detail and high standards of design encourage guests to relax in this peaceful setting among the vines. Takatu is a working vineyard where guests can appreciate fine wines to complement the food, with dinner available by arrangement. Meals are prepared with organic, regional and seasonal produce, and there is an extensive in-house wine cellar.

FACILITIES

- 4 super-king/twin ensuite bedrooms, all with rural views
- double baths, demist mirrors, hair dryers, toiletries, bathrobes, heated towel rails & heated floors
- yoga mats, essential oils, candles, cotton bed linen, writing desk, phone, tea/coffee & fridge with organic juices, fresh fruit & chocolate in each bedroom
- central heating; LCD TV available

- laundry service, extra
- full breakfast menu served
- dinner by request, extra
- complimentary pre-dinner Takatu wine & antipasti
- lounge with open fire, tea/coffee, Sky TV, video, DVD & writing desk
- email & fax available
- on-site parking; helipad

ACTIVITIES AVAILABLE

- on-site wine tours & tastings by arrangement
- beauty/masage therapy, extra
- beach, bush & ranges walks
- scenic flights, by arrangement
- art galleries & art tours
- golf course; horse riding
- garden walks & tours
- boutique vineyard tours
- Warkworth, 10-min drive

- restaurants & cafés, 2.5km
- Matakana village Saturday farmers' markets, 2-min drive
- glass-bottom boat & deep-sea diving; fishing; surfing; beaches
- organic & permaculture farm tours & workshops
- Auckland, 1-hour drive or 15 mins by helicopter
- Kauwau Island, 30-min trip from Sandspit via boat

The Castle Matakana

Hosts Val and Ross Sutherland

378 Whitmore Road, Matakana, R D 6, Warkworth
Phone 0-9-422 9288   *Fax* 0-9-422 9289
Email mail@the-castle.co.nz   *Website* www.the-castle.co.nz

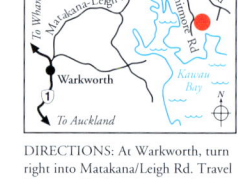

The Castle

DIRECTIONS: At Warkworth, turn right into Matakana/Leigh Rd. Travel 1km past Matakana & turn right at Omaha sign. Turn right into Takatu Rd, travel 2km, turn right into Whitmore Rd & travel 2.4km to The Castle on left.

3 bdrm	3 enst	Room rate $270–$342

Includes breakfast & apéritifs
Lunch, dinner & liquor extra

The Castle Matakana is a boutique lodge with vineyard in the Matakana Coast Wine Country near Warkworth. It is an easy hour north of Auckland and en route to the Bay of Islands. The contemporary architecture is designed to capture the rural and sea views over historic Kawau Bay, from every room. Upstairs is a spacious guest suite opening to a private balcony, with two further bedrooms in the guest wing on the ground floor, adjacent to the circular entrance lounge with log fire. Val's cuisine is a speciality at The Castle, featuring local produce and catering for individual requirements. Ross offers his own wines from his wine cellar, along with fine wines from Matakana's vineyards. Special occasions can be catered by arrangement.

FACILITIES

- 3 super-king/twin ensuite bedrooms, 1 with dual basins, bidet, dressing room, balcony
- cotton bed linen; iron & board
- hair dryers, heated floors, heated towel rails, toiletries & bathrobes
- fresh flowers, fruit, chocolates
- all rooms open to deck; views
- guest lounge with open fire, tea/coffee, music & artwork
- continental & cooked breakfasts served in dining room, or alfresco
- lunch/picnic on request, extra
- dinner, by prior arrangement, $75 pp, wine extra
- welcome tea/coffee on arrival
- laundry; central heating
- phone, fax & email access
- on-site parking

ACTIVITIES AVAILABLE

- giant chess board on balcony
- barbecue; pétanque/boules
- vineyard on site
- wine trail
- golfing
- art & craft galleries
- swimming; diving; sailing
- glass bottom boat trips
- ferry to Kawau Island
- local vineyard restaurant
- horse riding
- snorkelling
- Goat Island marine reserve
- white sand beaches
- surfing; wind surfing
- walking & tramping tracks
- Warkworth restaurants & township, 15-min drive
- Auckland, 1 hour south

The Castle

The Castle

MATAKANA, WARKWORTH
Rosemount Homestead

Host Libby Dykes

25 Rosemount Road, Matakana, Warkworth
Phone 0-9-422 2580   *Mobile* 027 496 6654   *Fax* 0-9-422 2583
Email enquiries@rosemount.co.nz   *Website* www.rosemount.co.nz

DIRECTIONS: Take SH 1 north to Warkworth. Turn right at traffic lights towards Matakana & Leigh. Pass Warkworth Golf Course on right, then turn left into Rosemount Rd. Travel up hill to Rosemount on right.

| 3 bdrm | 3 enst |

Room rate $195–$225   *Includes breakfast*

Originally built in 1900, Rosemount Homestead was constructed from a twin-trunk native kauri, felled by an early settler in the Matakana valley and sawn on the property. Libby and her late husband, Charlie, restored this two-storey villa with care and attention to detail to provide three ensuite guestrooms, each opening to a balcony. Set in a landscaped garden on six hectares (15 acres) of grazing land, Rosemount provides extensive rural views of rolling hillsides from its elevated site. Just one hour north of Auckland City, in the heart of the Matakana wine region, Rosemount is close to vineyards and Warkworth restaurants. A full breakfast is served in the dining room or alfresco by the swimming pool.

FACILITIES

- 2 queen ensuite bedrooms
- 1 twin ensuite bedroom
- cotton bed linen, writing desk, TV & tea/coffee in bedrooms
- heated towel rails & hair dryers in all 3 ensuites
- balcony opening from each bedroom with rural views
- fresh flowers
- unsuitable for children

- full country cooked breakfast
- email, fax & phone available
- lounge with open fire, Sky TV, CD-player & writing desk
- full wedding & honeymoon facilities available
- swimming pool & spa pool
- courtesy passenger transfer by arrangement
- on-site parking

ACTIVITIES AVAILABLE

- Matakana wine trail
- vineyards
- Ascension Vineyard music events & shows, 1km away
- many craft shops
- local produce stalls in surrounding area
- Sheep World
- Leigh fishing village
- Warkworth, 4km away

- several restaurants nearby, closest 5-min walk away
- Morris & James pottery
- Goat Island marine reserve with glass bottom boat trips
- walks & beaches on Tawharanui Peninsula
- Warkworth Golf Club & course, 3-min drive away
- Warkworth historical museum; kauri forest

WARKWORTH

Stargate Lodge

Hosts Tracie Lee and Kevin Martin

139 Clayden Road, Warkworth   *Postal* P O Box 275, Warkworth
Phone 0-9-425 9995   *Mobile* 021 665 401   *Fax* 0-9-425 0102
Email info@stargate-lodge.co.nz   *Website* www.stargate-lodge.co.nz

DIRECTIONS: From Auckland, take SH 1 north to Warkworth. Turn right at 2nd traffic lights & take left fork into Matakana Rd. Travel about 1km & turn left into Clayden Rd. Travel 1.4km, veering left to Stargate Lodge.

eftpos

4 bdrm	3 enst	1 prbth	1 pdrm

Room rate $230–$300

Includes breakfast
Lunch & dinner extra

In a peaceful setting with 360-degree rural vistas, Stargate Lodge is surrounded by a hectare of pastureland and three hectares of native bush, with walks throughout. Purpose-built in 2002 to provide contemporary accommodation, Stargate offers guests a choice of spacious ensuite bedrooms, each opening to a private balcony. Guests enjoy the gourmet cuisine prepared by Kevin, the in-house award-winning pastry chef, who is a leading cake designer. He provides daily menus to suit guests' requirements, with three-course dinner accompanied by wine from the bar beside the open fire in the guest lounge. Breakfast is chosen from the menu the evening before and served in the formal dining room, the breakfast nook, or in the guestrooms.

FACILITIES

- 1 king suite & bathroom, with queen sofa-bed in private lounge
- 3 super-king ensuite bedrooms
- hair dryers, toiletries & heated towel rails in all bathrooms; spa bath in 1 ensuite
- TV, tea/coffee, fridge & private balcony for each guestroom
- phone, fax & email available
- fresh flowers; laundry available
- cotton bed linen

- choice from full gourmet breakfast menu
- lunch by arrangement
- 3-course à la carte dinner, $50–$75 pp; wine extra
- guest lounge with open fire, bar, Sky TV, video, DVD & CD-player
- conference facilities
- on-site parking

ACTIVITIES AVAILABLE

- walks in 4-ha of native bush & pasture on site; star gazing
- BBQ area; 2 cats, 4 guinea pigs & 9 sheep on site
- wineries; golf courses
- swimming beaches
- snorkelling at Goat Island, a national maritime reserve
- boating, fishing & diving
- gardens open to visit

- restaurants, cafés & shopping at Warkworth, 10-min drive
- art galleries & antique shops
- Morris & James pottery
- museum at Warkworth
- Tawharanui Regional Park
- Sheep World; Honey Centre
- Ascension music events
- Waiwera hot pools, 25 mins
- Auckland, 1 hour south

MATAKANA, WARKWORTH
Ambiente

Hosts Patricia and Ron Ward

61 Golf Road, Matakana, Warkworth   *Phone* 0-9-422 2529
Postal P O Box 735, Warkworth   *Fax* 0-9-422 2529
Email ambiente@xtra.co.nz   *Website* friars.co.nz/hosts/ambiente.html

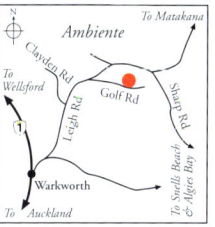

DIRECTIONS: From Auckland, take SH 1 north to Warkworth. Turn right at 2nd traffic lights & take left fork into Matakana-Leigh Rd. Travel about 2km & turn right into Golf Rd. Travel to Ambiente on left.

2 bdrm	1 enst	1 prbth

Apartment/room rate $175–$245

Includes continental breakfast
Self-catering in apartment

Located adjacent to an 18-hole golf course, Ambiente is set in over three hectares, including two hectares (five acres) of native bush. Guests are accommodated either in a self-contained apartment downstairs, or a separate queen-size bedroom and private bathroom. Ambiente is Italian for "ambience", the guestrooms featuring quality furnishings including silk cushions, with silk bathrobes and slippers for guest use. A continental breakfast is supplied on a trolley to the guestrooms, and the apartment has a self-catering kitchen. With views over native trees down into Matakana Valley and a nearby chestnut farm, Ambiente is situated in Matakana wine country, providing easy access for guests to the many vineyards, restaurants and cafés nearby.

FACILITIES

- apartment: 1 queen ensuite bedroom, dining area & lounge
- 1 queen bedroom with private bathroom
- quality cotton bed linen, TVs, phone jacks & tea/coffee
- hair dryers, toiletries, heated towel rails & bathrobes
- wheelchair access
- guest lounge with tea/coffee, artwork, books & magazines
- continental breakfast trolley to door
- full kitchen for self-catering in apartment
- email, & fax available
- self-serve laundry
- fresh flowers
- courtesy passenger transfer from Warkworth
- on-site parking

ACTIVITIES AVAILABLE

- bush walks on site
- 2ha native bush on site
- boat parking available
- Warkworth village, 3 mins
- shops & galleries
- linen specialist nearby
- 18-hole golf course, 500m
- surfing at Omaha, 10 mins
- Kawau Island ferry from Sandspit, 15-min drive
- restaurants & cafés, 3-min drive away
- wineries & vineyards
- gardens to visit
- Tawharanui Bird Sanctuary & Goat Island fish sanctuary, 20-min drive
- Leigh cafés & surfing
- Auckland City, 45 mins
- airport, 1-hour drive

© Friars' Guide to New Zealand Accommodation for the Discerning Traveller

55

SANDSPIT, WARKWORTH
The Saltings

Hosts Maureen and Terry Baines

1210 Sandspit Road, Sandspit   *Phone* 0-9-425 9670
Postal 1210 Sandspit Road, R D 2, Warkworth   *Mobile* 021 625 948
Fax 0-9-425 9674   *Email* relax@saltings.co.nz   *Website* www.saltings.co.nz

3 bdrm	3 enst

Room rate $225–$265   *Includes breakfast*

DIRECTIONS: From Auckland, take SH 1 north to Warkworth. At 2nd lights turn right towards Sandspit/ Snells Beach. Travel 5 mins then turn left into Sandspit Rd. Continue 2km to The Saltings driveway on right.

Located at Sandspit, overlooking the estuary, The Saltings was built in 1970 and converted to accommodation in 1996. The Mediterranean atmosphere is enhanced by the small vineyard, olive grove and lavender paths, complemented by the rustic interiors featuring oiled timber and plaster walls. French doors open from each of the three guestrooms to private patios, and the ensuites include tiled mosaics. Downstairs are the Tuscany Suite with its own lounge, the Palm Room, Lavender Room, and the guest coffee lounge. A full gourmet breakfast is served upstairs with sea views. Set in three hectares of landscaped gardens, The Saltings also offers self-contained accommodation at the Vintner's Haven (*see page 71 opposite*).

FACILITIES

- Tuscany Suite: 1 super-king ensuite bedroom with lounge, French doors to patio, writing desk, phone jack & tea/coffee
- Palm Room: 1 super-king ensuite bedroom opens to patio
- Lavender Room: 1 king ensuite bedroom opens to patio
- cotton bed linen; fresh flowers
- hair dryer, toiletries, bathrobes & heated towel rails
- full breakfast served upstairs in dining room with sea views
- private guest coffee lounge downstairs with TV
- email, fax & phone available
- German spoken
- private guest entrance
- on-site parking
- closed 24 Dec. – 2 January

ACTIVITIES AVAILABLE

- pétanque/boules on site
- 3ha (8 acres) landscaped grounds
- Matakana wine trail
- safe swimming at local beaches
- snorkelling at Goat Island Marine Reserve
- sea kayaking
- hiking in regional parks
- pottery & cafés
- mailboat cruise
- restaurants & cafés, 5 mins
- local artists
- antique shops
- Warkworth township, 10 mins
- 3 golf courses
- Kawau Island & historic Mansion House, by ferry
- gardens open to visit
- Waiwera hot pools, 25 mins
- Auckland, 1 hour south

The Saltings

SANDSPIT, WARKWORTH
The Vintner's Haven

Hosts Maureen and Terry Baines

1210 Sandspit Road, Sandspit, R D 2, Warkworth
Phone 0-9-425 9670   *Mobile* 021 625 948   *Fax* 0-9-425 9674
Email relax@saltings.co.nz   *Website* www.saltings.co.nz

DIRECTIONS: From Auckland, take SH 1 north to Warkworth. At 2nd lights turn right towards Sandspit/ Snells Beach. Travel 5 mins then turn left into Sandspit Rd. Continue 2km to The Saltings driveway on right.

3 bdrm	3 enst

Room/suite rate $200–$265   *Self-catering*   *Breakfast basket extra*
House rate $590–$675

The Vintner's Haven is a three-bedroom home built in 1980 and converted in 2003 to provide self-catering accommodation. Secluded and overlooking the small vineyard and estuary, this self-contained house extends the accommodation available next-door at The Saltings (*see opposite page 70*). The Bordeaux Suite includes a full kitchen, large decks for alfresco dining in summer, a log fire in the lounge for winter evenings, and a claw-foot bath. The Merlot Suite downstairs has a kitchenette, lounge and deck, and the Olive Room upstairs has a fridge and dining area. All three ensuites feature timber ceilings and local Morris and James tiles. Located in the heart of Matakana wine country The Vintner's Haven is close to restaurants and beaches.

FACILITIES

- Bordeaux Suite: 1 super-king bedroom upstairs, with claw-foot bath in ensuite, spacious kitchen, lounge, log fire, phone & balcony
- Merlot Suite: 1 queen bedroom downstairs, with ensuite, lounge, kitchenette & deck
- Olive Room: 1 super-king ensuite bedroom upstairs with fridge, tea/coffee, dining area & balcony
- self-service laundry

- breakfast basket by prior arrangement, $15 pp
- self-catering in both suites
- fresh flowers, bathrobes, cotton bed linen & phone jacks in all guestrooms
- hair dryers, heated towel rails & toiletries
- TV, CD-player & books in both lounges
- on-site parking

ACTIVITIES AVAILABLE

- 3ha (8 acres) of vines, olives & landscaped gardens
- Saturday morning markets at Matakana
- Matakana wine trail
- safe swimming at local beaches
- snorkelling at Goat Island Marine Reserve; sea kayaking
- hiking in regional parks
- local pottery

- restaurants & cafés, 5 mins
- mailboat cruise
- local artists; antique shops
- Warkworth township, 10 mins
- 3 golf courses
- Kawau Island & historic Mansion House, by ferry
- gardens open to visit
- Waiwera hot pools, 25 mins
- Auckland, 1 hour south

SANDSPIT, WARKWORTH
Sandspit Retreat

Hosts Sue and Dennis Anderson

18 Beach Street, R D 2, Sandspit, Warkworth
Phone 0-9-425 7128   *Mobile* 021 782 979   *Fax* 0-9-425 7128
Email sandspitretreat@value.net.nz   *Website* www.sandspitretreat.co.nz

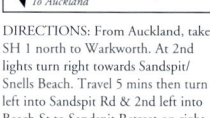

DIRECTIONS: From Auckland, take SH 1 north to Warkworth. At 2nd lights turn right towards Sandspit/Snells Beach. Travel 5 mins then turn left into Sandspit Rd & 2nd left into Beach St to Sandspit Retreat on right.

| 1 bdrm | 1 prbth | **Cottage rate $300**
Multiple night rates available | *Self-catering*
Includes breakfast provisions for 1st morning |

Set in a large subtropical garden, on the water's edge, Sandspit Retreat is a contemporary self-contained guesthouse. Designed with good utilisation of space, the retreat comprises a super-king/twin-size bedroom, private bathroom with garden view and open-plan lounge, dining and kitchen area. The bedroom opens onto a balcony where there is a spa pool with sea vistas. The spacious lounge is heated with a solid-fuel wood burner in winter, and the doors open to the decking with sea views for dining alfresco in the summer. Guests can self-cater and the gardens provide privacy from the hosts' residence. Guests have access to a gamesroom and indoor rock-climbing wall, and by arrangement the gymnasium and home theatre in the main house.

FACILITIES

- 1 private guesthouse for single-party bookings only
- 1 super-king/twin bedroom with Sky digital TV, DVDs & phone
- cotton bed linen; fresh flowers
- hair dryer, heated towel rails & toiletries in bathroom with 1-way glass garden view
- lounge with 2 double sofa-beds, wood burner & CD-player
- home theatre by arrangement

- breakfast provisions
- full self-catering kitchen
- phone & email available
- self-serve laundry
- children by arrangement
- spacious deck from lounge/ bedroom to spa pool
- gym by arrangement
- passenger transfer
- on-site parking

ACTIVITIES AVAILABLE

- gamesroom with X-box, table tennis & pool table; indoor rock climbing wall
- archery, sailing & kayaking from site
- beaches, fishing & wharf, within 2-min drive
- customised tours by hosts
- 3 golf courses; fishing trips
- Waiwera thermal pools, 20 mins
- Matakana wine trail

- restaurants, galleries, shops in Warkworth, 5-min drive
- Kauri Park; Sheep World
- horse riding; bush & beach walks; heritage trails
- Goat Island Marine Reserve snorkelling & boat trips
- white sand dune beaches
- cruises to Kawau Island
- Auckland, 50 mins south

MAHURANGI EAST, WARKWORTH
The Cottages

Hosts Marie Faith-Allen and Brian Allen   *Phone* 0-9-426 5605

91 Ridge Road, Scotts Landing, Mahurangi East, Warkworth
Mobile 027 326 8710   *Postal* 29 Chelverton Terrace, Red Beach, Orewa
Email faith-allen@xtra.co.nz   *Website* friars.co.nz/hosts/thecottages.html

DIRECTIONS: From Warkworth, at 2nd lights turn right into Sandspit Rd. Continue into Mahurangi East Rd. Travel past Algies Bay. Continue uphill & turn right into Ridge Rd. Travel 4.6km to The Cottages on right.

| 3 bdrm | 3 enst | Cottage rate $220 | *Self-catering* | *No meals available* |

Overlooking a large subtropical garden with native tui and fantails, hidden pathways and rest areas, The Cottages have rural views to the Mahurangi Harbour. Both cottages are self-contained with lounges opening to large private sundecks where alfresco dining is popular while enjoying the sunsets. The fully equipped kitchens enable guests to self-cater, and complimentary wine is provided. Opened in 2005, The Cottages feature a South Pacific flavour with artefacts from the Pacific Islands complementing the Maori and other New Zealand artworks. There are two queen-size ensuite bedrooms in Tui Cottage and one in Fantail Cottage, all bedrooms opening to separate private decks. Shops and restaurants are just a short drive away.

FACILITIES

- one-party booking per cottage
- Fantail Cottage: 1 queen ensuite bedroom
- Tui Cottage: 2 queen ensuite bedrooms
- cotton bed linen
- hair dryers, toiletries, heated towel rails, lavalavas & bathrobes
- private balcony from each bedroom
- self-serve laundry in each cottage
- full self-catering kitchen including dishwasher in each cottage
- complimentary wine
- lounge with Sky TV, DVD & CD-player, opening to large sundeck per cottage
- Sth Pacific & NZ artworks
- tiled patio per cottage
- on-site parking

ACTIVITIES AVAILABLE

- large subtropical garden with pathways & seats on site
- easy coastal walkways nearby
- safe beaches; golf course
- walk around Casnell Island
- historic buildings to visit
- Puhoi Historic Village & cheese factory
- Morris & James Pottery
- Waiwera hot pools
- restaurants & cafés, 15 mins
- Matakana market
- vineyard trips; wine trails
- ferry to Kawau Island
- Scandrett, Tawharanui, Mahurangi & Wenderholm Regional Parks nearby
- Goat Island marine reserve
- Orewa, 40-min drive
- Auckland, 1¼ hour drive

WARKWORTH
Waimana Point

Hosts Gloria and Geoff Collier

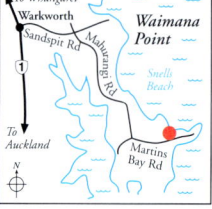

35 Martins Bay Road, R D 2, Warkworth
Phone 0-9-425 5102   *Mobile* 0274 971 535   *Fax* 0-9-425 5203
Email collier@xtra.co.nz   *Website* www.waimanapoint.co.nz

| 5 bdrm | 3 enst | 1 prbth | 1 pdrm |

Suite rate $450–$525

Includes breakfast options
Picnic lunch & dinner extra

Self-catering

DIRECTIONS: From Warkworth, at 2nd lights turn right to Snells Beach. Turn right into Mahurangi Rd & left into Martins Bay Rd. Travel past Algies Bay & continue 1km to Waimana Point on left. Travel 1.8km to lodge.

Waimana Point is located on a private secluded peninsula, not far from Warkworth. Maximising the sea views, the new lodge offers four self-contained suites, a conference room and lounge overlooking Kawau Bay to the island beyond. Set on seven hectares of pastureland and native bush, the lodge is constructed from cedar and riverstone. Each suite includes a kitchen and provisions, with breakfast options, and picnic lunches are available. The cuisine features local produce and seafood, and dinner can be served in the dining room, alfresco by a log fire or private dining can be arranged. There is a 20-metre heated lap pool and gym equipment, and the beach is just a two-minute walk away. The remnants of a Maori pa are visible on the site.

FACILITIES

- 3 suites with 1 super-king/twin ensuite bedroom in each
- 1 suite with 2 super-king/twin bedrooms & private bathroom
- Sky TV, DVD, writing desk, phone & internet connection
- hair dryers, toiletries, demist mirrors, bathrobes, heated floor & towel rails
- laundry available

- full kitchen for self-catering in each suite with provisions & full breakfast supplies
- cooked breakfast available
- picnic lunch, extra
- 4-course dinner with local produce & seafood, extra
- separate guest lounge with TV, DVD, wood fire, bar
- on-site parking; helipad

ACTIVITIES AVAILABLE

- conferences catered on site
- outdoor spa baths & sauna
- 20m heated indoor lap pool
- gym equipment; pétanque
- Maori pa remnants on site
- 7ha (18 acres) pasture/bush
- beach, 2-min walk
- watersports; launch cruises
- kayaking & dinghy sailing

- restaurants within 10 mins
- fishing; diving; swimming
- 2 local golf courses
- Scandrett Park, 2km away
- Goat Island marine reserve
- vineyards & wine tours
- Tawharanui Park, 20 mins
- boating in Kawau area; visits to Kawau Island
- Historic Mansion House

COWAN BAY, WARKWORTH
The Shanty

Hosts Megan Brice and Peter Sullivan

592 Cowan Bay Road, Pohuehue, Warkworth   *Postal* P O Box 387, Warkworth
Phone 0-9-425 0133   *Mobile* 021 806 060   *Fax* 0-9-425 0134
Email info.shanty@xtra.co.nz   *Website* www.cowanbayfarm.co.nz

DIRECTIONS: From Orewa take SH 1 north for 10 mins & turn right into Cowan Bay Rd. Travel 6km unsealed to Cowan Bay Farm at end. Veer left down to The Shanty. From Warkworth take SH 1 south for 5 mins & turn left.

| 3 bdrm | 1 prbth | Cottage rate $295 for 2 persons
Minimum 2-night stay on weekends | Extra persons $50 each
Self-catering | |

The Shanty

The Shanty, as the hosts affectionately call their restored beachfront cottage, is set in a secluded private bay on Mahurangi Harbour. High tide comes up to the sundeck, from where guests can watch fish jumping by day and the moonlight shining a path on the water at night. The sandy tidal beach is private for guest use only, offering safe swimming, fishing, kayaking and boating, with all equipment provided. The Shanty is suitable for families, where parents can relax on the deck and watch their children playing safely on the beach. Birdlife can be seen in the native bush on the 120-hectare farm, with bush walks in the adjacent reserve. The cottage is fully self-catering, with Warkworth township just 15 minutes' drive away.

FACILITIES

- 1 self-contained cottage
- single-party bookings only
- 1 king & 2 queen bedrooms
- 1 spacious bathroom with separate toilet
- hair dryer, toiletries & heated towel rails
- writing desk in 1 queen bedroom
- all bedrooms open to sundecks
- private beachfront location
- children welcome
- children's toys supplied
- full kitchen for self-catering
- basic supplies in pantry
- lounge with DVD, CDs, board games & books
- large sundeck opens from lounge & dining area
- pets welcome
- on-site parking

ACTIVITIES AVAILABLE

- 2 kayaks available for guest use
- high-tide boat launching available
- swimming & fishing from sandy beach on site; fishing net
- 120ha (300-acre) farm with rare cattle, sheep, 2 horses & 3 dogs
- bush walks & bird-watching, adjacent 160ha reserve
- gardens open to visit
- restaurants, cafés & shops in Warkworth, 15 mins north, or Orewa, 20-min drive south
- Matakana wine trail, weekend markets & Country Park
- Waiwera hot pools, cheese factory, Honey Centre, & Sheepworld
- Morris & James Pottery
- snorkelling at Goat Island
- Auckland City, 50 mins south

The Shanty

The Shanty

HATFIELDS BEACH, OREWA

Moontide Lodge

Hosts Ronnie and Andy Lee

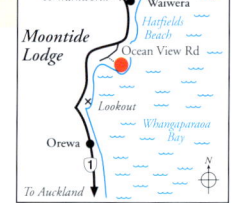

DIRECTIONS: From Auckland, take SH 1 north to Orewa. Continue north towards Hatfields Beach for 3km. Turn right into Ocean View Rd. Moontide Lodge on left, at end of driveway.

19 Ocean View Road, Hatfields Beach, Orewa
Phone 0-9-426 2374   *Mobile* 021 238 6010   *Fax* 0-9-426 2398
Email moontde@nznet.gen.nz   *Website* friars.co.nz/hosts/moontide.html

| 4 bdrm | 3 enst | 1 prbth | 1 pdrm |

Room rate $150–$200   *Includes breakfast*   *Lunch extra*

Moontide Lodge is perched on a clifftop overlooking Hatfields Beach and the ocean beyond. Only five minutes north of Orewa and south of the popular Waiwera hot pools, Moontide enjoys private access to the beach below. Renovated in 1998 to maximise the view, Moontide offers four guestrooms, each individually styled with ensuite or private bathroom. The Whangaparaoa Suite includes a private conservatory and deck, Hatfields Beach Room overlooks the beach below, Coromandel Room provides an ocean vista towards Coromandel, and Kauri View Room looks out on native bush and the beach. A full breakfast is served in the dining room or alfresco, lunch is also available, and there are small conference facilities at Moontide.

FACILITIES

- 4 queen bedrooms, 2 balconies
- 3 spacious ensuites & 1 private bathroom with robes & slippers
- phone, TV, desk, hair dryer & tea/coffee in each bedroom
- video & fax available
- guest lounge
- beach & ocean views
- children over 12 yrs welcome
- guest laundry, $10 per load
- continental or cooked breakfast served in dining room, or alfresco on deck
- lunch by arrangement, in garden, on decking, or picnic, extra
- complimentary drinks
- small conferences catered
- on-site parking
- passenger transfer arranged

ACTIVITIES AVAILABLE

- private access to beach
- boat ramp
- safe swimming from site, at Hatfields Beach
- horse trekking
- Waiwera hot pools, 5-min drive north
- Wenderholm Regional Park
- Puhoi historic village
- gardens open to visit
- choice of recommended restaurants nearby
- Orewa shops, 5 mins
- tennis
- golf courses & golf equipment available
- kayak tours
- Auckland City, 30 mins
- Auckland airport, 45-min drive south

WHANGAPARAOA
The Palms on Tindalls

Hosts Colleen and Graham Davies

75 De Luen Avenue, Tindalls Bay, Whangaparaoa
Phone 0-9-424 1930   *Mobile* 027 293 4929   *Fax* 0-9-424 1930
Email davies@palmsretreat.co.nz   *Website* www.palmsretreat.co.nz

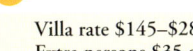

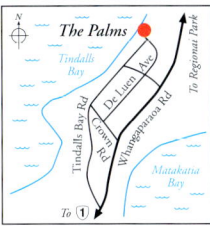

DIRECTIONS: From Auckland, take SH 1 north. Take Silverdale exit. Turn right into Whangaparaoa Rd. Travel through Manly village & turn left into Tindalls Bay Rd. At "T" junction turn left into De Luen Ave to The Palms.

| 2 bdrm | 1 prbth | Villa rate $145–$285
Extra persons $35 each | *Self-catering*
Long-term rates available | *Includes breakfast provisions* |

Located on the Whangaparaoa Peninsula, half an hour north of Auckland City, The Palms on Tindalls is a self-contained villa just 20 paces from the beach. Furnished with attention to detail, the villa provides a queen-size bedroom and, separate from the guest lounge, a private sun lounge with bed settee. Set in a private garden featuring a fish pond and waterfall, the villa has uninterrupted sea views of Tindalls Bay. French doors open from the lounge to the garden and beach beyond, and guests enjoy dining alfresco and barbecuing while watching the sunset over the bay. A self-service continental breakfast is provided and guests can self-cater in the fully equipped kitchen. There are restaurants in the village just three minutes' drive away.

FACILITIES

- one-party bookings only
- 1 queen bedroom
- 1 sunroom with double fold-out sofa
- 1 private bathroom
- hair dryer, toiletries, heated towel rails & bathrobes
- lounge with TV, DVD, CD-player & gas fire
- children welcome by request
- full kitchen for self-catering
- continental breakfast supplies, $15 pp, complimentary 1st night
- lounge & living areas opening to large courtyard with outdoor seating, barbecue & gardens
- self-serve laundry
- honeymoons catered for
- off-street parking

ACTIVITIES AVAILABLE

- spa pool & BBQ on site
- private garden with fish pond & waterfall on site
- safe swimming beach, 20m
- boating; watersports
- golf courses
- bush & coastal walks
- Wenderholm & Shakespear Park Regional Reserves
- Snowplanet, indoor snow dome
- restaurants in Manly Village
- Gulf Harbour Marina
- fishing, diving & cruising charters by arrangement
- ferries to bird sanctuary, Kawau Island & City
- Puhoi Village & cheese factory
- Waiwera Resort Hot Pools
- Orewa, 20 mins north
- Auckland, 30–40 mins south

Tindalls

TORBAY, AUCKLAND
The Bosuns Locker

Hosts Mandy and Clive Gumbley

11 Waiake Street, Torbay, Auckland
Phone 0-9-473 3713   *Mobile* 027 486 8520   *Fax* 0-9-473 3713
Email gums@xtra.co.nz   *Website* friars.co.nz/hosts/bosuns.html

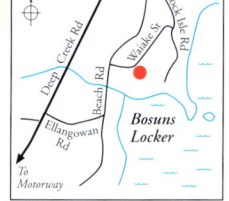

DIRECTIONS: From Auckland take SH 1 north. Take Albany exit into Oteha Valley Rd & then Carlisle Rd. Turn left into Deep Creek Rd, right into Ellangowan Rd, left into Beach Rd & right into Waiake St to cottage.

1 bdrm | 1 enst

Cottage rate $135–$245   *Includes breakfast*   *Self-catering*

The Bosuns Locker is a historic self-contained cottage originally built in 1930, just 80 metres from the beach. Recently renovated in a nautical theme, the cotttage provides accommodation for up to four guests with a super-king/twin bedroom and a sofa-bed in the lounge. There is a full kitchen for self-catering, and a welcome hamper is supplied, with extra provisions if required, by arrangement. The cottage is set in a private garden with sea views from the bedroom and kitchen. The hosts live in the house ajacent to the Bosuns Locker which has an interesting history. There is a walkway to the beach, where boat mooring is available, and restaurants are within walking distance. Auckland City is within half an hour's drive.

FACILITIES

- self-contained cottage with one-party bookings only
- 1 super-king/twin ensuite bedroom
- hair dryer, toiletries, heated towel rails & bathrobes
- fresh flowers; oil heaters
- lounge with tea/coffee, nibbles, TV, games, library & sofa bed
- phone in cottage for local calls only
- full kitchen for self-catering, with welcome hamper including home-baking, fruit & home-made chocolates
- extra provisions by request
- barbecue available
- laundry facilities in cottage
- children & pets welcome
- verandah in front of cottage
- on-site parking

ACTIVITIES AVAILABLE

- private garden on site
- beach 80m-walk away
- boat mooring
- local walks – bush walks, cliff-top beach walks
- swimming
- vineyards
- golf courses
- gardens to visit
- art galleries
- restaurants & cafés within walking distance
- historic homestead in local regional park
- horse riding
- Albany Sports Stadium
- Millennium Centre Sports Stadium
- Auckland City, 25 mins
- airport, 45-min drive

DEVONPORT, AUCKLAND
The Rainbow Villa

Host Judy McGrath

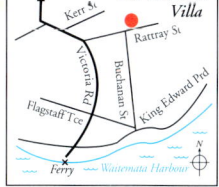

17 Rattray Street, Devonport
Phone 0-9-445 3597   *Email* rainbowvilla@xtra.co.nz
Fax 0-9-445 4597   *Website* friars.co.nz/hosts/rainbowvilla.html

DIRECTIONS: Travelling north, cross Auckland Harbour Bridge. Travel 1.5km & take Takapuna-Devonport exit. Follow signs to Devonport. Turn right into Victoria Rd & at village turn left into Rattray St. Rainbow Villa on left.

| 3 bdrm | 3 enst | **Double $130–$150** | **Single $100–$120** | *Includes breakfast* | |

This Victorian-style villa was built in 1885 for an engineer who came out from England to oversee the dockyard. The Rainbow Villa is so named because of the colourful stained-glass windows and it still features original fireplaces, tongue-and-groove ceilings, bay windows and carved archways. Judy, a sixth-generation New Zealander, has decorated the carefully restored villa in soft colours and uses the garden cottage as her art studio. Situated in a quiet cul-de-sac, close to the historic village of Devonport, The Rainbow Villa is set in a private garden, with a weeping elm in front of the villa and waterfall and small rock garden in the back of the garden. An ozone-purified spa pool offers a relaxing soak for guests in the garden setting.

FACILITIES

- 1 king, 1 queen & 1 twin ensuite bedroom, each with satellite TV
- hair dryers & toiletries
- bathrobes provided
- 100% cotton bed linen, white duvets & pillows, & Marcella bedspreads, with netting over each bed & electric blankets in winter
- guest lounge with satellite TV & complimentary sherry
- art studio

- breakfast – fresh orange juice, fruit platter, organic muesli, yoghurt, free-range eggs, lean bacon, & tomatoes
- tea/coffee & herbal teas
- phone & fax available
- ozone-purified spa pool
- pond in courtyard garden
- quiet cul-de-sac parking

ACTIVITIES AVAILABLE

- spa pool in garden
- sunny courtyard & pond
- many restaurants, wine bars & cafés within walking distance
- art gallery, museum, movies
- Windsor Reserve, safe swimming beach, 4-min walk
- 360° view over harbour from top of Mt Victoria
- harbour cruises from Devonport

- North Head historic gun emplacements
- tennis courts
- golf course
- bicycle riding
- private garden visits
- Devonport village shops
- exploring historic Devonport
- 10-min ferry to Auckland City shops, casino, etc

© Friars' Guide to New Zealand Accommodation for the Discerning Traveller

TAKAPUNA, AUCKLAND
Emerald Cottage

Manager Janice Heffernan

    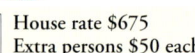

5 Alison Avenue, Takapuna   *Phone* 0-9-488 3500
Postal P O Box 33 303, Takapuna, Auckland   *Fax* 0-9-488 3555
Email info@emerald-inn.co.nz   *Website* www.emeraldcottage.co.nz

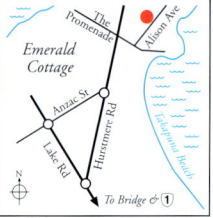

DIRECTIONS: Travelling north, cross Harbour Bridge. Take Takapuna exit. At 3rd set lights, turn left into Lake Rd. Next lights veer right into Hurstmere Rd. Turn right into The Promenade, then left into Alison Ave. Cottage on left.

| 3 bdrm | 1 enst | 1 prbth | **House rate $675** Extra persons $50 each | *Self-catering* **Long-term rates available** | *Breakfast extra* | |

The exclusive use of Emerald Cottage provides guests with privacy and seclusion overlooking Takapuna Beach with views to Rangitoto Island. This Cape Cod style home retains a seaside cottage ambience, but incorporates high quality fittings, furnishings and New Zealand artwork. Emerald Cottage is fully self-contained for self-catering or a chef can be arranged. A full cooked or continental breakfast is available in the Poolside Breakfast Room at The Emerald Inn adjacent. Next door, Emerald Villas are also available for accommodation (*see page 81 opposite*). An indoor spa pool is set in the conservatory looking out to the private landscaped garden. The downstairs lounge and upstairs honeymoon suite overlook the bay.

FACILITIES

- 1 king & 1 twin bedroom downstairs with bathroom including bath
- 1 super-king bedroom with double bath & double basin in ensuite, dressing room, fridge, tea/coffee, lounge & balcony
- heated towel rails, hair dryers & toiletries in all bathrooms
- TV & video in all bedrooms
- fresh flowers & original NZ art

- full kitchen for self-catering or chef by arrangement
- full breakfast at Emerald Inn, $10–$15 pp
- complimentary teas, coffee, fruit juice & cookies
- guest phone & fax
- guest laundry
- off-street parking
- passenger transfer arranged

ACTIVITIES AVAILABLE

- safe swimming beach, 50m
- indoor spa pool
- heated swimming pool adjacent
- 32 restaurants in walking distance
- downtown Auckland, 10-min drive, or 15 mins by ferry
- 6 golf courses
- tennis; cycling
- surfing; canoeing
- horse trekking

- Lake Pupuke nearby
- harbour cruises & boat trips to Rangitoto Island
- sea kayaking; jet-skiing
- fishing; parapenting
- 2 boating marinas
- coastal & bush walks
- gardens to visit
- art & craft galleries
- boutique shopping

TAKAPUNA, AUCKLAND
Emerald Villas

Manager Janice Heffernan

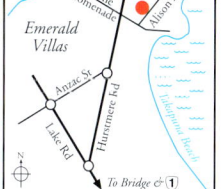

16 The Promenade, Takapuna   *Phone* 0-9-488 3500
Postal P O Box 33 303, Takapuna, Auckland   *Fax* 0-9-488 3555
Email info@emerald-inn.co.nz   *Website* www.emeraldcottage.co.nz

DIRECTIONS: Travelling north, cross Harbour Bridge. Take Takapuna exit. At 3rd set lights, turn left into Lake Rd. Next lights veer right into Hurstmere Rd. Turn right into The Promenade, then left into Alison Ave. Cottage on left.

 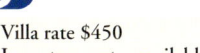

4 bdrm	2 prbth

Villa rate $450
Long-term rates available   *Self-catering*   *Breakfast extra*

Next door to Emerald Cottage (*see page 80 opposite*) are the Emerald Villas. These two villas offer spacious, fully self-contained accommodation, especially designed for families on transfer or holiday. Adjacent to Takapuna Beach, each holiday home is able to accommodate four people. Both family villas have a lounge, full kitchen for self-catering, bathroom including bath, guest laundry and two king-size bedrooms. Emerald Villas have private grounds with barbecue facilities, and are connected to The Emerald Inn complex for use of the heated swimming pool, spa pool, and the Poolside Breakfast Room where a full breakfast is available. The Takapuna business area, shops, cafés and restaurants are within walking distance of Emerald Villas.

FACILITIES

- single-party bookings per villa
- 2 self-contained villas
- 2 king bedrooms in each villa
- 1 bathroom, including bath, in each villa
- heated towel rails, hair dryers & toiletries in both bathrooms
- lounge with phone, Sky TV, video & CD-player in villas
- fresh flowers & original NZ art

- full kitchen for self-catering
- full breakfast at Emerald Inn, $10–$15 pp
- complimentary teas & coffee
- BBQ on site
- children welcome
- full laundry facilities
- off-street parking
- passenger transfer arranged

ACTIVITIES AVAILABLE

- safe swimming beach, 50m
- heated swimming pool adjacent
- 32 restaurants in walking distance
- downtown Auckland, 10-min drive, or 15 mins by ferry
- 6 golf courses
- cycling; horse trekking
- Lake Pupuke nearby
- sea kayaking; jet-skiing
- fishing

- 2 boating marinas
- harbour cruises & boat trips to Rangitoto Island
- coastal & bush walk
- tennis; surfing
- canoeing
- parapenting
- gardens to visit
- art & craft galleries
- boutique shopping

MATIATIA BAY, WAIHEKE ISLAND
The Moorings

Hosts Lyn and Warren Lincoln   *Phone* 0-9-372 8283

9 Ocean View Road, Matiatia Bay, Waiheke Island
Postal P O Box 377, Oneroa, Waiheke Island   *Fax* 0-9-372 8283
Email wlincoln@xtra.co.nz   *Website* www.themoorings.gen.nz

| 2 bdrm | 2 prbth | Studio rate $215–$280 | *Includes breakfast provisions* *Self-catering* |

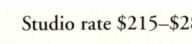

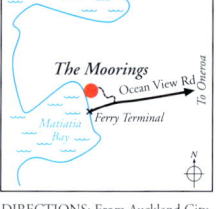

The Moorings
Ocean View Rd
Matiatia Bay
Ferry Terminal
To Oneroa

DIRECTIONS: From Auckland City in Quay St, take ferry to Waiheke Island. Take taxi or rental car up Ocean View Rd. Turn left into 1st driveway. Continue 100m to The Moorings at top. Well sign-posted.

Overlooking Matiatia Bay's moorings and the ferry wharf is The Moorings, purpose-built, self-contained accommodation. With uninterrupted views out to Rangitoto Island and the Hauraki Gulf to Auckland City beyond, The Moorings is popular for rest and recreation with constant boat activity to watch. Honeymooners find it a romantic retreat, yet still close to the amenities at Oneroa. The Moorings comprises two semi-detatched studio apartments, each open-plan with one king bed and a kitchette for self-catering. Continental breakfast provisions are supplied and the hosts live in the adjacent house. The entrance is through a private courtyard featuring lavenders, lemons and olives, and the studios open to private decks above the bay.

FACILITIES

- 2 studio apartments; one-party booking per studio
- each studio with 1 king bed & 1 private bathroom
- hair dryers, heated towel rails & toiletries in bathrooms
- spacious & sunny deck opening from each studio with seating, BBQ & panoramic sea views
- fresh flowers & magazines
- fax & email available
- self-contained kitchenette in each studio for self-catering
- continental breakfast provisions
- lounge area in each studio with Sky TV, stereo, CD-player, phone jacks & books
- laundry facilities available
- on-site parking; courtesy passenger transfer
- studio serviced on request, extra fee

ACTIVITIES AVAILABLE

- pétanque court on site
- bay access via private track
- honeymoons catered for
- guest barbecues on decks
- coastal walks; snorkelling
- rental cars, bikes & kayaks for hire at bottom of driveway
- fishing charters; fishing off rocks
- day trips around Waiheke
- gardens open to visit
- restaurant, 2-min walk away
- Oneroa beach, 10-min walk
- arts & crafts; olive groves
- wine tours & art tours
- restaurants, cafés, vineyards & shopping, 2-min drive
- Rangitoto Island, 20-min ferry
- Devonport, 30 mins by ferry
- Auckland City, 35 mins by ferry from Matiatia

CHURCH BAY, WAIHEKE ISLAND
The Estate, Church Bay

Hosts Helen and Julian Nalepa

56 Church Bay Road, Waiheke Island, Auckland
Email info@theestatechurchbay.co.nz   *Phone* 0-9-372 2637
Website www.theestatechurchbay.com   *Mobile* 021 048 4893

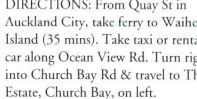

DIRECTIONS: From Quay St in Auckland City, take ferry to Waiheke Island (35 mins). Take taxi or rental car along Ocean View Rd. Turn right into Church Bay Rd & travel to The Estate, Church Bay, on left.

4 bdrm	2 enst	1 prbth

Double $400–$500
Single $350–$450

Includes breakfast
Lunch & dinner extra

The Estate, Church Bay is set in a commanding position on a ridge overlooking the Hauraki Gulf with 360-degree sea views. Surrounded by renowned vineyards and olive groves, hallmarks of Waiheke Island, The Estate is just over half an hour by ferry from Auckland City. The rose-lined courtyard is popular for weddings of up to 150 guests. Accommodation comprises four spacious bedrooms, two of which are in a guest wing with a private lounge. A full breakfast is served in the bedrooms, or alfresco on the balcony or in the courtyard. Adjoining The Estate is Mudbrick Vineyard and Restaurant which serves lunch and dinner, or these can be served in house by arrangement with the chef on call. Chelsea the labrador dog is in residence.

FACILITIES

- 2 super-king/twin bedrooms with ensuite bathrooms
- 1 wing with 2 super-king/twin bedrooms, inter-joining bathroom & private lounge
- cotton bed linen, TV, phone, tea/coffee & fridge in bedrooms
- bath, double basin, hair dryer, toiletries, bathrobes, heated floor & towel rails in bathrooms
- complimentary laundry service
- full cooked & continental breakfast by room service
- lunch & dinner in restaurant adjacent, or served in house by chef on call, extra
- lounge with open fire, Sky TV, video, DVD & bar
- email available; fresh flowers; children over 10 yrs welcome
- courtesy passenger transfer
- on-site parking

ACTIVITIES AVAILABLE

- pétanque & croquet on site
- bicycles & kayaks for guest use
- 4ha formal garden, native reserve, olive groves & pasture on site
- helicopter access; Mediterranean outdoor log fire & BBQ on site
- beauty & spa treatments, extra
- vineyards, wineries & olive grove tours by arrangement
- weddings, honeymoons & conferences catered for
- variety of restaurants & cafés within 10 mins
- safe swimming beaches
- horseback riding
- scenic walks & flights
- fishing, sailing & diving
- golf courses; paragliding
- arts & crafts; shopping
- WWII tunnels to explore
- ferry to Auckland, 35 mins

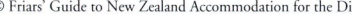

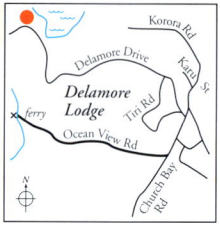

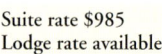

OWHANAKE BAY, WAIHEKE ISLAND
Delamore Lodge

Host Roselyn Barnett-Storey   *Mobile* 021 471 344

83 Delamore Drive, Owhanake Bay, Waiheke Island   *Phone* 0-9-372 7372
Postal P O Box 572, Oneroa, Waiheke Island   *Fax* 0-9-372 7382
Email reservations@delamorelodge.com   *Website* www.delamorelodge.com

4 bdrm	4 enst

Suite rate $985
Lodge rate available

Includes breakfast, hors d' oeuvres & apéritifs
Dinner extra

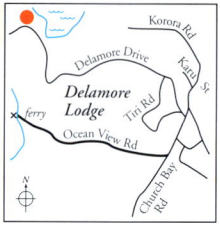

DIRECTIONS: From City, 35 mins by ferry to Waiheke Island. Take taxi or rental car along Ocean View Rd. Turn left into Korora Rd & left again into Delamore Dr. Delamore Lodge on right. 12 mins by helicopter.

Overlooking Owhanake Bay on Waiheke Island, Delamore Lodge was completed in 2003 without a straight wall in the entire complex. Built into the side of a rolling hill, leading directly to the beach, the curves and soft edges were designed to blend in with the sky, sea and earth. The interior walls and ceiling were all carefully hand-plastered and the result is an ambience that complements the sea vistas. Eight guests can be accommodated in the private suites, and special features include the starlit grotto, deep cave jacuzzi, sauna cove with all-over body shower, and the spa treaments available. Gourmet dining is enjoyed alfresco by the Mediterranean-style log fireplace, or indoors at individual dining tables or the shared table.

FACILITIES

- 4 super-king/twin suites with private courtyard gardens
- baths, double basins, heated towel rails, demist mirrors, hair dryers, toiletries, slippers & bathrobes
- phone, Sky TV, DVD, CDs, full mini-bar, teas/coffee, writing desk & artwork in suites
- wheelchair access; powder rooms
- open lounge with fire & sea vistas; Mediterranean outdoor log fire

- gourmet breakfast indoors, alfresco, or room service
- 5-course table d'hôte dinner with wine, extra
- fax & email available
- wedding ceremonies, honeymoons & functions catered
- 2 spa treatment rooms
- private guest entrance; on-site parking; helipad

ACTIVITIES AVAILABLE

- alfresco dining beside outdoor log fire
- grotto, jacuzzi, sauna, beauty & spa treatments on site
- lithos massage on site
- library & board games
- golf; beaches
- arts & crafts
- vineyard tours
- gardens; walks

- olive-grove cafés
- restaurants, 2-min drive
- music festivals
- kayaking; sailing; fishing
- wine festivals
- scenic flights
- scuba diving; paragliding
- tramping; horse riding
- Auckland City, 35 mins by ferry
- air services from Auckland

69

LITTLE ONEROA BAY, WAIHEKE ISLAND
The Boatshed

Host Jonathan Scott   Phone 0-9-372 3242

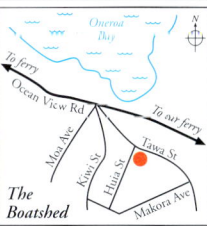

Corner of Tawa and Huia Streets, Waiheke Island   *Fax* 0-9-372 3262
Postal P O Box 91-742, Auckland Mail Centre   *Mobile* 021 512 127
Email enquiries@boatshed.co.nz   *Website* www.boatshed.co.nz

5 bdrm	5 enst	1 prbth

Room rate $600–$760

Includes breakfast
Lunch & dinner extra

DIRECTIONS: From Auckland City, take ferry to Waiheke Island. Take taxi or rental car along Ocean View Rd through Oneroa to Little Oneroa. Turn right into Tawa St. The Boatshed on right, on corner of Huia St.

The Boatshed, boutique seaside accommodation, is located on Waiheke Island's northern sun-drenched shores, set above the clear waters and white sandy swimming beaches of Oneroa. The contemporary architecture is designed to capture the feeling of Waiheke's historical boatsheds of the early 1900s. The five Boatshed guestrooms offer panoramic sea views, each with private balcony, open fire and ensuite bathroom. Fine dining is available with traditional and Pacific Rim cuisine matched to an extensive New Zealand wine list. A short walk takes guests to Oneroa village, with access to extensive coastal walks. Exclusive use of the Boatshed is available for family gatherings, small weddings, and management retreats.

FACILITIES

- 4 super-king/twin bedrooms, each with ensuite bathroom
- 3-storey Lighthouse, queen bed, ensuite & separate lounge suite
- cotton bed linen, writing desk, TV, CD, DVD, mini bar, open fire, IDD phone & wireless internet in all 5 guestrooms
- hair dryer, bathrobes, scuffs, heated floors, toiletries & beach bag of amenities
- full continental & cooked breakfast; lunch $25–$35 pp
- 4-course dinner, $85 pp
- guest lounge with open fire, tea/coffee, nibbles, bar, Sky TV, video & writing desk
- children by arrangement
- laundry available; wheelchair access
- courtesy passenger transfer; on-site parking

ACTIVITIES AVAILABLE

- pétanque/boules on site
- masseuse available on site by prior arrangement
- conferences, weddings, honeymoons catered for
- Little Oneroa Beach, 3-min walk; swimming
- coastal walks
- fishing & kayaking
- bicycle hire
- village, 8-min walk
- vineyard lunches & tours
- beaches & watersports
- art galleries & tours
- golf courses
- beauty therapy
- horse riding
- hiking
- passenger ferry wharf, 5-min drive
- Auckland City, 35 mins by ferry

TE WHAU POINT, WAIHEKE ISLAND
Te Whau Lodge

Hosts Liz Eglinton and Gene O'Neill

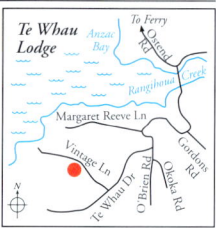

36 Vintage Lane, R D 1, Te Whau Point, Waiheke Island
Phone 0-9-372 2288   *Mobile* 027 430 8222   *Fax* 0-9-372 2218
Email lizandgene@tewhaulodge.co.nz   *Website* www.tewhaulodge.co.nz

DIRECTIONS: Take ferry to Waiheke Island. From Matiatia or Kennedy Pt, follow signs towards Rocky Bay. From O'Brien Rd, turn right into Te Whau Drive. Turn right again into Vintage Lane. Te Whau Lodge on left.

4 bdrm	4 enst	2 pdrm	Double $410	Single $360	*Includes breakfast & apéritifs*
			Double $610	Single $450	*Includes breakfast, apéritifs & dinner*

Surrounded by native planting and regenerating bush on Te Whau Peninsula, the Lodge features an outdoor spa pool and extensive decks, with outdoor seating overlooking Putiki Bay and the Waitemata Harbour. Panoramic views across the sea to Rangitoto Island and Auckland City beyond are complemented by the evening sunsets. Set in a rural location with vineyards and olive groves close by, Te Whau Lodge is a tranquil retreat, architecturally designed and purpose built in a contemporary New Zealand style. Te Whau accommodates up to eight guests in four ensuite bedrooms and offers fine food and wine. Dining is a key feature at Te Whau, with local produce used wherever possible, and Waiheke wines included on the wine list.

FACILITIES

- 4 super-king ensuite bedrooms
- hair dryers, toiletries, heated towel rails & wheelchair access
- cotton bed linen
- CD-player in each guestroom
- TV in rooms on request
- guest lounge with open fire, TV, video & CD-player

- full breakfast served in dining room or alfresco on spacious sundecks
- 4-course dinner served Saturday; other days by arrangement
- fully licensed
- phone, fax & email available
- complimentary laundry
- courtesy passenger transfer to & from ferry or local airfield

ACTIVITIES AVAILABLE

- outdoor spa pool with sea views
- in-house massage by arrangement
- pétanque/boules on site
- spacious decks for dining, relaxing & reading
- extensive library & CD collection
- conference facilities
- beaches; watersports
- many local walking trails
- art galleries & artist studios

- cafés & restaurants nearby
- vineyards
- golf
- boating; fishing
- shopping, 10-min drive
- Auckland City, 35 mins by passenger or car ferry
- Auckland International Airport, 12-min flight

72

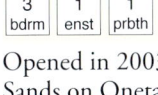

3 bdrm	1 enst	1 prbth

ONETANGI, WAIHEKE ISLAND
Waiheke Sands Apartment

Managers Tony and Raewyn Lancaster   *Phone* 0-9-372 4484

Apartment 16, 141–145 The Strand, Onetangi Beach, Waiheke Island
Postal P O Box 188, Oneroa, Waiheke Island   *Mobile* 027 448 5741
Email lansands@pl.net   *Website* www.waihekeluxury.com   *Fax* 0-9-372 4558

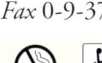

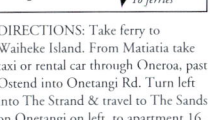

DIRECTIONS: Take ferry to Waiheke Island. From Matiatia take taxi or rental car through Oneroa, past Ostend into Onetangi Rd. Turn left into The Strand & travel to The Sands on Onetangi on left, to apartment 16.

Apartment rate $350–$450   *Self-catering*

Opened in 2003, Waiheke Sands Apartment is part of The Sands on Onetangi complex located on the sheltered quiet western end of the north-facing beach. The apartment commands panoramic views over Onetangi Beach from the lounge, dining room, two bedrooms and the deck. Designed in a contemporary style, the self-contained apartment provides quality fittings and furnishings including leather sofas and granite benches, and original New Zealand artwork is featured. Guests can self-cater in the fully equipped kitchen and alfresco dining can be enjoyed on the spacious terrace where there is a gas barbecue and outdoor furniture. There are many restaurants and wineries from five to 15 minutes away, and Auckland City is 35 minutes by ferry.

Waiheke Sands

Waiheke Sands

FACILITIES

- single-party bookings only
- 1 king ensuite bedroom
- 1 king & 1 twin bedroom share 1 bathroom
- king bedrooms open to deck
- hair dryer, toiletries & heated towel rails in both bathrooms
- lounge with tea/coffee, Sky TV, DVD, CD-player, artwork & magazines
- quality fittings
- self-service laundry
- fully equipped kitchen for self-catering
- large terrace with gas BBQ & outdoor furniture
- lift access
- wheelchair access
- children welcome
- sea views
- on-site parking

ACTIVITIES AVAILABLE

- direct beach access from apartment
- variety of restaurants, cafés & village shops, 5–15-min drive
- bush walks
- native bird-watching
- scenic drives
- wineries & tastings
- snapper fishing
- sea kayaking
- boating
- water skiing
- local art studios & art for sale
- bicycle hire
- golf course, 5-min drive
- horse trekking
- Waiheke Island tours
- Auckland City, 35 mins by passenger or car ferry
- Auckland International Airport, 12-min flight

Waiheke Sands

87

© Friars' Guide to New Zealand Accommodation for the Discerning Traveller

CONNELLS BAY, WAIHEKE ISLAND
Connells Bay

Hosts Jo and John Gow

Connells Bay, Cowes Bay Road, R D 1, Waiheke Island
Phone 0-9-372 8957   *Mobile* 021 363 613   *Fax* 0-9-377 4877
Email info@connellsbay.co.nz   *Website* www.connellsbay.co.nz

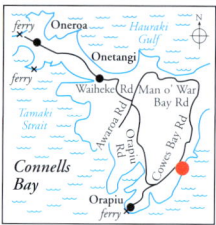

DIRECTIONS: Take ferry to Waiheke Island. Take hire vehicle on Waiheke Rd. Continue into Orapiu Rd. At "T" junction turn left into Cowes Bay Rd. Travel just over 1km to Connells Bay to yellow letterbox on left.

| 2 bdrm | 1 enst | 1 prbth | **Cottage rate $350** **Minimum 2-night stay** | *Includes breakfast provisions* *Self-catering* | |

Connells Bay

Sited at the historic trading depot in Connells Bay since circa 1890, the colonial guest cottage is one of three on 24 hectares (60 acres) at the privately owned bay on the eastern side of Waiheke Island. The century-old cottage has recently been restored and refurbished to provide self-contained accommodation just 10 metres from the beach, backed by native trees and rolling farmland. The guest cottage is set in a fenced garden, beyond which is a unique sculpture park comprising commissioned and purchased contemporary works by some of New Zealand's most renowned sculptors. Walking tracks are cut through the park and surrounding bush, which includes an ancient stand of kauri trees. Guests also enjoy kayaking to nearby islands.

FACILITIES

- one-party bookings only
- 2 double bedrooms, with ensuite or private bathroom, opening to deck
- hair dryer & quality toiletries in both bathrooms
- lounge with open fire, artwork, tea/coffee facilities, CDs, phone, books & magazines
- sunrise over sea from bedrooms & lounge
- full self-catering kitchen
- breakfast provisions
- outdoor BBQ area
- cotton bed linen
- fresh flowers
- self-serve laundry facilities
- on-site parking
- vehicle for hire, extra
- helipad; boat mooring

ACTIVITIES AVAILABLE

On site:
- pétanque or boules
- contemporary sculpture park
- walks in 24ha (60 acres) of bush & rolling farmland
- fishing boat with motor & gear; wharf
- 3 kayaks for guest use
- snapper fishing in bay
- safe swimming in bay

Off site:
- kayaking to nearby islands
- Stoney Batter historic site, 10-min drive
- vineyards; art galleries
- golf course, 20-min drive
- Waiheke Island tours
- Auckland airport, 12-min flight
- Auckland City, 35-min ferry

Connells Bay

Connells Bay

PATIO BAY, WAIHEKE ISLAND
Patio Bay

Hosts Frances and Ian McIndoe

Patio Bay, Waiheke Island   *Postal* 115 Victoria Avenue, Remuera, Auckland
Phone 0-9-524 7565   *Mobile* 021 728 829   *Fax* 0-9-520 5864
Email fox-home@xtra.co.nz   *Website* friars.co.nz/hosts/patiobay.html

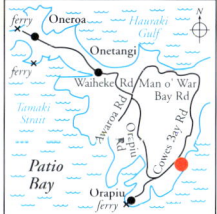

DIRECTIONS: From Quay St in City, take ferry to Waiheke Island. Take rental car on Waiheke Rd, into Orapiu Rd. At "T", turn left into Cowes Bay Rd. Take 5th drive on right at white cow letterbox to end of steep driveway.

5 bdrm	2 enst	1 shbth

House rate $1,200 up to 6 adults   *Self-catering, or qualified chef extra*
Minimum 3-night stay

Patio Bay

Patio Bay is a private holiday home available for self-contained accommodation for up to six adults for a minimum three-night stay. Situated on the eastern coast of Waiheke Island, Patio Bay is accessible by rental car or private transfer from the ferry terminals. The private sandy beach with deep safe anchorage offers secluded tranquillity, enhanced by pohutukawa trees, terraced garden, floodlit all-weather tennis court, golf chipping green and six hectares (15 acres) of land. The two-storey home built in a lodge style provides five bedrooms and three bathrooms. The king-size bedroom features a raised central spa bath, dual shower and private viewing balcony. All meals can be self-catered, using the fully equipped kitchen, although a professional chef is available if preferred.

FACILITIES

- private-group bookings
- 1 king ensuite bedroom, with double basins, dual shower, spa bath & balcony
- 1 queen ensuite bedroom
- 1 double & 1 twin bedroom & 1 bunkroom share 1 bathroom with bath & additional 2 toilets
- 3 hair dryers & 3 heated towel rails
- fully equipped kitchen, with walk-in coolroom, for self-catering & entertaining
- chef by arrangement
- lounge with open fire, large screen Sky TV, VCR, & hi-fi
- self-service laundry
- guest phone & fax
- unsuitable for children
- passenger transfer, extra

ACTIVITIES AVAILABLE

- boat mooring; rowboat
- indoor & outdoor BBQs
- spa pool & swimming pool
- floodlit all-weather tennis court & 4 racquets
- golf chipping green & clubs
- billiards, snooker, pool
- pétanque (boules)
- terraced garden
- swimming in bay
- restaurants & cafés, 20km
- fishing from bay
- Waiheke Channel
- Pakatoa Island, 2km by sea
- Ponui Island, 1km by sea
- 9-hole golf course, 20 mins
- Waiheke Island Walkways
- ferry from Orapiu Wharf, 2km
- ferry from Matiatia Wharf, 24km
- Auckland, 35-min ferry trip

Patio Bay

Patio Bay

TITIRANGI, WEST AUCKLAND
Titirangi Coastal Cottage

Hosts Fiona Jeaffreson and Mike Reynolds   *Mobile* 021 897 731

12 Opou Road, French Bay, West Auckland   *Phone* 0-9-817 8323
Postal P O Box 60 493, Titirangi, Auckland   *Fax* 0-9-817 8323
Email info@coastal-cottages.co.nz   *Website* www.coastal-cottages.co.nz

DIRECTIONS: From City take SH 16 & exit at Waterview. Travel to New Lynn & take Titirangi Rd. Turn left into Park Rd & left into Otitori Bay Rd. Turn left into Opou Rd & park outside #14. Take pathway down to Cottage.

2 bdrm	1 prbth

Cottage rate $450 for 2 persons
Extra persons $30 each

Includes breakfast provisions
Self-catering

Titirangi Coastal Cottage

Set in native bush at Titirangi, with views through nikau plams to the water beyond, Titirangi Coastal Cottage offers self-contained accommodation in a secluded spot only half an hour from Auckland City. The timbered cottage has been fully renovated and refurbished to provide two king-size bedrooms downstairs, both of which open to the lower deck where guests can relax in the spa pool beneath the native trees. Upstairs is a fully equipped kitchen for self-catering and a spacious living room with home theatre and original New Zealand artwork. The dining area opens to the upper deck from which guests can enjoy watching the native birds in the bush and the sea views while dining alfresco. Full breakfast provisions are supplied.

FACILITIES

- one-party bookings only
- 1 super-king/twin & 1 king bedroom with 1 bathroom including claw-foot bath
- hair dryer, toiletries, bathrobes, heated floor & towel rails
- both bedrooms open to deck overlooking bush & nikau palms
- lounge with wood fire, plasma-screen Sky TV, DVD, video & original NZ artwork
- fully self-contained kitchen for self-catering
- extensive breakfast provisions supplied
- self-serve laundry
- living area opens to deck with sea & bush views
- phone in cottage
- fresh flowers
- on-site parking

ACTIVITIES AVAILABLE

- sauna & spa pool on site
- private bush garden with native birds
- small conferences & honeymoons catered for
- barbecue available
- arts & crafts
- monthly Titirangi markets
- beaches
- vineyards
- restaurants & cafés nearby
- extensive bush walks
- horse riding
- theatre
- art gallery
- Waitakere ranges nearby
- gardens to visit
- Auckland City, 30 mins
- international airport, 40-min drive

WESTERN SPRINGS, AUCKLAND
Hastings Hall

Host Malcolm Martel

99 Western Springs Road, Western Springs, Auckland
Phone 0-9-845 8550   *Mobile* 021 300 006   *Fax* 0-9-845 8554
Email unique@hastingshall.co.nz   *Website* www.hastingshall.co.nz

DIRECTIONS: From city, take NW Motorway (SH 16). Take St Lukes exit & turn left into St Lukes Rd. Turn 1st left into Duncan McLean Link & veer right into Western Springs Rd. Hastings Hall on left.

| 10 bdrm | 6 enst | 2 prbth | 1 pdrm | **Double $165–$375** **Single $145–$325** | *Includes breakfast* *Breakfast for invited friends of guests, extra* | *Lunch extra* |

Hastings Hall is a heritage home, originally built in 1876, refurbished and now providing accommodation for 20 guests. The main house offers three bedrooms upstairs and two downstairs, with a further five guestrooms in the adjacent Stables. The colonial interiors are furnished with antiques, and each bedroom includes tea and coffee-making facilities, television and phone. The breakfast menu changes daily with a full range of dishes served in the dining room or spacious indoor/outdoor conservatory. Room service is offered, and lunch is available by request. A small conference or seminar room for staff-training sessions is available, and swimming and spa pools. Children are welcome, and there is a golden retriever, Barney, on site.

FACILITIES

- House: 1 king, 1 queen & 1 double ensuite bedroom upstairs; 1 king/twin & 1 queen bedroom with 1 private bathroom & wheelchair access downstairs
- Stables: 5 queen bedrooms, 3 with ensuites & 2 share 1 private bathroom
- cotton bed linen, phone, TV, tea/coffee, writing desk & fresh flowers in all bedrooms

- full breakfast menu
- lunch by arrangement
- private guest lounge with open fire, Sky TV, video, CD-player, grand piano, library & bar
- hair dryers, toiletries, heated towel rails, heaters & bathrobes
- powder room
- laundry, $5; fax & email
- off-street parking

ACTIVITIES AVAILABLE

- BBQ on site
- swimming & spa pools on site
- conference/seminar room on site
- in-house music lounge & library
- Auckland Zoological Gardens
- feeding ducks at Western Springs & chickens at Cornwall Park
- parks, reserves & private gardens
- museum & Auckland Domain
- art & craft galleries

- wide selection of cafés, restaurants & bars
- sightseeing & harbour tours
- Auckland City Centre & Viaduct Basin, 5–10 mins
- Sky Tower & casino
- Tahuna Torea Bird Sanctuary
- wine & antique shop trails
- Waitakere ranges, 30 mins
- airport, 30–45 mins

HERNE BAY, AUCKLAND
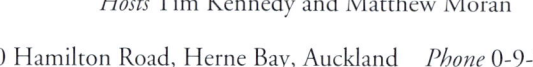
Moana Vista

Hosts Tim Kennedy and Matthew Moran

60 Hamilton Road, Herne Bay, Auckland   *Phone* 0-9-376 5028
Freephone 0800 213 761   *Mobile* 021 376 150   *Fax* 0-9-376 5025
Email info@moanavista.co.nz   *Website* friars.co.nz/hosts/moanavista.html

DIRECTIONS: From Ponsonby, take Jervois Rd & turn right into Hamilton Rd. Moana Vista on right. From Harbour Bridge, take 1st exit into Shelley Beach Rd. Turn right into Sarsfield St & left into Hamilton Rd.

| 3 bdrm | 2 enst | 1 prbth | **Double** $200–$240 | **Single** $160–$180 | *Includes breakfast* |

Moana Vista is located close to the Waitemata Harbour, in the prestigious suburb of Herne Bay. Originally built as a private residence in the 1890s, this two-storey villa has been renovated to offer accommodation. There are three guestrooms each with a bathroom, as well as an extra family bedroom, as Moana Vista is a child friendly establishment. Two of the upstairs bedrooms provide harbour views, which give Moana Vista its name. Guests can relax in two living areas, one with a grand piano, and the outside decking and subtropical sunken garden area are also popular. Breakfast includes fresh seasonal fruits, yoghurts and a bakery selection. A short evening stroll takes guests to a range of local award-winning restaurants in Ponsonby.

FACILITIES

- 2 queen ensuite bedrooms
- 1 queen bedroom with 1 private bathroom including bath
- extra family bedroom
- hair dryers, toiletries & heated towel rails
- cotton bed linen
- bathrobes
- children welcome

- continental breakfast served in dining room downstairs
- complimenary glass of wine
- TV, tea/coffee & mineral water available
- lounge with open fire, Sky TV, video, DVD, CD-player, grand piano & artwork
- high-speed wireless internet access in all rooms
- city location

ACTIVITIES AVAILABLE

- restaurants & cafés on Jervois & Ponsonby roads
- kayak available for guest use
- swimming & kayaking
- Waitemata Harbour & beach
- walk to city via waterfront, under harbour bridge, 20 mins
- boating/sailing
- private gardens open to visit
- Cornwall Park & One Tree Hill

- Sky tower restaurant & casino
- Auckland CBD, 20-min walk
- boutique shopping
- Britomart rail centre
- museum & art gallery
- The Domain
- antiques shops
- Viaduct Basin & America's Cup Village
- Auckland airport, 30 mins

PONSONBY, AUCKLAND

The Great Ponsonby B & B

Hosts Sally James and Gerard Hill

30 Ponsonby Terrace, Ponsonby, Auckland
Freephone 0800 766 792   *Phone* 0-9-376 5989   *Fax* 0-9-376 5527
Email info@greatpons.co.nz   *Website* www.greatpons.co.nz

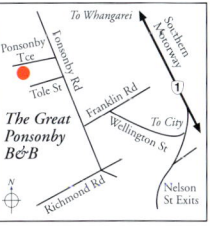

DIRECTIONS: Travelling north take Nelson St exit from Motorway. Turn into Wellington St, then left into Franklin Rd. Turn right into Ponsonby Rd, then left into Ponsonby Tce. Great Ponsonby on left, at bottom of road.

11 bdrm	11 enst	Suite rate $215–$350 Room rate $180–$220	*Includes breakfast*

This 1898 Victorian villa has been carefully restored to reflect the city's Pacific heritage, with bold use of colour and New Zealand artwork. Features include Pacific masks, tapa cloth, work by local ceramic artists, John Papas and Jeannie van der Putten tiles, sand-blasted windows by Kara Dodson, and floor rugs from Baluchistan. Soft leather couches create a comfortable lounge, and breakfast in the adjoining dining room ranges from self-serve continental to the Shearer's Special. Alternatively guests can enjoy their breakfast alfresco on the verandah overlooking the courtyard in the quiet cul-de-sac setting. The Great Ponsonby is within walking distance of many restaurants, cafés, shops, and city attractions, and not far from the beaches.

FACILITIES

- 1 large suite with balcony
- 5 super-king/twin suites, with ensuites & kitchenettes, 3 with baths
- 5 queen/twin ensuite bedrooms, with tea/coffee
- hair dryers, heated towel rails, demist mirrors & bathrobes
- cotton bed linen
- guest lounge with tea/coffee, music, artwork
- full breakfast cooked to order, from extensive menu
- morning paper
- direct dial phone in bedrooms
- fax, email & laundry available
- central heating
- children/dog by arrangement
- high-speed internet access
- quiet peaceful location
- off-street parking

ACTIVITIES AVAILABLE

- 2 bicycles available
- relaxing in sunny garden & courtyard on site
- beach towels available
- cat & dog on site
- pétanque in adjoining park
- bus passes every 10 mins
- Ponsonby historic walk
- Auckland CBD, 5-min drive
- motorway nearby
- large range of Ponsonby restaurants, outdoor cafés & bars in walking distance
- gym & swimming pool, 18-min walk
- art galleries nearby
- cinemas & museum nearby
- Herne Bay beaches nearby
- gardens open to visit
- airport, 30-min drive

The Great Ponsonby

PONSONBY, AUCKLAND
Amitees on Ponsonby

Hosts Ian Stewart and Jill Slee

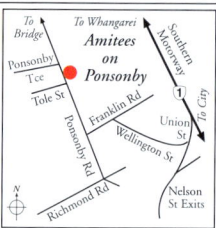

To Bridge • To Whangarei • Southern Motorway • Amitees on Ponsonby • Ponsonby Tce • Tole St • Franklin Rd • Wellington St • Union St • To City • Ponsonby Rd • Richmond Rd • Nelson St Exits

237 Ponsonby Road, Ponsonby   *Postal* Private Bag 47 900, Ponsonby, Auckland
Phone 0-9-378 6325   *Mobile* 021 661 999   *Fax* 0-9-378 6329
Email relax@amitees.co.nz   *Website* www.amitees.co.nz

DIRECTIONS: From south take Motorway to Nelson St exit. Turn left into Union St & Wellington St, & left into Franklin Rd. Turn right into Ponsonby Rd, to Amitees on right. From north take Shelley Beach Rd exit.

| 7 bdrm | 7 enst | **Room rate $180–$400** | *Includes continental breakfast* |

Located in the centre of Ponsonby's vibrant café and restaurant scene, Amitees On Ponsonby is an Edwardian villa with Queen Anne features. Originally built circa 1900, Amitees has been converted into a boutique hotel, now offering six ensuite bedrooms and a penthouse suite with city views. The interiors are designed in contemporary styling with antique furniture. There is an open fireplace in the guest lounge where a continental breakfast buffet provides a variety of breads, cereals, fresh fruit, yoghurt and juices. Complimentary snacks, juices, teas and coffees are available in the lounge at any time. Guests can also enjoy relaxing in the small garden and outdoor covered patio. Boutique shopping and the café culture are just a short walk away.

FACILITIES

- 1 super-king penthouse suite
- 1 king, 1 double, 1 twin & 3 queen ensuite bedrooms
- cotton bed linen, writing desk, TV, DVD & phone in bedrooms
- hair dryers, toiletries, heated towel rails & bathrobes in ensuites
- wheelchair access to 1 bathroom
- guest lounge with open fire, tea/coffee, nibbles, bar, Sky TV, DVD, books, magazines & writing desk
- full continental breakfast buffet in guest lounge
- computer with internet connection in guest lounge; fax available
- complimentary laundry
- private guest entrance
- outdoor covered patio
- on-site parking
- city location

ACTIVITIES AVAILABLE

- small garden on site
- boutique shopping
- gym
- Victoria Park Market
- Auckland City, 5 mins
- Harbour Bridge Climb
- bungy jump
- art galleries
- Auckland Museum, 5 mins
- range of restaurants, cafés & bars, nearby
- Sky Tower
- Sky City Casino
- Sky City Metro
- Aotea Square
- Viaduct Basin
- gardens to visit
- airport, 30-min drive

AUCKLAND CITY
Viaduct Landing

Manager Jennifer McBrearty   *Mobile* 027 542 4202   *Phone* 0-7-574 8054

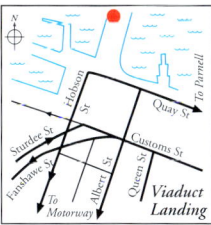

Apartment 32, Shed 24, Prince's Wharf, 147 Quay St, Auckland City
Postal P O Box 99 962, Newmarket, Auckland   *Freephone* 0800 ESSENCE
Fax 0-7-574 8096   *Email* stay@essencenz.com   *Website* www.essencenz.com

DIRECTIONS: From SH 1 Motorway, take exit to City Centre. Take Albert St to wharf at end. Turn left into Quay St and right onto Prince's Wharf. Viaduct Landing is Apartment 32 in Shed 24 on right.

3 bdrm	1 enst	1 shbth	**Apartment rate $889** for 4 persons	*Includes breakfast provisions*	
			Extra persons $100 each	*Chef service for meals extra*	*Self-catering*

Viaduct Landing is a boutique, seafront apartment on the north-west end of Prince's Wharf in downtown Auckland (*see above left*). Wrap-around decks on three sides allow for flexible outdoor living areas for alfresco dining, relaxing on loungers or in the spa pool, entertaining, and watching sunsets. Guests can enjoy the sea and city vistas, where harbour activity provides constant interest. This apartment also offers multi-room audio, home theatre and office facilities. Viaduct Landing is suitable for six guests, including children, and has a fully equipped kitchen for self-catering. Gourmet meals can be delivered, or a qualified chef can be arranged. There are 20 city restaurants, cafés and bars within walking distance of Viaduct Landing.

FACILITIES

- single-party bookings only
- 1 super-king/twin ensuite bedroom with bath, double basin & dressing room
- 1 super-king/twin & 1 queen bedroom share 1 bathroom
- designer cotton bed linen
- hair dryers, toiletries, demist mirrors, bathrobes, heated floors & heated towel rails
- self-serve laundry facilities
- full kitchen for self-catering with breakfast provisions
- pre-prepared gourmet meals delivered or chef services on site for lunch & dinner, extra
- multi-room audio
- broadband, laptop, printer, writing desk, phone, fax & email
- home theatre system
- on-site garaging; security

ACTIVITIES AVAILABLE

- outdoor entertaining area with BBQ & sun loungers
- spa pool for private use on site
- health & beauty spas adjacent
- fashion shops, duty free, CBD
- art galleries & museums
- theatre & shows
- Aotea Square markets
- sailing & fishing excursions
- Kelly Tarlton, free shuttle
- world-class restaurants, cafés & bars within 1km
- ferries, cruises, trains & buses, 5-min walk
- Harbour Bridge Experience
- Sky Tower, Casino, Sky Jump & Vertigo 10-min walk
- Ponsonby & Parnell, 10 mins
- golf courses; vineyards
- airport, 30-min drive
- coastal & bush walks

AUCKLAND CITY
Braemar on Parliament Street

Hosts Susan and John Sweetman   *Mobile* 021 640 688

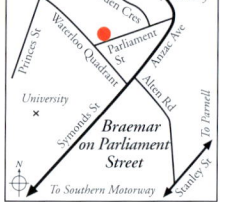

7 Parliament Street, Auckland City   *Phone* 0-9-377 5463
Email braemar@aucklandbedandbreakfast.com   *Fax* 0-9-377 3056
Freephone 0800 155 463   *Website* www.aucklandbedandbreakfast.com

DIRECTIONS: From Symonds St, continue into Anzac Ave. Turn sharp left into Parliament St. Braemar on Parliament Street on right towards top of street.

| 3 bdrm | 1 enst | 1 prbth | **Room rate $180–$295** | *Includes breakfast* |

Braemar on Parliament

Originally built in 1901 as a private residence, this Edwardian home now offers three guestrooms in a heritage setting in the heart of the Auckland CBD. Braemar on Parliament Street has been restored and renovated with attention to detail and furnished with antiques throughout. Upstairs the Batten Suite, Norman and Jenny's rooms offer accomodation in this historic listed home, where children and pets are welcome. There are two toy poodles and a cat in residence. A guest kitchenette opens from the lounge on the entrance floor and breakfast is served in the dining room downstairs from a full breakfast menu. There are many restaurants, cafés and bars within walking distance. Guests enjoy strolling downtown or through the university campus.

FACILITIES

- Batten Suite: 1 queen ensuite bedroom with heated towel rails & separate sitting room
- Norman's Room, with queen bed, & Jenny's Room, with double bed, share 1 bathroom
- bath, hair dryer, bathrobes & toiletries in both bathrooms
- cotton bed linen, TV & phone in bedrooms
- email & fax available
- full breakfast from menu served in dining room
- guest kitchenette
- guest lounge with open fire, tea/coffee, Sky TV, video, DVD, CD-player & artwork
- fresh flowers
- laundry available by request
- children & pets welcome
- honeymoons catered for

ACTIVITIES AVAILABLE

- Auckland CBD & Queen St, within 5–7-min walk away
- Auckland casino
- Sky Tower
- city bungy jump
- Waitemata Harbour
- health centres; gymnasiums
- swimming pools
- art galleries; library
- beaches; watersports
- many cafés, bars & restaurants, 5-min walk away
- boutique shopping within walking distance
- Viaduct Basin
- Auckland Museum, Domain & Winter Garden, 20-min walk
- public & private gardens; parks & reserves
- University of Auckland nearby
- airport, 30-min drive

Braemar on Parliament

Braemar on Parliament

PARNELL, AUCKLAND
St Georges Bay Lodge

Hosts Carol and Steven Quilliam   *Mobile* 021 214 1473

43 St Georges Bay Road, Parnell, Auckland   *Phone* 0-9-303 1050
Postal P O Box 42 036, Orakei, Auckland   *Fax* 0-9-360 7392
Email carol@stgeorge.co.nz   *Website* friars.co.nz/hosts/stgeorge.html

4 bdrm	4 enst

Double $215–$255
Single $195–$215

Includes breakfast

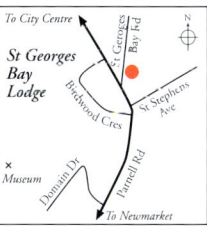

DIRECTIONS: From south take SH 1 Motorway to Khyber Pass exit. Turn right to Newmarket & then left into Parnell Rd. Turn right into St Georges Bay Rd. Lodge on right. From North, take Fanshawe St exit to Customs St.

St Georges Bay

One of the four original villas built in St Georges Bay Road in the 1890s, this Lodge has been totally renovated with tasteful modern amenities. Set in Parnell, a prestigious inner city location, this Victorian-style weatherboard villa, typical of the late 19th century, still includes original sash windows, turned verandah posts, fretwork detailing, bay windows and high ceilings. St Georges Bay Lodge now features native timber furniture and a new conservatory with arched windows, flowing on to a balcony overlooking a city park, with views of the central city, across the harbour to Rangitoto Island. A healthy breakfast is served alfresco on the balcony on sunny mornings, which is also a popular spot for night-time viewing of the harbour.

FACILITIES

- Gold Room: super-king/twin ensuite bedroom
- Blue Room & Cream Room: 2 king/twin ensuite bedrooms
- Lavender Room: double ensuite bedroom
- marble/tiled ensuites with toiletries & heated towel rails
- NZ woollen underlays
- library & private guest lounge
- full healthy continental & English-style cooked breakfast
- complimentary NZ port
- office facilities & PC with internet access
- central heating
- children by arrangement
- city & harbour views
- verandahs open to small private landscaped garden

ACTIVITIES AVAILABLE

- Parnell Village, 2-min walk
- Parnell cafés, restaurants, nightclubs, designer boutiques & speciality shops in Village
- Holy Trinity Cathedral, nearby
- Auckland City CBD, 1.5km
- world class yacht & tennis clubs, nearby
- health centres; gymnasiums
- swimming pools
- Parnell Rose Gardens, easy walk
- Auckland Museum, Domain & Winter Garden
- public & private gardens; parks & reserves
- sandy beaches; watersports
- art galleries; casino
- University of Auckland
- Waitemata Harbour
- airport, 30-min drive

St Georges Bay

PARNELL, AUCKLAND
Amersham House

Hosts Colleen and Gary Francis

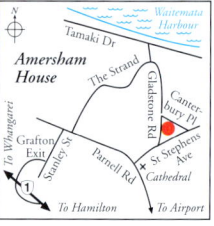

1 Canterbury Place, Corner Gladstone Road, Parnell, Auckland
Phone 0-9-303 0321   *Email* info@amershamhouse.co.nz
Fax 0-9-303 0621   *Website* amershamhouse.co.nz

DIRECTIONS: Take Grafton Rd exit from SH 1. Turn right into Grafton Rd, left into Stanley St, then right into Parnell Rd. Turn left into St Stephens Ave & left into Gladstone Rd. House on right, on corner of Canterbury Pl.

| 4 bdrm | 4 enst | 1 pdrm | Room rate $250–$400 | *Includes breakfast* | *Dinner extra* |

Amersham House is an elegant, 1930s residence renovated and refurbished to provide accommodation. The ground floor dining room and spacious guest lounge open into a private walled subtropical garden with all-day sun. The first floor includes three ensuite guestrooms, Skyline and Parnell Rooms with extensive city and harbour views and Rangitoto Room featuring a sauna. There is also a therapy room where guests can enjoy a massage or beauty treatment by arrangement. The third floor has one suite, the Regatta Room, with adjoining study and dressing room, ensuite with spa bath, and a balcony overlooking the Waitemata Harbour. A gourmet breakfast is prepared by the resident chef and served in the dining room or alfresco.

FACILITIES

- Regatta Room: king bed, ensuite, spa bath, dressing room, study & private balcony
- Rangitoto Room: queen bed, ensuite & sauna
- Parnell Room: super-king/twin bed & ensuite
- Skyline Room: queen bed, ensuite
- cotton bed linen; bathrobes; hair dryers & toiletries in ensuites
- in-room direct-dial phone
- continental & cooked breakfast selection
- dinner, by request, extra
- complimentary tea/coffee
- private guest lounge
- Sky TV, fax, laptops, email & Jetstream available
- laundry service, extra
- children by arrangement
- off-street parking

ACTIVITIES AVAILABLE

- outdoor spa pool on site
- heated swimming pool on site
- historic Parnell village, restaurants, cafés, art galleries, boutique shops, easy stroll
- Parnell Rose Garden nearby
- Newmarket shops, 5-min drive
- waterfront, scenic bays & eateries, in walking distance
- Viaduct Basin & super-yachts, 5-min drive
- Auckland City, shops, Sky City, 5-min drive
- Auckland Museum & Domain, in walking distance
- private gardens to visit
- motorway, 3-min drive away
- Auckland Explorer bus stop
- *Arcturus* schooner, previously owned by General Patton, preferential bookings, extra
- airport, 35-min drive

REMUERA, AUCKLAND
Aachen House Boutique Hotel

Hosts Joan and Greg McKirdy

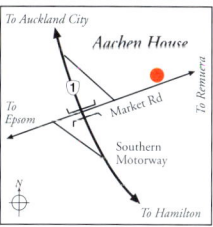

DIRECTIONS: Travelling either north or south on Southern Motorway, take Market Rd exits. Travel east towards Remuera for 100m. Aachen House Boutique Hotel on the left.

39 Market Road, Remuera, Auckland
Freephone 0800 AACHEN   *Phone* 0-9-520 2329   *Fax* 0-9-524 2898
Email info@aachenhouse.co.nz   *Website* www.aachenhouse.co.nz

  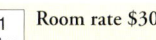

9 bdrm	9 enst	1 pdrm

Room rate $305–$530   *Includes breakfast & apéritifs*
Dinner extra

Aachen House

Aachen House, a restored Edwardian gentleman's residence, is nestled at the foot of the Mount Hobson reserve in the affluent suburb of Remuera. Sympathetically renovated to provide modern facilities, yet retaining the elegance of the Edwardian era with antique fittings and period pieces, Aachen House features many original details including ornate plaster ceilings, hand-carved fireplace mantels, timber wall-panels and the hand-crafted staircase. All nine bedrooms have large ensuite bathrooms, and five have direct access to private balconies and the garden. A gourmet breakfast selection is served in the spacious conservatory with its marble floor and antique furnishings, and an outlook over the private garden featuring an Edwardian-style pavilion.

FACILITIES

- 3 Californian-king, 2 super-king, & 2 king ensuite bedrooms
- 2 king single ensuite bedrooms, 1 with wheelchair access
- Egyptian cotton bed linen
- hair dryer, toiletries, bathrobes
- direct-dial phones, fax, modem
- 5 private balconies/verandahs
- powder room serves guest lounge
- children over 16 yrs welcome
- full gourmet breakfast
- dinner by request, extra
- complimentary tea/coffee & pre-dinner drinks
- satellite TV, classic films
- central heating
- laundry service; ironing
- conference facilities
- fire safety system
- ample on-site parking

ACTIVITIES AVAILABLE

- sheltered sunny garden, with Edwardian-style pavilion
- Mt Hobson park adjacent, with daffodils in springtime
- Mt St John walks & city views, easy 500m walk
- horse racing & trots, 5-min drive
- golf driving range & golf courses
- tennis & squash courts
- quality shopping, 10-min walk
- restaurants, 5–10-min walk
- antique shops, 300m walk
- City Centre, 10-min drive
- beaches, harbour, 10 mins
- museum & art galleries, 10-min drive away
- private gardens to visit
- bus transport, 300m away
- railway station, 300m away
- airport, 20-min drive

Aachen House

Aachen House

REMUERA, AUCKLAND
Amerissit

Host Barbara McKain

20 Buttle Street, Remuera, Auckland
Phone 0-9-522 9297   *Mobile* 027 284 4883   *Fax* 0-9-522 9298
Email barbara@amerissit.co.nz   *Website* www.amerissit.co.nz

3 bdrm	3 enst	1 pdrm

Room rate $180–$325
House rate $700

Includes breakfast
Self-catering available

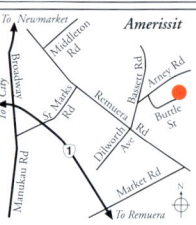

DIRECTIONS: Take SH 1 Motorway to Market Rd exit. Travel east towards Remuera. Turn left into Remuera Rd, right into Bassett Rd & 1st right into Arney Rd. Take 1st right into Buttle St to Amerissit at end.

Amerissit is architecturally designed and located in a quiet cul-de-sac near Newmarket. Although the emphasis is on privacy and tranquillity, Amerissit is only a few minutes' drive to restaurants, cafés, shopping, art galleries and museums. The motorways and beaches are also within easy access. The three individually designed bedrooms at Amerissit include slim-line televisions with Sky, DVD-players, in-wall or ceiling speakers, direct dial phone and high-speed internet access. Each room opens to a balcony or patio, offering total privacy with views over the peaceful garden surrounded by mature trees to Remuera and Mt Hobson beyond. A choice of continental or gourmet breakfasts are served in the guestrooms, dining room, or alfresco on the balcony.

FACILITIES

- Mt Hobson room, with king bed, ensuite, spa bath, dressing room & city views
- Remuera queen room, ensuite, reading room & tree views
- Newmarket king room, with underfloor heating in ensuite
- quality bed linen, Sky TV, DVD, CDs, videos, tuner, phone, tea/coffee, fridge & balcony for all 3 bedrooms
- gourmet breakfast menu; full kitchen available
- private guest lounge with open fire, tea/coffee, nibbles, bar, CD-player, piano, games, NZ artwork & magazines
- hair dryer, toiletries & heated towel rails in all 3 ensuites
- self-serve laundry, extra
- children welcome by request
- off-street & cul-de-sac parking

ACTIVITIES AVAILABLE

- Mt Hobson walks through daffodils in spring, 5-min walk
- golf courses & driving range
- horse racing & trotting
- art galleries & museums
- wine trails & harbour tours
- Parnell Rose Gardens, 5 mins
- local bush & beach walks
- watersports; sightseeing tours
- Sky Tower, 10-min drive
- restaurants, cafés, shopping & cinemas, in Newmarket, 10-min walk, & Parnell or Remuera, 5-min drive
- bus, railway & motorway nearby
- public & private gardens to visit
- Viaduct Harbour, 10-min drive
- Underwater World, 10 mins
- Auckland City CBD, 1.5km
- airport, 20-min drive
- Hauraki Gulf cruises, 10 mins

REMUERA, AUCKLAND
Cotter House

Host Gloria Poupard-Walbridge

4 Saint Vincent Avenue, Remuera, Auckland
Phone 0-9-529 5156   *Mobile* 027 567 2989   *Fax* 0-9-529 5186
Email info@cotterhouse.com   *Website* www.cotterhouse.com

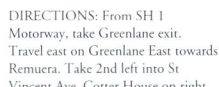

DIRECTIONS: From SH 1 Motorway, take Greenlane exit. Travel east on Greenlane East towards Remuera. Take 2nd left into St Vincent Ave. Cotter House on right.

4 bdrm	2 enst	1 prbth	1 pdrm	**Room rate $400–$590**	*Includes breakfast/brunch*
				Double $786–$1,015 Single $505–$550	*Includes all meals*

Cotter House has re-positioned itself as an inner city luxury retreat for pampered holidays, offering a secluded setting for weddings, honeymoons, business conferences and entertaining. Built in 1847 and carefully restored, preserving the original regency architecture, Cotter House features an 1892 ballroom, and is furnished with antiques complemented by Gloria's contemporary art collection. Guests are served four-course breakfasts or brunches, and enjoy access to the heated swimming pool, exercise pavilion and yoga classes. Either the bed and breakfast or all-meal option is available, the latter including gourmet dining accompanied by the extensive wine list from the house bar. In-room health spa treatments are available.

FACILITIES

- Suite: Bronze Room with queen bed & Empire Room with single bed; & 1 ensuite with bath
- Oriental Room: 1 double bedroom with ensuite
- Blue Provencal Room: 1 king/twin bedroom with private bathroom
- desks, Sky TVs, tea/coffee, DDI phones, CDs, DVDs, safes & irons
- hair dryers, toiletries, robes, slippers & turbans, heated floor/towel rails
- gourmet breakfast/brunch
- 4-course dinner, hors d'oeuvres with apéritifs; wine extra
- 2 guest lounges with open fires, Sky digital TV, CDs, DVDs & guest mini-fridges
- fluent French & Spanish, some Italian & Portuguese
- fully equipped guest office; laundry, dry cleaning available
- central heating; 7 carparks

ACTIVITIES AVAILABLE

- private bricked courtyard, heated swimming pool & BBQ area on site
- summer conferences, corporate seminars, banquets, weddings, receptions & other functions catered for guests only
- spa pool, massages, exercise pavilion & complimentary yoga classes available to guests
- Hauraki Gulf cruises
- wide selection of restaurants, bars & cafés, walking distance
- antique shops & cinemas
- Newmarket & Parnell shopping area, 5-min drive
- wine trail & harbour tours
- Auckland sightseeing tours
- CBD shopping, 10-min drive
- city museums & art galleries
- airport, 20-min drive

St Heliers Bay, Auckland
Cliff View

Hosts Jill Mathew and Geoff Annesley-Smith   *Mobile* 025 769 405

51 Cliff Road, St Heliers, Auckland   *Phone* 0-9-575 4052
Postal P O Box 25 233, St Heliers, Auckland   *Fax* 0-9-575 4051
Email cliffview@xtra.co.nz   *Website* friars.co.nz/hosts/cliffview.html

DIRECTIONS: From the City, take Tamaki Drive & travel around the waterfront for 8km. Continue past St Heliers Bay & into Cliff Rd. Cliff View on right at Ladies Bay.

| 1 bdrm | 1 enst | Room rate $250
Long-stay & off-season rates available | *Includes breakfast supplies*
Self-catering | |

With 180-degree uninterrupted harbour panorama, Cliff View offers a private king-size guest suite upstairs, with three balconies all providing different aspects of the view. Native pohutukawa trees on the cliff edge frame the vista and the spacious lounge invites relaxation and contemplation of the boating activities below. A secluded beach, Ladies Bay, is only a minute's walk down the hillside. A fully self-contained kitchen including breakfast supplies and dishwasher opens on to a sundeck for alfresco dining. The king-size bedroom has a private sundeck and ensuite bathroom, and a study provides a separate spot for letter writing, peace and quiet. Cliff View is only 11 kilometres from the City Centre, via a picturesque waterfront drive.

FACILITIES

- 1 self-contained private guest suite upstairs, with 1 king ensuite bedroom opening to sundeck
- heated towel rails, hair dryer & toiletries in ensuite bathroom
- TV, video & radio in lounge
- guest phones in bedroom & study
- complimentary guest laundry
- breakfast supplies include fresh fruit, orange juice, cereals, breads, yoghurt, cheeses, eggs, bacon
- fully equipped kitchen
- tea/coffee selection
- fresh flowers
- private guest lounge
- separate guest study
- 180° views over harbour
- 3 private sundecks
- non-smoking
- off-street parking

ACTIVITIES AVAILABLE

- swimming beach, 1-min walk
- St Heliers shops, 5-min walk
- restaurants & cafés, 5-min walk
- Kelly Tarlton's Underwater World, 4km away
- cliff edge walks adjacent
- Churchill & Glover Parks
- kayak & motor launch hire
- cycles & roller blades for hire on waterfront
- City & Sky Tower, 8km
- harbour cruises
- Tahuna Torea Bird Sanctuary
- fishing & sailing
- Auckland Museum
- gardens to visit
- golf courses
- Rangitoto & Waiheke Islands
- Tiritiri Matangi Island bird sanctuary

Point View Lodge

Hosts Tricia and Bruce Robertson

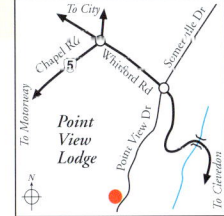

316 Point View Drive, Howick   *Phone* 0-9-537 5678   *Mobile* 021 935 780
Postal 316 Point View Drive, R D 1, Papatoetoe   *Fax* 0-9-537 5678
Email stay@pointview.co.nz   *Website* www.pointview.co.nz

DIRECTIONS: From City, take SH 1 motorway south. Take Eastern Highway exit. Turn right into Ti Rakau Dr. Turn left into Chapel Rd. Turn right into Whitford Rd & right into Point View Dr to Lodge on right.

| 3 bdrm | 2 enst | 1 prbth | 1 pdrm |

Room rate $320–$420   *Includes breakfast*   *Dinner extra*

Just half an hour south-east of downtown Auckland is Point View Lodge offering panoramic rural views to the city beyond. The purpose-built guest wing provides three bedrooms and bathrooms each opening to the deck and landscaped garden, surrounded by fields of sheep. Each bedroom is named after a volcanic cone, all visible from the Lodge. A buffet breakfast is supplemented with a choice of cooked gourmet dishes, either indoors or alfresco, and silver service dinner with complimentary local wine is also available in the formal dining room. Pre-dinner drinks are complimentary and restaurants are just a five-minute drive away. Tricia is a marriage celebrant and caters for small weddings at Point View Lodge.

FACILITIES

- 1 king/twin & 1 king ensuite bedroom, each with spa bath
- 1 queen bedroom with private bathroom
- cotton bed linen; bathrobes
- hair dryers, quality toiletries, heated towel rails & floors
- TV, DVD, CD-player, phone, tea/coffee, mineral water & air-conditioning in bedrooms
- laundry & dry cleaning, extra

- breakfast buffet with full cooked options
- 3-course dinner using local produce with wine, $85 pp
- apéritifs & hors d'oeuvres
- central heating; fresh flowers
- email & fax available
- children welcome in private-party bookings only
- off-street parking

ACTIVITIES AVAILABLE

- small weddings & honeymoons celebrated
- landscaped garden & fields with sheep on site
- guests' friends welcome for dinner parties
- sailing; fishing
- wine tours; shopping
- walking; treks
- beaches; watersports

- 25+ restaurants nearby
- vineyards; arts & crafts
- yacht racing; sightseeing
- art galleries; museum
- garden visits; golf courses
- Botany town centre, 5 mins
- Manukau City, 12 mins
- Botanic Gardens, 12 mins
- City Centre, 25 mins
- Auckland Airport, 25 mins

Point View Lodge

89

WHITFORD, AUCKLAND
Seafields

Hosts Stephanie Boyd-Dunlop and Doug Snelling

283 Broomfields Road, Whitford, Auckland *Phone* 0-9-530 8282
Postal 283 Broomfields Road, R D 1, Howick, Auckland *Fax* 0-9-530 9292
Email stephanie@seafields.co.nz *Website* www.seafields.co.nz

DIRECTIONS: From City, take SH 1 motorway south. Take Eastern Highway exit. Turn right into Ti Rakau Drive. Turn left into Chapel Rd. Turn right into Whitford Rd. Turn left into Broomfields Rd to Seafields on right.

| 6 bdrm | 3 enst | 1 prbth | 1 shbth |

Room rate $450–$550

Includes continental breakfast
Dinner extra

Seafields is a waterfront retreat on the shores of the Hauraki Gulf, offering secluded, peaceful accommodation, just half an hour from Auckland City by car or by ferry. With uninterrupted sea views overlooking the boats moored in the channel and beyond to islands in the Gulf, Seafields is an architecturally designed home providing four spacious guestrooms and a separate suite. There is an in-house spa bath and sauna room, where guests can enjoy therapeutic massage with essential oils by arrangement. The heated swimming pool, barbecue area and outdoor fireplace are also popular. A walk through the landscaped rock garden takes guests to the sea where watersports are at hand. A choice of restaurants are nearby.

FACILITIES

- 1 super-king bedroom, dressing room & ensuite with bidet, double bath & twin basin
- 2 king bedrooms with ensuites
- 1 queen suite with bathroom, TV room, kitchenette & patio
- 1 double & 1 twin bedroom in house share 1 bathroom
- hair dryers, toiletries, bathrobes heated mirrors & towel rails
- cotton bed linen; fresh flowers

- continental breakfast served
- dinner by arrangement, extra; qualified chef on call
- desk, phone, fridge, tea/coffee, safe, DVD & TV in bedrooms
- email; air-conditioning
- passenger transfer
- extensive verandahs with sea views; on-site parking
- helicopter transfers

ACTIVITIES AVAILABLE

- spa bath & sauna room
- heated swimming pool on site
- patio area with outdoor fireplace & BBQ; 2ha garden
- small weddings, conferences & seminars catered for
- fishing; harbour charter trips
- wine trails organised
- therapeutic massage, extra
- guided horse trekking

- restaurants, nearby
- horse riding & polo tuition
- golf; private garden visits
- art galleries; museums
- sea kayaking; water skiing
- flightseeing by helicopter; skydiving & gliding
- Auckland City, 30 mins by car or by ferry
- airport, 20-min drive

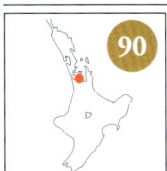

Papakura
Hunua Gorge Country House

Hosts Ben, Brandi and Joy Calway

482 Hunua Road, Papakura   *Postal* P O Box 27, Papakura
Phone 0-9-299 7926   *Mobile* 021 669 922   *Fax* 0-9-299 7926
Email hunuagorge@xtra.co.nz   *Website* friars.co.nz/hosts/hunua.html

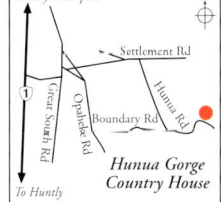

DIRECTIONS: From Auckland, take SH 1 south to Papakura exit. Turn left into Beach Rd. At lights continue ahead into Settlement Rd. Turn right into Hunua Rd. Travel across bridge & up gravel drive to house at top left.

| 5 bdrm | 1 enst | 1 prbth | 1 shbth |

Room rate $110–$150

Includes breakfast
Lunch & dinner extra

After crossing the gorge, guests reach this large country house set in 20 hectares (50 acres) with expansive rural views. Built in 1980, the architecture is simple country style in harmony with the rural location of Hunua Gorge, adjacent to the Hunua Ranges, popular for hiking and tramping, yet just 25 minutes from the airport. Night views are special with sunsets followed by the city lights and Manukau Harbour under the starry skies. Innovative meals include breakfast in bed if desired, or brunch, alfresco dining and picnics in the fresh country air. The best of seasonal produce is accessible daily, with regional wines and particular dietary needs Joy's speciality. Guests have the choice of four bedrooms, plus a bunkroom for children.

FACILITIES

- 1 king suite with ensuite
- 1 queen bedroom with private bathroom & bath
- 1 double & 1 twin bedroom & 1 bunk room with 1 bathroom
- cotton bed linen; fresh flowers
- hair dryers, toiletries & heated towel rails
- private guest lounge with open fire, tea/coffee, TV & video

- breakfast or brunch served
- lunch, $20 pp
- 3-course à la carte dinner, $35 pp
- wheelchair access
- email facilities
- complimentary laundry
- children & pets welcome
- verandah overlooking garden
- on-site parking

ACTIVITIES AVAILABLE

- pétanque/boules on site
- ponds, streams, bush & trees on site for walks
- slug-shot shooting
- pony rides
- picnicking spots
- golf courses
- fishing
- bush walking & hiking
- tramping in Hunua Ranges

- variety of restaurants, nearby
- shopping & cinemas, 10 mins
- scenic flights
- beaches for swimming, surfing & relaxing
- yachting
- gardens open to visit
- motorway (SH 1), 5-min drive
- airport, 25-min drive
- Auckland City, 30-min drive

DRURY, SOUTH AUCKLAND
The Drury Homestead

Hosts Carolyn and Ron Booker

349 Drury Hills Road, R D 1, Drury, Auckland South
Phone 0-9-294 9030   *Email* druryhome@paradise.net.nz
Fax 0-9-294 9035   *Website* friars.co.nz/hosts/drury.html

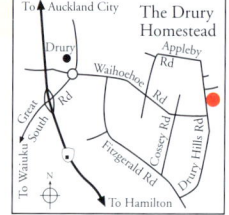

DIRECTIONS: Take SH 1 Southern Motorway to Drury exit. Turn nor'east & travel 800m to roundabout. Take Waihoehoe Rd east to "T" junction. Turn left into Drury Hills Rd. Drury Homestead 2nd driveway on right.

4 bdrm	3 enst	1 prbth	**Double $100–$130** *Includes breakfast or provisions in studio*
			Single $70 *Dinner extra* *Self-catering in studio*

This early colonial home, circa 1879, was built as the original homestead in the Drury area. It has been fully restored and refurbished to provide quality accommodation. The three upstairs bedrooms provide rural views, and downstairs there is a self-contained studio. A full cooked breakfast is served in the dining room and family dinner is also available. Studio guests can self-cater in their fully equipped kitchen if preferred, and restaurants are nearby. Guests enjoy relaxing on the deep verandahs, and for the more active, bush walks or jogging on the forested property. The Waihoehoe Stream in the garden features large rocks and the native bush attracts birdlife. Two dogs, a Jack Russell and a giant schnauzer, live on site.

FACILITIES

- 2 queen ensuite bedrooms upstairs
- 1 twin bedroom with private bathroom upstairs
- 1 self-contained queen studio
- hair dryers, heated towel rails & toiletries in all 4 bathrooms
- cotton bed linen; fresh flowers
- 2 lounges with tea/coffee, nibbles, TV & books
- children welcome

- full cooked or continental breakfast in dining room
- 3-course family dinner, $30–$40 pp; BYO
- breakfast provisions in full studio kitchen for self-catering
- fax, phone & email available
- self-serve laundry
- extensive verandahs with rural outlook; on-site parking

ACTIVITIES AVAILABLE

- garden & bushwalks on site
- farm animals, pasture, native bush & stream on site
- gliding club nearby
- Pukekohe township & motor racing, 15-min drive
- Auckland harbours & beaches for swimming & surfing
- gardens open to visit
- Manurewa Botanic Gardens, 15-min drive

- 3 restaurants within 2km
- variety of restaurants in Pukekohe & Bombay
- tramping in Hunua Ranges
- scenic flights
- yachting; fishing
- golf courses
- Auckland CBD, 35-min drive on southern motorway
- airport, 20-min drive

MIRANDA
Umoya Lodge

Host Johann van den Berg

30 Rataroa Road, Miranda   *Postal* 30 Rataroa Road, R D 3, Pokeno
Phone 0-9-232 7636   *Mobile* 021 655 599   *Fax* 0-9-232 7636
Email relax@umoyalodge.co.nz   *Website* www.umoyalodge.co.nz

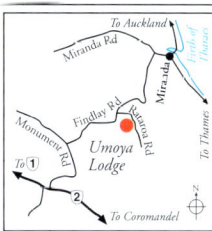

DIRECTIONS: From SH 1 turn off to SH 2 & travel east. Turn left into Monument Rd & travel 4km. Turn right into Findlay Rd & travel 4km. Turn right into Rataroa Rd & travel to Umoya Lodge on right.

| 2 bdrm | 2 enst | 1 pdrm | **Double $450–$650**
Single $360–$450 | *Includes breakfast*
Lunch & dinner extra |

Located on Mount Rataroa, set in 14 hectares (35 acres) of native bush, with sweeping mountain and sea views of the Firth of Thames and Coromandel Peninsula, Umoya Lodge was custom built to provide privacy and exclusivity. Accommodation is offered in both The Luxury Suite and the Retreat, which is adjacent to the main Lodge. A four-course gourmet dinner is available and can be served in the main Lodge, the conservatory or as room service. The contemporary rooms feature antiques, oriental rugs and international artwork and open to private gardens. The entire Lodge may be booked for private use, small conferences and weddings. Guests enjoy the extensive bush walks on site that abound with wood pigeons and other native birds.

FACILITIES

- 1 suite with 1 king bedroom, spa bath in ensuite; opens to private deck & watergarden
- 1 studio with king/twin ensuite bedroom, 2 decks & cast iron bath in tropical garden & views
- Sky TV, DVD, CD, writing desk, tea/coffee, bar, artwork & cotton bed linen in both suite & studio
- hair dryers, toiletries, heated towel rails, heated floor, bidets, demist mirrors & bathrobes

- full breakfast in guest suite
- gourmet meals, extra; licensed
- underfloor heating throughout
- guest lounge with open fire
- phone, fax & internet in lodge
- library; fresh flowers; sea views
- laundry service available
- separate guest entrance
- parking & garaging
- helipad & transfers to city

ACTIVITIES AVAILABLE

- fine dining indoors or alfresco
- in-house massage
- in-house art gallery
- pétanque on site
- extensive bush walks on site
- scenic flights; sky diving
- fishing
- horse riding
- ostrich farm
- hot pools

- bird sanctuary
- beach walks
- Hunua National Park
- wine & cheese tasting
- golf; squash
- antique stores
- gardens open to visit
- Auckland City, 55-min drive
- airport, 40-min drive or 10 mins by helicopter

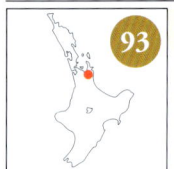

Te Puru, Thames
Te Puru Coast View Lodge

Host Bill and Bev Gausden

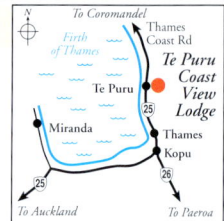

468 Thames Coast Road, Te Puru   *Postal* P O Box 241, Thames
Phone 0-7-868 2326   *Email* tepuru-lodge@xtra.co.nz
Fax 0-7-868 2376   *Website* www.tepurulodge.co.nz

DIRECTIONS: From Thames, take SH 25 north for 11km, to Te Puru. Te Puru Coast View Lodge on right up driveway.

| 4 bdrm | 3 enst | 2 prbth | 1 pdrm |

Room rate $120–$175   *All meals extra*

Built on a historic Maori pa site, Te Puru Coast View Lodge commands spectacular views of the Coromandel coastline, as the name suggests. This Mediterranean-style lodge was refurbished with hand-crafted native rimu and kauri furniture, before opening in 1989. Te Puru's award-winning licensed restaurant features premium New Zealand meats, Coromandel seafoods, and fine wines. After viewing panoramic sunsets, guests can enjoy intimate candlelit dining while the lights come on in the township below. Surrounded by native bush rich in history, the lodge is ideally sited for exploring the peninsula. The developing native heritage garden attracts varied birdlife, including the native kiwi, which can often be heard calling at night.

FACILITIES

- 4 ground-level bedrooms with views, TV, tea/coffee facilities, ceiling fans, electric blankets, & winter heating
- 1 ensuite king bedroom with sitting area & patio
- 1 ensuite queen bedroom
- 1 ensuite double bedroom
- 1 twin bedroom, with 2 double beds & 2 private bathrooms

- à la carte breakfast, served in dining room with coast view, or alfresco on sunny patio
- lunch by arrangement
- award-winning à la carte licensed restaurant with coast views, & log fire in winter
- spacious lounge with TV, VCR, stereo, library, open fireplace, & bar service
- on-site parking

ACTIVITIES AVAILABLE

- western gateway to scenic & historic Coromandel Peninsula
- full range shopping & services, in Thames, 10-min drive south
- Maori cultural heritage trail & site interpretation
- Thames Heritage Museum
- vineyard trail
- private gardens to visit
- beach & river swimming

- wide range of bush & beach walks close by
- historic walkways & sites
- arts & crafts trails
- rock prospecting
- bird-watching
- Coromandel forest park
- wading birds at Miranda
- special requests & activities organised

COROMANDEL
Driving Creek Villas

Host David Foreman

21A Colville Road, Coromandel
Phone 0-7-866 7755   *Email* reservations@drivingcreekvillas.com
Fax 0-7-866 7753   *Website* www.drivingcreekvillas.com

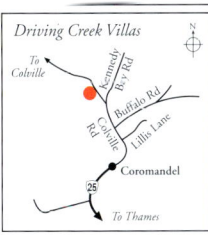

DIRECTIONS: From Coromandel township, take Rings Rd north for 2km. Continue left into Colville Rd to Driving Creek Villas on left. Take left fork of driveway to Villas.

4 bdrm	2 prbth

Villa rate $175–$245
Extra persons $25 each

Breakfast & dinner extra
Self-catering

Located on a stream in a native bush setting just north of Coromandel township, Driving Creek Villas were purpose-built and opened in 2005. These two self-contained villas are separate from each other to provide guest privacy and each has two bedrooms, the main one downstairs adjacent to the bathroom and an extra bedroom upstairs. The bedroom and living area open to a private deck with bush views and there is a fully equipped kitchen for self-catering in each villa. A breakfast tray is delivered by arrangement or there is a chef on call if required. Restaurants and cafés are just a five-minute drive away and guests can also enjoy the local history including an original gold-mining stamper battery. Bush walks and bird-watching are popular activities.

FACILITIES

- one-party bookings per villa
- 1 queen ensuite & 1 twin bedroom per villa
- Egyptian cotton bed linen
- phone in queen; writing desk & phone jack in twin bedroom
- wheelchair access in both villas
- hair dryers, toiletries, bathrobes, heated towel rails & heated floors
- heat pump & air-conditioning
- full kitchen in each villa for self-catering
- breakfast tray available indoors or alfresco, $15 pp
- dinner in villa by arrangement, extra
- fax & email available
- lounge in each villa with TV, DVD & CD-player
- courtesy passenger transfer; on-site parking

ACTIVITIES AVAILABLE

- mountain bikes available
- private garden & bush area with stream on site
- bird-watching on site
- bush & garden walks
- Barry Brickells Driving Creek Railway, 5-min walk
- wildlife sanctuaries
- beach, 7-min drive
- gardens to visit; fishing arranged
- restaurants in Coromandel township, 5-min drive
- gold stamper battery, 5 mins
- Coromandel township, 5-min drive away
- guided tour to historic house & garden
- Waiau Waterworks, 15 mins
- Whitianga, 40-min drive
- Thames, 1-hour drive

COROMANDEL
Buffalo Lodge

Host Evelyne Siegrist

Buffalo Road, Coromandel   *Postal* P O Box 11, Coromandel
Phone 0-7-866 8960   *Email* buffalo@wave.co.nz
Fax 0-7-866 8960   *Website* www.buffalolodge.co.nz

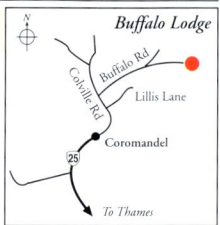

DIRECTIONS: From Coromandel, take Colville Rd north for 2km. Turn right into Buffalo Rd, continue past the Gold Stamper Battery & drive slowly on narrow road, following signs to Buffalo Lodge.

| 3 bdrm | 3 enst | 2 pdrm | **Room rate $220–$265** | *Includes breakfast* | *Dinner extra* |

Perched on a hillside with sweeping views over the Coromandel hills, Hauraki Gulf and as far as Waiheke Island, Buffalo Lodge is a contemporary country retreat, tucked away on two hectares (5 acres) of native bush. From here guests can explore the peninsula, and sample the superb sunsets, tranquil sounds of nature and native birdlife. The accent is on culture, with a contemporary art gallery displaying Evelyne and her late husband Raouf's paintings and sculptural work. Slippers are provided for guests to wear on the native miro floors. Buffalo Lodge is unsuitable for children and is open from October to the end of April. Evelyne recommends bookings of at least two days, to take in the scenic attractions of Coromandel and the surrounding area.

FACILITIES

- honeymoon queen suite, with panoramic view from bath
- 2 queen ensuite bedrooms
- heated towel rails, designer bathrobes & hair dryers
- private sundecks from bedrooms
- Swiss-quality bedding
- slippers provided
- 2 powder rooms
- contemporary art gallery
- Swiss-style breakfast
- cooked breakfast on request
- dinner by request, $85 pp
- BYO licence; no TV
- meals served in dining room with bush & ocean views
- extensive sundeck overlooking Hauraki Gulf
- German, French & Mandarin spoken

ACTIVITIES AVAILABLE

- Evelyne & Raouf's paintings for sale from on-site art gallery
- massage by arrangement
- bird-watching
- bush walking & climbing
- historic goldmine exploring
- gold stamper battery
- mining museum
- botanic & private gardens
- exploring Coromandel Peninsula
- restaurants, 5-min drive
- narrow-gauge railway
- swimming beaches
- golf course nearby
- fishing & diving
- native kauri tree grove
- pottery & craft trails
- horse riding
- historic township of Coromandel

WHITIANGA
Wairua Ora Creative Retreat

Hosts Louise McRae and Hamish Williamson

251 Old Coach Road, R D 1, Whitianga   *Postal* P O Box 186, Whitianga
Phone 0-7-866 0304   *Email* louise@wairuaretreat.co.nz
Fax 0-7-866 2304   *Website* www.wairuaretreat.co.nz

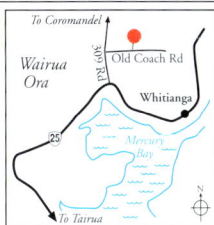

DIRECTIONS: From Tairua, take SH 25 north for 35km. Turn left into 309 Rd. Travel 4km to 2nd bridge & turn right into Old Coach Rd. Travel 1.5km to Retreat on left. Take driveway 200m, cross ford & travel to Retreat.

4 bdrm	4 enst	Room rate $1,000 for 2 persons for 2 nights	Includes all meals & creative workshop
		Room rate $280 *Includes breakfast*	*Dinner extra*

Wairua Ora Creative Retreat is set in over five and a half hectares (14 acres) of native bush bounded by two rivers. Exploration of the surrounding nature precedes artistic expression of discoveries, in the fully equipped art studio under the qualified eyes of the hosts, Louise and Hamish. Guests develop their artwork in the medium of their choice, completing a contemporary "masterpiece" by the end of their stay. The two-day customised workshops stimulate creativity and are complemented by relaxation for the body and mind with massage, yoga or reiki from on-site specialists. A private outdoor bath for two is a popular feature at Wairua Ora. Meals are a highlight, with locally grown and organic produce accompanied by fine New Zealand wines.

FACILITIES

- 2 king & 2 queen bedrooms
- extra double bed in mezzanine
- 4 ensuite bathrooms
- toiletries, hair dryers, heated towel rails, bathrobes
- 100% cotton bed linen
- guest lounge; DVDs; library
- fully equipped open art studio
- art for sale
- fresh flowers; games

- continental breakfast with fresh juices & home-made bread; alfresco dining
- lunch/picnic, extra
- 3-course dinner with fresh local produce & wine, included or $50 pp
- NZ wine list
- snacks with drinks available
- pure water; outdoor fires; on-site parking

ACTIVITIES AVAILABLE

- customised creative workshop
- outdoor bush spa bath for 2
- massage & therapy, extra
- yoga specialist, extra
- reiki or Hawaiian bodywork
- 5.6ha (14 acres) native bush, for walks & 2 rivers on site
- swimming holes; fruit trees
- bird-watching; glow-worms
- star-gazing by outdoor fire

- restaurants at Whitianga
- 18-hole golf course nearby
- boating; kayaking; fishing
- arts & crafts trail
- horse riding; hiking
- hot water beach nearby
- courtesy transfer to Auckland ferry terminal at Coromandel
- Whitianga airstrip, 10 mins
- Coromandel, 30-min drive

WHITIANGA
Villa Toscana

Hosts Giorgio and Margherita Allemano

Ohuka Park, Whitianga   *Postal* P O Box 43, Whitianga
Phone 0-7-866 2293   *Fax* 0-7-866 2269   *Mobile* 025 871 833
Email giorgio@villatoscana.co.nz   *Website* www.villatoscana.co.nz

 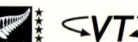

2 bdrm	1 prbth	1 pdrm	Suite rate $480–$720 for 2 persons	*Includes breakfast*
			Extra persons $120 each	*Dinner extra* *Self-catering*

DIRECTIONS: From Whititanga, take Buffalo Beach Rd (SH 25) north for 2km. Turn left into Centennial Dr. At top of hill, turn left into Rimu St. At Ohuka Park continue 1km, sign up private concrete drive to Villa Toscana.

Villa Toscana is a veritable piece of Tuscany imported from Italy, including 13 tonnes of Italian terracotta tiles, over 12 square metres of granite and marble slabs, Italian antique furniture and paintings, even a genuine terracotta pizza oven! Opened in 1998, this true Tuscan villa is set in two hectares of native bush with panoramic views over Whitianga and Mercury Bay to the islands beyond. Genuine Italian hosts, Giorgio and Margherita, with their young family, dog and cats, enjoy sharing their dream with guests. A fully self-contained suite provides guests with total privacy. Italian candlelit gourmet dinners, preceded by wine tasting, are served either on the terrace, in the suite, or in the cellar. Giorgio, who loves the sea, is also happy to take guests game fishing.

FACILITIES

- single-party bookings only
- 1 king/twin & 1 king bedroom
- 1 bathroom including bidet, hair dryer, heated towel rails, toiletries, bathrobes & slippers
- antique bed linen, fresh flowers, fruit & chocolates in suite
- fully self-contained guest kitchen
- self-serve guest laundry
- children welcome

- Italian continental breakfast, in suite, or alfresco on terrace
- 5-course dinner, $140 pp; wine from cellar, extra
- TV, VCR, DVD & CD-player in private guest lounge
- under-tile heating throughout
- Italian & French spoken
- airport courtesy transfer; security gates; helipad

ACTIVITIES AVAILABLE

- private outdoor spa pool with sea views
- Italian billiards table
- in-house art gallery
- guest BBQ; archery on site
- mountain bikes; tennis
- bush walks on site & peninsula
- duplicate bridge arranged
- horse riding on beach, 4-min drive away

- *Mamma Mia!* – 35 ft Bertram launch, available for skippered game fishing
- massage & beauty therapists
- swimming & watersports
- kayaking; windsurfing
- scenic flights
- Whitianga, 8-min drive
- 18-hole golf course, 12 mins
- Hot Water Beach, 30 mins

Villa Toscana

WHITIANGA
Driftwood Lodge B & B

Hosts Janice and Bruce Bell

167 Buffalo Beach Road, Whitianga   *Mobile* 021 716 769
Phone 0-7-866 5256   *Email* welcome@driftwoodnz.co.nz
Fax 0-7-866 5296   *Website* www.driftwoodnz.co.nz

DIRECTIONS: From Thames, take SH 25 to Whitianga. Continue north into Buffalo Beach Rd for 2km to Driftwood Lodge on left. Or from Coromandel, take take SH 25 to Whitianga. Driftwood Lodge on right.

| 3 bdrm | 3 enst | 1 pdrm | **Double $245** **Extra persons $50 each** | **Single $190** | *Includes continental breakfast* *Cooked breakfast, lunch & dinner extra* |

Located on the Coromandel Peninsula, on the outskirts of Whitianga, Driftwood Lodge is sited across the road from Brophy Beach Reserve. The guests have total use of the second floor above the hosts' residence. Purpose-built and opened in 2005, Driftwood Lodge provides three spacious ensuite super-king/twin guestrooms, each opening to a balcony. There is a private guest lounge with panoramic sea views, where breakfast can be served, or it can be enjoyed alfresco on the balconies, or room service is provided. Picnic baskets and barbecue evening meals are also available by arrangement. Watersports and the beach opposite the Lodge are popular with guests. Restaurants and cafés are just one kilometre away in Whitianga township.

FACILITIES

- 3 super-king/twin ensuite bedrooms with phone jacks, tea/coffee & fridge in each
- hair dryer, toiletries, heated floor & bathrobes in ensuites
- email, fax & phone available on request
- children & pets welcome
- private guest lounge with tea/ coffee, nibbles, bar, TV, video, artwork & book exchange
- continental breakfast served or $15 pp for full cooked
- picnic basket by request, extra
- BBQ dinner by arrangement, $20–$40 pp
- guest laundry, $10
- balcony from each bedroom
- private guest entrance
- courtesy passenger transfer
- off-street parking

ACTIVITIES AVAILABLE

- honeymoons catered for
- beach reserve across road
- beach & bush walks
- scenic boat trips
- fishing, big-game charter boats
- scenic flights
- art galleries; museum
- Hot Water Beach
- Cathedral Cove
- restaurants & cafés nearby
- diving; snorkelling
- golf; mini golf
- tennis; shopping
- yachting charters
- kayaking; windsurfing
- garden visits
- horse trekking
- Whitianga township, 1km

WHANGAMATA
Bushland Park Lodge

Hosts Reinhard and Petra Nickel

Wentworth Valley Road, Whangamata   *Phone* 0-7-865 7468
Postal P O Box 190, Whangamata   *Email* bushparklodge@xtra.co.nz
Fax 0-7-865 7486   *Website* www.bushlandparklodge.co.nz

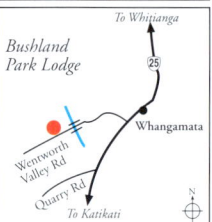

| 4 bdrm | 4 enst | 1 pdrm | Room rate $200–$350 | *Includes breakfast*
Dinner, sauna, spa & treatments extra |

DIRECTIONS: From Thames, take SH 25A south to SH 25. Turn right to Whangamata. Then turn right into Wentworth Valley Rd. Travel 5km & cross ford. Bushland Park on right. Or from Waihi take SH 25 north.

Bushland Park Lodge offers boutique accommodation with European old world charm for couples seeking a romantic escape. Petra and Reinhard have created their Nickel Strausse – a German Black Forest-style dining room for gourmet dining – featuring candlelit dinners beside a cosy firepace. Birthdays, anniversaries and other special events are popular celebrations at Bushland Park Lodge and Nickel Strausse. A range of special occasion and pamper packages with wellness treatments and dinner are available. The Lodge is set in two hectares (five acres) of native bushland park, the ambience enhanced by the water-lily pond, glow-worm grotto, and the tranquillity of the adjacent rainforest, close to Wentworth Falls, south of Whangamata.

FACILITIES

- 2 queen ensuite bedrooms with sunny balcony
- 2 super-king twin honeymoon suites with verandah
- hair dryers, heated towel rails, toiletries & bathrobes
- TV & video in suites
- phone, fax & email available
- tea/coffee facilities for rooms
- German & French spoken

- fully licensed Black Forest-style gourmet dining
- 3-course candlelit dinner, $75 pp
- special dietary needs catered, by prior arrangement only
- alfresco dining, open fireplaces
- Scandinavian sauna, $20 pp
- hydrotherapeutic spa pool, $10
- massage & beauty treatments

ACTIVITIES AVAILABLE

- in-house gourmet dining
- various games on site
- glow-worm grotto in 2ha park
- rainforest on site & walk to waterfall nearby
- safe beach & township at Whangamata, 10-min drive
- all outdoor & watersport activities arranged
- bush walks & beach walks for all fitness levels

- 18-hole golf course, 5km away
- Health Spa Treatments: massage, sauna, spa pool, beauty treatments & relaxation treatments, extra
- off-season package: 2 days with European "Culture & Cuisine" experience; pamper & wellness packages, & gift vouchers for corporate incentives, or personal gifts – www.bushlandparklodge.co.nz

Bushland Park

Above: Two hectares (five acres) of native bushland feature a water-lily pond, glow-worm grotto and outdoor sauna and spa pool.
Below: The Presidential Suite, with an open fireplace, is popular for special occasions at Bushland Park Lodge.
Opposite top: The Nickel Strausse is the boutique five-table gourmet dining room at Bushland Park Lodge for intimate dining.
Opposite bottom left: Bushland Park Lodge caters for all special celebrations, such as honeymoons, anniversaries and birthdays.
Opposite bottom right: The entrance to Bushland Park Lodge and Nickel Strausse with the accommodation facilities behind.

© Friars' Guide to New Zealand Accommodation for the Discerning Traveller

TAIRUA, COROMANDEL PENINSULA
Colleith Lodge

Hosts Maureen and Colin Gilroy

8 Rewa Rewa Valley, Tairua   *Postal* P O Box 25, Tairua
Phone 0-7-864 7970   *Mobile* 027 472 1423   *Fax* 0-7-864 7972
Email info@colleithlodge.co.nz   *Website* www.colleithlodge.co.nz

| 3 bdrm | 3 enst | 1 pdrm | **Room rate $325–$350** | *Includes breakfast & apéritifs* *Dinner extra* |

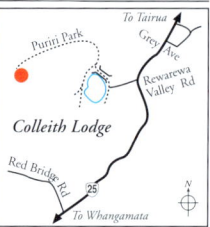

DIRECTIONS: From Whangamata, take SH 25 north towards Tairua. Just after 50km sign, turn left into Rewarewa Valley Rd. Turn right over causeway & right into Puriri Park. Travel up hill to Colleith Lodge at top on left.

Set in native bush full of birdlife, with views over the harbour and ocean to Slipper Island, Colleith Lodge was purpose built in 2002 from kiln-fired Hinuera stone. Three spacious ensuite bedrooms are available for guests, each opening to a private patio on the terrace overlooking the estuary. A full breakfast is served indoors or alfresco on the terrace, and a barbecue or full dinner is available by arrangement. A small wine cellar stocks a selection of New Zealand wines, and complimentary pre-dinner drinks and nibbles are offered to the guests each evening. Colin or Maureen will drive guests to the local restaurants at Tairua, or a ferry will provide transport to Paku. An outdoor border collie, Jip, complete the family.

FACILITIES

- 3 guest bedrooms: 1 super-king/twin & 2 queen bedrooms all with ensuite bathrooms
- all bedrooms open to private patios with sea views
- bathrobes, toiletries, heated floors & heated towel rails
- 1 guest lounge with wood fire, books, desk, phone & bar
- television lounge with Sky TV, video, DVD & CD-player

- breakfast indoors or alfresco
- complimentary apéritifs
- 3-course dinner, $65 pp, by arrangement
- wine cellar & list available
- phone jacks in bedrooms
- BBQ; tea/coffee available
- self-serve laundry
- email, phone & fax available
- fresh flowers; on-site parking

ACTIVITIES AVAILABLE

- easy bush walk on site
- 2 kayaks for guest use
- swimming & spa pools on site
- 1 outdoor dog Jip, a border collie
- bird-watching; fishing
- tramping, hiking & walking
- sightseeing; bush scenery
- golf; boating; goldmines

- Coromandel day tour, guided by hosts, extra
- restaurants at Paku via ferry 2km drive
- restaurants in Tairua, 1km
- cafés, crafts & galleries
- Hot Water Beach, 20 mins
- Cathedral Cove
- gardens to visit
- Whangamata town, 26km

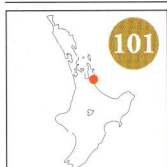

WAIHI BEACH
Cornucopia Villa Retreat

Host Cheryl Munro

Cornucopia Villa Retreat

50 Koutunui Road, R D 1, Athenree, Katikati
Phone 0-7-863 1162   *Mobile* 021 123 9868
Email cheryl@cornucopiavilla.com   *Website* www.cornucopiavilla.com

DIRECTIONS: From Waihi, take SH 2 south, past the Waihi Beach turn-off. Turn left into Athenree Rd. Travel 3km & turn left again into Koutunui Rd. Travel 500m to Cornucopia Villa Retreat on right.

4 bdrm	4 enst	Room rate $350–$450	*Includes breakfast*	*Lunch or picnic baskets extra*	

Opened in 2005, Cornucopia is a colonial villa built in 1880, with a new top storey added to provide four ensuite guestrooms. Retaining original features such as the stained glass and finials, the villa now has quality fittings and furnishings, with antiques complementing the native timber flooring. Breakfast is served in the dining room or alfresco on the wrap-around verandahs with views over farmland and hills to the ocean beyond. Set in almost a hectare, trees include a century-old oak, planted by the first owner on his wedding day, and the old orchard bears a variety of fruit – apples, pears, quinces, feijoas and almonds – a true cornucopia. Waihi Beach is just a five-minute drive away.

Cornucopia

Cornucopia

FACILITIES

- 1 king & 1 queen ensuite bedroom & upstairs balcony
- 1 king & 1 queen ensuite bedroom downstairs
- quality cotton bed linen, TV, tea/coffee & mineral water
- 1 cast iron bath; hair dryers, demist mirrors, heated towel rails, bathrobes & toiletries
- guest lounge with tea/coffee, nibbles, Sky TV, CD-player, library & writing desk
- full cooked or continental breakfast served
- lunch & gourmet picnic baskets, by request, extra
- guest laundry facilities
- fresh flowers
- massage & beauty therapy, in-house, extra
- BBQ; on-site parking
- light plane & helicopter access nearby

ACTIVITIES AVAILABLE

- 1ha (2 acres) grounds & orchard; croquet & pétanque
- telescope for star gazing
- Waihi surf beach, 5km
- natural hot mineral pools
- native bush walks
- bird-watching & photography
- boating, swimming, surfing & fishing; safe harbour
- Mayor Island – game & deep sea fishing
- restaurants nearby
- Pacifica golf course, 30 mins
- Morton Estate & Mills Reef wineries, 40 mins
- open cast working gold mine
- Katikati mural town – bird gardens, antiques, arts & crafts
- Karangahake Gorge walkway & steam train
- Coromandel Peninsula tours
- Rotorua, 1½-hour drive south

Cornucopia

WAIHI
Woodland Park Lodge

Hosts Barbara and Ken Hogg

418B Woodland Road, R D 2, Waihi

Phone 0-7-863 8168   *Email* barbara@woodlandpark.co.nz
Fax 0-7-863 8596   *Website* www.woodlandpark.co.nz

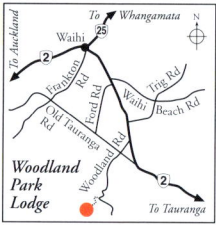

DIRECTIONS: From Waihi or Tauranga, take SH 2 & turn south into Woodland Rd. Travel 4km & turn right into 418B driveway. Travel 1km & take left-hand fork. Travel uphill & take middle fork to Lodge.

| 4 bdrm | 2 enst | 2 prbth | **Lodge room rate $425–$475**
Punga House rate $475–$795 | *Includes breakfast*
Minimum 2-night stay | *Lunch & dinner extra*
Includes breakfast or provisions | |

The philosophy of Woodland Park Lodge is to provide for guests' every need, from fine cuisine to health treatments in a relaxing environment. Set in a restful rural location, with views down the valley to the ocean beyond, Woodland Park is a 112-hectare farm with extensive native bush walks designed for rejuvenation. Guest are offered hosted accommodation in the Lodge, or self-contained privacy in the separate Punga House, both with quality furnishings and attention to detail. Breakfast provisions can be supplied in the Punga House if preferred, or breakfast is served in the dining room upstairs in the Lodge, with choices from a comprehensive breakfast menu the evening before. Lunch, gourmet picnic hampers and dinner can also be requested.

FACILITIES

- Lodge: 2 super-king bedrooms, 1 with ensuite & spa bath, 1 with private bathroom
- Punga House: 1 super-king bedroom with double bath & double shower in ensuite; & 1 queen bedroom with bathroom; self-catering kitchen; lounge; single-party bookings only
- hair dryer, bathrobes, toiletries, demist mirror & heated towel rails & floors in all 4 bathrooms
- full breakfast or provisions
- lunch, $20–$40 pp; dinner, $80–$95 pp; wine extra
- complimentary apéritifs; special diets catered for
- Lodge guest lounge & Punga lounge both with Sky TV, DVD, videos, music, games, books, artwork, bar & nibbles
- phone jacks; helipad

ACTIVITIES AVAILABLE

- in-house aromatherapy massage, extra
- personalised health & rejuvenation retreats
- gourmet picnicking; birdlife
- garden & bush walks on site
- seasonal farm activities on site
- beaches; watersports, 15 mins
- golf course adjacent
- Karangahake walkway, 20 mins
- guided beach & bush walks
- Coromandel Peninsula & Bay of Plenty nearby
- heritage sites & steam train
- gardens open to visit
- open-cast working goldmine; historic Waihi, 10 min drive
- wineries, collectables, antiques, art & craft trails
- murals at Katikati, 25 mins

Katikati
Matahui Lodge

Hosts Kay and Trevor Mitchell

187 Matahui Road, R D 2, Katikati, Bay of Plenty
Phone 0-7-571 8121   *Mobile* 021 416 632   *Fax* 0-7-571 8121
Email info@matahui-lodge.co.nz   *Website* www.matahui-lodge.co.nz

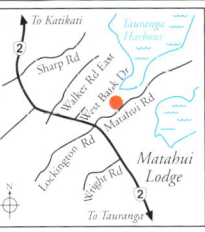

| 3 bdrm | 3 enst | 1 pdrm | **Room rate $325–$475** |

Includes breakfast & apéritifs
Lunch & dinner extra

DIRECTIONS: From Katikati take SH 2 south for 7.7km. Turn left into Matahui Rd. Travel 1.87km to Matahui Lodge on left. From Tauranga take SH 2 north, 500m past Morton Estate Vineyard. Turn right to Lodge.

North-facing with extensive rural views to Tauranga Harbour, Matahui Lodge is set in over two hectares (six acres) including a golf-driving range. Purpose built in 2001, the Lodge is designed for indoor/outdoor living, with a blend of contemporary and period furnishings and original New Zealand artwork. Two king-size bedrooms include mini-bars with complimentary juice, wine and beer. A queen-size bedroom overlooks the orchard. Guests enjoy the in-house library and gymnasium, and private golf lessons with Trevor are popular. Membership privileges are offered at the local championship golf course. Matahui is fully licensed and complimentary pre-dinner drinks can be followed by indoor or alfresco dining. There is light plane or helicopter access.

FACILITIES

- 2 super-king/twin bedrooms, each with ensuite, tea/coffee, fridge with courtesy drinks, iron, phone jack & views
- 1 queen ensuite bedroom upstairs with tea/coffee
- wheelchair access to 1 bedroom
- cotton bed linen; fresh flowers
- hair dryers, toiletries, heated towel rails & bathrobes
- laundry available
- breakfast served in dining room, alfresco or room service
- lunch indoors or alfresco, $20 pp
- 3–4 course dinner with wine, $65 pp; complimentary apéritifs
- lounge with open fire, Sky TV, video, DVD & CD-player
- library upstairs; original NZ art
- email, phone & fax available
- on-site parking; helipad

ACTIVITIES AVAILABLE

- in-house gym & massage
- outdoor fireplace & BBQ
- spa pool on site
- golf-driving range on site
- golf lessons from Trevor
- clay target shooting on site
- picnicking; scenic flights
- sea & freshwater fly fishing
- surfing beaches
- restaurants, 3–20 mins away
- Katikati murals, 4 mins north
- horse riding
- bush walking; gardens to visit
- vineyard tours & wine tasting
- kiwifruit & avocado orchards
- hot mineral pools, 16 mins south
- Mt Maunganui, 30 mins south
- Tauranga airport, 30 mins south

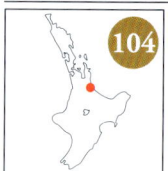

BETHLEHEM, TAURANGA
Hollies

Hosts Shirley and Michael Creak

Westridge Drive, Bethlehem, Tauranga
Phone 0-7-577 9678   *Email* stay@hollies.co.nz
Fax 0-7-579 1678   *Website* www. hollies.co.nz

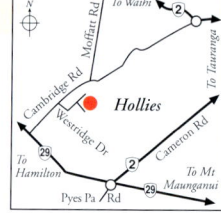

DIRECTIONS: From SH 2, turn into Cambridge Rd. Travel 4km, then turn left into Westridge Drive. Hollies on right. Or from SH 29, turn right into Cambridge Rd. Travel 2km, then turn right into Westridge Drive to Hollies.

3 bdrm	1 enst	2 prbth	Double $120–$250	*Includes breakfast*
			Single $95–$165	*Dinner extra*

Named after a family home in England, Hollies is set in almost half a hectare of landscaped gardens featuring roses, camellias, holly hedge, swimming pool with rock waterfall, gazebo and citrus trees. Hollies is a semi-rural contemporary home furnished in Mediterranean colours complementing tiled floors. The staircase sweeps up to the guest wing which comprises a spacious suite and two bedrooms overlooking the gardens. The suite includes kitchenette, bedroom, ensuite, lounge, balcony and guest entrance providing privacy suitable for honeymooners. The full gourmet breakfast menu offers fresh fruit, croissants, home-made jams and cooked dishes. Shirley will also serve dinner with New Zealand wine, by prior arrangement.

FACILITIES

- 1 king/twin suite (honeymoon) with lounge, TV, kitchenette, private balcony, & entrance
- 1 queen & 1 king/twin bedroom, each with private bathroom
- toiletries, hair dryers, robes
- guest lounge with TV, video, CD, opens to gardens & pool
- complimentary coffee/tea & home-made baking on arrival
- honeymoon packages available

- breakfast served alfresco in garden, family room, or suite
- dinner by arrangement, $40 pp
- teas/coffee, laundry, phone, fax, email facilities available
- fresh flowers
- children by arrangement
- Muffy, the white tabby cat
- courtesy passenger transfer
- secure off-street parking

ACTIVITIES AVAILABLE

- pétanque/boules on site
- in-ground swimming pool
- croquet on site
- viewing Michael's Jaguar cars
- hot mineral pools, 2-min drive
- canoeing & kayaking, 5 mins
- wineries nearby
- climbing Mt Maunganui, 15-min drive away
- safe beaches

- licensed award-winning restaurants, 3–6-min drive
- deep-sea fishing
- jet boating; horse racing
- private gardens to visit
- potteries; walks
- swimming with dolphins
- 5 18-hole golf courses
- kiwifruit & avocado orchards
- shopping in Tauranga, 7 mins

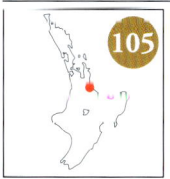

TAURANGA
Number Eight

Hosts Heather and John Gillies

8 River Oaks Drive, Woodford Park, Tauranga
Phone 0-7-543 4550   *Mobile* 021 618 806   *Fax* 0-7-543 4551
Email h.gillies@noeight.co.nz   *Website* www.noeight.co.nz

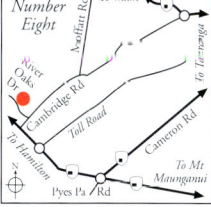

DIRECTIONS: From SH 2, turn south into Cambridge Rd. Travel 5km & turn right into River Oaks Drive. Number Eight on right. Or from SH 29, turn north into Cambridge Rd. Turn left into River Oaks Drive.

2 bdrm	2 enst	Room rate $200 Multiple-night rates available	*Includes breakfast* *Dinner extra*

Located in a semi-rural garden setting, just 10 minutes from Tauranga City, Number Eight provides hosted accommodation for four guests. Built in 2001, the two queen-size guestrooms each have an ensuite and there is a private guest lounge and adjoining dining room where meals are served. A full breakfast can be enjoyed at the dining table or alfresco in the courtyard, and three-course dinner is also available by arrangement. The hosts provide traditional New Zealand hospitality, and are happy to cater for small private functions. Many restaurants, cafés and shops are within 10 minutes' drive. There is a cat and Australian terrier on site. Number Eight is within easy access of Mount Maunganui, beaches, golf, fishing and kiwifruit orchards.

FACILITIES

- 2 queen ensuite bedrooms
- 1 bath available
- hair dryer, heated towel rails & bathrobes in ensuites
- cotton bed linen, dressing room, mineral water & TV in bedrooms
- fresh flowers, fruit & chocolates
- private guest lounge & shared lounge with tea/coffee, Sky TV, video, DVD, piano & CD-player
- full continental or cooked breakfast served
- 3-course dinner, $35 pp, wine extra
- email, fax, phone available
- laundry service, extra
- courtesy passenger transfer to restaurant & airport
- covered parking
- small private functions catered

ACTIVITIES AVAILABLE

- large landscaped gardens
- inner harbour & ocean beaches
- scenic walks; scenic flights
- fishing; boating
- swimming; snorkelling
- swimming with dolphins
- Mt Maunganui, 15 mins
- 20 golf courses within 1 hour
- thermal pools 4km
- café, 5-min walk
- restaurants, 5-min drive
- kiwifruit orchards, 20 mins
- gardens to visit & festivals
- arts & crafts
- vineyards; avocado orchards
- gliding; sky-diving
- Tauranga City, 10-min drive
- Rotorua City, 45 mins

TAURANGA
Frog Cottage

Host Sally Morrison

DIRECTIONS: From SH 2 turn south into Eleventh Ave. At round-about turn right into Devonport Rd. Frog Cottage on right.

379 Devonport Road, Tauranga   *Postal* 186 Devonport Road, Tauranga
Phone 0-7-571 5474   *Mobile* 025 963 916   *Fax* 0-7-578 2257
Email sally.morrison@xtra.co.nz   *Website* www.frogcottage.co.nz

| 2 bdrm | 1 prbth |

Cottage rate $385   *Includes breakfast provisions Self-catering*

Frog Cottage

Set in the heart of Tauranga, Frog Cottage was originally built in 1939 and has been totally renovated and refurbished to provide self-contained accommodation for single-party bookings. This traditionally designed cottage includes two bedrooms with Egyptian bed linen, bathroom with a double claw-foot bath, lounge with open fire, full kitchen for self-catering, and a laundry. Frog Cottage is just a short walk from the central business district of Tauranga City, with its many cafés and restaurants. Mount Maunganui with its surf beaches is nearby and Te Puke's kiwifruit and avocado orchards are a pleasant drive away. Breakfast provisions are supplied each day and guests enjoy privacy and independence at Frog Cottage.

FACILITIES

- self-contained cottage
- single-party bookings only
- 1 queen & 1 twin bedroom
- 1 private bathroom
- double claw-foot bath, hair dryer, toiletries & heated towel rails
- bathrobes
- Egyptian cotton bed linen
- fresh flowers
- full kitchen for self-catering
- breakfast provisions supplied
- phones in dining room & bedrooms
- lounge with open fire, Sky TV, DVD, CD-player, books & magazines
- self-serve laundry
- verandah
- on-site parking

ACTIVITIES AVAILABLE

- small garden on site
- swimming beaches nearby
- Memorial Hall
- wineries
- arts & crafts
- fishing
- CBD nearby
- boutique shopping
- kiwifruit & avocado orchards
- Tauranga restaurants & cafés, short walk away
- private gardens to visit
- golf courses, 15 mins
- Mt Maunganui, 15-min drive away
- Te Puke, 20-min drive
- Papamoa, 20 mins
- Auckland City, 2½-hour drive north

Frog Cottage

Frog Cottage

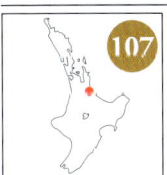

TAURANGA
Boscabel Lodge

Hosts Rosemary and Peter Luxton

98D Boscabel Drive, R D 3, Tauranga, Bay of Plenty
Phone 0-7-544 6647   *Mobile* 021 744 441   *Fax* 0-7-544 6647
Email boscabellodge@yahoo.com   *Website* friars.co.nz/hosts/boscabel.html

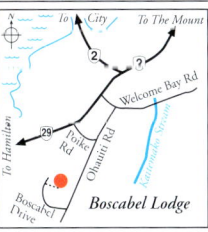

DIRECTIONS: From SH 29 or SH 2 travel towards Welcome Bay. Turn east into Welcome Bay Rd. Take 1st right into Ohauiti Rd. Travel 3km & turn right into Boscabel Dr. Towards end, turn right up a narrow right of way.

5 bdrm	1 enst	2 prbth	1 pdrm	Suite rate $150–$160	Includes continental breakfast in suite
				Apartment rate $150–$200	Self-catering Breakfast extra

Boscabel Lodge, meaning "beautiful wooded area" in Spanish, is set beside a native bush walk and surrounded with avocado trees from the orchard that originally occupied the site. Guests are offered the choice of a spacious suite in the house, or either of the two fully self-contained two-bedroom apartments with rural and sea views. The 12-metre solar-heated swimming pool and spa pool are popular on-site activities with vistas across the fields to Mt Maunganui and Mayor Island, which is visible in the distance. Continental breakfast is served in the suite, or available on request in the apartments, both of which include a fully equipped kitchen for self-catering. There are many restaurants 10 to 15 minutes' drive away in Tauranga and Mt Maunganui.

FACILITIES

- 1 queen bedroom with ensuite, dressing room & 4-poster bed
- 2 apartments each with 1 king or queen & 1 twin bedroom, private bathroom, lounge, & full kitchen with dishwasher, fridge & microwave
- hair dryers, heated towel rails, toiletries & cotton bed linen
- children welcome
- laundry facilities in apartments

- continental breakfast served in suite; extra for apartments
- phone, fax & email available
- German, Dutch/Flemish & French spoken by hosts
- separate guest entrances & terraces
- babysitting by arrangement
- off-street parking
- garaging

ACTIVITIES AVAILABLE

- 12-m solar-heated swimming pool on site
- heated spa pool; table tennis
- in-ground pétanque court
- avocado orchard on site
- landscaped garden
- native bush walk & stream, 2-min walk away
- fishing & big-game charters
- surf beaches, 15-min drive

- restaurants, cafés & bars, 15-min drive
- diving & hunting trips
- choice of golf courses
- scenic flights arranged
- swimming with dolphins
- shopping in downtown Tauranga or Mt Maunganui, 10–15-min drive
- Rotorua City, 45-min drive

WELCOME BAY, TAURANGA
Villa Collini

Hosts Margrit Collini and Andy Wurm

36 Kaiate Falls Road, R D 5, Welcome Bay, Tauranga
Phone 0-7-544 8322   *Mobile* 021 047 8394   *Fax* 0-7-544 8322
Email villacollini@pl.net   *Website* www.naturetours-nz.com

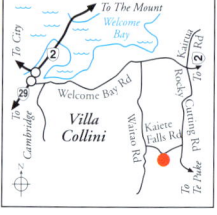

DIRECTIONS: From SH 29 or SH 2 turn east into Welcome Bay Rd. Travel 6.5km & turn right into Waitao Rd. Travel 5km then turn left into Kaiate Falls Rd. Travel 400m to Villa Collini on right.

| 2 bdrm | 1 enst | 1 pdrm | Double $110–$150 Single $80–$110 | *Includes breakfast Dinner extra* |

With panoramic views from the open-plan lounge over the surrounding valleys to the ocean and Mt Maunganui beyond, Villa Collini was architecturally designed in contemporary style in 1996. Accommodation is provided for single-party bookings only in two spacious bedrooms, sharing a private ensuite. A special continental breakfast, including home-made breads, fresh fruit and Italian coffee, is served alfresco on the terrace or indoors, where guests can enjoy the sea vistas. Dinner with wine is also available by arrangement, specialising in Mediterranean and international cuisine. Guests can relax in the spa pool and sauna on site, or take a bush walk to the Kaiate waterfalls close by. Andy and Margrit also operate guided nature tours.

FACILITIES

- one-party bookings only
- 1 super-king & 1 queen bedroom share ensuite with bath
- hair dryer, toiletries & heated towel rails in ensuite
- tea/coffee, TV, CD-player, music, books, magazines & writing desk in lounge
- 1 powder room
- German spoken by hosts

- continental breakfast with home-made breads
- dinner with wine, $40 pp
- self-serve laundry, $5
- email, fax & phone available
- children welcome
- set on hilltop with extensive lawns & garden on 1.5ha (4 acres) grounds
- on-site parking

ACTIVITIES AVAILABLE

- BBQ, spa pool & sauna on site
- boules/pétanque & basketball courts on site
- hosted nature tours
- bush walk to Kaiate waterfalls close by
- hot mineral pools, 5-min drive
- golf courses, 10–15-min drive
- Mt Maunganui & Papamoa
- sandy east coast surf beaches

- restaurants & shops, 15 mins
- dolphin watching
- gardens open to visit
- White Island by helicopter or boat
- Tauranga airport, 15 mins
- kiwifruit orchards & adventure park, at Te Puke, 20 mins
- Rotorua City, 50-min drive

WELCOME BAY, TAURANGA
Ridge Country Retreat

Hosts Joanne O'Keeffe and Penny Oxnam

300 Rocky Cutting Road, Welcome Bay, Tauranga
Phone 0-7-542 1301 *Email* relax@rcr.co.nz
Fax 0-7-542 2116 *Website* www.rcr.co.nz

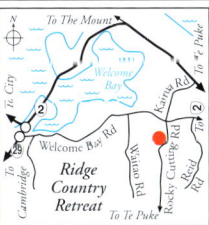

DIRECTIONS: From south take SH 2 thru Te Puke & travel 10km. Turn left into Welcome Bay Rd. Take 2nd turn on left into Rocky Cutting Rd for 3km to Retreat. From north turn right at roundabout, then left at 2nd roundabout.

5 bdrm	5 enst	1 pdrm	Double $950 Single $565	*Includes breakfast & dinner* **Off-season rates available**	*Lunch extra*

Ridge Country Retreat is set in native bush on 14 hectares (35 acres) of rural hills with panoramic views of Tauranga's coastline and farmland. Purpose built and opened in 2003, the Retreat offers five ensuite guestrooms, small conference facilities and a range of recreational opportunities including in-house beauty and body therapies. Ridge Country Retreat has been designed for guests with the motto in mind: "relax, reflect, replenish, recharge and revitalise". A full cooked breakfast is served in the dining room, then in the evening complimentary pre-dinner drinks and nibbles are followed by a five-course dinner served in the formal lounge, or alfresco on the private balcony. The Retreat is fully licensed and lunch is also available.

FACILITIES

- 5 super-king/twin bedrooms each with private bathroom & balcony
- cotton bed linen; powder room
- writing desk, TV, teas, ground coffee, mini-bar, phone, fax, email, iron & board in bedrooms
- bathrobes, hair dryers, toiletries, heated floors, heated towel rails, demist mirrors, double basins, spa baths with views in all ensuites
- laundry, $5; wheelchair access

- full gourmet breakfast menu
- 2-course lunch menu, $35 pp
- apéritifs & 5-course dinner
- guest lounge with open fire, Sky TV, DVD, CD-player, artwork, tea/coffee & fully licensed bar; library
- 2 Colourpoint Persian cats
- on-site parking; helipad
- local courtesy transfer

ACTIVITIES AVAILABLE

- corporate functions catered
- outside open stone fireplace with BBQ on site
- 15m heated lap & spa pools
- in-house gym & massage room
- strolls along native bush walks
- sandy east coast beaches
- Bayfair shopping centre
- kiwifruit orchards
- golf club with rural views, 3km

- cafés/restaurants with Japanese, Thai, Turkish, Chinese, Italian, Mediterranean & NZ cuisine
- deep-sea fishing; harbour cruises
- dolphin watching
- jet boating
- Tauranga City, 15-min drive
- Mt Maunganui, 10-min drive
- Rotorua thermal villages & trout fishing, 40 mins south

© Friars' Guide to New Zealand Accommodation for the Discerning Traveller

Pyes Pa, Tauranga
Cassimir Lodge

Host Reg Turner

20 Williams Road South, Pyes Pa, R D 3 Tauranga
Postal R D 3, Tauranga   *Phone* 0-7-543 2000   *Fax* 0-7-543 1999
Email cassimir@xtra.co.nz   *Website* www.cassimir.com

| 4 bdrm | 3 enst | 1 prbth | 2 pdrm |

Room rate $680–$1,000
Includes all meals & cocktail hour

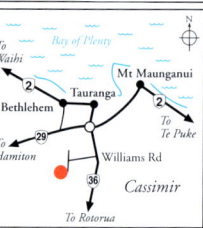

DIRECTIONS: From Auckland, take SH 2 to Bethlehem. Turn right into Moffat Rd, then left into SH 29. Turn right at roundabout into Pyes Pa Rd. Travel 12km & turn right into Williams Rd, then left to Lodge.

Originally built in 1890, Cassimir was totally redesigned in 1993, by the architect John Little of Ambientie, to feature early 19th-century colonial-style architecture, with Queen Anne-style turrets and dormer windows. Contemporary furnishings complement the native timber flooring, doors and furniture. Set in a private estate of 20 hectares with deer, sheep, cattle and horses, Cassimir offers a peaceful rural retreat. All meals are prepared by the host or chef. Five-course candlelit dinners specialise in fresh New Zealand seafood, lamb, venison and local wines. The East Wing comprises three suites and belvedere with expansive views to the Pacific Ocean, while the West Wing comprises a further suite, with similar attention to detail.

FACILITIES

- 4 king/twin bedrooms, 3 ensuites & 1 private bathroom in 2 guest wings
- bath in 1 marble bathroom
- spa bath in bathhouse
- solarium conservatory
- spacious bar lounge with grand piano & feature fireplace
- children with nannies welcome
- sea views from viewing belvedere
- full country breakfast, with any cooked preference
- light lunches, picnic hampers
- 5-course candlelit dinner, with local wines extra
- liquor licence
- library with fireplace
- phone, fax & email available
- laundry available
- on-site parking; helipad

ACTIVITIES AVAILABLE

- in-house board games
- lawn games – tennis, croquet, pétanque/boules
- telescope for star gazing
- native bird photography
- horse riding
- 9-hole pitch'n'putt
- trout fishing in estate stream
- gardens to visit
- bush walks
- wine trails
- mountain hiking
- deep-sea fishing
- white water rafting
- 2 golf courses
- shopping in Tauranga, 15km
- Mt Maunganui, 20 mins
- Rotorua lakes, 30-min drive
- Maori history at Rotorua

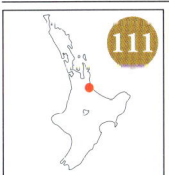

WHAKATANE
Motuhora Rise B & B

Hosts Toni and Jeff Spellmeyer

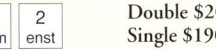

2 Motuhora Rise, Whakatane   *Postal* P O Box 553, Whakatane
Phone 0-7-307 0224   *Email* jtspell@xtra.co.nz
Fax 0-7-307 0541   *Website* friars.co.nz/hosts/motuhora.html

DIRECTIONS: From The Strand, turn right at roundabout into George St. Veer right into Hillcrest Rd, then turn right again into Waiewe St. Take 1st left into Motuhora Rise. 1st house on right at top of drive.

2 bdrm	2 enst		

Double $205
Single $190

Includes continental breakfast
Dinner extra

Nestled into the hilltops of Whakatane, Motuhora Rise overlooks the Rangitaiki Plains and Whale Island with the active volcanic White Island beyond. This purpose-built Bed and Breakfast offers an entire guest floor for peace and quiet, with only two guest bedrooms, an entertainment centre, and refreshment area. Guest privacy is ensured, with hosts Toni and Jeff living upstairs, accessible by intercom. Accommodation comprises two spacious bedrooms, each with ensuite bathroom featuring dual-headed showers. A hot tub/spa pool can be enjoyed on the guest decking under the stars. Toni serves guests fresh fruit with yoghurt, croissants or home-made muffins in the parlour, or alfresco. Dinner is offered, by request, and diets catered for.

FACILITIES

- 1 super-king/twin bedroom with wheelchair access, & 1 queen bedroom
- 2 ensuite bathrooms with double-headed showers
- hair dryers, toiletries, bathrobes & heated towel rails
- ceiling fans, chocolates & fresh flowers in bedrooms
- laundry available, $5
- fax & email available, extra

- continental breakfast served in parlour, or alfresco on guest patio
- 3-course dinner with lamb or venison & NZ wine, $45 pp
- cheeseboard on arrival
- refreshment centre with coffee, teas, fridge & microwave
- home theatre, VCR, DVD, satellite TV, CD, stereo
- off-street parking

ACTIVITIES AVAILABLE

- outdoor cat, Tigger, on site
- outdoor hot tub/spa pool on decking
- fishing rods & golf clubs available
- half-day walking tours
- 4 local golf courses
- White Island volcanic tour
- surf beaches; scuba diving
- swimming with dolphins

- restaurants & shops, 10-min walk
- beach walks; bush safaris
- museums; gardens open to visit
- trout & deep-sea fishing
- charter boats & cruises
- Tarawera Falls
- 4WD adventures; hunting
- gateway to East Cape
- Rotorua & Tauranga, each 1 hr

HAMURANA, ROTORUA
Panorama Country Homestay

Hosts Christine King and Dave Perry

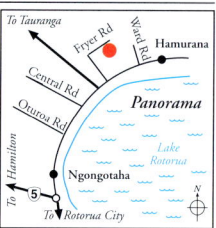

DIRECTIONS: Take SH 5 to round-about. Travel north round lake through Ngongotaha, towards Hamurana. Turn left into Fryer Rd & travel 1.5km, turning right at end of bitumen. Take 2nd driveway on right to Panorama.

144 Fryer Road, Hamurana   *Postal* 144 Fryer Road, R D 2, Rotorua
Phone 0-7-332 2618   *Mobile* 021 610 949   *Fax* 0-7-332 2618
Email panorama@wave.co.nz   *Website* www.babs.co.nz/panorama

3 bdrm	2 enst	1 prbth	**Double $150–$195**	**Extra person $50**	*Includes continental breakfast*
			Single $115	**Multiple-night rates available**	*Dinner extra*

Panorama is named for its panoramic views over Lake Rotorua and the surrounding countryside. Sited on two hectares of farmland, this architecturally designed cedar and brick home is set in landscaped gardens with private areas for guests to relax. Panorama features a private guest entrance and spacious rooms with native timber cathedral ceilings in the living areas. Panorama specialises in country hospitality offering dinner, with the emphasis on home-grown, home-made and local produce. Three-course dinners are served on the native rimu table in the formal dining room. Outdoor pursuits at Panorama include petting and feeding the sheep and working dog, playing a game of tennis, or relaxing in the therapeutic spa.

FACILITIES

- 1 super-king ensuite bedroom
- 1 super-king/twin bedroom with wheelchair access ensuite
- 1 queen bedroom with private bathroom & bath
- hair dryers, toiletries, heated towel rails & heaters
- cotton bed linen; fresh flowers
- children over 12 years welcome
- phone, fax & email available
- cooked breakfast, $15 pp
- 3-course dinner, $50 pp, with wine extra
- open fire in guest lounge
- Sky TV & wood fire in casual lounge
- laundry facilities available
- courtesy passenger transfer
- on-site parking
- lake views

ACTIVITIES AVAILABLE

- tennis court on site
- outdoor massage spa pool
- farm activities on site
- feeding pet sheep & dog
- fishing, boating on lake
- 3 golf courses, within 15 mins
- Maori culture, hangi, & concert
- geothermal attractions
- Hamurana & Rainbow Springs
- City restaurants, 15 mins
- Polynesian Spa
- Zorbs ball
- Skyline Gondola rides
- Agrodome
- Buried Village
- Redwood Grove walks
- Mt Tarawera
- Blue & Green Lakes

NGONGOTAHA, ROTORUA
Hamurana Country Estate

Hosts Kim and Andrew Martin

415 Hamurana Road, Ngongotaha   *Phone* 0-7-332 2222
Postal 415 Hamurana Road, R D 2, Rotorua   *Fax* 0-7-332 2284
Email stay@hcestate.co.nz   *Website* www.hcestate.co.nz

| 12 bdrm | 12 enst | Room rate $295–$550 | *Includes breakfast* | *Dinner extra* |

DIRECTIONS: From Rotorua take SH 5 north to Ngongotaha turn-off. Take SH 36 through Ngongotaha village & continue 5km around lake to Hamurana Country Estate on left.

Hamurana Country Estate is a secluded manor set in six hectares (15 acres) of farmland and gardens, with rural views to Lake Rotorua. Hosted by Kiwi owners, and extensively refurbished in 2004, Hamurana provides a peaceful country experience. The heated swimming pool is popular with guests, who also enjoy dining in the restaurant, or alfresco on the large balcony in warm weather. The resident chef prepares meals using fresh home-grown produce, complemented by a select range of New Zealand wines. Seven of the 12 individually furnished ensuite bedrooms include spa baths, and all have views of the lake, farm or gardens. Hamurana is an exclusive venue for conferences and weddings, just 15 minutes from Rotorua City.

FACILITIES

- 2 super-king suites, each with double spa bath in ensuite
- 5 Superior king/twin bedrooms, each with spa bath in ensuite
- 5 Standard king or queen bedrooms, each with ensuite
- toiletries, hair dryers, bathrobes
- phone, TV, tea/coffee in rooms
- laundry available
- guest lounge with open fire
- chef's à la carte breakfast
- à la carte restaurant, extra
- lunch by arrangement, extra
- licensed Rimu Bar
- balcony for alfresco dining
- guest & luggage lift; covered portico
- conference room for 20
- courtesy passenger transfer
- on-site parking; helipad

ACTIVITIES AVAILABLE

- BBQ areas on site
- heated swimming pool
- tennis court; farm walks
- home theatre room
- in-house billiards room
- pétanque terrain on site
- native bird-watching
- local trout guide
- kitchen & herb gardens
- 6ha farmland & gardens
- 6 golf courses, 3–15-min drive
- horse riding, 5-min drive away
- Hamurana springs & gardens
- Maori arts & crafts
- luge & gondola, 10-min drive
- Polynesian Spa, 15-min drive
- Hell's Gate thermal area, 20 mins
- redwood forest walks at springs
- Rotorua City & shops, 15 mins
- airport, 20-min drive

NGONGOTAHA, ROTORUA
Clover Downs Estate

Hosts Lyn and Lloyd Ferris

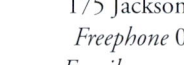

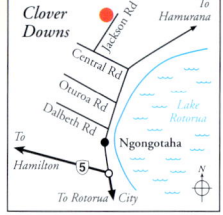

175 Jackson Road, Ngongotaha, R D 2, Rotorua   *Phone* 0-7-332 2366
Freephone 0800 3687 5323   *Mobile* 021 712 866   *Fax* 0-7-332 2367
Email reservations@cloverdowns.co.nz   *Website* www.cloverdowns.co.nz

DIRECTIONS: Take SH 5 to roundabout. Travel north round lake, through Ngongotaha, on Hamurana Rd. Take 3rd left into Central Rd, then turn right into Jackson Rd. Travel 1.75km to Clover Downs on left.

| 4 bdrm | 4 enst | 1 pdrm | Double $215–$305 Single $195–$290 | *Includes breakfast* |

Sited on a two-hectare (six-acre) deer and ostrich farm, Clover Downs is a brick ranch-style home built in 1987 with views to Lake Rotorua. The guest wing comprises the super-king/twin Governor's Suite, Gone Fishing Room, Rose Room and king-size Going Flying Room. All four bedrooms have ensuite bathrooms, and open to outdoor decks with lake or farm views. Rural vistas to the lake can also be enjoyed from the private guest lounge. A brick courtyard extends to a viewing deck overlooking the garden and farm. Lyn serves flexi-time full breakfasts with her home-made preserves and a variety of breads, croissants and muffins, and a cooked selection, either in the family room or alfresco overlooking the farm in summer.

FACILITIES

- 1 king & 3 super-king/twin ensuite bedrooms with decks
- bathrobes, hair dryers, toiletries, & heated towel rails in ensuites
- 1 bath & dual basins in suite
- cotton bed linen
- TV, video, ceiling fan, iron & ironing board in all 4 bedrooms
- fridge, tea/coffee, bottled mineral water, cookies, fruit & fresh flowers in each bedroom
- full continental breakfast, or cooked selection, extra
- private guest lounge with open fireplace
- decking for alfresco dining
- phone, fax, email available
- children welcome
- laundry available
- small conference facilities
- on-site parking

ACTIVITIES AVAILABLE

- pétanque/boules court
- deer & ostrich farm tour
- barbecue on site
- helicopter tours from site
- farm & forest horse riding
- 4 golf courses, 5–20-min drive
- clay-bird shooting
- guided fishing trips arranged
- traditional Maori hangi & Maori concerts
- city restaurants, 15-min drive
- watersports in lake
- 4WD tours & motorbikes – off-road, farm, bush or Mt Tarawera, 5–40 mins away
- gondola & luge
- private gardens to visit
- Agrodome
- thermal attractions
- Rotorua City shops, 15km

NGONGOTAHA, ROTORUA
Country Villa

Hosts Anneke and John van der Maat

351 Dalbeth Road, R D 2 Ngongotaha, Rotorua   *Fax* 0-7-357 5893
Phone 0-7-357 5893   *Local UK call phone* 0871 474 1573
Email countryvilla@xtra.co.nz   *Website* www.countryvilla.biz

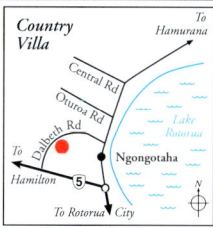

DIRECTIONS: From City, travel through Ngongotaha & over railway. Turn left into Dalbeth Rd & travel 3.5km to Villa on left. Or from SH 5, turn left after golf course into Dalbeth Rd. Travel 2.5km to Villa on right.

5 bdrm	3 enst	1 prbth	**Double** $215–$235 **Single** $195–$215	*Includes breakfast* **Extra persons** $85 each

This large Victorian-style villa was originally built in Auckland in 1906, and transported in 1996 to its present site in Ngongotaha, Rotorua. Totally renovated and refurbished, Country Villa offers three ensuite guestrooms downstairs, as well as an upstairs guest suite for single-party bookings. The turret provides rural views from the upstairs guest lounge, and there is another guest lounge downstairs with garden and lake views. Anneke serves breakfast in the conservatory with croissants or muffins, pancakes and fresh home-made bread and yoghurt, fresh fruit salad, and omelettes, or ham, cheese and tomatoes if preferred. Recommended restaurants are only a 10-minute drive away, and Ngongotaha village is just five minutes.

FACILITIES

- 3 queen bedrooms downstairs with ensuites, 2 with baths
- 1 suite upstairs with 1 queen/twin & 1 twin bedroom, 1 private bathroom & bath
- hair dryers, robes & toiletries
- wheelchair access to 1 ensuite
- private-party bookings upstairs; children welcome upstairs
- fluent Dutch & basic German spoken by hosts
- full breakfast, served downstairs in conservatory
- BBQ available for guest use
- turret lounge upstairs with tea/coffee, TV & writing desk
- guest lounge downstairs with piano, log fire & tea/coffee
- laundry service, extra
- phone, fax & email in office
- helicopter access on site
- on-site parking

ACTIVITIES AVAILABLE

- native bird-watching in large gardens
- feeding lambs in season; farm & garden walks on site
- trout fishing, 3-min drive
- golf, 3-min drive
- jetboats at Agrodome, 5 mins
- Maori cultural activities
- bungy jumping & Zorb
- 4WD at Mount Tarawera
- restaurants, 10-min drive
- Ngongotaha village, 5-min drive
- Rainbow & Fairy Springs, 7 mins
- Gondola, glass-blowing 7 mins
- Hamurana Springs, 8-min drive
- Redwood Grove, 15-min drive
- white water rafting & glow-worms at Okere Falls, 15 mins
- Rotorua City, 12-min drive
- airport, 20-min drive

NGONGOTAHA, ROTORUA
Nicara Lakeside Lodge

Hosts Heather and Mike Johnson

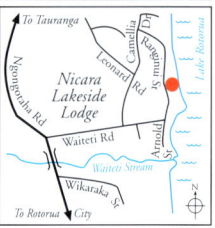

30–32 Ranginui Street, Ngongotaha   *Postal* P O Box 327, Ngongotaha
Phone 0-7-357 2105   *Mobile* 021 838 424   *Fax* 0-7-357 5385
Email info@nicaralodge.co.nz   *Website* www.nicaralodge.co.nz

DIRECTIONS: From north, take SH 5 to roundabout. Travel north round lake, through Ngongotaha village. Turn right into Waiteti Rd. At "T" junction turn left into Ranginui St to Nicara Lakeside Lodge on right.

| 4 bdrm | 4 enst | 1 pdrm | **Double $400–$450**
Single $350–$400 | *Includes breakfast & apéritifs* |

Overlooking Lake Rotorua, Nicara Lakeside Lodge is close to the Waiteti trout stream. Trout caught by guests can be prepared for breakfast, served in the dining room downstairs, or alfresco on the patio. Steps lead to the extensive grounds and private beach. This cedar, plaster and schist Lodge offers guests a place to relax inside or outdoors, to listen to music and enjoy the original art. Nicara provides four spacious ensuite guestrooms, all with lake views. Guests have the use of kayaks and bicycles, and a private jetty gives access for fishing and floatplane flightseeing excursions. Heather and Mike are willing to assist with all sightseeing and restaurant needs. Rotorua City, with its many attractions, is just a 12-minute drive away.

FACILITIES

- 4 king/twin ensuite bedrooms with panoramic lake views
- bathrobes, hair dryers, toiletries, heated towel rails & floors
- cotton bed linen, TV, phone, broadband, safe, trouser press, tea/coffee & fridge with soft drinks in all 4 bedrooms
- open fire, TV, video, DVD, CD-player, home theatre, piano, keyboard, games, artwork & books
- full breakfast menu can include local trout caught by guests
- patio for alfresco dining
- pre-dinner drinks served
- underfloor heating
- phone, fax & email available
- children over 12 yrs welcome
- laundry available
- pets on site
- on-site parking

ACTIVITIES AVAILABLE

- kayaks & bikes for guest use
- private beach & jetty
- assistance with activities/bookings
- Waiteti trout stream for fly fishing, 500m away
- fly-casting lessons arranged
- several golf courses nearby
- watersports on lake
- geothermal attractions
- scenic flights
- restaurants, 5–10km
- traditional Maori hangi & Maori concerts
- walkways & hikes
- Agrodome, Zorb & gondolas, 5-min drive
- horse riding
- hot pools
- gardens to visit
- Rotorua City, 10km

NGONGOTAHA, ROTORUA
Waiteti Lakeside Lodge

Hosts Brian and Val Blewett

2 Arnold Street, Ngongotaha   *Fax* 0-7-357 2311
Phone 0-7-357 2311   *Local UK call phone* 0871 474 1575
Email waitetilodge@xtra.co.nz   *Website* www.waitetilodge.co.nz

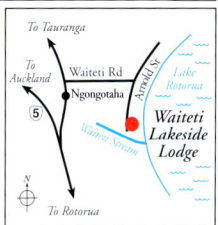

DIRECTIONS: From Rotorua City, take SH 5 to Ngongotaha. Continue to Waiteti Rd on right. Travel along Waiteti Rd to "T" intersection. Turn right into Arnold St. Waiteti Lakeside Lodge on the left.

| 5 bdrm | 3 enst | 1 shbth | Double $170–$270 Single $150–$250 | *Includes breakfast* Multiple-night rates available |

Right on the lake edge, at the mouth of the Waiteti Stream, Waiteti Lakeside Lodge has private access for trout fishing, with its own jetty. Brian and Val built their home from cedar timber and Hinuera stone, with pine wood panelling inside and native rimu stairs leading to the private guest floor. Neither traffic noise nor the characteristic Rotorua sulphur fumes intrude on the peaceful setting, with panoramic bedroom and balcony views over the lake to the city, forest and surrounding countryside. Rainbow and brown trout can be caught beneath the bedroom windows! Brian and his professional guides offer fly and boat fishing, and he enjoys taking guests on a scenic cruise to the Mokoia Island wildlife sanctuary with its endangered native birds.

FACILITIES

- 4 queen & 1 king/twin bedroom with heating, electric blankets & flyscreens
- 3 bedrooms with ensuites & TV
- 4 bathrooms with hair dryers & heated towel rails
- children over 10 yrs welcome
- spacious guest lounge overlooking lake, with Sky TV, video, pool table, library, fridge & tea/coffee facilities
- separate conservatory/ breakfast room with log fire
- continental or cooked breakfast selection
- phone & fax available
- laundry available
- wide, sunny verandahs
- stream & lake views
- gardens featuring natives, rhododendrons & azaleas

ACTIVITIES AVAILABLE

- guided boat trips to bird sanctuary
- year-round fishing on lake & in Waiteti Stream adjacent
- Canadian canoeing in stream & lake
- dinghy & outboard motor for hire
- guided fly fishing & charter boat with RPTFGA professional guides, equipment & licences provided
- restaurants & shopping, 5–10km
- Maori hangi & concert
- 5 golf courses nearby, golf clubs available
- 4WD fly fishing trips to remote streams
- hunting
- horse riding
- white water rafting
- helicopter tours
- gardens open to visit
- Rotorua City, 10km

NGONGOTAHA, ROTORUA
Ngongotaha Lakeside Lodge

Hosts Lyndsay and Graham Butcher

41 Operiana Street, Ngongotaha   *Phone* 0-7-357 4020
Freephone 0800 144 020   *Email* lake.edge@xtra.co.nz
Fax 0-7-357 4020   *Website* www.rotorualakesidelodge.co.nz

Ngongotaha Lakeside Lodge

DIRECTIONS: From Rotorua, take SH 5 to Ngongotaha. Travel through village. After railway crossing, take 1st right into Wikaraka St. Turn left into Okona Cres & left again into Operiana St. Lodge on right.

3 bdrm	3 enst	Double $150–$210 Single $130–$190	Includes breakfast Multiple-night rates available	Dinner extra

With lawn stretching to the lake edge, this contemporary home offers trout fishing in Lake Rotorua all year round. The quiet garden setting, free of sulphur fumes, is broken by the sounds of birds which frequent the sandspit. The upper floor of this two-storey home is designed for guests, including three ensuite bedrooms, dining room, large lounge and conservatory with panoramic views over the lake. Graham is willing to share his knowledge of fishing in the lake and at the mouth of the Waiteti Stream, only metres away, and enjoys cooking guests' catches. Fishing rods and canoe are available. Lyndsay serves a continental and cooked breakfast and is happy to provide an evening meal, by prior request. Activities can be arranged.

FACILITIES

- 1 king, 1 queen/twin & 1 twin ensuite bedroom
- toiletries, hair dryers & heated towel rails in all 3 ensuites; 1 demist mirror & heated floor
- tea/coffee, electric blanket, TV & flyscreens in all 3 bedrooms
- guest floor with lounge, TV, video, CDs, library & fridge
- conservatory overlooking lake
- children over 12 years welcome
- continental & cooked breakfast in dining room
- guests' catches cooked
- central heating
- phone & fax available
- laundry service available, extra
- lake edge site & lake views
- BBQ on site
- off-street parking

ACTIVITIES AVAILABLE

- fishing rods & canoe provided
- direct lake access from site
- trout fishing in lake & stream adjacent, all year round
- bird-watching
- guided fishing trips
- Ngongotaha village, 10-min walk
- agricultural Agrodome
- boiling mud pools & geysers
- thermal & volcanic areas
- Rotorua City, 10-min drive
- hot pools
- Maori hangi & concert
- gondola & luge
- white water rafting
- Redwood Memorial Grove in Whakarewarewa Forest
- walkways & tramping
- heli or float plane scenic flights

NGONGOTAHA, ROTORUA
Ariki Lodge

Hosts Wendy and Robert Forgie

2 Manuariki Avenue, Ngongotaha   *Postal* P O Box 578, Rotorua
Phone 0-7-357 5532   *Mobile* 027 288 6642   *Fax* 0-7-357 5562
Email rgforgie@xtra.co.nz   *Website* www.arikilodge.co.nz

DIRECTIONS: From Hamilton, take SH 5 towards Rotorua. Just before Agrodome turn left into Western Rd. At "T" junction turn left, then 1st right into Taui St. Turn right again into Manuariki Ave. Ariki Lodge on left.

| 3 bdrm | 3 enst | **Double $140–$230** | **Single $120–$210** | *Includes breakfast* | |

Set on the lake edge at Ngongotaha, with views across to Mokoia Island, Ariki Lodge offers accommodation for individuals or small groups. This single-storey home was built in the 1940s, but has been totally renovated to provide one suite with spacious ensuite, conservatory and private lounge, and two other guestrooms with two tiled ensuites in Italian marble and access to a spacious guest lounge. Breakfast is served in the dining room, or alfresco overlooking the lake. This lakeside accommodation is well suited for fishing from the Ngongotaha trout stream, just a few metres away, and the Waiteti trout stream, a short stroll along the beach. And yet the Lodge is sited only eight kilometres from Rotorua City Centre.

FACILITIES

- 1 suite with queen/twin bedroom, ensuite, spa bath, bidet, private sitting room, fridge, conservatory
- 1 super-king/twin & 1 queen bedroom, both with ensuites
- cotton bed linen
- electric blankets
- TV & video in both lounges
- tea/coffee facilities in each room
- breakfast served in dining room
- central heating
- hair dryer & toiletries in all 3 bathrooms
- fresh flowers
- phone, fax & email
- laundry available
- children welcome
- courtesy passenger transfer
- barbecue available on site
- off-street parking

ACTIVITIES AVAILABLE

- pétanque/boules on site
- trout fly fishing adjacent
- Agrodome
- Maori cultural performances; Maori arts & crafts
- Rainbow Springs
- geothermal attractions
- lake cruises
- scenic flights
- Polynesian Spa
- restaurants nearby
- 7 golf courses
- white water rafting
- tandem skydiving
- gondola & luge
- gardens open to visit
- 4WD tours; horse trekking
- Ngongotaha village, 5-min walk
- Ngongotaha trout hatchery
- Rotorua City, 8km away

NGONGOTAHA, ROTORUA
The Home of Hardy

Hosts Brent and Shirley Hardy

104 Parawai Road, Ngongotaha, Rotorua
Phone 0-7-357 4753   *Mobile* 021 959 192   *Fax* 0-7-357 4758
Email base@hardy.co.nz   *Website* www.hardy.co.nz

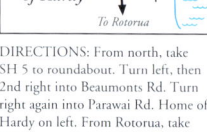

DIRECTIONS: From north, take SH 5 to roundabout. Turn left, then 2nd right into Beaumonts Rd. Turn right again into Parawai Rd. Home of Hardy on left. From Rotorua, take SH 5 to roundabout to Ngongotaha.

| 10 bdrm | 5 enst | 3 prbth | **Double** $220–$240 **Single** $190–$220 | *Includes continental breakfast* **Cottage rate** $235–$265 | *Lunch & dinner extra Self-catering in cottages* |

The Home of Hardy comprises a lakefront lodge and two self-contained cottages, built in 1995 from brick. Native rimu is used extensively on the interiors which creates a warm ambience. The hunting-fishing lodge theme throughout extends to the private jetty which provides lakeside moorings. Six guest bedrooms are offered within the lodge, with two further bedrooms in each cottage. Continental breakfast is served either in the main dining room, or alfresco on the deck beside the lake, or room service is available. Lunch or picnic hampers and dinner can also be provided by prior arrangement. The Home of Hardy offers a relaxing retreat on the shores of Lake Rotorua, both cottages and lodge set in quiet gardens with mature trees.

FACILITIES

- dinner by request, $60 pp, BYO
- lunch/picnic hamper, $20–$30 pp
- lodge: 1 twin & 3 queen ensuite bedrooms, 1 ensuite bunkroom with extra single bed, 1 single rm shares powder room/bathroom
- 2 cottages: each with 1 queen & 1 twin bedroom & 1 bathroom
- toiletries, hair dryers & heated towel rails in all 8 bathrooms
- TV in every bedroom
- single-party bookings in cottages include children
- complimentary morning & afternoon tea/coffee
- Sky TV, phone, fax, email
- 1 kitchen & 1 laundry in both cottages
- decking overlooking lake
- courtesy transfer
- off-street parking

ACTIVITIES AVAILABLE

- spa pool on site
- in-house billiards table
- croquet on site
- boules/pétanque
- boat jetty & moorings on site
- private access to lake
- fly, boat & helicopter fishing year-round in lake, professional guide available
- Indian-style canoe available
- trout stream nearby
- golf matches arranged
- rabbit shooting by arrangement
- Ngongotaha shops, 5-min drive
- restaurants, 15-min drive away
- agricultural Agrodome
- public & private gardens to visit
- Rotorua City, 15-min drive
- airport, 30-min drive away

Above: Lakeside lodge showing main lounge and dining room, looking through folding doors across decking to Lake Rotorua.
Below: One of the two cottages, showing open-plan lounge, dining area and kitchen with doors opening into private garden.
Opposite top: The lodge exterior, looking across the lawn from the lake to the main lounge, showing the garden and gazebo.
Opposite bottom left: Interior of one of the two cottages, showing a queen-size bedroom with its warm native rimu ceiling.
Opposite bottom right: The private driveway leads past the two brick cottages, set in private gardens, to the lakefront lodge.

ROTORUA
Peppers on the Point – Lake Rotorua

Host David Smail

214 Kawaha Point Road, Rotorua   *Mobile* 027 245 1101
Phone 0-7-348 4868   *Email* onthepoint@peppers.co.nz
Fax 0-7-348 1868   *Website* www.peppers.co.nz/onthepoint

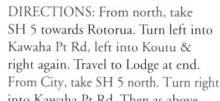

DIRECTIONS: From north, take SH 5 towards Rotorua. Turn left into Kawaha Pt Rd, left into Koutu & right again. Travel to Lodge at end. From City, take SH 5 north. Turn right into Kawaha Pt Rd. Then as above.

| 9 bdrm | 9 enst | 1 pdrm | Double $1,088 | Single $880 | *Includes breakfast* |
| Double $1,338 | Single $1,006 | *Includes breakfast & dinner* |

Peppers on the Point

Peppers on the Point is located on two hectares (five acres) of land at the end of Kawaha Point overlooking Lake Rotorua. With panoramic lake views to Mokoia Island, the lodge provides spacious bedrooms and a large guest lounge furnished with antiques. The Lake Villa, a four-bedroom contemporary home, is also available. The resident chef prepares all meals that are served around the lodge or in the privacy of the guests' suites. Fine dining is accompanied by a large selection of wines from the cellar. Guests enjoy the on-site facilities, including therapeutic massage and beauty treatments in the massage room, the gymnasium, and the tennis court. The expansive lakeside grounds feature gardens, native bush walks, a fishing jetty and private beach on the lake edge.

FACILITIES

- 1 twin with 2 double beds & 8 super-king/twin ensuite bedrooms
- cotton bed linen, TV, writing desk, phone, tea/coffee, fridge & decks opening from all bedrooms
- double basins, hair dryers, toiletries, bidets, demist mirrors, bathrobes, heated floors & heated towel rails
- spa baths & massage jet showers
- lounge with tea/coffee, nibbles, bar, Sky TV, DVD, CD-player & library

- full continental buffet & cooked breakfast served
- all-day lunch menu
- 4-course table d'hôte dinner
- qualified chef in residence
- laundry valet service
- email, fax & phone
- children welcome
- fresh flowers
- on-site parking

ACTIVITIES AVAILABLE

- tennis court & gymnasium
- massage/beauty therapy room
- conferences, weddings, special occasions & honeymoons catered
- library & wine cellar on site
- geothermal activity
- Maori cultural excursions
- fishing
- float plane & helicopter excursions, by arrangement

- boat cruises
- art galleries
- shopping
- golf courses
- arts & crafts
- hot pools
- gardens to visit
- Rotorua Centre, 10 mins
- airport, 30-min drive

Peppers on the Point

Peppers on the Point

KAWAHA POINT, LAKE ROTORUA
Koura Lodge

Hosts David and Gina Wells

DIRECTIONS: From north, take SH 5 towards Rotorua. Turn left into Kawaha Pt Rd, left into Koutu & right again. Travel to Lodge on right. From City, take SH 5 north. Turn right into Kawaha Pt Rd. Then as above.

209 Kawaha Point Road   *Postal* P O Box 1600, Rotorua
Phone 0-7-348 5868   *Mobile* 021 119 1000   *Fax* 0-7-348 5869
Email stay@kouralodge.co.nz   *Website* www.kouralodge.co.nz

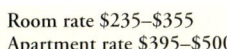

9 bdrm	8 enst	1 pdrm

Room rate $235–$355
Apartment rate $395–$500

Includes breakfast
Self-catering

Koura Lodge is a unique lakefront retreat situated near the tip of Kawaha Point, a leafy peninsula on Lake Rotorua, only five minutes' drive from the City Centre. Koura Lodge offers a range of bedrooms with ensuite bathrooms and terraces, and a spacious apartment, all with views over the lake to Mount Tarawera. Koura Lodge has direct lake access via its private jetty, with a boatshed housing a selection of watercraft, all available for guest use. There is also an on-site croquet lawn, and a championship-size astroturf tennis court can be used by arrangement. Guests can enjoy relaxing in the lakeside spa pool, or the Finnish sauna, and therapeutic massages are popular. Koura Lodge style breakfast is served in the lakeside dining room.

FACILITIES

- 2 Premium king bedrooms with ensuites & 1 spa bath
- 4 Standard queen/twin bedrooms with ensuites
- 1 Family suite with 1 queen, 1 twin bedroom & 1 ensuite
- 1 Penthouse Apartment with 1 king bedroom, ensuite, kitchen, fireplace, TV, phone, private balcony & family room
- extra child, $35 per night

- breakfast in dining room
- picnic hamper, extra
- email & internet access
- gymnasium
- on-the-lake spa pool
- Finnish sauna, extra
- therapeutic massage, extra
- boutique conference facility & functions, for up to 20 persons
- off-street parking

ACTIVITIES AVAILABLE

- direct lake access from site
- canoes & windsurfer
- Astroturf tennis court; croquet
- scenic helicopter & float plane flights, from Lodge jetty
- lake fishing, departing jetty
- free green fees at local golf club
- watersports; kayaking; jet boating & whitewater rafting
- mountain biking

- restaurants & shops, 5 mins
- horseback riding
- bush walks, all fitness levels
- geothermal areas & hot pools
- Maori culture & hangi
- gondola & Luge riding, 5 mins
- acrobatic plane & skydiving
- wildlife parks & farm shows
- Rotorua City Centre, 5 mins
- Rotorua Airport, 15 mins

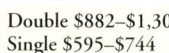

Kawaha Point Lodge

Hosts Margaret and Tony Seavill

171 Kawaha Point Road, Kawhaha Point, Rotorua
Phone 0-7-346 3602   *Email* inquire@kawahalodge.co.nz
Fax 0-7-346 3671   *Website* www.kawahalodge.co.nz

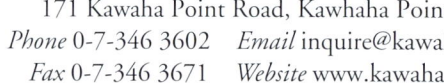

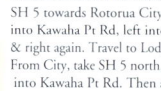

DIRECTIONS: From north, take SH 5 towards Rotorua City. Turn left into Kawaha Pt Rd, left into Koutu & right again. Travel to Lodge on right. From City, take SH 5 north. Turn right into Kawaha Pt Rd. Then as above.

8 bdrm	8 enst	1 pdrm	Double $882–$1,300	*Includes breakfast & dinner*	Double $880–$1100	*Includes breakfast*
			Single $595–$744	*Lunch extra*	Single $435–$544	*Lunch extra*

Set on the shores of Lake Rotorua, Kawaha Point Lodge provides panoramic views across the lake to Mt Tarawera. A private jetty enables professional fishing guides to collect guests interested in fishing for rainbow and brown trout. Alternatively guests can enjoy relaxing in the half-hectare (one-acre) mature gardens which feature statues, terracing, a gazebo and 1930s stone grotto. Additional on-site pursuits include swimming in the pool and unwinding in the sauna. The Lodge is licensed and five-course silver service dinner can be covered in the tariff and served in either the formal dining room, the more intimate library, the garden room, or alfresco on the wide verandah. Each of the eight ensuite guestrooms also has garden or lake views.

FACILITIES

- 8 king bedrooms, each with ensuite bathroom
- 2 spa baths, 5 baths, toiletries, hair dryers, heated towel rails
- 1 wheelchair access bathroom
- cotton bed linen, fresh flowers
- air-conditioning; lake views
- TV, music, library, garden room
- laundry available, extra
- chauffeur/guide accommodation

- full breakfast
- picnic baskets & buffet lunch available, $25–$35 pp
- 5-course dinner; fully licensed
- vegetarian alternatives
- fridge, tea/coffee, home-made biscuits in each room
- phone, fax & email
- off-street parking
- private jetty; helipad nearby

ACTIVITIES AVAILABLE

- lakeside setting & activities
- swimming pool & sauna on site
- mature garden, stone grotto on site
- pétanque & croquet on site
- private access to lake; lake cruises
- fishing guides & seaplane rides from private jetty on site
- trout fishing in lakes & rivers
- Rainbow Springs, Agrodome
- traditional Maori hangi & concert

- 3 professional golf courses
- Maori culture, arts & crafts
- helicopter & 4WD tours
- Polynesian Spa
- geothermal areas
- bush walks; horse riding; mountain biking
- gardens open to visit
- Rotorua City, 5-min drive
- airport, 15-min drive

ROTORUA
Robertson House

Hosts John Ballard and Patrice Legrand

70 Pererika Street, Rotorua
Phone 0-7-343 7559   *Email* info@robertsonhouse.co.nz
Fax 0-7-343 7559   *Website* www.robertsonhouse.co.nz

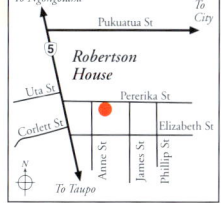

DIRECTIONS: From north, take SH 5 to Rotorua. Turn left into Pererika St to Robertson House on right. From south, take SH 5 to Rotorua & turn right into Pererika St to Robertson House on right.

| 4 bdrm | 3 enst | 1 prbth | **Room rate $110–$170** | *Includes breakfast* |

Originally built in 1905 for Edwin Robertson, a local coach company owner, this Victorian bay villa has been restored and refurbished to provide four guestrooms each with a bathroom. Roberston House, which has a Historic Places Trust classification, has colonial features including the fretwork around the verandah, finials, and polished timber flooring. Set in part of the original garden, Robertson House is located in the heart of Rotorua City, with cafés, restaurants and shops just 10 minutes' walk away. Breakfast is served in the dining room and there is a television in the adjoining guest lounge. Children and pets are welcome at Roberston House, which is central to Rotorua attractions such as the popular geothermal sights.

FACILITIES

- Hanimunu: queen ensuite bedroom with claw-foot bath
- Kikorangi: super-king/twin ensuite bedroom with extra single bed
- Kakariki: queen ensuite bedroom with extra single bed
- Mawhero: double canopy bed with private bathroom & robes
- hair dryers & toiletries in all 4 bathrooms
- email, fax & phone in office
- continental breakfast with cheese, cold meat & pastries served in dining room
- lounge with tea/coffee, nibbles, TV, DVD, books, CD-player & magazines
- guest laundry, $5
- central heating
- children & pets welcome
- 2 guest carparks on site

ACTIVITIES AVAILABLE

- bicycles for guest use
- large garden with seating
- geothermal sites
- scenic flights
- fishing
- walking
- Maori cultural shows
- horse riding
- rafting
- restaurants within 10-min walk
- off-road experiences
- trout fishing
- hot pools
- art galleries
- museums
- gardens open to visit
- Rotorua City Centre, 10-min walk away

ROTORUA CITY
Regal Palms

Hosts Alison and Graeme Pike

350 Fenton Street, Rotorua City   *Freephone* 0800 743 000
Phone 0-7-350 3232   *Email* experience@regalpalmsml.co.nz
Fax 0-7-350 3233   *Website* www.regalpalmsml.co.nz

DIRECTIONS: From north take SH 5 to Rotorua. Turn left into Devon St. Turn right into Fenton St to Regal Palms on left. From south, take SH 5 & veer right into Hemo Rd. Continue into Fenton St to Regal Palms on right.

52 bdrm	24 enst	23 prbth	1 pdrm	Suite rate $165–$275 Apartment rate $325–$345	*Self-catering Breakfast extra*

Regal Palms is a city resort, centrally located within walking distance of cafés, restaurants and shops, and with many on-site activities for all age groups. The first 26 suites were opened in 2001, then the south wing added in 2003 comprising 15 more suites and three two-bedroom apartments. All suites and apartments include indoor spa pools and full kitchens for self-catering, although meals are available with local restaurants offering a charge-back and delivery service. In-house facilities include the Phoenix Lounge with open fire, bar and internet café, which is used as a break-out room for boutique conferences in the Kentia Room above. Guests enjoy alfresco dining, the heated swimming pool, sauna, gym and playing mini-golf or tennis.

FACILITIES

- 3 apartments each including 2 king bedrooms, 2 bathrooms, laundry & original artwork
- 17 suites, 5 with 2 bedrooms & 12 with 1 bedroom, all with 1 bathroom & extra sofa-bed/s
- 24 studio-suites, 18 king & 6 queen/twin beds with ensuites
- spa pool, hair dryer, toiletries, heated towel rails & demist mirror in each suite/apartment
- room service meals available; breakfast, $11–$21.50 pp
- 44 full kitchens for self-catering, 11 with dishwasher drawers
- 44 lounges each with phone, mini-bar, digital Sky TV, video, CD-player & writing desk
- 18 DVDs/stereos; 18 bathrobes
- air-conditioners; double glazing
- guest laundry, extra; children welcome; parking on site

ACTIVITIES AVAILABLE

- 2 BBQ & outdoor dining areas
- heated swimming pool, sauna & gymnasium on site
- Phoenix Lounge, internet café & house bar opens to garden patio
- Kentia Room for boutique in-house conferences
- tennis court & mini-golf on site
- children's playground on site
- horse trekking; mountain biking
- restaurants & cafés, nearby
- Rotorua City, 2-min drive
- watersports at lake, 5 mins
- geothermal sights & pools
- Maori culture & hangi
- golf; gardens to visit
- gondola & luge; springs
- farm shows; trout fishing
- airport, 15-min drive
- Redwood Grove walks

LAKE ROTOITI, ROTORUA
Lakestay Rotoiti

Hosts Raewyn and Graeme Natusch

173 Tumoana Road, Lake Rotoiti, R D 4, Rotorua
Phone 0-7-345 4089   *Mobile* 0274 188 404   *Fax* 0-7-345 4089
Email lakestayrotoiti@xtra.co.nz   *Website* friars.co.nz/hosts/rotoiti.html

 3 bdrm   3 enst

Room/Studio rate $150
Off-season rates available

Includes breakfast
Self-catering in studio

Dinner extra

DIRECTIONS: North of airport turn east into SH 30. Travel 5.35km & turn left into pumice rd. Travel 100m, turn left into Main Race Rd, travel 1km & fork right into Tumoana Rd. Travel 1.73km to Lakestay Rotoiti on left.

Lakestay Rotoiti

One of just three lakefront sites on a secluded sandy beach bay, Lakestay Rotoiti offers two ensuite guestrooms as well as a fully self-contained studio only 26 metres from the lake edge. Built in 2004 to maximise lake views, Lakestay Rotoiti offers a peaceful quiet retreat, with both hosted and self-catering options available. The two guestrooms are upstairs in the main house, with elevated lake vistas, even from one of the ensuites, while the studio opens to a level grass lawn stretching to the lake shore. Guests have the use of kayaks, windsurfer and dinghy for exploring Lake Rotoiti, and bicycles are available for the bike tracks and forest walks. A full breakfast is served in the dining room or sunroom, and speciality vegetarian dinners are popular.

FACILITIES

- 2 queen ensuite bedrooms upstairs in house, with lake views
- 1 self-contained studio with queen bed, ensuite, writing desk, phone & kitchen, opens to garden & lake
- toiletries & heated towel rails in all 3 ensuites
- cotton bed linen, phone, TV & DVD in all 3 bedrooms
- TV, DVD, piano & wood burner in lounge in house

- continental & cooked breakfast for house guests, includes home-baked muesli, breads & muffins
- dinner by arrangement, extra – vegetarian speciality
- underfloor heating
- email, fax & phones
- on-site parking
- courtesy airport transfer

ACTIVITIES AVAILABLE

- dinghy, windsurfer, kayaks & bicycles for guest use
- private beach access from site
- bush & forest walks from site
- many cycling tracks
- trout fishing
- hot mineral pools, short boat trip away
- glow-worm caves by night
- Redwood Grove, 10-min drive

- restaurants & cafés, 15 mins
- safe swimming, windsurfing, sailing & water skiing on lake
- Maori cultural activities
- gondola rides
- geothermal areas – mud pools & geysers
- gardens open to visit
- airport, 8km
- Rotorua CBD, 20-min drive

Lakestay Rotoiti

Lakestay Rotoiti

HOROHORO, ROTORUA

Treetops Lodge

Hosts The Sax Family

351 Kearoa Road, Horohoro, R D 1, Rotorua
Phone 0-7-333 2066 *Email* info@treetops.co.nz
Fax 0-7-333 2065 *Website* www.treetops.co.nz

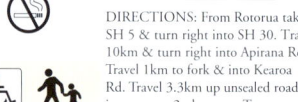

DIRECTIONS: From Rotorua take SH 5 & turn right into SH 30. Travel 10km & turn right into Apirana Rd. Travel 1km to fork & into Kearoa Rd. Travel 3.3km up unsealed road to intercom at 2nd gates to Treetops.

12 bdrm	12 enst	1 pdrm	Double $980–$1,930	*Includes breakfast & dinner*	*Lunch extra*
			Single $730–$1,680	**Extra persons in villa $350–$400 each**	

Located high in native flora on a 1,000-hectare (2,500-acre) eco and wilderness park, Treetops Lodge provides tranquillity only 50 minutes' drive from Rotorua City. Guest privacy is ensured with the siting of eight separate Villas, and a further four ensuite bedrooms in the Lodge. The chef provides a four-course menu for evening dining in the licensed dining room, and breakfast is served in the sunny conservatory or alfresco in the courtyard. Lunch is also available by arrangement. Small conferences, and weddings or other functions, can be catered for, either private, exclusive or formal as required. The many on-site activities include guided fly fishing, bird-watching, horse riding, abseiling and four-wheel drive experiences.

FACILITIES

- 8 Villas each with 1 super-king bedroom, ensuite, mini-bar, phone & lounge
- 4 super-king ensuite bedrooms in Lodge, each with phone
- cotton bed linen
- spa bath, double basin, hair dryer, toiletries, bidet, heated floors, heated towel rails & demist mirror in all ensuites
- children welcome
- full breakfast, indoors or alfresco
- lunch, $50 pp
- 4-course table d'hôte dinner served, wine extra
- open fire, Sky TV, video, CD-player in all Villas & Lodge
- fax & email available at Lodge
- laundry facilities
- on-site parking
- helipad

ACTIVITIES AVAILABLE

- 1,000ha (2,500-acre) eco park
- hiking on site
- in-house massage, extra
- fly fishing & tutorial, on site
- kayaking, archery & clay target shooting, on site
- horse riding; mountain bike riding, on site
- bird-watching & native animal spotting, on site
- eco tours, on site
- photographic safari, on site
- heli packages; cruises; golf
- sightseeing; cultural tours
- sailing & fishing in lake
- hot air ballooning
- tandem skydiving
- wilderness heli fishing
- big-game fishing; jet fishing
- water & snow skiing

LAKE TARAWERA, ROTORUA
Lake Tarawera Lodge

Hosts Jeff and Janine Oakes

19 Te Mu Road, R D 5, Rotorua
Phone 0-7-362 8754   *Email* stay@laketarawera.co.nz
Fax 0-7-362 8704   *Website* www.laketarawera.co.nz

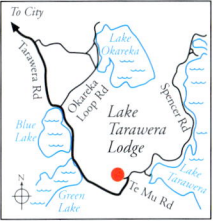

DIRECTIONS: From Rotorua take Te Ngae Rd (SH 30) towards airport. Turn right at 1st round-about into Tarawera Rd. Travel 11km & turn left into Te Mu Rd. Travel 200m to Lake Tarawera Lodge at end of road.

12 bdrm	6 prbth	1 pdrm

Cottage rate $260 for 2 persons
Extra persons $30 each

Self-catering
Breakfast provisions extra

Lake Tarawera

Overlooking Lake Tarawera to the mountain, the Lodge is built on the site of the historic Te Mu Mission Station, established in 1852. Surrounded by native forest, it includes six self-contained cottages and a communal guest lounge. Each cottage comprises two bedrooms, bathroom and self-catering kitchen, with a barbecue on the deck. Breakfast provisions or full supplies are available, and a qualified chef can be arranged. Families enjoy the child-friendly playground, pétanque, tennis court, volleyball and spa pool on site. There is a billiards table in the guest lounge, and bush walks enable guests to bird-watch by day and view glow-worms by night. Jeff is a trout fishing guide and can take guests boat fishing on the lake or fly fishing in the rivers.

FACILITIES

- 6 self-contained cottages:
  - 1 cottage with 1 king & 1 queen bedroom
  - 2 cottages with 2 queen bedrooms
  - 3 cottages with 1 queen & 1 twin bedroom in each
- 1 private bathroom per cottage with hair dryer, toiletries & heated towel rails in each
- lounge in each cottage with open fire, tea/coffee, TV, CD-player, music, artwork & writing desk
- full kitchen in each cottage for self-catering
- breakfast supplies, $15 pp
- qualified chef on call, extra
- self-service laundry, $4
- email, fax, phone in office
- drying room available
- courtesy passenger transfer
- on-site parking; garaging
- closed mid-July to mid-Sept.

ACTIVITIES AVAILABLE

- billiards table in guest lounge
- spa pool & tennis court on site
- beach volley ball on site
- pétanque & playground
- bush walk & glow-worm track
- massage treatments, extra
- black labrador & chickens
- bird-watching on site
- guided trout fishing, boat fishing & fly-fishing
- The Buried Village nearby
- restaurants, 5-min walk
- Rotorua City, 15-min drive
- scenic lake cruises
- helicopter flights
- guided tours to Mt Tarawera
- geothermal hot pools & cultural attractions, 15 mins
- Mt Maunganui, Taupo, Whakatane, 1-hour drive

Lake Tarawera

LAKE TARAWERA, ROTORUA
Spencer Lodge

Hosts Janet and Chris Watmore

144 Spencer Road, R D 5, Lake Tarawera, Rotorua
Phone 0-7-362 8153   *Email* chrisanjan@xtra.co.nz
Fax 0-7-362 8534   *Website* www.spencerlodge.com

DIRECTIONS: From Rotorua take Te Ngae Rd (SH 30) towards airport. Turn right at 1st roundabout into Tarawera Rd. Travel 13km then continue into Spencer Rd. Travel another 3km to Spencer Lodge on left.

4 bdrm	4 enst	1 pdrm	Double $1,050–$1,200 Single $590–$690	*Includes breakfast & dinner* *Picnic lunch extra*

Approached via a long driveway through trees, Spencer Lodge is backed by native bush, with views over Lake Tarawera. Extensively refurbished featuring custom-made oak furniture, quality furnishings and fittings and with high attention to detail throughout, Spencer Lodge now provides four spacious ensuite guestrooms with rural views of tree ferns on site to the lake below. There is also a spa pool with changing rooms in a setting to capture the lake views. Spencer Lodge stands in 14 hectares (35 acres) of paddocks and native trees with bush walks throughout. The resident chef provides a four-course dinner using hand-reared Highland beef, lamb, pork, chickens and eggs. Meals are served in the dining room or alfresco.

FACILITIES

- Kereru Room: 1 king bedroom with bath in ensuite
- Tui Room: 1 king ensuite bedroom opening to private balcony
- Fantail & Bellbird Rooms: 1 king ensuite bedroom each
- cotton bed linen, Sky TV, music centre, phone in all 4 bedrooms
- hair dryer, toiletries, demist mirror, bathrobes, heated floor & towel rails
- tea/coffee & balcony from mezzanine

- continental & cooked breakfast served
- picnic lunch, $30 pp
- 4-course dinner menu changes daily, included
- lounge with open fire, bar, tea/coffee, Sky TV, DVD
- fresh flowers; email & fax
- library; laundry available
- on-site parking

ACTIVITIES AVAILABLE

- large sundeck for relaxing
- extensive gardens with native bush & garden shade house
- spa pool on site
- fishing
- Maori cultural attractions
- thermal areas
- mineral spa
- historic Buried Village
- gardens open to visit

- Rotorua City, 20 mins
- boating
- watersports
- bush walks
- horse riding
- golf courses
- water rafting
- Redwood Grove in Whakarewarewa Forest
- airport, 20-min drive

LAKE TARAWERA, ROTORUA
Waitangi Lodge

Hosts Janet and Chris Watmore

303 Spencer Road, R D 5, Lake Tarawera, Rotorua
Phone 0-7-362 8913   *Email* chrisanjan@xtra.co.nz
Fax 0-7-362 8949   *Website* www.waitangilodge.com

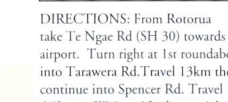

DIRECTIONS: From Rotorua take Te Ngae Rd (SH 30) towards airport. Turn right at 1st roundabout into Tarawera Rd. Travel 13km then continue into Spencer Rd. Travel 4.7km to Waitangi Lodge on right.

3 bdrm	1 enst	1 shbth	1 pdrm

Lodge rate $1,125–$1,750

Self-catering
All meals extra

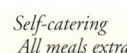

Waitangi Lodge

On the edge of Lake Tarawera, a couple of kilometres around the lake from Spencer Lodge, is Waitangi Lodge, a self-contained house. Set in over two hectares (six acres) of secluded gardens featuring a 12-metre waterfall, trout-spawning stream and glow-worm grotto, Waitangi Lodge is a Swiss-style home built from cedar and riverstone. There is an upstairs guest suite and also a downstairs suite with kitchenette, a full self-catering kitchen and lounge, all tastefully furnished with quality fittings and detailing. Guests can enjoy the on-site luxury boathouse with fully equipped lounge and bar, featuring a polished timber dance floor. The Lodge is serviced daily and a qualified chef is available if required. Rotorua City is 20 minutes' drive away.

FACILITIES

- single-party bookings only
- 1 self-contained house
- 1 downstairs suite with 1 king bedroom & ensuite
- 1 upstairs suite with 1 double bedroom & 1 twin bedroom sharing 1 bathroom
- spa bath, double basin, hair dryer, toiletries, bidet, heated towel rails & bathrobes in both bathrooms
- children welcome
- full self-catering kitchen
- all meals by request, extra; qualified chef on call
- cotton bed linen, tea/coffee & fridge in all 3 bedrooms
- lounge with open fire, bar, Sky TV, video & artwork
- heated ceiling panels
- on-site parking

ACTIVITIES AVAILABLE

- barbecue on site
- 2ha (6 acres) garden on site with 12m waterfall, streamside walkway & glow-worm grotto
- trout-spawning stream on site
- all-weather tennis court on site
- luxury boathouse on site
- spa pool on site
- fishing from site
- Lake Tarawera access from site
- restaurants, 5–20 mins
- swimming & watersports
- golf courses
- Maori cultural attractions
- geothermal sites
- arts & crafts
- vineyards
- Rotorua City, 20 mins
- Rotorua airport, 20 mins

Waitangi Lodge

Waitangi Lodge

LAKE TARAWERA, ROTORUA
Pukeko Landing

Manager Jennifer McBrearty

6 Ronald Road, Lake Tarawera, Rotorua   *Freephone* 0800 ESSENCE
Postal P O Box 99 962, Newmarket, Auckland 1031   *Mobile* 027 542 4202
Fax 0-7-574 8096   *Email* stay@essencenz.com   *Website* www.essencenz.com

DIRECTIONS: From Rotorua take Te Ngae Rd & turn right at the 1st roundabout into Tarawera Rd. Travel 13km then continue into Spencer Rd. Travel 7km & turn right into Ronald Rd. Travel 300m to Pukeko Landing on left.

| 3 bdrm | 1 enst | 1 prbth | **House rate $889–$1,114 for up to 4 persons**
Extra persons $100 each | *Self-catering*
Includes breakfast provisions |

Pukeko Landing

Pukeko Landing is a self-contained cottage overlooking Lake Tarawera. North-facing, the accommodation enjoys all-day sun with a garden walk through native bush and exotic plantings to the private jetty. Here guests can leave on chartered excursions, moor their boat, swim and fish. Bird-watching is a popular activity in this secluded location, the frequent visits of the native pukeko bird to the lawn that stretches to the edge of the lake inspiring the name of the cottage. A fully equipped kitchen allows for self-catering, with provisions and a qualified chef available by arrangement. Lodge-style dining is available within easy walking distance, while the shops, restaurants and thermal pools of Rotorua City are only 20 kilometres away.

FACILITIES

- self-contained cottage
- single-party bookings
- 1 super-king/twin bedroom with spa bath, double basin & demist mirror in ensuite
- 1 super-king/twin & 1 twin bedroom share 1 bathroom
- hair dryer, toiletries, heated towel rails, heated floor & bathrobes in each bathroom
- cotton bed linen; fresh flowers
- full kitchen for self-catering
- breakfast provisions supplied
- qualified chef available
- all meals by arrangement, extra
- open fire in lounge; tea/coffee, Sky TV, video DVD, CD-player
- computer, printer, phone & fax
- daily servicing; self-serve laundry
- on-site parking; security gates
- helipad by arrangement

ACTIVITIES AVAILABLE

- garden/bush walk & seating; bird-watching on site
- private jetty for swimming, fishing & boat mooring; row boat for guest use
- lawn area adjacent to lake edge
- pétanque on site
- massage by arrangement
- charter boat tours, pick-up from private jetty on site
- 'Hobbiton', 1-hr 20-min drive
- guided trout fishing in river, stream & lake
- self-drive or skippered pontoons
- fishing or scenic float plane & helitours
- water taxi to walks, hot water beach, or café
- jet-skiing; cultural experiences
- natural hot pools; buried village
- guided tours of Tarawera volcano
- Rotorua City shops, 20 mins

Pukeko Landing

Pukeko Landing

TE WHAITI, VIA ROTORUA

Hukitawa Country Retreat

Host Lesley Handcock

279 Minginui Road, Te Whaiti   *Phone* 0-7-366 3952
Postal Private Bag 3054, Te Whaiti, via Rotorua   *Fax* 0-7-366 3950
Email lesley@hukitawa.co.nz   *Website* www.hukitawa.co.nz

DIRECTIONS: From Rotorua, take SH 5 south to SH 38. Turn left & travel 60km to Te Whaiti. Turn right into Minginui Rd. Travel 2.79km to Hukitawa, on left. Travel 2.4km up drive.

| 3 bdrm | 3 enst | 1 pdrm | Double $390–$410 | Single $280 | *Includes all meals* |

Nestled in the Whirinaki Valley, Hukitawa is a rural retreat in a New Zealand home set on 92 hectares (233 acres) of farmland featuring deer, sheep and cattle. Nearby is the well-known Whirinaki rainforest forest where guests enjoy exploring the native bush, streams and waterfalls. Hukitawa is elevated above the surrounding farmland with views across the duck pond to the bush-clad Ikawhenua Ranges. Accommodation comprises three ensuite guestrooms, and an extra room for guides, pilots or children. From the privacy of the indoor spa pool, guests can enjoy panoramic views or star-gaze through the clear glass roof in the evening. All meals are included in the tariff, featuring New Zealand home-made cuisine and fresh produce served indoors or alfresco.

FACILITIES

- 1 super-king/twin, 1 king/twin & 1 double bedroom; 3 ensuites
- 1 extra king/twin bedroom & 1 shared bathroom for guides, pilots, or children
- hair dryers, heated towel rails, bathrobes & toiletries in ensuites
- open fire in lounge; tea/coffee, Sky TV, video & NZ art
- laundry, phone, fax & email available for guests

- full cooked breakfast served in dining room or patio
- light lunch or picnic wherever guests choose
- à la carte dinner, NZ style including roast meats, home-grown veges & BBQ
- cotton bed linen; flowers
- garaging; helicopter access on site; airstrip 7km
- courtesy passenger transfer

ACTIVITIES AVAILABLE

- indoor spa pool on site
- clay-target shooting on site
- garden & farm walks on site
- bird-watching on site – native birds, pond with ducks, stilts, herons & shags
- observing farming activities on neighbouring farmland
- painting & photography sites
- trout fishing, guide available

- guided horse riding
- 4WD tours, professional guide
- bush walking in Whirinaki podocarp forest 10km away, guided or independent, overnight trips available by prior arrangement
- Maori culture
- river rafting & kayaking, 25km
- Rotorua, 1¼ hrs north west; Lake Taupo, 1½ hrs south west

TAUPIRI RANGES, WAIKATO
Hillside Hotel and Nature Resort

Hosts Rosemary and Rod Leader   *Mobile* 027 499 0121

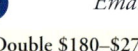

Hillside Station, via Tregoweth Lane, Huntly   *Phone* 0-7-824 9435
Postal c/- 50 Driver Road, R D 1, Hamilton   *Fax* 0-7-824 9436
Email info@hillsidehotel.co.nz   *Website* www.hillsidehotel.co.nz

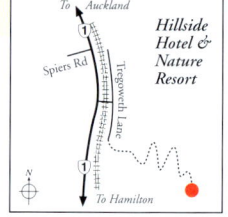

DIRECTIONS: From north, take SH 1 to Huntly. Continue past McDonald's for 700m & turn left into Tregoweth Lane. Cross railway & turn right up private road for 4km to Hillside Resort at top of hill.

| 27 bdrm | 27 enst | 1 pdrm | **Double $180–$275** **Single $165–$255** | *Includes breakfast* *Lunch & dinner extra* |

Hillside Hotel and Nature Resort was opened in 2003 on a hilltop overlooking the Waikato countryside. The 27 spacious guestrooms feature panoramic views and are located within the series of rustic-style buildings layered up the hillside to the restaurant at the top. While enjoying the fine dining, guests are treated to 360-degree rural views to Mt Ruapehu and to the Taupiri ranges. Also with sweeping views are the large conference room and supporting seminar rooms. Set on a 920-hectare farm including 120 hectares of native reserve, Hillside Hotel provides bush walks on site. The interiors are inspired by Charles Rennie MacIntosh's style with original artwork. The staff are happy to share their knowledge of local cultural heritage.

FACILITIES

- 2-bedroom suite with 1 king & 1 queen/twin; 2 king suites; 2 family king/queen/twin suites
- 4 king & 16 queen/twin bedrooms; 1 king studio
- 27 ensuite bathrooms, 3 with spa baths & 22 with baths
- cotton bed linen, TV, phone, fridge & tea/coffee in rooms
- hair dryers, heated towel rails, toiletries & bathrobes

- breakfast in restaurant, $15–$23; chef on call
- gourmet picnic lunch, $25 pp
- extensive 3-course à la carte dinner, $45–$55 pp
- room service, extra
- fax & broadband email
- laundry available
- children welcome

ACTIVITIES AVAILABLE

- conferences catered in large conference & seminar rooms
- 920ha farm with 120ha bush reserve on site
- pétanque on site
- bush walks on site
- cultural & heritage tours
- Coalfields Museum
- Candyland
- bush tramway

- Adventure Waikato – flying fox, Jurassic walk & glow-worm caves
- golf tours; river tours
- Kauri Grove; garden visits
- Rangiriri battle site
- pottery; thermal pools
- Mystery Creek Field-days
- Hamilton, 30 mins south
- Auckland, 1 hour north

MATANGI, HAMILTON
Matangi Oaks

Hosts Gloria and Clyde Morriss

634 Marychurch Road, R D 4, Hamilton
Phone 0-7-829 5765   *Mobile* 027 242 7429   *Fax* 0-7-829 5765
Email matangi.oaks@xtra.co.nz   *Website* www.matangioaks.co.nz

DIRECTIONS: From Hamilton, take SH 1 south towards Cambridge. At Tamahere cross-roads, turn left into Tauwhare Rd. Cross railway line at Matangi & turn right into Marychurch Rd. Matangi Oaks on left.

| 3 bdrm | 1 enst | 1 prbth | **Double $185**
Single $120 | *Includes breakfast*
Dinner extra |

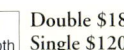   

Matangi Oaks is set in spacious gardens on 15 hectares with rural views, midway between Hamilton and Cambridge. Built in 1997, this two-storey home offers two upstairs bedrooms with one private bathroom, as well as a queen ensuite bedroom downstairs with underfloor heating. Gloria enjoys cooking, using fresh locally grown produce complemented by fine New Zealand wines. Matangi Oaks is surrounded by thoroughbred breeding stud farms, enabling guests to visit some of the country's famous horse studs. Mystery Creek is also nearby, where the annual agricultural field-days are held each June, with major indoor sports other times. Other local features include a well-known sporting memories collection and a military museum.

FACILITIES

- 1 queen bedroom with ensuite
- 1 super-king/twin bedroom with seating area & 1 double bedroom share 1 bathroom in single party, with bathrobes
- hair dryers, heated floor, heated towel rails & toiletries
- complimentary laundry
- fresh flowers in bedrooms
- complimentary tea & coffee
- TV in bedrooms & lounge
- full breakfast served in dining room or alfresco on patio
- dinner with wine, $50 pp
- central heating
- powder room
- private guest lounge
- email, fax & phone available
- unsuitable for pets
- children over 11 yrs welcome
- on-site parking

ACTIVITIES AVAILABLE

- Maungatautari Ecological Island Trust
- horse stud visits
- Hot Air Balloon Festival each April
- gardens open to visit
- Waikato University, 10 mins
- Mystery Creek, 10-min drive
- airport, 10-min drive
- Hamilton City, 10-min drive
- restaurants, 10-min drive
- 9 golf courses nearby
- Cambridge antique shops & activities, 10-min drive
- Waitomo Caves, 1-hr drive
- Raglan Beach for surfing & swimming, 1-hour drive
- Mount Maunganui, 1 hour
- Tauranga, 1-hour drive
- Rotorua, 1-hour drive

CAMBRIDGE
Thornton House

Hosts Christine Manson and David Cowley

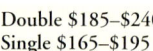

2 Thornton Road, Cambridge   *Phone* 0-7-827 7567
Postal P O Box 1037, Cambridge   *Fax* 0-7-827 7568
Email info@thorntonhouse.co.nz   *Website* www.thorntonhouse.co.nz

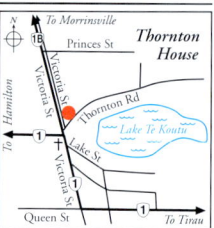

DIRECTIONS: Take SH 1 to Cambridge. On Victoria St, opposite St Andrews Church, turn right into Thornton Rd. Thornton House is 1st property on the left corner.

| 2 bdrm | 2 enst | **Double $185–$240**
Single $165–$195 | *Includes breakfast*
Lunch & dinner extra |

Originally built in 1902, this Queen Anne-style villa features a Marseilles tiled roof and was named "Orongo" by its first owners. Renamed, restored and renovated, Thornton House provides two ensuite guestrooms, the larger Garden Room opening to a private verandah. Set in landscaped gardens with mature trees and an abundance of roses, it is a peaceful location just minutes from the centre of Cambridge where guests can enjoy the antiques, craft shops and restaurants. A full breakfast menu is offered with breakfast served either in the guestrooms or alfresco on the sunporch, verandah or in the garden. Lunches and dinners are also available by prior arrangement. Three Burmese cats complete the family.

FACILITIES

- 2 queen ensuite bedrooms
- hair dryer, toiletries, heated towel rails & bathrobes
- 1 bath in Garden Room ensuite
- cotton bed linen
- tea/coffee, home-baked biscuits, TV & radio/CD/cassette-player in bedrooms
- lounge with open fire, Sky TV, video, CD-player, music, books, magazines & verandah
- full gourmet breakfast
- lunch or dinner by prior arrangement, extra
- picnic baskets available
- central heating
- fresh flowers
- phone, fax & email
- wine list
- off-street parking
- courtesy passenger transfer

ACTIVITIES AVAILABLE

- Burmese cats on site
- pétanque/boules on site
- wine cellar
- small weddings & honeymoons hosted
- relaxation massage by arrangement
- relaxing in garden on site
- antiques & craft shops
- Lake Te Koutu opposite
- farm & horse stud tours
- greyhound & harness racing
- restaurants nearby
- rowing & canoeing on Lake Karapiro
- garden & vineyard tours
- golfing
- Mystery Creek Field-days
- Hamilton City, 20-min drive
- airport, 15-min drive

CAMBRIDGE
Huntington Stables Retreat

Hosts Carol and Colin Townshend

106 Maungakawa Road, Cambridge   *Postal* P O Box 177, Cambridge
Phone 0-7-823 4120   *Mobile* 027 441 1425   *Fax* 0-7-823 4126
Email hunt.stables@xtra.co.nz   *Website* www.huntington.co.nz

DIRECTIONS: Take SH 1 south from Hamilton. At Cambridge, cross Victoria Rd into Thornton Rd. Travel to Robinson Rd. Continue right on Thornton Rd 2km. Turn left into Maungakawa Rd. Stables on right.

2 bdrm	2 prbth

Double $390
Single $350

Includes breakfast provisions
Self-catering

Huntington Stables Retreat accommodation is located adjacent to the Maungakawa Scenic Reserve, just five minutes from Cambridge village. The stables-style accommodation complex comprises two spacious self-contained studios. These open onto decks with rural vistas overlooking the pétanque court and horse paddocks beyond where Carol's Arab horse Springbok grazes. The South Stable is designed with romantic Caribbean-style bed linen in the king-size bedroom and the North Stable has a super-king/twin bedroom with paisley bed linen. A claw-foot bath is included in each studio's bathroom and both kitchens are fully equipped for self-catering and feature local pottery. Honeymooners enjoy a complimentary bottle of champagne.

FACILITIES

- 2 spacious self-contained studios
- South Stable: 1 king bedroom & Caribbean-style bed linen
- North Stable: 1 super-king/twin bedroom & paisley bed linen
- private bathroom in each studio with claw-foot bath, hair dryers, toiletries, robes & heated floors
- lounge in each studio with tea/coffee, nibbles, bar, Sky TV, video, CD-player, NZ artwork & books
- fully self-catering kitchen & dining area in each studio, with lavish provisions, utensils & local pottery; or breakfast by request
- wine cellar on site with wine for sale & BYO accepted
- central heating
- complimentary laundry
- 2 private guest entrances
- courtesy passenger transfer

ACTIVITIES AVAILABLE

- swimming & spa pools
- sauna & wine cellar on site
- barbecue & pétanque
- horses in adjacent paddock
- Maungakawa Scenic Reserve
- golf courses within 5km
- Cambridge village, 5 mins
- bush walk tracks
- Lake Karapiro for fishing, waterskiing & kayaking
- restaurants, 5-min drive
- jet boat & horse stud tours
- antique stores
- tennis & squash courts nearby
- harness racing
- Hamilton City, 20-min drive
- Airport, 15-min drive away
- *Waipa Delta* river boat tours
- Waitomo Glow-worm Caves, 30-min drive away

LAKE KARAPIRO
Maungatautari Lodge

Hosts Christine and Peter Scoular

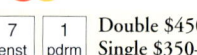

844 Maungatautari Road, Lake Karapiro   *Postal* P O Box 1060, Cambridge
Phone 0-7-827 2220   *Mobile* 021 866 873   *Fax* 0-7-827 2221
Email reservations@malodge.com   *Website* www.malodge.com

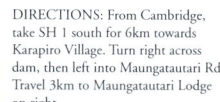

DIRECTIONS: From Cambridge, take SH 1 south for 6km towards Karapiro Village. Turn right across dam, then left into Maungatautari Rd. Travel 3km to Maungatautari Lodge on right.

| 7 bdrm | 7 enst | 1 pdrm | **Double** $450–$900 **Single** $350–$570 | *Includes breakfast, dinner & apéritifs* **Packages available** *Lunch extra* |

Maungatautari Lodge is an architecturally designed, purpose-built, boutique hotel, located one hour 45 minutes' drive south of Auckland City. The Lodge is situated on a 16-hectare working farm and throughbred horse stud, set in the lush green country-side of Waikato, overlooking Lake Karapiro. A fully equipped conference room can cater for 20 people. Apéritifs are served in the lounge, followed by table d'hôte fine dining prepared by the chef. Maungatautari is central to tourist attractions in Rotorua, Waitomo and Tauranga, all an easy one-hour drive away. Lake Taupo is one hour 30 minutes south. Activities available within half an hour of the Lodge include six golf courses, bush walks, horse treks, fishing and eco-tours, glow-worms, and winery tours.

FACILITIES

- 4 super-king/twin suites
- 3 super-king/twin villas
- cotton bed linen, dressing room, writing desk, phone, TV, fridge, minibar & tea/coffee in all suites
- spa baths, hair dryers, bathrobes, heated towel rails & toiletries
- wheelchair access to all villas
- guest lounge with open fire, Sky TV, music, writing desk & books
- email & fax available; fresh flowers

- full cooked & continental breakfast in conservatory
- lunch by request, extra
- 4-course dinner with home-grown veges, NZ organic beef, lamb, fish or game
- central heating throughout
- French spoken by hosts
- courtesy passenger transfer
- on-site parking

ACTIVITIES AVAILABLE

- in-ground swimming pool
- pétanque/boules on site
- chip & putt mini-golf
- croquet lawn on site
- 2.5ha (6-acre) park-like garden on 16ha farm
- massage, hair dressers & facials by arrangement
- Lake Karapiro adjacent
- stud tours; team building

- 6 golf courses within 30 mins
- fishing trips; canoeing
- gardens open to visit
- Maungatautari Mountain Reserve
- Cambridge, 5-min drive
- Karapiro Dam, 2-min drive
- Rotorua & Tauranga, 1 hour
- Waitomo Caves, 1-hr drive
- Lake Taupo, 1½-hour drive

TIRAU, WAIKATO
Oraka Deer Park

Hosts Linda and Ian Scott

71 Bayly Road, R D 1, Tirau   *Phone* 0-7-883 1382
Freephone 0800 835 838   *Mobile* 027 473 2657   *Fax* 0-7 883 1384
Email oraka@xtra.co.nz   *Website* www.oraka-deer.co.nz

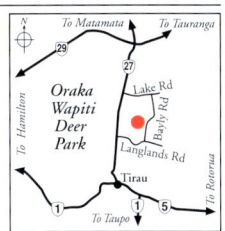

DIRECTIONS: From Hamilton take SH 1 or from Rotorua take SH 5 to Tirau. Take SH 27 north for 3km. Turn right into Langlands Rd. Travel 2km & turn left into Bayly Rd. Travel 710m to Oraka Deer Park on left.

2 bdrm	1 prbth

Cottage rate $200 for 2 persons
Extra persons $15 each

Self-catering
All meals extra

The cottage on Oraka Park Deer Farm is fully self-contained with a well equipped kitchen for self-catering. Farm vistas from every window ensure a tranquil stay on this 56-hectare farm. The 48 hectares of wapiti deer provide year-round interest for guests, from the growth of deer velvet in spring to the birth of fawns in summer and bottle feeding pet fawns, then the noisy mating roar of the stags in autumn. In addition there are walks in the large established garden, through the eight-hectare pine forest and beside Oraka Stream that borders the farm. The country cottage comprises two bedrooms, bathroom, fully appointed kitchen, lounge area and laundry. It is suitable for honeymooners or families, and meals can be catered by prior arrangement.

FACILITIES

- private-party bookings only
- 1 self-contained cottage
- 1 super-king & 1 double/twin bedroom in cottage
- 1 private bathroom with hair dryer & heated towel rails
- cotton bed linen
- lounge with TV & video
- full kitchen for self-catering
- guest phone & laundry

- breakfast, $15 pp
- lunch & dinner by arrangement, extra
- children's books, toys & playground available
- fresh flowers
- wheelchair access
- children welcome
- on-site parking; helipad
- swimming & spa pools

ACTIVITIES AVAILABLE

- walks in over 1ha (3 acres) garden, with 70-yr-old trees & roses
- tour of Deer Park; feeding deer
- 48ha deer farm & 8ha pine forest & stream on site
- deer roaring in autumn
- deer fawns born from mid-Nov.
- tennis court & croquet on site
- pétanque/boules on site
- shop & restaurant on site

- other restaurants nearby
- hot springs, 15km
- gliding
- 2 golf courses nearby
- antiques & collectables, 6km
- Tirau village, 6km
- Matamata township, 15km
- Rotorua, 50 mins south
- day trips to Tauranga beach, Hamilton, Waitomo caves

REWAREWA, OTOROHANGA
Kamahi Cottage

Hosts Evan and Elisabeth Cowan

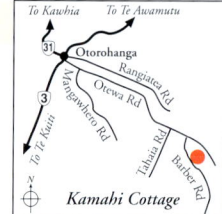

229 Barber Road, Rewarewa, R D 5, Otorohanga
Phone 0-7-873 0849   *Mobile* 021 055 1818   *Fax* 0-7-873 0849
Email enquiries@kamahi.co.nz   *Website* www.kamahi.co.nz

DIRECTIONS: Take SH 3 to Otorohanga. At south end of town, turn east into Otewa Rd, under railway bridge. Travel 12 km & turn right into Barber Rd. Travel 2.29km to Kamahi Cottage & homestead on left.

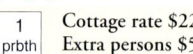

1 bdrm	1 prbth

Cottage rate $225 for 2 persons
Extra persons $55 each

Includes breakfast
Lunch & dinner extra   *Self-catering*

Kamahi Cottage

Set in over a hectare of landscaped garden, Kamahi Cottage was purpose built to blend into the surrounding countryside. This self-contained cottage opens to a verandah with hammock chairs. Uninterrupted panoramic views extend over rolling pastureland to Mount Pirongia and Kakapuka beyond. The hand-crafted cottage has been designed to be light and airy with wooden beams and staircase, concealed kitchen and mezzanine bedroom. A full breakfast is served in the homestead, or cottage if preferred, and lunch or picnic basket is available by prior arangement. Elisabeth enjoys serving two or three-course dinner with changing menus by prior request. Quality New Zealand wines are available for purchase.

FACILITIES

- 1 queen bedroom with cotton bed linen
- sofa bed in lounge
- private bathroom with hair dryer, heated towel rails, bathrobes & toiletries
- guest lounge with tea/coffee, home-made baking, sound system, CDs & writing desk
- laundry available, $10
- Swiss-German spoken by hosts

- full continental or cooked breakfast in homestead or in cottage if preferred
- picnic basket or lunch, $25 pp
- 3-course dinner with home-grown produce, $40 pp, BYO
- kitchenette for self-catering
- email, fax & phone available in homestead
- elderly cat in homestead
- on-site parking

ACTIVITIES AVAILABLE

- 1.25ha (3-acre) landscaped garden, native & exotic trees
- farm tours & walks on site
- deck area with hammock chairs
- honeymoons catered for
- professionally guided trout fishing tours, by arrangement
- black water rafting
- Waitomo caving & abseiling adventures, 30-min drive

- Otorohanga township & shops, 15-min drive
- Woodlyn Park Waitomo Farmshow
- Otorohanga kiwi house
- gardens open to visit
- Waitomo golf course
- Kawhia harbour & west coast beaches, 1 hr away
- Hamilton, 1-hour drive

WAITOMO
Tapanui Country Home

Hosts Sue and Mark Perry

Tapanui, 1714 Oparure Road, R D 5, Te Kuiti
Phone 0-7-877 8549   *Mobile* 027 494 9873   *Fax* 0-7-877 8541
Email info@tapanui.co.nz   *Website* www.tapanui.co.nz

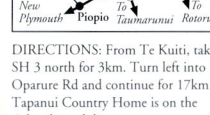

DIRECTIONS: From Te Kuiti, take SH 3 north for 3km. Turn left into Oparure Rd and continue for 17km. Tapanui Country Home is on the right, through limestone entrance.

2 bdrm	1 enst	1 prbth	Double $180–$195 Single $170–$185	*Includes breakfast Lunch & dinner extra*

After a dramatic entrance through the limestone outcrop, peace and quiet abound at Tapanui Country Home. Sue's extensive garden including rhododendrons and camellias bounded by a ha-ha provides uninterrupted views of the countryside. Designed to the Perrys' concept by Darryl Bell in 1982, the purpose-built homestead offers two spacious guestrooms, one in the main house with a private bathroom, and one with ensuite in the guest wing. Tapanui features exposed rimu ceilings, quiet-toned furnishings, Warner printed fabrics, original New Zealand art and handknotted oriental carpets. Guests enjoy meeting the family hand-reared sheep, kune pig and donkey on the 770-hectare (1900-acre) sheep and beef farm.

FACILITIES

- 2 super-king/twin bedrooms, with quality beds, feather or angora/wool mix duvets
- cotton bathrobes & slippers
- CD-player in both bedrooms
- toiletries, hair dryers, heaters & heated towel rails in both bathrooms
- central heating
- phone, fax & email available
- laundry available, extra
- continental/cooked breakfast
- lunch by arrangement
- dinner with NZ wine, $60 pp, by prior arrangement
- formal lounge with piano
- casual lounge with TV & leather couches
- separate dining room & patio
- outdoor furniture
- rural & mountain views

ACTIVITIES AVAILABLE

- Boots, the cat, on site
- garden & farm walks
- farm pets/activities when available, eg bottle-feeding lambs
- Waitomo Caves & glow-worms, 25-min drive
- BBQ luncheons at Roselands
- Waitomo Golf Course & horse trekking
- Natural Bridge walks, 4–25km from Waitomo Caves
- restaurants at Te Kuiti, 20km
- Kiwi House & native birds
- Marokopa Falls; Lost World
- Waitomo Museum of Caves
- private garden visits
- angora rabbit shearing
- black water rafting
- Altura gardens & wildlife park
- kiwi culture show at Woodlyn Park Waitomo

Taumarunui
Awarua Lodge

Hosts Raewyn and Jack Vernon   *Phone* 0-7-896 8100

1063 State Highway 4, Piriaka, Taumarunui   *Freephone* 0800 500 042
Postal c/- Piriaka Store, State Highway 4, Taumarunui   *Fax* 0-7-896 8102
Email info@awarualodge.co.nz   *Website* www.awarualodge.co.nz

| 2 bdrm | 1 prbth |

Guest wing rate $350
Multiple-night rate available

Includes breakfast hamper
Cooked breakfast & dinner extra

DIRECTIONS: From north, take SH 4 south to Taumarunui. Continue 10.63km south to Awarua Lodge on bend on left. Or from south, take SH 4 north to Piriaka. Continue over bridge to Awarua Lodge on right.

Awarua Lodge is set at the end of a tree-lined avenue in a large established garden bordered by the Whanganui River on two sides. Located on a five-hectare farm in park-like grounds, Awarua Lodge was architecturally designed by Graeme Johansen and offers a self-contained suite with two spacious bedrooms and a private bathroom in the guest wing. A kitchenette allows guests to self-cater, although meals are served in the dining room, guest wing or alfresco on the deck that opens from both bedrooms with views over the garden to the river beyond. Guests can enjoy relaxing in the landscaped garden and walking through the carefully planted trees which attract the birdlife. There are many walks in the surrounding hills of the King Country.

FACILITIES

- one-party bookings only
- 1 super-king/twin & 1 king bedroom in guest wing
- 1 private bathroom
- cotton bed linen
- hair dryer, toiletries, demist mirror, bathrobes & heated towel rails in bathroom
- laundry service, $10
- email & fax available
- breakfast hamper included; cooked breakfast $5 pp
- dinner by request, $40 pp, with complimentary wine
- kitchenette in guest wing
- guest lounge with Sky TV, video, tea/coffee & artwork
- decking opening from bedrooms & living room
- on-site parking

ACTIVITIES AVAILABLE

- 5ha farm & 1ha landscaped garden on site
- artist & photography opportunities on site
- bird-watching on site
- Whanganui River for tours, fishing & swimming
- milking in season
- tramping & hiking
- golf course, 10-min drive
- restaurants in Taumarunui, 10-min drive away
- sheep shearing
- gardens to visit
- lavender farm, 25 mins
- Raurimu Spiral lookout
- mountain walks, Tongariro Crossing
- skiing in winter
- Mt Ruapehu, 45 mins

LAKE TAUPO
Taupo Garden Lodge
FORMERLY AWAHURI GARDEN LODGE

Hosts William and Suzanne Hindmarsh

70 Hindmarsh Drive, Rangatira Park, Taupo

Freephone 0800 426 538   *Phone* 0-7-378 9847   *Fax* 0-7-378 5799

Email hindmarsh@taupogardenlodge.co.nz   *Website* www.taupogardenlodge.co.nz

3 bdrm	2 enst

Suite rate $400
2-night rate $650 per suite

Includes breakfast
Dinner & wine extra

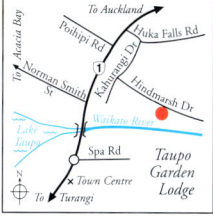

DIRECTIONS: Turn east from SH 1 into Huka Falls Rd, north of Taupo. Turn into Kahurangi Drive, opposite radio mast, to Rangatira Park, & left into Hindmarsh Drive. Taupo Garden Lodge is on the right, on lower terrace.

This peaceful, small fishing Lodge is set in over a hectare of colourful water gardens bordering the Waikato River, two kilometres north of Taupo. The garden, which features mature trees, rhododendrons, camellias, perennials and roses, is enhanced by the seclusion, views and rural tranquillity. The separate Garden Suite has a spacious super-king bedroom and single room, with a sunny private aspect. Its furnishings include Persian rugs and original oil paintings. The Heron Suite inside the Lodge is configured as a double or twin. Guests enjoy Suzanne's candlelit dinners, complemented by William's wine selection. As the hosts are fourth generation New Zealanders and have lived at Awahuri since 1963, they are well qualified to advise guests about local restaurants and attractions.

FACILITIES

- Garden Suite: 1 ensuite super-king/twin & 1 single bedroom, separate from Lodge
- Heron Suite: 1 double/twin ensuite bedroom in Lodge
- quality bed linen; fresh flowers
- hair dryer, toiletries & heated towel rails in both bathrooms
- tea/coffee, TV in Garden Suite
- complimentary laundry
- children welcome
- continental/cooked breakfast at times to suit, in dining room
- candlelit dinner, $65 pp, by arrangement
- vegetarians catered
- Suzanne can cook guests' trout catch, or William can smoke, vacuum pack & post to guests
- international wine selection, extra
- phone, fax & email available

ACTIVITIES AVAILABLE

- walks in over 1ha (3 acres) garden, with lawn, trees, 3 ponds & waterfall
- grass tennis court on site
- fishing & swimming in Waikato River on boundary
- river walks; hot thermal pools
- Huka Falls & Aratiatia rapids
- fly fishing & charter launches on Lake Taupo, 3-min drive
- recommended restaurants, 1km
- 3 golf courses, 3km, including Wairakei International
- guided deer hunting
- Classic Jaguar car tours & scenic river tours available
- hot-air ballooning
- mountain tramping & snow-skiing, 100km away
- warm clothing/gear available

Acacia Bay, Taupo
The Loft

Hosts Grace Andrews and Peter Rosieur

3 Wakeman Road, Acacia Bay, Taupo
Phone 0-7-377 1040   *Mobile* 027 485 1347   *Fax* 0-7-377 1049
Email book@theloftnz.com   *Website* www.theloftnz.com

DIRECTIONS: From SH 1, just north of Taupo, turn west into Norman Smith St. Turn left into Acacia Bay Rd & continue into Wakeman Rd. The Loft is immediately on left.

| 3 bdrm | 3 enst |

Room rate $130–$175

Includes breakfast
Lunch & dinner extra

Set in a small cottage garden, adjacent to a native bush reserve, The Loft was purpose built in 1999 to provide accommodation for up to six guests. The guest floor is upstairs, comprising three ensuite bedrooms, with the living rooms downstairs. Breakfast is a highlight, with fresh fruit, baking, and the guests' choice of a cooked option, served in the dining room or alfresco in the courtyard. Peter and Grace also enjoy providing home-cooked dinners and summer barbecues. They are happy to arrange guides and activities for their guests. Turtle, the red-eared turtle, completes the family. Lake Taupo, which is popular for its watersports, fishing and cruises, is only a few minutes' walk away and the township is just five minutes' drive.

FACILITIES

- upstairs guest floor
- 3 queen ensuite bedrooms with cotton bed linen, robes & TV
- single beds available
- hair dryer, heated towel rails & toiletries in all 3 ensuites
- tea/coffee, mini-fridge & bookshelf on landing
- full laundry service, extra
- children over 12 yrs welcome

- full continental & choice of cooked breakfasts
- home-cooked dinner, or summer BBQ, $30–$45 pp
- BYO or wine available for sale
- lounge with open fire, Sky TV & CD-player
- email, fax & phone available
- courtesy passenger transfer
- on-site parking

ACTIVITIES AVAILABLE

- small cottage garden on site, with courtyard for relaxing
- native bush reserve adjacent for bird-watching
- honeymoons catered for
- fly fishing, guides arranged
- Wairakei International Golf Course, 5 mins
- tramping & walking
- lake & river cruise

- restaurant, 200m away
- Taupo town centre, 5 mins
- kayaking; boating; rafting
- watersports; jet boating
- thermal activities
- gardens open to visit
- hunting tours
- horse riding, 5-min drive
- Lake Taupo, 7-min walk

ACACIA BAY, TAUPO
Tauhara Sunrise

Hosts Becky and Rob McEwen

38 Mapara Road, Acacia Bay, Taupo
Phone 0-7-376 8555   *Mobile* 021 177 3961   *Fax* 0-7-376 8557
Email rob@tauharasunrise.com   *Website* www.tauharasunrise.com

DIRECTIONS: From SH 1, cross bridge & turn left into Norman Smith St. Follow Acacia Bay signs & travel 5km to shops. Continue into Wakeman Rd & turn right into Mapara Rd. Tahaura Sunrise 200m on right.

| 3 bdrm | 3 enst | Room rate $300–$475 | *Includes breakfast & apéritifs* | Winter rates available |
| Room rate $460–$635 | *Includes breakfast, apéritifs, dinner & wine* |

The panoramic sunrises across Lake Taupo, viewed from all rooms in the lodge, give Tauhara Sunrise its name. The city lights of Taupo also reflect in the lake by night. Purpose built from stone and plaster in 2001, in contemporary style with original artwork, Tauhara Sunrise offers three ensuite guestrooms. The spacious upstairs room includes a double spa bath, and there is a guest kitchenette with fully stocked refrigerator between the two downstairs rooms. A full breakfast menu is provided and dinner is available after the happy hour. A state-of-the-art entertainment system, with plasma television, features in the media room, with open fire in the lounge/reading room. Becky offers therapeutic massage, and Pillpot, the cat, is also in residence.

FACILITIES

- 1 super-king ensuite bedroom, double basin & spa bath, upstairs
- 1 super-king/twin ensuite bedroom with wheelchair access, downstairs
- 1 queen ensuite bedroom downstairs
- hair dryers, toiletries, heated towel rails & demist mirrors
- cotton bed linen; robes & slippers; bedrooms open to patios
- entertainment room with CD-player, plasma Sky TV, video, DVD

- full breakfast menu
- complimentary apéritifs
- dinner with wine, extra
- guest kitchenette
- lounge with open fire
- high-speed internet, email, fax & phone available
- complimentary laundry
- courtesy passenger transfer
- off-street parking

ACTIVITIES AVAILABLE

- complimentary bar opening to spacious balcony & 6-person hot tub overlooking landscaped garden & lake
- in-house massage therapist
- weddings, honeymoons & conferences catered for
- tennis across road
- kayaking; rafting; lake cruises
- boutique shops; thermal resort

- sidewalk cafés & restaurants
- golf courses; hunting
- boat hire; fishing; sailing
- gliding; flight-seeing
- mountain biking & boarding
- gardens open to visit
- eco-tours; bush walking
- bungy jumping; skydiving
- skiing in winter, 1½ hours

Tauhara Sunrise

145

West Wellow Lodge

Hosts

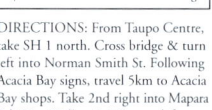

West Wellow

ACCOMMODATION NO LONGER AVAILABLE

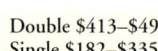

5 bdrm	4 enst	1 prbth	Double $413–$495	*Includes breakfast*	*Dinner extra*
			Single $182–$335	**House rate available**	

DIRECTIONS: From Taupo Centre, take SH 1 north. Cross bridge & turn left into Norman Smith St. Following Acacia Bay signs, travel 5km to Acacia Bay shops. Take 2nd right into Mapara Rd. West Wellow is 150m on left.

Set in a landscaped garden overlooking Lake Taupo, West Wellow is a tranquil venue for guests, just minutes' walk from Acacia Bay. Designed in historic style, West Wellow offers one ensuite guestroom downstairs and another three upstairs, each with access to the guest balcony with views across the lake to the township of Taupo and Mt Tauhara beyond. Guests enjoy the lights of Taupo by night. The close proximity to the lake enables guests easy access to the outdoor and watersports. Breakfast is usually served in the conservatory downstairs or alfresco, and dinner is available by prior arrangement. Tea and coffee facilities are provided on the landing, and a guest study includes a writing desk and television. Children are welcome in single-party bookings.

FACILITIES

- 1 super-king/twin bedroom & ensuite including bath & bidet
- 1 queen & 2 king ensuite bedrooms, 1 downstairs with wheelchair access
- 1 chauffeur or guide's single bedroom with private bathroom
- cotton bed linen; fresh flowers
- hair dryers, toiletries, heated towel rails & bathrobes
- children by arrangement
- complimentary wine bottle, cheese & fruit in bedrooms
- open fire, tea/coffee, Sky TV, video & writing desk
- phone, fax & email in study
- self-service laundry
- guest balconies overlooking Lake Taupo from bedrooms
- courtesy passenger transfer
- off-street parking

ACTIVITIES AVAILABLE

- BBQ for guest use, on site
- gourmet dinner by professional chef, by arrangement next-door, $150 pp, wine extra
- tennis court, 2-min walk
- hot mineral pools, 5km
- mini golf, 5km away
- Lake Taupo, 2-min walk
- Taupo shopping, 5-min drive
- scenic bush walks
- restaurants & bars, 1–5km
- trout fishing; lake & rivers
- golf courses, 5km away
- rafting; jet boats
- geothermal activity
- boating hire, 5-min walk
- Rotorua, 45-min drive
- ski-fields & mountain walks
- tandem skydiving

ACACIA BAY, TAUPO
Lake Taupo Lodge
Hosts Gary and Shirley Akers

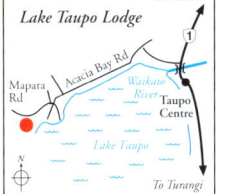

41 Mapara Road, Acacia Bay, Taupo   *Postal* P O Box 83, Taupo
Phone 0-7-378 7386   *Mobile* 027 453 3454   *Fax* 0-7-377 3226
Email lodge@reap.org.nz   *Website* friars.co.nz/hosts/laketaupo.html

DIRECTIONS: From Taupo Centre, take SH 1 north. Cross bridge, then turn left into Norman Smith St. Following Acacia Bay signs, travel 5km to Acacia Bay shops. Take 2nd right into Mapara Rd. Lodge is 200m on left.

7 bdrm	7 enst	Double $1,200–$1,500 Single $645–$745	*Includes breakfast & dinner* *Lunch extra*	

Lake Taupo Lodge

Sited above Acacia Bay on the north-western shores of Lake Taupo, the Lodge commands panoramic views over the water to the mountains beyond. Guests can relax in the quiet surroundings of the Lodge, yet it is only five minutes' drive from the centre of Taupo township. Built in 1984 in stone and mahogany timber, the Lodge was inspired by Frank Lloyd Wright architecture. The Art Nouveau interiors incorporate spacious living areas and seven guest suites. After dining on the chef's special cuisine, guests can enjoy themselves in the billiards room, music area, reading gallery, or in front of a log fire in winter. A stroll on the pathways through the park-like gardens is popular, with its ponds and mature trees attracting bellbirds and tui.

FACILITIES

- 7 super-king suites
- 7 ensuites, 5 include spa bath
- cotton bed linen
- private guest lounge, with log fire in winter
- laundry available
- music area includes grand piano
- reading gallery
- lake & garden views
- continental, or cooked breakfast prepared by chef
- lunch by arrangement, extra
- 4-course dinner included in tariff, wine extra, fully licensed
- vegetarian alternative available
- courtesy Taupo Airport transfer
- children 12 yrs & over welcome
- off-street carpark
- helipad

ACTIVITIES AVAILABLE

- in-house billiards room with full-size table
- park-like gardens with birdlife
- tennis court on site
- 3 golf courses nearby, including the Wairakei International Golf Course
- rainbow trout fishing in lake, rivers & streams
- watersports in Lake Taupo
- Lake Taupo township, 5 mins
- trekking
- bush walking
- boating
- Wairakei geothermal fields
- snow skiing at Mt Ruapehu, in winter, 60 mins away
- Taupo airport, 15-min drive

Lake Taupo Lodge

Lake Taupo Lodge

ACACIA BAY, TAUPO
The Gooses Roost

Hosts Ross and Kay Palmer

11 Glen Mohr, R D 1, Acacia Bay, Taupo
Phone 0-7-376 5000   *Fax* 0-7-376 5001   *Mobile* 029 376 5000
Email artroosting@actrix.co.nz   *Website* friars.co.nz/hosts/goosesroost.html

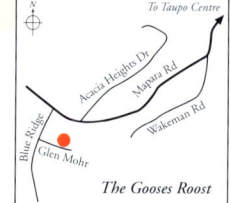

DIRECTIONS: From Taupo, take SH 1 north. Turn left into Norman Smith St & travel 5km to Acacia Bay shops. Take 2nd right into Mapara Rd. Turn left into Blue Ridge & left again into Glen Mohr to Gooses Roost on left.

1 bdrm	1 prbth

Double $250   Single $200   *Includes breakfast*

The Gooses Roost is an artists' retreat in a quiet rural location, just seven minutes from Taupo. This contemporary European-style home was built in 2003, sited to capture views towards Mt Tauhara. Accommodation comprises a guest suite with queen-size bedroom, bathroom and private sitting room. The bedroom opens onto the swimming pool area where guests can lounge or breakfast alfresco. Guests can choose a continental or full cooked breakfast which is served in the suite or on the patio. There are many restaurants in Taupo Centre and the lake with all its activities is nearby. The Gooses Roost features an in-house art gallery where guests can view and purchase Ross and Kay's paintings, and work can be commissioned.

FACILITIES

- 1 queen bedroom suite
- 1 private bathroom
- cotton bed linen & TV in bedroom
- bathrobes, hair dryer, toiletries, heated floor & towel rails in bathroom
- fresh flowers
- guest lounge with tea/coffee, TV, CD-player & artwork
- full cooked or continental breakfast served in suite or alfresco
- decking & patio area opening from bedroom
- phone available in house
- complimentary laundry
- art gallery of hosts' work for sale on-site
- on-site parking

ACTIVITIES AVAILABLE

- swimming pool on site
- large gardens on site for relaxing & walking
- Lake Taupo, 5 mins
- fishing
- boating
- jet skiing
- watersports
- horse riding
- many restaurants, nearby
- golf courses
- bush walks
- hot pools
- gardens to visit
- boutique shopping
- Taupo Centre, 7 mins
- ski-fields in winter
- Turangi, 45 mins

ACACIA BAY, TAUPO

The Top House

Hosts Jack and Margy Gower

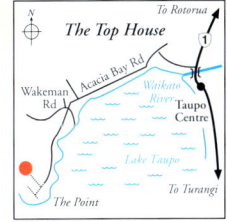

DIRECTIONS: From Taupo, take
SH 1 north. Turn left into Norman
Smith St. Follow Acacia Bay Rd to end
to The Point. At security gates punch
in code & continue uphill to end of
last drive on right to The Top House.

42 The Point, Taupo   *Postal* P O Box 104, Taupo
Phone 0-7-377 0169   *Email* bookings@thetophouse.co.nz
Fax 0-7-377 3134   *Website* www.thetophouse.co.nz

| 4 bdrm | 1 enst | 2 prbth | 1 pdrm | House rate $600–$1,500 | *Self-catering* |

With panoramic views over Lake Taupo to the mountains beyond, The Top House is set in private native gardens at The Point, near Acacia Bay. This award-winning Fraser Cameron designed house incorporates glass, timber and local stone to create a New Zealand ambience. The Top House offers self-contained accommodation with four bedrooms, three bathrooms, two spacious living rooms and a gamesroom. Ample living space and a well-appointed kitchen make this self-catering house suitable for small groups and families of up to 12 guests. Alfresco dining is popular with barbecue, two decks and secluded lawn. A chef can be arranged and restaurants are a short drive away. A golf buggy takes guests down to the on-site tennis courts and lake edge.

FACILITIES

- private-party bookings
- 4 super-king/twin bedrooms
- 1 ensuite with bath & 2 private bathrooms
- cotton bed linen
- hair dryers, toiletries, demist mirror, heated towel rails & double basin in all bathrooms
- children welcome
- NZ art throughout

- full self-contained kitchen for self-catering
- catering can be arranged
- living room with open fire, Sky TV, VCR & CD-player
- billiards table, Sky TV, CDs & DVDs in gamesroom & living room downstairs
- laundry; security gates
- on-site parking; helipad

ACTIVITIES AVAILABLE

- gas barbecue facilities
- in-house gamesroom
- fly fishing, guided by Jack, within 5-min walk away
- golf buggy available to go to tennis courts & fly fishing
- 2 boat ramps available
- beach access & summer swimming in sheltered harbour
- fishing from rocks; watersports

- restaurants, 5–10km
- bush walks nearby
- 4 golf courses, 3 international standard, 15–20 mins
- boutique shopping, 10 mins
- thermal pools, 10-min drive
- horse riding
- rope & rock climbing
- geothermal activities
- ski-field, 1 hour 20-min drive

© Friars' Guide to New Zealand Accommodation for the Discerning Traveller

LAKE TAUPO
Karaka Cottage

Host Delia Barnes

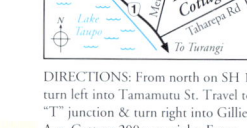

42 Gillies Avenue, Taupo   *Postal* P O Box 1622, Taupo
Phone 0-7-378 4560   *Mobile* 027 496 9432   *Fax* 0-7-378 3145
Email rugs@reap.org.nz   *Website* www.rugsoriental.co.nz

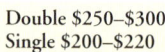

DIRECTIONS: From north on SH 1, turn left into Tamamutu St. Travel to "T" junction & turn right into Gillies Ave. Cottage 200m on right. From south, on SH 1, turn right into Rifle Range Rd, then right into Gillies Ave.

3 bdrm	3 enst	Double $250–$300 Single $200–$220	*Includes breakfast* **Winter rates available**	*Dinner extra* *Self-catering in cottage*

Set in a quiet garden with mature trees overhead, Karaka Cottage has been purpose-built to provide total guest privacy, adjacent to the main house. The deck from the cottage opens directly to the swimming pool, creating a relaxed atmosphere. Single parties can be accommodated in the super-king/twin bedroom of the self-contained cottage with its fully equipped kitchen for self-catering. Breakfast provisions are supplied for the cottage, or served in the dining room of the house or alfresco in the landscaped garden. Two bedrooms both with ensuite bathrooms are also available for guests in the house. Oriental rugs are a feature of both cottage and house. Dinner can also be provided – either in the dining room or in the cottage by arrangement.

FACILITIES

- private-party booking for cottage
- 1 super-king/twin ensuite bedroom in cottage
- 1 super-king/twin & 1 queen ensuite bedroom in house
- hair dryers, toiletries, heated towel rails, bathrobes & fresh flowers
- private lounge in cottage with TV
- tea/coffee & TV available in house
- self-catering kitchen in cottage
- breakfast served in house or alfresco, or provisions in cottage if preferred
- 3-course dinner with pre-dinner drinks, $60 pp
- open fire in lounge in house
- phone, fax, email & laundry available
- guest deck opens from cottage to swimming pool
- off-street parking

ACTIVITIES AVAILABLE

- swimming pool on site
- barbecue available
- restaurants, 1–2km away
- golf matches arranged – member Wairakei International Golf Course
- guided fishing
- boating trips arranged
- tourist shopping, 2km away
- sailing; paragliding
- Delia's *Rugs Oriental*, 2km
- thermal pools, 2km away
- Lake Taupo, 5-min walk
- lake activities – watersports
- jet skiing; water skiing
- gardens open to visit; horse riding & trekking
- Wairakei Park – jet boating
- Huka Falls – Aratiatia Rapids
- skiing in winter, 1-hour drive

LAKE TAUPO
Apartment Tekau Place

Host Margaret Hadwen   *Mobile* 0274 441 919

Waimahana, Apartment 10, 1 Lowell Place, Taupo   *Phone* 0-7-378 6095
Postal 106 Acacia Heights Drive, Taupo   *Fax* 0-7-378 6095
Email nhadwen@xtra.co.nz   *Website* friars.co.nz/hosts/tekau.html

DIRECTIONS: From Taupo township, travel south on SH 1 for 4 mins. At junction with SH 5, turn right into Lowell Place. Waimahana apartments on right. Tekau Place on 2nd floor.

3 bdrm	1 enst	1 prbth

Apartment rate $400
2-night minimum stay

Self-catering
Multiple-night rates available

Overlooking Lake Taupo, Tekau Place is a first floor apartment at Waimahana. With interiors designed in minimalist contemporary design, this thermally heated apartment features a spacious open-plan lounge and dining area opening to the balcony, with a view over the swimming pool to the lake beyond. The ensuite bedroom also opens to the balcony, and there is a bath in the second bathroom adjacent to the second bedroom. A third bedroom opens to the lounge, with a folding bed and sliding walls forming an extension to the living area. A fully equipped kitchen provides for self-catering, with restaurants and shops within walking distance. Guests enjoy Hot Water Beach which they can access directly in front of the apartment.

FACILITIES

- private-party bookings only
- 1 super-king bedroom, with plasma TV, dressing room & double shower in ensuite
- 1 queen bedroom with private bathroom including bath
- 1 extra bedroom/lounge with queen fold-down wall bed
- toiletries, hair dryer, heated floor & demist mirror in both bathrooms
- fully self-contained kitchen for self-catering
- spacious lounge with TV, sound system & phone
- air-conditioning
- central heating
- balcony with lake views
- children welcome
- self-service laundry
- garaging

ACTIVITIES AVAILABLE

- sauna & swimming pool on site
- private gym with treadmill, bike & elliptical trainer
- access to Hot Water Beach
- bush, mountain & lake edge walks
- scenic boat tours on Lake Taupo & river
- watersports on Lake Taupo
- trout fishing in lake & rivers
- restaurant, 50m away
- shop, 100m away
- Taupo town centre, 3-min
- thermal pools, 3-min drive
- golf courses of international standard
- gardens open to visit
- winter snow skiing, 1-hour drive south at Mt Ruapehu
- airport, 5-min drive

BONSHAW PARK, TAUPO
The Pillars

Hosts Ruth and John Boddy

7 Deborah Rise, Bonshaw Park, R D 3, Taupo
Freephone 0800 200 983   *Phone* 0-7-378 1512   *Fax* 0-7-378 1511
Email enquiries@pillarshomestay.co.nz   *Website* www.pillarshomestay.co.nz

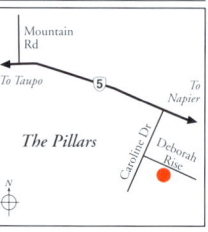

DIRECTIONS: Take SH 1 to Taupo. From Lake Tce, south of town, turn east into SH 5. Travel 5.7km towards Napier, then turn right into Caroline Drive. Take 1st turn on left into Deborah Rise. The Pillars on right.

4 bdrm	4 enst	1 pdrm	**Room rate $275–$475** **House rate $1,100**	*Includes breakfast* **Winter rates available**	*Lunch & dinner extra*

Overlooking Lake Taupo with views to Mount Ruapehu beyond, The Pillars was built in Mediterranean style. The landscaped gardens featuring a pond, gazebo and in-ground swimming pool enhance the tranquillity. Upstairs are the four ensuite guest bedrooms, three with private balconies, and one including a bath. A chauffeur's or guide's room is available downstairs. Breakfast and dinner on request are served in the dining room, conservatory or alfresco in the courtyard. But it is the extra little touches such as the complimentary writing paper and pens, chocolates, and wine that help make The Pillars special. Guests enjoy all-day sun and sunsets over the lake. The Pillars is an exclusive wedding venue and popular with honeymooners.

FACILITIES

- 1 super-king/twin, 1 king/twin & 2 Californian king/twin ensuite bedrooms; heated floors
- TV, radio-clock, tea/coffee, & fresh flowers in each guestroom
- fridge, fruit, wine, bottled water, & home-made biscuits in all bedrooms
- bathrobes, hair dryers, toiletries
- guide/chauffeur room available
- children over 13 years welcome

- 3-course dinner, with apéritifs, nibbles & nightcaps, $65 pp
- lunch & BBQ by request
- NZ continental breakfast alfresco on courtyard, or in dining room or conservatory
- phone, fax & email available
- complimentary laundry
- off-street parking
- courtesy passenger transfer

ACTIVITIES AVAILABLE

- swimming pool; pétanque
- all-weather tennis court, racquets & balls provided
- alpaca adjacent
- hot mineral pools, 5km
- Lake Taupo, 6km away
- Taupo shopping, 7km
- trout fishing in lake/rivers
- rafting; jet boats
- golf courses, 6km

- restaurants & bars 5–7km, transport provided
- bungy jumping; paragliding
- tandem skydiving
- horse trekking; mountain biking
- scenic bush walks; Mt Tauhara
- geothermal activity; hunting
- ski-fields, 1-hour drive away
- Rotorua, 45-min drive on SH 5
- Auckland, 3-hour drive on SH 1

Two Mile Bay, Taupo
Te Kowhai Landing

Manager Jennifer McBrearty   *Mobile* 027 542 4202

325 Lake Terrace, Two Mile Bay, Taupo   *Freephone* 0800 ESSENCE
Postal P O Box 99962, Newmarket, Auckland 1031   *Phone* 0-7-574 8054
Fax 0-7-574 8096   *Email* stay@essencenz.com   *Website* www.essencenz.com

DIRECTIONS: From north take SH 1 to Taupo. Continue on Lake Tce towards Turangi. Travel 5 mins to Te Kowhai on right. From south take SH 1 towards Taupo. Travel 5 mins past airport to Te Kowhai on left.

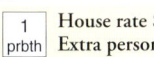
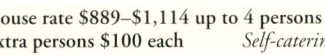

| 2 bdrm | 2 enst | 1 prbth | **House rate $889–$1,114 up to 4 persons** *Includes breakfast provisions* | **Extra persons $100 each** *Self-catering* *Chef service for meals, extra* |

Te Kowhai

Located on the shores of Lake Taupo, Te Kowhai Landing was purpose built in 2003 to provide state-of-the-art self-contained accommodation. Architectually designed to resemble a traditional New Zealand-style twin boatshed, this accommodation is "Smart Wired" to provide automated electronic fittings. With interiors designed by Sally Motion, Te Kowhai Landing features quality furnishings to complement the lake views from every room. There are two suites upstairs, with a balcony overlooking the lake, and below are the living and dining areas. The chef-designed kitchen enables guests to self-cater, or their dining needs can be catered for by a chef. The lounge opens towards the beach and a row boat is available for guest use.

FACILITIES

- single-party bookings only
- 2 super-king bedrooms upstairs, each with ensuite, dressing room, cotton bed linen, tea/coffee, fridge
- hair dryers, toiletries, heated floor, heated towel rails, demist mirrors & bathrobes; 1 double bath
- 2 lounges with wine, Sky TV, DVD, music, CD-player, games, artwork, books & writing desk
- central heating & log fire
- full kitchen for self-catering
- catered meals by arrangement
- computer, printer, broadband, fax & phones for guest use
- children welcome; twin beds in downstairs lounge
- conferences, weddings, cooking schools, product launches & art displays
- off-street parking; security gates

ACTIVITIES AVAILABLE

- spa pool; pétanque on site
- lake swimming & trout fishing direct access from site
- row boat for guest use
- customised scenic tours; wine tasting excursions
- guided trout fishing & hunting
- bush, mountain, lake-edge walks
- mineral pools, 3-min drive
- Huka Falls; aerial adventures
- Taupo shops, cafés & restaurants, 5-min drive
- golf courses; water pursuits
- mountain biking
- horse-riding; farm visits
- private gardens to visit
- wilderness & volcanic trips
- winter snow skiing, 1 hour
- "Middle-earth", 1½ hours
- airport, 5-min drive

Te Kowhai

Te Kowhai

© Friars' Guide to New Zealand Accommodation for the Discerning Traveller

LAKE TAUPO
Albion Lodge

Hosts David and Susie Pierce

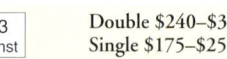

358 Lake Terrace, Two Mile Bay, Taupo   *Postal* P O Box 1810, Taupo
Phone 0-7-378 7788   *Mobile* 021 116 8496   *Fax* 0-7-378 2966
Email friars@albionlodge.co.nz   *Website* www.albionlodge.co.nz

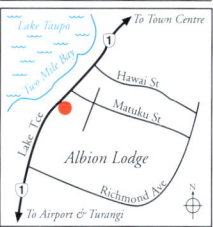

DIRECTIONS: From north take SH 1 to Taupo. Continue past SH 5 turn-off for 1.5km towards airport. Albion Lodge on left beside Anchorage. From south, take SH 1 to airport. Continue 2km to Albion Lodge on right

3 bdrm	3 enst	Double $240–$350 Single $175–$255	*Includes breakfast Lunch & dinner*

Albion Lodge is set in a native plant garden with views over Lake Taupo. Each of the three spacious guestrooms offer a super-king size bed and an ensuite including spa bath. Mealtimes are flexible and ingredients are fresh, and wherever possible, organic. A full cooked breakfast is served in the dining room, and a four-course table d'hôte dinner is offered. There is an extensive wine list featuring all the major varieties of New Zealand wines. An extensive collection of information on all the activities and attractions in Taupo is available. The lake is within walking distance from Albion Lodge. Hosts Susie and David are happy to advise on itineraries and arrange bookings for the guests during their stay in Taupo. Fishing guides can be arranged.

FACILITIES

- 3 super-king/twin bedrooms, all with ensuites & spa baths
- cotton bed linen
- hair dryer, toiletries, bathrobes, heated floor & towel rails
- lounge with gas fire, tea/coffee, nibbles, bar, CD-player, games, books & writing desk
- wheelchair access
- fresh flowers

- full cooked breakfast
- lunch hampers available
- 4-course table d'hôte dinner, $75 pp
- phone, fax, internet & email
- laundry available
- drying & ski storage room
- off-street parking
- central heating

ACTIVITIES AVAILABLE

- guided lake & fly fishing for rainbow & brown trout
- beach; watersports
- boat trips
- boat fishing
- rafting & kayaking
- parasailing; gliding
- sky diving
- floatplane, fixed wing & helicopter flights

- many restaurants, 10 mins
- shopping, 5-min drive
- bush walking
- bungy jumping
- horse riding
- 4 golf courses within 15 mins
- arts & crafts; volcanic centre
- 3 thermal parks within 30 mins
- Taupo town centre, 7-min drive

RAINBOW POINT, LAKE TAUPO
Tuscany on Taupo

Hosts Beryl and Richard Newman

28B Oregon Drive, Taupo   *Mobile* 021 063 2114
Phone 0-4-499 9309   *Email* c.newman@xtra.co.nz
Fax 0-4-384 8675   *Website* friars.co.nz/hosts/tuscany.html

DIRECTIONS: From north take SH 1 through Taupo township towards airport. Turn right into Rainbow Dr. Turn 2nd right into Oregon Dr. Tuscany on Taupo on left. From south turn left off SH 1 into Rainbow Drive.

VISA MasterCard

| 3 bdrm | 1 enst | 1 prbth | House rate $400 | *Self-catering* |

Set in a secluded garden, Tuscany on Taupo offers self-contained accommodation for up to six guests in a contemporary Mediterranean-style home. This four-level house provides three bedrooms, two bathrooms, and a full kitchen for self-catering. Basic provisions are supplied including the first morning breakfast. The dining room opens to a sheltered patio for alfresco dining and barbecues on the ground floor. There is a another barbecue on the first floor deck opening from the second lounge with adjacent kitchenette. The large bedroom on the top floor features a deck with a gimpse of the lake, the other floors looking onto the garden which shelters Tuscany on Taupo and provides lake access. Restaurants and shops are a few minutes away.

FACILITIES

- Top floor: 1 super-king/twin bedroom with ensuite, double basin, dressing room & patio
- First floor: 1 twin/king bedroom, lounge, kitchenette, computer with internet, patio
- Ground floor: 1 bathroom with spa bath & double basin, lounge with open log fire, TV, DVD & air-conditioning, full kitchen & dining area opening to patio
- Downstairs: 1 queen bedroom & full laundry
- phone on top & ground floors
- fax & email available
- hair dryers, toiletries, heated towel rails & demist mirrors
- cotton bed linen
- pets & children welcome
- single-party bookings only
- off-street parking; garaging

ACTIVITIES AVAILABLE

- 2 BBQs on patio/decks
- golf clubs for guest use
- fishing equipment & waders
- river or lake fishing
- Lions Lake Taupo walk
- watersports
- walks
- botanic gardens
- 4 golf courses within 10-min drive
- private gardens to visit
- restaurants, 2-min walk
- shopping, 5-min drive
- mineral pools, 3-min drive
- Taupo town centre, 5 mins
- prawn farm
- jet boating
- Huka Falls
- air sports
- winter skiing, 1-hour drive

Lake Taupo
Lakedge

Hosts Leone and Tim Graves

14 Oregon Drive, Taupo   *Phone* 0-7-378 7834
Mobiles 025 824 404 *and* 021 135 4290   *Fax* 0-7-378 7834
Email lakedge@reap.org.nz   *Website* www.reap.org.nz/~lakedge

DIRECTIONS: From north, take SH 1 to Taupo. Continue south on SH 1 & turn right into Rainbow Drive. Turn right again into Oregon Drive. Lakedge on left. From south, take SH 1 & turn left into Rainbow Drive.

| 2 bdrm | 1 enst | 1 prbth | **Double $340–$370** **Single $250–$280** | *Includes breakfast* *Dinner extra* |

Nestled on the shores of Lake Taupo, Lakedge features panoramic views across the water to Mount Ruapehu beyond. This architecturally designed award-winning home was purpose-built in June 2000 to provide two upstairs guestrooms with Italian tiled ensuite and tiled private bathroom. Both bedrooms open to a deck from where guests enjoy watching the ever-changing moods of the lake. Tim and Leone are born and bred New Zealanders and offer their guests Kiwi cuisine. Full breakfasts are served in the dining room or alfresco on the decking and three-course dinners are also available. The menu may include smoked fish and seafood chowder followed by herb encrusted rack of lamb, accompanied by local wines.

FACILITIES

- 1 super-king/twin ensuite bedroom upstairs
- 1 super-king/twin bedroom with private bathroom & spa bath
- both bedrooms include cotton bed linen, dressing room & TV
- hair dryer, toiletries, demist mirror, bathrobes, heated floor & towel rails in bathrooms
- tea/coffee & nibbles upstairs
- Sky TV, video, piano in lounge

- cooked breakfast served in dining room or alfresco
- 3-course dinner, $50 pp, wine extra
- pre-dinner drinks & nibbles
- large deck overlooking lake
- laundry available
- fresh fruit & flowers
- off-street parking
- courtesy passenger transfer

ACTIVITIES AVAILABLE

- kayaking – kayak available for guest use
- barbecue on site
- honeymoons & weddings catered for
- 3 golf courses including Wairakei – hosts are members
- golf rounds arranged with hosts or local members
- private tennis court nearby

- Taupo shops, cafés, bars & restaurants, 5-min drive
- thermal pools
- guided lake & river fly fishing
- bungy jumping
- sky diving
- trout fishing; lake walks
- Huka jet boats
- white water rafting
- winter snow skiing

LAKE TAUPO
Beside Lake Taupo

Hosts Irene and Roger Foote

8 Chad Street, Taupo
Phone 0-7-378 5847   *Mobile* 025 804 683   *Fax* 0-7-378 5847
Email besidelaketaupo@xtra.co.nz   *Website* besidelaketaupo.co.nz

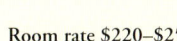

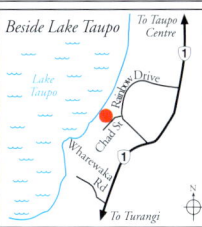

DIRECTIONS: From north, take SH 1 through Taupo township towards airport. Turn right into Rainbow Drive at 1st entrance. Turn right into Chad St. Homestead on right. From south, turn left off SH 1 into Rainbow Drive.

| 3 bdrm | 1 enst | 1 prbth | 2 pdrm | **Room rate $220–$250** | *Includes breakfast* |

Beside Lake Taupo is in fact located right on Lake Taupo. This two-storey home was architecturally designed for its lakeside setting and built in 1999. With lake views from all rooms, accommodation comprises a super-king/twin, a queen/twin and a queen bedroom, with two bathrooms, and balcony or terrace. Another terrace opens from the dining room, also overlooking the lake, where guests can breakfast alfresco and enjoy the view. Beside Lake Taupo is adjacent to a tranquil lakeside reserve and yet only 10 minutes' drive from Taupo centre to the north, and the airport to the south. The house is double-glazed and air-conditioned for guest comfort. An elevator takes guests and their luggage to the upstairs bedrooms.

FACILITIES

- 1 super-king/twin bedroom with ensuite & terrace
- 1 queen/twin & 1 queen bedroom with share bathroom & powder room for single-party
- TV & tea/coffee in bedrooms
- hair dryers, heated towel rails & toiletries in both bathrooms
- phone, fax & email available
- central heating; double glazing
- breakfast served in dining room or alfresco on terrace
- central lounge with sound system, Sky TV, video, CD-player & books
- air-conditioning
- laundry available
- internal elevator
- garage with direct internal access to house

ACTIVITIES AVAILABLE

- lake swimming from site
- fishing from site
- lakeside walks from site
- boating from site
- bush walks; tramping
- lake excursions; river cruises
- canoeing; kayaking
- trout fishing in lake & rivers
- horse trekking
- bike riding
- restaurants & shops nearby
- golf; bridge
- river rafting; rock climbing
- bungy jumping; sky-diving
- rainforests; hunting
- Tongariro National Park
- volcanic terrain, hot springs & pools
- airport, 10-min drive
- winter skiing

FOUR MILE BAY, LAKE TAUPO
Wharewaka Lodge

Hosts Susan and Tony Dalby

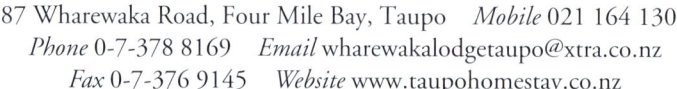

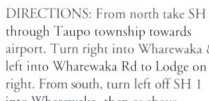

87 Wharewaka Road, Four Mile Bay, Taupo   *Mobile* 021 164 1308
Phone 0-7-378 8169   *Email* wharewakalodgetaupo@xtra.co.nz
Fax 0-7-376 9145   *Website* www.taupohomestay.co.nz

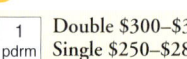

DIRECTIONS: From north take SH 1 through Taupo township towards airport. Turn right into Wharewaka & left into Wharewaka Rd to Lodge on right. From south, turn left off SH 1 into Wharewaka, then as above.

3 bdrm	3 enst	1 pdrm	Double $300–$320	*Includes breakfast*	*Lunch & dinner extra*
			Single $250–$280	**Off-season rates available**	

Wharewaka Lodge

Located on the lake edge with direct access to a safe swimming beach, Wharewaka Lodge is a contemporary home built in 2003 to provide accommodation for six guests in three ensuite guestrooms. A courtyard and small private garden are popular with guests and trout may be caught from the bottom of the landscaped garden. Each bedroom includes a seating area, fridge, tea/coffee facilities, home-made biscuits, juice and mineral water, and opens to a private balcony with lake views. Guests enjoy kayaking on the lake in front of the Lodge in the two kayaks provided. They also like walking and cycling the popular lakeside Lions Walk located on the Lake Taupo reserve adjoining Wharewaka Lodge. Two bicycles are available.

FACILITIES

- 1 super-king, 1 super-king/twin & 1 queen bedroom, all with TV, fridge, tea/coffee, private balcony & lake views
- 3 tiled ensuites, each with bath, hair dryer, toiletries, heated floor & heated towel rails
- cotton bed linen; bathrobes
- guest elevator to 1 queen bedroom
- central heating; double glazing
- fresh flowers
- breakfast indoors or alfresco
- lunch or picnic basket & dinner, by arrangement, extra
- lounge with open fireplace & Sky TV
- laundry facilities
- fax & internet available
- courtesy passenger transfer
- off-street parking

ACTIVITIES AVAILABLE

- beach & lake access from site
- 2 kayaks available
- swimming, kayaking, cycling, walking & fly fishing from site
- small business retreats catered
- boat tours on Lake Taupo
- 3 golf courses, 1 international
- hot mineral pools, 10 mins
- bush walks; horse trekking
- restaurants & shops, 7km
- watersports; trout fishing
- bungy jumping; parasailing
- sky-diving; airport, 5 mins
- jet boating to Huka Falls
- thermal areas, 15-min drive
- winter snow skiing, 1 hour
- Rotorua, 1¼ hours
- Hawke's Bay vineyard & gannet tours, 1½ hours
- Waitomo Caves, 1¾ hours

LAKE TAUPO
Lake Edge Lodge

Host Jean Russell

60 Mahuta Road, Five Mile Bay, R D 2, Taupo
Phone 0-7-378 0563   *Mobile* 021 780 563   *Fax* 0-7-378 0564
Email jean@lakeedgelodge.co.nz   *Website* www.lakeedgelodge.co.nz

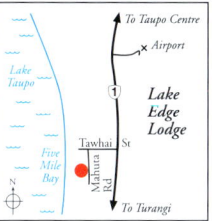

DIRECTIONS: From Taupo township take SH 1 south for 8km to Five Mile Bay. Turn right into Tawhai St & left into Mahuta St. Lake Edge Lodge halfway along on right. From Turangi, take SH 1 north towards airport.

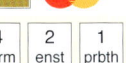

4 bdrm	2 enst	1 prbth

Room rate $180–$300
Seasonal or long-stay rates available

Continental breakfast hamper extra
Self-catering

Located right on the water's edge at Five Mile Bay on Lake Taupo, Lake Edge Lodge has been renovated and refurbished to provide three self-catering accommodation options. The Boat Shed is a totally self-contained apartment comprising two bedrooms, a bathroom and a full kitchen, and opens to a garden setting. The Kowhai and Tui Rooms have an ensuite bathroom and kitchenette each, and open directly to the lake, with views of Mt Ruapehu across the water. A continental breakfast hamper can be provided by arrangement. Restaurants and cafés are 10 minutes' drive north at Taupo town centre. A rowing boat and two canoes are available for guest use, and the beach is popular for swimming and watersports.

FACILITIES

- Boatshed apartment: 1 queen & 1 twin bedroom share 1 bathroom & double spa bath
- Kowhai: 1 king/twin ensuite bedroom with double spa bath
- Tui: 1 queen ensuite bedroom
- hair dryers, toiletries, heated towel rails & bathrobes
- fresh flowers
- central heating
- barbecues

- continental breakfast hamper by request, $12.50 pp
- kitchen or kitchenette
- open fireplace, nibbles, TV, video, CDs, games, artwork, books & desk in lounge
- email, fax & phone available
- laundry available, $5
- secure car & boat parking
- courtesy passenger transfer

ACTIVITIES AVAILABLE

- outdoor cocker spaniel on site
- rowing boat & 2 canoes available for guest use
- walks, swimming beach, watersports & fly fishing at lake edge from site
- white water rafting, transport available from door
- fishing pools at Waitahanui Stream, 2-min drive
- parasailing; bungy jumping
- bush walks; horse trekking

- Taupo restaurants & cafés, 10-min drive
- hot mineral pools
- scenic flights
- jet boating
- trout fishing at Tongariro River, 30-min drive south
- Tongariro National Park & skiing at Whakapapa, 1-hr drive

TURANGI
Ika Lodge

Hosts Suzanne and Kerry Simpson

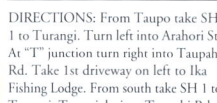

155 Taupahi Road, Turangi   *Postal* P O Box 259, Turangi
Phone 0-7-386 5538   *Fax* 0-7-386 5538
Email ikalodge@xtra.co.nz   *Website* www.ika.co.nz

| 4 bdrm | 2 enst | 1 prbth | Double $140–$180 Single $120–$140 | *Includes breakfast* **Apartment rate $160–$260** | *Lunch & dinner extra* *Self-catering in apartment* |

DIRECTIONS: From Taupo take SH 1 to Turangi. Turn left into Arahori St. At "T" junction turn right into Taupahi Rd. Take 1st driveway on left to Ika Fishing Lodge. From south take SH 1 to Turangi. Turn right into Taupahi Rd.

Originally designed as a fishing lodge in 1955, Ika was renovated and extended under the guidance of architect John Wilcox in 1998 to offer two guestrooms and two-bedroom self-contained apartment. The highlight for guests is fly fishing for trout with the resident guide Kerry, who is a member of the New Zealand Professional Fishing Guide Association. The Lodge has direct access to the Tongariro River, a haven for brown and rainbow trout, as well as being close to Lake Taupo. Guided river excursions are available for anglers of all levels of experience, or the Lodge's own six-metre boat can be used on the lake. Heli-fishing can also be arranged. Kerry's fishing is complemented by Suzanne's cuisine – as resident chef she offers all meals to suit guests' requirements.

FACILITIES

- 1 queen ensuite bedroom downstairs
- 1 queen/twin ensuite bedroom upstairs
- 1 self-contained apartment with 1 queen/twin & 1 king/twin bedroom
- hair dryers, toiletries & heated towel rails in all 3 bathrooms
- cotton bed linen, flowers, Sky TV & tea/coffee in all 4 bedrooms
- phone, fax & email in office
- open fire in guest lounge
- resident chef
- 3-course dinner, $50 pp, BYO
- lunch by request, $25 pp in guests' dining room
- full kitchen in apartment for self-catering
- powder room
- off-street parking
- courtesy passenger transfer

ACTIVITIES AVAILABLE

- garden seating on site
- direct river access from site
- fly fishing for trout in lake & rivers, resident guide
- raft & heli-fishing arranged
- golf course, 1km away
- white water rafting
- walking & hiking
- Turangi shopping centre & township, 5-min drive
- restaurants, walking distance
- Lake Taupo, 10-min drive
- thermal pools, 1km drive
- eco river raft tours
- Tongariro National Park, world heritage area
- horse trekking
- skiing, 30-min drive, July–October
- Taupo airport, 40-min drive

Ika Lodge

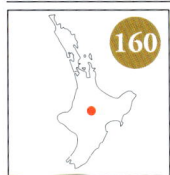

TURANGI
Tui Lodge

Hosts Ian and Frances Jenkins

196 Taupahi Road, Turangi
Phone 0-7-386 0840   *Mobile* 0274 411 625   *Fax* 0-7-386 0843
Email tui-lodge@xtra.co.nz   *Website* www.troutfishingguidesnz.com

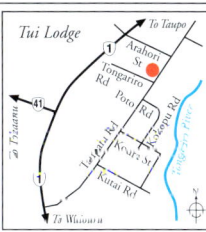

DIRECTIONS: From Taupo take SH 1 to Turangi. Turn left into Arahori St. At "T" junction turn right into Taupahi Rd. Tui Lodge on right. From south take SH 1 to Turangi. Turn right into Taupahi Rd. Tui Lodge on left.

4 bdrm	4 enst	1 pdrm

Double $300
Single $180

Includes breakfast
Group booking rates available

Tui Lodge is located near the Tongariro River, renowned for fly fishing for brown and rainbow trout. Ian, who is a member of the New Zealand Professional Guides Association, is happy to take guests fishing in the Tongariro, having been successful in catching many large trout including a 19-pounder in June 1990. He also takes guests fly fishing in some of the back country rivers. Purpose-built and opened in 2005, Tui Lodge is a blend of classic and contemporary design, offering four ensuite guest-rooms with views to Mt Pihanga and the Kaimanawa ranges. Guests enjoy watching the birdlife on river walks, especially the native tui which are plentiful throughout spring and summer when they feast first on kowhai blossom and then on the flax.

FACILITIES

- 4 king ensuite bedrooms
- cotton bed linen
- writing desk & mineral water in all 4 bedrooms
- hair dryer, toiletries, heated floor & towel rails in ensuites
- wheelchair access
- private guest lounge with open fire, tea/coffee, nibbles, Sky TV, artwork, library & books
- laundry facilities available

- full cooked or continental breakfast served in dining room
- fresh flowers
- email & fax, by request
- central heating
- powder room
- 2 friendly cats on site
- private guest entrance
- on-site parking

ACTIVITIES AVAILABLE

- in-house massage bookings
- barbecue available
- bird-watching on site & by river
- Tongariro Crossing
- guided river & lake fishing
- mountain & local river walks
- hot mineral pools
- Tongariro National Trout Centre
- sky diving; horse trekking
- bungy jumping; scenic flights

- restaurants, within walking distance
- heli fishing; rafting
- golf course
- Maori culture show
- 4WD adventures
- Huka Falls
- winter ski-fields
- Taupo, 45-min drive
- airport, 35-min drive

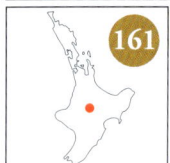

TURANGI
River Birches

Host Gill Osborne

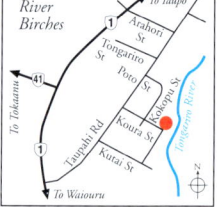

19 Koura Street, Turangi
Phone 0-7-386 0445   *Mobile* 027 406 3650   *Fax* 0-7-386 0442
Email reservations@riverbirches.co.nz   *Website* www.riverbirches.co.nz

DIRECTIONS: From Taupo take SH 1 to Turangi. Turn left into Arahori St. At "T" junction turn right into Taupahi Rd. Take 2nd left into Koura St, to River Birches on left. From south take SH 1 to Turangi. Turn right to Taupahi.

3 bdrm	3 enst	1 pdrm	Double $295–$325 Single $265–$295	*Includes breakfast* House rate $750	*Lunch & dinner extra*

Set on the banks of the Tongariro River, renowned for the Major Jones and Breakfast Pools adjacent to the property, River Birches is a boutique lodge just two minutes' walk to trout fishing. The three ensuite guestrooms are named after popular fishing spots on the river – Admiral (with hot tub), Duchess and Major – each opening to a private verandah and the award-winning garden. Guests can stroll beneath the mature birch trees frequented by native birds beside the river, and there is an enclosed garden outside the bathrooms. Guests enjoy using the fully equipped fitness room, and relaxing on the decking with apéritifs in summer or in the drawing room in front of the fire in winter. Meals are served in the dining room, or alfresco, and room service is available.

FACILITIES

- Admiral: 1 super-king ensuite bedroom with TV, DVD, mini-bar & hot tub
- Duchess: 1 super-king/twin ensuite bedroom
- Major: 1 super-king/twin ensuite bedroom
- 100% cotton bed linen; down duvet, bathrobes & slippers, tea/coffee, IDD phone, writing desk, broadband & iPOD music station in each bedroom
- baths, hair dryers, toiletries, heated towel rails & floor
- full cooked breakfast
- lunch, $25 pp; 3-course dinner with wine, $50 pp; wine extra
- open fire, tea/coffee, nibbles & bar in lounge & family room
- Sky TV, DVDs in family room
- air conditioning; heating; WiFi
- courtesy passenger transfer to/from Taupo; on-site parking

ACTIVITIES AVAILABLE

- direct river access from garden
- fully equipped fitness room
- BBQ & mountain bikes available
- fishing gear available & guiding arranged
- fly fishing & heli-fishing
- Tongariro River walks adjacent
- rafting & kayaking
- 18-hole golf course
- bush walks
- horse riding
- winter skiing/snowboarding
- 4 restaurants, 5-min drive
- hot thermal pools, 7-min drive
- scenic flights; jet boating
- boating & fishing on Lake Taupo, 10-min drive
- hiking & tramping
- Turangi township, 5-min drive
- Taupo airport, 40-min drive

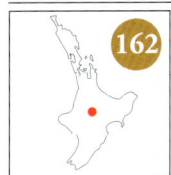

PUKAWA BAY, LAKE TAUPO
Paratiho-by-the-Lake Cottage

Hosts John and Valda Milner

10 Kowhai Drive, Upper Pukawa Bay, R D 1, Turangi
Phone 0-7-386 6318   *Email* milners@paratihonz.co.nz
Fax 0-7-386 6418   *Website* www.paratihonz.com

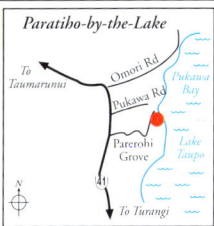
Paratiho-by-the-Lake

DIRECTIONS: From Turangi, take SH 41 north for 14km. Turn right into Parerohi Grove. After 300m, turn left into Kowhai Drive. Continue 100m to drive on left, to Paratiho-by-the-Lake. Cottage on right.

| 2 bdrm | 1 prbth | Cottage rate $160 for 2 persons
Extra persons $50 each | *Self-catering*
No meals available | |

Meaning "Paradise", Paratiho-by-the-Lake is located overlooking the western shores of Lake Taupo with views to Taupo township with relected lights at night in the distance. Purpose-built in 1996, this self-contained cottage is 100 metres from the main homestead, which ensures guest privacy for single-party bookings. A full kitchen enables guests to self-cater. French doors open to a large sundeck with a gas barbecue and outdoor furniture for alfresco dining. Paratiho is set in 2.6 hectares (6.5 acres) of developing gardens including 7,000 trees, a small vineyard, olive grove and pond, with native trees attracting birdlife. John is a retired fishing guide, and enjoys assisting fishing enthusiasts. Turangi township is just 14 kilometres' drive south.

FACILITIES

- private party bookings only
- 1 self-contained cottage with 2 super-king/twin bedrooms & 1 private bathroom
- hair dryers, toiletries, heated towel rails, bath & bathrobes
- panoramic lake views
- self-serve laundry facilities
- phone, fax, email available
- children & pets welcome

- full kitchen for self-catering
- breakfast basket, $15 pp
- lounge with log fire & TV
- gas BBQ & loungers on patio
- garaging
- boat parking
- friendly labrador retriever dog, Travis, on site
- courtesy guest transfer to & from Taupo Airport

ACTIVITIES AVAILABLE

- 2.6ha developing gardens with small vineyard & olive grove
- fly fishing for trout in Tongariro River & streams, resident guide
- guided trout fishing by boat on Lakes Taupo or Otamangakau
- watersports – white water rafting, kayaking, canoeing, yachting, waterskiing & swimming
- private gardens open to visit
- horse trekking

- restaurants, Tokaanu 8km & Turangi 14km
- choice of local bush/lake & Tongariro National Park walks
- thermal pools, 8km; scenic flights
- 18-hole golf course
- Tongariro National Trout Centre complex, 15 mins
- snow skiing, July–Sept

Paratiho-by-the-Lake

Paratiho-by-the-Lake

MANUTUKE, GISBORNE
Opou – A Country House

Hosts Robyn Bickford and Manav Garewal

95 Whakato Road, Manutuke   *Postal* P O Box 139, Manutuke, via Gisborne
Phone 0-6-862 8732   *Mobile* 025 209 6431   *Fax* 0-6-862 8042
Email stay@opoucountryhouse.co.nz   *Website* www.opoucountryhouse.co.nz

DIRECTIONS: From Gisborne take SH 2 south for 13.5km to turnoff for Manutuke. Turn right past church into Manutuke. Turn right into Whakato Rd & cross 2 cattle stops to Opou – A Country House.

| 4 bdrm | 2 enst | 2 prbth | 2 pdrm | **Double $420–$675** **Single $420–$506** | *Includes breakfast* **House rate $1,690 up to 8 persons** | *Lunch & dinner extra* |

Opou was built in the 1880s by Captain Read, a well known trader in Gisborne. From 1910 it has been owned by the Clarks, a pioneering landowning family of the Gisborne area. Opou is set in almost two hectares of garden surrounded by a further 12 hectares (30 acres) of farmland. This large house is suitable for family groups, small conferences and retreats, as well as individual travellers. The four bedrooms are upstairs, spacious and furnished with an eclectic mix of furniture. A full Western or Asian breakfast is served downstairs or alfresco, and lunch or picnics are available by arrangement. Opou is licensed, and complimentary pre-dinner drinks can be folllowed by dinner, or a driver can take guests into the restaurants 15 minutes away.

FACILITIES

- 2 super-king/twin ensuite bedrooms
- 2 super-king/twin bedrooms with private bathrooms
- bathrobes, demist mirrors, hair dryers, double basins & toiletries
- cotton bed linen, fresh flowers, chocolates, tea/coffee in rooms
- Sky TV, video, DVD, CDs, library, nibbles, licensed bar
- 4 open fireplaces
- Western or Asian breakfast
- picnic/lunch menu $55 pp
- 3–4-course dinner, $80 pp
- courtyard with open fire for alfresco dining
- phone, fax & email available
- children welcome
- laundry available, extra charge
- Hindi, Urdu & Malay spoken
- on-site parking; helipad

ACTIVITIES AVAILABLE

- swimming pool on site
- garden tours, pheasant, quail, 2 dogs & 1 cat on site
- croquet & pétanque on site
- in-house beauty treatments, massage & cooking classes
- Gisborne Wine & Food Festival in October
- vineyards; farm activities
- sea & river fishing; boat tours
- restaurants, Gisborne, 15-min drive, driver available
- shopping; arts & crafts; golf
- safe beaches; horse trekking
- Maori culture & arts; picnics
- Eastwood Hill Arboretum
- back country 4WD adventures
- helicopter tours; charter flights
- airport, 12-min drive
- Gisborne City, 13.5 km north

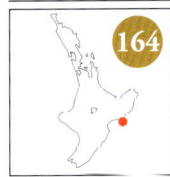

OPOUTAMA, MAHIA
Tunanui Station Cottages

Hosts Leslie and Ray Thompson

1001 Tunanui Road, Nuhaka R D 8, Opoutama, Mahia, Northern Hawke's Bay
Phone 0-6-837 5790   *Mobile* 027 240 2421   *Fax* 0-6-837 5791
Email tunanui@xtra.co.nz   *Website* www.tunanui.co.nz

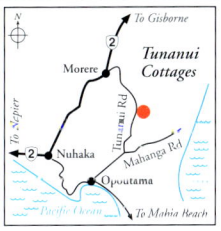

DIRECTIONS: Take SH 2 to Nuhaka. Travel east to Opoutama. Continue straight ahead into Mahanga Rd. Travel 2km, then turn left into Tunanui Rd. Travel 4km to Tunanui Station on the right.

4 bdrm	2 prbth	3 bdrm	1 prbth	Cottage rate for 2 persons $195	Low-season weekly rates	*Self-catering*
				Extra adults $50 each, children $30	*Breakfast provisions & dinner extra*	

Tunanui Station is a 2,000-hectare sheep and cattle farm in the hills overlooking Mahia Peninsula, in Northern Hawke's Bay. Owned and hosted by a third-generation farming family, Tunanui offers two separate fully self-contained cottages providing guests with privacy and seclusion. The Cottage (*above*) is nestled among trees, backed by five hectares of native bush. Built in 1898, The Cottage still features the Edwardian layout of the rooms, with original kauri doors, rimu flooring and open fireplace in the lounge. A few hundred metres down the road, set in its private garden, is The Farmhouse (*below*) with panoramic views of farmland, the peninsula and the ocean beyond. The Farmhouse, built in 1975, is larger and more spacious than The Cottage. Both are well-appointed and furnished in a comfortable country style with some antique furniture. They are suitable for longer stays to provide time for unwinding in the seclusion of Tunanui Station and for exploring the farm and surrounding region.

FACILITIES

- 2 self-contained cottages
- single-party bookings
- 3 bedrooms & 1 bathroom with dual-shower in The Cottage
- 4 bedrooms & 2 bathrooms with bath in The Farmhouse
- cotton bed linen, hair dryers, feather & wool bedding
- fresh flowers & fresh herbs
- lounges with open fire, TV, video, CD & NZ books
- children welcome
- phone card guest phones
- fax available
- guest laundries with irons
- 2 full kitchens for self-catering
- breakfast provisions, by arrangement, extra
- dinner/BBQ with hosts, by arrangement, extra
- verandahs with BBQs
- underfloor heating, separate dining room & dishwasher in The Farmhouse only
- secure parking
- 2 car garaging with The Farmhouse
- helipad
- farm airstrip
- low-season May-September weekly rates available

ACTIVITIES AVAILABLE

On site:
- 2,000-ha (5,100-acre) farm
- seasonal farm activities with sheep, cattle, working dogs & horse-riding for advanced riders arranged, extra
- farm roads for scenic walks & mountain biking
- secluded river valley
- private river swimming
- picnics; trout fishing
- historic concrete viaduct
- indigenous forest & birds
- guests' horses welcome
- grass tennis court

Off site:
- Mahia Beach; fishing charters
- hot mineral pools at Morere
- private gardens to visit
- guided caving trips
- 9-hole golf course, clubs hire
- guided tours to carved Maori meeting house on marae
- marae community dinners
- wineries, 60-min drive north
- 2 arboretums, 90-min drive
- Lake Waikaremoana, 90 mins
- bar at Bistro at Mahia Beach
- Gisborne City, 60 mins north
- Wairoa town, 40 mins south

MAHIA, GISBORNE

The Quarters

Hosts Malcolm and June Rough

867 Mahanga Road, Mahia   *Postal* R D 8, Nuhaka
Phone 0-6-837 5751   *Email* m.rough@xtra.co.nz
Fax 0-6-837 5721   *Website* www.quarters.co.nz

DIRECTIONS: From Gisborne, take SH 2 south to Nuhaka. Turn left towards Mahia. Travel to Opoutama. Continue straight on & do not cross railway line. Continue past Mahanga Beach turn-off to Te Au farm at end.

| 2 bdrm | 1 prbth | Double $165–$185 Extra persons $25–$30 each | Self-catering Breakfast provisions & dinner extra |

With unimpeded ocean views, the site on Te Au Farm was carefully chosen for The Quarters. The fully renovated shearers' quarters were relocated to this coastal farm to provide total privacy and comfort for those wanting to get away from it all. Single-party bookings of eight people can be accommodated. The queen-size bedroom, designer bunkroom and living room all open to the large deck for dining and taking in the truly panoramic sea vistas. A fully equipped kitchen makes self-catering easy, with fresh crayfish when available. Home-cooked meals can also be provided. Guests can join in activities on the sheep and beef farm. Fishing from the rock is popular and there are extensive marked walks with coastal, farm and bush views.

FACILITIES

- self-contained accommodation
- single-party bookings only
- 1 queen bedroom
- 1 twin room with 2 sets of designer bunks
- 1 private bathroom
- toiletries & heated towel rails
- self-serve laundry
- panoramic views over ocean
- children welcome
- fresh bread & crayfish (when available) on arrival
- fully equipped kitchen for self-catering
- breakfast provisions by arrangement, extra
- dinner by arrangement: frozen home-made meals or BBQ with hosts, extra
- large glass doors opening to peaceful deck

ACTIVITIES AVAILABLE

- BBQ with hosts, by request
- walks on 711ha sheep & beef farm & Bush Reserve
- viewing sunrise over ocean
- mountain bikes for hire
- limestone tennis court
- farm activities on site
- hunting – pig & goat
- crayfish & paua collecting
- marae visits; golf courses
- trout fishing & river swimming
- Mahanga Beach, nearby, 2-min drive to 6km sandy shoreline for swimming, surfing, boogie boarding & walking
- social excursions around Mahia Peninsula
- 2 restaurants & cafés, 15 mins
- wineries; Morere Hot Pools
- Gisborne City, 1-hour drive

The Quarters

BLUFF HILL, NAPIER
Freemans on Clyde

Hosts Anthony and Sue Freeman

17 Clyde Road, Bluff Hill, Napier

Phone 0-6-835 9124   *Mobile* 021 171 0209   *Email* freemo@iprohome.co.nz
Fax 0-6-835 9129   *Website* hawkesbaynz.com/pages/freemansonclyde

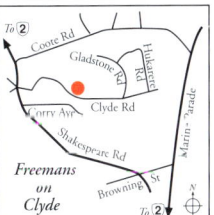

DIRECTIONS: From north take SH 2 to Hyderabad roundabout. Turn left into SH 50. Turn right into Coote Rd, left into Shakespeare Rd & left into Clyde Rd. From south, take Marine Pde & turn left into Coote Rd as above.

3 bdrm	3 enst

Room rate $180   **Winter rates available**   *Includes breakfast*

Originally built in 1854, Freemans on Clyde is one of Napier's earliest farmhouses that has survived the devastating 1931 earthquake. Located on Napier Hill, this colonial farmhouse features Cape Cod-style settler architecture and now offers three ensuite guestrooms. Guests enjoy relaxing on the large verandah and patio in the summer and beside the open fire in the guest lounge in winter. An extensive cottage garden includes an orchard of citrus trees, plums, olives and avocados. For breakfast guests wander five minutes down the hill to the city to Sue and Anthony's *Caffe Aroma*. Here they can choose from the full café menu included in the room rate. Waffles, bagels, a full English breakfast, Eggs Benedict or other cooked options are available.

FACILITIES

- 3 queen ensuite bedrooms
- heated towel rails
- cotton bed linen
- private guest lounge with open fire, tea/coffee & herbal teas
- phone in family room
- TV, CD-player, library, artwork, games & magazines
- historic architecture
- breakfast in *Caffe Aroma*, hosts' café downtown, with full cooked & continental breakfast menu
- email available
- fresh flowers
- private guest entrance
- off-street parking
- Molly the fox terrier in residence

ACTIVITIES AVAILABLE

- large cottage garden on site & orchard with citrus trees, olives, avocados & plums
- downtown Napier shops, 5-min walk away
- bush walks
- Art Deco walks
- gardens to visit
- golf courses
- vineyard tours
- many restaurants, bars & cafés within walking distance
- gannet colony
- national aquarium of NZ
- marineland
- public gardens
- earthquake exhibition
- Hastings, 20 mins
- Taupo, 1½-hour drive
- Gisborne, 2½-hour drive

NAPIER
The County Hotel

Hosts Christopher and Angela Barons

12 Browning Street, Napier   *Postal* P O Box 345, Napier
Phone 0-6-835 7800   *Freephone* 0800 THE HOTEL   *Fax* 0-6-835 7797
Email countyhotel@xtra.co.nz   *Website* www.countyhotel.co.nz

18 bdrm	18 enst	1 pdrm	**Room rate $150–$550**	*All meals extra*
			Seasonal and B&B rates available	

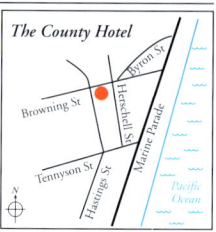

The County Hotel

DIRECTIONS: In the CBD of Napier. Follow "Port" signs to Marine Pde. Turn west into Browning St. The County Hotel & Anatole's Café are on the left.

The County Hotel

Originally built in 1909, The County Hotel is the only example of the Victorian-Edwardian classical revival style that survived the devastating 1931 Napier earthquake. Redevelopment since 1993 has transformed the former County Council building into the boutique hotel as well as Chambers Fine Dining and Seafood Restaurant and the Churchill's Champagne and Snug Bar. Historic Edwardian Gothic features with Art Deco influences have been preserved, such as the high ceilings and wood panelling. The 18 bedrooms include the Regal Suite opening to a spacious balcony, and many of the ensuite bathrooms feature a therapeutic spa bath. The County Hotel is close to all of Napier City's attractions and the nearby vineyards are popular.

FACILITIES

- 2 twin & 16 king & queen ensuite bedrooms, many with spa baths
- 1 Regal Suite with 1 king & 1 queen bedroom, 2 bathrooms, lounge with fireplace & large balcony
- each bedroom includes writing bureau, Sky TV, phone, modem, fax & electric blanket
- 2 wheelchair-access rooms
- all rooms air-conditioned
- children welcome

- Chambers Fine Dining & Seafood Restaurant on site
- Churchill's Champagne & Snug Bar
- complimentary newspaper
- guest library with port
- function rooms
- business centre
- foreign currency exchange
- 18 carparks

ACTIVITIES AVAILABLE

- Chambers Fine Dining & Seafood Restaurant on site
- Napier city shopping precinct
- Art Deco walk
- theatres
- Ocean Spa swimming pool complex
- Marineland
- fountains; aquarium
- Kiwi House

- restaurants & cafés
- vineyards & orchards
- private gardens to visit
- public parks & seaside gardens
- beach; fishing
- heritage trails
- art galleries
- museums
- 1 of only 3 mainland gannet colonies in NZ & the world

NAPIER
Apartment at the Dome

Manager Russell Angus

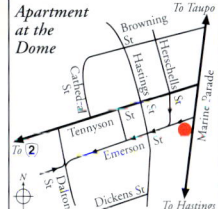

Dome Apartments, Level 1, Corner Marine Parade and Emerson Street, Napier
Postal 10 Cobden Road, Napier   *Phone* 0-6-835 8770   *Fax* 0-6-835 8770
Email rangus@xtra.co.nz   *Website* friars.co.nz/hosts/dome.html

DIRECTIONS: Take SH 2 to Napier and follow "Port" signs to Marine Pde. Apartment at the Dome on corner of Emerson St, on west side of Parade, opposite soundshell & ocean.

| 2 bdrm | 2 enst | Apartment rate $425 for 2 persons
Extra room $50 | *Includes continental breakfast provisions*
Long-stay rates available | *Self-catering* |

Located on Marine Parade in the heart of Napier City is the Art Deco building of The Dome Apartments. Upstairs, above a café, is this self-contained apartment with its spacious rooms and high ceilings. The rooms are furnished with attention to detail including Art Deco features of the era in which it was built after the devastating Napier earthquake of 1931. The living room opens into a private sunroom, and there is an extra day bed in the second bedroom. Guests can self-cater in the well equipped kitchen or dine at the many cafés and restaurants within walking distance. Popular activities are strolling along Marine Parade beside the ocean, taking an Art Deco tour of the city, and visiting the award-winning wineries of the district.

FACILITIES

- one-party bookings only
- 1 king & 1 double bedroom
- 2 ensuites, each with double shower, hair dryer, toiletries, heated towel rails & bathrobes
- Egyptian cotton towels
- cotton bed linen; fresh flowers
- lounge with Sky TV, video, DVD, CD-player, music, writing desk, books & phone
- laundry facilities in apartment
- children over 10 yrs welcome
- full kitchen for self-catering
- continental breakfast provisions supplied
- email facilities; elevator
- living room opens to sunroom
- Spanish spoken by host
- courtesty passenger transfer
- covered carpark nearby

ACTIVITIES AVAILABLE

- seashore & bush walks
- private gardens to visit
- national aquarium
- Art Deco architecture tours
- earthquake museum
- art studios & galleries
- award-winning wineries
- 4 championship golf courses
- heritage trails
- cafés, bars, brasseries, alfresco restaurants & shops at doorstep
- 1 of only 3 mainland gannet colonies in NZ & world
- swimming beaches
- horse riding
- public parks & gardens
- guided fly & deep-sea fishing
- flightseeing; hot air ballooning
- gliding & paragliding

© Friars' Guide to New Zealand Accommodation for the Discerning Traveller

PUKETAPU, NAPIER
Silverford

Hosts Diana & Grant Roberts

358 Dartmoor Road, Puketapu, Napier
Phone 0-6-844 5600   *Email* homestay@paradise.net.nz
Fax 0-6-844 4423   *Website* www.silverford.co.nz

DIRECTIONS: From Napier, travel west to Puketapu. Turn left into Dartmoor Rd. Travel 3.5km to Silverford on right, & up oak driveway. From Hastings, cross bridge into Swamp Rd, turn right, then left twice.

3 bdrm	1 enst	1 prbth	Double $260–$285	Single $215	*Includes breakfast*

Built from native kauri in 1906, with Tudor-style architecture, Silverford is a paradigm country residence designed by Tilleard Natusch to suit New Zealand timbers and conditions. The original rimu interiors with panelling and fireplaces remain intact, as does the inner courtyard garden. The deep verandahs provide shade from Hawke's Bay sunshine and open to the extensive garden. Guests are served breakfast in the country kitchen or alfresco on the verandah. Sited at the end of a half-kilometre oak-lined driveway, Silverford is set in seven hectares (17 acres) where guests enjoy the spacious lawns, established trees, ponds and orchards, in the quiet of the countryside, yet within easy access of the nearby cities. Dinner is available at The Mission Winery nearby.

FACILITIES

- 1 queen bedroom with ensuite bathroom
- 1 king & 1 double bedroom share 1 guest bathroom
- 1 bath available
- heated towel rails & hair dryer in both bathrooms
- electric blankets
- central heating
- fresh flowers
- breakfast served in kitchen, or alfresco on verandah
- tea & coffee available
- phone, fax, email available
- laundry available
- historic architecture
- garden setting with ponds, mature trees & orchards
- rural views
- on-site parking

ACTIVITIES AVAILABLE

- swimming pool on site
- friendly farm animals
- à la carte dinner at The Mission Winery, 8km
- horse trekking
- golf courses
- gardens open to visit
- hot air ballooning
- paragliding
- bush walks; beaches
- Taradale restaurants, 10-min drive
- restaurants at Napier & Hastings, 20-min drive
- wine tasting & vineyard lunches
- trout fishing
- aquarium
- gannet colony
- Napier airport, 25 mins

NAPIER, CAPE KIDNAPPERS
Merriwee Country Home

Host Jeanne Richards

29 Gordon Road, Te Awanga, Hawke's Bay
Phone 0-6-875 0111   *Mobile* 021 214 5023   *Fax* 0-6-875 0111
Email merriwee@xtra.co.nz   *Website* www.merriwee.co.nz

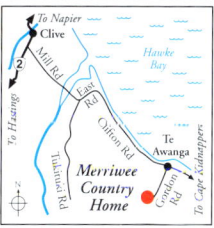

DIRECTIONS: From Napier, take SH 2 south through Clive & turn left into Mill Rd. Follow signs towards Cape Kidnappers. Take Clifton Rd to Te Awanga village. Turn right into Gordon Rd to Merriwee at end.

| 5 bdrm | 2 enst | 1 prbth | Room rate $150–$240
House rate $1,000 | *Includes breakfast*
Self-catering in suite | *Dinner extra* |

Set in a rural garden surrounded by two hectares of apricot orchards, Merriwee Country Home is an original villa built in 1908 on an elevated site overlooking the ocean. Te Awanga beach is just a stroll away, while the mainland gannet colony and new golf course at Cape Kidnappers is nearby. Merriwee offer guests four spacious bedrooms, and a self-contained suite, with French doors opening to large verandahs and a courtyard. A full breakfast with crêpes and other cooked options is served in the large country kitchen, and dinner is available by arrangement. Three wineries are within walking distance and restaurants at Napier, Hastings and Havelock North are all 15 minutes' drive away. Guests enjoy relaxing in the swimming pool area on site.

FACILITIES

- 1 self-contained suite with queen bedroom, ensuite, sitting room, kitchenette & private entrance
- 2 queen bedrooms with ensuite
- 1 king, 1 twin bedroom share 1 private bathroom
- hair dryer, toiletries & heated towel rails in all 3 bathrooms; 1 with wheelchair access
- cotton bed linen; fresh flowers
- children welcome; cat & dog on site

- full breakfast served
- 3-course dinner & glass of wine, $45 pp; BYO
- tea/coffee, fruit, nibbles & home baking
- 3 living rooms with open fireplaces, TV, CDs, piano, games, artwork, books & writing desk
- email, fax & phones
- off-street parking

ACTIVITIES AVAILABLE

- salt-water swimming pool, pétanque, cricket & soccer on site
- walks in 2ha grounds with gardens, lawns & apricot orchard on site
- wineries & vineyards, within walking distance
- new Cape Kidnappers golf course & mainland gannet colony nearby
- beach walks & ocean swimming
- hot pools; theatre & galleries

- restaurants & cafés, 15 mins
- guided walking, wine & art trails; horse riding
- gardens open to visit
- hot air balloons
- fishing – river & beach
- Art Deco Napier, 15 mins
- National Aquarium of NZ
- Marineland & model railway town, Lilliput

Te Awanga
Cape Estate – Te Awanga Downs

Hosts Marki and Chris Nilsson

34 Gordon Road, Te Awanga, Hawke's Bay
Phone 0-6-875 0419   *Mobile* 027 421 0016   *Fax* 0-6-875 0419
Email info@teawangadowns.com   *Website* www.teawangadowns.com

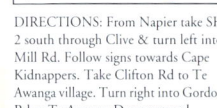

DIRECTIONS: From Napier take SH 2 south through Clive & turn left into Mill Rd. Follow signs towards Cape Kidnappers. Take Clifton Rd to Te Awanga village. Turn right into Gordon Rd to Te Awanga Downs at end.

6 bdrm	3 enst	2 prbth	1 shbth	1 pdrm	House rate $900 up to 6 persons Extra persons $100 each	*Includes breakfast for 1st morning* *Self-catering Lunch & dinner extra*

Te Awanga Downs at Cape Estate is a fully self-contained farm homestead for single-party bookings. It is located 15 minutes south of the Art Deco city of Napier, and just five minutes from the entrance to the mainland gannet colony and the new international standard golf course, both at Cape Kidnappers. Set in nearly two hectares (four acres) of lawns and garden, with views overlooking vineyards to Hawke Bay and the sea beyond, Te Awanga Downs offers two grass tennis courts, a swimming pool and farm walks for guests. Furnished with antiques, the formal dining room caters for up to 10 guests, with a qualified chef on call. There are restaurants, cafés, bars and wineries nearby, and guests can self-cater in the fully equipped kitchen if desired.

FACILITIES

- one-party bookings only
- 2 super-king/twin ensuite bedrooms in homestead
- 1 super-king ensuite bedroom in separate garden "courthouse" with fridge & tea/coffee
- 3 single bedrooms with 1 share bathroom; 2 extra bathrooms
- cotton bed linen; hair dryers, toiletries, heated towel rails, bathrobes & wheelchair access
- full kitchen for self-catering; breakfast for 1st morning & bottle of local wine
- lounge with open fire, Sky TV, video, CD-player, piano, artwork & library
- fax & phone; fresh flowers
- extensive outdoor living area
- self-serve laundry
- on-site parking; helipad
- children welcome

ACTIVITIES AVAILABLE

- games room with billiards table & grand piano
- swimming pool on site
- wood-fired & gas BBQs
- 2 grass tennis courts on site
- pétanque/boules & croquet
- farm & garden walks on site
- 4 golf courses, including Cape Kidnappers Golf Course, 5 mins
- gannet colony transport, 5 mins
- restaurants & cafés nearby
- 3 neighbouring vineyards, wineries & cafés
- beaches nearby
- arts & crafts tours
- Art Deco buildings, 15 mins
- Summer Festival Weekends
- Havelock North, 10 mins
- Napier City, 15-min drive
- Hastings City, 15 mins

HAVELOCK NORTH
Weldon Boutique Bed & Breakfast

Host Pracilla Hay

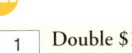

98 Te Mata Road, Havelock North   *Postal* P O Box 8170, Havelock North
Freephone 0800 206 499   *Phone* 0-6-877 7551   *Fax* 0-6-877 7051
Email pracilla@weldon.co.nz   *Website* www.weldon.co.nz

DIRECTIONS: Take SH 2 to Havelock North. From roundabout in centre of village, take Te Mata Rd north for 0.9km. Opposite St Hill Lane, turn right into driveway to Weldon Boutique B&B.

5 bdrm	2 prbth	1 shbth	Double $130–$150	*Includes breakfast*
			Single $100–$120	*Dinner extra*

Originally built circa 1906, Weldon offers a peaceful setting with French Provençale style ambience. Accommodation is provided in spacious bedrooms elegantly furnished with period and antique furniture. Television, tea and coffee facilities, fresh flowers, fine linen and fluffy towels are supplied in all five bedrooms. Breakfast of fresh local fruits and gourmet cooked options is served alfresco in the garden in summer, or in the dining room during winter. Dinner is also available by arrangement. Two toy poodle dogs, James and Thomas, love to greet the guests. Weldon is located within easy walking distance of the cafés, restaurants and Irish pub in the village of Havelock North. Napier City is just 20 minutes north.

FACILITIES

- 1 single & 2 double bedrooms with bathroom upstairs, heated towel rails & toiletries
- 1 queen & 1 twin bedroom with 1 private bathroom & clawfoot bath downstairs
- cotton bed linen & bathrobes
- hair dryer, fresh flowers, TV, tea/coffee, biscuits, water & port in each bedroom
- laundry available
- full breakfast with fresh local fruits & cooked option
- 2-course dinner with wine, $45 pp, by arrangement
- guest lounge with tea/coffee, TV, video, library & piano
- phone, fax & email available
- courtyard to relax in
- private guest entrance
- off-street parking

ACTIVITIES AVAILABLE

- wineries tours
- arts & crafts trails
- garden visits
- beaches
- walking
- golf courses
- bush walks
- Te Mata peak
- horse riding
- 20 mins village cafés, restaurants & shops, within walking distance
- golden beaches, 20 mins away
- paragliding
- gannet safari tours
- Havelock North, 10-min walk away
- Hastings, 10-min drive
- Art Deco Napier, 20 mins

HAVELOCK NORTH
Telegraph Hill Villa

Hosts Rose and Jeremy Gresson

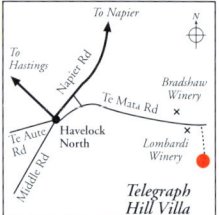

334 Te Mata Road, R D 12, Havelock North   *Mobile* 025 243 0508
Freephone 0800 672 681   *Phone* 0-6-877 5140   *Email* gresson@xtra.co.nz
Fax 0-6-877 5508   *Website* friars.co.nz/hosts/telegraph.html

DIRECTIONS: From Napier, travel south towards Havelock North. Turn left into St Hill Lane. At "T" turn left again into Te Mata Rd. Continue to Bradshaw Estate Winery on left. Turn right up 0.8km drive to Telegraph Hill.

2 bdrm	1 enst

Villa rate $230 for 2 persons
Extra persons $30 each

Includes breakfast provisions
Self-catering, or dinner extra

Set in the heart of Hawke's Bay's renowned wine country, on an olive grove, Telegraph Hill Villas offer a peaceful hilltop retreat with panoramic views over the plains to the mountains and ocean beyond. The self-contained 1996 Villa provides total privacy, separated from the hosts' house by an olive grove of 100 trees. The two bedrooms each have an adjoining dressing room and direct access to the ensuite bathroom. A fully equipped kitchen allows for self-catering, with breakfast provisions supplied. The barbecue is popular for alfresco dining and the north-facing verandah catches all-day sun. The adjacent floodlit tennis court and the hosts' swimming pool provide exercise for the more active. A second larger Villa is being built for summer 2005.

FACILITIES

- single-party bookings
- 1 queen & 1 twin bedroom
- dressing room with each bedroom
- cotton bed linen
- 1 ensuite bathroom, directly accessible from both bedrooms
- hair dryer, toiletries, heated towel rail & heated mirror
- Sky TV, phone, & ironing facilities
- laundry available in house
- breakfast provisions
- dinner by arrangement, extra
- fully equipped kitchen for self-catering
- fresh flowers; stereo
- guest barbecue
- fax & email available
- children welcome
- off-street parking

ACTIVITIES AVAILABLE

- BBQ on Villa site
- pétanque/boules on site
- floodlit tennis court
- swimming pool on site
- walks among 2,000 olive trees on 7ha olive estate on site – olive products for sale
- wine trails
- fishing
- scenic flights
- restaurants & shopping
- golf
- gardens to visit
- rivers, beaches & mountain walks close by
- gannets at Cape Kidnappers
- Splash Planet
- Napier, 28km
- Hastings, 10km
- Havelock North, 4km

HAVELOCK NORTH
The Barn

Hosts Don, Jean and Nicole Brown   *Mobile* 021 490 414

62 St Andrews Road, Havelock North   *Phone* 0-6-877 8801
Postal P O Box 8716, Havelock North, Hawke's Bay   *Fax* 0-6-877 7002
Email reservations@thebarn.co.nz   *Website* www.thebarn.co.nz

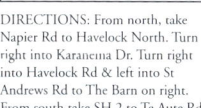

DIRECTIONS: From north, take Napier Rd to Havelock North. Turn right into Karanema Dr. Turn right into Havelock Rd & left into St Andrews Rd to The Barn on right. From south take SH 2 to Te Aute Rd.

| 3 bdrm | 1 enst | 2 prbth | Cottage rate **$290 for 2 persons** Extra rooms **$115 each** | *Includes breakfast hamper* **Minimum 2-night stay** | *Self-catering* |

The Barn

The Barn offers self-contained accommodation in a spacious new retreat, designed in the style of a traditional American barn. Named after the original barn on the two-hectare (six-acre) property, The Barn is set in extensive gardens and orchards with rural views towards Te Mata peak and the Ruahine Range beyond. Six guests can be accommodated in The Barn, in three bedrooms, each with its own bathroom. A fully equipped kitchen enables guests to self-cater if they wish. A breakfast hamper is delivered to The Barn each morning with home-baked bread, home-made jams, juice, cereal, fresh fruit and free-range eggs from the chickens on site. Guests can enjoy alfresco dining, and the restaurants in Havelock North are just three minutes away.

FACILITIES

- single-party bookings only
- 1 queen ensuite bedroom with tea/coffee facilities
- 1 double & 1 twin bedroom each with private bathroom
- cotton bed linen
- hair dryer, toiletries, heated towel rails & bathrobes in 3 bathrooms
- lounge with Sky TV, video, DVD, surround-sound system, CD-player & magazines
- full kitchen for self-catering
- full breakfast provisions delivered in hampers
- self-serve laundry
- email & fax by request
- air-conditioning & central heating; fresh flowers
- rural views
- on-site parking with garaging & carport

ACTIVITIES AVAILABLE

- over 2ha (6 acres) private gardens & orchards on site
- pétanque on site
- barbecue & courtyard
- vineyard tours
- safe-swimming rivers
- golf courses
- gardens open to visit
- fishing
- flightseeing
- restaurants, cafés, boutique shops & art galleries in Havelock North village, 3-min drive
- award-winning wineries
- beaches; walks
- mainland gannet colony
- airport, 20-min drive
- Hastings, 5-min drive
- Napier City, 15-min drive

The Barn

The Barn

© Friars' Guide to New Zealand Accommodation for the Discerning Traveller

HAVELOCK NORTH
Endsleigh Cottages

Hosts Margie and Denis Hardy

22 Endsleigh Road, Havelock North   *Postal* P O Box 8218, Havelock North
Phone 0-6-877 7588   *Mobile* 027 444 3800   *Fax* 0-6-876 0275
Email endsleigh.cottages@xtra.co.nz   *Website* www.endsleighcottages.co.nz

DIRECTIONS: From Havelock North, take Middle Rd south for 3km. Cross intersection with Gilpin & Iona Rds, then turn left into Endsleigh Rd. Endsleigh Cottages are on the right.

| 4 bdrm | 2 enst | 2 prbth | **Cottage rate $100–$200** **Extra persons $50 each** | *Includes breakfast* *Self-catering in 2 larger cottages* |

The three Endsleigh Cottages are located adjacent to the 1914 homestead set in an established garden among rural hills. The smallest cottage (*see above and below left*) dates from the early 1900s, while the middle cottage (*above right*) is a classic 1920s Arts and Crafts-style construction. The largest cottage (*below right*) has been constructed more recently with recycled components. Guests enjoy the mature garden that Margie and Denis have created since 1967. The two larger cottages are self-contained, each with a fully equipped kitchen for self-catering. All three cottages feature verandahs with garden views to the valley and mountains beyond. The smallest cottage is popular with honeymooners and the two larger cottages are suitable for entertaining.

FACILITIES

- smallest cottage: 1 king ensuite bedroom
- middle cottage: 1 king bedroom, 1 bathroom, 2 extra beds in sitting room
- largest cottage: 1 ensuite king, 1 queen bedroom with bathroom, 1 extra bed
- 8-seat dining table & piano in largest cottage
- phone in each cottage
- dinner by arrangement, $50 pp
- breakfast provisions supplied
- fully equipped kitchen & guest laundry in 2 larger cottages
- fresh flowers, cotton bed linen, claw-foot baths, toiletries, pedestal basins & hair dryers
- open fires, Sky TV, videos, VCR, CDs, cassettes, books & magazines in 2 larger cottages
- single-party bookings per cottage

ACTIVITIES AVAILABLE

- entertaining in 2 larger cottages
- gas BBQs & outdoor furniture
- 1ha garden on site with mature trees, lawns, borders, ponds, shrubberies & large aviary
- pétanque/boules, croquet & grass tennis court on site
- 6 mountain bikes available
- Kidnappers international golf course, 30-min drive
- restaurants, cafés & shopping in Havelock North
- best trout fishing river in region close by, guide available
- country walks; garden visits
- vineyard trails & restaurants
- watersports; beaches
- Art Deco Napier, 20 mins
- gannet colony at Cape Kidnappers, 30 mins

HAVELOCK NORTH
Muritai

Hosts Margie and Denis Hardy   Mobile 027 444 3800

68 Duart Road, Havelock North   *Phone* 0-6-877 7588
Postal P O Box 8218, Havelock North   *Fax* 0-6-876 0275
Email endsleigh.cottages@xtra.co.nz   *Website* www.muritai.co.nz

DIRECTIONS: From Havelock North village roundabout, take Te Mata Rd north-east. Turn right into Duart Rd. Muritai on right.

| 6 bdrm | 4 enst | 1 prbth | 1 pdrm | **House rate $700 per night** Multiple-night rates available | *Includes breakfast provisions* *Self-catering* |

Endsleigh Cottages

Muritai is one of several major houses established in Hawke's Bay in the 1890s. It now offers self-contained accommodation for up to 10 guests in four king-size and two single bedrooms with four bathrooms. There are quality furnishings including many antiques and notable contemporary paintings. Muritai is suitable for entertaining indoors in the spacious living rooms or outdoors where there is a large barbecue facility. Verandahs on all sides open to the established gardens surrounding the house, with views over Havelock North village and out to the coast. Generous breakfast provisions are supplied, with a full kitchen for self-catering, or catering services are available. Restaurants in Havelock North village are within walking distance.

FACILITIES

- single-party bookings only
- 4 king ensuite bedrooms
- 2 single bedrooms & 1 private bathroom
- cotton bed linen
- hair dryers & toiletries in all 5 bathrooms
- sitting room with open fire, Sky TV & music system to all main rooms
- fully equipped kitchen for self-catering
- breakfast provisions supplied
- catering services available by arrangement, extra
- full laundry facilities
- guest phone; fresh flowers
- children welcome
- central heating
- on-site parking & garaging

ACTIVITIES AVAILABLE

- barbecue area with outdoor furniture
- croquet on site
- professionally developed chip & putting green on site
- pétanque on site
- extensive garden on site
- Kidnappers international golf course, 30-min drive
- watersports
- restaurants in Havelock North, in walking distance
- best trout fishing river in region close by, guide available
- beaches
- vineyard trails & restaurants
- gardens to visit
- Art Deco Napier, 20 mins
- gannet colony at Cape Kidnappers, 30 mins

Endsleigh Cottages

Endsleigh Cottages

TUKITUKI VALLEY, HAWKE'S BAY
Tom's Cottages

Hosts Linda and Van Howard

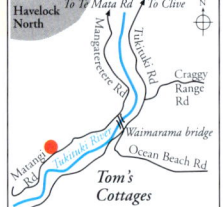

116 Matangi Road, Tukituki Valley, Havelock North   *Phone* 0-6-874 7900
Postal P O Box 8642, Havelock North, Hawke's Bay   *Mobile* 027 431 9086
Email vanh@clear.net.nz   *Website* www.tomscottages.co.nz   *Fax* 0-6-874 7909

DIRECTIONS: From Havelock North take Te Mata Rd for 3km. Turn right into Mangateretere Rd. Travel 4km towards Waimarama bridge & turn right into Matangi Rd. Travel 1km to Tom's Cottages on right.

3 bdrm   3 enst   **Cottage rate $200–$350**   *Includes breakfast provisions*   *Self-catering*

With rural views over the Tukituki River valley to Te Mata peak, Tom's Cottages are tucked away in a secluded spot just eight kilometres from Havelock North. The two cottages, built in 1920 and 1940, are fully restored and self-contained, offering total privacy by being set 500 metres apart from each other. The larger of the two, Big Tom's Cottage, provides two ensuite bedrooms, a bath, laundry, kitchen and living room including television and DVD-player. The smaller, Tom's Cottage, has one ensuite bedroom, kitchen and separate living room with television. Both cottages feature an additional open air bathtub, for wood-fired alfresco bathing, overlooking the river below. Farm fresh breakfast provisions are supplied daily.

FACILITIES

Big Tom's Cottage:
- 1 king & 1 queen bedroom & 2 ensuites, 1 with bath
- open-plan kitchen & living room with open fire, TV & DVD; self-service laundry
- phone jack

Tom's Cottage:
- 1 queen ensuite bedroom
- self-catering kitchen
- living room with TV

Both cottages:
- breakfast provisions daily
- hair dryer, toiletries & bathrobes in ensuites
- cotton bed linen; fresh flowers
- CD-player, books & magazines
- children & pets welcome
- cot or crib available
- 2 secluded outdoor baths
- on-site parking

ACTIVITIES AVAILABLE

- alfresco dining on decks
- BBQ on site
- local rivers & beaches
- farm, bush & mountain walks
- trout fishing
- wineries & wine trails
- private gardens to visit
- golf courses
- Splash Planet
- scenic flights
- restaurants & cafés nearby
- orchard & olive grove tours
- Havelock North village, 8km
- historic homes to visit
- Cape Kidnappers gannet colony
- Hastings, 20-min drive
- Art Deco Napier, National Aquarium of NZ & Marineland, 30-min drive
- Wellington, 3 hours south

WAIPUKURAU
Mynthurst Farmstay

Hosts Annabelle and David Hamilton

912 Lindsay Road, Waipukurau, R D 3, Hawke's Bay
Phone 0-6-857 8093   *Mobile* 027 2322458   *Fax* 0-6-857 8093
Email mynthurst@xtra.co.nz   *Website* friars.co.nz/hosts/mynthurst.html

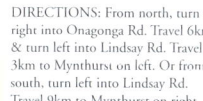

DIRECTIONS: From north, turn right into Onagonga Rd. Travel 6km & turn left into Lindsay Rd. Travel 3km to Mynthurst on left. Or from south, turn left into Lindsay Rd. Travel 9km to Mynthurst on right.

3 bdrm	1 enst	1 prbth	1 pdrm	Double $175 Single $90	*Includes breakfast* Extra children $35 each	*Lunch & dinner extra*

Mynthurst Farmstay is a family homestead on a working 560-hectare sheep and beef farm. Three guestrooms with two bathrooms are available for accommodation in this farmstay. Guests are welcome to observe farm activities, participate in farm tours, walk on the farm, or relax on the extensive terrace overlooking the garden with views to the Ruahine Range.

A separate sitting room is also available for relaxation. Annabelle serves a continental breakfast of seasonal fruits, cereals, scones or muffins alfresco on the terrace in summer, with eggs or other cooked dishes on request. Three-course dinner featuring local produce and wine is also available, by prior arrangement. Alternatively there are restaurants 10 minutes away in Waipukurau.

FACILITIES

- 1 super-king/twin, 1 double & 1 single bedroom
- 2 bathrooms, each with hair dryer, heated towel rails, bathrobes & toiletries
- cotton bed linen; fresh flowers
- children welcome, cot available
- central heating
- open fire, tea/coffee, TV, & artwork in sitting room
- powder room
- continental breakfast served in dining room or alfresco on terrace, cooked on request
- lunch by arrangement, extra
- 3-course dinner with wine, by arrangement, $35 pp
- complimentary laundry
- email facilities available
- courtesy passenger transfer
- on-site parking

ACTIVITIES AVAILABLE

- farm walks & tours
- observing 560-ha sheep, bull & beef farm activities
- trout fishing, guide available
- tennis court on site
- trampoline on site
- private gardens to visit
- bush walks
- 3 golf courses, within 10km
- local beaches, 30km drive
- restaurants, 9km
- wineries & wine trails
- orchard tours
- hot air ballooning
- helicopter sightseeing arranged
- Waipukurau & Waipawa, 9km
- gannet colony at Cape Kidnappers, 60km drive
- Art Deco Napier, 55km drive
- Wellington, 3 hours south

179

AWAKINO, TARANAKI
Awakino Estate – Rosegarden Homestead

Hosts Gaby and Karl Heinz Reipen

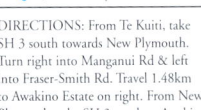

148 Fraser-Smith Road, Awakino-Mokau R D 1, Taranaki
Phone 0-6-752 9142 or 0-6-752 9117   *Fax* 0-6-752 9142
Email awakinoestate@hotmail.com   *Website* www.awakinoestate.co.nz

eftpos
VISA MasterCard

| 3 bdrm | 1 prbth | **Double $150**
Single $110 | *Includes breakfast*
Minimum 2-night stay |

DIRECTIONS: From Te Kuiti, take SH 3 south towards New Plymouth. Turn right into Manganui Rd & left into Fraser-Smith Rd. Travel 1.48km to Awakino Estate on right. From New Plymouth, take SH 3 north to Awakino.

Awakino Estate is a combination of two farms, Awakino Heads and Pioi Station, covering 1,320 hectares. The Estate offers accommodation for up to 26 guests, the main house, Rosegarden Homestead, providing bed and breakfast, for one party at a time. Home to the internationally successful Welsh pony and cob stud, Awakino Estate features an Angus and Hereford stud. Guests are welcome to bring their own horses for farm and beach rides and can use the riding arena on site. Overlooking the Tasman Sea, Awakino Estate has eight kilometres of coastline where guests can walk, and a forest with native birdlife to view. Other popular pursuits on site at Awakino include swimming and kayaking, fishing, hunting and photography.

FACILITIES

- 2 queen bedrooms
- 1 twin bedroom
- 1 private bathroom
- cotton bed linen
- bathrobes
- hair dryers & toiletries
- fresh flowers
- fruit basket in bedrooms
- guest lounge with Sky TV & CD-player
- gourmet breakfast served indoors or alfresco
- phone, fax & email available
- laundry available, extra
- garden setting
- mountain views
- swimming facilities
- rural location
- German spoken by hosts
- on-site parking

ACTIVITIES AVAILABLE

- garden on site
- swimming pool on site
- forest walks on site
- horse riding arena
- kayaking, with 4 kayaks available for guest use
- fishing from site
- whitebaiting
- bush walking
- photo-shooting
- restaurants, 5-min drive
- bird-watching
- pig hunting
- Mokau River boat tours by arrangement, 5 mins
- golf course nearby
- swimming beaches, on site
- New Plymouth, 1 hour
- Waitomo Caves, 1-hour drive away

AWAKINO, TARANAKI
Awakino Estate – Ponga House

Hosts Gaby and Karl Heinz Reipen

148 Fraser-Smith Road, Awakino-Mokau R D 1, Taranaki
Phone 0-6-752 9142 or 0-6-752 9117   *Fax* 0-6-752 9142
Email awakinoestate@hotmail.com   *Website* www.awakinoestate.co.nz

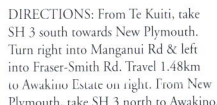

DIRECTIONS: From Te Kuiti, take SH 3 south towards New Plymouth. Turn right into Manganui Rd & left into Fraser-Smith Rd. Travel 1.48km to Awakino Estate on right. From New Plymouth, take SH 3 north to Awakino.

2 bdrm	1 enst	1 prbth	House rate $220	*Self-catering*	Minimum 2-night stay

Ponga House is part of Awakino Estate, set in native bush abounding with birdlife and with ocean views. Guests are offered total privacy at Ponga House, which is fully self-contained and provides panoramic views over Awakino River. The entire Estate of 1,320 hectares is available for guests to explore, including quiet swimming beaches, native bush, lakes and waterfalls. Awakino Estate's own whitebait stands give guests the opportunity for whitebait fishing, and they can enjoy riding their own horses on the beach and farmlands. Guests can self-cater in the well-equipped kitchen and there is also a barbecue outdoors, popular for alfresco dining. A golf course is nearby, and the city of New Plymouth is 60 minutes' drive south of Awakino.

FACILITIES

- 1 self-contained house
- one-party bookings only
- 1 queen ensuite bedroom
- 1 queen bedroom with private bathroom
- toiletries & hair dryers
- cotton bed linen
- fresh flowers
- separate lounge with open fire, TV & CD-player
- full kitchen for self-catering with dishwasher
- laundry facilities
- outdoor entertaining area with barbecue
- mountain & river views
- children welcome
- native bush setting
- German spoken by hosts
- on-site parking

ACTIVITIES AVAILABLE

- 8km beaches & coastline
- native bush on site
- lakes on site
- waterfalls on site
- variety of walks
- swimming on site
- fishing from site
- whitebaiting on site
- kayaking
- restaurants, 5-min drive
- bird-watching
- pig hunting
- horse riding
- Mokau River boat tours by arrangement
- golf course nearby
- swimming beaches
- New Plymouth, 1 hour
- Waitomo Caves, 1-hr drive

181

Awakino, Taranaki
Awakino Estate – Sunset View Houses

Hosts Gaby and Karl Heinz Reipen

148 Fraser-Smith Road, Awakino-Mokau R D 1, Taranaki
Phone 0-6-752 9142 or 0-6-752 9117   *Fax* 0-6-752 9142
Email awakinoestate@hotmail.com   *Website* www.awakinoestate.co.nz

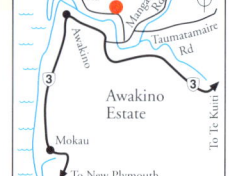

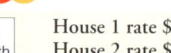

| 4 bdrm | 3 prbth | House 1 rate $250 House 2 rate $230 | Both houses $450 Minimum 2-night stay | *Self-catering* |

DIRECTIONS: From Te Kuiti, take SH 3 south towards New Plymouth. Turn right into Manganui Rd & left into Fraser-Smith Rd. Travel 1.48km to Awakino Estate on right. From New Plymouth, take SH 3 north to Awakino.

Awakino

Sunset View Houses are perched directly above the sandy swimming beach at Awakino with uninterrupted views over the Tasman Sea to the west and towards Mount Taranaki to the south. Watching the sunsets is a tranquil way to end each day, spent swimming in the lagoon, fishing for snapper, diving for crayfish, or just relaxing to the sounds of the ocean. The two Sunset Houses are self-contained and both offer privacy and peace and quiet with all facilities provided. Guests can self-cater in the fully equipped kitchens and dine alfresco using the barbecue. One house includes a spacious rimu lounge room, and the other has two lounges and a large kitchen. The Sunset View Houses are accessible only by four-wheel drive vehicles.

FACILITIES

- one-party booking per house
- House 1: 2 queen bedrooms & 1 private bathroom; large rimu lounge with open fireplace
- House 2: 2 queen bedrooms & 2 private bathrooms; 2 lounges & large kitchen with open fire
- toiletries & hair dryers
- cotton bed linen; fresh flowers
- self-service laundry per house
- full kitchen for self catering in each house
- TV & CD-player in lounge in both houses
- outdoor entertaining area with barbecue per house
- children welcome
- sea & mountain views
- German spoken by hosts
- 4-wheel drive access only

ACTIVITIES AVAILABLE

- native bush on site
- lakes & waterfalls on site
- variety of walks on site
- swimming in lagoon
- watching sunsets
- sandy swimming beach
- snapper fishing from site
- diving for crayfish
- horse riding arena
- restaurants, 5 mins away
- bird-watching
- whitebaiting
- kayaking
- pig hunting
- Mokau River boat tours by arrangement
- golf course nearby
- New Plymouth, 1 hour
- Waitomo Caves, 1-hr drive

Awakino

Awakino

© Friars' Guide to New Zealand Accommodation for the Discerning Traveller   198

OKATO, TARANAKI

Patuha Farm Lodge

Hosts The Henderson Family

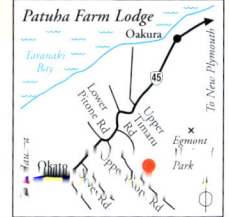

575 Upper Pitone Road, Okato   *Postal* R D 4, New Plymouth
Phone 0-6-752 4469   *Email* patuha.farm.lodge@clear.net.nz
Fax 0-6-752 4470   *Website* www.patuhafarmlodge.co.nz

| 10 bdrm | 10 enst | 1 pdrm | **Double $210**
Single $115 | *Includes breakfast & dinner*
Lunch extra |

DIRECTIONS: Take SH 3 to New Plymouth. Travel south-west on SH 45 for 15km to Oakura. Travel another 10km & turn left into Upper Pitone Rd. Travel 5.75km & turn into Lodge driveway on left. Travel 2km to Lodge.

Patuha is a third generation family farm, taking its name from the highest peak of the nearby Kaitake Range. The 160-hectare (400-acre) sheep and beef farm provides a peaceful site for guests and seasonal farming activities. Twenty hectares of native rainforest surround the lodge which borders Egmont National Park, with a 20-minute bush walk leading guests to the renowned Pukeiti Rhododendron Gardens. Built in the 1980s, Patuha Farm Lodge *(see centre of photo above)* is being progressively updated and caters for small conferences, with 10 ensuite bedrooms comprising four queen and six twin, three with double and single beds. Meals feature traditional farm cuisine which is served in the dining room, adjacent to the licensed bar.

FACILITIES

- 4 queen & 6 twin bedrooms, including electric blankets
- 10 ensuite bathrooms
- 1 separate spa bathroom
- TV & phone in each bedroom
- central heating
- seasonal flowers
- children welcome
- conference room & facilities
- fax & email available

- continental & cooked breakfast
- 3-course dinner included
- traditional farm cuisine
- lunch or picnics available by request, extra
- wood burner in lounge & dining area; licensed bar
- tea/coffee & cookies area
- courtesy passenger transfer
- on-site parking

ACTIVITIES AVAILABLE

- games room in-house
- farm walks on site
- seasonal farm activities eg shearing, docking, haymaking, stock work
- native bush walks on site
- bird-watching on site
- Pukeiti Rhododendron Gardens adjacent
- snow skiing at Mt Egmont

- surf-casting from beach, 10km
- trout fishing at Stoney River
- golf course, 12km away
- Egmont National Park
- private gardens open to visit
- Rhododendron Week, Oct./Nov.
- short local walks & day tramps
- New Plymouth, 30-min drive
- ski-field in winter, 1-hour drive

NEW PLYMOUTH
Oak Valley Manor

Hosts Paul and Pat Ekdahl

248 Junction Road, R D 1, New Plymouth
Phone 0-6-758 1501   *Mobile* 027 442 0325   *Fax* 0-6-758 1052
Email kauri.holdings@xtra.co.nz   *Website* www.oakvalley.co.nz

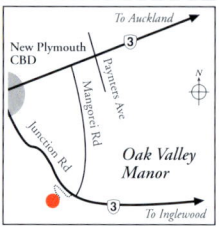

2 bdrm	2 enst

Double $150
Single $65–$125

Includes breakfast
Multiple-night rates available

DIRECTIONS: Take SH 3 towards New Plymouth. From south, travel to Junction Rd. Oak Valley Manor is on left. From north, turn left into Mangorei Rd. Turn right into Junction Rd. Oak Valley Manor is 50m on left.

Oak Valley Manor was purpose-built in 1995 to provide a private wing for guests. Comprising two bedrooms with ensuite bathrooms, and a private lounge, the wing offers views of Mt Egmont/Taranaki on one side, and opens to a private courtyard on the other. Guests can choose their own privacy or are welcome to socialise with Pat and Paul in the shared lounge. The breakfast menu is provided the night before and is served in the dining room. Animals on this two-hectare rural property include donkeys, pigs, peacocks, hens and Yale the dog. Ducks and geese enjoy the lake which is surrounded by a developing oak grove and landscaped garden. Tours through the family owned and operated organic brewery are available.

FACILITIES

- 2 queen/twin bedrooms
- cotton bed linen
- 2 ensuite bathrooms
- private lounge in guest wing with TV, tea/coffee, phone
- 1 shared lounge with hosts
- children
- pets welcome
- laundry available
- continental breakfast served in dining room
- fax available
- private guest entrance
- guest courtyard
- landscaped garden
- courtesy passenger transfer
- animals on site
- on-site parking

ACTIVITIES AVAILABLE

- organic brewery tours
- winery, 1.5km away
- renowned surf beaches
- surfing & windsurfing
- 2 golf courses, 4km
- Tupare Gardens, 1km
- Pukekura Park
- Brooklands Bowl for outdoor summer concerts
- restaurants/shopping, 5-min drive
- private gardens to visit
- New Plymouth, 5-min drive
- walking & hiking at Mt Egmont
- Pukeiti Rhododendron Gardens & Restaurant, 30-min drive away
- Rhododendron Week, Oct./Nov.
- Festival of Lights, 24 Dec.–Feb.
- snow skiing at Mt Egmont, learning & advanced ski tows

EGMONT NATIONAL PARK
Mountain House Motor Lodge
and Andersons' Alpine Lodge

Host Berta Anderson

Pembroke Road, Stratford   *Postal* P O Box 303, Stratford   *Mobile* 025 412 372
Mountain House Phone and Fax 0-6-765 6100 *or Andersons' Phone* 0-6-765 6620
Freephone 0800 MOUNTAIN   *Email* mountainhouse@xtra.co.nz

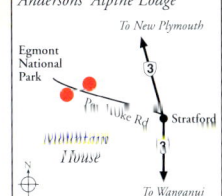

DIRECTIONS: From New Plymouth or Wanganui, take SH 3 to Stratford. Turn west into Pembroke Rd. Travel 9km to Andersons' Alpine Lodge on right, or another 5km to Mountain House Motor Lodge on the left.

| 13 bdrm | 13 enst | Room rate $165–$205 | *All meals extra* |

Set five kilometres apart on the edge of the Egmont National Park, at the foot of Mt Taranaki, are Andersons' Alpine Lodge and the Mountain House Motor Lodge. Offering diverse accommodation, these venues provide spectacular views of the mountain, sunsets and native bush. Andersons' is a three-storey, Swiss-style lodge featuring oil paintings by the late Keith H. Anderson. The Mountain House comprises a 10-bedroom lodge, family chalet and à la carte licensed restaurant, winner of many awards, with an extensive game menu. Restaurant meals are available at the Summit and Egmont Rooms with adjoining lounge bar. Sited on the eastern flank of Mt Egmont/Taranaki, this is an ideal base for mountain walks from 15 minutes' to five days' duration.

FACILITIES

- Mountain House restaurant with full à la carte menu for all meals, licensed lounge bar & open fire
- continental breakfast at Andersons'
- 1 king & 2 twin ensuite bedrooms at Andersons', king with spa bath
- 10 king, queen, double & twin bedrooms at Mountain House
- art by the late Keith H. Anderson
- sauna & spa complex at Mountain House
- children welcome at Mountain House
- pets welcome at Andersons'
- laundry available
- farm pets at Andersons'
- mountain views
- German spoken
- courtesy passenger transfer
- helipad
- on-site parking

ACTIVITIES AVAILABLE

- east Egmont bush walks
- family tramping
- guided summit climbs
- trout stream, opposite
- 3–5-day round mountain trek
- rainforest walking tracks
- walks from Plateau
- Heritage Trails
- Taranaki Rhododendron Week, October/November annually
- scenic helicopter flights
- Manganui Ski-field, 3km
- golf courses
- museums
- Stratford, 5–10-min drive
- Taranaki Pioneer Village, 15km north
- Hollard Gardens, 20km
- Dawson Falls, 20km away
- beach, 40km away

ELTHAM, TARANAKI
Caniwi Lodge on the Lake

Hosts Jean and Maureen Gauvin

505A Aorere Road, R D 19, Eltham, Taranaki
Phone 0-6-764 7577   *Email* caniwi@xtra.co.nz
Fax 0-6-764 7578   *Website* www.caniwilodge.co.nz

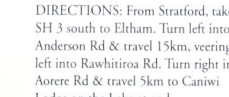

Caniwi Lodge

DIRECTIONS: From Stratford, take SH 3 south to Eltham. Turn left into Anderson Rd & travel 15km, veering left into Rawhitiroa Rd. Turn right into Aorere Rd & travel 5km to Caniwi Lodge on the Lake at end.

6 bdrm	2 enst	2 prbth

Suite/room rate $200–$250
Chalet rate $200 for 2 persons

Includes breakfast or basket
Extra persons $15 each

Lunch & dinner extra
Self-catering

Located on 40 hectares (100 acres) of Taranaki farmland overlooking Lake Rotorangi, Caniwi Lodge on the Lake is set in a landscaped garden and lawns with a large redwood grove on site for guests to enjoy. Caniwi offers a guest suite and bedroom for one-party bookings in the house, as well as two private new self-contained chalets closer to the lake. A full breakfast is either served in the breakfast room or a breakfast basket is provided by room service. Jean has 20 years' restaurant experience and he will serve lunch alfresco in fine weather, and four-course dinner using organically grown seasonal farm produce, by request. A boat ramp and jetty enable guests to enjoy watersports such as kayaking and power-boating on the lake.

FACILITIES

- one-party booking per chalet/house
- 1 queen suite: spa bath in ensuite, dressing room, TV, DVD, phone & tea/coffee, opens to 2 verandahs
- 1 queen ensuite bedroom & TV
- 2 self-contained chalets with 1 queen bedroom & 3 singles in mezzanine; 1 private bathroom & full self-catering kitchen in each
- self-serve laundry
- fresh flowers
- full cooked or continental breakfast served or basket
- light cooked lunch, $20 pp
- 4-course dinner in dining room, $40 pp, wine extra
- lounge with open fire, Sky TV, DVD & CD-player
- hair dryers & toiletries
- French & Spanish spoken
- on-site parking; helipad

ACTIVITIES AVAILABLE

- 2 cats, dog, magpie & pig on site
- clay-bird shooting on site
- power boating & kayaking
- pétanque court on site
- extensive grounds with gardens, redwoods & walks on site
- jetty & boat ramp on site
- tramping & hiking
- scenic helicopter flights
- museum
- restaurants, 30 mins
- Mt Taranaki
- fishing; hunting
- golf courses
- gardens to visit
- Eltham, 25-min drive
- Stratford, 30-min drive
- New Plymouth, 1 hr north
- Wanganui City, 1 hour 40 min-drive south

Caniwi Lodge

Caniwi Lodge

RANGATAUA, OHAKUNE
Whare Ora Lodge

Hosts Diana and Tiri Sotiri

1 Kaha Street, Rangataua, Ohakune, Central Plateau
Phone 0-6-385 9385   *Mobile* 027 481 5667   *Email* whareora@xtra.co.nz
Fax 0-6-385 9385   *Website* www.whareoralodge.co.nz

To Turoa Ski-field
Dreadnought Rd
To National Park
Ohakune
Miharo St
Kaha St
49A *49*
Waiouru
To Wanganui
Whare Ora

DIRECTIONS: From Waiouru, turn off SH 1 into SH 49. Travel 21km to Rangataua. Turn right into Piwari St, left into Kaha St. Whare Ora at end on right. From Taumarunui, take SH 4 to SH 49A to Ohakune. Continue 5km.

2 bdrm	2 enst

Suite rate $195–$225   *Includes breakfast*   *Lunch & dinner extra*
Extra persons $70 each   **Seasonal rates available**

Maori for "place of well-being", Whare Ora Lodge is located 20 minutes from the Turoa Ski-field and only five minutes from an entrance to the Tongariro World Heritage Site where much of the filming of *The Lord of the Rings* was shot. Originally built in 1910, Whare Ora Lodge was architecturally redesigned in 1997, blending the existing home with contemporary accommodation facilities. Two guest suites are now available. The quietness is enhanced by the garden setting, framing views of Mt Ruapehu in its varied moods, with Mt Taranaki also visible to the west. Tiri and Diana have a large library and wide music selection. Their New Zealand art collection includes hand-blown glass. Himalayan Persian cats are in residence.

FACILITIES

- 1 upstairs queen suite with lounge, ensuite & 2 extra single beds
- 1 downstairs queen suite with ensuite & spa bath, lounge & undercarpet heating
- demist mirror & heated towel rail in downstairs ensuite
- fresh flowers, hair dryer, TV, radio & toiletries in both rooms
- cotton bed linen & goosedown duvets on all beds in winter

- 3-course dinner with wine, by request, $50–$80 pp
- lunch by arrangement
- tea/coffee available
- phone, fax & email
- complimentary laundry
- children by arrangement
- lock-up ski cupboard & drying room
- garaging; cats on Site

ACTIVITIES AVAILABLE

- pétanque & croquet lawn
- native bird-watching
- native bat colony
- 2 ski-fields in winter
- Tongariro World Heritage site
- Mt Ruapehu walks
- Waimarino Golf Course, 10 mins
- squash courts, 5-min drive
- scenic flights over volcanoes

- cafés & restaurants
- night club in winter
- Ohakune, 5-min drive
- snow-boarding
- NZ beech forest walks
- trout fishing; horse treks
- Karioi Lake
- garden visits
- Waiouru Army Museum, 20-min drive away

WANGANUI
Arles B & B

Hosts Sue and Tom Day

50 Riverbank Road, State Highway 4, R D 3, Wanganui
Phone 0-6-343 6557   *Mobile* 021 257 8257   *Fax* 0-6-343 6557
Email sue@arles.co.nz   *Website* www.arles.co.nz

DIRECTIONS: Take SH 3 to City. Travel north on Anzac Pde, to SH 4. Travel 4km from Dublin St bridge to Arles B&B on right. Or from National Park, take SH 4 towards Wanganui to B&B on left.

| 6 bdrm | 2 enst | 2 prbth | 1 pdrm |

Room rate $120–$160
Apartment rate $120–$240

Includes breakfast
Self-catering in apartment

Arles is a large comfortable country home originally built in the 1880s on 400 hectares (over 1,000 acres) of farmland, less than one hectare of gardens now remaining. The spacious grounds feature many mature native and exotic trees, wisteria softens the front of the homestead and an indoor grapevine in the conservatory bears grapes in summer. The original kauri staircase takes guests to their upstairs bedrooms. Downstairs, guests can relax in the rimu-panelled guest lounge with a complimentary glass of wine and a book, game or puzzle from the library. There is a fully equipped guest kitchen/laundry and a barbecue and swimming pool for the summer months. Treetops is a separate two-bedroom apartment with kitchen, living/dining room and balcony.

FACILITIES

- 1 king with private balcony & 1 queen ensuite bedroom
- 1 double & 1 twin bedroom family suite, with 1 bathroom, claw-foot bath & bathrobes
- Treetops: self-catering apartment with 1 queen & 1 twin bedroom; sofa bed in lounge & 1 bathroom
- tea/coffee in bedrooms & both guest kitchens
- full breakfast includes home-made bread, jams & baking
- TV & CD-player in both guest lounges
- central heating in homestead
- phone, fax & email available
- families welcome; cot & highchair available
- secure garaging for guests on river trips; on-site parking

ACTIVITIES AVAILABLE

- swimming pool & BBQ on site
- garden ramble & bird watching on site
- historic *Waimarie* paddle steamer on river
- art galleries & museums
- scenic drive along Whanganui River across road
- river & beaches nearby
- Cooks Gardens & Splash Centre
- restaurants, shops & historic buildings, 6-min drive
- renowned children's play area at Kowhai Park, 4km – bumper boats, mini-golf, train rides & go carts
- Virginia & Westmere lakes
- jet boating, 2 hour to full day trips; canoeing on river
- 3 golf courses within 15km
- ski-fields, 1½-hr drive north

The Rutland Arms Inn

Hosts Peter and Judy Jefferson   *Phone* 0 6 347 7677

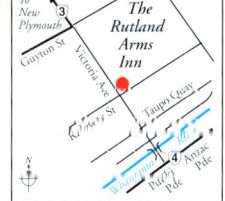

48–52 Ridgway Street, Wanganui   *Postal* P O Box 499, Wanganui
Freephone 0800 RUTLAND   *Mobile* 021 331 338   *Fax* 0-6-347 7345
Email enquiries@rutland-arms.co.nz   *Website* www.rutland-arms.co.nz

DIRECTIONS: From New Plymouth, take SH 3 to Victoria Ave. Turn left into Ridgway St. Inn on corner. From Wellington take SH 3, or from Ohakune take SH 4 to Victoria Ave. Turn right into Ridgway St.

8 bdrm	8 enst	1 pdrm

Room rate $130–$180

Continental breakfast included
Cooked breakfast, lunch & dinner extra

Named after the Rutland Stockade which was erected in 1847 on the hill in the centre of Wanganui, the original Rutland Hotel was built in 1849. A colourful history includes two fires destroying the wooden building, which was first rebuilt in 1869, then the present brick building in 1904. This central city hotel has been totally restored and refurbished, retaining the Edwardian architectural features with an old English-style pub downstairs. Imported English beers are offered with à la carte meals, served by the open fire or in the courtyard café which includes the original well. The upstairs guest accommodation comprises eight bedrooms carefully finished in early-colonial design with ensuite bathrooms and Victorian-style mahogany furniture throughout.

FACILITIES

- 6 queen & 2 queen/twin ensuite bedrooms, 4 with spa baths
- special suite includes double spa bath, twin basins & bidet
- tea/coffee, writing desk, Sky TV, minibar, direct-dial phone, fax
- 100% cotton bed linen
- laundry & dry cleaning service, extra
- broadband connection available
- private guest entrance

- licensed restaurant & bar, with open fire
- à la carte dinner, extra
- à la carte lunch, extra
- full cooked breakfast, extra
- continental breakfast served in suite or restaurant
- powder room downstairs
- central heating
- off-street carpark

ACTIVITIES AVAILABLE

- licensed restaurant on site
- wishing well on site
- historic riverboat cruise
- historic opera house
- unique Durie Hill elevator
- art gallery & museum, 500m
- library, 500m away
- Central City shopping
- Kowhai Park

- Wanganui in Bloom, Dec.–Feb.
- Belmont Golf Course
- Virginia Lake Reserve & Bason Botanic Gardens
- private gardens to visit
- Whanganui River walks; canoeing
- Cooks Gardens
- Kai-iwi beach
- historic Bushy Park homestead
- Mt Ruapehu ski-field, 1½-hr drive

WESTMERE, WANGANUI
Arlesford House

Hosts June and George Loibl

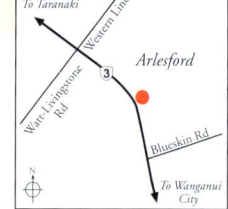

202 State Highway 3, R D 4, Westmere, Wanganui
Phone 0-6-347 7751 *Mobile* 025 852 922 *Fax* 0-6-347 7561
Email arlesford.house@xtra.co.nz *Website* arlesfordhouse.co.nz

DIRECTIONS: From Wanganui City, take SH 3 towards New Plymouth. Travel for 8km to Arlesford House on right.

4 bdrm	2 enst	2 prbth

Double $165–$230   **Single $135–$180**   *Includes breakfast*

Designed by Wanganui architect Bob Talboys and built from native heart rimu by Joseph Gopperth in 1934, Arlesford House is located just eight kilometres north of the city. Set in established landscaped gardens with mature trees, Arlesford is furnished with antiques and original New Zealand artwork. This two-storey Georgian-style homestead now offers accommodation comprising four guestrooms, each with its own bathroom and rural or garden views. Open fires warm the lounge and drawing room with an adjacent sunroom. A leisurely breakfast is served downstairs in the dining room or alfresco beside the swimming pool in the park-like gardens. There is also a three-bedroom, two-bathroom self-contained cottage available on site.

FACILITIES

- Regency Room: 1 super-king ensuite bedroom & spa bath
- Victoria Room: 1 super-king/twin ensuite bedroom & bath
- Ruapehu & Anne Rooms: each with queen/twin or king/twin bedroom & private bathroom
- hair dryer, toiletries, heated towel rails & bathrobes; baths in Anne & Victoria bathrooms
- children welcome
- full cooked or continental breakfast buffet; afternoon tea on arrival
- cotton bed linen, tea/coffee, desk & TV in bedrooms
- guest lounge with open fire, tea/coffee, TV, video, phone & writing desk
- complimentary laundry service
- on-site parking
- courtesy passenger transfer

ACTIVITIES AVAILABLE

- swimming pool on site
- flood-lit tennis court
- pétanque
- barbecue available
- small conference room
- Westmere Lake Wildlife Reserve, 2-min drive
- Bason Botanical Gardens
- Virginia Lake
- Mowhanau Beach
- Wanganui restaurants, cafés & shops, 10-min drive
- canoeing
- jet boating
- paddle steamer on river
- museum
- Sarjeant Art Gallery
- 4 golf courses nearby
- gardens open to visit
- New Plymouth, 2 hrs north

MANGAWEKA, RANGITIKEI
Mairenui Rural Retreat

Hosts Sue and David Sweet

Ruahine Road, Mangaweka
Phone 0-6-382 5564   *Mobile* 025 517 545   *Fax* 0-6-382 5564
Email mairenui@xtra.co.nz   *Website* www.mairenui.co.nz

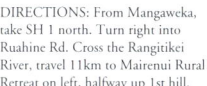

DIRECTIONS: From Mangaweka, take SH 1 north. Turn right into Ruahine Rd. Cross the Rangitikei River, travel 11km to Mairenui Rural Retreat on left, halfway up 1st hill.

10 bdrm	2 enst	3 shbth

The Homestead: *Includes breakfast*
Double $130–$280, Single $95–$140

The Retreat: *Meals extra*
Double $150, Extras $50

The Villa: *Meals extra*
Double $80, Extras $40

The century-old farm homestead has been in the Sweet family for four generations. David and Sue chose a Comesky design from the Athfield architectural school for their 1970s self-contained Retreat, built among a stand of 700-year-old native trees, apart from the homestead. The multi-storey Retreat features an open-plan design around a circular staircase, with polished floors, brickwork, 1970s' furnishing, memorabilia and refurbished interiors. The original homestead, built in 1896, has been totally restored as a self-contained colonial villa, also set in the expansive park-like grounds featuring ponds, rhododendrons, camellias and old roses. The spacious lounge in The Villa includes a small pool table, plenty of games and books and a wind-up gramophone. Guests enjoy relaxing on the large sunny verandah with its rural outlook. Both The Retreat and The Villa are self-catering, but meals are also available at the homestead, which is hung with original artwork by New Zealand and European artists. Its furniture in native timbers is hand-crafted by a German craftsman who lived on the 310-hectare sheep and cattle

FACILITIES

- The Homestead: 1 double & 1 twin bedroom with ensuites, 1 including sunken bath, sitting area & verandah
- The Retreat: 1 twin & 2 double bedrooms with 1 shared bathroom & 2 toilets
- The Villa: 3 double & 2 twin bedrooms, with 2 guest-share bathrooms, & 1 original claw-foot bath
- cotton bed linen, duvets &/or blankets in Homestead
- single-party bookings for The Retreat & The Villa
- Retreat & Villa self-contained with full kitchens for self-catering
- Retreat & Villa breakfast, served at Homestead, $10–$15 pp
- 3-course dinner served at Homestead, $40 pp; wine extra
- lunch on request $12.50 pp
- lounge facilities in Homestead bedrooms, with tea/coffee
- spacious lounges in Homestead, Retreat & Villa, with open fires
- pool table & gramophone in Villa
- French & German spoken
- on-site parking

ACTIVITIES AVAILABLE

- barbecues at each house
- pétanque court at Villa
- croquet on Homestead & Villa lawns
- concrete tennis court
- Homestead garden, 1.6ha
- farm & bush walks
- four-wheel-drive farm tours
- horses for experienced riders
- river swimming
- Rangitikei private garden visits
- Rangitikei historic home tour
- bird-watching
- white water & float rafting
- bungy jumping & flying fox
- on-farm catch & release trout fishing
- 4 scenic golf courses
- wool warehouse, craft shops
- café & restaurants, 30km away
- Waiouru Army Museum, 45km
- Ohakea Airforce Museum, 80km
- Rugby Museum, PN, 80km
- winter ski areas, 90 mins away
- Wellington or Rotorua, 3-hour easy drive away

Mairenui

HUNTERVILLE, RANGITIKEI
Rathmoy Garden Cottage

Hosts Susanna and Christopher Grace

Rangatira Road, Hunterville   *Postal* Rathmoy, R D 6, Hunterville
Phone 0-6-322 8334   *Email* sgrace.rathmoy@xtra.co.nz
Fax 0-6-322 8380   *Website* www.rathmoy.co.nz

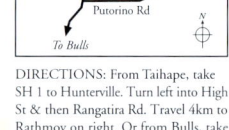

DIRECTIONS: From Taihape, take SH 1 to Hunterville. Turn left into High St & then Rangatira Rd. Travel 4km to Rathmoy on right. Or from Bulls, take SH 1 north. Turn right into Putorino Rd. Travel 12km to Rathmoy on left.

| 2 bdrm | 1 prbth | Cottage rate $275–$330 for 2 persons
Extra persons $60 each | *Self-catering*
Includes breakfast provisions |

Set in the well-known Rathmoy Garden in the Rangitikei, this self-contained cottage is located on the far side of the lake, ensuring guest privacy and peaceful garden views. Built in 1990, Rathmoy Cottage provides two guest bedrooms and a wheelchair access bathroom for private-party bookings only. A fully equipped kitchen with well-stocked pantry enables guests to self-cater, although breakfast provisions are supplied. Guests also enjoy using the gas barbecue for alfresco dining beside the lake, which is home to waterfowl. Other popular on-site activities include bird-watching, feeding the friendly farm animals and pets, wandering in the 2.4-hectare garden, and farm and bush walks for all fitness levels.

FACILITIES

- single-party bookings only
- 1 super-king/twin & 1 twin bedroom
- 1 wheelchair access bathroom
- quality linen, hair dryer, bathrobes & heated towel rails
- antiques, books & flowers
- log fire, TV, CD, tape-player, writing desk & guest phone
- underfloor heating

- breakfast provisions supplied
- complimentary beverages
- fully equipped kitchen for self-catering including bread-making machine, microwave & dishwasher
- fax & email available
- guest laundry
- garaging
- helipad; private airstrip

ACTIVITIES AVAILABLE

- multiple-night rate available
- established garden on site
- farm & bush walks for all fitness levels
- farming activities
- friendly farm animals & pets
- Rangitikei River access on farm for swimming, picnicking & trout fishing
- mountain bikes & dinghy available

- bird-watching & waterfowl
- restaurants, 5-min drive
- antiques & crafts shops
- white water & float rafting
- historic house tours
- private gardens to visit
- golf courses 10-min drive, clubs available
- bungy jumping; jet boat rides
- snow skiing, 1½-hour drive

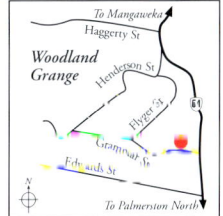

DIRECTIONS: From Feilding, take Kimbolton Rd north for 28km to Kimbolton village. Turn left into Grammar St & travel 100m to Woodland Grange on right. Follow driveway to cottage.

KIMBOLTON, MANAWATU

Woodland Grange

Hosts Juanita and Scott Curry

13 Grammar Street, Kimbolton   *Postal* P O Box 71, Kimbolton
Phone 0-6-328 9667   *Mobile* 021 142 9570   *Fax* 0-6-328 9614
Email hotcurry@xtra.co.nz   *Website* friars.co.nz/hosts/woodland.html

1 bdrm	1 enst

Cottage rate $180 for 2 persons
Extra persons $30 each

Includes continental breakfast provisions
Self-catering

Set in a rambling woodland garden of almost two hectares (four acres), the self-contained cottage at Woodland Grange provides a quiet retreat for honeymooners and garden lovers. Located in the upper Manawatu, on the outskirts of Kimbolton village, Woodland Grange is just minutes from the renowned Cross Hills Gardens and the Heritage Park of the Rhododendron Association. The cottage includes a queen-size bedroom, with an extra sofa-bed in the living room. Provisions for self-catering are supplied. Juanita and Scott, who live adjacent, also cater for weddings in their chapel on site and guests are welcome to play the organ. Originally designed as a nursery, the garden now features mature trees and ponds with seating areas.

FACILITIES

- single-party bookings only
- 1 queen ensuite bedroom in self-contained cottage
- bathrobes, hair dryer, toiletries & heated towel rails
- dressing room
- phone jack in bedroom
- night-store heater
- lounge with open fire, TV, CD-player, games & books
- continental breakfast provisions supplied
- small kitchen with basic provisions for self-catering
- fresh flowers; confectionery
- fax available in house
- self-serve laundry in cottage
- iron & ironing board
- extensive garden setting
- on-site parking

ACTIVITIES AVAILABLE

- guest BBQ in secluded cottage courtyard
- 2ha (4-acre) woodland garden ramble on site
- chapel on site for weddings
- organ in chapel for guest use
- heated outdoor shower & bath
- swimming; trout fishing
- rhododendron gardens nearby: Cross Hills & Heritage Park, 3–5-min drive north
- historical café & wine bar, 3-min walk away
- dinner at Cheltenham Hotel, 10-min drive
- Kimbolton village, 3-min walk
- walkways; picnic areas
- gardens open to visit
- Feilding, 20-min drive
- Palmerston North City, 35-min drive south

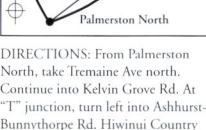

PALMERSTON NORTH
Hiwinui Country Estate

Hosts Jan and Dave Stewart

465 Ashhurst-Bunnythorpe Road, Hiwinui, R D 11, Palmerston North
Phone 0-6-329 2838   *Mobile* 025 268 0173   *Fax* 0-6-329 2828
Email jan@hiwinui.co.nz   *Website* www.hiwinui.co.nz

3 bdrm	3 enst

Double $280–$360
Single $220

Includes breakfast & apéritifs
Dinner extra

DIRECTIONS: From Palmerston North, take Tremaine Ave north. Continue into Kelvin Grove Rd. At "T" junction, turn left into Ashhurst-Bunnythorpe Rd. Hiwinui Country Estate on right (15 mins from city).

Hiwinui Country Estate is set on 450-hectares (1,100 acres) of the Stewart family's farming properties on the northern outskirts of Palmerston North. Guests can choose from three bedrooms with ensuites. A large schist fireplace opens both to the lounge and the dining room. The underground cellar offers an extensive range of wines from New Zealand's leading vineyards. Nestled close to the lodge, in a secret garden for privacy, is an outdoor spa pool and open log fireplace for guests seeking relaxation. Hiwinui Country Estate has its own in-house beauty therapist who offers body treatments. Guests can also enjoy one of New Zealand's renowned river trips through the dramatic Manawatu Gorge, aboard the Lodge's private jet boat.

FACILITIES

- 1 super-king ensuite bedroom with spa bath & double basin
- 1 king ensuite bedroom with double shower & 1 queen ensuite bedroom
- cotton bed linen, fresh flowers, phone, tea/coffee, mineral water & TV in bedrooms
- hair dryers, toiletries, bathrobes & heated flooring
- children over 8 yrs welcome
- cooked or continental breakfast
- formal dinner by arrangement, $70 pp; complimentary apéritifs & hors d'oeuvres; licensed
- phone, fax & email
- lounge with open fire, Sky TV, video, CDs, piano & artwork
- laundry; wheelchair access
- courtesy airport transfer
- on-site parking; helipad

ACTIVITIES AVAILABLE

- BBQ & outdoor spa pool on site
- pets welcome, kennels supplied
- guided tours of farm
- feeding calves & lambs in season
- in-house massage & beauty therapy
- private hosted jet boat
- pétanque court
- golf-driving pad
- duck shooting parties
- restaurants in Palmerston North, 15-min drive
- helicopter flights arranged
- trip to windfarm
- Manfield Autocourse
- walks in Ruahine Ranges
- Feilding saleyards
- Victoria Esplanade gardens
- fly fishing
- airport, 10-min drive

PALMERSTON NORTH
The Palm and Oaks

Hosts Heather and Michael Rogers

183 Grey Street, Palmerston North
Phone 0-6-359 0755 *Email* enquiries@thepalm-oaks.co.nz
Fax 0-6-359 0756 *Website* www.thepalm-oaks.co.nz

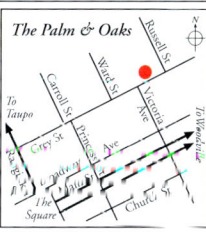

The Palm & Oaks

DIRECTIONS: From north, take Rangitikei St to Grey St. Turn left & travel to The Palm & Oaks on left. From south, turn left at The Square, then left into Rangitikei St. Turn right into Grey St. The Palm & Oaks on left.

4 bdrm	3 enst	Room rate $250–$350	*Self-catering*	*Includes provisions for 1st morning*

The Palm & Oaks

The Palm & Oaks is a self-contained inner city villa, nestled between an established orchard and lawn tennis court in a garden setting. This understated Italian-style villa is architecturally designed, with elegant lines and striking contrasts. Purpose built in 2000, the villa incorporates walled courtyards for privacy, in keeping with the Mediterranean theme. Indoor/outdoor living is enhanced with lighting and water features. There are four sunny bedrooms, the master suite including a spacious balcony and dressing room. The kitchen, with kauri benches and rimu joinery, is fully equipped for self-catering. The Palm & Oaks is popular for special occasions and long stays, and is within easy walking distance of quality restaurants, theatres and shops.

FACILITIES

- 2 queen ensuite bedrooms upstairs, 1 extra queen shares 1 ensuite if required
- 1 twin ensuite bedroom with bath & wheelchair access
- cotton bed linen, fresh flowers, phone & Sky TV in bedrooms
- hair dryers, toiletries, bathrobes & heated towel rails
- children over 12 yrs welcome
- honeymoon/conference venue

- exclusive use of villa
- breakfast provisions for 1st morning supplied
- full kitchen for self-catering
- alfresco dining facilities
- formal lounge/dining room
- underfloor gas heating
- self-serve laundry
- security system; garaging
- bookings essential

ACTIVITIES AVAILABLE

- tennis court in garden setting
- spa pool in private courtyard
- barbecue on site
- gardens & orchard on site
- Manawatu Gorge walk
- Science Centre
- wind farm
- gardens to visit
- Herb Farm visits

- restaurants, bars & cafés, within walking distance
- 4 golf courses nearby
- downtown movie theatre
- CBD & shopping malls
- reserve & bush walks
- Victoria Esplanade Gardens
- arts & crafts
- art galleries & museums
- theatres

The Palm & Oaks

The Palm & Oaks

WOODVILLE

Otawa Lodge

Hosts Del and Sue Trew

132 Otawhao Road, Kumeroa, R D 1, Woodville
Phone 0-6-376 4603 *Mobile* 027 230 1327 *Fax* 0-6-376 5042
Email rest@otawalodge.co.nz *Website* otawalodge.co.nz

DIRECTIONS: From Woodville take
SH 2 north for 4.1km. Turn right
into Hopelands Rd, travel 6.1km &
cross river. Turn left into Kumeroa Rd
& travel 6.7km through Kumeroa.
Continue into Otawhao Rd to Lodge.

| 2 bdrm | 2 prbth | Room rate $215–$265 | *Includes breakfast* | *Lunch & dinner extra* | |

Set on 32 hectares, in the rolling hills at the head of the Otawhao Valley, Otawa Lodge is an original example of Art Nouveau architecture. Built in 1914, this single-storey Edwardian homestead features a Marseilles tiled roof and stained glass leadlight windows. The intricate plasterwork of the ceilings and walls in the entrance hall and sitting room are complemented by native rimu dados and panelling. Guests dine on fresh organic produce and speciality fish dishes. The Queen Anne-style turret serves as an octagonal guest library with views of the surrounding garden. Guests enjoy the six hectares of native bush with tui, bellbirds and native pigeons. The house is heated by hot water radiators and both of the two guestrooms have private bathrooms.

FACILITIES

- 1 super-king/twin & 1 queen bedroom with cotton bed linen & mineral water
- 2 private bathrooms with hair dryer, bathrobes, heated towel rails & toiletries
- guest sitting & dining room with piano & writing desk
- library; TV on request
- laundry available
- email, fax & phone available
- choice of full cooked or continental breakfast
- 4-course dinner with apéritifs & coffee, $70 pp
- selected NZ wine list
- fresh flowers
- central heating
- private guest entrance
- on-site parking; garaging
- courtesy passenger transfer

ACTIVITIES AVAILABLE

- conferences, honeymoons & formal dinners catered for
- pétanque & croquet on site
- hill & bush walks on site
- 1ha (2-acre) garden, 26ha (64-acre) farmland & 6ha (14-acre) native bush & creek on site
- farm visits; tennis courts nearby
- Manawatu Gorge – for jet boats, abseiling & kayaking
- visits to Te Apiti & Tararua wind farms
- Gottfried Lindauer Studio
- golf course; horse riding
- fishing; swimming
- antiques shopping
- sky diving; quad-bike trips
- tramping; hunting
- lavender farm
- Mt Bruce Wildlife Centre

MASTERTON, WAIRARAPA

Camellia Estate

Hosts Ray and Liz Piper

39 Renall Street, Masterton, Wairarapa   *Fax* 0-6-370 9055
Phone 0-6-370 9088   *Mobiles* 027 488 8921 *and* 025 888 922
Email camellia@wise.net.nz   *Website* friars.co.nz/hosts/camellia.html

   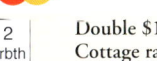 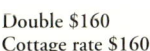

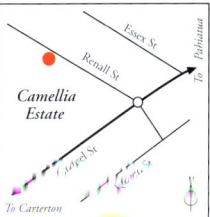

DIRECTIONS· From north, take SH 2 to Masterton. Continue into Chapel St. Turn right into Renall St. Camellia Estate on left. From south, take SH 2 to Masterton. Continue into High St, veer left into Chapel St.

| 4 bdrm | 2 prbth | **Double $160** **Cottage rate $160** | **Single $90** | *Includes breakfast* *Self-catering in cottage* | *Dinner extra* | |

This historic villa, built in 1903, still features the original finials, high ceilings, stained-glass doors and tiled fireplace. Camellia Estate is set in a half-hectare woodland garden, which features a stream running through it and a fountain on the lawn. Accommodation in the villa comprises three bedrooms, including a king-size four-poster bed, and spa bath in the guest bathroom, with single-party bookings ensuring privacy. A full breakfast is served either indoors or alfresco overlooking the swimming pool and tennis pavilion. Dinner with wine is available by prior request, or a barbecue can be arranged in the summer months. Then, in winter, guests can enjoy the log fire in the sitting room. A new self-catering cottage is also available.

FACILITIES

- private-party bookings
- 1 king, 1 queen & 1 twin bedroom & 1 private bathroom
- 1 self catering cottage with 1 queen bedroom
- cotton bed linen & bathrobes
- hair dryer, toiletries, heated towel rails & spa bath
- fresh flowers in rooms
- central heating
- 11am checkout time

- continental/cooked breakfast
- dinner with wine, $35 pp
- log fire, Sky/Digital TV, DVD, video & music in guest lounge
- grand piano in lounge
- phone, fax & email facilities
- complimentary tea/coffee
- children over 10 years welcome
- complimentary laundry
- off-street parking

ACTIVITIES AVAILABLE

- 0.5ha garden with stream
- barbecue on site
- tennis court & pavilion
- pétanque/boules court
- swimming pool
- hot air ballooning, adjacent
- antique shops
- historic town tours
- vineyards
- town centre, 5-min walk

- restaurants, 5-min walk
- beaches
- gardens open to visit
- horse riding
- bush walks
- golf
- fishing
- caving
- Mt Bruce Wildlife Centre
- Wellington City, 2-hr drive

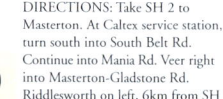

Riddlesworth Estate

Hosts Adrienne Avery and Stuart Forbes

61 Masterton-Gladstone Road, R D 4, Masterton
Phone 0-6-378 0130   *Mobile* 021 705 007   *Fax* 0-6-378 0131
Email adrienne.avery@xtra.co.nz   *Website* www.riddlesworth.com

DIRECTIONS: Take SH 2 to Masterton. At Caltex service station, turn south into South Belt Rd. Continue into Mania Rd. Veer right into Masterton-Gladstone Rd. Riddlesworth on left, 6km from SH 2.

    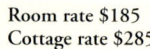

3 bdrm	3 enst	Room rate $185	Includes breakfast for all guests
		Cottage rate $285	2-night minimum stay Self-catering for lunch & dinner

Bounded on two sides by the Ruamahanga River, Riddlesworth is a 24-hectare (60-acre) farm, offering views of the Tararua Range. This extensive property was a former thoroughbred stud farm, named after an early racehorse imported from England. Built in 2001 in American southern colonial style, the house provides two queen-size ensuite guestrooms with rural views. A separate self-contained cottage also has a queen-size bedroom, as well as a fully equipped kitchen for self-catering if desired. A gourmet breakfast is served in the house dining room, or alfresco on the patio. Restaurants are only six kilometres away in Masterton, and winery tours throughout the Wairarapa vineyard region are always popular with guests.

FACILITIES

- House: 2 queen bedrooms, both with baths in ensuites
- Cottage: 1 queen bedroom, with spa bath in ensuite
- hair dryers, demist mirror, bathrobes & heated towel rails
- central heating & air conditioning in house
- fresh flowers
- email, fax & phone facilities
- billiards/snooker room
- gourmet breakfast
- full kitchen for self-catering in cottage only
- lounge with open fire & tea/coffee in house
- media room with big-screen Sky TV, DVD & video in house
- rural & mountain views
- courtesy passenger transfer from railway station
- on-site parking

ACTIVITIES AVAILABLE

- swimming pool
- BBQ available for guest use
- tennis court on site
- 24ha (60 acres) on site with mature trees, orchard, vegetable garden & river
- guided fishing on local rivers
- bird-watching on site
- river walks & bicycling on site
- antique shops, 6km
- restaurants, 6km
- laundry, 6km
- mountain hiking
- river rafting
- golf
- hot air ballooning
- gardens open to visit
- horse riding
- wine tasting & wine tours
- Wellington City, 1½ hrs

Above: The Ruamahanga River flows adjacent to Riddlesworth Estate, providing popular areas for walking.
Below: One of the two queen-size guest bedrooms in the main house, looking into the ensuite which includes a bath.
Opposite top: The exterior of the main house at Riddlesworth Estate, built in southern colonial American style in 2001.
Opposite bottom left: The separate self-contained guest cottage at Riddlesworth, where guests can self-cater in the full kitchen.
Opposite bottom right: The queen-size bedroom in the guest cottage opens into an ensuite bathroom with a spa bath.

Gladstone Vineyard Apartment

Hosts Christine and David Kernohan

20 Gladstone Road, R D 2, Carterton
Phone 0-6-379 8563   *Email* info@gladstone.co.nz
Fax 0-6-379 8564   *Website* www.gladstone.co.nz

DIRECTIONS: From Greytown or Masterton, take SH 2 to Carterton. Turn east into Park Rd. At "T" junction turn left into Carters Rd. Take 1st right into Gladstone Rd. Travel 3 mins to Vineyard on right.

| 1 bdrm | 1 enst | **Apartment rate $215** | *Includes breakfast provisions* | *Self-catering* |  |

Set in the thriving wine-growing area of the Wairarapa, Gladstone Vineyard Apartment is situated above the Gladstone winery. The apartment offers a queen-size bed with double settee for additional guests. The lounge area is warmed by a wood burner and a spacious deck is popular for alfresco dining in the summer. Guests enjoy the views over the vineyard to the hills beyond, or for the more active walks around the vineyard and pond or through the native bush adjacent. Country breakfast supplies and a bottle of wine are provided and dinner can be delivered by arrangement. A lunchtime café operates on site from October to March, on Friday, Saturday and Sunday. The hosts live in a separate Victorian house about 200 metres from the winery.

FACILITIES

- private-party bookings only
- 1 queen ensuite bedroom
- phone, TV & tea/coffee in bedroom; fresh flowers
- hair dryer, heated towel rails, bathrobes, bath & toiletries
- double bed settee for extras
- email, fax & phone available
- laundry by arrangement
- complimentary bottle of wine
- full kitchen for self-catering
- provisions – mushrooms, eggs, bacon, fruit, cereal, fresh bread/croissants & tea/coffee
- café on site, Oct–Easter
- wine for sale
- private guest lounge with wood burner, nibbles, TV & CD-player
- on-site parking; helipad

ACTIVITIES AVAILABLE

- pamper weekend package, by request with theraputic massage, manicures & dinner for 2
- pétanque court on site
- vineyard, wine tastings & winery tours on site
- pond & garden walks
- small dogs welcome
- honeymoons catered for
- Carters Reserve with board walk through native bush next door
- restaurants nearby
- adventure activities
- wheelwright
- cheesemaker
- museum
- ostrich farm
- antique shops
- wineries
- bush walks
- gardens open to visit

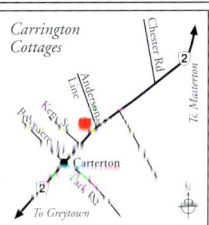

CARTERTON, WAIRARAPA

Carrington Cottages and Gardens

Hosts Shirley and John Cameron

High Street North, State Highway 2, Carterton
Phone 0-6-379 7039   *Mobile* 027 445 6409   *Fax* 0-6-379 7039
Email cameron@wise.net.nz   *Website* www.carringtoncottages.co.nz

3 bdrm   **2** enst

Cottage rate **$150 for 2 persons**
Extra persons **$45 each**

Includes breakfast provisions
Self-catering

DIRECTIONS: From Greytown take take SH 2 north through Carterton. Turn left into Carrington House on corner of Andersons Line. From Masterton take SH2 south towards Carterton. Carrington on right

Carrington Cottages are set in eight hectares (20 acres) of park-like grounds and gardens designed by the renowned New Zealand landscape architect, Alfred Buxton, in the early 1900s. Original features can still be seen including the lake and the driveway that winds through mature exotic trees to arrive at the house. Accommodation is offered in two separate self-contained cottages tucked away on the northern sunny side of the property. Carrington Farm Cottage (*above*) was originally built in 1860 and is now restored and refurbished with colonial furniture to provide two double bedrooms, a bathroom, laundry and full kitchen. Carrington House Cottage (*below*) was relocated in the 1970s and furnished in Italian designer style. This cottage comprises one queen-size bedroom and ensuite, with laundry facilities, a full kitchen and mountain views. Guests can self-cater in both cottages, and dine beside the open fire or alfresco looking out to the daffodil fields and garden.

FACILITIES

- 2 self-contained cottages
- single party bookings per cottage
- House Cottage: 1 queen bedroom, 1 ensuite with shub, video & mountain views
- Farm cottage: 2 double bedrooms, 1 bathroom with heated towel rails & wheelchair access
- hair dryer, toiletries & bathrobes in both cottage bathrooms
- fresh flowers
- lounge with open fire, TV, books & artwork in both cottages
- phone jacks in cottages for laptop computer connection

- full kitchen for self-catering in both cottages
- breakfast provisions supplied
- laundry facilities in both cottages
- views of mountain ranges or garden
- colonial furniture in Farm Cottage
- Italian designer furnishings in House Cottage
- pet sheep, cats & dogs on site
- children by arrangement
- historic garden setting
- private location
- off-street parking

ACTIVITIES AVAILABLE

- garden seats on site
- garden walks on site
- vineyards, 10-min drive
- wine trails
- sports ground
- Clareville showground
- antiques shop, 2-min drive
- antiques trail
- local crafts
- museum
- arts studio
- historic town tours
- restaurants nearby
- gardens open to visit
- plant nurseries

- cheesemaker to visit
- east coast beaches
- fishing
- swimming
- bush walks
- Tararua Forest Park
- caving
- adventure activities
- Mt Bruce Wildlife Centre
- hot air ballooning
- Carterton township, within walking distance
- Masterton, 7-min drive
- Greytown, 5 mins south
- Wellington City, 1½ hrs

GREYTOWN, WAIRARAPA
Briarwood

Host Liz Kennedy

21 Main Street, Greytown
Phone 0-6-304 8336   *Mobile* 027 252 4902   *Fax* 0-6-304 8316
Email briarwood@xtra.co.nz   *Website* www.briarwood.biz

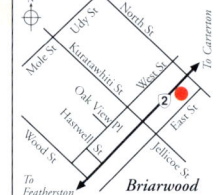

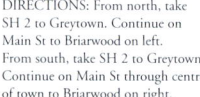

DIRECTIONS: From north, take SH 2 to Greytown. Continue on Main St to Briarwood on left. From south, take SH 2 to Greytown. Continue on Main St through centre of town to Briarwood on right.

| 2 bdrm | 2 enst | **Double** $195–$250
Single $150–$215 | *Includes breakfast*
Lunch & dinner extra | *Self-catering* |

 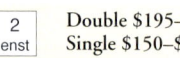 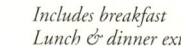 

Built circa 1867, Briarwood is a colonial townhouse in Greytown's historic Main Street offering bed and breakfast in two suites, one fully self-contained. Extensive renovations retain many original features. The two private bedrooms, with quiet acoustics, feature Egyptian bed linen, mohair wraps, and an eclectic mix of antiques and contemporary artwork. Both ensuites include a clawfoot bath, and aromatherapy products. Guests can enjoy breakfasts and dégustation dinners in the formal dining room upstairs, by the fire in winter, or alfresco in the private courtyards in summer. There is a full kitchen in one suite for self-catering, and platters or picnic hampers are available by arrangement. Wairarapa vineyard tours are popular with guests.

FACILITIES

- 1 super-king/twin & 1 queen suite, each with ensuite, private courtyard, lounge & dining area
- bathrobes, clawfoot bath, double shower, hair dryer, toiletries, heated floor & towel rails in both ensuites
- Egyptian cotton bed linen
- wheelchair access
- keypad entry to each suite

- fresh flowers; fax & phone
- complimentary laundry
- café-style breakfast menu
- lunch or picnic hamper by arrangement, $35 pp; dinner with wine, $85 pp
- full self-catering kitchen
- tea/coffee, nibbles, bar, Sky TV, video, DVDs, CDs, desk, artwork, books & internet access in both suites

ACTIVITIES AVAILABLE

- pétanque/boules & BBQ on site
- vineyard tours
- paua factory
- golf courses
- tennis courts
- adventure sports
- hot air ballooning
- mountain hiking
- horse trekking
- gardens open to visit

- beaches & scenic coastal tours
- award-wining restaurants
- museums & historic buildings
- antique shops & galleries
- colonial heritage walks
- hunting & fishing, guides available
- spectacular river gorge
- Martinborough, 15 mins
- Masterton, 20 mins

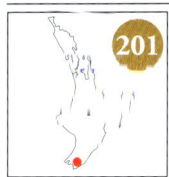

GREYTOWN, WAIRARAPA
Westwood Country House

Ann Jill Kemp

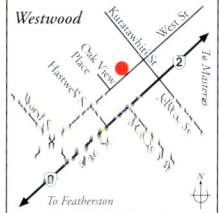

DIRECTIONS: From Featherston, take SH 2 north to Greytown. Turn left into Wood St, then right into West St. Westwood on left. From Carterton, take SH 2 south to Greytown. Turn right into Kuratawhiti St, then left.

82 West Street, Greytown   *Postal* P O Box 34, Greytown
Phone 0-6-304 8510   *Mobile* 027 471 6466   *Fax* 0-6-304 8610
Email westwood.kemp@xtra.co.nz   *Website* westwood.greytown.co.nz

   Double $195–$275   **Single $170–$225**   *Includes breakfast*

4 bdrm	3 enst	1 prbth

A top category award winner in New Zealand House of the Year, Westwood has been designed to blend with the surrounding trees, stream and mountain views. The guest wing provides spacious bedrooms for up to seven guests, with dressing rooms, large ensuites or private bathrooms and adjoining verandahs opening into the garden. Each bedroom also includes tea and coffee-making facilities, a fridge and Sky television. Breakfast is served alfresco by the pool in summer, in the dining room in winter, or in the guests' rooms if preferred. Guests enjoy the formal Italian-inspired herb garden and landscaping, playing croquet and pétanque, swimming in the pool, picking raspberries in season, or viewing the animals on the four-hectare (nine-acre) site.

FACILITIES

- 3 super-king/twin & 1 single bedroom
- 3 ensuites & 1 private bathroom
- hair dryers, bathrobes & wheelchair access
- heated towel rails & heated floors
- 1 bath & double basin
- 2 dressing rooms
- fresh flowers in rooms
- breakfast served in dining room, bedrooms, or by pool
- tea/coffee, fridge & Sky TV in all 3 bedrooms
- guest lounge with open fire
- phone, fax & email facilities
- laundry available
- private guest entrance
- off-street parking
- barbecue available

ACTIVITIES AVAILABLE

- swimming pool on site
- in-ground croquet lawn
- pétanque/boules on site
- exclusive garden tours on site
- raspberry picking in season
- nearly 4ha (9 acres) with formal herb garden on site
- sheep & hens on site
- golf courses & tennis courts
- gardens open to visit
- restaurants, 3-min stroll
- antique shops, nearby
- hiking on mountain & river walks
- horse trekking
- adventure sports
- Greytown shops, 3-min walk
- Martinborough's world renowned vineyards, 20 mins
- Wellington City, 1-hour drive

MARTINBOROUGH, WAIRARAPA
Riverside Retreat

Hosts Christine and Derek Douché

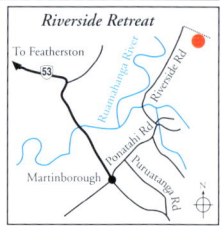
Riverside Retreat

2894c Riverside Road, Martinborough   *Postal* 19 Pownall Street, Masterton
Phone 0-6-377 3035   *Mobile* 027 230 7241   *Fax* 0-6-377 3035
Email cridding@infogen.net.nz   *Website* www.riverside.co.nz

DIRECTIONS: From Martinborough take Princess St & continue into Ponatahi Rd. Travel 2km & turn left into Riverside Rd. Travel 4.5km to end of road & turn right uphill through gate to Riverside Retreat on left.

| 2 bdrm | 1 prbth | 1 pdrm | House rate $280 for 2 persons Extra persons $35 each | *Includes breakfast provisions* Winter rates available | *Self-catering* |

Riverside Retreat

Overlooking the Ruamahanga River as it winds through the South Wairarapa valley, Riverside Retreat provides self-contained accommodation with panoramic rural views to the Tararua Range beyond. Newly built in innovative design as a circular arch barn house, Riverside Retreat features high quality fittings and furnishings and a mezzanine bedroom suitable for honeymooners. There is a fully equipped kitchen and basic provisions for self-catering, and lunch and dinner can be arranged. A large deck is popular for alfresco dining, and the restaurants of Martinborough village are only 10 minutes' drive away. Guests can enjoy the hillside walks on site through emerging fig and olive groves, to secluded outlooks over vineyard, river and farmland.

FACILITIES

- one-party bookings only
- 2 queen bedrooms
- 1 bathroom with bath & toiletries
- 1 powder room downstairs
- cotton bed linen
- self-serve laundry
- 2 living areas with tea/coffee, Sky TV, video, CD-player, music, writing desk, books & magazines
- decking with extensive views

- self-serve continental breakfast supplies
- full kitchen for self-catering with provisions
- lunch & dinner by qualified chef, by prior arrangement
- air-conditioning
- unsuitable for young children
- on-site parking; helipad

ACTIVITIES AVAILABLE

- developing olive & fig groves
- walks on site
- barbecue available
- vineyards nearby
- wine tasting & tours
- arts & crafts
- gardens open to visit
- fishing in river
- Mt Bruce Wildlife Centre

- restaurants & cafés, 10 mins
- alpaca farm tours
- helicopter flights arranged
- Martinborough Square, 10-min drive away
- Greytown, 20-mins
- Carterton, 25-mins drive
- Masterton township, 40-mins
- Wellington City, 1¼-hour drive away

Riverside Retreat

Riverside Retreat

MARTINBOROUGH, WAIRARAPA
Margrain Vineyard Villas

Hosts Daryl and Graham Margrain

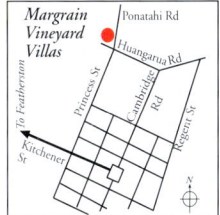

Margrain Vineyard Villas

Ponatahi Rd
Huangarua Rd
To Featherston
Princess St
Kitchener St
Kansbridge Rd
Regent St

DIRECTIONS: From Featherston, travel towards Martinborough. On edge of township turn left into Princess St. Continue to Huangarua Rd. Cross intersection to Margrain driveway, 200m past left corner of Ponatahi Rd.

Ponatahi Road, Martinborough   *Postal* P O Box 97, Martinborough
Phone 0-6-306 9292   *Email* margrain@xtra.co.nz
Fax 0-6-306 9297   *Website* www.margrainvineyard.co.nz

15 bdrm	15 enst

Room rate $160–$300   *Includes continental breakfast provisions*

The four-hectare Margrain Vineyard was first planted in 1992. Three years later the first wines from the estate were produced, coinciding with the opening of the first eight of the 15 Margrain Vineyard Villas, sited adjacent to the terraced vineyard. The architecture was designed by Roger Walker, with interior design by Decor Trends. Each villa comprises a king/twin or queen-size bed, ensuite bathroom with wheelchair access, and lounge area (one separate suite), with French doors opening to a spacious balcony overlooking the rural pastureland of the Huangarua River valley, to the Tararua Range beyond. This is a favourite spot for watching pukeko. Facilities are available for small conferences adjacent to the wineshop and winery with its three-vault cellars.

FACILITIES

- 15 separate villas
- single-party bookings for each villa
- each villa comprises 1 bedroom, 1 spacious bathroom, sitting area & extensive private balcony
- 9 king/twins & 6 queen bedrooms, all with ensuites
- 15 ensuite bathrooms with heated towel rails
- continental breakfast provisions
- tea/coffee-making facilities
- TV in each villa
- iron & board in each villa
- cotton bed linen
- wheelchair access to 1 villa
- balconies overlook river valley
- children by arrangement
- off-street parking
- developing garden

ACTIVITIES AVAILABLE

- wine tasting, winery & vineyard
- Old Winery Café on site
- pukeko watching on site
- pétanque/boules on site
- trout fishing in adjacent river
- good restaurants, 5-min drive
- Wairarapa wine trail
- tennis & squash courts
- 18-hole golf course
- private gardens to visit
- antiques & craft shops
- colonial museum
- glow-worm caves
- horse trekking
- canoeing; caving
- chasm walkway; seal colony
- abseiling, rafting
- Putangirua Pinnacles
- Ngawi fishing village
- Palliser Bay coast

MARTINBOROUGH
The Old Manse

Hosts Sandra and John Hargrave

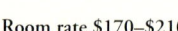

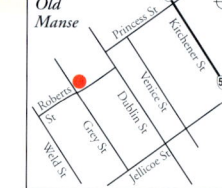

19 Grey Street, Martinborough *Freephone* 0800 399 229
Phone 0-6-306 8599 *Mobile* 027 439 9229 *Fax* 0-6-306 8540
Email info@oldmanse.co.nz *Website* www.oldmanse.co.nz

6 bdrm	6 enst	1 pdrm

Room rate $170–$210 *Includes breakfast*

qualmark ★★★+

DIRECTIONS: From Featherston, take SH 53 to Martinborough. Turn right into Princess St. At "T" junction turn left into Dublin St, then right into Roberts St. The Old Manse on right corner of Grey St.

The Old Manse

Originally built in 1876, The Old Manse was the Presbyterian manse of Martinborough for 80 years. Fully restored in 2000, The Old Manse now offers six ensuite guestrooms and a spacious lounge with open fireplace and verandah looking out to the on-site vineyard and the large garden and lawns. A gazebo provides a peaceful spot in the garden for relaxing, and the verandah is a sunny area for alfresco breakfasting. Continental and cooked breakfast can also be served in the dining room. Restaurants and cafés are just a five-minute walk away in Martinborough village. Guests can enjoy the outdoor spa pool and croquet on the lawn, or the billiards room indoors. Vineyard walks and wine tasting are popular activities in the Martinborough region.

FACILITIES

- 5 queen ensuite bedrooms
- 1 twin ensuite bedroom
- bath in 1 ensuite bathroom
- cotton bed linen
- hair dryer, toiletries, bathrobes & heated towel rails
- email, fax & cordless phone
- guest lounge with open fire, tea/coffee, nibbles, Sky TV, video, DVD, CD-player & writing desk
- continental & cooked breakfast served in dining room or alfresco on deck
- laundry available
- verandah opening to garden
- historic architecture
- vineyard on site
- private guest entrance
- on-site parking
- courtesy passenger transfer

ACTIVITIES AVAILABLE

- spa pool on site
- pétanque & croquet on site
- billiards room on site
- large garden & lawn area with gazebo for relaxing
- 18-hole golf course
- tennis courts
- wine tasting; antique shops
- fishing; canoeing
- Mt Bruce Wildlife Centre
- restaurants, 5-min walk
- horse trekking
- 4WD quad bikes; mountain biking
- vineyard walks
- seal colony
- hot air ballooning
- jet boat tours
- clay bird shooting
- glow-worm caves

The Old Manse

The Old Manse

PALLISER BAY, WAIRARAPA
Pounui Homestead

Hosts Ju and Nick Allen

2110 Western Lake Road, R D 3, Featherston
Phone 0-6-307 7687   *Email* pounui@xtra.co.nz
Fax 0-6-307 7686   *Website* www.pounuihomestead.co.nz

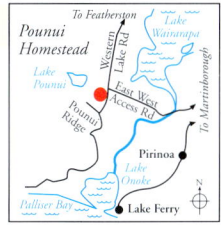

DIRECTIONS: From Wellington take SH 2 over Rimutaka hill to Featherston. Take Western Lake Rd & travel 33km to Pounui on right. Homestead at top of drive. (Pounui is 1½-hour drive from Wellington.)

4 bdrm	2 enst	1 shbth	1 pdrm

House rate $250–$350 for 2 persons   Multiple-night rates available
Extra persons $50 each   Children under 10 years $30 each   *Self-catering*

Pounui Homestead

Located in a rural setting with lake and sea views, Pounui Homestead is a self-contained house set in 13 hectares (33 acres) of mature gardens, lawns and covenanted first-generation native bush. The hosts live on site in an adjacent historic cottage and welcome the opportunity to provide guests with information about activities, the property and local history. Pounui Homestead offers four bedrooms, a bunkroom and three bathrooms, as well as two lounges and a fully equipped kitchen for self-catering. Two bedrooms and both lounges access private garden and lawn areas from separate verandahs. Breakfast provisions for the first morning are supplied and further provisions can be arranged. A chef is available for catered meals if required.

FACILITIES

- private-party bookings only
- 1 king & 1 king/twin bedroom
- 2 ensuites with claw-foot baths
- 1 queen & 1 queen/twin bedroom share 1 bathroom
- cotton bed linen, hair dryers, heated towel rails; fresh flowers
- children welcome; cots available
- self-serve laundry
- 1 powder room
- full kitchen for self-catering
- 1st morning breakfast supplies
- chef by arrangement, extra
- 2 lounges with open fireplace & woodburner
- Sky TV, CD & video players, books, magazines & artwork
- phone, email & fax available
- private tree-lined guest entrance
- on-site parking, garaging; helipad

ACTIVITIES AVAILABLE

- farm/bush walks on neighbouring Pounui farm by arrangement
- in-season feeding lambs/calves
- garden & native bush walks
- croquet & pétanque/boules
- 4WD vehicle & ATV/quad bike tours, extra charge:
  – Lake Pounui & bushland tours
  – sheep/dairy farm guided tours
- Cape Palliser seal colony & lighthouse
- jet boat tours, extra charge:
  – Lake Onoke/Lake Ferry
  – Ruamahanga River
- Putangirua Pinnacles
- surfing, fishing & diving at Ocean Beach
- Martinborough vineyards
- tramping & hunting in 2 forest parks in area
- spit walk at Lake Onoke
- canoeing; horse trekking

PALLISER BAY, WAIRARAPA
Wharekauhau Country Estate

Hosts Kristy and Nico de Lange

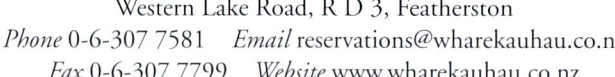
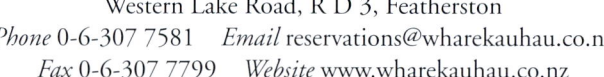

Western Lake Road, R D 3, Featherston
Phone 0-6-307 7581   *Email* reservations@wharekauhau.co.nz
Fax 0-6-307 7799   *Website* www.wharekauhau.co.nz

DIRECTIONS: Take SH 2 to Featherston. Then take Western Lake Rd south & travel for 40km. Wharekauhau at end of road. (50km south-west of Martinborough also.) Or 10 mins by helicopter from Wellington.

| 12 bdrm | 12 enst | 1 pdrm | Double $1,375–$2,105 | *Includes breakfast & dinner* |
| Single $915–$1,655 | *Lunch & activities extra* |

Wharekauhau is a luxury lodge, set on 2,200 hectares of farmland overlooking the rugged coastline of Palliser Bay on the southern tip of the North Island, providing uninterrupted panoramic ocean views from every guestroom. Opened in 1998, the Edwardian-style main lodge is within walking distance of 12 cottage suites, each comprising a king/twin bedroom, lounge area featuring an open fireplace, walk-in dressing room, ensuite bathroom, mini-bar and fridge. A full buffet and à la carte cooked breakfast is served in the country kitchen. Pre-dinner drinks and a four-course table d'hôte dinner are included in the tariff and served in the licensed lodge dining room. Private dining is also available in the Drawing Room or Palliser Room, by request.

FACILITIES

- 12 cottage suites, each with 1 king/twin ensuite bedroom
- 1 bath, dual basins, hair dryer, toiletries, heated floor, heated towel rails & demist mirror in each ensuite bathroom
- phone, open fireplace, walk-in dressing room, tea/coffee, mini-bar & fridge in each cottage suite
- Egyptian cotton bed linen
- fresh fruit

- tariff includes full buffet & à la carte breakfast, apéritifs & 4-course dinner
- fully licensed
- à la carte light lunch, extra
- modem & fax line in suites
- TV available on request
- laundry charged per item
- children welcome
- on-site parking

ACTIVITIES AVAILABLE

On site complimentary:
- health facility:
  – all-weather tennis court,
  – indoor heated pool,
  – outdoor spa pool,
  – gym
- helipad for heli-tours
- pétanque/boules & croquet
- mountain biking
- hiking

On site charged:
- massages; 4WD safaris; ATV bike tours
- sheep farm tours; jet boating
- sporting clay-field; hunting
- surf-casting; horse riding

Off site:
- seal colony; wine tasting
- golf; gardens to visit
- Martinborough vineyards

Te Horo, Kapiti
Bixley House – Country Retreat

Hosts Angela and Derek Perkins

255 Old Hautere Road, Te Horo, Kapiti   *Freephone* 0800 4 BIXLEY
Phone 0-6-364 3969   *Mobiles* 021 459 004 or 027 624 7457
Email enquiries@bixleyhouse.co.nz   *Website* www.bixleyhouse.co.nz

DIRECTIONS: From north, take SH
1 south to Otaki. Turn left into Otaki
Gorge Rd. Travel 3km & turn right
into Old Hautere Rd. Travel 500m to
Bixley House on right. From south,
take SH 1 towards Otaki. Turn right.

3 bdrm	1 enst	2 prbth	Double $195–$250 Single $145–$210	*Includes breakfast* *Dinner extra*

Bixley House

Set in extensive landscaped gardens, Bixley House was built in a traditional English style with dormer leadlight windows. There is a native forest remnant on the property, attracting birdlife, with a backdrop of the Tararua Range. Three spacious guestrooms with bathrooms are offered for accommodation, and there is a family room with a woodburner fire, as well as a private guest lounge. There are also in-house facilities for small conferences. Continental and full cooked breakfasts are served in the breakfast room, formal dining room or alfresco on the patio. Dinner is available by prior arrangement. There are several restaurants within a few minutes' drive of Bixley House. A German Shepherd dog, Blaze, completes the family.

FACILITIES

- Foxhall: 1 super-king/twin ensuite bedroom with patio
- Purdis: 1 king/twin bedroom with writing desk, private bathroom, bath
- Rushmere: 1 king bedroom with private bathroom & spa bath
- hair dryer, toiletries, bathrobes, heated floor & heated towel rails
- lounge with woodburner, Sky TV, video, DVD, CD-player, tea/coffee, nibbles, artwork & writing desk

- continental & full cooked breakfast
- 3-course dinner with wine, $45 pp
- cotton bed linen, TV, tea/coffee in bedrooms
- laundry service, $5
- email & broadband
- small conferences catered
- on-site parking

ACTIVITIES AVAILABLE

- barbecue available
- native forest remnant on site
- large landscaped gardens
- Otaki Forks
- Tararua Range
- Kapiti Island bookings
- Ruth Pretty Catering School
- The Lindale Centre
- Ferndale Equestrian Centre
- Southward Car Museum

- restaurants, 5 mins
- Kapiti 4WD adventures
- Foxton windmill
- Nga Manu Nature Reserve
- 4 golf courses; beaches
- art galleries; museum
- gardens open to visit
- air shuttle
- Otaki township, 5 mins
- Wellington, 1 hour south

Bixley House

Bixley House

Te Horo, Kapiti Coast
Te Horo Lodge

Host Craig Garner

109 Arcus Road, Te Horo   *Postal* P O Box 43, Te Horo   *Mobile* 027 430 6009
Freephone 0800 483 467   *Phone* 0-6-364 3393   *Fax* 0-6-364 3323
Email reservations@tehorolodge.co.nz   *Website* www.tehorolodge.co.nz

4 bdrm	4 enst	1 pdrm	**Double $195–$330**	*Includes breakfast*
			Single $150–$240	*Dinner extra*

DIRECTIONS: From Otaki, take SH 1 for 8km south. At Te Horo, turn left across railway into School Rd. Turn left again into Arcus Rd. Te Horo Lodge at end of road on left. Or from Waikanae, take SH 1 for 9km north.

Designed by architect Gary Cullen and purpose-built in 1998, Te Horo Lodge offers four ensuite guestrooms with a conservatory, private lounge and boutique conference room. A roaring open fire in the stone fireplace in the lounge in winter and the spa and swimming pool in summer make Te Horo a suitable get-away for Wellingtonians all year round. Set in two hectares (five acres) of gardens and developing orchard, and surrounded by another two hectares of native bush, Te Horo provides peace and tranquillity for rest and recreation. A full breakfast is served in the dining room and dinner is also offered in this fully licensed Lodge. Alfresco barbecues in the gazebo are popular or, alternatively, restaurants are just a 10-minute drive away at Waikanae.

FACILITIES

- 1 wheelchair access guestroom
- 3 super-king/twin bedrooms with ensuites & verandahs
- 1 super-king/twin upstairs suite with ensuite & bush views
- hair dryers, toiletries, heated towel rails, demist mirror, bathrobes & heated floor
- carafe of port, chocolates & fresh flowers in bedrooms
- laundry available, $10

- 3-course dinner, by arrangement only, $55 pp
- conservatory, BBQ & gazebo
- guests' tea/coffee facilities
- business & conference room for up to 12 people
- lounge with open fire, TV, DVD, video, CD-player, books
- phone & fax available
- on-site parking
- courtesy passenger transfer

ACTIVITIES AVAILABLE

- conferences for up to 12 people
- outdoor swimming & spa pools
- pétanque court on site
- 2ha-gardens & orchard with tamarillos & olives on site
- 2ha native bush on site
- Ruth Pretty's cooking classes, booking essential
- 5 golf courses within 30 mins
- Te Horo Beach, 10 mins

- Waikanae restaurants, 10 mins
- 4WD adventures, 20 mins
- garden visiting; biking; fishing
- Nga Manu Nature Reserve
- Southwards Car Museum
- Lindale Centre, including Kapiti cheeses & Kapiti ice cream
- Kapiti Island excursions
- Wellington, 1 hour south

Te Horo, Kapiti Coast
Pateke Lagoons Wetlands

Hosts Peter and Adrienne Dale

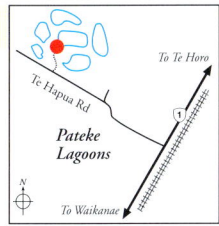

152 Te Hapua Road, Te Horo, R D 1, Otaki, Kapiti Coast
Phone 0-6-364 2222   *Mobile* 021 439 661   *Fax* 0-6-364 2214
Email peter@pateke-lagoons.co.nz   *Website* www.pateke-lagoons.co.nz

DIRECTIONS: From north, take SH 1 to Te Horo & continue 2km south. Turn right into Te Hapua Rd. Travel 1.52km to Pateke Lagoons on right. From south, take SH 1 to Waikanae & continue 8km north. Turn left.

| 2 bdrm | 2 enst | Room rate $195 | *Includes breakfast* | *Lunch & dinner extra* | |

In a secluded spot overlooking 14 hectares (35 acres) of wetland, guests at the lodge at Pateke Lagoons can walk through the native flora protected by the QEII National Trust and watch waterfowl and other birdlife. Endangered species such as dabchicks nest on the lagoon, and royal spoonbills can be seen over the summer. A deserted west coast beach can be reached by a private walking track and bird sanctuaries can also be visited. Accommodation comprises two queen-size downstairs bedrooms, each opening to a private courtyard with wetland views. Meals are served as needed in the dining room overlooking the lagoons, or in the guest courtyards or library. Picnic lunches and dinner featuring fresh local produce are also available.

FACILITIES

- 1 queen ensuite bedroom
- 1 queen/twin ensuite bedroom
- bath in one ensuite
- hair dryer, heated towel rails, demist mirror, toiletries & bathrobes in both ensuites
- tea/coffee, wine, cheese, biscuits, phone jacks, fridge & cotton bed linen in bedrooms
- private courtyards open from both bedrooms

- full cooked breakfast using local produce served
- picnic lunch by request, extra
- à la carte dinner using local produce with wine, $60 pp
- laundry available
- library; fresh flowers
- courtesy passenger transfer
- on-site parking
- helicopter access

ACTIVITIES AVAILABLE

- 20ha wetland wildfowl refuge with native trees on site
- bush & wetland walks on site
- native flora
- bird & waterfowl watching – estuarine, coastal & bush
- barbecue available
- deserted beach, 1km walk via private track
- Kapiti coast gardens to visit

- restaurants nearby
- Nga Manu Bird Sanctuary, 10-min drive away
- Kapiti Island trips, by prior arrangement only
- Manawatu Estuary, 30 mins
- Tararua Forest Park, 30 mins
- Lake Papaitonga, 30 mins
- railway station, 15 mins
- Wellington City, 1 hour south

Pateke Lagoons

© Friars' Guide to New Zealand Accommodation for the Discerning Traveller

210

WAIKANAE, KAPITI COAST
Hurunui Homestead Boutique Lodge

Hosts Erica and Geoff Lineham

15 Hurunui Street, Waikanae   *Postal* P O Box 81, Waikanae
Phone 0-4-902 8571   *Email* relax@hurunuihomestead.co.nz
Fax 0-4-902 8572   *Website* www.hurunuihomestead.co.nz

4 bdrm	3 enst	1 prbth	1 pdrm

Double $195–$300
Single $145–$260

Includes breakfast
Packages available

DIRECTIONS: From Wellington or Otaki, take SH 1 to Waikanae. Turn west into Ngaio Rd, then 1st right into Parata St. Turn left into Sylvan Ave, then right into David St. Turn left into Hurunui St to Lodge at end.

Nestled in secluded park-like gardens, with a private bush walk and adjoining eco-heritage reserve, Hurunui Homestead is under an hour's drive from downtown Wellington. Accommodation includes a spacious suite in the private downstairs wing, and upstairs are two further guestrooms with a mezzanine sitting room. Two guest living rooms featuring original artworks and antiques open to an expansive sun-drenched courtyard. Breakfast time is flexible with seasonal fruits and home-made specialities presented on different fine china each morning. Guests enjoy the extensive grounds with solar-heated outdoor swimming pool, private aromatherapy spa pool, tennis court, pétanque piste, gazebo, water gardens and native birdlife.

FACILITIES

- Water Garden suite: 1 super-king/twin bedroom, dressing room, ensuite, tea/reading room & 1 double bedroom with bathroom
- 2 queen ensuite bedrooms upstairs, 1 with dressing room
- cotton bed linen, goosedown duvets, TV, iron & board, & garden views
- robes, slippers, hair dryer, toiletries, heated towel rails & ensuite heating
- cable TV, video, CD-player, piano

- breakfast in dining room
- sherry, port, chocolates, tea/coffee, cookies, mini-fridge, filtered water
- 2 open fires in lounges
- artwork & fresh flowers
- WiFi, guest computer with broadband; fax
- laundry service, extra
- off-street parking

ACTIVITIES AVAILABLE

- heated pool (summer), on site
- private spa pool/jacuzzi room
- all-weather tennis court on site
- pétanque court; bird-watching
- 0.8ha native bush walk on site
- Lindale Tourist Centre – Kapiti cheeses, speciality shopping, farm walk & demonstrations
- Paraparaumu Beach golf course
- bush/river walks; Saturday market

- restaurants & cafés, 2 mins
- Waikanae shops, 2-min drive
- Nga Manu Nature Reserve & nocturnal house, 5-min drive
- safe swimming & sand beaches, 5-min drive
- Kapiti Island visits arranged
- Wellington-Picton interisland ferries, 50-min drive south
- Wellington City, 50 mins

Waikanae, Kapiti Coast
Te Nikau Forest Retreat

Owners Noel and Helen Trustrum   *Local hosts* Patricia and Murray Cardie

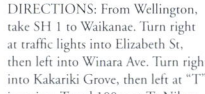

Kakariki Grove, Waikanae   *Postal* 42 Mortimer Terrace, Brooklyn, Wellington
Owners' Phone   0-4-938 7774   *and Fax* 0-4-938 9994   *Email* info@tenikau.co.nz
Hosts' Phone and Fax 0-4-293 5737   *Website* www.tenikau.co.nz

DIRECTIONS: From Wellington, take SH 1 to Waikanae. Turn right at traffic lights into Elizabeth St, then left into Winara Ave. Turn right into Kakariki Grove, then left at "T" junction. Travel 100m to Te Nikau.

| 2 bdrm | 1 prbth | House rate $255–$295 for 2 persons Extra persons $45 each | *Includes breakfast provisions* 2-night minimum | *Self-catering or catering arranged* Long-stay rates available |

Set in a clearing of a native coastal forest, on a terrace above a mountain stream, Te Nikau Forest Retreat offers total self-contained privacy. The seclusion of Te Nikau makes it suitable for honeymooners and romantic weekends. Local hosts, Patricia and Murray, welcome guests to Te Nikau. The chef from Rumours, a well-known Waikanae restaurant, will tailor dinner requirements to suit individual needs, or guests may choose to self-cater using the well-equipped kitchen. Built in 1997, Te Nikau borders Hemi Matenga Nature Reserve, which features abundant birdlife and the largest remnant stand of kohekohe forest in New Zealand. Guests enjoy relaxing in the spa pool on the deck, surrounded by the native forest.

FACILITIES

- self-contained forest retreat
- single-party bookings only
- 1 king & 1 single bedroom, & double sofa-bed in study
- 1 private bathroom
- large open fire, TV & DVD
- hair dryer, toiletries, heated towel rails & bathrobes
- guest balcony & decks
- clothes dryer
- fully equipped kitchen for self-catering
- continental & cooked breakfast provisions
- catered dinner tailored to needs of guests, extra
- complimentary bottle wine
- unsuitable for young children
- native forest setting
- off-street parking

ACTIVITIES AVAILABLE

- tree house spa pool on site
- bird-watching on site
- native forest walks & mountain stream on 0.5ha site
- Nature Reserve adjacent, with native forest walks
- wildlife reserves; horse riding
- Kapiti coast beaches & rivers
- restaurants & cafés, 5 mins
- Paraparaumu Beach golf course
- Waikanae shops, 5-min drive
- Lindale tourist complex
- Southwards Motor Museum
- pottery & craft shops
- Kapiti Island bird sanctuary, prior bookings necessary
- Wellington-Picton interisland ferries, 45-min drive
- Wellington City, 45-min drive
- babs.co.nz/tenikau

WAIKANAE, KAPITI COAST
Broadeaves

Hosts Liz and Andrew Kirkland

24 Ngarara Road, Waikanae, Kapiti Coast, Wellington
Phone 0-4-293 1483   *Mobile* 027 554 5175   *Fax* 0-4-293 1583
Email stay@broadeaves.co.nz   *Website* www.broadeaves.co.nz

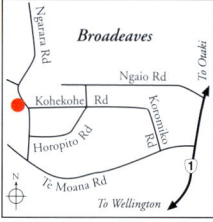

DIRECTIONS: From Wellington, take SH 1 to Waikanae. Turn left at 1st traffic lights into Te Moana Rd. Turn right into Ngarara Rd. Travel past T-junction to Broadeaves on left.

3 bdrm	1 enst	1 prbth	1 pdrm	Room rate $120–$225 Children $25 each	Includes breakfast & apéritifs Family package available	Dinner extra

Located in a peaceful garden setting in a quiet neighbourhood, Broadeaves provides accommodation for two separate parties. The main ensuite guestroom opens to its private spa pool deck surrounded by trees. There is also a spacious guest bedroom, opening to a verandah, that shares a bathroom with the third guestroom if needed. Continental and cooked breakfast is served in the dining room, or alfresco on the verandah looking out to the garden. A complimentary platter and wine are offered before dinner. While guests dine in the village nearby, Liz is happy to baby-sit their children, or dinner is available at Broadeaves by arrangement. Two retriever dogs and a cat are part of the family. Broadeaves is less than an hour north of Wellington City.

FACILITIES

- 1 queen bedroom with ensuite, dressing room & tea/coffee opens to private spa pool
- 1 super-king/twin opening to verandah & 1 queen bedroom share 1 private bathroom, in single-party bookings only
- bathrobes, double basins, hair dryer, toiletries, heated floor & towel rails in bathrooms
- cotton bed linen; fresh flowers

- full breakfast; complimentary pre-dinner wine & platter
- 3-course dinner in dining room, $35 pp; wine extra
- games, artwork, books, Sky TV, video, DVDs, CDs, tea/coffee & fresh baking in lounge
- complimentary laundry
- basic German spoken
- off-street parking
- children welcome

ACTIVITIES AVAILABLE

- garden, pétanque court & gym equipment on site
- children's play area with toys
- swimming pool, gym & park, all 3-min walk
- Kapiti coast beach, 4-min drive
- river walks & whitebaiting, 3-min drive
- native birds at Nga Manu Nature Reserve, 5-min drive

- restaurants, 5-min drive, or courtesy transfer available
- golf, bowls, croquet, 4–5 mins
- horse riding, 5-min drive
- Waikanae village, 5-min drive
- art galleries; gardens to visit
- Southwards Motor Museum, 7-min drive
- Lindale tourist centre, 8 mins
- Wellington City, 45 mins south

Waikanae Beach
Toheroa

Hosts Perrin and Ann Kirby

15 Oratia Street, Waikanae Beach   *Phone* 0-4-802 4707
Postal P O Box 12200, Thorndon, Wellington   *Mobile* 021 421 397
Email kapt@kapt.co.nz   *Website* friars.co.nz/hosts/toheroa.html

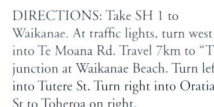

| 3 bdrm | 1 enst | 1 shbth | House rate $300 for 2 persons
Extra persons $50 each | *Includes breakfast provisions for 1st morning*
Minimum 2-night stay | *Self-catering*
Weekly rates available |

DIRECTIONS: Take SH 1 to Waikanae. At traffic lights, turn west into Te Moana Rd. Travel 7km to "T" junction at Waikanae Beach. Turn left into Tutere St. Turn right into Oratia St to Toheroa on right.

With uninterrupted views over Waikanae Beach to Kapiti Island, Toheroa is situated for viewing sunsets every evening from the house, the large deck or the beach. Toheroa is a self-contained holiday home with alfresco beach living on the doorstep. Named after the historically abundant supply of shellfish to be gathered at Waikanae Beach, Toheroa is an architecturally designed house with three bedrooms and two bathrooms. There is an open fireplace in the living room and a full kitchen for self-catering. Breakfast is supplied for the first morning, and local restaurants and a shop are just a stroll along the beach. Trips to the bird sanctuary of Kapiti Island are a highlight for guests, but need to be booked well in advance.

FACILITIES

- self-contained holiday house
- 1 queen ensuite bedroom with dressing room
- 1 queen & 1 twin bedroom share 1 private bathroom
- cotton bed linen
- hair dryers, toiletries, bathrobes, & heated towel rails
- phone available
- children welcome
- full kitchen for self-catering
- basic provisions & breakfast for 1st morning supplied
- living room with open fire, Sky TV, DVD, CD-player, music, books, artwork & writing desk
- large decking with sea views to Kapiti Island & sunsets
- beach access from deck
- on-site parking

ACTIVITIES AVAILABLE

- canoe & bicycles available for guest use
- direct beach access from site
- beach walks
- swimming
- kayaking
- golf course, 3 mins away
- Kapiti Island, booking needed
- Nga Manu Bird Sanctuary
- horse riding
- 2 restaurants, 5-min walk
- local store, 2-min drive or 10-min beach walk
- 4-wheel bike excursions
- Lindale Farm experience
- bowling & croquet
- art galleries
- gardens to visit
- Waikanae township, 7km
- Wellington City, 50 mins

RAUMATI SOUTH, KAPITI COAST
Sea Spirit Boutique Accommodation

Hosts Debbie Young and Campbell Thomson

1 Forest Lane, Raumati South, Kapiti Coast   *Phone* 04-902 3114
Postal 1 Karekare Road, Raumati South, Kapiti Coast   *Mobile* 029 902 3114
Email debbie@seaspirit.co.nz   *Website* www.seaspirit.co.nz   *Fax* 04-902 3114

DIRECTIONS: From Wellington, take SH 1 towards Paraparaumu. Turn left at Raumati South turn-off into Poplar Ave. At "T" junction, turn left into Kainui Rd, then 2nd right into Forest Lane. Sea Spirit is 1st on right.

2 bdrm	1 prbth

House rate $295 for 2 persons
Extra persons $45 each

Self-catering
Includes breakfast provisions

Sea Spirit offers self-contained contemporary boutique accommodation with sea views. Using timber lining and with careful attention to detail, Sea Spirit was purpose built in 2004. Featuring views to Kapiti Island, the upstairs floor comprises a spacious king-size bedroom opening to a balcony with café-style table and chairs. There is a massage table and professional massage therapists can be arranged. Downstairs is an extra single bedroom, bathroom, and full kitchen with high-quality appliances. There is also a separate office including a guest computer, and a laundry. The dining room opens to a courtyard with South-East Asian influence, where from an outdoor bathtub guests can view the sea through a courtyard wall window.

FACILITIES

- single-party bookings only
- 1 king bedroom upstairs with foot massager, massage table & oils; opens to balcony
- 1 single bedroom downstairs
- 1 bathroom with spa bath, hair dryer, toiletries, heated floor, mirror & towel rail; slippers
- cotton bed linen; bathrobes
- office with computer, internet access, fax & phone

- full breakfast supplies
- complimentary wine & Kapiti cheese platter on arrival
- full self-catering kitchen
- lounge with wide-screen TV, DVDs, CDs & local artwork
- self-service laundry; beach bag
- off-street parking
- outdoor bathtub in courtyard; 3-flame gas fire, grasses, native flax & hammock

ACTIVITIES AVAILABLE

- professional massage therapist by arrangement, extra
- tarot-card & clairvoyant readings on site, extra
- beach, short walk, for sunsets, swimming, surf, sea kayaking
- kayaks, surfboards & mountain bikes available
- Kapiti Island tour bookings
- shopping centre; Raumati village boutique shops

- restaurants & cafés
- international golf course
- Southwards Motor Museum
- 4WD tours; 4WD quad
- horse trekking
- river kayaking; fishing; mountain biking
- Queen Elizabeth Park
- Lindale farm complex
- Wellington, 45 mins south

UPPER HUTT, WELLINGTON
Eiréné Rural Apartment

Hosts Mary and David Beachen

1029 Akatarawa Road, Upper Hutt, Wellington
Phone 0-4-526 3638   *Mobile* 021 107 6949   *Fax* 0-4-526 3628
Email beachen@paradise.net.nz   *Website* www.eirene.co.nz

DIRECTIONS: From Wellington, take SH 2 to Upper Hutt. Turn left into Akatarawa Rd (signposted to Staglands). Travel 2km across Hutt River to Eiréné on left (before cemetery).

2 bdrm	1 prbth	Double $185 Single $160	*Includes breakfast* Children $40 each	*Dinner extra* *Self-catering*

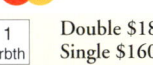 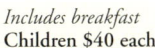

Eiréné is located in Akatarawa Valley, with private access to the crystal clear Akatarawa River. A bush track on site leads guests to the scenic swimming hole and fishing in the river is popular. Eiréné Rural Apartment provides Mediterranean-style self-contained accommodation with two bedrooms. There is a fully equipped kitchen for self-catering and home baking is included. Breakfast, chosen from the menu the night before, is served in the apartment and dinner is also available. Guests enjoy the hedged ozone-purified spa pool, and pony rides, feeding the sheep and Shetland pony are other on-site activities. The well-known private gardens, Moss Green and the Efil Doog sculpture gardens, are further along the Akatarawa Valley.

FACILITIES

- single-party bookings only
- 1 self-contained apartment
- 1 queen & 1 twin bedroom
- 1 private bathroom
- cotton bed linen; fresh flowers
- hair dryers, toiletries, heated floor, demist mirror & bathrobes
- children welcome
- lounge with Sky TV, video, CDs, games, magazines & artwork
- full kitchen for self-catering
- breakfast served in apartment
- 3-course dinner including complimentary wine, $35 pp
- mini-bar, tea/coffee, Milo, plunger coffee, home baking
- phone in kitchen
- courtesy passenger transfer
- laundry available in house
- on-site parking

ACTIVITIES AVAILABLE

- BBQ & private walled courtyard
- private ozone-purified spa pool
- mountain bikes available
- croquet & grass tennis court
- pony rides on site
- feeding shetland pony & sheep
- fishing in river
- swimming & diving in private swimming hole
- Upper Hutt, 6-min drive
- restaurants, 6-min drive
- sculpture garden, 5 mins
- private gardens to visit
- Settlers' Museum
- golf courses
- bush walks
- Staglands animal park
- sandy beaches, 30 mins
- interisland ferries, 35 mins
- Wellington City, 35 mins

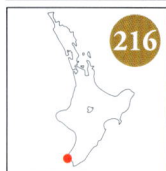

OHARIU VALLEY, WELLINGTON
Woodhaven

Hosts Anne and James Conder

20 Riflerange Road, Ohariu Valley, Wellington
Phone 0-4-477 4047   *Email* anne@woodhaven.co.nz
Fax 0-4-477 4047   *Website* www.woodhaven.co.nz

DIRECTIONS: From Wellington take motorway to Johnsonville exit. At 2nd roundabout turn left into Ironside Rd. Continue into Ohariu Valley for 5km. At cross-roads turn left into Rifle Range Rd. Woodhaven 200m on right.

   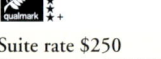

4 bdrm	1 enst	2 prbth

Suite rate $250   Apartment rate $200   *Includes breakfast or provisions*   *Lunch & dinner extra*
Cottage rate $230 for 2 persons   Extra persons $30 each   *Self-catering*   *Includes breakfast provisions*

Woodhaven is set in a two-hectare (almost five-acre) garden, featuring a pond with birdlife, in the rural location of Ohariu Valley, just 20 minutes from Wellington City. In the homestead, designed and built in French Farmhouse style in 1999, guests are offered the spacious Chateau Suite including a lounge, balcony and French antiques, or the self-contained apartment with full kitchen and breakfast provisions. Features include Egyptian cotton bed linen and furniture from native timbers. A self-catering cottage with king and queen beds in the large mezzanine is also offered. It opens to the potager where guests are welcome to the organic vegetables grown. There is a barbecue on the large private deck behind the cottage for alfresco dining.

FACILITIES

- 1 king suite with dressing room, ensuite & private lounge
- 1 self-catering apartment: 1 queen bedroom with bathroom & kitchen
- 1 self-catering cottage: 1 king & 1 queen in mezzanine bedroom, sofa-bed in lounge, bathroom with claw-foot bath, full kitchen, log fire, laundry & deck with BBQ
- hair dryers, toiletries, heated towel rails, heated floors & bathrobes

- continental or full breakfast to suite; or provisions to apartment & cottage
- lunch/picnic by request, extra
- 3-course dinner & wine, $60 pp, or formal dinner by chef, by prior arrangement
- fresh flowers
- email, phone & fax in office
- on-site parking
- children welcome

ACTIVITIES AVAILABLE

- BBQ & pétanque on site
- Oscar, the cat, Doris, the pet sheep, lambs & chickens on site
- 1.6ha of gardens to explore
- pond with birdlife on site
- horse trekking stables, 2-min walk
- 9-hole golf course, 3-min drive
- Old Coach Road heritage trail walk
- local gardens open to visit
- Karori wildlife reserve

- restaurants, 10–15 mins
- valley café, 2-min walk
- farm visits
- mountain biking
- fishing
- snorkelling
- bush walks
- Te Papa
- Botanic Gardens
- Wellington City, 20 mins

LOWER HUTT, WELLINGTON
Coopers Manor

Hosts Shirley and Alan Davis

132 Woburn Road, Lower Hutt, Wellington
Phone 0-4-566 2272   *Fax* 0-4-569 2426
Website friars.co.nz/hosts/coopersmanor.html

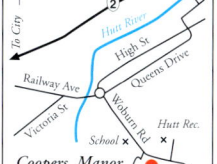

DIRECTIONS: From Wellington, take SH 2 motorway. Take Petone exit & cross overbridge into Hutt Rd. Turn right into Railway Ave. At roundabout, turn right into Woburn Rd. Coopers Manor on right.

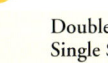

2 bdrm	2 prbth

Double $285
Single $200

Includes breakfast
Dinner extra

Built in 1921 as a residence for English seed merchant Fred Cooper, this English-style manor was totally restored in the 1990s to accommodate guests. Original features such as the timber panelling and 2.8-metre stud have been retained, including the polished matai floor and oak panelling in the entrance hall. Guests have the choice of a queen or twin room upstairs, with an adjacent private bathroom, or a super-king-size bedroom downstairs also with a private bathroom. The ground floor also includes the formal lounge, sunroom and dining room. Coopers Manor is set in English-style gardens featuring oak trees, roses and spacious lawns where guests can relax or alternatively enjoy the tennis court, swimming pool, and sauna.

FACILITIES

- 1 super-king bedroom downstairs with private bathroom
- 1 queen or twin bedroom upstairs with private bathroom, bath & heated towel rails
- hair dryers & toiletries in both bathrooms
- cotton bed linen
- fresh flowers
- children by arrangement
- continental/cooked breakfast, served in dining room
- dinner by request, extra
- tea & coffee available
- Sky TV & video available
- central heating
- open fireplaces
- laundry available, extra
- quiet garden setting
- off-street parking

ACTIVITIES AVAILABLE

- in-house sauna room
- in-ground swimming pool
- tennis court on site
- bars & restaurant 1-min walk
- art gallery, 5-min walk
- bowling club, 5-min walk
- Riddiford Gardens, 5-min walk
- shopping centre, 5-min drive
- Settler's Museum, 5-min drive
- charter clubs, 5-min drive
- 4 golf courses, 5-min drive
- watersports, 10-min drive
- trout & sea fishing
- Hutt recreation ground opposite
- Te Papa Museum of NZ, 15 mins
- Trentham Racecourse, 20 mins
- Heretaunga Golf Course, 20 mins
- Wellington City, 20-min drive
- interisland ferries, 15-min drive
- airport, 25-min drive

LOWRY BAY, WELLINGTON
The Gatehouse

Hosts Lisa and Philip Andrew

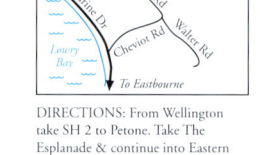

57 Cheviot Road, Lowry Bay, Wellington
Phone 0-4-568 7600   *Mobile* 021 527 600   *Fax* 04-568 7601
Email stay@thegatehouse.co.nz   *Website* www.thegatehouse.co.nz

DIRECTIONS: From Wellington take SH 2 to Petone. Take The Esplanade & continue into Eastern Bays Marine Drive towards Eastbourne. At Lowry Bay, turn left into Cheviot Rd & travel to The Gatehouse on left.

| 1 bdrm | 1 prbth | Apartment rate $355–$395 for 2 persons Extra persons $60 each | *Includes breakfast* *Self-catering* *Dinner extra* |

Located in quiet, leafy Lowry Bay, two minutes' walk from the beach, The Gatehouse is part of a larger property built in 1929 by well-known architect Natusch and based on another home in Cornwall, England. The Gatehouse was formerly a coach house until its transformation in 2001, and now provides boutique accommodation completely detached from the main house. Upstairs the super-king/twin bedroom overlooks the parterre garden and opens onto a balcony. Downstairs the spacious lounge includes a sofa bed for extra guests, while the fully equipped kitchen enables self-catering. A full breakfast is served in The Gatehouse apartment at a time to suit guests, and three-course dinner including wine is also available by arrangement.

FACILITIES

- private-party bookings only
- 1 self-contained apartment
- 1 super-king/twin bedroom upstairs with cotton bed linen, feather duvets, TV & phone
- 1 sofa bed available downstairs
- 1 bathroom downstairs with hair dryer, heated towel rails, demist mirror, beach towels, toiletries & bathrobes
- children over 7 yrs welcome
- flexi-time full breakfast served; 3-course dinner with wine, $70 pp, by request
- full kitchen for self-catering; coffee, range of teas, nibbles & home baking
- lounge with fresh flowers, fire, TV, CDs, DVD-player & complimentary mini-bar
- phone, fax & email available
- courtesy laundry service

ACTIVITIES AVAILABLE

- heated outdoor swimming pool & jacuzzi
- seashore & native forest walking trails
- beach swimming
- historic Eastbourne village, restaurants, cafés, art galleries, 7-min drive
- gardens open to visit
- stadium, 15-min drive
- bus stop at end of street
- 18-hole golf course & mini-golf, 10-min drive
- yacht moorings at Lowry Bay Marina, 5-min drive
- Lower Hutt City, shopping, indoor pool, 10-min drive
- Interislander terminal, 15 mins
- Wellington City, shopping, Te Papa Museum & restaurants, 20-min drive
- Days Bay ferry to Wellington City

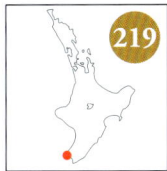

219

KOROKORO, WELLINGTON
Sea Breeze

Hosts Bronnie and Craig Lyne

4 Green Park Lane, Korokoro, Petone, Wellington   *Phone* 0-4-586 0025
Mobiles 021 453 743 *and* 021 877 333   *Fax* 0-4-586 0026
Email info@seabreezehomestay.co.nz   *Website* www.seabreezehomestay.co.nz

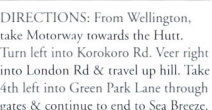

DIRECTIONS: From Wellington, take Motorway towards the Hutt. Turn left into Korokoro Rd. Veer right into London Rd & travel up hill. Take 4th left into Green Park Lane through gates & continue to end to Sea Breeze.

eftpos
VISA MasterCard

| 2 bdrm | 1 enst | 1 prbth |

Room rate $275   *Includes breakfast*   *Lunch, dinner & tours extra*

Sea Breeze overlooks Wellington Harbour and City with balconies opening from the lounge and guestrooms. Built in 1999, this three-storey Mediterranean-style home provides a king-size ensuite guest bedroom, with a twin room and bathroom if required. Guestrooms are downstairs, with single-party bookings ensuring maximum privacy. Bronnie serves breakfast in the dining room upstairs, or alfresco on the courtyard. She prepares lunches by arrangement or picnic hampers if needed and enjoys serving à la carte evening meals. Bronnie is also a beauty therapist and offers treatments in-house by arrangement. Sea Breeze features panoramic views of the ocean and bush, and the interisland ferries are only seven minutes away on the motorway.

FACILITIES

- one-party bookings only
- 1 king ensuite & 1 twin bedroom with bathroom
- cotton bed linen, phone & mineral water in bedrooms
- bath, hair dryer, demist mirror, heated floor, toiletries & robes
- guest lounge with tea/coffee, Sky TV, video, CD-player & piano
- office available with fax, computer & email access
- continental or cooked breakfast served
- light or cooked lunch, extra
- 3-course à la carte dinner with wine, extra
- balconies with wide views
- central heating; sea views
- children welcome; laundry
- guest garaging
- courtesy passenger transfer

ACTIVITIES AVAILABLE

- personalised tours for up to 10 guests, see www.nzluxurytours.co.nz
- beauty therapist on site
- table tennis on site
- sunny, spacious courtyard & barbecue area
- honeymoons catered for
- shopping centre nearby
- bush walks, 2-min drive
- selection of restaurants, 5–10-min drive
- beaches, 5-min drive
- swimming pools, 5–10 mins
- tennis court & selection of golf courses nearby
- Picton ferries, 7-min drive
- Wellington City & Te Papa Museum, 10-min drive
- airport, 30-min drive

© Friars' Guide to New Zealand Accommodation for the Discerning Traveller

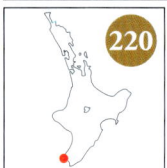

KHANDALLAH, WELLINGTON
Homebush House

Hosts Judy and Peter Devane

75 Homebush Road, Khandallah   *Phone* 0-4-471 0362   *Mobile* 027 416 3155
Postal 9 Tinakori Road, Thorndon, Wellington   *Fax* 0-4-471 0363
Email surgjw@xtra.co.nz   *Website* friars.co.nz/hosts/homebush.html

DIRECTIONS: From SH 1 motorway towards Wellington, take Ferry exit to Hutt Rd. Travel 2km & turn right into Onslow Rd. Travel 1km uphill & turn right into Homebush Rd. Travel 1km to Homebush House.

4 bdrm	2 prbth	House rate $450 for 2 persons Extra adults $40 each	*Includes continental breakfast provisions* *Self-catering*
		Extra children $25 each	

High on the hills above Wellington Harbour, Homebush House features unobstructed panoramic views of Wellington City and the surrounding hills. Set in landscaped gardens with courtyards designed for alfresco entertaining overlooking the harbour, Homebush offers self-contained accommodation for single-party bookings of up to eight guests. Sea views are captured from every angle throughout the house which includes spacious living areas, hardwood floors, French doors, Italian-tiled bathrooms and gas fireplaces. A large fully equipped kitchen with continental breakfast supplies enables self-catering, and other provisions can be arranged. Homebush is a suitable venue for small conferences. There are restaurants nearby, and a city bus service.

FACILITIES

- single-party bookings only
- 1 king, 1 queen & 2 single bedrooms
- 2 private bathrooms with hair dryers, toiletries & heated towel rails; spa bath in 1 bathroom
- bottle NZ wine, tea/coffee, fruit bowl & chocolates
- cotton bed linen; fresh flowers
- full laundry; central heating

- continental breakfast
- full kitchen for self-catering
- Sky TV, DVD, videos, CDs, artwork, books, desk, phones
- 2 large living rooms, each with gas fireplace; sofa bed; separate dining room & study
- large deck around ground level
- double garage, 4 off-street carparks, electric gates & security system; transport extra

ACTIVITIES AVAILABLE

- courtyards for alfresco dining
- harbour & hillside walks
- Khandallah village, 2km
- Te Papa Museum of NZ
- Embassy theatre, home of *The Lord of the Rings*
- Westpac Trust Stadium, 5 mins
- cable car; golf courses
- regular bus service to city, 50m
- City Centre, 10-min drive

- restaurants & shops nearby
- fishing; cycling; waterfront
- sandy beach & swimming at Oriental Bay; harbour cruises
- Courtenay Place – cinemas, concerts, live theatre, ballet, galleries, national orchestra
- private & Botanic Gardens; zoo; Karori Wildlife Sanctuary
- ferry terminal, 5-min drive; airport, 20-min drive

KHANDALLAH, WELLINGTON
Khandallah Bed and Breakfast

Hosts Margaret and Tim Fairhall

50 Clark Street, Khandallah, Wellington
Phone 0-4-479 5578   *Email* fairhall@paradise.net.nz
Website friars.co.nz/hosts/khandallah.html

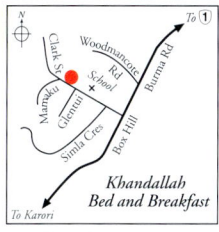

DIRECTIONS: From SH 1 Motorway, take Johnsonville exit & follow signs towards Khandallah & Karori. Turn right off Box Hill into Clark St. Khandallah B&B on right. (4km from SH 1.)

| 2 bdrm | 1 enst | 1 prbth | Room rate $200–$230 | *Includes breakfast* |

Khandallah Bed and Breakfast is set in large grounds with formal rose gardens and box hedging, with views over Wellington and the bush-clad Mount Kaukau that guests often enjoy climbing. The heated swimming pool and tennis court are also popular and Tim is happy to arrange a round of golf with guests. The house was built in 1926 in double brick and has weatherboard additions. Both rooms have french doors opening on to a balcony where guests can watch the sunset. Margaret provides fresh home baking and serves full breakfasts including fresh muffins and croissants in the formal dining room using antique silver and chinaware. Tim runs a large model railway, set in southern Germany in the 1930s to 1950s.

FACILITIES

- 1 twin ensuite bedroom & 1 queen bedroom with private bathroom; cotton bed linen
- TV, tea/coffee, home baking & fridge with wine/lemonade in bedrooms
- hair dryer, heated towel rail & bathrobes in both bathrooms
- balcony opening from ensuite bedroom, with table & chairs
- email, fax & phone available

- full or continental breakfast including home-made jams, preserved fruit & fresh baking, served in formal dining room
- lounge with open fire, Sky TV, video, CDs & writing desk
- laundry available
- central heating; fresh flowers
- antiques & NZ paintings
- friendly cat, Samantha
- off-street parking

ACTIVITIES AVAILABLE

- tennis court on site, tennis racquets & balls provided
- heated swimming pool, towels provided
- formal garden with roses & box hedging on site
- watching sunset from balcony
- native bush walk to top of Mt Kaukau, 1 hour return
- regular bus & rail service, 5-min walk away

- restaurants, 5-min walk
- golf courses nearby, rounds arranged
- Otari Native Botanic Garden
- Wellington Botanic Gardens
- Te Papa Museum, 15 mins
- Karori Wildlife Sanctuary
- sports stadium, 10-min drive
- interisland ferry, 8-min drive
- airport, 25-min drive

222

THORNDON, WELLINGTON
Kauri Trees House

Hosts Daniel McKeown and Gerard Walsh

35 Hobson Street, Thorndon, Wellington
Phone 0-4-472 5675   *Email* enquiries@kauritrees.com
Website www.kauritrees.com

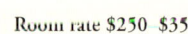

DIRECTIONS: From Wellington, take Motorway (SH 1) towards the Hutt. Take Tinakori Rd exit & turn right into Hobson St to Kauri Trees House, just past first Hobson Cres turn-off.

2 bdrm	2 enst	Room rate $250-$350	Includes breakfast

Kauri Trees is a colonial villa, built circa 1901 as a private residence, in what is now a leafy inner city area of ambassadors' residences and embassies. Wellington City is right on the doorstep. The central location enables guests to walk to restaurants and Parliament. Kauri Trees offers two ensuite guestrooms and a spacious lounge featuring Gerard's grand piano, which guests can enjoy listening to or playing. Gerard also speaks French. Danny serves a full breakfast in the dining room, where small conferences can be held. Named because of the native kauri trees recently planted in the street-front garden, Kauri Trees House is a piece of yesteryear with today's facilties. The interisland ferries to Picton are just a five-minute drive away.

FACILITIES

- 1 king & 1 twin bedroom, both with ensuite bathrooms
- Sky TV, phone jacks & tea/coffee in both bedrooms
- hair dryers & toiletries in both ensuites
- 1 bath & 1 double basin
- open fire, grand piano, artwork & books in lounge
- quiet central city location
- cooked/continental breakfast served in dining room
- central heating
- phone available
- broadband access available
- children welcome
- French spoken by Gerard
- complimentary laundry
- secure off-street parking

ACTIVITIES AVAILABLE

- playing or listening to grand piano in lounge
- small conference room
- Parliament, within walking distance
- art galleries
- concerts
- embassies nearby
- City shops, 5-min walk
- sandy beaches
- cafés & restaurants
- historic buildings in Thorndon, short walk
- private gardens open to visit
- Botanic Gardens
- Carter Observatory
- Westpac Stadium, 5-min walk away
- interisland ferry, 5-min drive
- airport, 25-min drive

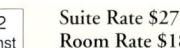

<small>KELBURN, WELLINGTON</small>

Sommerville House

Hosts Lynda and Wally Sommerville

30 Clermont Terrace, Kelburn, Wellington   *Mobile* 021 121 5272
Phone 0-4-973 0094   *Email* info@sommervillehouse.com
Fax 0-4-973 8584   *Website* www.sommervillehouse.com

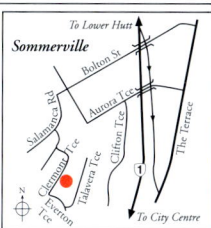

DIRECTIONS: From SH 1 Motorway take Terrace/Kelburn exit, turn left into The Terrace at lights & left into Bolton St. Clermont Tce is 2nd on left & Sommerville House has sign on garage at number 30 (next to number 27).

| 2 bdrm | 2 enst | **Suite Rate $275** **Room Rate $180** | *Includes breakfast* **Long-term rates available** | *Self-catering in suite* | |

Within walking distance of downtown Wellington, Sommerville House provides a spacious, fully self-contained suite that occupies the top floor, including a conservatory with panoramic views over the city and harbour. Downstairs is a queen-size ensuite bedroom opening to a private courtyard garden. Built circa 1900, this Victorian villa was renovated in the mid 1980s, retaining original features such as the high ceiling. Guests are served a full breakfast downstairs in the dining room, or upstairs by request. Basic cooking ingredients are supplied in the suite, which has a full kitchen for self-catering, making it suitable for longer stays. Both lounges include Sky television, DVD and CD-players, with a piano for guest use in the downstairs lounge.

FACILITIES

- 1 self-contained super-king suite upstairs with dressing room, desk, phone, kitchen, lounge, TV, conservatory, deck
- 1 queen ensuite bedroom downstairs with walk-in wardrobe, fridge, tea/coffee
- hair dryers, toiletries, heated towel rails & bathrobes
- cotton bed linen; fresh flowers
- email & phone available
- breakfast served in downstairs dining room, or in suite
- complimentary bar, tea/coffee, nibbles, Sky TV, DVD, CDs, piano, games, artwork, books & writing desk in lounge
- children welcome in suite; extra beds available
- central heating; complimentary laundry
- off-street parking; garaging

ACTIVITIES AVAILABLE

- courtyard garden with BBQ
- panoramic city & harbour views
- cable car to city, 2-min walk
- Botanic Gardens, 3-min walk
- Wellington Stadium & Te Papa Museum of NZ, 15-min walks
- Wellington Carter Observatory, 5-min walk
- concerts; art galleries
- beaches; bush walks
- Wellington shops, restaurants, night life & Victoria University, all 5-min walks away
- private gardens open to visit
- Karori Wildlife Sanctuary, 5-min drive
- interisland ferry terminal, 3km
- railway station, 1½km
- airport, 10km away

KELBURN, WELLINGTON
Rawhiti Boutique Bed and Breakfast

Host Annabel Leask

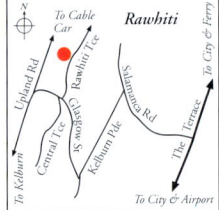

40 Rawhiti Terrace, Kelburn, Wellington
Phone 0-4-934 4859   *Fax* 0-4-972 4859
Email rawhiti@paradise.net.nz   *Website* www.rawhiti.co.nz

DIRECTIONS: From City, take The Terrace & turn north into Salamanca Rd. Turn left into Kelburn Pde, right into Glasgow St, then right again into Rawhiti Tce. Rawhiti on left. Or take Cable Car from City to Rawhiti Tce.

Room rate $190–$265   *Includes breakfast*
Corporate & off-season rates available

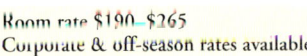

Meaning "the rising sun" in Maori, Rawhiti faces east so that both guest bedrooms are warmed by the morning sun. Both bedrooms have views over the city and harbour by day and city lights at night, as does the sunny breakfast room. This historical home, built in the early 1900s, has been refurbished to retain original features such as the sash windows and open fireplace. Sited high above the university, Rawhiti is within walking distance of the city, yet provides a peaceful retreat, with a private garden overlooking the city and harbour vistas. Annabel is a born and bred Wellingtonian, having lived in Kelburn most of her life, but with many years overseas as well. She speaks French and her oil paintings feature on the walls of Rawhiti.

FACILITIES

- 1 king ensuite bedroom with bath, writing desk, cable TV, fridge, iron & small balcony with night views of city lights
- 1 super-king/twin ensuite bedroom with TV & views
- bath, hair dryer, demist mirror, heated towel rails, bathrobes & toiletries
- tea/coffee, filtered water, phone jacks, fresh flowers & cotton bed linen in both bedrooms
- full cooked breakfast, served in dining room upstairs
- upstairs sitting room with open fire, piano, artwork, library, complimentary port & views
- NZ artwork; French spoken
- children by arrangement
- central heating
- laundry, phone & fax available
- garage space available

ACTIVITIES AVAILABLE

- garden with harbour views on site
- walking track to Upland Rd & village
- 2-min walk to Cable Car to city
- 5-min walk to restaurants, cafés, bars & shopping
- 5-min walk to Botanic Gardens & Carter Observatory
- 2-min walk to Victoria University
- Central Business District
- restaurants, 5-min walk
- beaches
- art galleries; concerts
- Te Papa Museum of NZ
- historic buildings
- private gardens to visit
- railway, 5-min drive
- airport, 20-min drive
- interisland ferries, 8-min drive away

KELBURN, WELLINGTON
Ruby House

Host Elizabeth Barbalich   *Phone* 0-4-934 7930

14B Kelburn Parade, Kelburn, Wellington   *Fax* 0-4-934 7935
Postal 35 Rawhiti Terrace, Kelburn, Wellington   *Mobile* 021 483 980
Email elizabeth@rubyhouse.co.nz   *Website* www.rubyhouse.co.nz

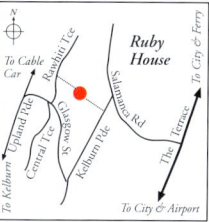

DIRECTIONS: From City, take The Terrace & turn north into Salamanca Rd. Turn left into Kelburn Pde. Narrow Lane between #10 & 14 to Ruby House. Drive down narrow lane to unload bags. Sign high on lamppost.

| 3 bdrm | 3 enst | Room rate $185–$230 Minimum 2-night stay | *Includes continental breakfast* |

Nestled among native trees, Ruby House offers guests comfort and privacy in a central location. A self-contained villa-style guesthouse provides three spacious bedrooms with antique furniture, ensuite bathrooms, television, and phone and modem lines. The guesthouse has been purpose-built for maximum privacy, with entry via a security keypad at the front door. Guests may choose a country-style bathroom complete with claw-foot bath and French doors opening to a private courtyard, a sunny loft bedroom overlooking the garden, or an elegant room with sash windows and stained glass.

FACILITIES

- 1 super-king/twin, 1 queen & 1 king ensuite bedroom
- toiletries & heated towel rails in all 3 ensuites
- 1 claw-foot bath
- quality cotton bed linen & down duvets on all beds
- antique furniture, writing desk, phone, TV & iron in all 3 bedrooms
- kitchenette in central living area
- healthy continental breakfast buffet provided
- quiet acoustics
- fax facility available
- children by arrangement
- 1 bedroom opens onto private courtyard
- sundecks & balcony
- private guest entrance
- off-street site with garaging

ACTIVITIES AVAILABLE

- rear garden with lavender, roses & kowhai trees on site
- Cable Car, 3-min walk
- Victoria University, 2-min walk
- Italian, Mediterranean & Indian restaurants in local Kelburn village
- Club Kelburn for gym, squash & tennis courts, 3-min walk
- Kelburn village with cafés & restaurants, 10-min walk
- botanical gardens, 3-min walk
- Carter Observatory, 6-min walk
- CBD, 5 mins by Cable Car
- private gardens open to visit
- art galleries
- Te Papa Museum of NZ, 10-min walk away
- native botanic garden, 5 mins
- harbour cruises
- interisland ferries, 7-min drive
- airport, 15-min drive

MOUNT VICTORIA, WELLINGTON
Villa Vittorio

Hosts Annette and Logan Russell

6 Hawker Street, Mount Victoria, Wellington
Phone 0-4-801 5761   *Mobile* 027 432 1267   *Fax* 0-4-801 5762
Email villa@villavittorio.co.nz   *Website* friars.co.nz/hosts/vittorio.html

DIRECTIONS. From City Centre, take Courtenay Pl & continue along Majoribanks St. Turn left into Hawker St. Villa Vittorio on right. From airport, take Cambridge Tce. Turn right into Majoribanks St, then as above.

1 bdrm	1 prbth	**Double $180–$220** **Single $120–$135**

Includes breakfast
Dinner extra

Centrally located in the heart of the capital city, Villa Vittorio is a late 1890s character cottage featuring the original native kauri floors, and offering a sitting room, and bedroom with private bathroom for accommodation. Views over the city can be enjoyed from the sitting room and front balcony. Annette delights in preparing gourmet dishes, and serves breakfast in their Italian-style dining room which has been painted by a local artist. The Mediterranean-style courtyard catches the morning sun, making it a favourite spot for alfresco breakfasts. Villa Vittorio caters for special occasions and small intimate weddings, and dinner accompanied by a complimentary bottle of New Zealand wine can be served in the dining room by arrangement.

FACILITIES

- 1 double bedroom & 1 private bathroom including bath
- hair dryer, heated towel rails, demist mirror, robes & toiletries
- cotton bed linen & fresh flowers
- guest sitting room with gas fire, TV, radio, music system, tea/coffee, bar & balcony
- complimentary port & sherry in guest sitting room
- phone, fax & email available

- full breakfast served in Italian-style dining room, or alfresco in private courtyard
- 3-course gourmet dinner & bottle NZ wine, $65 pp
- laundry available, extra
- city views
- small weddings catered
- garaging, extra
- courtesy passenger transfer

ACTIVITIES AVAILABLE

- personally escorted tours arranged
- Te Papa Museum, 5-min walk
- Wellington shops, 5-min walk
- conference & civic centres
- concerts, theatres, ballet, national orchestra & cinemas
- Oriental Bay & waterfront
- parliament; old St Paul's
- Wellington Sports Stadium
- Basin Reserve

- restaurants close by
- Wellington Arts Festival
- several golf courses nearby
- Cable Car
- Botanic Gardens
- Wairarapa vineyards, 1-hour drive away
- railway station, 5-min drive
- airport, 8-min drive
- interisland ferries, 7 mins

ORIENTAL BAY, WELLINGTON
298 Oriental Parade

Hosts Susan Bilbie and family

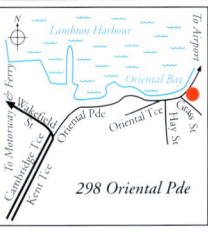

298 Oriental Parade, Oriental Bay, Wellington
Phone 0-4-384 4990   *Mobile* 021 113 5960   *Fax* 0-4-384 4990
Email 298@298.co.nz   *Website* www.298.co.nz

298 Oriental Pde

DIRECTIONS: From Motorway, take Aotea exit. Keep left along waterfront to Oriental Bay, to 298 on right. From airport, follow signs towards City. Continue along waterfront to 298 Oriental Pde on left.

2 bdrm	2 enst	1 pdrm	Double $500 Single $450

Includes breakfast & apéritifs
Lunch & dinner extra

298 Oriental Pde

Built in 1928 in the style of a Parisian townhouse, 298 Oriental Parade was the Japanese Embassy for about 30 years. It has been in the Bilbie family since 1980. It now offers 2 ensuite guestrooms – the Summer House with open fire and the Forget Me Not Room. Set in a private walled garden featuring a pond and fountain, 298 provides water's edge, harbour and city views and guests can enjoy watching sunsets from the balconies. Original ornate plaster ceilings, stained glass windows and wood panelling feature throughout. Complimentary wine and hors d'oeuvres are offered in the evening, and a full breakfast is served each morning. Lunch and dinner are also available. The airport is 10 minutes' drive away and City Centre just two minutes.

FACILITIES

- Summer House: 1 queen ensuite bedroom with open fire
- Forget Me Not Room: 1 king ensuite bedroom with balcony
- cotton bed linen, dressing room & stereo in bedrooms
- hair dryers, toiletries & bathrobes in both ensuites
- 3 lounges include open fire, Sky TV, video, library, writing desk, CD-player & piano

- continental or cooked breakfasts, served anywhere
- lunch, $25 pp
- 3–4-course dinner with wine, $75 pp
- complimentary laundry
- children by arrangement
- central heating; garaging
- private guest entrance
- courtesy passenger transfer

ACTIVITIES AVAILABLE

- in-house billiards table
- gym equipment on site
- garden with pond & fountain
- beach, across road
- jogging & roller blading
- swimming pool & gym, within walking distance
- Oriental Bay Marina
- live theatre, walking distance
- Te Papa, walking distance

- City Centre for shopping, cafés & bars, nearby
- harbour cruises
- town belt scenic walks
- golf course, 10-min drive
- Opera House
- Maritime Museum
- harbour activities, eg: kayaking, sailing
- airport, 10-min drive

298 Oriental Bay

298 Oriental Pde

SEATOUN, WELLINGTON
Edgewater Wellington

Host Stella Lovering

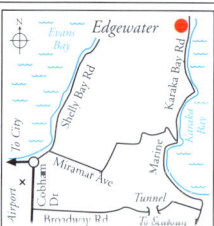

459 Karaka Bay Road, Karaka Bay, Seatoun, Wellington   *Phone* 0-4-388 4446
Faxes 0-4-388 4446 *and* 0-4-388 4649   *Email* edgewaterwellington@xtra.co.nz
Mobile 021 613 357   *Website* www.edgewaterwellington.co.nz

DIRECTIONS: From City, follow signs towards Airport & Seatoun. Turn left into Broadway Rd. Travel through Tunnel to Seatoun. Continue to waterfront. Turn left & follow water's edge to Edgewater on left.

4 bdrm	4 enst	Double $190–$290 Single $150	*Includes breakfast* *Lunch & dinner extra*

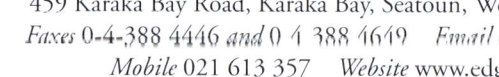

Seatoun is a historic seaside village where waterfront houses were originally built as holiday homes. Located at the water's edge in Karaka Bay, Edgewater was used for accommodation during the filming of *The Lord of the Rings*. This Mediterranean-style home was built to an award-winning design in 1976. Featuring expansive ocean views, Edgewater offers four ensuite bedrooms with peaked cedar ceilings beneath separate roofs. Stella serves fresh fruits, home-made breads, pancakes and egg dishes for breakfast in the dining room or alfresco in the inner courtyard or on the guest balcony. Dinner is also offered, specialising in premium quality meats, seafood and game. As ex-owner/chef of an award-winning Wellington restaurant, Stella's motto is "fresh is best".

FACILITIES

- 1 queen, 1 king/twin & 2 super-king bedrooms, all with ensuite bathrooms
- hair dryers, toiletries, heated towel rails & heated floor
- cotton bed linen; fresh flowers
- tea/coffee & Sky TV in all 4 bedrooms
- 4 private guest entrances
- laundry available, $10
- children welcome

- gourmet breakfast
- lunch, $30 pp
- à la carte dinner, $80 pp
- comprehensive wine selection
- meals served in dining room, or alfresco in courtyard or balcony
- phone & fax available
- central heating
- guest balcony
- off-street parking

ACTIVITIES AVAILABLE

- restaurant nearby
- seashore strolls
- fishing
- swimming
- snorkelling
- diving by arrangement
- historic seaside village, within walking distance
- cycling
- walks

- Te Papa Museum of NZ
- golf club, 10-min drive
- harbour cruises
- shopping, 10-min drive
- NZ's only cable car
- parks & gardens to visit
- galleries
- City Centre, 10-min drive
- airport, 5-min drive
- interisland ferries, 15 mins

Seatoun, Wellington
Villa Karaka Bay

Host Stella Lovering

387 Karaka Bay Road, Karaka Bay, Seatoun, Wellington
Phone 0-4-388 4446   *Mobile* 021 613 357   *Fax* 0-4-388 4446
Email edgewaterwellington@xtra.co.nz   *Website* www.villakarakabay.co.nz

2 bdrm	2 enst

Villa rate $300–$350 for 2 persons
Extra persons $100 each

Self-catering
Dinner extra

DIRECTIONS: From City, follow signs towards Airport & Seatoun. Turn left into Broadway Rd. Travel through Tunnel to Seatoun. Continue to waterfront. Turn left & follow water's edge to Villa Karaka Bay on left.

Located on the sea front at Karaka Bay, this French-style villa was originally built in 1898 as a holiday and convalscent home beside the sea. Featuring twin bay windows with sash panes and stained glass sky-lights, Villa Karaka Bay has a distinctive colonial gabled roofline topped by finials, and has been carefully restored to provide self-contained accommodation. Guests have two bedrooms, each with its own ensuite bathroom including a bath, and a separate lounge. A fully equipped kitchen enables guests to self-cater, and dinner is available by arrangement at Edgewater (*see opposite page 244*), a short stroll along the road. With panoramic harbour views, the villa's courtyard and balcony are popular spots for alfresco breakfast in the sun.

FACILITIES

- self-contained cottage; one-party bookings only
- 1 king & 1 twin bedroom, each with ensuite bathroom
- hair dryer, toiletries, bath & bathrobes in both ensuites
- cotton bed linen
- tea/coffee, nibbles, bar, phone, Sky TV, CD-player & books in lounge
- children welcome
- full self-catering kitchen
- à la carte dinner on request at Edgewater, $80 pp (*see p. 244*)
- alfresco dining
- balcony & courtyard
- fresh flowers
- ocean views
- email & laundry available
- hosts live off-site nearby
- on-site parking

ACTIVITIES AVAILABLE

- seaside strolls from site
- historic seaside village nearby
- homes of *The Lord of the Rings* directors nearby
- swimming beaches
- snorkling
- cycling
- fishing
- art galleries
- golf club, 10-min drive
- restaurant within short stroll
- shopping, 10-min drive
- Te Papa Museum of NZ
- parks & botanic gardens
- private gardens to visit
- harbour cruises
- NZ's only cable car
- City Centre, 10-min drive
- airport, 5-min drive
- interisland ferries, 15 mins

South Island

Vintners Retreat, in Blenheim – for accommodation see page 272.

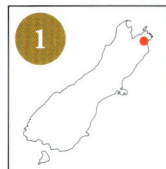

MARLBOROUGH SOUNDS
Forsyth Island

Hosts Jan and Peter Hood

Postal Private Bag, Havelock, Marlborough
Phone 0-3-579 8018   *Email* info@forsythisland.co.nz
Fax 0-3-579 8218   *Website* www.forsythisland.co.nz

DIRECTIONS: Access by sea or air only. From Wellington, 20 mins by helicopter; take ferry to Picton, then 15 mins by seaplane; or fly to Blenheim, then drive to Havelock, then 1 hour by boat to Forsyth Island.

| 3 bdrm | 3 enst | Lodge rate $900 for up to 6 persons | *Self-catering* | *All meals extra* |

Forsyth Island in the Marlborough Sounds is available for private accommodation. The entire island of 840 hectares (2,100 acres) is for single parties to enjoy. Up to eight guests can be accommodated in Paruparu Lodge, either catering for their own needs, or with all meals provided to their requirements. Forsyth Island is just 300 metres from the mainland and can be accessed via a 20-minute helicopter ride from Wellington, or 15 minutes by plane from Picton, or a one-hour boat trip from Havelock. Watersports are favourite activities, with dolphins and whales often glimpsed nearby. Guests can explore the 33 kilometres of shoreline and the many walking tracks throughout the island with its native flora, including the rare milktree.

FACILITIES

- one-party bookings only
- 1 king, 1 queen & 1 twin bedroom, each with ensuite
- sofa bed on mezzanine
- cotton bed linen, dressing room, TV & phone in all 3 bedrooms
- hair dryers, toiletries, demist mirrors, heated towel rails & floor
- email, fax & phone available; fresh flowers
- full kitchen for self-catering
- shopping list for groceries for self-catering option
- individualised menus for all meals prepared by qualified chef, by arrangement, extra
- lounge with tea/coffee, bar, nibbles, Sky TV, video, DVD, library & CD-player
- laundry facilities; barbecue
- children welcome; helipad

ACTIVITIES AVAILABLE

- private use of entire island for Lodge guests
- BBQ on large decking with panoramic views
- weddings & honeymoons catered for
- 50km of walking tracks
- sea kayaking from site
- mountain biking; hiking
- fishing & boating
- seal, dolphin & whale watching on site
- diving & snorkelling from site
- swimming & surfing at beach
- bush & beach walks
- bird-watching on site
- native flora including milktree
- boat tours in island's boat
- Wellington, 20 mins by helicopter

MARLBOROUGH SOUNDS
Pohuenui Island – Garden Bay Estate

Host Nigel Mitchell

Pohuenui Island

Postal Pohuenui Nature Resort, Private Bag, Havelock, Marlborough
Phone 0-3-579 8161   *Email* pohuenui.island@xtra.co.nz
Fax 0-3-579 8162   *Website* www.pohuenui.com

DIRECTIONS: Access by sea or air only. From Wellington, 20 mins by helicopter; or take ferry to Picton, then 15 mins by seaplane; or fly to Blenheim, then drive to Havelock, then 1 hr by boat to Pohuenui Island.

| 3 bdrm | 2 prbth | **Lodge rate $900 for up to 6 persons** | *Self-catering* | *BBQ extra* | |

Pohuenui Island

Pohuenui Island is located in the Marlborough Sounds and offers Garden Bay Estate on its eastern coast for single-party bookings. One of the largest privately owned islands in the South Pacific, Pohuenui covers 2,166 hectares, with 45 kilometres of pathways throughout for guests to explore the island. Built in one of the sandy coves on Pohuenui, Garden Bay Estate provides self-contained accommodation for up to six guests, with a fully equipped kitchen for self-catering. Guests can enjoy hiking over the green hillsides among native flora, with peaks up to 600 metres high opening up vistas over the Sounds below. Watersports are always popular, from swimming with the dolphins and kayaking, to fishing and diving in the clear waters.

FACILITIES

- one-party bookings only
- 1 king bedroom with private bathroom
- 2 queen bedrooms share 1 private bathroom
- cotton bed linen & phone in all 3 bedrooms
- hair dryers, toiletries, demist mirrors, heated towel rails & floor
- lounge with tea/coffee, TV, DVD, CD-player, books & writing desk
- full kitchen for self-catering if desired
- shopping list for guests' choice of groceries
- special BBQs, extra
- fresh flowers
- email, fax & phone available
- laundry facilities
- helipad

ACTIVITIES AVAILABLE

- private use of entire island for Estate guests
- large decking with barbecue area & panoramic views
- weddings & honeymoons catered for
- 45km walking tracks
- sea kayaking on site
- mountain biking
- fishing & boating on site
- seal, dolphin & whale watching on site
- diving & snorkelling
- swimming & surfing at bay on site
- bush & beach walks
- bird-watching on site
- hiking on site
- native plants & trees
- boat tours

Pohuenui Island

Pohuenui Island

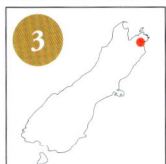

Host Nigel Mitchell

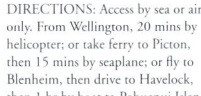

Postal Pohuenui Nature Resort, Private Bag, Havelock, Marlborough
Phone 0-3-579 8161   *Mobile* 025 798 131   *Fax* 0-3-579 8162
Email pohuenui.island@xtra.co.nz   *Website* www.pohuenui.com

4 bdrm	2 enst	1 prbth

Lodge rate $900 for up to 8 persons   *Self-catering*   *All meals extra*

DIRECTIONS: Access by sea or air only. From Wellington, 20 mins by helicopter; or take ferry to Picton, then 15 mins by seaplane; or fly to Blenheim, then drive to Havelock, then 1 hr by boat to Pohuenui Island.

Pohuenui Island

Pohuenui Island Farmhouse is located on the western shore, surrounded by garden and orchard. Macadamia nuts, walnuts, lemons and grapefruit can be gathered in season. Guests can either self-cater using the Farmhouse kitchen, or meals can be provided, featuring the freshest seafood and accompanied by Marlborough wines. The Farmhouse is available for single-party bookings only, and guests have full access to the island's extensive walking tracks and 50 kilometres of coastline, including several private sandy coves. Watersports throughout the summer are popular, and guests can experience the working farm of 3,500 sheep, as well as a small ostrich farm and a herd of alpacas. Pohuenui Island is just 20 minutes from Wellington by air.

FACILITIES

- one-party bookings only
- 1 king & 1 queen bedroom, both with ensuites
- 1 double & 1 twin bedroom share 1 private bathroom
- cotton bed linen, dressing room, & tea/coffee in rooms
- hair dryer, toiletries, bidet, demist mirror, heated towel rails & floor in all bathrooms
- email, fax & phone available
- full kitchen for self-catering
- shopping list for groceries for self-catering option; BBQ
- individualised menus for all meals prepared by a qualified chef, by arrangement, extra
- laundry facilities
- lounge with open fire, bar, tea/coffee, nibbles, TV, video, DVD, music & writing desk
- fresh flowers; helipad

ACTIVITIES AVAILABLE

- private use of entire island for Farmhouse guests
- working farm activities with sheep, ostriches, alpacas
- weddings & honeymoons catered for
- 45km walking tracks
- sea kayaking on site
- mountain biking
- fishing & boating on site
- seal, dolphin & whale watching on site
- diving on site
- swimming & surfing at beach on site
- bush & beach walks
- bird-watching on site
- hiking; native flora
- boat trips
- Wellington, 20 mins by air

Pohuenui Island

Pohuenui Island

SOUTH ISLAND
Luxury Chauffeurs

Host Neil Anderson

14a Harrow Street, Dunedin   *Postal* P O Box 7035 Dunedin
Phone 0-3-477 3144   *Email* neil@luxurychauffeurs.co.nz
Fax 0-3-477 3145   *Website* www.luxurychauffeurs.co.nz

DIRECTIONS:
Guests can be collected from accommodation throughout the South Island.

8 vehicles

Rates available

Luxury Chauffeurs welcomes guests to the South Island of New Zealand. Guests are chauffeured through the highways and byways of the South Island to destinations of their choice by experienced professional drivers. Luxury Chauffeurs features an extensive fleet of classic cars. Offering personalised tours of Dunedin heritage icons, viewing birdlife on the Otago Peninsula, driving through Central Otago, the southern lakes or Fiordland, Luxury Chauffeurs can also arrange scenic flights by fixed wing or helicopter. Guests can travel south to Mandeville by Rolls Royce or Bentley and fly in a classic aircraft. For wedding packages cars are dressed with silk ribbons. Ski adventure tours in a Range Rover or four-wheel-drive coach are also available.

FACILITIES

- Corporate Class: pair of BMW 7 series – both vehicles long-wheelbase for maximum comfort; seating 1–4 passengers
- 4WD vehicles: Range Rover 4.6 HSE, especially suited for corporate or touring/ski travel; seating 1–4 passengers
- 4WD tour coach, suited for winter/outdoor pursuits, ski adventure tours & families; seating 1–6 passengers

- Luxury Class: 2 Rolls Royce Silver Spirits, matching pair; seating 1–4 passengers
- Rolls Royce Corniche Coupé, classic touring in a 2-door coupé; seating 1–4 passengers
- 1955 Bentley S1, classic motoring – specialised wedding car with silk ribboning; seating 1–4 passengers

ACTIVITIES AVAILABLE

- personalised tours created
- corporate airport transfers
- meet & greet services
- half, full & numerous day tours created, including scenic flights
- city & heritage tours of Dunedin
- accommodation & lodge transfers
- Otago Peninsula wildlife tours – albatross & penguin viewing
- hunting/pheasant shoots in seasons

- Oamaru – Victorian tours, Moeraki Boulders
- Mandeville Tours
- wine & golf tours through Central Otago
- ski tours by 4WD
- Middlemarch Farm Tours
- wedding packages
- business & family reunions
- individualised schedules

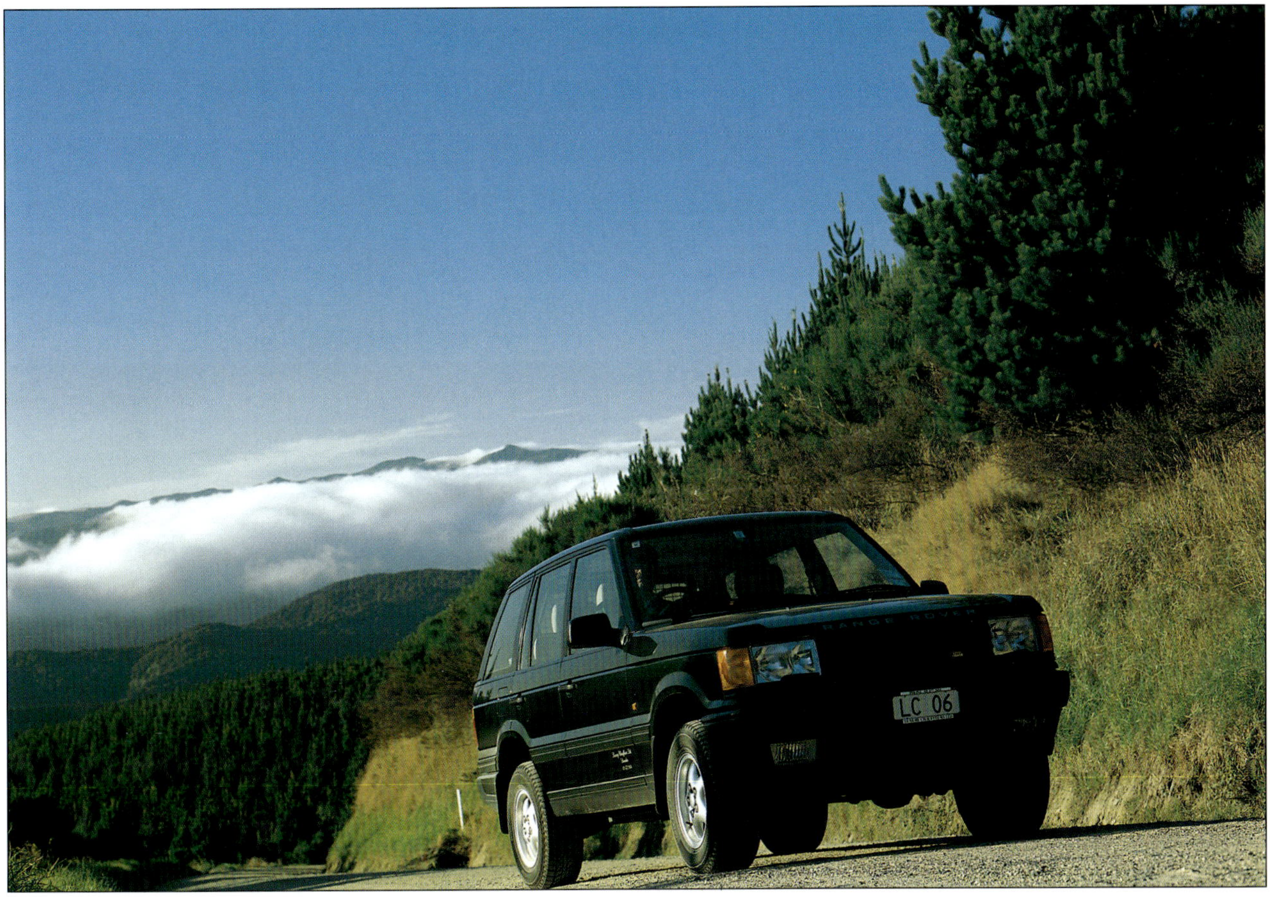

Luxury Chauffeurs

Above: From 1 to 4 guests can travel the byways throughout the South Island in a 4WD Range Rover with Luxury Chauffeurs.
Below: A Rolls Royce or Bentley chauffeurs guests to Mandeville for a nostalgic flight in a surviving 1936 Dragonfly bi-plane.
Opposite top: Scenic fly/drive tours of Dunedin area with Mainland Air complemented by BMW 7 series long-wheelbase sedans.
Opposite bottom left: The 1955 S1 Bentley in front of the heritage stone Dunedin Railway Station can be dressed for weddings.
Opposite bottom right: Classic touring for 1 to 4 passengers in a Rolls Royce Corniche two-door coupé on the Otago Peninsula.

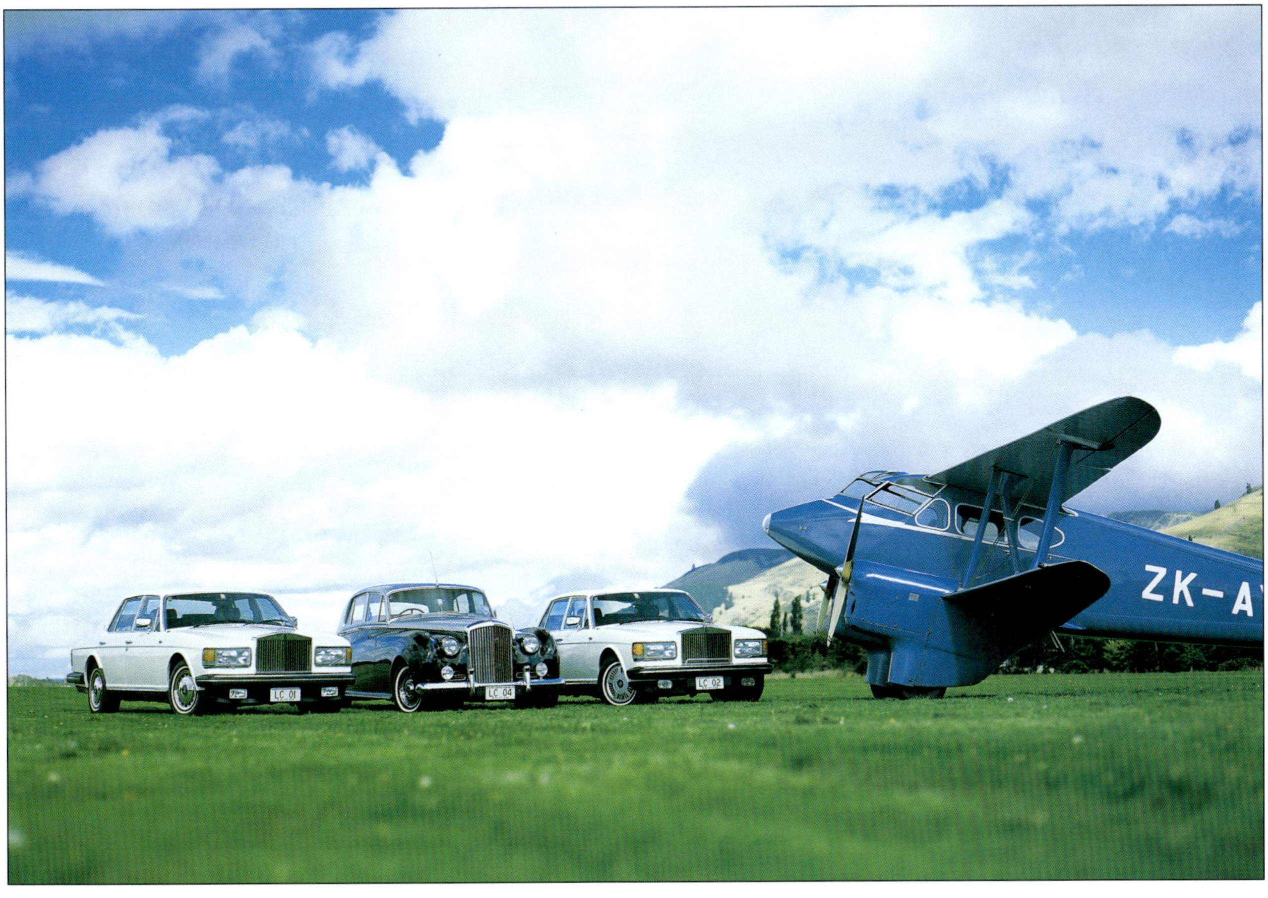

Luxury Chauffeurs

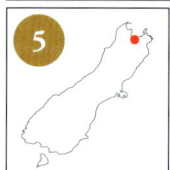

PICTON, MARLBOROUGH SOUNDS
M.Y. Galerna

Hosts Dick Wheeler and Karen Errey

Picton, Marlborough Sounds   *Postal* P O Box 17 570 Christchurch
Phone 0-4-494 0250   *Mobile* 027 499 4299   *Fax* 0-3-326 6989
Email galerna@xtra.co.nz   *Website* www.nzyachtcharters.com

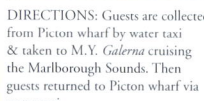

DIRECTIONS: Guests are collected from Picton wharf by water taxi & taken to M.Y. *Galerna* cruising the Marlborough Sounds. Then guests returned to Picton wharf via water taxi.

| 3 cabins | 3 enst | Cabin rate $1,750–$2,200 Yacht rate $2,700–$3,900 | *Includes all meals* Minimum 2-night stay | Tour rates available |

M.Y. *Galerna* is a newly arrived 87-foot motor yacht, built in classic style for Scandinavian royalty in 1973. Guests can book on a per cabin basis or by exclusive charter. The timbered interiors provide a comfortable traditional ambience and every convenience is included from central heating and air-conditioning to a sauna attached to the main ensuite cabin. The cuisine features local seafood and fresh game. Available for customised cruises, *Galerna* plies the Marlborough Sounds in summer, as well as Fiordland and Fiji. A water taxi from Picton wharf delivers guests to private moorings wherever the *Galerna* is cruising, providing opportunities to discover the scenic history of the Sounds. A 160-hectare (400-acre) estate offers a tennis court, heated swimming pool and forest walks.

M.Y. Galerna

M.Y. Galerna

FACILITIES

- 3 cabins for 3 couples; extra beds by arrangement
- 1 queen cabin with ensuite including bath
- 2 double/twin cabins each with ensuite
- hair dryers & toiletries in all 3 ensuite bathrooms
- sauna for queen cabin
- air-conditioning
- central heating
- satellite TV, DVD-player & books
- children welcome by arrangement
- full continental or cooked breakfast served in saloon or alfresco on deck
- lunch included in tariff
- dinner using a range of local seafood & fresh game with complimentary wine included in tariff

ACTIVITIES AVAILABLE

- barbecue on board
- fishing; kayaking
- diving with dive compressor
- bird-watching
- bush walks
- private walking tracks at Tory Channel mooring
- private tennis court at mooring
- private heated swimming pool at mooring
- customised charters
- Marlborough Sounds cruises
- water taxi to & from Picton & M.Y. *Galerna*, included in tariff
- West Coast Tours, including cruise in Marlborough Sounds, nights at luxury lodges on west coast, then join yacht again in Fiordland
- Stewart Island tours
- cruises to Fiji islands
- interisland ferries from Picton

M.Y. Galerna

M.Y. Galerna

Above: The saloon on M.Y. *Galerna* is spacious and centrally heated. Here guests can relax and dine together in comfort.
Below: The spacious main cabin has a queen-size berth, adjoining sauna, and includes a bath in the ensuite bathroom.
Opposite top: The centrally heated guest cabins include two with a double and single berth in each and adjoining ensuites.
Opposite bottom left: M.Y. *Galerna* is an 87-foot ocean-going motor yacht with Norwegian hull, available for customised cruises.
Opposite bottom right: Guests can dine alfresco on the deck while cruising through the scenic Marlborough Sounds or Fiordland.

M.Y. Galerna

© Friars' Guide to New Zealand Accommodation for the Discerning Traveller

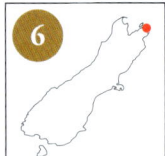

Raetihi Lodge

Hosts Margaret and Dexter Taylor

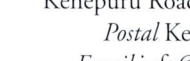

Kenepuru Road, Double Bay, Kenepuru Sound *Phone* 0-3-573 4300
Postal Kenepuru Road, R D 2, Picton *Fax* 0-3-573 4323
Email info@raetihilodge.co.nz *Website* www.raetihilodge.co.nz

| 14 bdrm | 14 enst | 1 pdrm | **Room rate $215–$330**
Seasonal rates & special packages available | *All meals extra* |

DIRECTIONS: From Picton ferry, take water taxi, if pre-arranged. Or take Queen Charlotte Dr to Linkwater. Turn right & travel to Te Mahia. Take water taxi to Double Bay. Raetihi Lodge adjacent to jetty. Moorings.

Raetihi Lodge was redesigned and rebuilt in 2000, to provide relaxation in a tranquil environment. Nestled in native bush on the waterfront, it offers 14 ensuite guestrooms, each opening to a private deck, with nine of the bedrooms featuring views out to Kenepuru Sound. Raetihi is an isolated retreat which can be reached by water taxi, air, or road. The Lodge also incorporates conference facilities and is available for secluded weddings. Meals are served in the dining room, with a selection of regional and international wines to complement the chef's cuisine. The on-site sauna, spa pool and aromatherapy massages are popular, after a day exploring the Sounds. Guests also enjoy walking beside the seashore and on the hillsides, or fishing in Kenepuru Sound.

FACILITIES

- 9 sea view rooms, 2 garden view rooms & 3 hillside rooms, each with super-king, king, queen or twin beds
- 14 ensuites each with bathrobes, heated towel rails, hair dryer & toiletries
- mini-bar, tea & coffee-making facilities in 11 bedrooms
- individual heating in bedrooms
- wheelchair access
- continental or English breakfasts, extra
- lunch & dinner, extra, daily menus
- fully licensed bar & restaurant
- guest lounge with open fireplace & library
- conference room & business centre with email facilities
- weddings catered for

ACTIVITIES AVAILABLE

- gymnasium, sauna & spa pool
- aromatherapy massage on site
- courtesy use of fishing tackle, mountain bikes, kayaks & dinghies
- scenic walks from Lodge
- mooring available
- fishing trips; yachting
- 9-hole golf course, 4km
- local garden tours
- visits to local artist
- scenic boat cruises & mussel farm visits
- water skiing; sea kayaking
- dolphin watching
- snapper fishing trips
- scenic flights to/from Picton or Wellington
- Picton by water taxi, 45 mins; by air, 10 mins; by road, 2½-hour drive

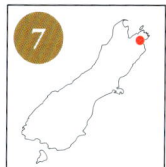

QUEEN CHARLOTTE SOUND
Double Cove Retreat

Hosts Matthew and Rose Montgomery

Double Cove, Queen Charlotte Sound, Marlborough
Phone 0-3-577 6940   *Mobile* 027 483 6380   *Fax* 0-3-577 6940
Email unwind@doublecoveretreat.co.nz   *Website* www.doublecoveretreat.co.nz

DIRECTIONS: Access by sea only, from Picton or Waikawa marinas. Transfers from all arrival points to Retreat provided or arranged. Double Cove Retreat is 10 mins from Picton by private boat or water taxi.

| 4 bdrm | 2 enst | 1 shbth | **House rate $950–$1,450** | *Self-catering* | *All meals extra* | | |

Double Cove Retreat

A short scenic boat ride takes guests to Double Cove Retreat, tucked away in the Marlborough Sounds, providing privacy and tranquillity for self-contained holidays. Up to 12 guests have sole use of this contemporary four-level Retreat with views over the sea to the bush-clad hills. Designed for unwinding and enjoying the on-site activities, guests enjoy the watersport equipment provided, the jetties and spacious decking for alfresco dining. A chef can be arranged by request, and two boats are also available – a Naiad inflatable, or a luxury launch skippered by Matthew. Guests can relax with the library of books and DVDs in the comfortable lounge or games room, or take a glass of champagne down to the spa pool at the water's edge.

FACILITIES

- one-party bookings only
- 1 king ensuite bedroom on top floor with spa bath, TV, phone & balcony
- 1 queen & 1 twin bedroom mid-floor share 1 bathroom
- 2 double & 4 single fold-out beds in downstairs gamesroom
- hair dryer, toiletries & heated towel rails in all 3 bathrooms
- bathrobes & cotton bed linen
- full self-catering kitchen
- chef for meals by arrangement
- open fire, Sky TV, video, DVD, CD-player, games, books, artwork, writing desk & computer/internet in lounge
- TV, DVD, CDs, PlayStation 2 & table tennis in gamesroom
- laundry, fax & phone; central heating & air-conditioning
- courtesy passenger transfer

ACTIVITIES AVAILABLE

- in-house TV & gamesroom
- new waterfront deck area with BBQ, hot tub, outdoor heaters, alfresco dining table & boatshed
- 5 kayaks for guest use
- helipad on site
- 4.8m Naiad boat with 90hp Yamaha outboard available for sight-seeing, water skiing, sea biscuiting, extra
- skippered launch available, extra
- restaurants, cafés, aquarium, playground & ferries at Picton, 10 mins by boat
- winery tours & wine tasting
- nature tours to Motuara Island – native birdlife, seals & dolphins to view
- fishing; hiking & tramping
- Queen Charlotte Track
- Ship Cove – site of Captain Cook's arrival

Double Cove Retreat

Double Cove Retreat

QUEEN CHARLOTTE SOUND
The Lazy Fish Retreat

Hosts Rosie and Steve George

Kahikatea East Bay, Marlborough Sounds   *Phone* 0-3-573 5291
Postal Private Bag 429, Picton   *Fax* 0-3-573 5291
Email relax@lazyfish.co.nz   *Website* www.lazyfish.co.nz

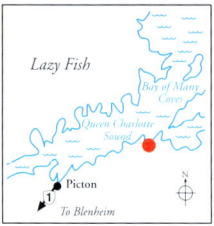

Lazy Fish

DIRECTIONS: Boat service leaves from Picton wharf or ferry terminal twice daily or by arrangement to The Lazy Fish Retreat. From south, take SH 1 to Picton wharf.

4 bdrm	4 prbth	1 pdrm	Double $445–$495 Single $395–$445	*Includes all meals* *Water taxi extra*

Lazy Fish

The Lazy Fish Retreat provides quality accommodation in a beachfront lodge, located right on the water's edge, in the heart of the Marlborough Sounds. A scenic boat trip from Picton wharf takes guests to The Lazy Fish Retreat, set in a private bay flanked by pohutukawa and palm trees. Guests have a choice of four private bungalows, each with four-poster queen-size bed, outdoor bath, terrace and private garden. All four bungalows have sea or garden views. The resident chef provides all meals, served in the dining room or alfresco. The Lazy Fish Retreat is a popular get-away for honeymooners. Guests enjoy the watersports available and fishing from the site, or chartered fishing trips and sailing can be arranged.

FACILITIES

- 4 bungalows: each including 1 queen bedroom, private bathroom, outdoor bath, private terrace & garden
- cotton bed linen; fresh flowers
- toiletries & bathrobes
- 2 lounges, tea/coffee, CDs, piano, library, games & artwork
- self-serve laundry
- sea & garden views

- tariff includes all meals
- continental or cooked breakfast served
- buffet-style lunch
- dinner served in main dining area, or alfresco
- vegetarians catered for
- honeymoons catered for
- email & phone available
- beachfront setting

ACTIVITIES AVAILABLE

- water taxi fares extra
- well stocked library
- BBQ on site
- kayaks & row boat available
- swimming & snorkelling
- fishing from site
- charter fishing trips available
- Queen Charlotte Track day walks
- hiking & tramping

- Marlborough Sounds scenic cruises
- sailing charters on request
- eco tours
- nature tours to Motuara Island – birdlife, seals, & dolphins to view
- Ship Cove – site of Captain Cook's arrival
- Picton, 12km by sea

Lazy Fish

Lazy Fish

PICTON
Sennen House

Hosts Imogen and Richard Fawcett

9 Oxford Street, Picton   *Mobile* 021 035 9956
Phone 0-3-573 5216   *Email* enquiries@sennenhouse.co.nz
Fax 0-3-573 5216   *Website* www.sennenhouse.co.nz

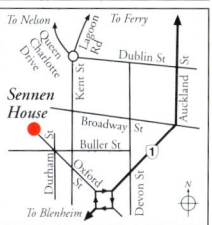

DIRECTIONS: From Picton ferries, travel into Kent St. Turn right into Buller St, right into Durham St & left into Oxford St. Sennen House at end. From Blenheim, turn left into Kent St & 2nd left into Oxford St.

5 bdrm	4 enst	1 prbth

Apartment rate $275–$345
Suite rate $395–$675

Includes breakfast hamper
Self-catering

Sennen House

Sennen House was built in 1886 by Englishman George Smith, a local timber merchant. Rescued from demolition in 1965, and restored to its former glory in 2002, this colonial villa now offers three self-contained apartments and a spacious suite. The Victoria, Banks' and Cooks' apartments open to balconies with views of sheep on the native bush-clad hills, gardens or Picton and the sea beyond. The suite has exclusive use of the formal lounge and front entrance-way, as well as the private brick courtyard beneath a century-old camellia. Generous continental breakfast hampers are provided daily to each apartment or the suite, and guests can self-cater in the apartments using their fully equipped kitchens, or enjoy the range of nearby restaurants.

FACILITIES

- 3 apartments: 1 king/twin, 1 queen/twin & 1 queen ensuite bedroom, each with lounge, kitchen, balcony & views
- 1 suite: 1 super-king/twin & 1 king bedroom, 1 ensuite & 1 private bathroom & bath
- hair dryers, toiletries, bathrobes & heated towel rails
- children welcome by request
- laundry $15; phone, internet
- breakfast hamper for private or alfresco dining
- port in winter, or wine with hosts in summer
- pure cotton bed linen
- multi-channel TV, tea/coffee, chocolates & cookies in all apartments & suites
- luggage storage available
- courtesy passenger transfer

ACTIVITIES AVAILABLE

- native bush & birds on site
- cats & sheep on site
- strolling on foreshore nearby
- local shops nearby
- kayaking; sailing; fishing
- local walks to lookouts
- Edwin Fox & Picton museums
- boat trips in Sounds
- Picton restaurants within easy walking distance
- wine tours of Marlborough vineyards
- dolphin & bird watching
- Queen Charlotte track
- Picton ferries, 10-min walk
- horse trekking in Blenheim & Pelorus
- Blenheim, 20-min drive
- Rainbow ski-field, 1 hour
- Nelson City, 2-hour drive

PICTON
McCormick House

Hosts Jeanne and Carl Beaumont

21 Leicester Street, Picton
Phone 0-3-573 5253 *Mobile* 025 327210 *Fax* 0-3-573 5263
Email enquiries@mccormickhouse.co.nz *Website* www.mccormickhouse.co.nz

DIRECTIONS: From Picton ferries, travel into township & turn left into Waikawa Rd. Travel 1.6km & turn right into Leicester Rd. McCormick House on right.

| 3 bdrm | 3 prbth | Double $220–$370 | Single $190–$340 | *Includes breakfast & apéritifs* |

Not far from the Picton ferry terminal is historic McCormick House, set in an established native garden with views to a native bush reserve. After extensive renovations, McCormick House retains many original features, including the native rimu panelled staircase and fireplace. Architecturally designed in 1914, the house now offers three guestrooms, each with distinctive individual interior design. The Captains Room is spacious and incorporates a claw-foot bath; the Boatshed Room is designed with vibrant South Pacific colouring; and the Palm Room, with four-poster bed and curved-wall marble ensuite with muti-jet double shower, opens to a sunroom with double spa bath. The Queen Charlotte track and kayaking in the Sounds are popular.

FACILITIES

- 1 super-king/twin with claw-foot bath, 1 king with double spa bath & 1 queen bedroom
- 3 ensuites with heated floor, heated towel rails, hair dryer, toiletries & bathrobes
- 100% cotton bed linen
- TV, DVD, direct dial phone in all 3 bedrooms; fresh flowers
- 2 resident cats, Ashlee & Cuddles, on site

- continental & cooked breakfast served in dining room or alfresco on terrace
- pre-dinner drinks served
- guest lounge with open fire, tea/coffee, fridge, CDs, books & internet access
- private guest entrance
- courtesy passenger transfer
- off-street parking

ACTIVITIES AVAILABLE

- pétanque terrain on site
- native garden on site
- swimming
- boating & sailing
- sea kayaking
- diving; fishing
- Queen Charlotte Track day walks
- hiking & tramping
- eco tours

- restaurants within walking distance (1.5km)
- Marlborough Sounds scenic cruises
- local golf course
- winery tours
- performing arts
- art galleries, 1.6km
- Picton township, 1.6km
- interisland ferries,1.7km

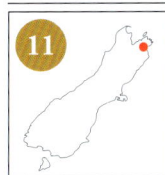

WHATAMANGO BAY, PICTON
A Sea View

Hosts Christine and Dave Grigg

424 Port Underwood Road, Whatamango Bay, R D 1, Picton 7372
Phone 0-3-573 8815   *Email* aseaview@paradise.net.nz
Fax 0-3-573 8815   *Website* www.aseaview.co.nz

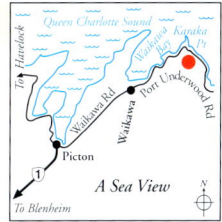

DIRECTIONS: From Picton, take Waikawa Rd for 8km to Karaka Point. Continue 1km on Port Underwood Rd to sign *Sea View* on right (about 15-min drive from Picton). Turn right into driveway to A Sea View.

3 bdrm | **3 enst** | Room rate $130–$199 | *Includes breakfast* | *Lunch & dinner extra* | *Self-catering*

Set on the slopes above Whatamango Bay, A Sea View offers expansive views over Queen Charlotte Sound from the deck and guestrooms. The large terraced garden features native plants which attract abundant birdlife. The three ensuite guestrooms have sea views and private entrances, and two offer self-catering facilities. Guests are served a continental or full cooked breakfast including bacon, eggs, tomatoes, mushrooms, fruit, home-made jams, yoghurt, muesli and bread, in the main house, or alfresco while enjoying the view from the deck. Christine and David welcome the opportunity to help guests with their holiday plans and arrange activities in the Marlborough Sounds. An evening meal and lunch are available by prior arrangement.

FACILITIES

- 2 king ensuite bedrooms
- 1 queen ensuite bedroom
- toiletries & hair dryers
- cotton bed linen, TV, tea/coffee & mineral water in bedrooms
- sea & garden views
- laundry available
- email, fax & phone available in main house
- 2-tonne registered boat mooring
- continental or full cooked breakfast served in main house or alfresco on deck
- lunch, $10 pp on request
- 3-course dinner with wine, $65 pp, by arrangement
- kitchenette for self-catering in 2 rooms
- courtesy passenger transfer from Picton airport or ferry; on-site parking

ACTIVITIES AVAILABLE

- winery tours
- boat trips in Sounds
- dolphin & penguin watching
- fishing
- kayaking; sailing
- diving
- restaurants, nearby
- hiking to nearby Maori pa site
- golf course
- swimming
- Queen Charlotte Track
- trekking
- day trips to Kaikoura & Nelson Lakes
- Picton ferries, 15-min drive
- Blenheim, ½-hour drive
- Nelson City, 2-hour drive

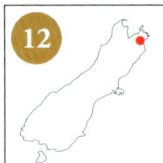

PICTON
Koro Park Lodge

Hosts Diane Purkis and Brian Martin

779 State Highway 1, Koromiko, R D 3, Blenheim
Phone 0-3-573 5542   *Email* koropark@actrix.co.nz
Fax 0-3-573 5548   *Website* friars.co.nz/hosts/koro.html

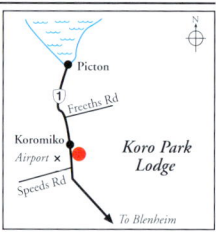

DIRECTIONS: From the Picton ferry terminal, take SH 1 south for 9km to Koromiko. Koro Park Lodge on left, sign at gate. From Blenheim, take SH 1 north for 19km. Koro Park Lodge on right.

3 bdrm	2 enst

Double $115–$170   Single $95–$150   *Includes breakfast*

Situated in the Koromiko Valley, nine kilometres south of Picton on State Highway One, Koro Park Lodge is centrally located for guests to visit the many wineries, arts and crafts, restaurants, shopping facilities, golfing, and scenic and fishing boat trips available in the Marlborough region. Not far from the Picton ferry terminal or airport, Koro Park Lodge is set on a hectare of park-like grounds, with mature trees and sweeping lawns surrounded by rural views of the valley and bush-clad hills beyond. A full continental or cooked breakfast is served downstairs in the guest lounge by Diane and Brian. Guests are offered a two-bedroom suite upstairs with its own bathroom, and a queen suite downstairs which includes a spa bath, opening to a private courtyard.

FACILITIES

- 1 queen & 1 single bedroom suite upstairs, with ensuite
- 1 queen suite downstairs, with spa bath in ensuite, opening to private courtyard
- hair dryer, toiletries & heated towel rails in both bathrooms
- TV, music, & tea/coffee facilities provided
- complimentary laundry
- fresh flowers
- full continental or cooked breakfast served in guest lounge
- phone, fax & email available on request
- garden setting
- rural views
- courtesy passenger transfer
- on-site parking

ACTIVITIES AVAILABLE

- Picton Airport close by
- golf course, 1km away
- fishing & cruising trips in Marlborough Sounds
- wine trail & wine tasting
- arts & crafts trail
- private gardens to visit
- alpaca & llama farm
- numerous walking tracks
- Blenheim, 19km
- licensed restaurants nearby
- white water rafting
- yacht & launch charter
- Marlborough Sounds Adventures, 15-min drive
- Old Beaver Town, 15-min drive to Blenheim
- dolphin-watching eco tours
- Rainbow Ski-field, 1 hour
- Picton interisland ferries, 9km

BLENHEIM
Opawa Lodge

Hosts Lesley Tuckett and Ross Connochie

143A Budge Street, Blenheim
Phone 0-3-577 9989   *Mobile* 025 411 214   *Fax* 0-3-577 9949
Email opawalodge@xtra.co.nz   *Website* www.marlborough.co.nz/opawa

DIRECTIONS: Take SH 1 to Blenheim. On the northern outskirts, just south of Opawa River bridge, turn east into Budge St. Travel 1.1km to Opawa Lodge on left.

| 3 bdrm | 1 enst | 1 prbth | Double $140–$180 Single $100–$125 | *Includes breakfast* | *Dinner extra* |

Set on the outskirts of Blenheim, Opawa Lodge is close to Marlborough vineyards, yet within minutes of the township. This riverside accommodation comprises three guest bedrooms and two bathrooms, with views of the Opawa River even from the ensuite! Adjacent is the guest conservatory, where a continental or full cooked breakfast is served overlooking the garden that slopes down to the river, with rural vistas to the fields and Richmond Range beyond. Lesley and Ross specialise in local cuisine, offering informal dining in the evening by prior arrangement. Guests enjoy the on-site access to the Opawa River, with fishing rods and rowboat available and there is also an in-ground pool for summer swimming.

FACILITIES

- 1 queen bedroom with TV, & spa bath in ensuite
- 1 queen & 1 twin bedroom with private bathroom
- bathrobes, hair dryers, toiletries & heated towel rails
- TV in conservatory
- complimentary laundry
- luggage/vehicle storage for overnight trips away

- full breakfast in conservatory
- informal dinner with wine in conservatory, by arrangement
- tea/coffee in conservatory
- powder room; fresh flowers
- phone, fax & email available
- children over 10 yrs welcome
- rail & airport courtesy passenger transfers
- ample off-street parking

ACTIVITIES AVAILABLE

- swimming pool on site
- river fishing access on site, fishing rods available
- barbecue on site
- fresh & saltwater fishing trips
- row boat & canoes available
- arts & crafts trail
- personal wine tours arranged
- restaurants, only minutes away
- adventure activities in Sounds

- Blenheim town for shopping
- private garden tours
- golf courses
- white water rafting
- Queen Charlotte Walkway
- Kaikoura whale watching
- Marlborough Sounds, 30km
- Nelson Lakes National Park for winter skiing
- interisland ferries, 25 mins

BLENHEIM
Old St Mary's Convent

Host Christine Webber

776 Rapaura Road, R D 3, Blenheim
Phone 0-3-570 5700 *Email* retreat@convent.co.nz
Fax 0-3-570 5703 *Website* www.convent.co.nz

7 bdrm	7 enst

Room rate $450–$550

Includes breakfast
Dinner extra

DIRECTIONS: From the Picton ferry, take SH 1 south towards Blenheim. Turn right at Spring Creek into Rapaura Rd. Travel 5km to Convent on left. Or from Blenheim, take SH 1 north 3km to Spring Creek.

In 1994 the Old St Mary's Convent was relocated on its eight-hectare (20-acre) park-like setting in the heart of Marlborough's wine district. Built in 1901, the Convent is now restored to its former glory with the ground floor interiors replicating the century-old layout with antique furnishings. The original chapel upstairs has been transformed into an apartment-size executive or honeymoon suite, retaining the arched, stained-glass windows and cathedral ceilings. All seven bedrooms are spacious and airy, with full ensuite bathrooms including claw-foot baths, and with balconies overlooking the gardens to the surrounding hills. A separate historic chapel, complete with original pews, pulpit and organ, is available for weddings in its garden setting.

FACILITIES

- 1 super-king/twin, 1 super-king & 5 queen bedrooms
- 7 ensuites, each with claw-foot bath, toiletries, hair dryer, robes
- executive/honeymoon suite in original chapel upstairs
- guest balconies & verandahs
- garden views
- heating & air-conditioning
- internet terminal for guests

- breakfast served in formal dining room
- dinner by request, extra
- guest kitchenette
- guest lounge
- fresh flowers
- guest library with ornate kauri fireplace
- laundry facilities
- on-site parking

ACTIVITIES AVAILABLE

- 8-ha garden & birdlife on site
- spring-fed stream & trout on site
- complimentary bicycles
- grass tennis courts next door
- golf courses close by
- wineries tours nearby
- arts & crafts trail
- private gardens to visit
- trout fishing, guide available

- restaurants nearby
- sailing
- horse trekking
- mountain biking
- Marlborough Sounds fishing trips & kayaking
- scenic walks in Marlborough Sounds
- Rainbow Ski-field, 1½-hour scenic drive

Above: The private lounge in the honeymoon suite, formerly the chapel, looking through the arched doorway to the bedroom.
Below: Old St Mary's Convent, built in 1901, is set in large gardens and lawns, with a separate chapel for garden weddings.
Opposite top: Old St Mary's Convent is situated in eight hectares of park-like grounds, with views to the surrounding hills.
Opposite bottom left: Guests enjoy relaxing at Old St Mary's Convent on the second-storey verandah overlooking the garden.
Opposite bottom right: The spacious Mother Superior's Room, looking through to the large ensuite with its claw-foot bath.

© Friars' Guide to New Zealand Accommodation for the Discerning Traveller

BLENHEIM
The Peppertree
Luxury Accommodation

Hosts Heidi and Werner Plüss

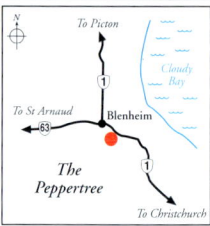

3284 State Highway 1, Riverlands, Blenheim   *Postal* P O Box 279, Blenheim
Phone 0-3-520 9200   *Email* info@thepeppertree.co.nz
Fax 0-3-520 9222   *Website* www.thepeppertree.co.nz

5 bdrm	3 enst	2 prbth	Double $350–$370 Single $310–$330	*Includes breakfast* *Dinner extra*

DIRECTIONS: 25 mins from the Picton ferry. Take SH 1 south to Blenheim. Continue for another 5km to Cob Cottage, on the right. The Peppertree is next door on the south side.

The Peppertree takes its name from the pepper-trees (*Schinus molle*) lining the driveway. Built as a farmhouse in 1901 for Adam Bell, this Edwardian villa was converted into a restaurant in 1984. Then, 10 years later, The Peppertree was transformed into boutique accommodation. Constructed from the native timbers rimu, kauri and matai, the interior has been refurbished in sympathy with the era of the home. The five bedrooms are individually designed, three with private verandahs. Alfresco country breakfasts can be served on the sunny wisteria-clad verandah, which opens to almost a hectare (two acres) of mature garden, surrounded by The Peppertree's boutique vineyard and olive grove. Guests enjoy tasting its own Chardonnay and olive oil.

FACILITIES

- 1 king, & 2 king/twin & 2 queen bedrooms, 3 with private balcony or verandah
- 5 bathrooms, 1 with spa bath
- toiletries, hair dryers, bath-robes & central heating
- fresh flowers, chocolates & coffee/tea facilities in rooms
- phone & TV in bedrooms
- open fires in guest lounge, dining room & bedrooms
- country breakfast in dining room or alfresco on verandah
- fax & wireless internet/email
- complimentary port & sherry in lounge or on verandah
- fully licensed, with NZ wines
- walnut pillars, kauri archway, stained glass in entrance hall
- small conference venue
- safe on-site parking; helipad

ACTIVITIES AVAILABLE

- vineyard & olive grove on site
- pétanque/boules & croquet lawn
- swimming pool & gym facilities
- Cob Cottage colonial museum adjacent
- Marlborough wine trails & tasting, with lunches available
- historic Brayshaw Park
- golf courses nearby; walking
- visiting private gardens
- restaurants, 5-min drive
- freshwater & sea fishing
- summer sailing; horse riding
- Blenheim Airport, 10-min drive, transport if required
- Marlborough Sounds, 30km
- interisland ferries, 25 mins
- winter skiing, 1½-hour drive
- whale watching at Kaikoura, 1½-hour drive south

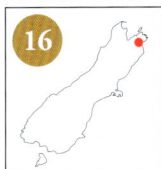

BLENHEIM
St Leonards Vineyard Cottages

Hosts Jeanette and Steve Parker

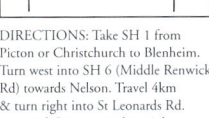

18 St Leonards Road, R D 1, Blenheim
Phone 0-3-577 8328   *Mobile* 025 686 1636   *Fax* 0-3-577 8329
Email stay@stleonards.co.nz   *Website* friars.co.nz/hosts/stleonards.html

DIRECTIONS: Take SH 1 from Picton or Christchurch to Blenheim. Turn west into SH 6 (Middle Renwick Rd) towards Nelson. Travel 4km & turn right into St Leonards Rd. Vineyard Cottages 2nd on right.

| 5 bdrm | 2 enst | 2 prbth | **Room rate** $100–$270 **Extra persons** $35–$50 each |

Includes continental breakfast provisions
Self-catering

The four St Leonards Vineyard Cottages are set in two hectares (approximately five acres) surrounding the original homestead of the area, circa 1884. The hosts, the Parker family, occupy the homestead. The Stables is converted into a self-contained cottage overlooking the lemon grove and animal paddocks, to the distant Wither Hills. A barbecue can be enjoyed in a private garden and a pot-belly stove provides added warmth in winter. The architecturally restored Woolshed overlooking the vineyards sleeps five guests and features rustic recycled materials, an open fire in the lounge area opening to decking with a barbecue and an outdoor bath. A smaller annexe adjacent to the house, separated by the carport, is also self-contained with a kitchenette for self-catering. The newest addition is a character one-bedroom cottage reminiscent of colonial New Zealand, with extra beds, full kitchen, pot-belly stove, verandah and barbecue. Guests enjoy the tennis, pétanque and swimming pool on site.

FACILITIES

- Woolshed: 1 queen & 1 twin bedroom, private bathroom, extra toilet, lounge with divan & open fire, deck & outdoor bath
- Stables: 1 queen ensuite bedroom, lounge, pot-belly & patio
- Cottage: 1 queen bed, 2 fold-away beds, divan bed in lounge, bathroom, pot-belly & verandah
- Annexe: 1 double bedroom with ensuite bathroom
- all 4 cottages include TV, microwave & BBQ
- hair dryers, heated towel rails & toiletries in all bathrooms
- children & pets welcome
- breakfast provisions in all 4 cottages, including home-made preserves
- wine in guest fridges, extra
- full kitchens in Woolshed & Cottage for self-catering
- kitchenettes in Stables & Annexe for self-catering
- email, fax & phone available in main house
- self-serve laundry
- orchard & gardens
- local artwork
- on-site parking
- courtesy airport transfer

ACTIVITIES AVAILABLE

- in-ground lawn tennis court
- farmyard animals to pet
- pétanque & croquet on site
- swimming pool on site
- 2ha (5-acre) garden on site
- picking fruit & walnuts from trees in season, on site
- surrounded by vineyards
- wineries, 3-min drive
- shopping, 5-min drive
- trout fishing nearby
- bush walks
- horse trekking
- fishing in Marlborough Sounds, 30-min drive
- restaurants, 5-min drive
- golf courses
- gardens open to visit
- airport, 3-min drive
- Blenheim township, 5 mins
- scenic flights
- boat trip through Malborough Sounds
- Picton ferries, 25-min drive
- Rainbow Ski-field, 1 hour
- Nelson, 1 hr 20-min drive
- dolphin swimming in Kaikoura, 2-hour drive
- whale watching in Kaikoura, 2-hour drive

St Leonards

BLENHEIM
Uno Più

Hosts Gino and Heather Rocco

75 Murphys Road, Blenheim
Phone 0-3-578 2235 *Mobile* 021 174 4257 *Fax* 0-3-578 2235
Email stay@unopiu.co.nz *Website* www.unopiu.co.nz

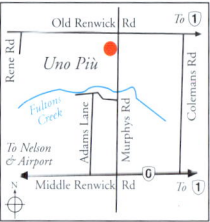

DIRECTIONS: Take SH 1 from Picton or Christchurch to Blenheim. Turn west into SH 6 (Middle Renwick Rd) towards Nelson. Turn right into Murphys Rd. Uno Più on left. (3km from town centre.)

| 2 bdrm | 2 enst | Double $240–$350 | Single $180–$290 | Includes breakfast Dinner extra |

Uno Più, meaning "One Plus" in Italian, provides Italian-style hospitality set on a farmlet of almost two hectares, where horses and sheep graze in the paddocks surrounding the historic homestead. Built in 1917, this private residence has been renovated to offer guest accommodation comprising two king bedrooms with ensuites. The swimming pool is enclosed with roses and a predominantly white garden. Special features include the baby grand piano in the guest lounge, a sauna, a guest office with broadband internet access, an outdoor chess set, pétanque court and, of course, the Italian cuisine. Gino's home-made pasta is as popular as his Italian breakfast platter with hot rolls, to complement his pancakes with maple syrup, strawberries and cream.

FACILITIES

- 1 super-king/twin & 1 king bedroom, each with ensuite
- claw-foot bath in 1 ensuite
- tea/coffee, fridge, iron, phone, CDs, DVDs & Sky TV in bedrooms
- hair dryers, toiletries, demist mirrors, heated floors & heated towel rails
- bathrobes; fresh flowers
- high-speed internet access

- breakfast served in dining room or alfresco
- 3-course Italian dinner with wine by arrangement, $70 pp
- guest lounge with open fire & baby grand piano
- complimentary laundry; fax & email available
- established trees & gardens
- off-street parking

ACTIVITIES AVAILABLE

- Marshall & Rose baby grand piano for guest use
- pétanque court & outdoor chess set on site
- 10m swimming pool on site
- 1.5ha farmlet with horses, 2 collie dogs, 1 cat & Oswald the sheep
- private gardens to visit
- arts & crafts

- walks & tramping
- wine trail, 5-min drive away
- tennis courts nearby & croquet, 1.5km away
- Blenheim township, 3km
- river & sea fishing
- Queen Charlotte walkway
- Marlborough Sounds
- Picton ferry, 30-min drive

BLENHEIM
Ancora Uno Più

Hosts Gino and Heather Rocco

75 Murphys Road, Blenheim
Phone 0-3-578 2235   *Mobile* 021 174 4257   *Fax* 0-3-578 2235
Email stay@unopiu.co.nz   *Website* www.unopiu.co.nz

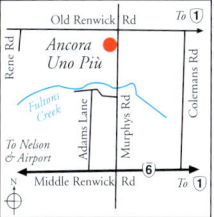

DIRECTIONS: Take SH 1 from Picton or Christchurch to Blenheim. Turn west into SH 6 (Middle Renwick Rd) towards Nelson. Turn right into Murphys Rd. Uno Più on left. (3km from town centre.)

| 2 bdrm | 1 prbth | Cottage rate $240–$380 for 2 persons
Extra persons $60 each | *Includes breakfast*
Self-catering | *Dinner extra* |

Ancora Uno Più, meaning "Yet Another One Plus" in Italian, is a self-contained cottage set among olive trees in the garden of Uno Più homestead. This mud-block cottage features a cathedral ceiling and restored native kauri doors and surrounds which complement the natural mud-block interiors. The cottage provides two bedrooms, a super-king size and a queen/twin, and private bathroom with a 1920 claw-foot bath. A fully equipped kitchen allows for self-catering, the lounge features a Victorian fireplace and French doors open to a sunny patio where a barbecue is located. Breakfast is delivered to the cottage, or guests are welcome to breakfast in the homestead (*see opposite page 268*), and Gino's Italian dinners are also available by request.

FACILITIES

- single-party bookings only
- 1 super-king & 1 queen/twin bedroom & 1 private bathroom
- claw-foot bath in bathroom
- bathrobes, hair dryer, toiletries, heated floor & towel rails
- open fire, CDs, DVDs, phone & Sky TV in lounge
- fresh flowers & complimentary drinks; self-serve laundry

- full kitchen for self-catering
- breakfast supplied
- 3-course Italian dinner with wine, $70 pp, by arrangement
- garden views
- phone, fax & email available
- high-speed internet access
- serviced daily
- children by arrangement
- off-street parking

ACTIVITIES AVAILABLE

- outdoor chess set on site
- BBQ on patio
- 10m swimming pool on site
- 1.5ha farmlet, horses, sheep
- friendly sheep (Oswald), 1 cat, 2 collie dogs & pétanque court on site
- tennis courts nearby
- croquet, 1.5km away
- private gardens open to visit

- wine trail, 5-min drive away
- public gardens & parks
- arts & crafts
- walks & tramping
- Blenheim township, 3km
- river & sea fishing
- Queen Charlotte walkway
- Marlborough Sounds
- Picton ferry, 30 mins north

WAIRAU VALLEY, BLENHEIM
Glenavy Vineyard Apartment

Hosts Jackie and Trevor McGarry

1046 State Highway 63, R D 1, Blenheim
Phone 0-3-572 9562   *Email* glenavy@mlb.planet.gen.nz
Fax 0-3-572 9567   *Website* glenavy-vineyard.co.nz

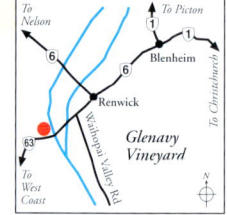

DIRECTIONS: From Blenheim, take SH 6 towards Nelson. Turn left onto SH 63 towards West Coast. Travel 10.46km, crossing Waihopai River bridge to Glenavy on right. Turn sharp right & travel along drive 1.2km.

1 bdrm	1 enst

Apartment rate $200–$230   *Includes continental breakfast provisions*   *Self-catering*

Set on a working vineyard, Glenavy provides a self-contained upstairs apartment which is detached from the main house to ensure guest privacy. Located in the Wairau Valley, just 20 minutes from the township of Blenheim, Glenavy is a peaceful retreat set in a garden on 16 hectares (40 acres) beside the Wairau River, with rural views to the Wither Hills and the Richmond Range. The hot dry climate is ideal for growing grapes, and Trevor enjoys taking guests on a vineyard tour of Glenavy and answering their enquiries about grape growing. Jackie provides continental breakfast provisions to the apartment, enabling guests to breakfast at their leisure. Guests are also invited to happy hour. Restaurants and shops are only a 10-minute drive away.

FACILITIES

- 1 upstairs apartment with 1 queen ensuite bedroom
- hair dryer & toiletries in ensuite bathroom
- quality bed linen
- phone jack
- guest balcony opening from lounge
- fresh flowers; rural views
- quiet vineyard setting
- continental breakfast provisions provided
- fully equipped kitchen for self-catering
- Marlborough wine tasting
- Sky TV, video & CD-player
- fax & email available
- complimentary laundry
- hosts in main house
- on-site parking

ACTIVITIES AVAILABLE

- guided tour of 8ha (20-acre) vineyard on site, by Trevor
- extensive garden on site
- Wairau River access on site
- trout fishing from site
- swimming in river
- winery tours & tastings
- 5 golf courses, 10-min drive
- boating
- bush walks
- restaurants, 10-min drive
- Renwick, 10-min drive
- Blenheim, 20-min drive
- boating in Marlborough Sounds, 40-min drive
- whale watching, 1½-hr drive
- skiing, 2-hour drive away
- Picton ferries, 40-min drive
- airport, 15-min drive
- Nelson, 1½-hour drive

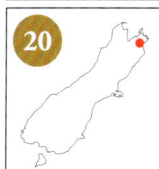

RENWICK, BLENHEIM
LeGrys Vineyard Cottage

Hosts Jennifer and John Joslin

Conders Bend Road, Renwick, Blenheim   *Postal* P O Box 65, Renwick
Phone 0-3-572 9490   *Mobile* 021 313 208   *Fax* 0-3-572 9491
Email stay@legrys.co.nz   *Website* friars.co.nz/hosts/legrys.html

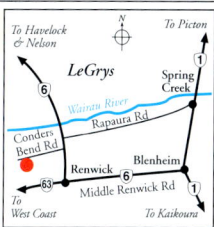

| 2 bdrm | 1 prbth | Cottage rate $250 for 2 persons
Extra persons $50 each | *Includes breakfast hamper* | *Self-catering* |

DIRECTIONS: From Blenheim, take SH 6 towards Nelson. Travel through Renwick & continue 1.5km. Turn left into Conders Bend Rd. Travel 1km to LeGrys on left. From Nelson take SH 6, cross Wairau River & turn right.

Set in a private vineyard, with rural views to the Richmond Range, the accommodation at LeGrys was purpose-built in 1993. Both the main house and adjacent cottage are constructed from mudbricks, complemented by contemporary interiors. The self-contained cottage features a cathedral ceiling and provides two guest bedrooms, a bathroom and kitchenette for self-catering. All guests are offered a complimentary platter and tasting of LeGrys and Mudhouse wine on arrival. The vineyard setting, with backdrop of hills, ensures quietness, and a stream runs past the cottage door. On-site activities include swimming in the solar-heated indoor pool and touring LeGrys Vineyard.

FACILITIES

- single-party bookings for self-contained cottage only
- 1 queen & 1 twin bedroom, with 1 bathroom in cottage
- email, fax & phone available
- hair dryers, heated towel rails, bathrobes & toiletries
- cotton bed linen
- fresh flowers
- children welcome

- full breakfast provisions delivered daily in hamper to cottage
- kitchenette in cottage
- music, tea/coffee; gas BBQ
- TV & CDs
- log burner in cottage
- complimentary platter & wine on arrival
- Alice, Airedale dog on site

ACTIVITIES AVAILABLE

- indoor solar-heated swimming pool on site
- pétanque/boules on site
- Mudhouse & LeGrys Wines, complimentary tasting at cellar door
- vineyard tour on site
- day tours/activities, with transport to & from LeGrys
- winery visits

- 6 golf courses; horse trekking
- restaurants, 5–10-min drive
- pony-&-trap winery trail
- sailing; garden visits
- bush walks in hills
- guided trout fishing
- mailboat trips at Kenepuru & Marlborough Sounds
- Rainbow Ski Field, 1½ hours

RENWICK, BLENHEIM
Vintners Retreat

General Manager Stewart Milne

55 Rapaura Road, Blenheim   *Postal* P O Box 109, Renwick
Freephone 0800 484 686   *Phone* 0-3-572 7420   *Fax* 0-3-572 7421
Email info@vintnersretreat.co.nz   *Website* www.vintnersretreat.co.nz

DIRECTIONS: From Picton take SH 1 towards Blenheim. At Spring Creek turn right into Rapaura Rd. Travel 5.5km to Vintners Retreat on left. From Nelson take SH 6 towards Blenheim & turn left into Rapaura Rd.

30 bdrm	28 prbth

Villa rate $200–$360 for 2 persons
Extra persons $35 each

Self-catering
Breakfast extra

Located in the heart of Marlborough's renowned wine region, Vintners Retreat is set in nearly two hectares (four acres) of park-like grounds surrounded by vineyards. The accommodation comprises 14 individual European-style villas separate from each other, each with two or three bedrooms and two bathrooms. Catering for a maximum of 60 guests, Vintners Retreat provides full self-catering facilities, with a well equipped kitchen in each villa and barbecue on each patio. Breakfast can be provided by arrangement and there are many restaurants in the surrounding area. Guests enjoy the on-site activities such as pétanque, tennis, and swimming in the pool. Bicycles are available for hire and wine trails nearby are popular with guests.

FACILITIES

- 14 separate self-contained villas
- 4 Stables & 4 Lodges: each with 2 bedrooms & 2 bathrooms
- 2 Lodges: 3 bedrooms & 2 bathrooms in each
- 4 Manors: 2 bedrooms & 2 bathrooms & balcony in each
- cotton bed linen & phone in all villas & 1 spa bath per villa
- hair dryer, toiletries & heated towel rails in all 28 bathrooms
- fully equipped kitchen for self-catering in all 14 villas
- continental or cooked breakfast by request, extra
- barbecue on private patio area of each villa
- laundry facilities in each
- lounge area in each villa
- internal garaging per villa
- courtesy passenger transfer

ACTIVITIES AVAILABLE

- nearly 2ha park-like grounds on site
- vineyards adjacent
- swimming pool on site
- pétanque/boules on site
- tennis court on site
- bike hire available
- wine trails in vicinity
- golf courses
- fishing
- restaurants, nearby
- sailing in Sounds
- guided trout fishing
- horse trekking
- gardens open to visit
- Kenepuru & Marlborough Sounds day trips
- airport, 10-min drive
- Blenheim, 20-min drive
- Rainbow Ski Field, 1½ hours

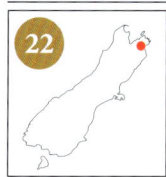

RENWICK, MARLBOROUGH SOUNDS
Jefferswood

Hosts Sandra and Jeff Sewell

Camerons Road, R D 1, Havelock, Marlborough
Phone 0-3-572 8081   *Email* jefferswood.sewell@xtra.co.nz
Fax 0-3-572 8091   *Website* www.jefferswood.co.nz

DIRECTIONS: From Blenheim, take SH 6 towards Nelson. Travel through Renwick & cross Wairau River bridge. Continue on SH 6 & turn left into Camerons Rd. Travel 300m to Jefferswood on right.

| 2 bdrm | 2 enst | Double $225 Single $175 | *Includes breakfast* *Picnic hampers, BBQ & dinner extra* |

 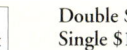

Jefferswood is an eco-friendly adobe, timber and schist homestead, opened in 2003. A verandah surrounds the homestead, and the two guestrooms open to a gallery with bi-fold windows providing rural views to the foothills of Mt Riley. The organic property includes a two-hectare developing arboretum and a pond to attract the birdlife. Sandra serves a full breakfast which includes home-grown produce in season. Afternoon tea on arrival and pre-dinner wine with nibbles are served in the evening. Wineries and restaurants are five minutes' drive away. Guests can enjoy a barbecue under the native totara trees or picnicking beside the pond. Jefferswood offers peaceful rural accommodation just 20 minutes from the township of Blenheim.

FACILITIES

- 1 super-king/twin & 1 queen ensuite bedroom
- double shower, hair dryer, demist mirror, toiletries, bathrobes in both bathrooms
- cotton bed linen; fresh flowers
- underfloor heating
- wheelchair access; wake-up calls
- complimentary laundry
- solar-heated hot water
- full breakfast in dining room, or on verandah
- picnic hampers, BBQ & dinner on request, extra
- home baking; kitchen available; all day refreshments
- lounge with gas fire, daily newspaper, music centre, books & games
- email, fax & phone available
- garaging; courtesy transfer

ACTIVITIES AVAILABLE

- picnicking, bird-watching & 2ha arboretum, on site
- jogging local trails with host; local bush walks
- private farms, wineries, gardens & scenic day tours; guide available
- landing strip nearby; airport, 15-min drive
- arts & crafts; horse riding
- Havelock marina
- restaurants, cafés & shopping in Havelock/Blenheim, 15–20 mins
- Marlborough Sounds for fishing, walks, boating, touring, kayaking
- trout fishing; guide available
- Gold-mining at Wakamarina
- Queen Charolotte Track
- whale watching arranged
- Picton ferries, 40-min drive; Nelson City, 1¼-hour drive

HAVELOCK, MARLBOROUGH SOUNDS
Pelorus Lodge

General Manager Tim Smith

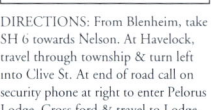

Clive Street, Havelock, Marlborough Sounds   *Phone* 0-3-574 2999
Postal P O Box 9304, Wellington   *Fax* 0-4-385 3175
Email service@peloruslodge.com   *Website* www.peloruslodge.com

DIRECTIONS: From Blenheim, take SH 6 towards Nelson. At Havelock, travel through township & turn left into Clive St. At end of road call on security phone at right to enter Pelorus Lodge. Cross ford & travel to Lodge.

4 bdrm	4 enst

Room rate $1,800–$2,250   *Includes breakfast, apéritifs, dinner & luncheon cruise*
Lodge rate $6,750

Ensconced within 12 hectares (30 acres) of grounds, overlooking Havelock Marina and the Marlborough Sounds, is Pelorus Lodge, completed in 2002. A Mercedes ML320 will transport guests to the entrance, through the security gates, across the waterfall to the seclusion of the lodge. Inside, the focal point of the spacious conservatory is a ceiling height waterfall, tumbling over rocks. Personally designed five-course dinner, with Pacific Rim cuisine, is served in the adjacent dining room with panoramic views of the Sounds. Downstairs is a separate guest lounge separating two of the ensuite bedrooms. A luncheon cruise on the 14-metre (42-foot) *Lady Karita*, built in 1939, is included in the tariff. Exclusive use of the Lodge is available.

FACILITIES

- Pelorus: king ensuite bedroom, spa bath, dressing room, TV
- Forest: super-king bedroom, ensuite & hydrotherapy spa bath
- Rewarewa: queen bedroom, ensuite includes spa bath
- Rata: queen bedroom with TV & private bathroom
- Egyptian cotton bed linen, safe, phone, fridge & tea/coffee; toiletries, heated towel rails & bathrobes

- breakfast served in conservatory
- 5-course gourmet dinner
- complimentary cocktail hour
- luncheon included on cruise
- 2 guest lounges with open fire, tea/coffee, Sky TV & video
- business service available
- complimentary laundry
- courtesy transfer; security system
- on-site parking; helipad nearby

ACTIVITIES AVAILABLE

- sauna on site
- 2ha of native planting on site with waterfall
- garden walks
- complimentary 5-hr launch cruise & seafood luncheon
- honeymoons catered for
- barbecue available
- fishing tours
- gold-mining

- cafés for lunch within walking distance
- scenic drives
- museum; wineries
- Havelock shops & township, within walking distance
- airport, 20-min drive
- Blenheim, 25-min drive
- Picton ferries, 45-min drive
- Nelson, 45-min drive

Pelorus Lodge

Pelorus Lodge

Above: The waterfall tumbles down the garden, over the driveway and into the pool, in the peaceful two-hectare setting.
Below: Pelorus Lodge overlooks the marina where *Lady Karita* is moored, awaiting guests for their luncheon cruise in the Sounds.
Opposite top: The spacious dining room and upstairs guest lounge provide panoramic views of the Marlborough Sounds.
Opposite bottom left: The upstairs Pelorus guestroom includes a king-size bed, with dressing room, ensuite and sea views.
Opposite bottom right: Dining is a highlight at Pelorus Lodge with resident chef providing Pacific Rim cuisine and fine wine.

© Friars' Guide to New Zealand Accommodation for the Discerning Traveller

RAI VALLEY, MARLBOROUGH SOUNDS
Mudbrick Lodge

Host Tania Lawrence

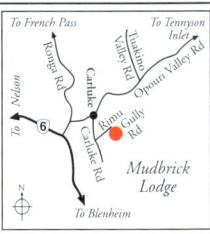

150 Rimu Gully Road, Rai Valley   *Postal* P O Box 92, Rai Valley, Marlborough
Phone 0-3-571 6147   *Mobile* 027 251 3867   *Fax* 0-3-571 6147
Email tania@mudbricklodge.co.nz   *Website* www.mudbricklodge.co.nz

DIRECTIONS: From Blenheim, take SH 6 towards Nelson. Turn right towards French Pass. Take 1st right over bridge, then right into Carluke Rd. Take 1st left into Rimu Gully Rd. Travel to end to Mudbrick Lodge.

| 3 bdrm | 3 ensl | 1 pdrm | Double $195–$250 Single $150 | *Includes breakfast Lunch & dinner extra* |

Constructed from mudbricks and macrocarpa in 1996, Mudbrick Lodge is located in a secluded 400-hectare (1,000-acre) valley. Set in almost two hectares (four acres) of landscaped gardens, the separate guest accommodation comprises two ensuite bedrooms upstairs and a deluxe guestroom downstairs opening to a verandah. Guests are welcome to relax in the garden or, for the more active, two local hunting and fishing guides will take them hunting, fishing, diving, horse trekking or following wine and art trails. Tania is a professional chef who serves full cooked breakfasts, including home-made preserves, in the conservatory, homestead, garden or room service. She is happy to prepare lunch and dinner to a personalised menu too.

FACILITIES

- 2 super-king/twin ensuite bedrooms upstairs
- 1 super-king/twin ensuite bedroom with bath, wheelchair access & verandah downstairs
- percale bed linen, Egyptian cotton towels & down duvets
- tea/coffee, mineral water, phone & writing desk in bedrooms
- hair dryers & toiletries
- wheelchair access

- full breakfast indoors, in conservatory or alfresco
- picnic or light lunch, $25 pp
- 3-course dinner, $50 pp
- licensed; fresh flowers
- lounge with open fire, Sky TV, DVD, CDs & bar
- children welcome
- phone, fax, email; laundry
- on-site parking; helipad

ACTIVITIES AVAILABLE

- spa pool & BBQ on site
- pet dog, cats, pigs & chickens on site
- guided hunting & fishing
- fly fishing at end of driveway
- native bush walks
- fly & salt-water fishing
- scuba & free diving
- sea kayaking
- wine trails

- horse treks; golf courses
- historic gold trails
- art & craft trails
- guided tramping
- Queen Charlotte track
- Abel Tasman National Park
- Havelock, 20-min drive
- Okiwi Bay & Duncan Bay, 20-min drive
- Blenheim & Nelson, 40 mins

Mudbrick

Okiwi Bay, Marlborough Sounds
Croisilles Villa

Hosts Marie and Peter Hill

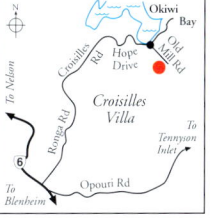

Old Mill Road, Okiwi Bay   *Phone* 0-3-544 8343
Postal 86 Patons Road, Hope, Nelson   *Fax* 0-3-544 8333
Email pmhill@ts.co.nz   *Website* friars.co.nz/hosts/croisilles.html

4 bdrm	2 enst	1 shbth

House rate $350
Extra persons $45 each

Self-catering
3-night minimum stay

DIRECTIONS: From Blenheim, take SH 6 towards Nelson. Turn right into Ronga Rd towards French Pass. Continue into Croisilles Rd & Hope Drive to Okiwi Bay. Turn right into Old Mill Rd to Villa on right.

Set on almost two hectares on a hillside overlooking Okiwi Bay, Croisilles Villa was built as a holiday home in 2003. Croisilles Villa is a fully self-contained house, accommodating up to eight guests in a single-party booking. Located halfway between Blenheim and Nelson, Okiwi Bay is a secluded holiday spot popular for watersports. The Villa provides guests with two canoes for kayaking and fishing gear is available. Guests also enjoy the outdoor bathtub at Croisilles Villa overlooking the bay, and the barbecue on the spacious decking area is popular for alfresco dining. There is a fully equipped kitchen for self-catering, with basic provisions supplied and a complimentary bottle of wine. The local restaurant is just five minutes' walk away at Okiwi Bay.

FACILITIES

- one-party bookings only
- 1 king ensuite bedroom with dressing room, TV & phone
- 1 queen ensuite bedroom
- 1 queen & 1 twin bedroom share 1 bathroom
- cotton bed linen
- hair dryers, heated towel rails, toiletries & bathrobes
- self-serve laundry
- full kitchen for self-catering, with breakfast provisions
- complimentary bottle of wine
- lounge with gas fire, Sky TV, video, DVD & CD-player
- guest phone in kitchen
- children over 8 yrs welcome
- barbecue available
- 2 outside fires & seating
- on-site parking; garaging

ACTIVITIES AVAILABLE

- outdoor bath overlooking bay on site
- fishing gear, 2 mountain bikes & 2 canoes available for guest use
- walking track to beach
- Durville Island charters
- watersports
- Okiwi Bay
- kayaking; mountain biking
- restaurant, 5-min walk away
- wineries; arts & crafts
- waterskiing & jet skiing
- fishing & diving trips
- wind-surfing; swimming
- gardens open to visit
- walking; boating
- French Pass, 1¼-hour drive
- Blenheim & Nelson City, 1 hour

Croisilles

NELSON
Retiro Park Lodge

Hosts Robbert de Jongh and Victor Flores

152 Teal Valley, R D 1, Nelson
Phone 0-3-545 0118   *Email* info@retiroparklodge.co.nz
Website www.retiroparklodge.co.nz

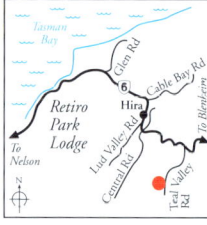

DIRECTIONS: Take SH 6 from Picton or Blenheim towards Nelson, or from city, travel 14km north. Turn south into Teal Valley Rd. Travel 1.4km to private road & continue 200m to Retiro Park Lodge on right.

3 bdrm	2 enst	1 prbth

Double $195–$275
Single $135

Includes breakfast
Lunch & dinner extra

Set in a peaceful valley 15 minutes from Nelson City, Retiro Park Lodge (*see centre of photo above*) offers guests a quiet get-away with rural views. Spanish for "retreat", Retiro Park Lodge provides a spacious converted barn as well as accommodation in the Lodge. Victor, a trained chef, serves breakfast or dinner by arrangement in the garden conservatory, or alfresco in the vine-clad courtyard opening onto the large garden. Victor can also provide picnic baskets. Guests can enjoy relaxing in the extensive garden setting and viewing the llamas, alpacas and donkeys. There are walking tracks throughout the almond and olive groves on site to the new vineyard. Cable Bay, a popular attraction, is just 12 kilometres away for kayaking and visiting local crafts and artists.

FACILITIES

- 1 queen ensuite bedroom & 1 double bedroom with 1 private bathroom in Lodge
- 1 queen ensuite bedroom & kitchenette in converted barn
- toiletries & heated towel rails in all 3 bathrooms; 2 baths
- bathrobes, cotton bed linen & fresh flowers in bedrooms
- fridge & tea/coffee in bedrooms, opening to balconies

- English/continental breakfast
- lunch basket & wine, $75 for 2
- dinner with wine, $90 pp, by arrangement; licensed
- kitchenette in Lodge & lounge with open fire, bar, Sky TV, CD-player, artwork & books
- phone, email & laundry
- Dutch & Spanish spoken
- courtesy transfer; parking

ACTIVITIES AVAILABLE

- swimming pool & BBQ on site
- pets, donkeys, alpacas & llamas on site
- walks on site through olive & almond groves & boutique vineyard
- Nina Davis & Creative Earth potteries, short drive
- Happy Valley 4WD adventures & flying fox, 6km
- horse treks

- restaurants, 14km
- Cable Bay, 12km
  – kayaking
  – local artists
  – scenic & estuary walks
  – David Haig Furniture
- gardens open to visit
- Nelson City, 15-mins south
- Picton ferries, 1¾-hr drive
- Nelson Lakes, Kahurangi & Abel Tasman national parks

NELSON CITY
Parautane Lodge

Hosts Candace and Alan Donovan

137 Parautane Way, R D 1, Nelson   *Mobile* 021 052 6842
Phone 0-3-545 2959   *Email* parautaneinfo@paradise.net.nz
Fax 0-3-545 2958   *Website* www.nelsonlodge.co.nz

DIRECTIONS: From Nelson City, take SH 6 north towards Blenheim for 12 mins. Turn left into Todd Bush Rd. At end turn right into Parautane Way. Travel 1.5km uphill to signposted Parautane Lodge on left, to carpark.

4 bdrm	4 enst	Single $200–$220 Double $260–$290	*Includes breakfast* *Dinner extra* **Low-season & corporate rates available**

Located high on a hillside above Tasman Bay, Parautane Lodge was built in 2004 in the style of a Canadian mountain lodge. Set in four hectares (10 acres) with panoramic views over the bay to the western ranges beyond, Parautane Lodge offers four ensuite guestrooms, all with sea veiws – three queen-size opening to decking above the ocean, and upstairs a separate king-size room including an extra sofa bed. There are steps down to a spa pool on the hillside and guests can also enjoy therapeutic massage from Candace, the resident masseuse. Continental and cooked breakfast is offered to guests in the dining room that opens on to the spacious deck. Parautane Lodge is located just 12 minutes north of Nelson City, with its many cafés and restaurants.

FACILITIES

- 3 queen, 1 king bedrooms, with ensuites, each opens to deck
- heated towel rails & floor, hair dryer, demist mirrror, toiletries & bathrobes in all 4 ensuites
- 100% cotton bed linen
- phone, jackpoint, writing desk, tea/coffee, TV & DVDs in all 4 bedrooms
- central heating
- children by arrangement
- full breakfast in dining room or alfresco on deck
- 3–4-course dinner & wine, $60 pp, by arrangement
- guest fridge in dining room
- Candace speaks French
- outdoor seating areas & deck
- private guest entrance
- on-site parking area
- courtesy passenger transfer

ACTIVITIES AVAILABLE

- spa pool on site
- BBQ on site
- in-house masseuse
- small conferences
- kayaking
- 4-wheeling adventures
- flying fox
- horseback riding
- mountain biking
- City Centre, restaurants, cafés, shops, 12-min drive
- vineyards
- tramping, hiking
- WOW museum
- gardens to visit
- airport, 15-min drive
- 3 National Parks, within 1½-hour drive away
- interisland ferries, 2 hours

NELSON CITY
Muritai Manor

Hosts Jan and Stan Holt

48 Wakapuaka Road, Wakapuaka, R D 1, Nelson   *Mobile* 027 437 0622
Freephone 0800 260 662   *Phone* 0-3-545 1189   *Fax* 0-3-545 0740
Email stay@muritaimanor.co.nz   *Website* www.muritaimanor.co.nz

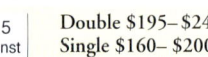

DIRECTIONS: Take SH 6 from Picton or Blenheim towards Nelson. At Wakapuaka, 5 mins north of city, Muritai Manor well signposted on left (Signs illuminated at night.) From Nelson, take SH 6 past Atawhai.

5 bdrm	5 enst	**Double $195–$240**	*Includes breakfast*	*Dinner extra*
		Single $160–$200	**Off-peak rates available**	

This Edwardian colonial house, built in 1903 for the local archdeacon, was renovated by Jan and Stan in 1997, the new extensions blending with the original style. Muritai means "sea breeze" in Maori, referring to its setting above the ocean. Sited just five minutes north of Nelson on a north-west facing elevation, Muritai Manor looks across Tasman Bay to Abel Tasman National Park in the distance. Guests have the choice of five ensuite bedrooms furnished with antiques, and can enjoy the outdoor facilities, including the heated swimming pool, spa and croquet lawn. Flower beds line the driveway and mature English oaks and lime trees provide summer shade and autumn colour. Jess, Dande and Flora are the three canine family members.

FACILITIES

- 2 king/twin, 1 king & 2 queen ensuite bedrooms
- 5 ensuites, 2 with baths
- toiletries & heated towel rails
- cotton bed linen & electric blankets
- antiques; fresh flowers
- all rooms serviced daily
- guest balconies; sea views
- laundry available
- cooked or continental breakfast in dining room
- lunch or dinner by request, $30–$95 pp
- tea/coffee facilities & TV
- guest lounge with open fire
- children by arrangement
- phone, fax & email available
- guest parking for 5 cars
- airport or bus depot transfer

ACTIVITIES AVAILABLE

- solar-heated swimming pool
- Nelson restaurants 5-min drive
- spa pool, robes provided
- BBQ available
- croquet lawn on site
- pétanque/boules on site
- public Japanese stroll garden, 5-min drive away
- vineyards
- arts & crafts
- Nelson City, 5-min drive
- horse riding; golf
- gardens open to visit
- fishing
- Nelson Lakes
- skiing in winter
- 3 National Parks – Abel Tasman, Kahurangi & Nelson Lakes
- Picton ferry, 2-hour drive

NELSON CITY
California House Inn

Hosts Janice and Ray Evans

29 Collingwood Street, Nelson
Phone 0-3-548 4173   *Email* info@californiahouse.co.nz
Fax 0-3-548 4184   *Website* www.californiahouse.co.nz

DIRECTIONS: Take SH 6 to Nelson roundabout & turn into Trafalgar St towards City Centre. Turn 1st left into Wainui St, then 1st right into Collingwood St. California House Inn on left. (1-min drive from City Centre.)

6 bdrm	6 enst

Room rate $185–$295

Includes breakfast
Packed lunches & dinner extra

Built as a large family home in 1893, this Victorian villa has been completely renovated and refurbished. Original features include the impressive English oak-panelled entrance hall, fireplaces with carved kauri surrounds, and 24 stained-glass windows with a central skylight that gives a sense of spaciousness to the house. Native timbers, colonial furnishings and fine English antiques feature throughout, with books and photographs from the early 1900s, and an extensive local contemporary art collection. Sunny verandahs offer relaxation in the quiet garden setting. Speciality breakfasts are a highlight and may include home-made Bircher muesli, smoked salmon crêpes, mushroom and spinach frittata or French toast with manuka dry-cured bacon.

FACILITIES

- 1 twin with 2 queen beds, 1 queen & 4 king bedrooms, each with ensuite, 2 with baths
- heated towel rails, hair dryers, locally hand-made toiletries
- winter heating & electric blankets; quality bed linen
- hi-speed internet access, tea/coffee, chocolates & fresh flowers in bedrooms
- fluent French spoken
- full breakfast served; gourmet packed lunches & dinner, extra
- guest sitting room with wood-burning stove, desk, grand piano, library & wine
- computer, fax, TV/DVD/VCR & laundry service available
- guest fridge; guest parking
- activity planning assistance
- all trips collect from door

ACTIVITIES AVAILABLE

- short walk from house to:
  – City Centre, cinema
  – restaurants, cafés, shops
  – Central Business District
  – arts & crafts galleries
  – geographical centre of NZ
- running, walking or biking on Matai riverside path
- Saturday morning market
- 3 golf courses; gear hire
- river & ocean fishing
- range of waterfront restaurants; Tahunanui Beach, 5-min drive
- vineyard & Macs Brewery tours
- Abel Tasman kayaking & walks
- yacht cruising & sail racing
- public parks & gardens
- airport, 15-min drive
- interisland ferries, 1¾ hours
- 3 National Parks, within 1½-hour drive away

California House

California House

NELSON CITY
Riverside Apartment

Hosts Alison Phillips and Robin White

Riverside, Nelson   *Postal* 45 Collingwood Street, Nelson
Phone 0-3-548 9418   *Mobile* 025 678 1170   *Fax* 0-3-548 9418
Email waimarie.motel@xtra.co.nz   *Website* www.riversideapartments.nelson.co.nz

DIRECTIONS: From SH 6, turn left into Trafalgar St. Turn left into Halifax St & continue into Riverside. Apartment 1st on left. From airport take Wakefield Quay into Haven Rd. Turn left into Halifax St.

| 2 bdrm | 1 prbth | 1 pdrm | Apartment rate $160–$200 for 2 persons $200–$280 for 4 persons | *Self-catering* Minimum stay may apply | *Breakfast extra* Corporate & long-stay rates |

Overlooking the Maitai River, Riverside Apartment provides peace and quiet, just one block from the City Centre. This self-contained apartment includes a full kitchen for self-catering, with a terrace opening from the lounge where guests enjoy alfresco dining above the river, close enough to see trout jumping! Native birds such as the tui, heron and kingfisher feed on the river, and there is a formed walkway along the riverside. Upstairs in the apartment is a queen-size bedroom and bathroom, and downstairs are a twin bedroom and powder room. There are many restaurants a few minutes' walk away, and a heated swimming pool, sauna and gym are a 200-metre walk along Riverside.

FACILITIES

- 1 self-contained apartment for one-party bookings only
- 1 queen bedroom upstairs & 1 twin bedroom downstairs share upstairs bathroom
- bath, hair dryer & toiletries
- TV & phone in queen bedroom, opens to balcony
- cotton bed linen
- double sofa-bed & TV in downstairs lounge opening to verandah
- continental breakfast on request, extra, in 6-seater dining room or alfresco on terrace overlooking river
- full self-catering kitchen with phone
- fresh flowers; powder room
- laundry available
- children under 10 years, by arrangement
- off-street parking; 1-car garage

ACTIVITIES AVAILABLE

- bird-watching from site
- Maitai River access from site for fishing, walkway, native birds
- heated swimming pool, sauna & gym, 200m walk
- Within 5–10-min walk:
  - pottery, craft & art galleries
  - Nelson Cathedral
  - Nelson School of Music
  - restaurants, cafés & shopping
  - Queens Gardens
  - Suter Art Gallery
  - Saturday craft & produce market
  - movie theatre
  - Maitai River walkway
  - track to centre of NZ lookout
- 3 golf courses, 10–20-min drive
- sailing, kayaking
- wineries, beaches, fishing
- airport, 15-min drive
- Abel Tasman National Park, 1hr
- interisland ferries, 2-hr drive

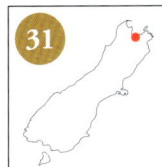

NELSON CITY
Baywick Inn

Hosts Janet Southwick and Tim Bayley

51 Domett Street, Nelson

Phone 0-3-545 6514   *Mobile* 027 454 5823   *Fax* 0-3-545 6517
Email baywicks@iconz.co.nz   *Website* www.baywicks.com

3 bdrm	2 enst	1 prbth

Double $140–$165
Single $110–$130

Includes breakfast
Dinner extra

DIRECTIONS: From Picton or Christchurch, take SH 6 to Nelson. Turn left into Trafalgar St. Turn left again into Hardy St & continue to river. Turn right into Domett St. The Baywick Inn on right.

Overlooking Maitai River and bordering Brook Stream, this restored Victorian villa was built in 1885 and features native rimu panelling and tiled carved fireplaces. Guest accommodation comprises three spacious upstairs bedrooms: Parkdale, named after Janet's Toronto neighbourhood, includes a sunroom; Burnside, the original name of the house, has its own balcony; and Greenwood with river views. Guests enjoy the private garden beside the Brook where they can feed eels, trout and ducks. Janet, a chef by profession, serves gourmet breakfasts in the sunny dining room, and her menu includes fresh fruit salad, toasted pecan muesli, and smoked salmon or other speciality omelettes. The Baywick is also home to Mombozzie, the wire-haired fox terrier.

FACILITIES

- Parkdale: 1 queen bedroom with ensuite including claw-foot bath, & sunroom
- Burnside: 1 queen/twin ensuite bedroom with private balcony
- Greenwood: 1 queen bedroom with private bathroom
- bathrobes, toiletries & hair dryer in all 3 bathrooms
- turn-down service, chocolates
- tea/coffee/cappuccino downstairs

- House Special breakfast
- 3-course dinner, with wine, by arrangement, $40–$50 pp
- open fire & complimentary sherry & port in guest lounge
- TV, fresh flowers in bedrooms
- high-speed internet
- off-street parking
- peaceful residential setting
- Canadian/NZ hospitality

ACTIVITIES AVAILABLE

- City Centre, 5-min walk
- pétanque/boules on site
- feeding wildlife in the Brook
- Tim's classic MGs to view
- Baywick's Wine Cellars showroom on site
- Maitai River walkway
- Polytechnic, walking distance
- wine & arts & crafts trails
- art gallery & gardens

- restaurants & shopping within walking distance
- golf links, 5-min drive
- cathedral; beaches nearby
- sailing & kayaking
- Founders Park
- Centre of NZ trail
- Japanese gardens
- Abel Tasman National Park day trips

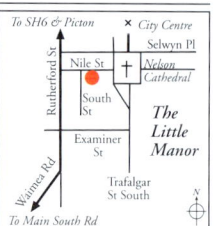

NELSON CITY
The Little Manor

Hosts Angela Higgins and Christopher Geen

12 Nile Street West, Nelson   *Postal* P O Box 767, Nelson
Phone 0-3-545 1411   *Mobile* 021 247 1891   *Fax* 0-3-545 1417
Email the.little.manor@xtra.co.nz   *Website* friars.co.nz/hosts/littlemanor.html

DIRECTIONS: From SH 6, turn left into Trafalgar St, then right into Halifax St. Turn left into Rutherford St, then left again into Nile St West. The Little Manor is on the right.

| 2 bdrm | 1 prbth | Cottage rate $195–$240 for 2 persons
Extra persons $45 each | *Self-catering*
Includes breakfast basket |

The Little Manor is self-contained accommodation set in the historic precinct of inner Nelson. Built in 1863, this colonial Victorian home has been elegantly renovated to provide two upstairs bedrooms, sundeck, and extra sofa-bed in the reading room. The bathroom features a claw-foot bath downstairs. The breakfast basket comprises a fruit bowl, cereals, eggs, bagels, croissants or other fresh breads, home-made jams and sauces. Other meals can be self-catered in the fully equipped kitchen. A dining room, lounge, and full laundry are also downstairs and the spacious entrance hall includes a writing desk. Antiques enhance the quiet old-world ambience.

FACILITIES

- fully self-contained house
- single-party bookings only
- 1 king & 1 queen bedroom with bathrobes
- 1 bathroom, claw-foot bath, toiletries & hair dryer
- 100% cotton bed linen
- double sofa-bed, magazines in reading room upstairs
- 2 TVs, video & CD-player
- fresh flowers
- private sundeck balcony
- full kitchen for self-catering
- selection of teas & coffees
- breakfast basket & pantry
- open fire & central heating
- phone, fax & writing desk
- complimentary guest laundry, or valet service
- masseuse & hairdresser available, by arrangement

ACTIVITIES AVAILABLE

- City Centre, 2-min walk
- Nelson Cathedral, 2-min walk
- award-winning restaurants & cafés, 2–3-min walk
- shopping, 3-min walk
- golf courses, 10–20-min drive
- harbour cruises & watersports
- art galleries & pottery studios
- local markets
- parks & public gardens to visit
- private gardens open to visit
- wineries
- 4WD biking in native NZ forest
- trout & sea fishing
- Tahunanui & Kaiteriteri Beaches
- Golden Bay cruises
- Nelson Lakes – walks, skiing
- Abel Tasman & Kahurangi National Parks
- airport, 12-min drive

NELSON CITY

SouthHaven

Hosts Jeanette and Peter Hancock   *Mobile* 027 436 3858

2B South Street, Nelson   *Email* info@cottageaccommodation.co.nz

Postal Pomona Road, Ruby Bay, R D 1, Upper Moutere, Nelson

Phone 0-3-540 2769   *Fax* 0-3-540 2769   *Website* www.cottageaccommodation.co.nz

| 2 bdrm | 1 enst | 1 prbth | **Apartment rate $180–$210**
Extra persons $35 each | *Includes breakfast provisions*
2-night minimum stay on weekends & public holidays | *Self-catering* | |

DIRECTIONS: Take SH 6 to Nelson City. Turn left into Trafalgar St, & right into Halifax St. Turn left into Rutherford St, then left again into Nile St West. Take 1st right into South St. SouthHaven on corner on right.

SouthHaven was built in 1998 atop the corner of historic South Street, the oldest fully preserved street in New Zealand. This two-storey self-contained townhouse is sited overlooking the street, with French doors opening from the lounge on to the spacious garden balcony for alfresco dining. From here the spire of Trafalgar Cathedral can be seen and its carillon bells enjoyed. The well-equipped rimu kitchen is designed for self-catering for single-party bookings. The spacious main bedroom is upstairs, with queen-size bed, ensuite, television and chaise longue. A second double bedroom below has a separate toilet. Within minutes of SouthHaven, guests can wander through art and craft galleries or dine at award-winning restaurants and cafés.

FACILITIES

- single-party bookings only
- 1 queen ensuite bedroom
- 1 double bedroom & toilet
- TV, phone & chaise longue in upstairs queen bedroom
- cotton bed linen, hair dryers, bathrobes, toiletries
- fresh flowers
- self-serve laundry
- secure garaging

- breakfast provisions, including cereals, eggs, bread, home-made jams, teas & plunger coffee
- full kitchen for self-catering
- balcony suitable for alfresco dining overlooking street
- living room with gas fire, Sky TV, video, CD-player, music, games, phone, fax & writing table

ACTIVITIES AVAILABLE

- relaxing on spacious balcony
- award-winning restaurants, cafés & wine bars, 2-min walk
- pottery & craft galleries
- shopping; theatres
- Nelson Cathedral
- golf courses; trout fishing
- mountain climbing; hiking
- Miyazu Japanese Gardens
- Queens Gardens

- City Centre, 3-min walk
- private garden tours
- Maitai River walks
- wine tours; glass blowing
- golden beaches; safe swimming
- sailing; kayaking; windsurfing
- heritage trail; Nelson Lakes
- 3 National Parks, 1-hr drive
- Nelson airport, 10-min drive
- interisland ferries, 1¾ hours

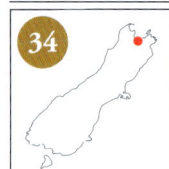

NELSON CITY
Alma Cottage

Hosts Susan and Chris White-Johnson

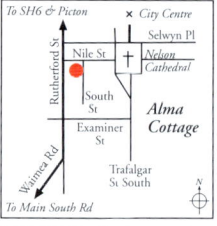

2C South Street, Nelson   *Postal* 7 Dumont Place, Kaiteriteri, R D 2, Motueka
Phone 0-3-527 8558   *Mobile* 021 393 351   *Fax* 0-3-527 8558
Email almacottage@ihug.co.nz   *Website* www.almacottage.co.nz

DIRECTIONS: Take SH 6 to Nelson City. Turn left into Trafalgar St, & right into Halifax St. Turn left into Rutherford St, then left again into Nile St West. Take 1st right into South St. Alma Cottage on right.

| 2 bdrm | 1 prbth | Cottage rate $180 for 2 persons
Extra persons $25 each | *Includes continental breakfast provisions*
Self-catering |

Alma Cottage is a self-contained townhouse in a central city location in Nelson. It was built in 1998 in the style of the other early colonial cottages in historic South Street, a cul-de-sac preserved in a 130-year-old time warp. This two-storey townhouse provides total privacy and independence for single parties of up to four guests in two bedrooms. The bathroom includes a bath, and the kitchen is fully equipped for self-catering. Complimentary breakfast provisions of fruit, cereals, yoghurt, bacon, eggs, toast, jams, juice, teas and coffee are supplied sufficient for at least two mornings. There is also a barbecue and outdoor furniture for alfresco dining in the cottage garden. Many restaurants, cafés and bars in Nelson City are just a few steps away.

FACILITIES

- single-party bookings only
- self-contained townhouse
- 1 queen & 1 twin bedroom upstairs
- 1 private bathroom upstairs
- bath, hair dryer & toiletries
- cotton bed linen, duvets & electric blankets on all beds
- phone in queen bedroom
- children welcome

- continental breakfast provisions for 2 mornings
- full kitchen with dishwasher for self-catering
- guest lounge downstairs with TV, video, CD-player, books, writing desk & phone
- guest laundry
- outdoor furniture & BBQ
- cottage garden; off-street carport for 2 cars

ACTIVITIES AVAILABLE

- BBQ in courtyard
- heritage trail
- potters adjacent
- art galleries adjacent
- Nelson City Centre, just 2-min walk away
- Nelson Cathedral
- craft shops
- Rutherford Conference Centre
- movie theatres

- restaurants, cafés & bars within walking distance
- parks & public gardens
- private gardens to visit
- Maitai River walk
- wine trail
- beaches
- National Parks
- Nelson Lakes
- Picton ferries, 1¾ hours

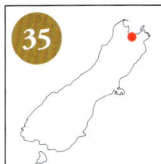

NELSON CITY
South Street Cottages

Hosts Jeanette and Peter Hancock   *Mobile* 027 436 3858

1, 3 and 12 South Street, Nelson   *Website* cottageaccommodation.co.nz
Postal Pomona Road, Ruby Bay, R D 1, Upper Moutere   *Fax* 0-3-540 2769
Phone 0-3-540 2769   *Email* info@cottageaccommodation.co.nz

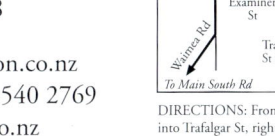

DIRECTIONS: From SH 6, turn left into Trafalgar St, right into Halifax St, then left into Rutherford St. Turn left into Nile St West, then 1st right into South St. Biddle & Dillon Cottages on left, & Briar Cottage at end on right.

6 bdrm	3 enst	Cottage rate $160–$175 for 2 persons *Includes breakfast provisions* *Self-catering*
		Extra adults $30 each Children $15 each 2-night minimum stay on weekends

Biddle, Dillon and Briar Cottages are three of the restored residences in historic South Street, the oldest preserved precinct in New Zealand. These cottages were built around 1864 and are now available for single-party bookings, being self-contained and private, with two double bedrooms in each. Biddle Cottage *(see photographs above)* was named after a local pharmacist who began the restoration work in the 1980s, which Peter and Jeanette completed. Dillon Cottage *(see right below)* is named after Constantine Augustus Dillon who in 1851 bought the town acre which now includes South Street. Briar Cottage *(see left below)* is larger, although it was originally only a two-room cottage, before being transformed briefly into a gallery in the 1970s. Each cottage is designed for guests' independence, with dining room, lounge, fully equipped kitchen and paved garden seating area. Jeanette supplies breakfast provisions, including fresh fruit, home-made jams, bread and eggs, for guests' use.

FACILITIES

- 3 self-contained cottages:
  – Biddle Cottage (no. 1)
  – Dillon Cottage (no. 3)
  – Briar Cottage (no. 12)
- single-party bookings only in each cottage
- 2-night minimum stay on weekends & public holidays
- fully fenced – children & pets welcome in all 3 cottages
- 2 double bedrooms & fold-down sofa in each cottage
- cotton bed linen
- 1 private bathroom with heater, hair dryer & toiletries in each cottage
- full laundry in each cottage
- breakfast provisions supplied
- full-sized fully equipped kitchen including microwave in each cottage, for self-catering & entertaining
- guest phone, log burner, & dining room in each cottage
- lounge with books, TV, stereo, CDs & tapes in each cottage
- fresh flowers & window boxes in each cottage
- garden courtyard with outdoor furniture & BBQ per cottage
- private independent locations
- historic setting
- quiet cul-de-sac location

ACTIVITIES AVAILABLE

- relaxing in private cottage garden at each cottage
- restaurants, cafés & wine bars, 2-min walk away
- City Centre, 3-min walk
- pottery & craft galleries in South Street & region
- historic buildings/precinct
- shopping
- theatres
- golf links
- trout-fishing rivers
- private gardens to visit
- Miyazu Japanese Stroll Gardens
- mountains & skiing in winter
- wine trails
- Heritage Trail
- Maitai Valley walks
- Queens Gardens
- swimming; beaches
- sailing; sea kayaking
- skydiving
- caving
- mountain biking
- glass blowing
- arts & crafts trails
- Nelson Lakes
- Abel Tasman National Park day trips

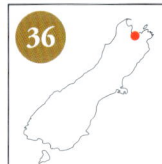

NELSON CITY
Cathedral Inn

Hosts Judith Nicholas and Joy Nimmo

369 Trafalgar Street South, Nelson
Freephone 0800 883 377   *Phone* 0-3-548 7369   *Fax* 0-3-548 0369
Email info@cathedralinn.co.nz   *Website* cathedralinn.co.nz

| 7 bdrm | 7 enst | **Double $210–$290** **Single $190** | *Includes breakfast* **House rate available** |

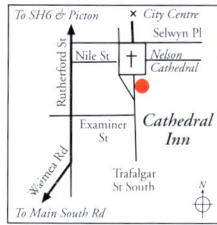

DIRECTIONS: From Picton, travel into City. Take Rutherford St, then turn left into Examiner St. Turn left into Trafalgar St. Cathedral Inn up driveway on right. From south, turn right into Examiner St, then as above.

Set on a rise at the edge of the Cathedral gardens, the Cathedral Inn was once the home of Bishop Andrew Suter, founder of the City's art gallery. Located in the quiet residential heart of the City, the 130-year-old building has been sensitively restored. The broad staircase takes guests to seven sunny bedrooms upstairs, each with fresh flowers, writing desk and ensuite. Refreshments and ironing facilities are provided. Below are the living areas, including the spacious dining and living room with open fireplace, drinks cabinet and writing desk. This opens to a covered terrace and sunny courtyard where guests enjoy socialising in summer. Full breakfasts feature fresh local produce, home-made baking and a cooked speciality daily, with dietary requests catered for.

FACILITIES

- Superior: 4 king/twin, 1 queen Standard: 1 queen, 1 twin all ensuite bedrooms
- 7 ensuite bathrooms – bathrobes, toiletries, heated towel rails
- desk, TV, direct dial phone, tea/coffee, electric blankets, hair dryer, fresh flowers & home-made chocolates in all bedrooms
- under-carpet heating, open fires
- books, magazines, periodicals

- full breakfast options
- complimentary sherry, port, chocolates, cookies & tea/coffee-making facilities
- fax & email facilities, & computer ports available
- guest luggage elevator; all rooms fully serviced daily
- covered terrace & private courtyard with table & chairs
- 6 guest carparks

ACTIVITIES AVAILABLE

- outdoor spa pool/hot tub for guest use on site
- Nelson City, easy 4-min walk
- art galleries, cinemas, shopping, restaurants & cafés within walking distance
- Saturday craft/produce market
- public Japanese stroll gardens, 5-min drive away
- wine trail
- arts & crafts trails

- trout fishing; hunting
- range of adventure activities
- horse trekking
- kayaking; beaches
- watersports
- private gardens open to visit
- 3 golf courses, 10–20-min drive
- 3 National Parks, 1-hr drive
- winter skiing, 1½-hour drive

NELSON CITY
Shelbourne Villa

Hosts Val and Wayne Ballantyne

21 Shelbourne Street, Nelson
Phone 0-3-545 9059   *Email* beds@shelbournevilla.co.nz
Fax 0-3-546 7248   *Website* www.shelbournevilla.co.nz

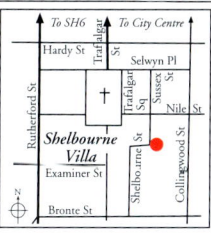

DIRECTIONS: Take SH 6 to Nelson. Turn into Trafalgar St. At "T" junction, turn left into Selwyn Pl. Take 1st right into Trafalgar Sq. Turn 1st left into Nile St East & 1st right into Shelbourne St. Villa on left.

4 bdrm	4 enst	Double $195–$295 Single $175–$275	*Includes breakfast Self-catering suite*

Shelbourne Villa is in a quiet suburban location, yet within five minutes' walk of the City Centre. Originally built in 1929, this classic villa has been refurbished, still in New Zealand genre, and is set in an English style garden with separate seating areas including a terrace with small pond and waterfall. Accommodation comprises four guestrooms: the Master Suite, Newby Suite, Super-king Loft, and self-contained Garden Suite with patio seating. Continental breakfast options include cereals, yoghurt, sliced fresh fruit, fresh fruit juice, and coffee or tea. A cooked café-style breakfast option is also offered. Coffees, teas and baked goodies are available in the guest lounge, and the Garden Suite has a kitchenette for self-catering if desired.

FACILITIES

- 1 king-size Garden Suite with ensuite & full kitchenette for self-catering; children over 11 yrs
- 1 super-king ensuite loft with deck
- 2 king ensuite bedrooms
- hair dryers, curling irons, heated towel rails, toiletries, 2 double basins
- phone, writing desk & TV in all bedrooms; cotton bed linen & bathrobes; fresh flowers
- 2 verandahs overlooking garden
- continental & cooked breakfast served
- complimentary apéritifs
- guest lounge with tea/coffee & baking, TV, VCR & CDs
- heating & air-conditioning
- laundry available
- fax & email available
- off-street parking
- courtesy passenger transfer

ACTIVITIES AVAILABLE

- seating areas in gardens for reading, lounging & relaxing
- craft studios
- cinemas in walking distance
- cafés & restaurants, short walk
- city shopping, 5-min walk
- Cathedral & churches
- Nelson School of Music
- Queens Gardens
- Suter Art Gallery
- Maitai River walks close by
- Grampian Trail nearby
- trail to centre of New Zealand within 5-min walk
- full exercise facility, 5 mins
- Tahuna Beach
- Stonehurst Farm horse treks
- Höglund glass blowing
- wineries
- tour planning, extra charge

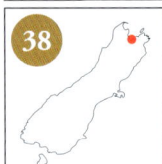

NELSON CITY
Grampian Villa and Cottage

Hosts Jo and John Fitzwater

209 Collingwood Street, Nelson   *Mobile* 021 459 736
Phone 0-3-545 8209   *Email* stayinnelson@grampianvilla.co.nz
Fax 0-3-548 7888   *Website* www.grampianvilla.co.nz

DIRECTIONS: Take SH 6 to Nelson roundabout & turn into Trafalgar St. Turn 1st left into Wainui St, then 1st right into Collingwood St. Cross bridge & continue to Grampian Villa & Cottage on corner of Bronte St.

8 bdrm	8 enst	Room rate $115–$350	*Includes breakfast*	*Dinner extra*	

Originally built in 1895 for a pioneer botanist and arts supporter, Grampian Villa is a two-storey Victorian villa, across the road from Grampian Cottage, built in 1910. Both are located on a tree-lined street on the lower slopes of The Grampians hills, five minutes' walk to the City Centre. The Villa's spacious Deluxe guestrooms have French doors opening to verandahs with views to the city and sea. An open fire warms the guest lounge during winter evenings. Native timbers are used extensively. A healthy gourmet breakfast of freshly baked croissants and local produce is served on the villa verandah or in the guest dining room overlooking the English garden. In-room continental breakfast is served to Grampian Cottage guests. Dinner is also available.

FACILITIES

- Grampian Villa: 3 super-king ensuite Deluxe bedrooms & 1 queen ensuite Deluxe bedroom with claw-foot bath downstairs
- Grampian Cottage: 4 queen Standard bedrooms with 4 ensuite bathrooms
- bathrobes, toiletries & hair dryers in all bathrooms
- quality linen, phone, TV & desk in each bedroom

- gourmet breakfast in Villa; continental in Cottage
- dinner by arrangement, extra
- tea/coffee, port & cookies
- Sky TV, VCR, DVD, CDs, movies & open fire in Villa
- fax & computer available; wireless broadband internet access thoughout Villa
- off-street under-cover parking for Villa

ACTIVITIES AVAILABLE

- garden on site
- City Centre, 5-min walk
- range of restaurants, cafés & wine bars, easy walk
- Grampian, Centre of NZ & Maitai Walkways nearby
- Fairfield Park/Melrose House
- arts & crafts galleries within walking distance
- wine tours of Nelson

- Saturday market
- Höglund glass blowing studio
- World of Wearable Arts
- range of motorcycles to hire
- horse trekking; kayaking
- cathedral, churches & School of Music, within 5-min walk
- full exercise facility, 5 mins
- 3 golf courses; polytechnic
- airport, 12-min drive

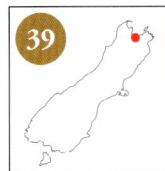

NELSON CITY
Warwick House

Hosts Jenny and Nick Ferrier

64 Brougham Street, Nelson   *Mobile* 021 688 243
Freephone 0800 022 233   *Phone* 0-3-548 3164   *Fax* 0-3-548 3215
Email enquiries@warwickhouse.co.nz   *Website* www.warwickhouse.co.nz

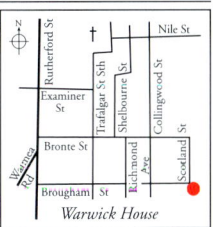

DIRECTIONS: Take SH 6 to Nelson roundabout & turn into Trafalgar St. Turn 1st left into Wainui St, then 1st right into Collingwood St. Continue to Brougham St & turn left to Warwick House at end on right.

| 3 bdrm | 3 enst | Room rate $250–$395 Guest wing rate $1,200 | *Includes breakfast Lunch & dinner extra* | |

Designed in Gothic Revivalist style and built in the mid 1800s for Alfred Fell and his family, Warwick House was named after Warwickshire in England, where the Fells emigrated from in 1842. Recently restored to offer guest accommodation in the former ballroom wing, Warwick House retains many original features such as the castle-like four-storey tower and the polished native matai flooring throughout including the sprung dancing floor in the ballroom where the full cooked breakfast is served. Jenny has used her interior design skills to ensure comfort for all guests. Dinner can be arranged for four or more guests. Set in traditional rose gardens with heritage trees, Warwick House provides garden, rural and city views that extend to the Tasman Sea.

FACILITIES

- Tower Suite: queen bedroom, ensuite with claw-foot bath, 2-storey octagonal lounge in upper tower & rural views
- Bayview Suite: king 4-poster bed & large private lounge, ensuite with claw-foot bath, city & sea views
- Peacock Garden Room: super-king bedroom, ensuite with claw-foot bath, rural views & opens to garden

- cooked breakfast served; lunch & dinner for 4+ guests, extra
- self-catering apartment available
- ballroom with sprung floor, open fire, TV, CDs & DVDs
- phone, fax & email available
- extra single bed for both suites
- cotton bed linen, TV, writing desk, fridge, tea/coffee in rooms
- bathrobes, hair dryers, toiletries & heated towel rails

ACTIVITIES AVAILABLE

- aromatherapy, massage & reflexology, by arrangement
- ballroom for hire
- group bookings available
- BBQ & gardens on site
- bicycles available for guest use
- walking labrador, Victoria
- beaches & lakes nearby
- bush walks; golf; pottery
- Nelson Cathedral, 5-min walk

- Nelson City, 5–10-min walk via riverside "Willowwalk"
- wine tours & art tours
- weekend markets; galleries
- Brook & Maitai river walks, 5–10-min walk from site
- sailing; kayaking; caving
- trout fishing & fishing tours
- private scenic flights; skiing
- Centre of NZ walk

© Friars' Guide to New Zealand Accommodation for the Discerning Traveller

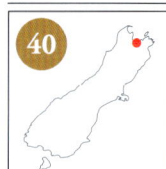

NELSON CITY
Sunnybank Homestead

Hosts Margaret and Robbie Johnston

156 Nile Street, Nelson

Phone 0-3-548 1971   *Email* relax@sunnybank.co.nz
Fax 0-3-548 1973   *Website* www.sunnybank.co.nz

DIRECTIONS: Take SH 6 to Nelson roundabout & turn into Trafalgar St. Turn 1st left into Wainui St, then 1st right into Collingwood St. Continue & turn left into Nile St. Sunnybank on left on corner of Mayroyd Tce.

3 bdrm	2 enst	1 prbth	**Room rate $325**	*Includes breakfast*	*Lunch & dinner extra*

Located in the heart of Nelson City, Sunnybank Homestead is one of Nelson's protected heritage homes. Originally built circa 1856 and now restored to its Victorian grandeur, Sunnybank offers guests three spacious bedrooms and bathrooms. Sunnybank features original imported marble and slate fireplaces, gilt mirrors and ornate plaster cornices. Margaret is a working artist and her paintings and sculptures are displayed at Sunnybank, along with many antiques and other New Zealand artworks. Set in large gardens, restored and developed, the Homestead provides quality accommodation in a central location, with city shops only 10 minutes' walk away. Margaret serves a leisurely breakfast using fresh local produce.

FACILITIES

- Annies Room: 1 super-king/ twin bedroom with private bathroom & clawfoot bath
- Magnolia & Milner Suites: 1 queen ensuite bedroom in each
- cotton bed linen, phone, TV, tea/coffee & mineral water
- hair dryer, heated towel rails, toiletries & bathrobes
- laundry available, extra
- email & fax facilities available

- continental or cooked breakfast served
- lunch by arrangement, extra
- 3-course dinner with wine, by arrangement, extra
- sitting room upstairs with tea/coffee, fridge & port
- family lounge with Sky TV, video, CD-player & books
- courtesy airport transfer; off-street parking

ACTIVITIES AVAILABLE

- large gardens & grounds featuring mature trees
- BBQ on sundeck
- honeymoons & small weddings catered for
- walking/running tracks nearby
- Abel Tasman National Park, 1 hr
- local wineries, 15 mins
- many galleries, arts & crafts
- gardens open to visit

- city restaurants & cafés, 10-min walk
- World of Wearable Art museum; Tahuna Beach
- Rainbow Ski-field
- trout fishing
- mountain biking
- City Centre for shopping & cafés, 10-min walk
- airport, 10-min drive

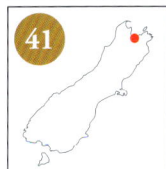

NELSON CITY
Manuka Cottage

Hosts Alison Phillips and Robin White

3 Manuka Street, Nelson   *Postal* 45 Collingwood Street, Nelson
Phone 0-3-548 9418   *Mobile* 025 678 1170   *Email* manukacottage@xtra.co.nz
Fax 0-3-548 9418   *Website* www.manukacottage.nelson.co.nz

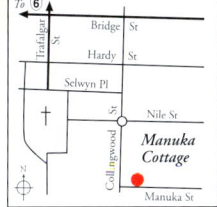

DIRECTIONS: Take SH 6 to Nelson roundabout & turn south into Trafalgar St. Travel to cathedral steps & turn left into Selwyn Place. Take 2nd right into Collingwood St & turn left into Manuka St. Cottage on left.

2 bdrm	1 prbth	Cottage rate $190–$240 for 2 persons *Includes continental breakfast provisions* *Self-catering*
		$250–$320 for 4 persons Corporate & long-stay rates available Minimum stay may apply

Originally built circa 1890, Manuka Cottage has been restored to provide accommodation in the heart of Nelson City. This historic self-contained cottage still retains the native totara and kauri flooring and now offers a king-size bedroom and private bathroom featuring a claw-foot bath downstairs. Up the spiral staircase is a loft with queen and single beds. A separate living area includes a wood burner and opens to a sundeck and bricked courtyard bordered by a small private cottage garden. A continental breakfast basket is provided for the first morning, and guests enjoy alfresco dining in the sunny courtyard where a gas barbecue is available. A full kitchen enables guests to self-cater, with shops and restaurants just a short walk away.

FACILITIES

- one-party bookings
- 1 king bedroom downstairs with phone & TV
- 1 queen & 1 single bed in upstairs loft bedroom, access via spiral staircase
- 1 bathroom downstairs including claw-foot bath
- toiletries, hair dryer & heated towel rails in bathroom
- bathrobes; cotton bed linen
- continental breakfast basket supplied for 1st morning
- full kitchen for self-catering
- TV, DVD, CD-player, music, books, nibbles & wood burner in lounge, opening to deck
- phones & fax; self-service laundry
- children under 10 years by arrangement
- bicycle & kayak storage

ACTIVITIES AVAILABLE

- gas BBQ area in bricked courtyard bordered by private cottage garden
- Within 5–10-min walk:
  – pottery, craft & art galleries
  – Cathedral & School of Music
  – restaurants, cafés & shopping
  – Queens Gardens
  – Suter Art Gallery
  – Saturday craft & produce market
  – movie theatre
  – Maitai River walkway
  – track to centre of NZ lookout
- wineries
- gardens open to visit
- 3 golf courses, 10–20-min drive
- sailing; kayaking
- beaches; fishing
- airport, 15-min drive
- Abel Tasman National Park, 1-hour drive
- interisland ferries, 2 hrs

Manuka Cottage

Long Lookout Gardens

Hosts Yvonne and David Trathen

60 Cleveland Terrace, Nelson
Phone 0-3-548 3617   *Mobile* 021 152 3321   *Fax* 0-3-548 3127
Email enjoy@longlookoutgardens.co.nz   *Website* www.longlookoutgardens.co.nz

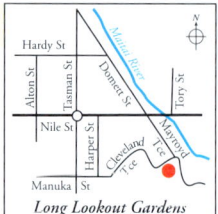

Long Lookout Gardens

DIRECTIONS: Take SH 6 to Nelson, turn into Trafalgar St, 1st left into Wainui St & 1st right into Collingwood St. Turn left into Nile St. Turn right into Mayroyd Tce & right into Cleveland Tce. Long Lookout on left.

2 bdrm	2 enst	Room rate $295–$350	*Includes breakfast*	*Dinner extra*

Named in 1866 because of the extensive views across the landscaped garden to Tasman Bay in the distance, Long Lookout Gardens is located in the foothills overlooking Nelson City. This English two-storey residence was originally built in 1864, for J.C. Richmond, a local politician and engineer. The house was rebuilt in 1936 and now offers two ensuite guestrooms, a queen-size downstairs and a super-king/twin upstairs. The classic English interiors include richly coloured fabrics and under-carpet heating. An English-style breakfast is served in the formal dining room, in the kitchen, or alfresco on the patio, and dinner is also available, by prior arrangement. There are many restaurants and cafés within walking distance.

FACILITIES

- 1 queen ensuite bedroom with bath, downstairs
- 1 super-king/twin ensuite bedroom, upstairs
- cotton bed linen, tea/coffee, mineral water, nibbles, fridge, wine, port & chocolates
- bathrobes, hair dryer, toiletries, heated floor & towel rails
- iron, ironing board & security safe available to guests

- English-style full cooked or continental breakfast
- dinner by request, extra
- vegetarians catered for
- laundry service, $15
- fresh flowers; email, fax & phone available
- private guest entrance
- courtesy passenger transfer
- off-street parking

ACTIVITIES AVAILABLE

- large (over 0.5ha) garden on site for walking & relaxing
- Nelson City, 10-min walk
- golf course, 5-min drive
- Maitai River walks
- Centre of NZ walk
- fishing charters to Abel Tasman National Park; wine tours
- private gardens open to visit
- public gardens & parks

- many restaurants, cafés & bars, 10-min walk
- horse trekking
- trout fishing
- sailing
- sea kayaking
- skydiving
- mountain biking
- ski-field, 1½-hour drive
- Picton ferries, 1¾ hours

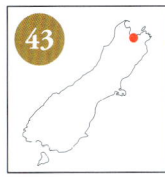

43

Maitai River Lodge

Hosts Cathie and Bob Bowley

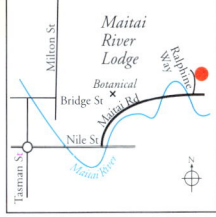

14 Ralphine Way, Maitai Valley, Nelson   *Phone* 0-3-548 8999
Freephone 0800 MAITAI   *Mobile* 021 548 899   *Fax* 0-3-548 3830
Email enquiries@maitai.co.nz   *Website* www.maitai.co.nz

DIRECTIONS: Take SH 6 towards Nelson. Turn left into Atawhai Drive. Continue into Milton St. Turn right into Bridge St, left into Tasman St, left into Nile St East & left into Maitai Rd. Turn left into Ralphine Way.

| 5 bdrm | 5 enst | **Room rate $250–$350** | *Includes breakfast & bottle of wine* | *Supper platter extra* |

Set in almost a hectare (two acres) in the Maitai Valley, surrounded by farmland, river flats and native bush, Maitai River Lodge is only three kilometres from Nelson City Centre. There are two spacious bedrooms upstairs opening to the terrace, and three bedrooms downstairs, two with garden access. Guest safes are provided in the fully hosted Lodge which features local clay art, paintings and glass art throughout. A gourmet breakfast selection is served in the upstairs dining room or alfresco on the terrace. Guests can relax there or in the garden with a glass of local wine and listen to the native birdlife as the sun sets. Guests also enjoy soaking in the therapeutic spa pool. Pepper, the cat, Herculette, the goat, and lambs complete the scene.

FACILITIES

- 1 super-king/twin & 2 super-king ensuite bedrooms downstairs, 2 with garden entrances
- 2 super-king ensuite bedrooms upstairs with bathrobes, port/ sherry & safe, open to terrace
- cotton bed linen, writing desk, phone, tea/coffee, heater, iron & ironing board in bedrooms
- hair dryer, heated towel rails & toiletries in all 5 ensuites

- continental & cooked breakfast
- bottle of wine & nibbles
- supper platter by request, extra
- formal guest lounge downstairs with bar, video, TV, DVD, CDs & artwork, opens to garden
- informal lounge upstairs
- broadband internet & fax
- laundry available, extra
- on-site parking

ACTIVITIES AVAILABLE

- 2 BBQs on site
- honeymoons catered for
- pétanque & croquet
- therapeutic spa pool
- feeding pet lambs & goat
- swimming in Maitai River
- Centre of NZ lookout
- golf course; farm walks
- Maitai River walks
- Abel Tasman National Park

- restaurants & cafés, 3km
- sailing & fishing charters
- helicopter scenic tours
- guided fly fishing & hunting
- *Lord of the Rings* jeweller & filming sites
- vineyards, arts & crafts tours
- ski-field; Nelson Lakes
- Saturday market; quad biking
- longest flying fox in world

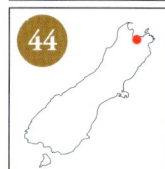

PORT HILLS, NELSON
Wakefield Quay House

Hosts Woodi and John Moore

385 Wakefield Quay, Port Hills, Nelson
Phone 0-3-546 7275   *Email* wakefieldquay@xtra.co.nz
Mobile 027 265 7547   *Website* www.wakefieldquay.co.nz

DIRECTIONS: From Nelson City, take Haven Rd (SH 6) to Wakefield Quay. Wakefield Quay House on waterfront on left. From airport, take Rocks Rd towards city. Continue into Wakefield Quay to Wakefield House.

| 3 bdrm | 3 enst | Double $225–$275 Single $175–$245 | *Includes breakfast* **Low-season rates available** | |

Wakefield Quay House is a classic colonial villa with a Historic Places category A rating. Built in 1905, the house now offers accommodation in three ensuite queen-size guestrooms, retaining the original native rimu timber throughout. Sited directly opposite the boat harbour entrance, with spacious deck areas where guests can relax and enjoy watching the ships and yachts, Wakefield Quay House is just three minutes from either Tahunanui Beach or Nelson City. Artwork is a special feature, and Woodi can personally introduce guests to Nelson artists, while Johnny is a qualified skipper and can take guests out on his yacht for a sail or tuition. Antique silverware and linen napkins are used on the large rimu dining table at breakfast time.

FACILITIES

- 3 queen ensuite bedrooms
- hair dryers, heated towel rails, bathrobes & toiletries
- chocolates & tea/coffee
- artwork throughout
- complimentary laundry
- lounge with open fire, nibbles, bar, Sky TV, video, CD player, library & books
- fresh flowers
- full cooked or continental breakfast served
- complimentary pre-dinner drinks & nibbles
- fax & phone available
- children over 12 yrs
- wireless internet & computer for guest use
- garaging by request
- large deck & garden

ACTIVITIES AVAILABLE

- sea swimming from site
- 34-ft yacht available for charter & sailing courses
- bicycles for guest use
- watching ships & yachts with on site binoculars
- Wednesday night yacht racing
- waterfront walks; sunsets
- Cable Bay kayaks
- Abel Tasman National Park
- 5 restaurants within 5-min walk away
- personal introductions to Nelson artists
- arts & crafts; wine tours
- gardens to visit
- Nelson City, 5 mins
- Nelson Airport, 10 mins
- winter skiing
- Picton ferries, 2-hr drive

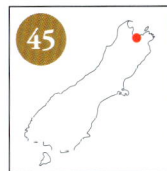

PORT HILLS, NELSON
Penthouse 11

Hosts Sue and John O'Riordan

309 Wakefield Quay, Nelson
Phone 0-3-545 2275   *Mobile* 025 401 181   *Fax* 0-3-545 2205
Email info@penthouse11.com   *Website* www.penthouse11.com

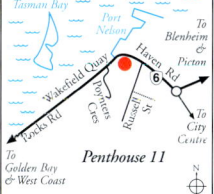

DIRECTIONS: From Blenheim, take SH 6 to Nelson. At 2nd roundabout turn left into Haven Rd. Continue into Wakefield Quay to Penthouse 11 on left.

2 bdrm	1 enst	1 prbth	Room rate $250–$350	*Self-catering*

With uninterrupted panoramic views of the sea below to the snow-capped mountains beyond, Penthouse 11 is a fully self-contained apartment right on the waterfront. Located at the top of the Waterfront Apartments, Penthouse 11 is literally across the road from the sea, just two kilometres from Tahunanui Beach in one direction and the same distance from the City Centre in the opposite direction. This architecturally designed apartment provides two spacious bedrooms each with a bathroom, and an extra third bedroom on request. Baby equipment is also available if required. The fully equipped kitchen and gas barbecue allow guests to self-cater, and there are award-winning restaurants and bars within walking distance along the waterfront.

FACILITIES

- 1 super-king/twin ensuite bedroom with balcony
- 1 super-king bedroom with private bathroom & bath
- hair dryers, bathrobes, heated towel rails & toiletries
- sheepskin underlays; rollaway bed & porta-cot available
- lounge with phone, LCD Sky TV, DVD, stereo, CD-player, books & artwork
- full kitchen for self-catering
- fresh fruit bowl; fresh flowers
- air-conditioning
- central heating
- complimentary laundry
- children welcome
- small pets by arrangement
- 2 secure undercover parking spaces on site
- stairs & lift

ACTIVITIES AVAILABLE

- watching boats, yachts & ships from site
- gas barbecue on site
- yachting, boating
- canoeing, kayaking
- wind surfing
- watersports
- wineries; arts & crafts
- glass blowing; potteries
- Saturday morning market
- waterfront restaurants, cafés & bars within walking distance
- Abel Tasman National Park
- Skywire
- bush walks
- gardens to visit
- 4WD motorbikes
- City Centre, 5-min drive
- Nelson Airport, 5 mins
- interisland ferries, 1¾ hours

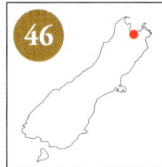

PORT HILLS, NELSON
Waterfront Penthouse

Hosts Alison Phillips and Robin White

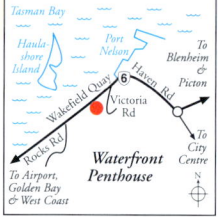

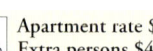

14/311 Wakefield Quay, Nelson   *Postal* 45 Collingwood Street, Nelson
Phone 0-3-548 9418   *Mobile* 025 678 1170   *Fax* 0-3-548 9418
Email water.front@xtra.co.nz   *Website* www.waterfrontpenthouse.nelson.co.nz

DIRECTIONS: From Nelson City, take Haven Rd towards airport. Continue into Wakefield Quay. Penthouse is on left, opposite Yacht Club. From airport, take Rocks Rd towards city & continue into Wakefield Quay.

| 3 bdrm | 2 enst | 1 prbth | Apartment rate $290–$350 for 2 persons   *Includes breakfast basket*   *Self-catering*
Extra persons $40–$50 each   Long stay & winter rates   Minimum stay may apply |

Maximising the extensive harbour views from every room, Waterfront Penthouse is the largest apartment of the complex that was opened in 2003. With secure garaging beneath, the spacious living areas on the first floor open to a balcony, across the road from the yacht club, providing guests with continual boating activities to watch. Fully self-contained, the Waterfront Penthouse has a well-equipped kitchen for self-catering and large living room with telescope for watching ships coming through The Cut. As well as the main ensuite bedroom on the first floor, there are two further bedrooms and bathrooms upstairs, with an office too. Restaurants are within walking distance along the waterfront, and the city is just a short drive away.

FACILITIES

- private-party bookings only
- 2 super-king/twin ensuite bedrooms, 1 with bath
- 1 twin bedroom & private bathroom on top floor
- hair dryers, toiletries, heated floor & heated towel rails
- study/office with writing desk
- bathrobes; cotton bed linen
- fresh flowers; nibbles; phone
- full self-catering kitchen
- continental breakfast basket provided for 1st morning
- lounge with TV/DVD/CD, NZ artwork & magazines
- air-conditioning/heat pump in each room
- self-serve laundry
- children welcome
- secure garaging

ACTIVITIES AVAILABLE

- small conference/meeting venue
- alfresco dining, bird-watching, harbour sunset & yacht race viewing from balcony
- fishing opposite site, or tours
- swimming beach, easy walk
- Trafalgar Centre, 15-min walk
- helicopter rides; art tours
- walking tracks; wineries
- adventure activities
- award-winning waterfront restaurants & cafés, 2-min walk
- 3 golf courses, 10–20 mins
- boating; sailing
- Abel Tasman National Park, 1-hour drive
- City Centre, 5-min drive
- airport, 10-min drive
- interisland ferries, 1¾ hours

47

PORT HILLS, NELSON
Harbour View Apartments

Hosts Penny Adams and John Rowburrey

3 Harbour Terrace, Nelson
Phone 0-3-545 7044   *Mobile* 021 299 4307   *Fax* 0-3-548 8420
Email hva@paradise.net.nz   *Website* www.harbourviewapartments.co.nz

DIRECTIONS: From Nelson City, take Haven Rd (SH 6) into Wakefield Quay. Turn left into Poynters Cres. Turn sharp left into Harbour Tce. Turn right up steep drive to Harbour View Apartments.

VISA MasterCard

3 bdrm 2 prbth

Apartment rate $200–$250 for 2 persons
Extra adults $40 each   Children over 5 years $20 each

Self-catering
No meals available

Harbour View

Opened in 2003, Harbour View Apartments offer uninterrupted views of Nelson's harbour entrance, known as "The Cut", to Tasman Bay and the western ranges beyond. Harbour View comprises two self-contained apartments, the first with one bedroom and the second with two. Both apartments include spacious living areas which open onto large decks edged with glass balustrades. Guests can also enjoy the views from the private outdoor spa pool beneath a maple tree. Contemporary furnishings and Persian rugs complement the native rimu hardwood flooring. The fully equipped kitchen in each apartment enables guests to self-cater, or they can dine at restaurants only a few minutes' walk along Nelson's waterfront.

FACILITIES

- single-party bookings
- 2 self-contained apartments
- 1st apartment: 1 queen bedroom
- 2nd apartment: 1 queen & 1 king/twin bedroom
- cotton bed linen; fresh flowers
- 1 bathroom per apartment
- hair dryer & toiletries in bathrooms
- heat pump & air-conditioner
- full kitchen per apartment for self-catering
- biscuits & fresh fruit
- living room per apartment with queen bed-settee, TV, video, CD-player, music, phone, artwork & magazines
- spacious decks; sea views
- laundry available
- off-street parking

ACTIVITIES AVAILABLE

- private outdoor spa pool on site
- alfresco dining on deck
- watching ships & yachts from site
- arts & crafts trail
- cinema
- sailing; rafting
- 3 national parks
- fishing; hunting
- hiking; kayaking
- beaches
- restaurants, bars & cafés, within walking distance
- live music in Nelson City, 5-min drive
- wineries
- golf courses
- mountain biking
- horse trekking
- winter skiing
- Picton ferries, 2-hr drive

Harbour View

Harbour View

© Friars' Guide to New Zealand Accommodation for the Discerning Traveller

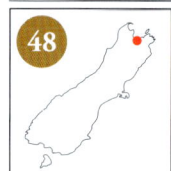

48

Kimberley House Nelson

Hosts Jenny Wilson and Chris North

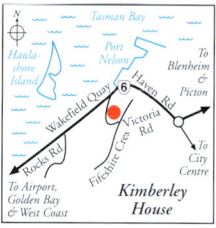

25 Victoria Road, Nelson   *Postal* P O Box 26–126, Epsom, Auckland
Phone 0-3-546 8965   *Fax* 0-3-548 7645
Email j-wilson@clear.net.nz   *Website* www.kimberley.co.nz

DIRECTIONS: From Nelson City, take Haven Rd (SH 6) to Port. Turn left up Victoria Rd. Kimberley House 400m on left – 2 entrances. From airport, take Rocks Rd towards city. Turn right up Victoria Rd.

6 bdrm	5 enst	1 prbth	**Apartment rate $180–$300** **Extra persons $50 each**	*Includes continental breakfast provisions* **Low-season rates available**	*Self-catering*

Overlooking "The Cut" in Nelson Harbour, Kimberley House features panoramic sea views and endless hours of interest for guests watching the boats and ships below and the sunsets each evening. Originally built in 1964 and extensively renovated in 2001 to offer guest accommodation, Kimberley House now provides three self-contained apartments, a three-bedroom upstairs and a two and one-bedroom apartment downstairs. Each apartment features native timber furniture, an outside deck with barbecue, and a private entrance. Guests can self-cater in the fully equipped kitchen in each apartment, and continental breakfast provisions are supplied daily. A 400-metre walk down the hill takes guests to top seaside restaurants.

FACILITIES

- 2 downstairs apartments with 1 or 2 super-king/twin ensuite bedrooms; 1 large bathtub
- 1 upstairs apartment with 3 king/twin bedrooms, phone, fax, writing desk, 2 ensuites & 1 bathroom with bidet & bath
- hair dryer, heated towel rails & toiletries in all bathrooms
- cotton bed linen
- children welcome – steep site

- continental breakfast provisions per apartment
- self-contained kitchen per apartment for self-catering
- lounge in each with Sky digital TV, video & music
- central heating & air-conditioning per apartment
- serviced daily if required
- private guest entrances & decks; off-street parking

ACTIVITIES AVAILABLE

- spa pool & 3 barbecues on site
- viewing sunsets over harbour
- bird & boat watching from site
- Tahunanui Beach
- swimming; sailing
- windsurfing; water skiing
- sea & white water rafting
- golfing; roller blading
- mountain biking; hiking
- wineries trail

- Boat Shed Café & 3 top restaurants, short walk
- central Nelson restaurants, cafés & bars, 5-min drive
- wilderness park walks
- arts & crafts; art galleries
- Nelson's weekend market
- winter snowboarding & skiing at Nelson Lakes National Park & Rainbow ski-fields

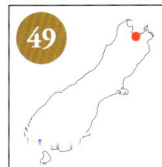

PORT HILLS, NELSON
Abel Tasman Villa

Host Nicola Clinton

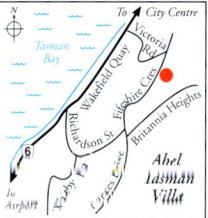

31A Fifeshire Crescent, Nelson

Phone 0-3-548 8533   *Mobile* 027 289 8982   *Fax* 0-3-548 8533

Email clinton@abeltasmanvilla.co.nz   *Website* www.abeltasmanvilla.co.nz

DIRECTIONS: From City, take Wakefield Quay & turn left into Victoria Rd. Turn right into Fifeshire Cres. Villa on left. From airport, take Rocks Rd towards City. Turn right up into Richardson St. Turn left into Fifeshire.

2 bdrm	1 enst	1 prbth	Villa rate $275–$445 Extra persons $45 each	*Includes breakfast provisions* Multiple-night & corporate rates available	*Self-catering*

Abel Tasman Villa is self-contained accommodation set high above the harbour with panoramic sea views. This architecturally designed purpose-built apartment provides privacy and independence for guests and is suited to long-term stays. Breakfast provisions are supplied according to a previously chosen menu, and a fully equipped open-plan kitchen enables guests to self-cater. Single parties of up to four guests can be accommodated in two bedrooms each with its own bathroom. A lock-up garage is available for roadside parking, then a stairway leads up to the villa, which is unsuitable for children. Overlooking "The Cut", guests can enjoy viewing the setting sun across Tasman Bay, while ships and pleasure craft provide endless interest.

FACILITIES

- private-party bookings only
- 1 queen bedroom with ensuite including bath
- 1 queen bedroom & bathroom
- cotton bed linen; fresh flowers
- hair dryer & toiletries
- phone jacks; phone available
- fax & email in office
- complimentary fruit bowl & bottle of wine
- breakfast provisions, pre-faxed or emailed choices
- self-contained with full kitchen for self-catering
- lounge with open fire, Sky TV, DVDs & music
- heat-pump/air-conditioning
- unsuitable for children
- decking surrounding villa
- self-serve laundry; garaging

ACTIVITIES AVAILABLE

- patio area for entertaining
- boat watching with binoculars
- WOW complex
- walks; golf courses
- day trips to Abel Tasman National Park, Mapua cruise, Nelson Harbour curise
- wineries; kayaking
- arts & crafts; art galleries
- Nelson's Saturday flea-market
- waterfront restaurants, cafés & bars, within 5-min walking distance
- Haulashore Island ferry trips
- horse trekking; fishing
- winter skiing
- Nelson City Centre, 5-min drive away
- airport, 10-min drive
- Picton ferries, 1¾ hours

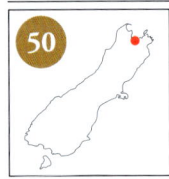

PORT HILLS, NELSON
Te Puna Wai

Hosts Richard Hewetson and James Taylor

24 Richardson Street, Port Hills, Nelson
Phone 0-3-548 7621   *Mobile* 021 679 795   *Fax* 03 548 7645
Email stay@tepunawai.co.nz   *Website* www.tepunawai.co.nz

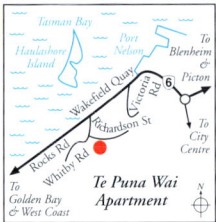

DIRECTIONS: From Nelson City, take Wakefield Quay towards airport. Opposite Haulashore Island, turn left uphill into Richardson St. Continue left. Te Puna Wai is 2nd drive on right. From airport, take Rocks Rd.

3 bdrm	3 enst	Double $160–$260 Single $120–$195	*Includes breakfast*

Te Puna Wai offers boutique accommodation, with panoramic sea and mountain views from Nelson's Port Hills. This restored 1857 three-storey villa offers three different accommodation options. At ground level are the Haulashore apartment and Wakatu room, with marble-tiled bathrooms. Haulashore has a designer kitchen, includes laundry and opens to a verandah and courtyard. The Fifeshire suite occupies the top floor, and comprises a spacious queen-size bedroom with picture window, ante-room with extra double bed and large newly renovated bathroom. All rooms have fridges and tea/coffee facilities. Guest areas include lounge, verandah and elevated lawn. Broadband, WiFi and a guest computer is available. Nelson City Centre is a three-minute drive.

FACILITIES

- 1 self-contained apartment with queen ensuite bedroom
- 1 upstairs suite with queen & double beds & ensuite
- 1 queen ensuite bedroom
- marble-tiled bathrooms with heated floors
- TV, phone, fridge & tea/coffee in all bedrooms
- central heating & open fireplaces; art collection
- full breakfast, served alfresco, weather permitting
- high-speed (wireless) internet access; computer available
- children & well-behaved pets welcome
- Richard speaks Portuguese, French, German, Spanish & Danish
- off-street parking
- friendly pets on site

ACTIVITIES AVAILABLE

- foreshore walks to beach
- 7-mins walk to waterfront restaurants, cafés, bars
- 10-min drive to airport
- 3-min drive to Nelson City
- swimming at bottom of Richardson St & nearby at Tahunanui Beach
- local arts community
- gardens & parks to visit
- Nelson Saturday morning market
- Wearable Arts centre
- wineries; quad biking
- walks, hiking, bike hire & scenic flights
- mountain climbing & hiking
- sailing & fishing charters; kayaking
- kayaking at Cable Bay & Abel Tasman National Park
- Picton train or ferry, 1½ hours

Te Puna Wai

PORT HILLS, NELSON

The Wheelhouse Inn
and Captain's Quarters

Hosts Ralph and Sally Hetzel

41 Whitby Road, Port Hills, Nelson
Phone 0-3-546 8391   *Mobile* 027 449 3380   *Fax* 0-3-546 8391
Email wheelhouse@ts.co.nz   *Website* wheelhouse.nelson.co.nz

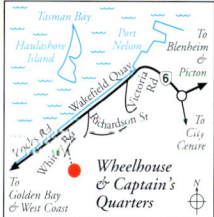

DIRECTIONS: From Nelson City, take Haven Rd & continue along the waterfront. Turn left up Richardson St & veer right into Whitby Rd. Take drive to left at end of road up to The Wheelhouse Inn & Captain's Quarters.

| 3 bdrm | 2 prbth | 1 prbth | **Apartment rate $130–$190 for 2 persons** **Extra persons $15 each** | *Self-catering* *Breakfast extra* |

Overlooking the harbour entrance and Tasman Bay are these two totally separate self-contained apartments. The Wheelhouse Inn was built first in 1997, followed by the Captain's Quarters two years later. The nautical theme harmonises with the seascapes and the enthusiasm of the hosts who sailed to New Zealand in 1974. North-facing, the apartments enjoy all-day sun and the seaward windows and decking afford wonderful views of not only the boating activites below, but also the sunsets. The bedrooms in these two multi-level apartments are located upstairs, with the living areas below. Full kitchens provide for self-catering, although meals can be served by prior arrangement. Restaurants are on the waterfront within walking distance.

FACILITIES

- 2 self-contained apartments
- Wheelhouse Inn: 1 queen bedroom with private bathroom
- Captains Quarters: 1 queen bedroom & 1 bunkroom, with private bathroom
- children welcome
- basic Spanish spoken
- off-street parking

In both apartments:
- single-party bookings only
- breakfast on request, $15 pp
- full kitchen for self-catering
- lounge with TV, CDs, stereo, DVD, phone & writing desk
- extra fold-out sofa beds
- hair dryer & toiletries
- guest laundry
- sea views

ACTIVITIES AVAILABLE

- binoculars for enjoying sea views from apartments
- dining available on request
- barbecue available
- mountain bikes available
- viewing sunsets
- watersports
- arts & crafts
- wineries
- beaches; fishing

- restaurants nearby
- waterfront, 2-min drive
- cultural events
- gardens open to visit
- walking
- National Parks
- Nelson City, 5-min drive
- Marlborough Sounds, 1 hour
- airport, 5-min drive
- Picton ferries, 1¾-hour drive

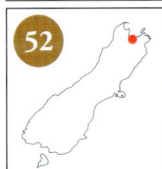
RICHMOND, NELSON
Althorpe

Hosts Jenny and Bob Worley

13 Dorset Street, Richmond, Nelson
Phone 0-3-544 8117   *Email* stay@althorpe.co.nz
Fax 0-3-544 8117   *Website* friars.co.nz/hosts/althorpe.html

DIRECTIONS: From Nelson City, or from Motueka or West Coast, take SH 6 to Richmond, via deviation. Turn south into Church St & then continue into Dorset St. Althorpe on right.

| 2 bdrm | 1 enst | 1 prbth | Double $140–$160 Single $110–$130 | *Includes breakfast* |

Althorpe was built circa 1887 for Richard Weston Dyson and remained in his family for over 70 years. The Worleys began restoration in 1982, original features retained including spacious entrance hallways, high ceilings, native rimu woodwork and open fireplaces. The two guest bedrooms and the private lounge have been designed with guest privacy in mind, verandahs opening to secluded gardens with the mature trees framing a distant sea view. Access to spa pool and swimming pool via guest lounge. Jenny serves her special breakfast selection in the informal dining area in the large kitchen. Period and antique furniture complement the warm atmosphere of this colonial homestead. Restaurants are within walking distance.

FACILITIES

- 1 double bedroom with writing desk & ensuite bathroom
- 1 king/twin bedroom with private bathroom
- cotton bed linen, down duvets & electric blankets
- laundry, for multiple nights
- children over 12 yrs welcome
- central heating
- open fireplaces
- special breakfast with fresh fruit platter, omelettes, crêpes, croissants, muffins, pastries, etc
- tea/coffee & other refreshments in guest lounge at all times
- email facilities available on request
- large quiet garden with mature trees & rose beds
- off-street parking

ACTIVITIES AVAILABLE

- swimming & spa pools on site
- restaurants within 5-min walk
- Richmond Tavern, 5-min walk
- shopping ccntrc, including antique shops, 5-min walk
- arts & crafts trails
- wine trails
- golf links, 10-min drive
- beaches, 10km
- trout fishing
- pottery, 5-min drive
- glass blowing, 10-min drive
- public parks & gardens
- caving, horse trekking
- sailing, sea kayaking
- private gardens to visit
- Abel Tasman National Park
- Nelson Lakes National Park 40–50-min drive away
- Nelson City, 15-min drive

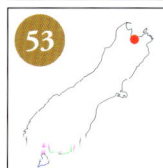

RICHMOND, NELSON
Kershaw House

Hosts Nicky Watson and Ian Hannell

10 Wensley Road, Richmond, Nelson

Phone 0-3-544 0957   *Email* info@kershawhouse.co.nz
Fax 0-3-544 0950   *Website* www.kershawhouse.co.nz

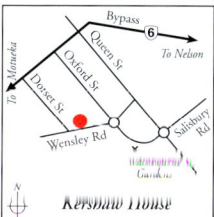

DIRECTIONS: From Nelson City, take SH 6 south to Richmond. Turn left at Mobil Service Station into Oxford St. Then turn right at roundabout into Wensley Rd. Kershaw House on right.

| 4 bdrm | 4 enst | Room rate $150–$275 | *Includes breakfast* | |

Kershaw House is a character home built in 1929 and has a Historic Places Trust Category Two classification. Historic features include the oak-panelled entrance hall, its wooden staircase ascending to the gallery with the original Art Deco leadlight window. Providing accommodation for up to eight guests, Kershaw House offers four ensuite guestrooms. Located close to local beaches, golf courses and Nelson City, Kershaw House is a convenient base for excursions to Abel Tasman and Nelson Lakes National Parks, award-winning vineyards and restaurants, and the region's many artisan galleries. Nicky and Ian serve breakfast, the menu changing daily, either in the dining room or alfresco in the garden. The new cat, Dougal, is in residence.

FACILITIES

- 1 super-king, 1 double & 2 king air-conditioned ensuite bedrooms
- 4 ensuites, each including toiletries & hair dryer
- tea & coffee-making facilities, ports & sherries in all bedrooms
- private garden & relaxation area
- guest lounge with well-stocked library & satellite TV
- unsuitable for children

- full continental or cooked breakfast served in dining room or alfresco in garden
- complimentary email & internet workstation for guest use
- Nicky speaks German
- young cat, Dougal, on site
- courtesy airport transfer
- secure off-street parking

ACTIVITIES AVAILABLE

- boutique vineyards nearby
- local pottery, handicraft & glass-blowing studio nearby
- hiking trails & nature walks
- parks & gardens to visit
- horse trekking
- sailing & fishing charters
- fishing/hunting guides available
- adventure sports – skydiving, kayaking, white water rafting

- award-winning restaurant & café, 5-min walk
- 2 local beaches 10-min drive
- tour bus stops, 2-min walk
- Nelson Airport, 10-min drive
- Nelson City, 15-min drive
- Abel Tasman National Park, 40-min drive
- Nelson Lakes, 1-hour drive
- interisland ferries, 2-hr drive

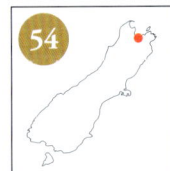

BRIGHTWATER, NELSON
Athenry Lodge

Hosts Deborah and Brett Mytton

Clover Road East, Brightwater, Nelson
Phone 0-3-544 1772   *Mobile* 025 442 766   *Fax* 0-3-544 1773
Email athenrylodge@xtra.co.nz   *Website* www.athenrylodge.co.nz

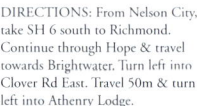

DIRECTIONS: From Nelson City, take SH 6 south to Richmond. Continue through Hope & travel towards Brightwater. Turn left into Clover Rd East. Travel 50m & turn left into Athenry Lodge.

5 bdrm	5 enst	2 pdrm

Double $250–$300
Single $230–$250

Includes breakfast, apéritifs & hors d'oeuvres
Picnic hampers extra

Constructed from natural earth block, New Zealand native timbers and Australian jarrah, Athenry Lodge is designed with spacious open-plan living areas and four ensuite bedrooms upstairs. A music theme is featured throughout the Lodge which includes a pianola downstairs. There is also a separate and private loft over the garage. Located less than half an hour south of Nelson City, Athenry Lodge is set in private gardens on 17 hectares of farmland. Guests enjoy the easy access to activities that can be arranged, with picnic hampers available. Continental buffet and cooked options are served at the dining table or alfresco in the courtyard, and complimentary pre-dinner drinks and nibbles are also offered.

FACILITIES

- 1 twin & 3 queen ensuite bedrooms upstairs in house
- private loft over garage with 1 queen ensuite bedroom, spa bath, TV, fridge & microwave
- hair dryer, toiletries, heated floor & bathrobes; bath in 2 ensuites
- musical interior design theme
- lounge with tea/coffee, nibbles, mineral water, bar, Sky TV, video, CD-player & pianola
- continental breakfast buffet with cooked options
- picnic hampers, extra
- pre-dinner drinks & nibbles included; in-house bar
- self-serve laundry; helipad
- central heating; fresh flowers
- phone, fax & email
- on-site parking; helipad
- courtesy passenger transfer

ACTIVITIES AVAILABLE

- private gardens surrounded by 17ha farmland
- barbecue available
- picnicking on site
- fishing
- pottery; arts & crafts
- private gardens to visit
- National Park
- private gardens to visit
- horse trekking
- restaurants & cafés at Richmond, 5-min drive
- parks & gardens
- walking tracks
- wineries
- bungy jumping
- ski-field in winter
- Richmond, 5 mins north
- Airport, 20 mins north
- Nelson City, 25 mins north

RICHMOND, NELSON
Nelson Country Retreat

Hosts Kate Lovell and John Perrin

94 Hoult Valley Road West, R D 1, Wakefield, Nelson
Phone 0-3-541 8860   *Mobile* 021 260 7448   *Fax* 0-3-541 8860
Email jksh.farm@actrix.co.nz   *Website* www.nelsoncountryretreat.com

Nelson Country Retreat

DIRECTIONS: From Nelson City take SH 6 south to Wakefield. Continue for 4km & turn right into Hoult Valley Rd West. Turn right at letter boxes & travel to wooden gate. Cross new bridge & continue to Nelson Country Retreat.

| 2 bdrm | 2 enst | Double $220 / Single $150 | Includes continental breakfast / Dinner extra | Self-catering |

Nelson Country Retreat is located on a 40-hectare (100-acre) wapiti deer (elk) farm and provides self-contained accommodation in a converted hop barn. Sited on a terrace overlooking the hop farm, river and native trees, the hop barn provides spacious luxury and 360-degree rural views to the Richmond Range beyond. Guests enjoy the farm tours on site and can hand-feed wapiti deer. Accommodation comprises two king-size ensuite bedrooms on the second floor of the barn which features native beech timber flooring, exposed beams and tiled bathrooms. Breakfast is served in the barn accompanied by the morning paper, and dinner with wine is available in the hosts' home adjacent. There is also a full kitchen for self-catering if preferred.

FACILITIES

- one-party bookings only
- 2 king ensuite bedrooms
- cotton bed linen, electric blankets & writing desk in bedrooms
- double showers, hair dryers, toiletries & heated towel rails
- guest lounge with gas fire, tea/coffee, nibbles, bar, TV, video, CD-player & magazines
- laundry service, $15

- continental breakfast served in Hop Barn
- dinner with wine, $30 pp
- full kitchen for self-catering, with dishwasher
- email, fax & phone
- courtesy passenger transfer
- children welcome
- on-site parking
- garaging; helipad

ACTIVITIES AVAILABLE

- farm tour on site
- native bush walk on site
- hand feed deer on site
- helicopter charters by arrangement from site
- 2 golf courses
- driving range
- heated swimming pool
- tennis courts
- steam museum

- restaurants, nearby
- antique shops; vineyards
- swimming
- trout fishing; rivers
- horse riding; kayaking
- Nelson City, 30 mins
- Nelson Lakes, 40 mins
- Abel Tasman National Park, 40-min drive away
- ski-field, 1½-hour drive

Nelson Country Retreat

Nelson Country Retreat

© Friars' Guide to New Zealand Accommodation for the Discerning Traveller

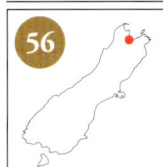

TASMAN BAY, NELSON
Istana Coastal Cottage

Hosts Sara and Bernard Isherwood

Coastal Highway, R D 1, Richmond
Phone 0-3-544 1979   *Mobile* 021 255 1555   *Fax* 0-3-544 1979
Email info@istana.co.nz   *Website* friars.co.nz/hosts/istana.html

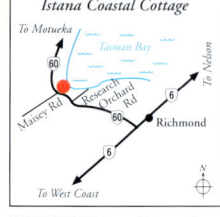

DIRECTIONS: From Nelson, take SH 6 south to Richmond. Continue & turn right into SH 60. Travel on this Coastal Highway 9.6km to Istana Coastal Cottage on right.

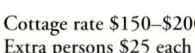

1 bdrm	1 prbth

Cottage rate $150–$200
Extra persons $25 each

Includes continental breakfast provisions
Self-catering

Istana Coastal Cottage is located on the Waimea Estuary. The name Istana is the Malay word for "palace". The hosts lived for some years in Malaysia. Designed in 1985 by Graham Postles, the cottage was built with rammed earth and New Zealand native rimu and matai, then furnished with Asian furniture. Accommodation comprises one queen-size bedroom and a separate alcove with double sofa bed. A full kitchen allows guests to self-cater, and continental breakfast provisions are supplied. The estuary provides guests with the opportunity for kayaking, sailing and bird-watching. Rabbit Island beach and a choice of golf courses are nearby. Istana Coastal Cottage is set in the heart of the Nelson wine and café area and Nelson City is only 20 minutes away.

FACILITIES

- private-party bookings only
- 1 self-contained cottage
- 1 queen bedroom
- double sofa bed in alcove
- writing desk in bedroom
- private bathroom with hair dryer, toiletries, heated towel rails & bathrobes
- phone & fresh flowers
- self-serve laundry
- continental breakfast provisions supplied
- full kitchen for self-catering
- TV, stereo, books & games
- smoking area outside on terrace
- children over 11yrs welcome
- on-site parking
- garaging
- www.istana.co.nz

ACTIVITIES AVAILABLE

- almost 2ha (4 acres) on site, with estuary access
- bird-watching
- swimming pool on site
- tennis court on site
- pétanque/boules on site
- kayaking & sailing from site
- Rabbit Island beach, 10-min drive away
- bush & beach walks
- award-winning cafés to visit, 2-min drive away
- 5 golf courses within 30-min drive; courtesy clubs
- wine trails; arts & crafts
- sea kayaking
- trout fishing
- Abel Tasman National Park, 40-min drive
- Nelson City, 20-min drive

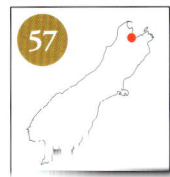

TASMAN BAY, NELSON
Kimeret Place

Hosts Clare and Peter Jones

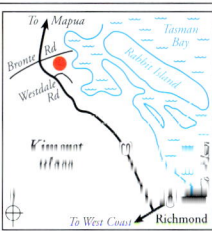

Bronte Road East, near Mapua, Nelson   Phone 0-3-540 2727
Postal Bronte Road East, R D 1, Upper Moutere, Nelson   *Fax* 0-3-540 2726
Email stay@kimeretplace.co.nz   *Website* www.kimeretplace.co.nz

DIRECTIONS: From Nelson City, take SH 6 past Richmond, & turn right into SH 60. Travel 12km towards Motueka & turn right at top of hill into Bronte Rd East. Travel 750m to Kimeret Place on right.

4 bdrm	4 enst

Double $185–$340   Single $145–$270
Cottage rate $240–$320
Includes breakfast
Self-catering available in cottage

Kimeret Place is set on two hectares (five acres) of sloping land overlooking the Waimea Inlet to the Richmond Range beyond. The upper guest floor in the main house comprises the spacious Edwin and Alexander suites, both opening to a balcony with views over the garden and inlet to the mountains. Native rimu timber and leadlights feature throughout the house. Located separately from the house are a studio and adjoining one-bedroom apartment, which can also be booked as a two-bedroom cottage. Each has an ensuite and private deck. The apartment includes cooking facilities for self-catering. A full breakfast is served for all guests either in the house, or alfresco on the large main deck overlooking the heated swimming and spa pools.

FACILITIES

- Alexander Suite: 1 California king/twin bedroom with Sky TV & DVD; Edwin Suite: 1 king/twin bedroom
- ensuite with spa bath, bathrobes, sitting area, desk, TV, video, hi-fi, dressing room, fridge, mini-bar & balcony in both suites
- 1 apartment with self-catering kitchen & 1 studio – each with 1 king/twin ensuite bedroom, sitting area, TV, hi-fi & fridge
- continental or cooked breakfast in house lounge or on deck; daytime snack menu
- hair dryers, toiletries, heated towel rails, cotton bed linen & tea/coffee in all bedrooms
- laundry available, $5
- email, fax & phone available
- airport/bus station/restaurant transfer service, from $5
- on-site parking

ACTIVITIES AVAILABLE

- heated swimming pool
- spa pool & pétanque on site
- paintings, by Clare, for sale
- large deck area with BBQ for guest use
- Abel Tasman & Kahurangi National Parks; sandy beaches
- sea & fly fishing
- kayaking; walking tracks
- arts & crafts

- 5 restaurants nearby
- winery & gallery, 500m
- Seifried Vineyard, 4km
- 20 wineries within 10km
- olive groves to visit
- gardens open to visit
- Mapua, 4km north
- 4 golf courses, 10–20 mins
- Golden Bay or Marlborough Sounds, 2-hour drive away

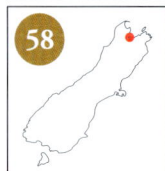

Tasman Bay, Nelson
Brontë Lodge

Hosts Margaret and Bruce Fraser

Bronte Road East, off Coastal Highway 60, near Mapua, Nelson
Phone 0-3-540 2422   *Email* margaret@brontelodge.co.nz
Fax 0-3-540 2637   *Website* brontelodge.co.nz

DIRECTIONS: From Nelson City, take SH 6 south past Richmond. Turn right into SH 60. Continue 10 mins to Bronte Rd East on right. Travel 1.5km to end of road. Brontë on left. Helicopter site available.

4 bdrm	4 enst	Double $440–$540	Single $425–$525	*Includes breakfast*

The homestead at Brontë is set in mature gardens adjacent to the boutique vineyard and orchards. Garden pathways lead to the shores of the Waimea Estuary, where the two adjoining guest suites are sited, with the two guest villas nearby. Here, in the quiet of the inlet, white herons, royal spoonbills and oystercatchers can be observed. Each suite or villa is tastefully decorated and includes king-size bed, quality bed linen, lounge area with sofa, writing desk, commissioned New Zealand artworks, dressing room and ensuite. À la carte breakfast is served at the homestead, alfresco in warm weather on the decks overlooking the garden to the estuary, or in the Edwardian dining room with its polished wood, leadlights and open fire.

FACILITIES

- 2 separate suites & 2 villas, with king & king/twin beds
- each suite & villa includes 1 dressing room & 1 private bathroom with spa bath
- separate lounge facilities in suites/villas with Sky TV & phone; kitchenette with fridge, tea/coffee & microwave
- portable BBQ on request
- original local artwork
- full breakfast at homestead or continental breakfast in suites & villas, by arrangement
- complimentary beverages & home-baking in suites & villas
- phone/fax & CD in villas; wheelchair access to 1 villa
- binoculars for viewing birdlife
- native & villa watergardens
- private driveways to villas & suites; helipad available

ACTIVITIES AVAILABLE

- pétanque/boules on site
- heated swimming pool & all-weather tennis court
- relaxing in homestead garden
- boutique vineyard on site
- walks through orchard along estuary shoreline; swimming
- Canadian canoeing, sailing & windsurfing from site
- hunting & fishing guides
- restaurants 5–10-min drive
- 5 award-winning wineries
- 3 golf links, 7–15-min drive
- sea kayaking; golden beaches
- swimming at Rabbit Island
- craft trail; skiing in winter
- hiking in Abel Tasman National Park, 45-min drive
- Nelson Airport, 20-min drive
- Picton ferry, 2½ hours away

Above: The two villas are purpose-built for estuary views, with a driveway for easy access. The two suites have a similar vista.
Below: Bi-fold windows of the villas open to the lawn overlooking Waimea Estuary, for indoor/outdor living and alfresco dining.
Opposite top: In summertime, breakfast is served alfresco on the deck of the homestead at Brontë Lodge overlooking the garden.
Opposite bottom left: The bedroom in the Hamilton Villa features a king-size bed and quality linen as do all four bedrooms.
Opposite bottom right: Guests enjoy the new heated swimming pool at Brontë Lodge, where they can also relax on deckchairs.

TASMAN BAY, NELSON
Atholwood Country Accommodation

Hosts Robyn and Grahame Williams

Bronte Road East, R D 1, Upper Moutere
Phone 0-3-540 2925   *Mobile* 025 310 309   *Fax* 0-3-540 3258
Email atholwood@xtra.co.nz   *Website* www.atholwood.co.nz

DIRECTIONS: From Nelson City, take SH 6 south past Richmond. Turn right into SH 60. Continue 10 mins to Bronte Rd East on right. Travel 1km to Atholwood Country Accommodation on right.

3 bdrm	3 enst	Double $180–$200	Single $150	*Includes breakfast*	*Lunch & dinner extra*
		Extra adult $50, children $30 each	Weekly rate available		*Self-catering in apartment*

Atholwood offers two accommodation options – The Gatehouse, a separate self-contained apartment (*see below right*), and an upstairs guest wing in the main house overlooking Waimea Inlet. The Gatehouse is the converted ground floor of the original pottery, built at the driveway entrance. It includes a spacious bedroom, bathroom, lounge, a full kitchen for self-catering, and indoor and alfresco dining areas. Built in 1982, the contemporary-style timbered house features high ceilings and native rimu interiors. Set in almost one hectare of landscaped gardens on the edge of the inlet, Atholwood affords water views across the surounding orchards and olive groves to the mountains beyond. Guests enjoy the hidden walks in the garden and watching the tides ebb and flow from the gazebo. Both accommodation options provide guests with privacy and seclusion. Within the house, breakfast, at a time to suit, is served in the dining room, upstairs in the guest lounge, or on the deck. Home-made muesli and fruit, or a special cooked selection, are offered. Picnic lunches and a three-course dinner with local wine can be arranged.

FACILITIES

- The Gatehouse: 1 king/twin bedroom with single trundler, 1 bathroom with wheelchair access, laundry, full kitchen, dining/lounge & outdoor area
- 1 guest wing upstairs in house:
  – opens to balcony
  – 1 queen & 1 queen/twin bedroom, each with ensuite
  – bath in 1 ensuite
- open fire, organ & Sky TV in downstairs lounge in house
- cotton bed linen; fresh flowers
- hair dryers, toiletries, heated towel rails & bathrobes
- breakfast selection in house
- picnic lunches, $12 pp
- 3-course à la carte dinner with local wine, $50 pp
- fruit, teas/coffee & home baking in both guest lounges
- self-service laundry both in house & in Gatehouse
- children/pets by arrangement
- Carlos, the cat, in residence
- basic German spoken
- email, fax & cordless phone
- courtesy car available
- on-site parking

ACTIVITIES AVAILABLE

- spa pool & swimming pool
- croquet lawn on site
- BBQ available on site
- canoe available for Inlet
- sea & native bird-watching
- garden walks on site
- Mapua Village, nearby
- watersports
- swimming
- fishing
- boating
- kayaking
- walking
- selection of restaurants
- award-winning wineries
- golf club, 10-min drive
- charter boats
- dolphins
- arts & crafts trail
- gardens open to visit
- Richmond, 10-min drive
- Motueka, 20-min drive
- Abel Tasman National Park, 40-min drive away
- day tours arranged
- skiing in winter, 1½ hrs

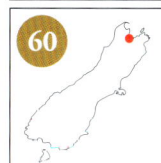

UPPER MOUTERE
Maple Grove Cottages

Hosts Judy Straford and George Page

72 Flaxmore Road, R.D.2, Upper Moutere, Nelson
Phone 0-3-543 2267   Mobile 025 618 8641   Fax 0-3-543 2267
Email george1judy@xtra.co.nz   *Website* www.maplegrove.co.nz

DIRECTIONS: From Richmond take SH 60 towards Mapua. Turn west into Seaton Valley Rd. Continue into Gardner Valley Rd. Turn right into Moutere Highway. Take 1st right into Flaxmore Rd to Maple Grove on right.

| 4 bdrm | 2 prbth | Double $160 Single $150 | *Includes breakfast hamper Cooked breakfast extra* | *Self-catering* |

Located in rural seclusion in the countryside of Upper Moutere, Maple Grove Cottage is set in nearly two hectares (four acres) of landscaped grounds including a mature acer grove. Purpose built in 2002 in pioneer style, Maple Grove Cottage provides self-contained accommodation for up to four guests. The cottage features a colonial-style verandah overlooking the pond, with views to Mt Arthur and the western ranges. A breakfast hamper is supplied daily and cooked breakfast is also available. Guests can self-cater in the kitchenette and a gas barbecue is popular for alfresco dining by the brook under the trees. Restaurants, cafés and vineyards are a short drive away. There is a second new self-contained cottage also now available for accommodation.

FACILITIES

- single-party bookings only
- 2 self-contained cottages each with 2 bedrooms
- 1 bathroom each with double shower, hair dryer, toiletries & bathrobes
- cotton bed linen; fresh flowers
- Sky TV, video, CD-player, music, games, artwork, books, writing desk & nibbles in lounge
- breakfast hamper includes continental, fresh farm eggs, home-made bread & jams
- cooked breakfast, extra
- kitchenette for self-catering
- hosts live in main house
- self-service laundry
- phone, fax & email in cottage
- verandah; garaging
- courtesy passenger transfer

ACTIVITIES AVAILABLE

- nearly 2ha (4 acres) land with gas BBQ, mature trees, garden walks, pond & farm animals
- tramping on Mt Arthur & at Kahurangi National Park
- Abel Tasman National Park walkways & sea kayaking
- jet boating
- mountain biking
- golf; fishing
- award-winning restaurants & cafés at Mapua, 5-min drive
- Kaiteriteri & Tahunanui beaches
- vineyards, wine tasting & olive groves
- arts, crafts & galleries
- local potters
- Motueka, 10-min drive north
- Nelson & airport, 30 mins

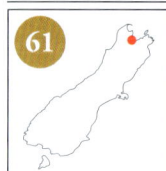

UPPER MOUTERE, NELSON
Mahana Escape

Hosts Gloria Eggeling and Steven Edwards

750 Old Coach Road, R D 1, Upper Moutere, Nelson
Phone 0-3-540 3090   *Mobile* 025 289 0060   *Fax* 0-3-540 3090
Email gloria@mahanaescape.co.nz   *Website* www.mahanaescape.co.nz

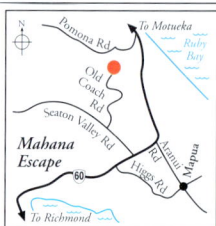

DIRECTIONS: From Richmond, take SH 60 towards Motueka. Turn left into Seaton Valley Rd, then right into Old Coach Rd. Mahana Escape at end of road (6 mins from SH 60 turn-off).

5 bdrm	1 enst	2 prbth	Room rate $160–$250	*Includes breakfast* *Lunch & dinner extra*
			Apartment rate $310	*Self-catering in apartment*

Set on two hectares (five acres) of developing land, Mahana Escape features panoramic views overlooking the Tasman Sea. Mahana is Maori for "a warm place to rest", and provides accommodation with a Mediterranean ambience, comprising three upstairs guestrooms and a downstairs two-bedroom apartment. Gloria serves a full breakfast in the dining room, or alfresco on the deck, and she offers picnic lunch by arrangement. She will also prepare two or three-course dinners, with whitebait a speciality, and wheat-free or gluten-free meals can be arranged. Guests enjoy the Abel Tasman National Park nearby, and Gloria offers a luggage-minding service for her guests. The cafés and art studios at Mapua village are just a short drive away.

FACILITIES

- 1 king bedroom upstairs, with dressing room, spa bath & dual basin in ensuite, TV, phone jack
- 1 queen & 1 twin bedroom upstairs, with bath in bathroom
- 1 apartment downstairs, with 1 queen & 1 twin bedroom, 1 bathroom, kitchenette, lounge, TV & phone jack
- bathrobes, hair dryers, toiletries, heated floor & heated towel rails

- full breakfast choice
- 2–3 course à la carte dinner with wine, $35–$60 pp; lunch/picnic by request, extra
- open fire, Sky TV/video/DVD CDs, & art in upstairs lounge
- nibbles & home-made cookies
- phone, fax & email available
- children welcome; fresh flowers
- courtesy laundry; parking

ACTIVITIES AVAILABLE

- guest BBQ on site, with salads by request
- small weddings catered
- courtesy passenger transfer
- pétanque/boules on site
- garden walks on site
- neighbouring alpaca farm
- golf courses
- local potteries & artists
- award-winning wineries

- Mapua village restaurants, cafés & art studios, 6-min drive
- horse riding, 15-min drive
- walking/trekking in Abel Tasman National Park & Kahurangi National Park, 30 mins; transport arranged & luggage minded
- gardens open to visit
- Motueka, 16-min drive
- Nelson City, 45-min drive

RUBY BAY
Sandstone House

Hosts Jenny and John Marchbanks

30 Korepo Road, Ruby Bay, Nelson   *Phone* 0 3 540 3251
Postal Korepo Road, R D 1, Upper Moutere, Nelson   *Fax* 0 3 540 3251
Email sandstone@rubybay.net.nz   *Website* rubybay.net.nz

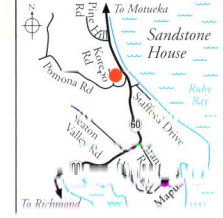

   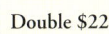

DIRECTIONS: From Nelson take SH 6 past Richmond & turn right into SH 60. Travel past Mapua turn-off. Turn left into Pomona Rd & then 1st right into Korepo Rd. Travel 300m to Sandstone House on right.

2 bdrm	2 enst	1 pdrm	Double $220	Single $200	*Includes breakfast*

Purpose built from imported Australian sandstone in 2001, Sandstone House is located above Ruby Bay with panoramic views over the Tasman Sea. The Australian ambience is enhanced by the deep verandahs surrounding the house, the high ceilings and clay-tiled roof. Guests can enjoy the privacy of their own wing, with private verandahs opening from both bedrooms, each including a writing desk, tea and coffee-making facilities and fridge. Breakfast is prepared according to guests' wishes and is served in the dining room or on the decking overlooking the sea. The guests have a private entrance, and upstairs are the hosts, who have lived in the area since 1970. Restaurants are only five minutes' drive away at the village of Mapua.

FACILITIES

- 2 queen ensuite bedrooms
- bedrooms open to verandah
- hair dryer, toiletries, bathrobes, demist mirror & heated towel rails in both bathrooms
- writing desk, phone, TV, tea/coffee, fridge, fruit, mineral water & juice in each bedroom
- Sky TV, video & CD in lounge
- open fire in lounge

- continental or cooked breakfast in dining room or alfresco on verandah
- guest barbecue
- 1 powder room
- fresh flowers
- central heating
- fax & email available
- on-site parking
- private guest entrance

ACTIVITIES AVAILABLE

- self-serve BBQ
- track to beach, 5-min walk
- flat-bottomed scenic boat
- jet boating
- watersports; swimming
- fishing; aquarium
- gardens open to visit
- award-winning wineries, 10-min drive away
- Mapua village, 5-min drive

- restaurants, 2km away
- horse riding, 5-min drive
- arts & crafts
- Motueka, 15-min drive away
- sea kayaking
- trout fishing rivers, 30-min drive
- Abel Tasman & Kahurangi National Parks, 30–50 mins
- Nelson City, 30-min drive

RUBY BAY
Ruby Bay Lodge & Vineyard Cottage

Hosts Audrey and Sam Watt

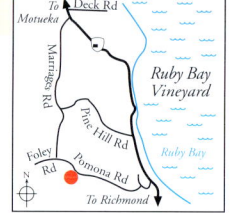

271 Pomona Road, Ruby Bay, R D 1, Nelson
Phone 0-3-540 3938   *Mobile* 027 454 0393   *Fax* 0-3-540 3938
Email stay@rubybaylodge.co.nz   *Website* www.rubybaylodge.co.nz

DIRECTIONS: From Nelson, take SH 6 past Richmond & turn right into SH 60. Travel 25 mins to Ruby Bay & turn 1st left into Pomona Rd. Travel uphill 2.5km to Ruby Bay Lodge & Vineyard Cottage on left.

4 bdrm	2 enst	1 prbth	Cottage rate $225–$300 Extra persons $50 each 2-night minimum stay *Self catering*	
			Room rate in Lodge $275–$350 *Includes breakfast or provisions for cottage* *Lunch extra*	

Ruby Bay Lodge

Purpose built in 2004 with panoramic views over the boutique vineyard and landscaped parklands of almost 10 hectares, to Tasman Bay beyond, the accommodation comprises a self-contained cottage and a guest wing in the Lodge. The cottage includes a bedroom and mezzanine, with full kitchen and stocked chef's pantry for self-catering. Breakfast provisions are supplied daily and there is a barbecue for guest use. The Lodge offers two ensuite bedrooms, guest lounge and viewing tower. Lodge guests are served a full gourmet breakfast, with lunch by arrangement, and complimentary apéritifs and hors d'oeuvres. A welcome platter and wine is provided for all guests and there is a range of award-winning restaurants just a few minutes' drive away.

FACILITIES

- single-party bookings in cottage
- Cottage: 1 king bedroom & 1 double bed in mezzanine with 1 private bathroom; gas log fire
- Lodge: 2 king ensuite bedrooms with tea/coffee, minibar, balcony
- cotton bed linen & writing desks
- hair dryers, heated towel rails, bathrobes & toiletries; flowers
- speciality honeymoons & romantic breaks catered

- kitchen in cottage for self-catering, with full provisions
- full breakfast for Lodge
- packed/alfresco lunch with wine by request, $30 pp
- DVD/CD/Sky TV in lounges
- email, fax & phone available
- self-serve laundry
- courtesy passenger transfer by request; on-site parking

ACTIVITIES AVAILABLE

- guided vineyard tours & wine tasting on site; BBQ
- open-top car hire available
- picking fruits in season
- movie library on site
- 2 small French bulldogs, Louis & Rory on site
- arts & crafts trail
- Mapua Wharf
- boat trips & fishing

- Mapua restaurants, 5 mins
- Abel Tasman & Kahurangi National Parks
- Motueka trout fishing
- 9-hole Tasman golf course
- beach walks
- helicopter flights; sky diving
- Nelson Airport & WOW complex, 25 min drive
- Picton Ferry, 2-hr drive

Ruby Bay Lodge

Ruby Bay Lodge

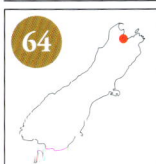

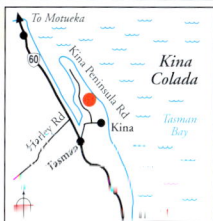

Kina Peninsula, Tasman Bay
Kina Colada Holiday & Health Retreat

Hosts Christine and Franz Lieber

Kina Peninsula Tasman   *Postal* R.D.1 Upper Moutere, Nelson
Phone 0-3-546 6700   *Email* info@kinacolada.co.nz
Fax 0-3-526 6770   *Website* www.kinacolada.co.nz

DIRECTIONS: Take scenic coastal highway, SH 60, from Nelson & travel 40km towards Motueka. At Tasman, turn right into Kina Rd. Travel 1km & turn left. Kina Colada is 1st driveway on right.

3 bdrm	3 enst	Double $195–$490	Includes continental breakfast
		Single $110–$180	Lunch, dinner & treatments extra

Kina Colada

Kina Colada is a European-style holiday and health retreat sited on eight hectares on a cliff-top on Kina Peninsula overlooking Tasman Bay. Built in 1997 with Mediterranean architecture complemented by timber floors and ceilings, ensuites with heated tile floors, and double-glazed windows, Kina Colada combines relaxation with the opportunity for spa treatments. The uniquely designed health treatment rooms offer a choice of beauty treatments, massages, marine bodyworks, antique mud room, oxygen therapy and marine baths. Guest facilities include European sauna, and large salt-water swimming pool with ha-ha blending into the bay vista. As well as healthy continental breakfasts, Franz serves Mediterranean-style lunch or dinner, by arrangement.

FACILITIES

- 1 king & 2 king/twin upstairs suites
- 3 ensuites with heated floors, toiletries & hair dryers
- tea/coffee, fridge, TV & phone in all 3 bedrooms
- health treatment rooms
- double glazing
- sea & mountain views
- guest lounge
- healthy continental or cooked breakfast served
- 2-course dinner, by request, $45–$65 pp
- laundry available
- children over 10 years welcome
- German spoken by hosts
- massages & treatments, extra
- salt-water swimming pool
- on-site parking

ACTIVITIES AVAILABLE

- aromatic massage, $95/1 hr
- eyelash tint, eyebrow tint & tidy, $32/30 mins
- Flash Soleil/Sun Kiss, $95/1 hr
- Jambes Toniques, $90/45 mins
- Le Grand Classique, $140/ 1¼–1½ hours
- optimizer, $125/1¼–1½ hrs
- phyto-bain/bath, $15/any time
- phyto-marine, $120/1¼ hours
- plaisir d'arômes, $95/1 hr
- soin velours, $125/1 hr
- spa manicure, $55/1 hr; spa pedicure, $65/1 hr
- wineries; restaurants
- tidal inlet for motor boating
- 9-hole golf course, 1.5km
- swimming beaches; walks
- arts & crafts; gardens to visit
- kayaking; fishing

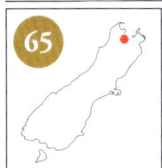

KINA BEACH, TASMAN BAY
Old Schoolhouse Vineyard Cottage

Hosts Dave Birt and Pam Robert

Dee Road, Kina Beach, R D 1, Upper Moutere, Nelson
Phone 0-3-526 6252   *Mobile* 027 281 2425   *Fax* 0-3-526 6252
Email kinabeach@xtra.co.nz   *Website* www.kinabeach.com

DIRECTIONS: Take scenic coastal highway, SH 60, from Nelson & travel 40km towards Motueka. At Tasman, turn right into Kina Beach Rd. Take 1st right into Dee Rd. Kina Beach Vineyard 1st on left to Cottage.

1 bdrm	1 prbth

Cottage rate $200–$250
Extra persons $25 each

Includes continental breakfast provisions
Self-catering

Sited on Kina Beach Vineyard Estate, the Old Schoolhouse Vineyard Cottage has been carefully restored and transformed into self-contained accommodation. Originally built in 1934, the Redwoods Valley Schoolhouse was moved to the vineyard in 1999 and retains the native heart matai floors, tongue and groove walls and ceilings. Guests enjoy the panoramic views over Tasman Bay, the sunrises and sunsets being especially popular. Vineyard tours are also available to guests. Breakfast provisions are supplied, sufficient for two days, and a fully equipped kitchen enables guests to self-cater. A barbecue is also available for alfresco dining, and restaurants are not far away. The cottage can accommodate honeymoon couples and a sunroom provides an extra single divan.

FACILITIES

- single-party bookings only
- self-contained cottage
- 1 queen bedroom
- sunroom with single daybed
- toiletries, hair dryer & heated towel rail in bathroom
- cotton bed linen
- fresh flowers
- babies or children over 14 years welcome
- continental breakfast provisions for 2 mornings
- full kitchen, including dishwasher, for self-catering
- open fire, bar, writing desk, books & CDs in lounge
- guest laundry
- wrap-around decks
- fax & phone in main house
- outdoor furniture & BBQ

ACTIVITIES AVAILABLE

- vineyard tours on site
- relaxing in NZ native & cottage garden on site
- Kina Beach, 200m walk
- Tasman Golf Course, 5 mins
- craft shops nearby
- Rabbit Island; gardens to visit
- safe swimming beaches
- watersports
- winery tours, by arrangement
- restaurants nearby
- Mapua village, 10-min drive
- Kaiteriteri Beach, 30-min drive
- Tahunanui Beach, 30-min drive
- kayaking, 40-min drive
- Abel Tasman walks, 40-min drive
- Rainbow Ski-field, 2-hour drive
- Motueka, 10-min drive
- Nelson City & airport, 30 mins

TASMAN
Wairepo House

Hosts Joyanne and Richard Easton

Weka Road, Marini, Coastal Highway, Nelson
Phone 0 3 526 6865   *Mobile* 021 801 044   *Fax* 0-3-526 6101

Email joyanne@wairepohouse.co.nz   *Website* www.wairepohouse.co.nz

5 bdrm	4 enst	1 prbth	**Double** $350–$595	
			Single $325–$570	*Includes breakfast*

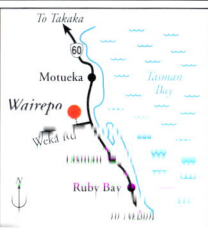

DIRECTIONS: From Nelson City, travel on SH 60 towards Motueka for 45km. Continue 3km past Tasman township, then turn left at Weka Rd. Wairepo House is the stone entrance 1st on the right.

Wairepo House is a three-storey colonial homestead with views towards Tasman Bay. The rural setting is complemented by Wairepo's fourth-generation apple and pear orchard and the 7,000 peonies grown for export. Wairepo House features warm native timbers, chapel ceilings, and sundecks. Four suites have been designed and furnished for guest comfort and privacy with rich-coloured fabrics, antiques and local artwork. Flexi-time gourmet breakfast or brunch can be served on the sundeck overlooking the heated pool. Almost a hectare (two acres) of woodland garden is planted for all seasons with established trees and rambling perennial borders. Guests can enjoy the grass tennis court, pétanque lawn, and refreshments in the summer house.

FACILITIES

- 1 upstairs suite: 1 super-king/twin & 1 super-king bedroom, desk & balcony, ensuite with double spa bath & bidet, kitchenette, lounge, open fire, TV & private balcony
- 1 downstairs suite: 1 super-king bedroom, private bathroom, sun-room with TV, tea/coffee, desk
- 1 downstairs suite: 1 super-king bedroom, spa bath in ensuite, lounge, kitchenette, wheelchair access
- full flexi-time breakfast

- complimentary drinks, alcohol, nibbles & platters
- heated tiled floors & demist mirrors in all bathrooms
- 1 extra suite available with ensuite & private lounge
- CDs, cassettes, radios, hair dryers, flowers & chocolates
- original NZ art, leadlights, rimu panelling, throughout
- fax, email, laundry available

ACTIVITIES AVAILABLE

- heated swimming pool; tennis court
- chess set in garden, pond, summer house & peony garden walk
- croquet & pétanque/boules
- orchard & packhouse tour
- vineyard next door
- good restaurants nearby
- wine trails & craft trails
- Motueka, 6km north
- Nelson City, less than 50km

- windsurfing & water skiing according to tides
- trout fishing guides available
- golden beaches; kayaking
- golf courses at Tasman & Motueka, 4-min drive away
- lakes & mountains; walks
- Abel Tasman & Kahurangi National Parks
- winter snow skiing & Picton, 2-hour drive

MOTUEKA

Copper Beech Gallery

Hosts John and Carol Gatenby

240 Thorp Street, Motueka, Nelson
Phone 0-3-528 7456   *Mobile* 021 256 0053   *Fax* 0-3-528 7456
Email copper.beech.gallery@xtra.co.nz   *Website* www.copperbeechgallery.co.nz

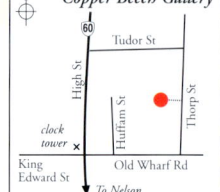

DIRECTIONS: From Nelson City, travel on SH 60 towards Motueka for about 45 mins. At clock tower corner, turn right into Old Wharf Rd. Then turn 2nd left into Thorp St. Copper Beech Gallery is 100m on left.

| 2 bdrm | 2 enst | Double $250–$320 | Single $210–$250 | *Includes breakfast* |

Copper Beech Gallery is the home of landscape artist John R Gatenby. His paintings are exhibited throughout the house and in his adjacent studio and gallery. The rooms in this contemporary home open onto extensive patios and a hectare of park-like gardens. Nelson's fresh fruit and seafood feature on the breakfast menu and are served alfresco beneath a pergola, in the court-yard, or more formally in the sunlit dining area. Copper Beech Gallery is a semi-rural retreat offering mountain views, peace, relaxation and recreation, just 10 minutes' drive from Motueka River's renowned trout fishing. Located on the outskirts of Motueka township, it is 20 minutes to Kaiteriteri's golden beaches and half an hour to Abel Tasman or Kahurangi National Park.

FACILITIES

- 1 queen & 1 twin bedroom, each with ensuite bathroom
- hair dryers, toiletries, heaters, heated towel rails & bathrobes
- bedrooms open to sundecks
- private guest lounge
- phone & fax facilities
- TV in the Snug
- fresh flowers & chocolates in both bedrooms
- full breakfast with selection of fresh local produce – fruit platters & seafood
- tea/coffee & guest fridge with quality refreshments
- original NZ paintings – tuition available on request
- tranquil garden overlooking bird & water fowl sanctuary & estuary
- level access – no stairs
- off-street parking beside door

ACTIVITIES AVAILABLE

- art gallery; summer house in garden & outdoor golden labrador, Abbi, on site
- beach, 5-min walk
- golf course, 2-min drive
- restaurants/shops, 2 mins
- scenic flights, tandem skydiving, 5-min drive
- wineries, 20-min drive
- arts & crafts trails, pottery, woodwork available
- golden sandy beaches & coastal tracks, 20-min drive
- marine reserve & helicopter fishing trips, guide available
- kayaking/walks/tramps/boat trips into Abel Tasman & Kahurangi National Parks, 30-min drive
- Marble Mountain – extensive limestone cave systems, 40 mins
- Nelson City, 45-min drive
- Picton interisland ferry, 2½ hours

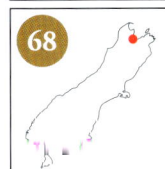
KAITERITERI, MOTUEKA

The Haven

Hosts Allean and Tom Rowling

Bay View Road, Kaiteriteri   Postal Kaiteriteri, R.D. 2, Motueka
Phone 0-3-527 0005   *Email* the.haven@internet.co.nz
Fax 0-3-527 8065   *Website* friars.co.nz/hosts/thehaven.html

The Haven

DIRECTIONS: Take SH 60 to Motueka. Continue through Riwaka, turn right & travel 6km to Kaiteriteri. Travel 0.5km up hill & turn left into Rowling Heights, then left into Bay View Rd. The Haven is 1st on left.

| 2 bdrm | 1 enst | 1 prbth | House rate $200 2-night minimum stay | Extra couple $50 Multiple–night rates available | *Includes breakfast provisions* *Self-catering* |

The Haven was designed in nautical style in 2000, reflecting Tom's seafaring career as captain of many vessels. Tom's great-great grandfather was the first European to land in Kaiteriteri. With panoramic views over Tasman Bay, The Haven provides self-contained accommodation for four guests in the ensuite Captain's Cabin and Crews Quarters with private bathroom. The fully equipped "galley" for self-catering includes breakfast provisions, local produce and home baking. A barbecue and two decks make alfresco dining popular with guests. The hosts live adjacent, their house set in a large garden with a swimming pool for guest use, and a woodland track leading down to Kaiteriteri Beach where a dinghy is available for the more adventurous.

FACILITIES

- private-party bookings only
- 1 king ensuite bedroom
- 1 twin bedroom with private bathroom
- cotton bed linen
- fresh flowers
- hair dryer, quality toiletries, heated towel rail & bathrobes
- self-service laundry
- lounge with pellet fire, TV, video & phone
- breakfast provisions
- fully self-contained kitchen for self-catering
- nibbles, home-baking & organic local produce
- 2 sundecks
- unsuitable for small children
- courtesy passenger transfer
- on-site parking

ACTIVITIES AVAILABLE

- swimming pool on site
- Oscar, the elusive cat, on site
- barbecue available
- private bush walk to beach
- dinghy available
- line fishing from rocks
- sea kayaking
- ocean swimming
- snorkelling; horse trekking
- water taxis & tourist launches
- restaurants, 10-min drive
- wine trails
- bush walks; tramping
- potters; arts & crafts trail
- gardens open to visit
- Abel Tasman National Park gateway
- Kahurangi National Park tours
- Motueka, 30-min drive
- Nelson City, 1-hour drive

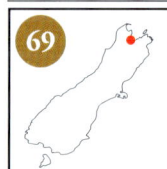

KAITERITERI
Te Hiwi

Hosts Val and Mike Swatridge

151 Sandy Bay Road, Kaiteriteri   *Phone* 0-3-527 8524
Postal 151 Sandy Bay Road, R D 2, Motueka   *Mobile* 027 286 5431
Email info@tehiwi.co.nz   *Website* www.tehiwi.co.nz

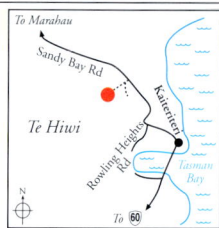

DIRECTIONS: Take SH 60 to Motueka. Continue through Riwaka, turn right & travel 6km to Kaiteriteri. Continue uphill towards Marahau. After 1km turn left up private road. Follow signs to Te Hiwi on left.

2 bdrm	1 enst	1 prbth

Apartment rate $200
Extra persons $25 each

Includes breakfast provisions
Self-catering

With 270-degree sea views over Tasman Bay to the Richmond Range, Te Hiwi provides self-contained accommodation in a contemporary apartment built in 2004. Located separately from the hosts for total privacy, Te Hiwi offers two ensuite guestrooms and spacious living areas overlooking the beaches at Kaiteriteri. The king-size bedroom opens to a private garden featuring a waterfall, and the apartment ensures privacy high above the bay in a bush setting on the ridge, which translates as Te Hiwi. Daily breakfast provisions in the pantry include pickles, jam and home baking. Guest can self-cater in the fully equipped kitchen and fresh vegetables are available in the garden. The apartment opens to a paved patio with seating to enjoy the panoramic ocean vistas.

FACILITIES

- single-party bookings only
- 1 king ensuite bedroom with writing desk, phone jack & opens to private garden with waterfall
- 1 twin bedroom with private bathroom, opens to deck
- cotton bed linen
- hair dryers, bathrobes, toiletries, heated floor & towel rails
- fax & computer available for guest use in house
- self-catering with full kitchen including dishwasher
- breakfast provisons included
- lounge with Sky TV, DVD, video, music & CD-player
- fresh flowers
- children over 10yrs welcome
- self-serve laundry
- 270-degree sea views

ACTIVITIES AVAILABLE

- walks in secluded garden on site
- bush walks adjacent on ridge
- sea kayaking; sailing
- golf courses
- wineries; arts & crafts trail
- tramping, bush & coastal walks
- river or sea fishing
- horse trekking
- potters; arts & crafts trail
- selection of restaurants & cafés, short drive away
- gardens open to visit
- art studios & galleries
- gateway to Abel Tasman National Park
- Kahurangi National Park tours, 35-min drive
- Motueka, 20-min drive
- Nelson City 1-hour drive

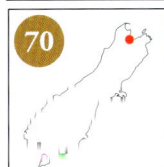

Bellbird Lodge, Kaiteriteri

Hosts Anthea and Brian Harvey

Sandy Bay Road, Kaiteriteri *Postal* Kaiteriteri, R D 2, Motueka
Phone 0-3-527 8555 *Mobile* 021 037 1470 *Fax* 0-3-527 8556
Email stay@bellbirdlodge.com *Website* www.bellbirdlodge.com

DIRECTIONS: Take SH 60 to Motueka. Continue through Riwaka, turn right & travel 6km to Kaiteriteri. Continue uphill towards Marahau. After 1.5km turn right into private road. Lodge is 3rd house on left.

| 3 bdrm | 1 enst | 1 prbth | 1 pdrm | **Double $165–$250** **Single $120–$180** | *Includes breakfast* *Dinner (in winter) extra* | | |

Bellbirds sing in the garden and native bush behind the Lodge above Tasman Bay. Built in 1998, the house was remodelled in 2001 for ground-floor accommodation. Set on a quiet hillside just minutes' drive from Kaiteriteri Beach, Bellbird Lodge features sea or bush views from the spacious Magnolia Room, and both bedrooms in the Rosewood Suite. Anthea and Brian offer home baking with complimentary afternoon tea, and are happy to book local activities for their guests. The continental breakfast buffet is complemented by a hot speciality, such as grilled local nectarines with mascarpone served on toasted fruit bread in the dining room, or alfresco overlooking the ocean. Quality local restaurants offer lunch and dinner.

FACILITIES

- 1 super-king/twin ensuite bedroom
- 1 queen & 1 twin bedroom with private bathroom & spa bath
- hair dryer, toiletries & bathrobes
- tea/coffee & mineral water in all 3 bedrooms
- TV, video, books, games, music, CD-player & piano in lounge
- fresh flowers; guest fridge
- children over 10 yrs welcome

- continental breakfast buffet & cooked course each day
- complimentary afternoon tea provided; home baking
- 4-course dinner with wine, $50 pp by prior arrangement, May – Oct.
- phone, fax & email available; complimentary laundry
- courtesy passenger transfer; on-site parking

ACTIVITIES AVAILABLE

- gas barbecue on sun terrace
- golden beaches; swimming
- water taxis; yacht charter & launch cruises
- skydiving; flying fox
- scenic helicopter flights
- tramping, bush & coastal walks
- horse trekking; caves, 25 mins
- sea kayaking; sailing; snorkelling & river or sea fishing

- 4 restaurants 3–10-min drive
- potters; arts & crafts trail
- golf courses; mini golf
- wineries; gardens to visit
- gateway to Abel Tasman National Park
- Kahurangi National Park tours, 35-min drive
- Motueka, 20-min drive
- Nelson 1-hour drive away

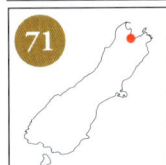

RIWAKA VALLEY, MOTUEKA
The Resurgence

Hosts Clare de Carteret-Bisson and Peter Adams

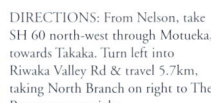

574 Riwaka Valley Road, R D 3, Motueka
Phone 0-3-528 4664   *Email* info@resurgence.co.nz
Fax 0-3-528 4605   *Website* www.resurgence.co.nz

DIRECTIONS: From Nelson, take SH 60 north-west through Motueka, towards Takaka. Turn left into Riwaka Valley Rd & travel 5.7km, taking North Branch on right to The Resurgence on right.

6 bdrm	6 enst	2 pdrm

Lodge room rate $245–$495
Cottage suite rate $245–$395

Includes breakfast, apéritifs & dinner   *Picnic extra*
Self-catering   *Includes welcome basket*   *All meals extra*

Located in the Riwaka River valley, The Resurgence offers tranquillity enhanced by 20 hectares of the surrounding native bush, with walking tracks and views to the Kahurangi National Park. With architect-designed renovations, The Resurgence was opened in 2003, providing guests with four ensuite queen-size bedrooms upstairs, and two separate self-contained cottage suites. Clare and Peter, both trained in French cuisine, serve a full breakfast in the dining room, or alfresco on the verandah. They offer lunch as required, and four-course dégustation dinner matched with fine Nelson wines. Guests enjoy the swimming pool, spa pool, and the walk to the crystal pools at the Riwaka Resurgence, where the river emerges from a marble cave.

FACILITIES

- 4 queen ensuite bedrooms upstairs in main house
- 2 self-contained cottages: 1 super-king/twin & 1 queen ensuite bedroom, self-catering kitchen & BBQ in each
- all rooms open to balconies
- massage showers, hair dryers, toiletries, demist mirrors, heated floor & towel rails
- cotton bed linen; bathrobes
- cooked & continental breakfast
- picnic, $15 pp; 4-course table d'hôte dinner, $50 pp; wine extra
- open fire, tea/coffee, bar, books & guides in lounge & maproom; TV on request, videos, DVDs, CDs, music, games, artwork
- phone, fax, modems in all bedrooms, email & laundry
- French spoken; wheelchair access; on-site parking; helipad

ACTIVITIES AVAILABLE

- spa pool, swimming pool, hammocks & bicycles
- 20ha (50 acres) native bush
- picnicking, swimming hole, native bush walks & fishing at Riwaka Resurgence, 2 mins
- kayaking, walking & sailing in Abel Tasman National Park, 20-min drive away
- eco tours & bird-watching
- wineries, arts trail & markets
- walking, tramping, horse riding, fishing & river canoeing in Kahurangi National Park
- Golden Bay/Farewell Spit tours
- safe swimming beaches
- golf at Motueka & Tasman
- Motueka, 20-min drive away
- Nelson airport, 50-min drive
- Nelson City, 1-hr drive away

Resurgence

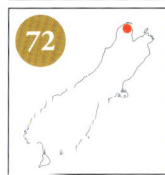
POHARA, GOLDEN BAY

Bay Vista House

Hosts Sue and Ian McCracken

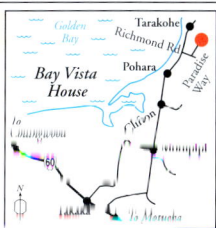

Paradise Way, Pohara   *Postal* Paradise Way, R.D.1, Golden Bay
Phone 0-3-525 9772   *Mobile* 021 378 736   *Fax* 0-3-525 9772
Email hosts@bayvistahouse.co.nz   *Website* www.bayvistahouse.co.nz

DIRECTIONS: Take SH 60 to Takaka. Turn right into Motupipi St. At roundabout turn right into Abel Tasman Dr. At "T" junction, turn left to Pohara. Turn right into Richmond Rd, then left into Paradise Way to end.

| 3 bdrm | 3 enst | Double $195–$250 | Single $175–$220 | *Includes continental breakfast* | |

Bay Vista House is situated on the hillside above Pohara Beach, one and a half hours' drive from Nelson City. The setting takes advantage of the sun and the views across Golden Bay to Collingwood and Farewell Spit. The activities and scenic sites of Golden Bay are within easy reach, and Abel Tasman National Park is just 20 minutes' drive away through Wainui Bay. All three guestrooms enjoy panoramic views of Golden Bay and open to the terrace where Sue and Ian serve continental breakfast alfresco, while guests enjoy the native birds from the adjacent nature reserve. The spa pool in the garden is popular with guests in the evenings, for relaxing and watching the sun set over the mountains of Kahurangi National Park.

FACILITIES

- 1 king suite & 2 queen bedrooms
- 3 ensuite bathrooms with hair dryer, toiletries, heated towel rails, iron & ironing board in each
- fridge, TV, tea, coffee & lounge chairs in all 3 guestrooms
- all bedrooms open to terrace
- phone, fax & email available
- fresh, healthy continental breakfast served
- outdoor spa pool with view
- landscaped gardens with views & native birdlife
- native bush reserve adjacent
- day tours/activities arranged
- courtesy passenger transfers from/to buses & shuttles
- on-site parking

ACTIVITIES AVAILABLE

- 3 restaurants within 5-min walk for evening meals
- Pohara beach, 5-min walk
- Pohara tennis court, 2 mins
- Pohara golf course, 5-min drive
- Tarakohe boat harbour, 5 mins
- Takaka township, 10-min drive
- arts & crafts of Golden Bay
- Te Waikoropupu Springs, 20-min drive away
- Farewell Spit 4WD tours from Collingwood, 30 mins
- Abel Tasman National Park, 20-min drive; Kahurangi National Park access
- golden sand swimming beaches; horse trekking
- sea kayaking & fishing; bird-watching
- bush walks; coastal walkways
- Nelson Airport, 1½ hours

Bay Vista

COLLINGWOOD, GOLDEN BAY
Collingwood Homestead

Hosts Maggie and Adrian Veenvliet

Elizabeth Street, Collingwood, Golden Bay
Phone 0-3-524 8079   *Email* maggie@collingwoodhomestead.co.nz
Fax 0-3-524 8979   *Website* www.collingwoodhomestead.co.nz

DIRECTIONS: From Nelson City, take SH 60 south over Takaka Hill to Golden Bay. At Collingwood village, turn right at beginning of Elizabeth St into driveway at sign, to Collingwood Homestead.

| 4 bdrm | 3 enst | 1 prbth | **Double $265** | **Single $245** | *Includes breakfast* |

This turn-of-last-century colonial home was built as a private residence when Collingwood was a thriving gold town of three thousand people. Adrian extended the drawing room and added decking using the original verandah posts. The leadlight windows, polished matai floors, high ceilings and open fire are also original features. Sited across the road from the beach, Collingwood Homestead overlooks the Aorere River Estuary, with a backdrop of mountain ranges. The house is set in a cottage garden with climbing roses and native tree ferns. Maggie enjoys serving elaborate gourmet breakfasts in the dining room or alfresco on the decking overlooking the sea. Two cats, the tortoise-shell Poppy and ginger Boris, complete the family.

FACILITIES

- 2 king ensuite bedrooms
- 1 queen ensuite bedroom
- 1 twin bedroom with spacious private bathroom
- drawing room with antiques, piano, open fire & verandah
- Dutch & some German spoken
- courtesy passenger transfer
- old china & glass collection
- children over 11 yrs welcome
- gourmet breakfasts served in dining room or alfresco on decking
- phone, fax & email available
- laundry available, extra
- sea views
- Boris, the ginger cat & Poppy, the tortoiseshell cat, in residence
- off-street parking

ACTIVITIES AVAILABLE

- relax on decking, opposite beach
- swimming beach, only 300m away across road
- fishing boat trips
- Farewell Spit trip
- guided walks on tracks
- bungy jumping
- squash & tennis courts
- Pupu Springs
- Settlers' Museum
- guided trout fishing
- surf-casting
- shellfishing
- Te Anaroa caves
- Begonia House
- scenic tour to West Coast & Westhaven Inlet
- Cob Valley tour to glacial north range
- Takaka, 27km away

WHANGANUI INLET

Westhaven Retreat

Hosts Monika and Bruno Stompe

Te Hapu Road, Westhaven Inlet, Collingwood, Golden Bay

Fax 0-3-524 8354   *Website* www.westhavenretreat.com

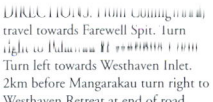

7 bdrm	3 enst	2 prbth	**Double $175–$255**	*Includes breakfast*	**Cottage rate $280 for 1–2 persons**	
			Single $155–$235	*Lunch & dinner extra*	**Extra persons $22 each**	*Self-catering*

DIRECTIONS: From Collingwood travel towards Farewell Spit. Turn right to Pakawau 11 minutes from. Turn left towards Westhaven Inlet. 2km before Mangarakau turn right to Westhaven Retreat at end of road.

The drive from Collingwood takes guests off the beaten track through the Scenic Reserve of forests, streams and lakes to the untouched wilderness at Westhaven *(see above)*. Panoramic views are captured from both the octagonal dining and living room windows in the house overlooking the ocean, and from the self-contained cottage below. Set on a 500-hectare peninsula, Westhaven includes private beaches, caves, eye-catching rock formations, rainforest, hundreds of native nikau palms and 55 llamas for guests to feed and trek with. A new highlight is the two-kilometre track through native bush to the western beach. Breakfast in the house is guests' choice of cooked or buffet breakfast. Picnic lunches and Austrian dinner menus are also available.

FACILITIES

- self-catering cottage with 1 king & 1 twin bedroom & sofa bed
- 1 twin, 1 super-king/twin & 3 king bedrooms in house
- 3 ensuites & 1 private bathroom in house, 1 with dual basins
- hair dryers, toiletries & bathrobes
- laundry available
- phone, fax, email & computer
- German spoken

- European breakfast
- lunch by arrangement
- 3-course dinner, with NZ wine selection, $45 pp
- tea/coffee, juice & soft drinks available
- crayfish, crabs, mussels
- TV in both lounges
- panoramic ocean views
- passenger transfer; helipad

ACTIVITIES AVAILABLE

- 500 ha (1,250 acres) with private beaches & secluded swimming pool
- 55 friendly llamas on site to feed, groom & for trekking
- fishing for snapper & blue jackfish
- bush walks through rainforest & natural nikau palm groves on site
- seals & penguins in season
- complimentary 4WD tour
- charter boat for fishing/sightseeing

- swimming & surfing
- private caves on site
- hiking & diving
- bird-watching
- photography
- rock climbing
- horse riding arranged
- Cape Farewell, 45 mins
- Collingwood, 1 hour
- Nelson, 3-hour drive

Westhaven

Westhaven

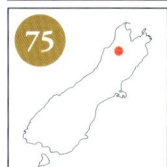

MURCHISON
Owen River Lodge

Host Felix Borenstein

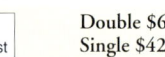

Owen Valley East Road, Murchison   *Postal* CMB 7, R D 3, Murchison
Phone 0-3-523 9075   *Email* stay@owenriverlodge.co.nz
Fax 0-3-523 9076   *Website* www.owenriverlodge.co.nz

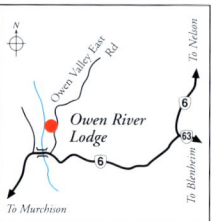

DIRECTIONS: From Murchison, take SH 6 north 20km towards Nelson. At Owen River Bridge, turn left into Owen Valley East Rd. Travel 2km to Owen River Lodge on left. Or from Nelson take SH 6 south for 110km.

4 bdrm	4 enst

Double $660
Single $425

Includes all meals
Wine extra

Set in landscaped gardens surrounded by six hectares (16 acres) of farmland overlooking the Owen River, this new lodge features almost a kilometre of river frontage. Guests are accommodated in four semi-detached suites, with all meals included in the tariff and prepared by the qualified resident chef. Full cooked breakfasts and four-course dinners, complemented by wine from the in-house cellar, are served in the dining room with views down the Owen River valley. Picnic lunches are also provided, for guests enjoying the renowned fly fishing, the local walks, mountain bike riding, or just relaxing by the river. Owen River Lodge was purpose built in 2003 and is open each October through to April, closed May to September.

FACILITIES

- 4 super-king/twin ensuite bedrooms
- 1 double ensuite bedroom for guide/chauffeur
- hair dryer, toiletries, heated towel rails, bathrobes in all 4 ensuites
- tea/coffee & fresh fruit in all 4 bedrooms
- phone, fax & email available
- children over 12 years welcome, by arrangement

- resident chef
- full cooked breakfast served
- lunch or picnic provided
- 4-course dinner served; wine from cellar, extra
- private guest lounge & bar
- central heating
- laundry available
- passenger transfer arranged
- on-site parking; helipad

ACTIVITIES AVAILABLE

- BBQ on site
- fly-fishing gear supplied
- 3 mountain bikes available
- guided full-day fly fishing tours, $625 per day
- massage arranged, extra
- bush walking; tramping
- kayaking; white water rafting
- caving; hunting
- horse riding

- bird-watching
- arts & crafts
- golf course
- Sunday markets
- local museums
- art galleries
- vineyard & winery tours
- Murchison, 15 mins
- Nelson City, 1½-hour drive north

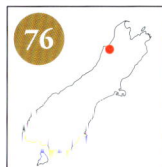

WESTPORT
River View Lodge

Host Noeline Biddulph

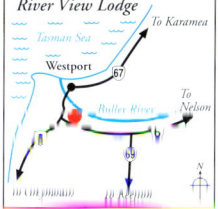

River View Lodge

Store Highway 6, Buller Gorge Road, Westport   *Postal* P O Box 229, Westport
Freephone 0800 184 656   *Phone* 0-3-789 6037   *Fax* 0-3-789 6037
Email info@rurallodge.co.nz   *Website* www.rurallodge.co.nz

DIRECTIONS: From Nelson City, take SH 6 south towards Westport. Drive through the Buller Gorge almost to Westport. River View Lodge on the right.

4 bdrm	4 enst

Double $190
Single $170

Includes breakfast
Lunch & dinner extra

River View

Overlooking the Buller River, seven kilometres from Westport, River View Lodge is located in the Lower Buller gorge, off the Nelson/Picton highway. With picturesque views of the large garden and over the river to the surrounding mountains, the contemporary guest wing comprises three king-size ensuite bedrooms, one with wheelchair access, and all opening to a verandah. There is also one queen-size bedroom in the house with a small lounge which looks onto a private courtyard. Guests are offered both buffet and cooked breakfasts, and all meals are served in the lounge/dining room in the house, with panoramic views of the river and garden. A three-course table d'hôte dinner with New Zealand wine is available, by arrangement.

FACILITIES

- 1 king/twin & 2 king ensuite bedrooms in guest wing
- 1 queen bedroom with 1 ensuite bathroom in suite in house
- hair dryer, toiletries, heated towel rails, bathrobes & heater in all 4 ensuite bathrooms
- 1 wheelchair access bathroom
- TV, radio/clock, tea/coffee, sweets, fresh flowers, electric blankets & seating area in all 4 bedrooms
- breakfast by room service
- lunch available, $10–$15 pp
- 3-course dinner & wine, $45 pp, by arrangement
- laundry, $5 per load
- phone & fax available
- children by arrangement
- panoramic river views
- barbecue available
- on-site parking; helipad

ACTIVITIES AVAILABLE

- established English-style garden
- grass tennis court on site
- therapeutic massage by arrangement, extra
- Buller River adjacent
- bush walks; golf course
- fishing
- gardens to visit
- jet boating
- heated swimming pool, 7km
- restaurants nearby
- picture theatre
- underwater & white water rafting
- beaches; seal colony
- coaltown museum
- horse trekking
- Westport, 7km away
- pancake rocks
- sightseeing by arrangement

River View

River View

Archer House

Host Kerrie Fairhall

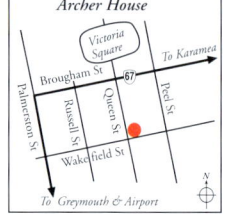

Archer House

75 Queen Street, Westport   *Mobile* 027 260 3677
Freephone 0800 789 877   *Phone* 0-3-789 8778   *Fax* 0-3-789 8763
Email accom@archerhouse.co.nz   *Website* www.archerhouse.co.nz

DIRECTIONS: From Greymouth & airport, cross bridge over Buller River into main street of Westport (Palmerston St). Turn right into Wakefield St. Archer House on left, on right-hand corner of Queen St.

| 3 bdrm | 2 enst | 1 prbth | **Double $150** | Single $140 | *Includes breakfast* |

Archer House is a Category 1 New Zealand Heritage Home, built in 1890 as an Italianate villa for Robert Taylor, a prosperous Westport grocer. It was used by the Sisters of Mercy from 1947 for 34 years, until Paul Archer bought and renovated it for accommodation. Now offering three queen-size guestrooms, with bathrooms and original open fireplaces, Archer House also retains leadlighting throughout and is furnished with antiques and artwork. A full cooked breakfast is served in the dining room or the conservatory with views to the mature garden. The spaciousness of Archer House makes it suitable for weddings, private functions, and small business conferences, or the entire house can be booked for privacy. Kerrie, the host, lives off-site.

FACILITIES

- 1 queen bedroom with private bathroom
- 2 queen/twin bedrooms with ensuite bathrooms
- cotton bed linen, TV & tea/coffee in bedrooms
- hair dryer, toiletries, heated floor & heated towel rails
- open fires in 1 lounge & 2 bedrooms
- email, fax & phone
- full cooked breakfast, with daily specials, served in dining room or conservatory
- 2 lounges with TV & piano & conservatory with verandah opening to garden
- fresh flowers; artwork
- laundry available
- children welcome
- off-street parking
- host lives off-site

ACTIVITIES AVAILABLE

- weddings, functions & conferences catered for
- large mature garden on site
- Tauranga Bay
- heated swimming pool nearby
- town centre, short stroll away
- walkways & tracks
- Coaltown Museum
- beach & bush walks
- Kawatiri Golf Links
- Bay House & other restaurants nearby
- seal colony; jet boating
- Underworld Rafting
- white water rafting
- horse trekking
- fishing; whitebaiting
- Hector Pottery
- Karamea Limestone Caves
- Pancake Rocks

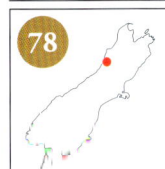

PUNAKAIKI, BULLER
Hydrangea Cottages

Hosts Karen Dickson and Neil Mouat

4224 Main Road, Punakaiki   *Postal* P O Box 47, Punakaiki, Westland
Phone 0 3 731 1839   *Email* punakaiki@xtra.co.nz
Fax 0-3-731 1838   *Website* www.pancake-rocks.co.nz

DIRECTIONS: From Greymouth, take SH 6 north towards Punakaiki. 700m north of Punakaiki Bridge to Hydrangea Cottages on right. From Westport, take SH 6 to 700m south of Pancake Rocks on left.

5 bdrm	4 prbth

Cottage rate $175–$275 for 2 persons
Extra persons $20–$30 each

Self-catering
No meals available

Just a short walk from the Pancake Rocks and Blowholes, the Hydrangea Cottages enjoy panoramic views overlooking the Tasman Sea. Built among limestone outcrops surrounded by native bush and wild hydrangeas, the four self-contained cottages comprise a two-bedroom cottage, one-bedroom studio, and two-storey house with two apartments. Each cottage is individually designed and carefully created using native timber, and sited for privacy as well as sea views. Kitchens enable self-catering in each cottage, and there is a restaurant and café just minutes walk away. Located on the rugged west coast at Punakaiki, the Hydrangea Cottages provide a peaceful escape from city life; the nearest shop is half an hour south at Greymouth.

FACILITIES

- single-party bookings per cottage
- 4 cottages, each with 1 or 2 queen bedrooms & 1 bathroom:
  – Rata: upstairs apartment & bath
  – Mamaku: downstairs apartment
  – Rimu: 1-bedroom studio
  – Nikau: 2 bedroom cottage
- hair dryers & toiletries
- Nikau includes CDs, heated towel rails & mirror
- fresh flowers; decks with sea views
- kitchenette for self-catering in all 4 cottages
- lounge in each cottage, with TV, DVD, artwork & books
- guest laundry; dryer, $2
- on-site parking
- courtesy coach to gate
- phone & internet café, 700m walk away
- hosts live adjacent

ACTIVITIES AVAILABLE

- horse trekking on site, novice to experienced; 19 horses
- swimming in river mouth, 150m
- Pancake Rocks at beach opposite
- glass blowing & craft gallery within walking distance
- dolphin swimming nearby
- canoeing, 2km north; caving
- golf courses, 30 mins – 1 hour
- west coast gardens open to visit
- restaurants, 200m – 1.5km
- greenstone/jade carving, 30 mins – 1 hour south
- tramping/hiking in Paparoa National Park
- seal colony, 1-hour drive
- Greymouth, 30 mins south
- Hokitika or Westport, 1 hr
- Franz Josef Glacier, 3 hours
- Nelson, 3½-hour drive

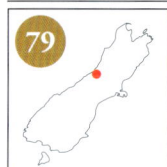

NINE MILE CREEK, GREYMOUTH
Breakers Seaside Bed & Breakfast

Host Jan Macdonald

Nine Mile Creek, State Highway 6, Greymouth   *Postal* P O Box 188, Greymouth
Freephone 0800 350 590   *Phone* 0-3-762 7743   *Fax* 0-3-762 7733
Email stay@breakers.co.nz   *Website* www.breakers.co.nz

DIRECTIONS: From Greymouth, take SH 6 north 10.5km to Rapahoe. Continue 4km over Nine Mile Creek to Breakers Seaside B&B on left. (29km south of Pancake Rocks at Punakaiki.)

| 4 bdrm | 4 enst | Double $150–$235 | Single $125–$175 | *Includes breakfast* |

Breakers

Designed to maximise the panoramic views over the Tasman Sea and Paparoa National Park, Breakers Seaside Bed & Breakfast provides direct access to a secluded West Coast beach. Recently refurbished, Breakers offers two ensuite guestrooms upstairs in the main house and two new ensuite guestrooms in the garden annex, all with sea views. Guests enjoy falling asleep to the sound of waves on the beach below. Cooked or buffet breakfast is served in the dining room downstairs in the main house. Located in a quiet setting on almost a hectare (two acres) of land on the rugged unspoiled West Coast, Breakers is only 14 kilometres north of the township of Greymouth, and close to many tourist activities. The Pancake Rocks at Punakaiki are half an hour north.

FACILITIES

- 2 queen ensuite bedrooms upstairs in main house
- 2 king ensuite bedrooms in garden annex
- hair dryers & toiletries
- cotton bed linen, TV & tea/coffee in bedrooms
- all rooms opening to balcony or deck area overlooking the ocean
- cooked or buffet breakfast available in dining room
- lunch & picnic hampers by arrangement
- guest lounge with tea/coffee, library & magazines
- internet, fax & phone on request
- laundry available, extra
- sea views from every room
- on-site parking

ACTIVITIES AVAILABLE

- private beach access for beach walks
- 0.8ha (2-acre) coastal garden
- surfing & surf-casting
- black water rafting
- caving
- sea kayaking
- seal colony
- quad-bike bush tours
- Croesus Track
- restaurants, 14km south
- Shanty Town
- Lake Brunner
- gardens open to visit
- Jade Trail at Jade Boulder gallery
- Pancake Rocks & blowholes at Punakaiki, 30km north
- Paparoa National Park
- Greymouth township, 14km south, for shopping

WESTLAND
Lake Brunner Lodge

Hosts Janice and Gary Hopper

Mitchells, Lake Brunner • Postal Mitchells, R D 1, Kumara, Westland
Phone 0 3 738 0163 • Email info@lakebrunner.co.nz
Fax 0 3 738 0163 *Website* www.lakebrunner.com

DIRECTIONS: Take SH 73 to the West Coast. From Greymouth, turn off at Kumara, & travel 22km to Mitchells & Lake Brunner Lodge. From Christchurch turn off at Jacksons & travel 17km to Lodge.

11 bdrm	11 enst	Double $533–$700	*Includes breakfast & dinner*
		Single $295–$420	**Long-term & off-season rates available**

Lake Brunner

Lake Brunner Lodge offers peace and seclusion on the shores of Lake Brunner amid temperate rainforest. Constructed from local rimu, this 1930s bungalow still generates its own hydro power and reticulates its own water. Original native timber panelling features throughout the Lodge, which has recently been refurbished. The villa behind has been built in harmony with the existing Lodge. Lake Brunner Lodge provides professional fishing and conservation expertise, with brown trout fishing a speciality and guided environmental explorations. The chef prepares a daily changing menu using fresh meat, fish and produce, which is served table d'hôte to guests on the large dining-room table with premium New Zealand wines.

FACILITIES

- 7 ensuite bedrooms in Lodge, 4 in villa – doubles & twins; lounges in 2, verandahs on 5
- views of Lake Brunner
- separate library with trophies
- guest drawing room with open fire, separate bar & wine list
- fishing & environmental guides available for discussions, by request
- landscaped garden
- professional chef in house
- tariff includes table d'hôte dinner of NZ meat & fish, classic sauces & fresh produce, premium NZ wines, extra
- continental/cooked breakfast
- separate dining room
- Donna, the boxer dog, a playful extra
- float plane & boat charter service available on site

ACTIVITIES AVAILABLE

- qualified guide services available
- fly & spin fishing – qualified guides available
- guided botanical photography
- guided bird-watching
- walking tracks
- mountain biking; golf
- canoeing; horse trekking
- trophy brown trout & salmon
- black water rafting
- visits to skilled craftspeople – woodturners, jade sculptor & spinners
- kiwi nesting sanctuary
- black petrel nesting sanctuary
- Hector's dolphin, spotted shag & seal colonies
- duck shooting in autumn
- close to Arthur's Pass & Paparoa National Parks

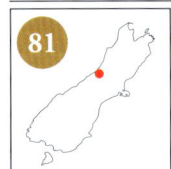

GREYMOUTH–HOKITIKA
Kapitea Ridge

Hosts Trixie and Murray Montagu

Chesterfield Road, Kapitea Creek, R D 2, Hokitika
Phone 0-3-755 6805   *Fax* 0-3-755 6895
Email stay@kapitea.co.nz   *Website* www.kapitea.co.nz

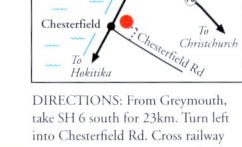

DIRECTIONS: From Greymouth, take SH 6 south for 23km. Turn left into Chesterfield Rd. Cross railway line & take 1st driveway on left, signposted to Kapitea Ridge. From Hokitika, take SH 6 for 17km.

7 bdrm	7 enst	1 pdrm	Room rate $385–$495	*Includes breakfast & interpreted coastal walk*
				Supper platter extra

Overlooking the Tasman Sea, Kapitea Ridge is nestled into the coastal landscape, with native bush and rural farmland, and provides easy access to West Coast activities. The curved roofline of each guestroom enhances the panoramic views of the ocean and mountains. The furnishings reflect New Zealand landscape colours, and one ensuite features paua shell and tiles. Guests can relax in front of the log fire, the bay window or within the large native garden. Pacific Rim cuisine, focusing on seasonal fresh local fare and fine wine, is served alfresco or in the conservatory. Early evening is a favourite time for guests to stroll on the deserted beach with Bella, a young sheepdog, or unwind in the hot tub with a complimentary glass of bubbly.

FACILITIES

- 1 suite sleeps 3 guests
- 4 super-king/twin, 1 double & 2 queen bedrooms
- 7 ensuites with hair dryers, heaters, demist mirrors, toiletries, 1 with bath & 1 with claw-foot bath
- bathrobes, fresh flowers, phone, chocolates, tea/coffee, port, TV & seating area in each bedroom
- balconies/patio with sea views
- children over 12 years welcome
- gourmet breakfast buffet
- 3-course platter-style evening supper, $40–$65 pp
- alfresco fireside BBQ
- wine cellar & liquor licence
- NZ art & gift gallery
- hydrotherapy hot tub
- native birds in coastal garden
- on-site car park
- helipad

ACTIVITIES AVAILABLE

- weddings catered, with Murray, a marriage celebrant
- reflexology treatments, extra
- mountain bikes, gold panning, pétanque/boules & clay-bird shooting on site
- fishing guide available
- 2 golf courses, complimentary fee
- dolphins & seal colonies
- Shanty town & Punakaiki Pancake Rocks tours
- restaurants, 15-min drive
- white heron sanctuary
- coastal fauna & flora walk; historic gold tunnel walk
- alpine & coastal national parks
- local artisans – in wood, greenstone/jade, gold, fibre
- scenic flights to Franz Josef & Fox Glacier tours
- white water & cave rafting

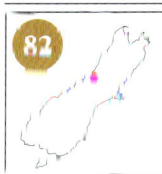

AWATUNA, WESTLAND
Awatuna Homestead

Hosts Pauline and Hemi Te Rakau   Phone 0-3-755 6834

9 Stafford Road, Awatuna, R D 2, Hokitika   *Postal* P O Box 25, Hokitika, Westland
Freephone 0800 006 888   *Email* reception@awatunahomestead.co.nz
Fax 0-3-755 6876   *Website* www.awatunahomestead.co.nz

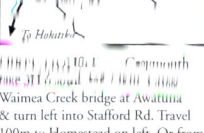

Waimea Creek bridge at Awatuna
& turn left into Stafford Rd. Travel
100m to Homestead on left. Or from
Hokitika, take SH 6 north for 12km.

| 5 bdrm | 3 enst | 1 prbth | 1 pdrm | **Double $195–$300** | **Single $175** | *Includes breakfast, dinner extra* |
| | | | | **Apartment rate $200** | **Extra persons $25 each** | *Self-catering* |

Awatuna

Awatuna Homestead is a peaceful private coastal retreat with river frontage. It is set in extensive gardens featuring natives and conservation planting including traditional harakeke or flax gardens. Pauline and Hemi are happy to share the Maori and European cultural heritage of the site and surrounding area with their guests. Timber is used throughout the colonial homestead and the wood stove provides heating and cooking facilities. Accommodation comprises three ensuite bedrooms in the house as well as a separate self-contained apartment with a further two guestrooms. French doors open from all bedrooms onto the verandahs. Farmhouse-style dining is available using home-grown produce in season. Self-catering is optional for apartment guests.

FACILITIES

- 1 super-king/twin, 1 queen & 1 twin bedroom, with 3 ensuite bathrooms, in homestead
- self-contained apartment: 1 queen & 1 twin bedroom, with 1 bathroom & full kitchen
- TV, clock-radio, seating & electric blankets in bedrooms
- hair dryers, bathrobes, toiletries, heated tiled floors & towel rails
- 1 spa bath & heated mirror

- continental or special breakfast served
- 3-course table d'hôte dinner, $55 pp, by request
- extensive wine list
- private hot tub/spa pool in bush setting
- guest laundry, fax & phone use, extra
- on-site parking & helipad

ACTIVITIES AVAILABLE

- cultural interpretative talks by Hemi
- garden walks; bird-watching
- small friendly dogs, 2 cats, horses & free-range chickens
- canoes available on site
- vintage Morris cars on site
- evening glow-worm tour
- beachcombing, walking distance
- tours & scenic flights arranged
- fishing, hunting, eco tours

- award-winning cafés nearby
- greenstone, gold, wood, pottery & fibre artists
- golf course in Hokitika
- garden tours
- paddle boat; gold panning
- historic walking tracks
- Shantytown; Pancake rocks
- glaciers; National Parks
- lakes; white herons

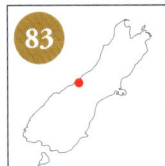

RIMU, HOKITIKA
Rimu Lodge

Hosts Helen and Peter Walls

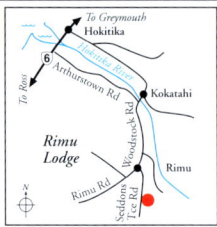

DIRECTIONS: From Hokitika, take SH 6 south. Cross Hokitika River & turn left into Arthurstown Rd. Turn right into Woodstock-Rimu Rd. Travel 2km to Rimu & turn left into Seddons Tce Rd. Rimu Lodge on left.

33 Seddons Terrace Road, Rimu, Hokitika   *Postal* P O Box 65, Hokitika
Phone 0-3-755 5255   *Mobile* 025 648 7060   *Fax* 0-3-755 5237
Email rimulodge@xtra.co.nz   *Website* www.rimulodge.co.nz

| 4 bdrm | 4 enst | **Room rate $225–$275** | *Includes breakfast* | *Dinner extra* |

Purpose built in 2004, Rimu Lodge is a contemporary retreat featuring views over the landscaped gardens blending into the native bush, across the Hokitika River valley and farmland to mountains beyond. Architecturally designed to reflect the mountains and valleys, interior colours are in soft earth tones, with four ensuites bedrooms for accommodation. A full cooked breakfast is served downstairs in the Great Room with its large stone fireplace, or alfresco on the spacious decking to which it opens, overlooking the river. Dinner with wine is available by arrangement, or restaurants are just 10 minutes north in the township of Hokitika. Guests enjoy the bush walks on site, and half or full-day trout fishing tours are popular nearby.

FACILITIES

- 4 queen ensuite bedrooms
- bathrobes, demist mirror, hair dryer, heated towel rails & toiletries in all 4 ensuites
- Egyptian cotton bed linen
- tea/coffee, fridge & tea/coffee in all 4 bedrooms; TV available
- private guest lounge with open stone fireplace, tea/coffee, video, CDs, piano
- fresh flowers

- full cooked breakfast with daily specials & fresh fruit
- 3-course dinner with wine, by arrangement, extra
- central heating
- complimentary laundry
- wheelchair access to 1 queen
- email & fax in office
- courtesy transfer from airport
- on-site parking

ACTIVITIES AVAILABLE

- BBQ available
- bush walks on site
- ½–full day trout fishing tours
- Links golf course, 10 mins
- Shanty town
- Lake Kaniere
- scenic flights to glaciers
- White Heron Sanctuary tours
- local artisans in wood, jade, gold, paua shell & glass

- Hokitika restaurants, 10km
- gardens open to visit
- airport, 10-min drive north
- Hokitika, 10 mins north
- Ross, 22km south
- Greymouth, 40 mins north
- Franz Josef & Fox glaciers, 1¾–hour drive south
- Christchurch, 3-hour drive
- Nelson, 4 hours north

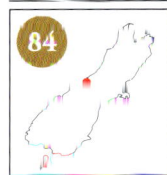

HARIHARI, SOUTH WESTLAND
Wapiti Park Homestead

Hosts Bev and Grant Muir   *Mobile* 021 385 252

State Highway 6, R D 1, Harihari, South Westland
Freephone 0800 WAPITI   *Phone* 0 3-753 3074   *Fax* 0-3-753 3024
Email wapitipark@xtra.co.nz   *Website* www.wapitipark.co.nz

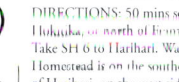

DIRECTIONS: 50 mins south of Hokitika, or north of Franz Josef. Take SH 6 to Harihari. Wapiti Park Homestead is on the southern edge of Harihari, on the west side of the state highway.

| 5 bdrm | 4 enst | 1 prbth | **Double $525**
Single $360 | *Includes breakfast & dinner*
B&B rates available | *Lunch extra* |

Kiwi Hosts Bev and Grant provide rural accommodation set in the remote south of Westland, at the gateway to the Franz Josef Glacier, 68km south. Their spacious country homestead overlooks their deer farm which specialises in the breeding of wapiti (Rocky Mountain elk), and is near the renowned brown trout fishery, Lafontaine Stream. The award-winning landscaped garden includes native ferns and flora, azaleas, rhododendrons, camellias and old roses, and a pond with an island is home to duck, swans and native birds. A convenient West Coast stop-over between Queenstown and Christchurch or Picton, this neo-colonial homestead was built in 1978 on the site of the original 1908 boarding house, coach stop and post office.

FACILITIES

- 4 king/twin ensuite bedrooms
- 1 king/twin bedroom with bathroom & wheelchair access
- fridge, fan, TV, tea/coffee, fruit basket, electric blankets, wool underlays & hair dryer
- phone, fax, email & complimentary laundry
- 2 guest lounges & trophy/games room with pool table
- off-season rates available
- full cooked or continental breakfast; B&B available
- 5-course table d'hôte dinner included in tariff
- unsuitable for young children
- award-winning garden with stone patios, pond & fountain
- elk farm & glow-worm tours
- on-site parking
- helipad

ACTIVITIES AVAILABLE

- guided hunting safaris
- guided fishing for brown trout, salmon & saltwater surf-casting
- treks & nature tours arranged
- glow-worm walk; horse treks
- bush/rainforest walks
- white heron sanctuary
- historic goldfields
- community tennis & squash court; golf course, 25 mins
- mountain climbing
- National Park tracks
- photographic opportunities
- glacier walks
- scenic flights
- heliskiing in winter
- canoeing; white water rafting
- National Park attractions
- greenstone crafts, 78km north in Hokitika

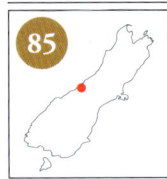

Franz Josef
Westwood Lodge

Hosts Janet and Bill Gawn

State Highway 6, Franz Josef   *Postal* P O Box 37, Franz Josef
Phone 0-3-752 0112   *Email* westwood@xtra.co.nz
Fax 0-3-752 0111   *Website* www.westwood-lodge.co.nz

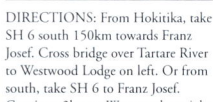

DIRECTIONS: From Hokitika, take SH 6 south 150km towards Franz Josef. Cross bridge over Tartare River to Westwood Lodge on left. Or from south, take SH 6 to Franz Josef. Continue 2km to Westwood on right.

9 bdrm	9 enst	1 pdrm	Room rate $295–$495	*Includes breakfast* *Dinner extra*
			Room rate $395–$595	*Includes breakfast & dinner*

Westwood Lodge offers eight spacious bedrooms and one suite. The large guest lounge features a picture window with alpine views. Located on one hectare in a rural setting on the outskirts of Franz Josef village, Westwood Lodge is close to the glaciers. A full breakfast is served and a three-course table d'hôte dinner is available from the chef's menu in the licensed dining room. There is a bar in the guest lounge and a full-size snooker table in the billiards room. The bedrooms and suite each have a super-king/twin bed, ensuite bathroom and include tea and coffee facilities, television, writing desk, and lounge area opening to a verandah with outdoor seating. Six of the guest bedrooms have mountain views and two open on to a courtyard.

FACILITIES

- 8 bedrooms & 1 suite, each with super-king/twin bed, TV, phone, writing desk & tea/coffee
- bath, dual basin, demist mirror, hair dryer, toiletries, heated floor & wheelchair access in 9 ensuites
- guest lounge with mountain views, open fire & writing desk
- conservatory area with mountain view & private dining by request
- children over 12 yrs welcome
- continental or cooked breakfast in dining room
- 3-course table d'hôte dinner, $45 pp
- resident chef; guest bar
- fax available
- laundry service available
- 2 cats on site
- on-site parking
- courtesy passenger transfer

ACTIVITIES AVAILABLE

- white water rafting, grade 2 to grade 5 rivers
- glacier walks
- heli-hiking
- kayaking
- bush walks
- guided bush hikes
- lake, river & sea fishing
- Franz Josef Glacier, 10-min drive south
- lunch cafés in Franz Josef village, within walking distance, or 1-min drive south
- Fox Glacier, 30-min drive south
- bird-watching
- scenic flights
- rugged West Coast scenic route
- lake paddle-boat cruises
- Hokitika township, 150km north

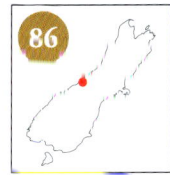

FOX GLACIER
Te Weheka Inn

Host Guy Sanders

DIRECTIONS: From Franz Josef travel south on SH 6 for 23km to Fox Glacier village. Te Weheka on left, opposite Department of Conservation Information Centre.

State Highway 6, Fox Glacier   *Postal* P O Box 90, Fox Glacier
Freephone 0800 913 414   *Phone* 0-3-751 0730   *Fax* 0-3-751 0731
Email stay@teweheka.co.nz   *Website* www.teweheka.co.nz

| 20 bdrm | 20 enst | 1 pdrm | **Double** $310 **Single** $290 | *Includes breakfast* *Dinner extra* |

Purpose-built in November 2001 at Fox Glacier township, Te Weheka Inn provides accommodation in 20 super-king/twin-size ensuite guestrooms. Each bedroom features full amenities including phone, Sky television, tea and coffee-making facilities, writing desk, ironing facilities and easy chairs. All 20 bedrooms and the upstairs guest lounge open to individual balconies, some with views over the Lower Fox and Cook River Valley. A full breakfast is included in the tariff and served in the dining room downstairs. There is a breakfast buffet as well as a variety of cooked dishes. Packed lunches are available by request, and dinner is offered during the summer season only. Guests enjoy exploring Fox Glacier and the nearby walking tracks.

FACILITIES

- 20 king/twin ensuite bedrooms
- 2 sets of interconnecting rooms
- cotton bed linen, writing desk, phone, Sky TV, tea/coffee & balcony from each bedroom
- baths, hair dryers, toiletries
- wheelchair access
- self-serve laundry facilities
- underfloor heating
- fax & email available
- self-serve continental or full cooked breakfast; vegetarians catered for
- dinner available from November to April, extra
- guest lounge upstairs with music, artwork, library, magazines, writing desk, internet access & balcony
- internal elevator/lift
- on-site under-cover parking

ACTIVITIES AVAILABLE

- guided glacier walks
- local day & half-day walks
- Lake Matheson walks
- Gillespies Beach walks
- ice climbing instruction
- scenic flights
- Fox Glacier & walks, 5-min south of village
- Franz Josef Glacier & village, 30-min drive north
- restaurants, gift shop & viewing Mt Cook, 2-min walk
- West Coast scenic route
- fishing; hunting
- bush walks; bird-watching
- heli-hiking; mountain trekking
- art & crafts at Franz Josef
- Hokitika, 2-hour drive north
- Haast, 1½-hour drive south
- Wanaka, 3-hour drive south

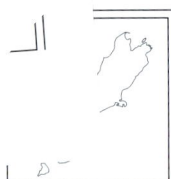

Wilderness Lodge Lake Moeraki

Hosts Dorothy Piper and Malcolm Edwards

State Highway 6, Haast   *Postal* Private Bag 772, Hokitika
Phone 0-3-750 0881   *Email* lakemoeraki@wildernesslodge.co.nz
Fax 0-3-750 0882   *Website* www.wildernesslodge.co.nz

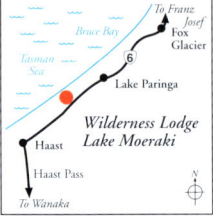

| 28 bdrm | 28 enst | Double $500–$700 Single $320–$395 | *Includes breakfast, dinner & guided activity programme* **Low-season rates available** |

DIRECTIONS: From Haast, take SH 6 north for 30km. Wilderness Lodge on left of highway. From Fox Glacier, take SH 6 south for 90km. Wilderness Lodge on right of highway.

This Wilderness Lodge is located on the southern West Coast, on the banks of the Moeraki River where it flows from Lake Moeraki, only two kilometres from the Tasman Sea. Its very remoteness is its prime feature, giving access to a pristine area of New Zealand including 1,000-year-old native trees, rare Fiordland crested penguins and elephant seals in season, or fur seals year round. This was the original road camp site in the 1960s when the Haast Road was built. In 1989 Dr Gerry McSweeney and Anne Saunders developed it into a premier nature lodge. The surrounding wilderness can be explored on foot, by vehicle or by canoe. Guided group walks and tours for a minimum of four people are offered daily at extra cost, as below.

FACILITIES

- the Wilderness Lodge mission is "to combine quality hospitality with nature discovery & conservation"
- 4ha grounds set in rainforest World Heritage Park
- 18 Lodge & 10 Garden bedrooms, all with ensuites
- spacious guest lounge, with open log fire, overlooking river
- wine cellar, liquor licence
- continental buffet of cereals, yoghurts, fruit & home-style cooked breakfast served in Riverside Restaurant
- 4-course dinner with choices
- vegetarian option on request
- restaurant or picnic lunch available for guests, extra
- guest laundry
- Lodge shop with local souvenirs

ACTIVITIES AVAILABLE

- complimentary daily naturalist-guided programme of 2 activities eg rainforest & bird discovery walks, lake canoeing, giant eel feeding & glow-worm/night sky walks
- network of forest, lake & sea-coast short to full-day walks, penguin walks & canoe trips; kayaks & canoes for guest use
- DOC Guiding Licence WC 14903

Optional guided adventures extra:

- guided 4–5 hr seal & penguin walks
- guided 4-hr sea-coast, rainforest, Hector's dolphin & historic goldminers walk
- guided ½-day canoe safaris
- trout fishing gear hire
- Fox Glacier & Lake Matheson, 1-hour drive north

Wilderness Lodges
Lake Moeraki and Arthur's Pass

(See pages 340 and 342)

New Zealand's only two Wilderness Lodges, established and owned by biologists Anne Saunders and Dr Gerry McSweeney, are a day's drive apart in dramatically contrasting natural settings. Guided activities explore the forests, rivers and wildlife around both Lodges. West of the Southern Alps, Wilderness Lodge Lake Moeraki features towering rainforest, pristine seacoast, Fiordland crested penguins and fur seals. The Lodge lies on the lake shore, 30 minutes' forest walk from the Tasman Sea. Wilderness Lodge Arthur's Pass is in the heart of the Southern Alps amid a landscape of wild rivers, tawny tussock, snow-capped peaks, beech forest, kea parrots and alpine flowers. This Lodge is located on a 2,400-hectare (6,000-acre) sheep station and nature reserve.

Above: Upper Otira Valley in Arthur's Pass National Park. Daily guided walks from both Lodges take guests into the mountains, forests, rivers & coast to discover unique native flora and fauna.

Right top: Moeraki seacoast – just 30 minutes easy walk from the Wilderness Lodge. Fiordland crested penguins, elephant seals, fur seals, Hector's dolphins and marine life are found on this coast.

Right centre: Tawaki – Fiordland crested penguin on the Moeraki coastline. Only 6,000 of these rare penguins remain in the entire world. They breed at Moeraki from July to early December.

Right bottom: Kea – the world's only mountain parrot. Cheeky and intelligent, they have little fear of humans and feed on fruit, insects and worms at Arthur's Pass, and flax nectar at Moeraki.

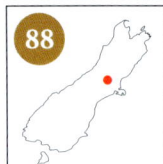
ARTHUR'S PASS
Wilderness Lodge Arthur's Pass

Hosts Kathy Dunn & David Webster

State Highway 73, Arthur's Pass   *Postal* P O Box 33, Arthur's Pass
Phone 0-3-318 9246   *Email* arthurspass@wildernesslodge.co.nz
Fax 0-3-318 9245   *Website* www.wildernesslodge.co.nz

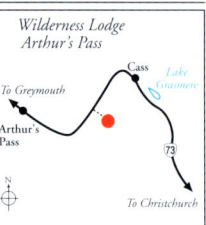

DIRECTIONS: From Christchurch, take SH 73 for 130km west. 16km before Arthur's Pass, turn left into the Wilderness Lodge driveway. Travel 1km to Lodge. Well signposted. From Greymouth travel 130km to driveway.

| 24 bdrm | 24 enst | Double $590–$980 Single $395–$690 | *Includes breakfast, dinner & guided activity programme* **Low-season rates available** |

Built in 1996, this Wilderness Lodge lies between Arthur's Pass National Park and Craigieburn Forest Park, surrounded by 2,000 hectares of native beech forest, tussock grasslands and a small lake. The Lodge is sited on the historic 2,400-hectare high-country Cora-Lynn Station, farmed since 1860, and invites guests to experience high-country nature and merino sheep farming. A network of mountain, forest, river and farm walks and complimentary guided activities introduce visitors to high-country ecology and wildlife in a wilderness setting. Day walks, and canoe and fishing trips, are optional extras. Wilderness Lodge Arthur's Pass nestles into the natural landscape and every room enjoys sunshine and alpine views.

FACILITIES

- the Wilderness Lodge mission is "to combine quality hospitality with nature discovery & conservation"
- 20 queen/twin bedrooms, each with ensuite shower & bath
- 4 king-size lodges, each with spa
- spacious mountain view lounge with fireplaces, library of NZ books
- historic David McLeod library

- 4-course dinner choices; vegetarian by arrangement
- continental or home-style cooked country breakfast
- picnics & lunches, $18–$32 pp
- Black Range conference room
- children 2–12 yrs, half rates when sharing with 2 adults
- passenger transfers from Tranz Alpine Train available

ACTIVITIES AVAILABLE

- 30km of mountain, forest & farm self-guided nature walks
- complimentary daily guided programme of 2 activities eg bird-watching, forest, wetlands, tussockland walks, shearing & spinning; night sky walks
- DOC Guiding Licence CA 15048
- picnic areas & lookouts
- trout fishing, guided by prior arrangement

Optional guided adventures extra:
- Southern Alps Otira Glacier & wildflower expedition
- Limestone Castles & lake canoeing
- Torlesse Tussockland Park traverse
- West Coast rainforests & Granite Island canoe safari
- Southern Alps waterfalls, pygmy forest & giant buttercup walk

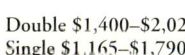

ARTHUR'S PASS
Grasmere Lodge

Hosts Oliver and Vicki Newbegin

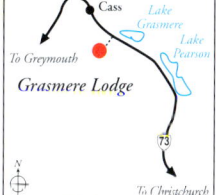

State Highway 73, Cass   Postal Private Bag 55 009, Christchurch
Phone 0-3-318 8407   *Email* retreat@grasmere.co.nz
Fax 0-3-318 8263   *Website* grasmere.co.nz

DIRECTIONS: From Christchurch take SH 73 towards Arthur's Pass. Travel past Lake Pearson for 5km. Follow Grasmere Lodge sign on left

13 bdrm	13 enst

Double $1,400–$2,025
Single $1,165–$1,790

*Includes breakfast & dinner
Lunch extra*

Surrounded by snowcapped mountains and alpine lakes, Grasmere Lodge is a high-country retreat, not far from Arthur's Pass, sited on a merino sheep station 700 metres above sea level. The Lodge now combines the old station homestead built in 1858, with new buildings which feature 13 luxurious guest bedrooms, each with a tiled ensuite including a spa bath. Before dinner, guests gather around the log fires in the spacious panelled lounge or the library and sample wines from Oliver's extensive underground cellar. The resident chefs offer a daily five-course table d'hôte menu, serving candlelit dinner to guests in the formal dining room. Breakfast and lunch are served in the conservatory or Verandah Restaurant looking out to the garden.

FACILITIES

- 13 king/twin bedrooms, each with ensuite bathroom
- all 13 ensuite bathrooms include spa bath, heated mirror, underfloor heating, hair dryer & quality toiletries
- 1 spa studio with resident therapist available
- cotton bed linen, bathrobes & slippers in each bedroom
- laundry available
- spacious lounge & bar with stone fireplace, billiards table, grand piano & original artwork
- library with stone fireplace
- French & German spoken
- children welcome, by arrangement
- covered garage parking
- helipad
- small conference boardroom

ACTIVITIES AVAILABLE

- outdoor heated swimming pool
- relaxing & enjoying views from loungers on private guest patios opening from each guestroom
- 3 pianos for guests' use
- picnicking – lunch available, extra charge
- 2ha garden & lawns
- tennis courts
- guided horse trekking
- pétanque/boules on site
- clay pigeon shooting on site
- fly fishing
- kayaks available
- mountain bikes available
- nearby lakes
- tramping in Arthur's Pass National Park
- Arthur's Pass 30km away
- Christchurch, 1½ hours away

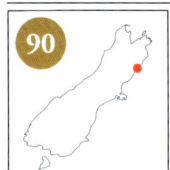

KEKERENGU, MARLBOROUGH
Kulnine Homestead

Hosts Helen and John Cundall

Kulnine Homestead

5 Kekerengu Valley Road, Kekerengu, Marlborough   *Mobile* 021 272 5761
Postal P O Box 17, Kekerengu   *Phone* 0-3-575 8911   *Fax* 0-3-575 8911
Email cundall@ake.quik.co.nz   *Website* www.kulninehomestead.co.nz

DIRECTIONS: From Kaikoura, take SH 1 north towards Blenheim for 70km to Kekerengu. Turn left into Kekerengu Valley Rd & travel 80m to Kulnine Homestead on left. From Blenheim take SH 1 south for 70km.

| 2 bdrm | 2 enst | Room rate $320–$375 | *Includes breakfast* *Dinner extra* |

Kulnine Homestead

Halfway between Kaikoura and Blenheim is Kulnine Homestead, with views to the mountains in the west and the Pacific Ocean just 180 metres to the east. Built in 1869, Kulnine now offers two spacious ensuite guestrooms, both with garden views. Set in almost a hectare (two acres) of park-like gardens, with mature native trees that attract the birdlife, Kulnine Homestead provides a tranquil escape in a rural location. The Matai Room opens to a verandah, garden and green tennis court. Breakfast is served alfresco or in the formal dining room, and complimentary canapés and boutique wine are offered before dinner, which is also available. Small weddings and honeymoons can be catered, with John as the resident chef and Helen the marriage celebrant.

FACILITIES

- 2 queen ensuite bedrooms
- hair dryer, toiletries & heated towel rails in both bathrooms
- bathrobes, cotton bed linen & writing desk in bedrooms
- Sky TV & video in TV lounge
- open fire, CDs, piano, nibbles, tea/coffee, artwork & books in formal lounge
- phone, fax & email available
- full breakfast served indoors or alfresco on verandah
- 3-course dinner with NZ wines, by request, $60 pp, in formal dining room
- pre-dinner canapés & wine
- fresh flowers & fruit bowl
- courtesy passenger transfer
- laundry; on-site parking
- closed July & August

ACTIVITIES AVAILABLE

- small in-house weddings
- James, a cat, on site
- lawn tennis court, pétanque & croquet on site
- river walks on site
- petting sheep on site
- Pacific Ocean 180m away
- back-country safaris
- whale & seal watching
- high-country activities
- award-winning restaurant nearby
- fishing trips; horse riding
- smallest church in NZ
- gardens open to visit
- Kaikoura, 1-hour drive south
- Blenheim, 1-hour drive north
- interisland ferries, 1¼ hrs north
- Christchurch & international airport, 3-hour drive south

Kulnine Homestead

Kulnine Homestead

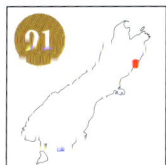

KAIKOURA
Hapuku Lodge

Manager Justin Stafford-Wilson

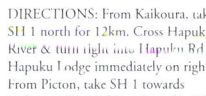

Corner Hapuku Road and State Highway 1, RD 1, Kaikoura
Freephone 0800 KAIKOURA   *Phone* 0-3-319 6559   *Fax* 0-3-319 6557
Email info@hapukulodge.com   *Website* www.hapukulodge.com

DIRECTIONS: From Kaikoura, take SH 1 north for 12km. Cross Hapuku River & turn right into Hapuku Rd. Hapuku Lodge immediately on right. From Picton, take SH 1 towards Kaikoura. Turn left into Hapuku Rd.

| 7 bdrm | 7 enst | 1 pdrm | **Room rate $320–$350**
 Apartment & tree house rate $390 | *Includes breakfast* | *Lunch & dinner extra*
 Self-catering in apartment |

Purpose-built in 2003, Hapuku Lodge provides contemporary accommodation in six spacious ensuite guestrooms and a separate fully self-contained apartment. The Lodge features a spacious guest lounge with double fire and custom-designed hand-crafted furniture throughout. The on-site multi-award winning Hapuku Café specialises in local seafood, venison and vegetarian fare. Guests can also dine alfresco on the second-storey lookout of the Lodge, and enjoy the ocean views from upstairs with the backdrop of snow-capped mountains. Set on a deer farm with a landscaped organic wind garden and olive grove, Hapuku Lodge is just 10 minutes north of Kaikoura township. Five luxury tree houses will be opened in January 2006.

FACILITIES

- 3 super-king/twin, & 3 queen ensuite bedrooms in Lodge
- 1 separate self-catering upstairs apartment including spa bath
- Sky TV, DVD, CDs, phone, tea/coffee & fridge in bedrooms
- hair dryer, toiletries, bathrobes, heated towel rails, heated floors
- fresh flowers; fax & email
- open double fire, CDs, artwork, books & desk in guest lounge
- full continental breakfast buffet for Lodge guests
- complimentary refreshments
- lunch & dinner in apartment or Lodge, or at adjacent café & licensed restaurant, extra
- laundry available, none
- courtesy transfers, helipad
- on-site parking/garaging
- 5 luxury tree houses opening 2006

ACTIVITIES AVAILABLE

- guests' pets by arrangement; cat, chickens, goat, deer on site
- BBQ on site
- bicycles & picnics available
- entertainment in Hapuku Café on occasions, on site
- diving, kayaking & fishing in ocean
- swimming with dolphins
- horse riding
- shopping & art galleries in Kaikoura township, 12km
- whale watching; bird-watching
- golf course
- 4WD tours; scenic flights
- gardens open to visit
- tramping in Arthurs Pass National Park
- Interisland ferry, 2 hours north
- Christchurch, 2 hours south

345

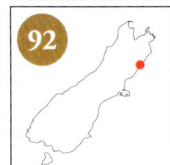

KAIKOURA
Kincaid Lodge

Hosts Helen and Judith Costley

611 Main North Road, State Highway 1, Hapuku, R D 1, Kaikoura
Phone 0-3-319 6851 *Mobile* 021 062 3600 *Fax* 0-3-319 6801
Email helen@kincaidlodge.co.nz *Website* www.kincaidlodge.co.nz

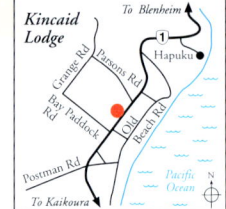

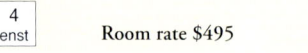

eftpos
VISA MasterCard

| 4 bdrm | 4 enst |

Room rate $495 *Includes breakfast*

DIRECTIONS: From Kaikoura, take SH 1 north towards Blenheim for 6km. Pass Hapuku School on right of main road. Driveway to Kincaid Lodge immediately on left of main highway at wine barrel letterbox.

After a century in one family, the historic homestead of the original farm, Kincaid Downs, has been totally renovated to provide accommodation. Mother and daughter team, Judith and Helen, born and bred New Zealanders, welcome guests to Kincaid Lodge, set in a large garden, with bush walks and mountain views. The four ensuite bedrooms each open to a private verandah, with garden outlooks. Helen gives sheepdog displays with Bonnie rounding up the coloured sheep, Helen was formally a shepherd in the southern alps and Foalie the horse is a favourite with guests. Just five minutes north of Kaikoura township, Hector's dolphins can be seen swimming most mornings, 20 minutes' walk away, and whale-watching can be booked.

FACILITIES

- 2 super-king & 2 queen ensuite bedrooms
- hair dryers, toiletries, heated towel rails & demist mirrors
- bathrobes & slippers; cotton bed linen; fresh flowers
- spa bath in honeymoon room
- sofa, tea/coffee & fridge in all 4 bedrooms
- children over 12 yrs welcome

- full breakfast served indoors or alfresco on verandah
- 2 open fires, nibbles, TV, CDs, piano, guitar, artwork & books in lounge
- wine list available
- complimentary laundry
- courtesy passenger transfer
- on-site parking
- helipad

ACTIVITIES AVAILABLE

- all-weather tennis court, pétanque, badminton, croquet & clay-bird shooting on site
- garden, bush & farm on site with cattle & old horse, Foalie
- sheepdog displays with Bonnie & coloured sheep on site
- mountain bikes & golf clubs available for guest use
- hunting; quad biking
- whale watching tour bookings

- restaurants within 6km
- Hector's dolphins at beach, 20-min walk or 5-min drive
- diving; kayaking; surfing
- bush walks; Mt Fyffe walks
- art galleries; winery
- Mt Lyford ski-field, 1 hour
- scenic & whale flights
- Kaikoura, 5-min drive south
- Christchurch, 2 hours south

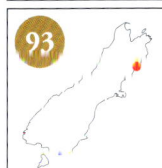

KAIKOURA
Miharotia House

Hosts Polly and Trevor Ruawai

274 Scarborough Street, Kaikoura
Phone 0-3-319 7497   *Email* bestviewsmiharotia@xtra.co.nz
Fax 0-3-319 7498   *Website* www.miharotia.co.nz

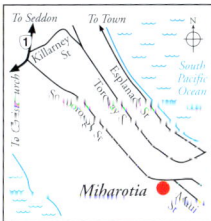

DIRECTIONS: From Blenheim take SH 1 to Kaikoura. Travel 1.7 3km past Caltex & turn left then right into Scarborough St. Miharotia on right. From Christchurch, take SH 1 north. Turn 1st right past Southbay Pde.

4 bdrm	4 ensl

Room rate $180–$290

Includes continental breakfast
Cooked breakfast extra

Miharotia is Maori for to admire, or to wonder at, with panoramic views over the Pacific Ocean and Kaikoura township to the Southern Alps beyond. Set in a landscaped garden, Miharotia offers four individually designed ensuite guestrooms with individual temperature control, opening to a private balcony. Continental breakfast includes home-made yoghurt, a platter of seasonal fruits and muffins, or cooked options are available such as fresh locally farmed eggs and local fish. Breakfast is served in the upstairs dining room, alfresco on the balcony, or room service if desired. Whale and bird watching by boat or air are popular, and guests enjoy swimming with dolphins and seals. Polly has Ngai Tahu ancestry and is happy to arrange Maori tours.

FACILITIES

- 1 super-king/twin & 3 queen ensuite bedrooms, each opening to private balcony
- cotton bed linen; fresh flowers
- phone, TV & tea/coffee in rooms
- hair dryer, toiletries, heated floor, heated towel rails & bathrobes
- wheelchair access
- phone & fax available
- laundry, $5; 1 powder room
- continental breakfast served in dining room, on balcony, or room service
- full cooked breakfast, $10 pp
- lounge with tea/coffee, Sky TV, video, CDs, books & writing desk
- email, phone & fax available
- courtesy passenger transfer
- private guest entrance; on-site parking

ACTIVITIES AVAILABLE

- spa pool on site
- native bird-watching
- swimming with dolphins or seals
- whale watching by boat or air
- peony garden flowering November/December
- conservational walkway
- groper or crayfishing trips
- art galleries
- Maori tours
- restaurants & cafés, 2 mins
- fur seal colony
- mountain climbing; hiking
- swimming; scuba diving
- golf course
- horse trekking
- skiing in winter
- Kaikoura township, 2 mins
- Christchurch, 2 hours south

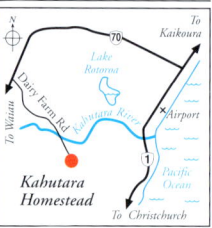

KAIKOURA
Kahutara Homestead

Hosts Nikki and John Smith

Dairy Farm Road, Kaikoura   *Postal* P O Box 9, Kaikoura
Phone 0-3-319 5580   *Freephone* 0800 273 351   *Fax* 0-3-319 5580
Email kahutarahomestead@xtra.co.nz   *Website* friars.co.nz/hosts/kahutara.html

2 bdrm	1 enst	1 prbth

Double $230–$250
Single $180

Includes breakfast
Dinner extra

DIRECTIONS: From Kaikoura, take SH 1 south for 5km. Turn right into SH 70 & travel 11km. Turn left into Dairy Farm Rd & travel nearly 6km, crossing bridge over Kahutara River to Kahutara Homestead at end of road.

Kahutara Homestead was built in 1910 on the 1,100-hectare (2,600-acre) farm that runs Corriedale sheep and Angus cattle. Named after the Australasian harriers (kahu) that live among the rocky outcrops (tara), Kahutara Homestead affords views to the Seaward Kaikoura Range and out to sea towards Christchurch. John enjoys taking guests on the 1880s horse mail route to a lookout point 500 metres above sea level, and farm activities can be viewed in season. The homestead features native rimu panelling and offers two guestrooms – a queen/twin with ensuite, and a queen/twin with a private bathroom including a claw-foot bath. Nikki serves meals in the country kitchen, with fresh New Zealand lobster a speciality.

FACILITIES

- 1 queen/twin bedroom with ensuite bathroom
- 1 queen/twin bedroom with private bathroom, claw-foot bath & bathrobes
- toiletries & heated towel rails
- hair dryers available
- fresh flowers
- phone & fax available
- complimentary laundry

- full cooked breakfast served in country kitchen
- 3-course dinner, apéritifs & NZ wine with hosts, $50–$70 pp; NZ lobster/crayfish or venison by arrangement
- tea & coffee available
- Sky TV & open fire in private guest lounge
- on-site parking
- helipad

ACTIVITIES AVAILABLE

- native birds in extensive garden
- viewing seasonal farm activities
- farm walks on almost 1,100ha hill country, includes extensive areas of native bush
- peony garden flowering November/December
- horse stud on site
- bookings for whale watching, dolphin swimming, ocean wings & albatross tours

- bookings for horse trekking
- located on scenic Alpine Pacific Triangle Route, linking to Hanmer Springs
- sea fishing trips for crayfish/lobster & groper
- trout fishing
- seal colony
- Kaikoura, 20-min drive
- Christchurch, 2 hours south

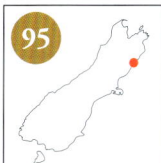

KAIKOURA
Fyffe Country Lodge

Hosts Christine Rye and Colin Ashworth

State Highway 1, R D 2, Kaikoura
Phone 0-3-319 6869   *Fax* 0-3-319 6865
Email fyffe@xtra.co.nz   *Website* fyffecountrylodge.com

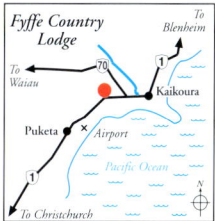

DIRECTIONS: From Blenheim, take SH 1 south to Kaikoura. Continue for 5km on SH 1. Fyffe Lodge on right of SH 1. From Christchurch, take SH 1 north towards Kaikoura. Pass airport on right, to Fyffe Country Lodge on left.

| 6 bdrm | 6 enst | 1 pdrm | **Double** $495–$867 **Single** $250–$475 | *Includes breakfast, dinner & drinks* *Lunch extra* |

This adobe country lodge was built in 1994 from rammed earth bricks and roofed with hand-split Canadian cedar shakes. Set in an English-style cottage garden beneath the snow-capped mountains of the rugged Kaikoura coastline, Fyffe Country Lodge provides uninterrupted rural views of Mt Fyffe. Only five minutes south of Kaikoura on the main highway, the Lodge offers two executive suites and four ensuite bedrooms, all with mountain vistas. Breakfast can be served in the guestrooms, and meals are available in the licensed award-winning restaurant downstairs or alfresco in the north-facing courtyard that captures the all-day sun. Seafood is a favourite, with fresh crayfish and local produce complemented by Marlborough wines.

FACILITIES

- 2 king suites with ensuite, 1 with jacuzzi, video & library
- 2 king & 2 queen ensuite bedrooms with tea/coffee
- chauffeur's ensuite bedroom
- hair dryer, cotton bed linen, robes, toiletries, TV in rooms
- laundry & dryer available
- pure artesian bore water
- tea/coffee; video library

- award-winning licensed gourmet restaurant serving fresh crayfish/ lobster daily with "Fyffe" brand Seafood Chowder
- à la carte dinner, licensed bar
- complimentary pre-dinner drinks
- continental breakfast in guest-rooms, dining room, courtyard
- phone, fax, email & photocopying available
- courtesy car; helipad

ACTIVITIES AVAILABLE

- 100-guest functions – garden parties, family reunions, weddings, small conferences catered for
- courtesy mountain bikes
- barbecue on site
- beach walks, 200m away
- arts & crafts; seal colonies
- 4WD treks; hunting deer
- swimming with dolphins

- Kaikoura shops, 5-min drive
- quad bikes for famland tours, 20-min drive south
- hiking & mountain climbing
- scenic helicopter flights; golf
- horse trekking; whale watching
- ski-field in winter, 1-hour drive to Mt Lyford
- Blenheim, 1½-hour drive north
- Christchurch, 2-hr drive south

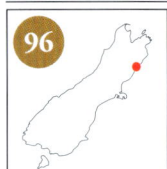

KAIKOURA
Greystones

Hosts Jane and Tony Henderson

Boat Harbour, State Highway 1, Oaro, R D 2, Kaikoura
Phone 0-3-319 5299   *Mobile* 025 640 5110   *Fax* 0-3-319 5049
Email hendersons@greystones.co.nz   *Website* www.greystones.co.nz

DIRECTIONS: From Kaikoura, take SH 1 south for 20km. Greystones on left. Or from Christchurch, take SH 1 north towards Kaikoura. Travel through Oaro & continue past Oceanview Restaurant for 100m to Greystones.

2 bdrm	2 enst	Double $845 Single $570	*Includes breakfast, dinner & drinks Lunch extra*

Uniquely located on the seaward side of State Highway One, just 20 kilometres south of Kaikoura, is Greystones, overlooking the South Pacific Ocean. Purpose-built in 1999 and true to its name, the ground floor at Greystones is clad in grey riverstone, with the upper storey in rough-sawn board and batten, roofed in slate. A spacious deck overlooks the sea, just 20 metres away at high tide, where breakfast with home-made bread is served alfresco, weather permitting. Guests can choose from an in-house dinner menu which includes New Zealand crayfish, accompanied by New Zealand cheeses, fresh fruit and vegetables, apéritifs and wine. Fur seals can be observed on the rocks in front of the house and dolphins swim by for seven months of the year.

FACILITIES

- 1 queen/twin & 1 queen ensuite bedroom
- hair dryers & heated towel rails
- cotton bed linen; fresh flowers
- lounge with open fire, tea/coffee, TV, video, CDs, writing desk & billiards room
- air-conditioning; central heating & double glazing
- email, fax & phone in office
- continental/cooked breakfast served in dining room or alfresco on decking
- 3-course dinner with NZ wine & apéritifs, in tariff
- lunch by arrangement, extra
- rooms overlooking ocean
- large deck & rock garden
- unsuitable for children
- on-site parking

ACTIVITIES AVAILABLE

- in-house billiards room
- relaxing on deck; enclosed courtyard garden
- watching sunrise over ocean
- fur seals adjacent
- ocean, 20 metres below
- whale-watching
- dolphin-watching in season from site (7 months/year)
- 4WD quad bike treks
- swimming with dolphins
- sea kayaking
- fishing; scuba diving
- 18-hole golf course
- scenic flights
- horse riding & trekking
- Kaikoura township, shops & activities, 20km north
- Christchurch City, 1½-hour drive south

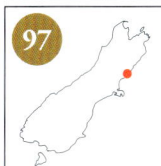

CHEVIOT
Gore Bay Lodge

Hosts Jillian and Lyndon Sigglekow

716 Gore Bay Road, R D 3, Cheviot, North Canterbury
Phone 0-3-319 8870   *Mobile* 027 233 4633   *Fax* 0-3-319 8870
Email gorebaylodge@xtra.co.nz   *Website* www.gorebaylodge.co.nz

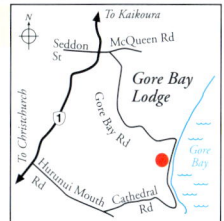

DIRECTIONS: From Christchurch, take SH 1 north for 1¼ hours to Cheviot. Turn right into Gore Bay Rd & travel 8km to Gore Bay Lodge on right. From Picton, take SH 1 south for 3 hours to Cheviot & turn left.

| 3 bdrm | 3 enst | Suite rate $160 | *Includes continental breakfast* | *Self-catering* |

Gore Bay Lodge

Gore Bay Lodge is located right on the beachfront of one of New Zealand's popular surfing beaches. Built in 2005, Gore Bay Lodge provides three self-contained suites, each with uninterrupted sea views. Continental breakfast is served in the suites, and a kitchenette in each enables guests to self-cater if desired. There is a barbecue area on site, and decking from each suite overlooking the beach is popular for alfresco dining. Alternatively, restaurants at Cheviot township are just ten minutes' drive away. From Gore Bay Lodge it is an easy drive to Kaikoura for whale and dolphin experiences, or to Hanmer Springs to enjoy the hot pools. Waipara wineries are also accessible, while closer at hand are tennis courts and a golf course.

FACILITIES

- 2 suites with 1 queen ensuite bedroom in each
- 1 suite with 1 twin ensuite bedroom
- TV, tea/coffee, mineral water & fridge in all bedrooms
- toiletries & bathrobes
- lounge with tea/coffee, TV, artwork & books per suite
- shared self-serve laundry facilities
- continental breakfast served in guestrooms
- kitchenette for self-catering in all 3 suites
- fax & email available
- fresh flowers; sea views
- guest barbecue area
- decking opening from each suite
- on-site parking

ACTIVITIES AVAILABLE

- large garden on site
- tennis court, 100m
- surfing beach
- safe swimming
- diving
- nature walks
- fishing
- swimming with dolphins
- whale watching, 45 mins
- hot pools, 1-hour drive
- restaurants, nearby
- Waipara wineries
- Cheviot township, 8km
- golf course, 10 mins
- Kaikoura, 45 mins north
- Hanmer Springs, 1 hour
- ski-field, 1-hour drive
- Christchurch City, 1¼-hour drive south
- Picton ferries, 3 hrs north

Gore Bay Lodge

Gore Bay Lodge

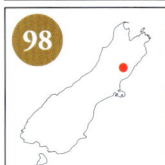

HANMER SPRINGS
Albergo Hanmer Lodge

Hosts Bascha and Beat Blattner

88 Rippingale Road, Hanmer Springs   *Postal* P O Box 79, Hanmer Springs
Freephone 0800 342 313   *Phone* 0-3-315 7428   *Fax* 0-3-315 7428
Email albergo@paradise.net.nz   *Website* www.albergohanmer.com

| 3 bdrm | 3 enst | 1 pdrm | **Double $140–$280**
Single $100–$220 | *Includes breakfast*
Off-peak & house rates available | *Dinner extra*
Self-catering |

DIRECTIONS: From Christchurch, take SH 7 to Hanmer Springs turn-off on right. Continue 9km towards Hanmer village. Turn left into Argelins Rd, then 2nd left into Rippingale Rd. Albergo Hanmer is 700m on left.

With uninterrupted mountain views, Albergo Hanmer & Alpine Villa are set in almost a hectare of alpine gardens, two minutes' drive from the centre of Hanmer. Italian for "boutique hotel", Albergo Hanmer was purpose-built in Hacienda style to catch all-day sun and features an eclectic interior design. Constructed from Oamaru stone, the Lodge and Villa include double-glazing, underfloor heating and quality fittings. Bascha and Beat specialise in designer breakfasts, providing over 10 choices to start the day: Swiss Birchermuesli, Spanish Summer Frittata, wafer-thin sweet or savoury French crêpes, or a full English breakfast. Cuisine du Marché dinners offer a blend of European and Pacific Rim cuisine, with Swiss Surprise Desserts.

FACILITIES

- 3 super-king/twin ensuite bedrooms; 1 double spa bath
- all rooms with air-conditioning, in-room tea/coffee, TV & fridge
- alpine views from all windows, sunsets & stars over Lewis Pass
- 3 living areas: formal lounge, sunny conservatory, chat-lounge with internet & coffee
- Feng shui sunken courtyard, BBQ area, waterfall & love swing
- flexitime 3-course gourmet breakfast, extensive menu
- 3–7-course tailored silver service dinner by arrangement, extra
- full kitchen for guest use
- phone, fax & email available
- Swiss/German, French, Italian & Spanish spoken by hosts
- courtesy passenger transfer

ACTIVITIES AVAILABLE

- healing retreats available
- on-site motivational workshops, exclusive "Soul for Women" retreats
- pamper packages & gift vouchers
- massage & beauty treatments on site
- honeymoons & events catered
- 18-hole golf course, adjacent
- squash & tennis courts nearby
- Hanmer thermal pools & day spa
- fishing/hunting, guides available
- restaurants, cafés, boutique shops & gym
- family maze & mini golf
- mountain bike & hiking trails; bungy jumping; jet boating; scenic flights
- guided forest/nature walks
- Kaikoura: whale watching, dolphins, kayaking & paragliding, 1½-hour drive
- 2 ski-fields, within 1 hour

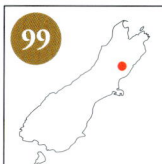

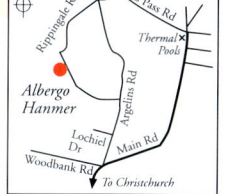

HANMER SPRINGS
Albergo Hanmer Alpine Villa

Hosts Bascha and Beat Blattner

88 Rippingale Road, Hanmer Springs   *Postal* P O Box 79, Hanmer Springs
Freephone 0800 342 313   *Phone* 0-3-315 7428   *Fax* 0-3-315 7428
Email albergo@paradise.net.nz   *Website* www.albergohanmer.com

DIRECTIONS: From Christchurch, take SH 7 to Hanmer Springs turn-off on right. Continue 9km towards Hanmer village. Turn left into Argelins Rd, then 2nd left into Rippingale Rd. Albergo Hanmer is 700m on left.

| 1 bdrm | 1 enst | Villa Rate $280–$525 for 2 persons Extra persons $80 each | *Includes breakfast* Off-peak rates available | *Dinner extra* *Self-catering* | |

The new stand-alone Alpine Villa has been built in Oamaru stone to complement Albergo Lodge (*see opposite page 352*). The villa includes a full apartment-style kitchen with double doors leading to the spacious bedroom featuring an American king bed, raised ceiling, in-room DVD/cinema system and suspended cupid sculptures created by Bascha. The large marble ensuite has a dedicated wet area and a high panorama window for uninterupted mountain views while showering. Guests have private access to the split-level courtyard featuring a jacuzzi, which is popular on starry nights. Bascha and Beat's three-course designer breakfast is served in either the privacy of the suite, alfresco, or in the main lodge at a time to suit guests.

FACILITIES

- all facilities at Albergo main Lodge (*page 354*) available for Villa guests' use also
- 1 American king/twin bedroom with ensuite bathroom
- dual basins, bidet, heated towel rail, demist mirrors & heated floor in marble ensuite
- hair dryer, toiletries, bathrobes
- double glazing, insect screens, heated floors & air-conditioning

- flexi-time 3-course gourmet breakfast, extensive menu
- in-room tea/coffee, wine list, Albergo Special Tinto drink
- dining room & lounge with double sofa-bed
- in-room DVD/cinema
- split-level courtyard with tables, sun loungers & private jacuzzi
- phone, fax & email available

ACTIVITIES AVAILABLE

- honeymoons & events catered
- in-house massage & beauty treatments; aromatherapy
- 18-hole golf course, adjacent; 'hole-in-one' golf challenge
- village cruisers & quad bikes
- argo (8WD) & 4WD tours
- back-country Molesworth farm 4WD tours
- adventure activities

- cafés, boutique shops, art galleries & museum, nearby
- night spot, bar & dancing, 10-min walk
- horse trekking
- river rafting & jet boating
- heli-tours: scenic & skiing
- local taxi service, all hours
- Maruia Springs Japanese bathhouse & restaurant, 50-min drive

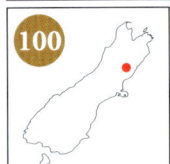

HANMER SPRINGS
Rippinvale Retreat

Hosts Helen and John Beattie

68 Rippingale Road, Hanmer Springs
Phone 0-3-315 7139   *Email* rippinvale123@xtra.co.nz
Fax 0-3-315 7139   *Website* www.hanmersprings.net.nz

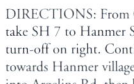

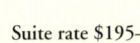

| 2 bdrm | 2 enst | **Suite rate $195–$285** | *Includes breakfast* | *Picnic hampers & massage extra* |

DIRECTIONS: From Christchurch, take SH 7 to Hanmer Springs turn-off on right. Continue 9km towards Hanmer village. Turn left into Argelins Rd, then left again into Rippingale Rd. Rippinvale on right.

Nestled in a secluded one-hectare wooded garden in a 20-hectare (50-acre) lifestyle block adjacent to the Hanmer Springs golf course, Rippinvale Retreat is located two minutes' drive from the village with its thermal springs. This country lodge was built in 2000 in traditional New Zealand colonial style with mudbrick and boasts uninterrupted alpine views. A separate guest wing provides total privacy with two cosy apartment-style queen suites. Each centrally heated suite has French doors opening to a private courtyard garden. A gourmet breakfast menu of the freshest produce can be served in the guest suites, or alfresco. Helen, who is a massage therapist, can provide in-house therapeutic massages. John can arrange free chase hunting/fishing trips.

FACILITIES

- 2 apartment-style suites: each with 1 queen bedroom, ensuite & sitting room
- cotton bed linen; bathrobes
- hair dryer, heated towel rails & toiletries in ensuites
- TV, phone, games & ironing facilities in both suites; all suites open to verandahs
- fax & email available
- laundry service available

- full gourmet breakfast in suite or alfresco in garden
- kitchenette in each suite with teas, percolator coffee, iced water, nibbles, fruit
- fresh flowers
- outdoor alpine jacuzzi
- private guest entrances
- on-site parking
- courtesy passenger transfer

ACTIVITIES AVAILABLE

- in-house therapeutic massage, by Helen, massage therapist
- black labrador, Zac, & Burmese cat, Lily, on site
- tennis court & pétanque on site
- picnicking, hampers available
- hunting, hiking & 4WD treks, with John (professional hunting guide)
- winter pamper package, extra
- village & thermal pools, 2-min drive

- restaurants nearby
- mountain biking
- bungy jumping
- jet boating; golf
- horse riding
- camera treks
- kayaking; rafting
- fishing; hunting
- winter skiing

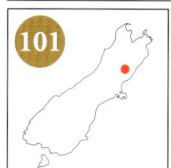

HANMER SPRINGS
Cheltenham House

Hosts Maree and Len Earl

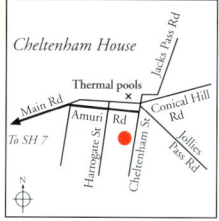

Cheltenham House

DIRECTIONS: From Christchurch, take SH 7 to Hanmer Springs turn-off on right. Continue 9km to Hanmer village. Turn right into Cheltenham St. Cheltenham House on right. From north take Lewis Pass to Hanmer.

13 Cheltenham Street, Hanmer Springs
Phone 0-3-315 7545   *Email* enquiries@cheltenham.co.nz
Fax 0-3-315 7645   *Website* www.cheltenham.co.nz

6 bdrm	5 enst	1 prbth	Double $170–$210 Single $150–$190	*Includes breakfast*

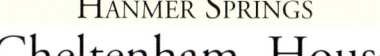

In a quiet setting in the heart of Hanmer Springs alpine village is Cheltenham House, with its extensive garden of spacious lawns, flower beds and mature trees which attract native birdlife. This double-gabled, bungalow-style residence, built in the 1930s, has been restored by the Earls since 1996. Constructed from native heart rimu, Cheltenham House features the original billiards room with rimu timber panelling, open fireplace, piano and full-size billiards table. Guests are accommodated in six spacious bedrooms with seating and dining areas, and all house rooms can be configured as twin facilities. Two bedrooms open to private sunrooms, and two are located in the garden. A full range of breakfasts is served in the guests' private rooms.

FACILITIES

- 2 queen ensuite garden rooms
- 1 queen/twin ensuite bedroom upstairs under eaves in house
- 2 super-king/twin ensuite bedrooms downstairs with private sunrooms
- 1 queen/twin bedroom & private bathroom with wheelchair access
- breakfast area with table & chairs, couch, TV, coffee/tea & electric blanket in each bedroom
- Siamese cat, Phoebe, on site
- room service – large choice of cooked breakfasts served in dining area in bedrooms
- local wine offered with hosts each evening
- open fireplace, piano & full-size biliards table in lounge/billiards room
- central heating
- laundry available
- off-street parking

ACTIVITIES AVAILABLE

- in-house billiards
- pétanque/boules on site
- high country station tours
- restaurants, 1-min walk away
- 2-min stroll to thermal pools
- shops, an easy walk away
- 18-hole golf course, 3-min drive
- tennis courts; horse trekking
- historic home & garden tours
- Christchurch, 1½ hours south
- salmon & trout fishing
- helicopter scenic flights
- kayaking; paragliding
- bungy jumping
- river rafting; jet boating
- massage & beauty therapy
- mountain bike rides
- 2 ski-fields, within 1 hour
- extensive range of forest walking & tramping

Cheltenham

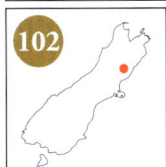

WAIPARA GORGE, WAIPARA
Claremont Country Estate

Hosts Richard and Rosie Goord

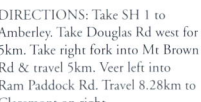

828 Ram Paddock Road, Waipara Gorge, Amberley, R D 2, North Canterbury
Phone 0-3-314 7559   *Email* relax@claremont-estate.com
Fax 0-3-314 7065   *Website* www.claremont-estate.com

 eftpos
 VISA MasterCard

5 bdrm	3 enst	2 prbth	Double $650–$1,350	*Includes breakfast & dinner*
			Single $540–$1,070	*Includes tour for 2-night stays*

DIRECTIONS: Take SH 1 to Amberley. Take Douglas Rd west for 5km. Take right fork into Mt Brown Rd & travel 5km. Veer left into Ram Paddock Rd. Travel 8.28km to Claremont on right.

Claremont Country Estate is located on the spectacular Waipara Gorge, close to the Waipara wineries, 45 minutes north of Christchurch Airport. Set on a 1,100-hectare farm that runs deer, sheep and cattle, the 1866 homestead was carefully restored in 2000 as a Lodge, and is now furnished with antiques. Guests enjoy two living rooms, a pavilion dining room, vine-clad verandahs and five bedrooms, each with a spacious bathroom. Family accommodation is available within a separate three-bedroom self-contained cottage. The Estate features a limestone escarpment and unique rock formations, including the giant sculptural "Bishop's Head" rock (*see opposite*) and ancient "God's marbles" – one-metre spheres found within the river bank.

FACILITIES

- 1 queen suite, dressing room, lounge, spa bath in ensuite, hot tub on balcony, kichenette
- 1 super-king/twin ensuite bedroom downstairs with dressing room
- 3 queen bedrooms upstairs, 2 with ensuites & 1 with private bathroom, all 3 with baths
- hair dryers, toiletries, demist mirrors & heated towel rails
- hosted apéritifs & fine dining
- family accommodation in 3-bedroom, 2-bathroom self-contained cottage
- bathrobes & slippers; cotton bed linen
- 2 guest living rooms with open fires, library, verandahs & stone-walled courtyard
- Sky TV, video, DVD & CD-player; multi-room audio

ACTIVITIES AVAILABLE

- guided 4WD tour of estate, Waipara Gorge & limestone cliffs; complimentary for 2-night stay
- scenic walks through 700ha farm with 10km of river
- hard tennis court, badminton, lawn croquet & garden spa pool
- corporate retreats & small conferences catered for
- golf course at Amberley Beach
- Amberley award-winning restaurant & shops, 12 mins
- Waipara vineyards, wine tasting & café lunches, 10–15 mins
- guided fishing – ocean & river; guided horse trekking trips
- Christchurch City, 1 hr south
- Hanmer Springs thermal pools, 1-hr drive
- Kaikoura whale watching, 1½-hour drive north

Above left: Claremont offers a four-wheel-drive safari of the Estate with its natural rock formations, such as the "Bishop's Head".
Above right: The dramatic Waipara Gorge is on site with its natural clear water swimming pool in the river.
Below: Claremont enjoys 10 kilometres of direct river frontage, with scenic walks and colourful autumn foliage.
Opposite top: The Claremont Country Estate historic homestead was built in 1886 from locally handcut limestone blocks.
Opposite bottom left: The guestrooms are individually themed, and three of the adjoining bathrooms include claw-foot baths.
Opposite bottom right: Four-course dinner is offered, including home-produced venison, lamb and garden-fresh vegetables.

© Friars' Guide to New Zealand Accommodation for the Discerning Traveller

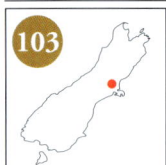

RANGIORA
Okuku Country Estate

Hosts Lorraine and Robert Smith

Rakahuri Road, Rangiora, R D 4, North Canterbury
Phone 0-3-312 8740   *Email* enquiries@okukulodge.co.nz
Fax 0-3-312 8122   *Website* www. okukulodge.co.nz

DIRECTIONS: From Christchurch, travel north to Rangiora. Take Ashley St through Loburn. Turn left at Ashley Gorge & Oxford signpost, then travel 15km, crossing Okuku & Garry Rivers. Turn left into Rakahuri Rd.

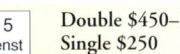

5 bdrm	5 enst	**Double $450–500** **Single $250**	*Includes breakfast & dinner* *Lunch extra*

Okuku Country Estate is set in four hectares of well-established park-like grounds with century-old trees, nestled in the North Canterbury foothills of the Southern Alps. Built in 1920 as the Rakahuri homestead for the Ensor family, Okuku has been fully renovated and now provides five guest bedrooms, mostly upstairs, with spacious dining, entertainment and living areas downstairs. Breakfast is served in the elegant dining room or alfresco, and a gourmet evening meal is included in the tariff. Guests enjoy the billiards room with its full-size table and the bar facilities. The indoor swimming pool is also popular, with adjoining barbecue and outdoor entertaining area. Christchurch City is just 45 minutes' drive away.

FACILITIES

- 2 king, 1 double & 2 queen bedrooms, all with ensuites
- fresh flowers, toiletries, hair dryers & bathrobes in bedrooms
- guest lounge with open fireplace
- tea/coffee available
- phone & fax available
- rooms serviced daily
- afternoon tea served on guests arrival
- continental & cooked breakfast, served indoors or alfresco
- lunch by request, extra
- evening meal included
- billiards room
- barbecue & outdoor dining area
- garden setting
- on-site parking

ACTIVITIES AVAILABLE

- exclusive use for conferences
- in-house full-size billiards table
- indoor spa pool
- indoor swimming pool
- in-ground croquet lawn
- in-ground tennis court
- 4ha mature gardens, with ponds, 100-year-old trees, & parkland
- bush walks on site
- fishing in river on site
- jet boating
- horse trekking
- country walks
- gardens open to visit
- golf courses
- off-site fishing
- restaurants/shops at Rangiora, 15-min drive
- Christchurch City, 45-min easy drive away

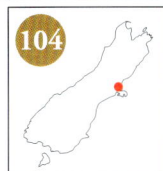

OHOKA, NORTH CANTERBURY
Stoneleigh Lodge

Hosts Liz and Chris Strack

55 Threlkelds Road, R D 2, Ohoka, North Canterbury
Phone 0-3-313 3832   *Mobile* 027 229 9954   *Fax* 0-3-365 2118
Email info@stoneleighlodge.co.nz   *Website* www.stoneleighlodge.co.nz

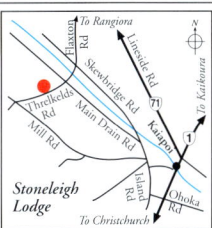

DIRECTIONS: From Christchurch, take SH 1 north. Take Kaiapoi exit & turn left into Ohoka Rd overpass. Turn right into Island Rd, then left into Mill Rd. Turn right into Threlkelds Rd to Stoneleigh on left.

2 bdrm	2 enst

Room & suite rate $295–$395   *Includes breakfast*

Stoneleigh

Featuring an alpaca farm and formal gardens, Stoneleigh Lodge is set in eight hectares (20 acres) in North Canterbury with views over the plains to the Southern Alps beyond. Designed in French chateau style, Stoneleigh was built in 2002 and offers two spacious ensuite guestrooms. A seasonal breakfast menu is offered, with a choice of breakfasts served in the formal dining room. There is a barbecue for guest use and restaurants are nearby. Christchurch City and International Airport are an easy 20-minute drive via the motorway. Guests enjoy exercising in the heated indoor swimming pool on site and relaxing in the spa pool. Bicycles are available for guest use and there are a number of private gardens open to visit in the vicinity, as well as a golf course.

FACILITIES

- 1 super-king/twin suite with spa bath in ensuite
- 1 king ensuite bedroom
- cotton bed linen, dressing room, TV, writing desk & phone
- hair dryer, toiletries, bathrobes, heated floors & towel rails
- 2 guest lounges, Sky TV, video, DVD, piano, library & writing desk
- complimentary tea/coffee, wine & nibbles
- full cooked & continental breakfast menu served
- central heating
- email, fax & phone available in library
- complimentary laundry
- children over 10 years or by arrangement
- garaging; helipad
- on-site parking

ACTIVITIES AVAILABLE

- 8ha (20-acre) alpaca farm
- formal garden on site
- heated indoor swimming & spa pools on site
- bicycles for guest use
- gardens open to visit
- horse trekking; wineries
- swimming beaches; jet boating
- international golf course
- Wilson Mill Gardens
- restaurants nearby
- historic steam boat rides
- hot air ballooning
- Willowbank wildlife reserve
- Orana Park; salmon fishing
- TranzAlpine railway
- ski-fields in winter
- airport & Antartic Centre, 20-min drive south
- Christchurch City, 20km

Stoneleigh

Stoneleigh

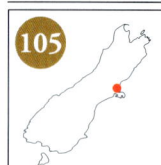

RANGIORA, CHRISTCHURCH

Frantoio Cottage

Host Barbara Smith

94 Isaac Road, Eyrewell, R D 1, Rangiora, Christchurch
Phone 0-3-310 6144   *Mobile* 027 251 1959   *Fax* 0-3-310 6133
Email bvtaylor@xtra.co.nz   *Website* friars.co.nz/hosts/frantoio.html

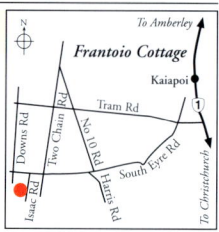

DIRECTIONS: Take SH 1 north over Waimakariri bridge. Take Tram Rd exit. Travel 0.5km & turn left into South Eyre Rd. Travel 12–15 mins & turn left into Isaac Rd. Turn right into driveway. Frantoio Cottage at end.

1 bdrm	1 enst

Cottage rate $195–$225

Includes breakfast provisions

Self-catering
Lunch hamper & dinner extra

Located on a 20-hectare (50-acre) olive grove and nut orchard, Frantoio Cottage provides self-contained accommodation for one couple in a rural setting, 30 minutes north of Christchurch City. Purpose built in 2003, this contemporary cottage is named after an Italian variety of olives grown on the property. Adjacent are vineyards and there are many other activities within half an hour's drive. The cottage comprises one super-king/twin bedroom opening to private decking, an ensuite including a bath, a lounge which also opens to the deck, and a fully equipped kitchen complete with dishwasher. Breakfast provisions are supplied, and dinner can be served at the cottage by arrangement. Restaurants are just a short drive away.

FACILITIES

- 1 self-contained cottage with 1 super-king/twin bedroom
- 1 ensuite bathroom includes bath, hair dryer & toiletries
- cotton bed linen; bathrobes
- fresh flowers
- original artwork
- sundeck from lounge & bedroom
- log fire, TV, CD, DVD in lounge
- Italian & basic Japanese spoken

- breakfast provisions supplied
- lunch hamper, extra
- dinner, $25–$40 pp
- full kitchen for self-catering
- basic provisions, nibbles, wine & mineral water supplied
- laundry service available
- pets on site
- on-site parking

ACTIVITIES AVAILABLE

- wildlife reserve nearby
- Clydesdale wagon trips
- gardens & nurseries to visit
- 3 safe swimming beaches
- trout & salmon fishing
- horse riding & trekking
- jet-boating
- hot air ballooning
- wine trails, 40-min drive
- Antarctic Centre, 25 mins

- vineyard restaurant, 7 mins
- Kaiapoi/Rangiora/Oxford, 15 mins
- golf courses including Clearwater Resort International, 20 mins
- Christchurch & airport, 30 mins
- Port of Lyttelton cruises, 45 mins
- Hanmer Springs thermal alpine village; Akaroa, each 80 mins
- TranzAlpine scenic train day trip
- 4 ski-fields, 1-hour drive

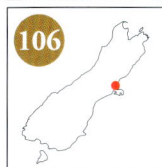

BELFAST, CHRISTCHURCH
Devondale House

Hosts Sue and Stuart Fox   *Phone* 0-3-323 6616

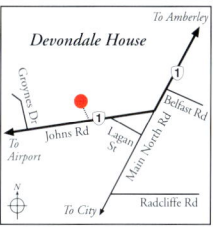

66 Johns Road, Belfast, Christchurch
Freephone 0800 167 735   *Mobile* 027 200 7236   *Fax* 0-3-323 8723
Email info@devondalehouse.co.nz   *Website* www.devondalehouse.co.nz

DIRECTIONS: From north take SH 1 right into Johns Rd. Devondale House on right by statue. Take private road towards security gate. Intercom on right, 3m before gate. Press Fox button. From airport, take Johns Rd for 6km.

| 2 bdrm | 2 enst | Room rate $210–$275 | *Includes breakfast* | *Dinner extra* |

Devondale House is a rural retreat, just minutes from the city, yet in a quiet location behind security gates adjacent to a peaceful walkway through farmland. Set in extensive gardens, complete with tennis court, Devondale offers guests spacious ensuite bedrooms with views to the Southern Alps, quality linen, tea and coffee-making facilities, writing desks and fresh flowers. A traditional English breakfast is served in the sunny breakfast room or alfresco on the terrace. Popular activities with guests include a fireside evening meal at Willowbank wildlife restaurant, with deer outside the window, followed by a guided night tour to see live kiwi. Clearwater Golf Resort nearby also offers fine dining. Molly, a West Highland White terrier, is a friendly extra.

FACILITIES

- East Room: spacious queen bedroom & spa bath in ensuite
- West Room: spacious king/twin bedroom with colonial bed & mist-free mirrors in ensuite
- hair dryers, toiletries & heated towel rails in both ensuites
- TV, phone, writing desk, fresh flowers, chocolates & tea/coffee in both bedrooms
- quality bed linen; fresh flowers
- breakfast served in dining room or alfresco on terrace
- dinner by request, extra
- complimentary sherry or port
- views to Southern Alps
- private guest lounge
- security gate
- statue marks entrance
- secure off-street parking

ACTIVITIES AVAILABLE

- tennis court on site
- Clearwater Golf Course & restaurant adjacent
- Willowbank restaurant & wildlife reserve, includes kiwi
- Groynes recreation/picnic area with fish & birdlife, nearby
- Antarctic Centre, 6-min drive
- Orana Park
- jet boating on Waimakariri River
- Rosebank winery & restaurant, 2-min drive
- Russley Golf Course
- seasonal trout fishing
- guided salmon fishing
- Botanic Gardens, 12 mins
- private gardens to visit
- airport 7–8-min drive
- City Centre, 15-min drive
- local ski-field, 1¼ hours

Devondale

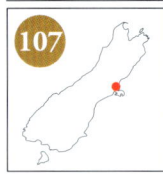

HAREWOOD, CHRISTCHURCH
Clearview Lodge

Hosts Sue and Robin Clements

8 Clearwater Avenue, Christchurch
Phone 0-3-359 5797   *Mobile* 021 727 883   *Fax* 0-3-358 9131
Email relax@clearviewlodge.com   *Website* www.clearviewlodge.com

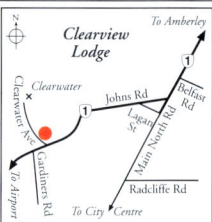

DIRECTIONS: From north, follow SH 1 right into Johns Rd. Turn right into Clearwater Ave. After 50m turn right into Clearview driveway. From airport, take Russley Rd/Johns Rd (SH 1) for 6km to Clearwater Ave.

| 3 bdrm | 3 enst | Room rate $225–$325 | *Includes breakfast Lunch & dinner extra* |

Clearview Lodge

Set in four hectares (10 acres), surrounded by an olive grove, vineyard and apple orchard, at the entrance to Clearwater Golf Resort, Clearview Lodge was built in 2001 in French chateau-style. With views to the Port Hills and Southern Alps beyond, Clearview offers three ensuite guestrooms. The Pinot and Frantoio Rooms are upstairs adjacent to the guest lounge opening to a large balcony. Downstairs is the Braeburn Room with wheelchair access and the guest dining room. The Pinot and Braeburn ensuites include a bath and the showers have massage nozzles. A full breakfast including home baking and home-made jams is served in the conservatory, dining room or alfresco on the patio in summer. Lunch and dinner are available by arrangement.

FACILITIES

- Pinot Room: 1 super-king/twin ensuite bedroom & bath upstairs
- Braeburn Room: 1 super-king/twin ensuite bedroom with bath & wheelchair access downstairs
- Frantoio Room: 1 super-king/twin ensuite bedroom upstairs
- cotton bed linen, phone & TV
- hair dryers, heated floors & bathrobes in all 3 ensuites
- fresh flowers

- continental & cooked breakfast served
- lunch & dinner, by prior arrangement, extra
- email & fax available
- guest lounge with open fireplace, opens to balcony
- guestrooms serviced daily
- private guest entrance
- on-site parking

ACTIVITIES AVAILABLE

- 8-seater spa pool
- pétanque on site
- barbecue available
- honeymoons, weddings & conferences catered for
- Clearwater Golf Resort, 2-min drive away
- Groynes park & picnic area
- Willowbank Wildlife Reserve with kiwi house

- restaurants, nearby
- seasonal trout/salmon fishing
- St Helena Vineyard
- wineries; berry farm
- Orana Park
- International Airport & Antarctic Centre, 10 mins
- City Centre, 15-min drive
- Waimakariri River jet boating
- ski-fields, 1 hr 15-min drive

Clearview Lodge

Clearview Lodge

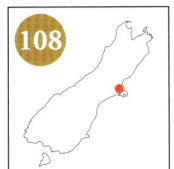

UPPER RICCARTON, CHRISTCHURCH
Huntley House

Manager David French

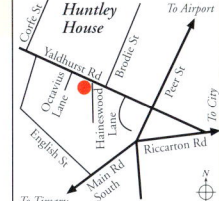

67 Yaldhurst Road, Upper Riccarton, Christchurch
Phone 0-3-348 8435   *Email* reservation@huntleyhouse.co.nz
Fax 0-3-341 6833   *Website* www.huntleyhouse.co.nz

 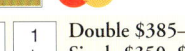

DIRECTIONS: From airport take Memorial Ave & turn right into Grahams Rd. Turn left into Waimairi Rd. Veer right into Peer St & turn right into Yaldhurst Rd. Travel to Huntley House on left.

17 bdrm	17 enst	1 pdrm

Double $385–$535
Single $350–$480

Includes breakfast
Self-catering option in apartments

Dinner extra

Huntley House

Huntley House is a colonial homestead built in 1876 for an early settler, JH Twentyman, and set in a mature hectare of park-like gardens fringed by established English trees. Now converted into a boutique hotel, but retaining many historical features, Huntley House offers 17 well-appointed ensuite guest bedrooms, including two self-contained garden apartments with two bedrooms in each. A breakfast buffet is complemented with a cooked menu selection to order, prepared by the resident chef, who also provides dinner for guests as required. There are many popular on-site activities such as playing snooker or darts indoors, and enjoying the garden, swimming pool or pétanque outdoors. The City Centre is just 10 minutes' drive away.

FACILITIES

- 4 homestead bedrooms, 4 garden bedrooms, 4 garden suites, 2 garden 2-bedroom apartments & 1 cabin
- spa bath, double shower, hair dryer, toiletries, bidet, bathrobes, wheelchair access, heated mirror, floor & towel rails in 17 ensuites
- cotton bed linen, Sky TV, DVD, CDs, writing desk, phone, broadband, fan, central heating/gas fire, tea/coffee, mineral water, mini-bar & fridge in 17 bedrooms

- full breakfast served
- 4-course dinner, $75 pp
- kitchens in 2 apartments
- guest lounge with open fire, bar, tea/coffee, nibbles, Sky TV, video & DVD
- laundry; fresh flowers
- email, fax & phone
- courtesy passenger transfer
- on-site parking

ACTIVITIES AVAILABLE

- swimming pool on site
- pétanque & croquet on site
- darts & snooker on site
- 1ha mature gardens
- tennis courts
- golf courses & mini-golf
- public parks
- gardens open to visit
- flying
- walks

- restaurants, within 3km
- hot air ballooning
- wildlife park
- museum & art gallery
- Hagley Park & Botanic Gardens
- Riccarton shopping nearby, or in City Centre, 7km
- Christchurch International Airport & Antarctic Centre, 10-min drive

Huntley House

Huntley House

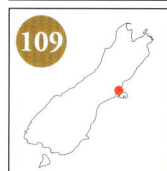

FENDALTON, CHRISTCHURCH

Tangley on Clyde

Hosts Janet and Ian Wallace

193 Clyde Road, Fendalton, Christchurch
Phone 0-3-351 8940   *Mobile* 027 290 9441   *Fax* 0-3-351 8941
Email stay@tangley.co.nz   *Website* www.tangley.co.nz

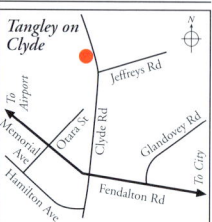

DIRECTIONS: From Christchurch International Airport, take Memorial Ave & travel to end at cross-roads. Turn left into Clyde Rd & travel to Tangley on Clyde on left.

2 bdrm	2 enst

Room rate $400–$495   *Includes breakfast*

Tangley On Clyde is an Edwardian homestead set in an English garden in the heart of Christchurch. Originally built in 1906, Tangley on Clyde has been restored and renovated extensively to provide accommodation. The Gunwalloe suite includes a king-size bedroom, an adjoining sunroom, and an ensuite with a spa bath. The Ardlochan room has a spacious super-king/twin bed and ensuite. Breakfast is served in the dining room with an open fireplace to warm it in winter, and there is a grand piano for guests to play in the living room, which opens to a sun terrace and the sheltered garden with its mature specimen trees and birdlife. Many ethnic restaurants are a short walk away and all Christchurch amenities are within easy access.

FACILITIES

- Gunwalloe suite: 1 king bedroom with spa bath in ensuite & 2 singles in adjoining sunroom
- Ardlochan room: 1 super-king/twin bedroom with ensuite
- cotton bed linen
- hair dryer, toiletries, bathrobes, demist mirror, heated floor & towel rails in all bathrooms
- living room with open fire, piano, tea/coffee, video & DVD
- full cooked or continental breakfast served
- email, fax & phone available
- fresh flowers
- laundry facilities
- children welcome
- 1 friendly cat on site
- honeymoons catered for
- on-site parking

ACTIVITIES AVAILABLE

- large cottage garden on site
- buses to CBD from front gate
- Central City, 5-min drive
- Avon River, 10-min walk
- Canterbury University, 10-min walk away
- Arts Centre
- Hagley Park
- gardens open to visit
- Antarctic Centre, 5 mins
- many restaurants, cafés & bars, 5-min walk away
- Cathedral Square, 10 mins
- Christchurch Botanic Gardens, 5-min drive
- wineries
- heritage tram rides
- beaches
- Christchurch International Airport, 5-min drive

PAPANUI, CHRISTCHURCH
Heatherston

Hosts Jan and Murray Binnie

46 Searells Road, Papanui, Christchurch
Phone 0-3-355 3239   *Fax* 0-3-355 3259   *Mobile* 027 418 8961
Email enquiries@heatherston.co.nz   *Website* www.heatherston.co.nz

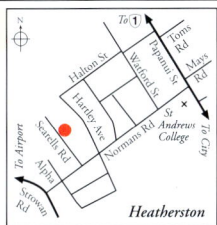

DIRECTIONS: From Christchurch airport, take Memorial Ave. Turn left into Glandovey Rd, thru roundabout, then left into Strowan Rd. Turn left into Normans Rd & 2nd left into Searells Rd, to Heatherston on right.

3 bdrm	3 enst	Double $150–$200	Single $120–$160	*Includes breakfast*

Set in a quiet suburban street in Christchurch, Heatherston was purpose-built in 2003 to offer boutique accommodation. Professionally designed, Heatherston provides an upstairs guest floor with three ensuite bedrooms, separated by a relaxing area with a balcony. Peace and quiet is ensured by the double-glazed windows, and quality furnishings include a claw-foot bath in the queen ensuite. Breakfast is served downstairs, at separate tables in the dining room, with a continental buffet and cooked options. The front garden at Heatherston features a fountain that is lit at night. Just 10 minutes' drive from the City Centre, and 10 minutes from the airport, guests at Heatherston are within walking distance of restaurants and close to bus routes.

FACILITIES

- upstairs guest floor
- 1 queen ensuite bedroom upstairs, with claw-foot bath
- 2 king/twin ensuite bedrooms upstairs, 1 with extra single bed
- hair dryer, toiletries, demist mirror, heated towel rails & heated floor in all 3 ensuites
- TV & tea/coffee in bedrooms
- cotton bed linen; fresh flowers

- continental/cooked breakfast served in dining room
- relaxing upstairs area with fridge, books, games, phone & opens to small balcony
- piano in lounge downstairs
- powder room; central heating
- basic French spoken
- fax & email available
- 2 off-street car parks

ACTIVITIES AVAILABLE

- Merivale Mall, 2 blocks away
- local bars, cafés & restaurants
- small boutique local shops
- City Centre, 10-min drive
- Cathedral Square, 10 mins
- Arts Centre, 10 mins
- weekend markets
- Avon River & Hagley Park
- Christchurch Botanic Gardens

- wineries; Orana Park
- private gardens open to visit
- gondola rides with city views
- Antarctic Centre, 10 mins
- airport, 10-min drive
- TranzAlpine express
- Akaroa day trips
- ski-fields, 1 hour away
- Hanmer Springs, 1½ hours

The Charlotte Jane

Hosts Moira and Siegfried Lindlbauer

110 Papanui Road, Merivale, Christchurch
Phone 0-3-355 1028   *Email* charjane@ihug.co.nz
Fax 0-3-355 8882   *Website* friars.co.nz/hosts/charlottejane.html

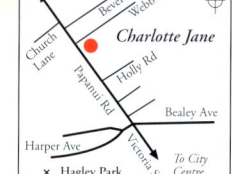

DIRECTIONS: Within walking distance of Christchurch City Centre. Take Victoria St to Bealey Ave. Travel along Papanui Rd for 4 blocks to Webb St on right. The Charlotte Jane is on corner of Papanui Rd & Webb St.

12 bdrm	12 enst

Double $355–$495
Single $200–$250

Includes breakfast
Dinner extra

The original Rangi Ruru School, built in 1891, has been transformed into a boutique hotel with adjacent Alexander Lawrence conservatory restaurant. An etched-glass window depicts the *Charlotte Jane*, one of the First Four Ships to Christchurch in 1850. Colonial antiques, claw-foot baths and a four-poster bed in the honeymoon suite complement the ornate arched windows and original open fireplaces, now gas. Other bedrooms feature sleigh beds and bedheads, and four rooms include writing desks. Eleven ensuites incorporate bidets and three feature spa baths. Attention to detail is evident throughout, with native kauri and rimu used extensively. Although within walking distance of the City Centre, double glazing ensures peace and quiet.

FACILITIES

- 10 king bedrooms, including 1 honeymoon suite with 4-poster
- 2 twin bedrooms with king singles
- 12 ensuite bathrooms with hair dryers, heated towel rails & toiletries, 11 bidets, 3 spa baths & 2 antique claw-foot baths
- cotton bed linen; fresh flowers
- 2 wheelchair access bedrooms
- phones, TV, videos & latest movie cassettes in bedrooms
- full breakfast buffet
- à la carte dinner in restaurant
- BBQ courtyard; licensed
- tea/coffee in dining room
- private guest lounge & library; reception area
- fax & computer available
- children over 14 yrs welcome
- German, French & Spanish spoken; off-street parking

ACTIVITIES AVAILABLE

- range of gourmet restaurants & cafés, within walking distance
- Merivale Village, an easy walk
- Victoria St premier shops
- Arts Centre, 12-min walk
- 12-hole Hagley golf course
- Christchurch Casino
- Botanic Gardens, 10-min walk
- riverside jogging track
- Avon River, 10-min walk
- City Centre, 15-min walk
- airport, 15-min drive
- Antarctic Centre
- hot air ballooning
- museum
- gondola
- gardens open to visit
- Ferrymead Historic Park
- day trips to Akaroa & Banks Peninsula

Charlotte Jane

Charlotte Jane

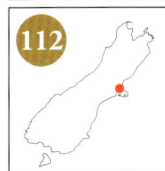

MERIVALE, CHRISTCHURCH
Elm Tree House

Hosts Karen and Allan Scott

236 Papanui Road, Merivale, Christchurch
Phone 0-3-355 9731   *Mobile* 025 232 5058   *Fax* 0-3-355 9753
Email stay@elmtreehouse.co.nz   *Website* www.elmtreehouse.co.nz

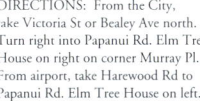

DIRECTIONS: From the City, take Victoria St or Bealey Ave north. Turn right into Papanui Rd. Elm Tree House on right on corner Murray Pl. From airport, take Harewood Rd to Papanui Rd. Elm Tree House on left.

6 bdrm	6 enst

Room rate $235–$325 for 2 persons
Seasonal rates available   *Includes breakfast*

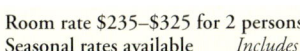   

Elm Tree House, named after the large weeping elm on the front lawn, has a Historic Places classification. Built in 1920 by the England Brothers, this home was later owned by a former Canterbury Member of Parliament. Native timbers and leadlight windows are used throughout both storeys. Set in a large Merivale garden, this large English colonial-style house is only 15 minutes' walk from the City Centre, or 15 minutes' drive from the airport and Tranz Alpine rail station. A continental or cooked breakfast is served in the dining room, where French doors open to the lawn. Licensed restaurants and cafés are 200 metres away in Merivale Village. Complimentary tea and coffee are available in guests' bedrooms and the spacious guest lounge.

FACILITIES

- 2 king/twin, 1 super-king/twin & 2 queen ensuite bedrooms upstairs
- 1 super-king/twin bedroom downstairs
- hair dryer & heated towel rails in all 6 ensuite bathrooms
- electric blankets & hypo-allergenic pillows on all beds
- laundry & dry cleaning available
- fresh flowers & direct-dial phones in all bedrooms
- breakfast in dining room
- outdoor dining area
- complimentary tea/coffee, port & sherry in bedrooms & lounge
- spacious lounge with gas fire, TV & Wurlitzer
- double glazing
- fax, email & internet
- off-street parking

ACTIVITIES AVAILABLE

- walled garden on site
- Merivale Mall, 200m walk
- antique shops
- 6 licensed restaurants
- turn-of-century large timber homes in area
- Hagley Park, 15-min walk
- City Centre, 15-min walk
- Tranz Alpine express, 15-min drive
- airport, 15-min drive
- private gardens open to visit
- golf
- Arts Centre
- Cathedral Square
- Botanic Gardens
- Christchurch Casino
- Avon River
- assistance with South Island itineraries

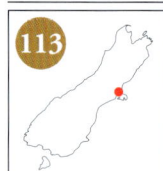

CHRISTCHURCH CITY
Springfield Cottage

Hosts Noeleen and Michael Clarke

137 Springfield Road, St Albans, Christchurch
Phone 0-3-377 1368   *Email* relax@springfieldcottage.co.nz
Website www.springfieldcottage.co.nz

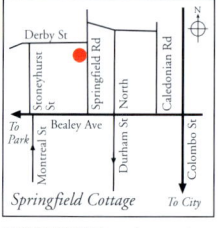

1 bdrm	1 prbth

Cottage rate $150–$250
2-night minimum stay

Breakfast provisions extra
Self-catering

DIRECTIONS: From airport, take Memorial Ave & continue into Fendalton Rd. At "T" junction, turn left into Harper Ave & continue into Bealey Ave. Turn left into Springfield Rd. Springfield Cottage on left.

Originally built in the 1870s, Springfield Cottage was completely renovated in 2002 for guest accommodation. This self-contained heritage cottage is located only two kilometres from the City Centre, yet guests enjoy the quietness of its private garden. Springfield Cottage offers a queen-size bedroom and private bathroom for one couple. The living area includes a gas fire, television, DVD-player, CD-player, games, and small library of books, CDs and DVDs. Breakfast provisions can be supplied or all meals can be self-catered in the fully equipped kitchen. A sunroom looks into the garden courtyard where alfresco dining and the gas barbecue are popular with guests. Local restaurants and cafés are within walking distance.

FACILITIES

- single-party bookings only
- 1 self-contained heritage cottage with 1 queen bedroom
- 1 private bathroom
- hair dryer, toiletries, & heated towel rails
- bathrobes
- lounge area with TV, DVD, music, CD-player & books
- 1 sunroom with writing desk

- provisions for continental & cooked breakfasts, extra
- full kitchen for self-catering
- gas fire & electric heating
- guest phone
- fresh flowers
- laundry facilities
- gas BBQ in garden courtyard with outdoor furniture
- hosts live off-site

ACTIVITIES AVAILABLE

- pétanque/boules on site
- cottage garden on site
- golf course; fitness track; horse riding; boating in Hagley Park
- carriage rides; historic trams
- Botanic Gardens
- private gardens open to visit
- punting on Avon River
- Arts Centre
- art galleries; museums

- restaurants at Merivale Mall & City Centre
- Cathedral Square, 2km
- guided city walking tours
- boutique shopping
- Christchurch Casino
- theatres; night clubs & wine bars
- Antarctic Centre, 20 mins
- airport, 20-min drive

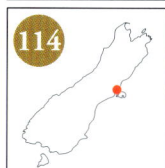

CHRISTCHURCH CITY
Hambledon

Hosts Jo and Calvin Floyd

103 Bealey Avenue, Christchurch
Phone 0-3-379 0723   *Email* hambledon@clear.net.nz
Fax 0-3-379 0758   *Website* www.hambledon.co.nz

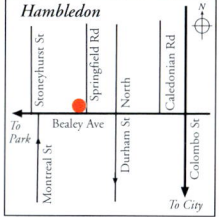

DIRECTIONS: From the City, take Colombo St north to Bealey Ave. Turn left & travel to Springfield Rd on right. Hambledon is on the corner of Bealey Ave & Springfield Rd.

| 5 bdrm | 4 enst | 1 pdrm | **Room rate $250–$295** | *Includes breakfast* | *Self-catering in cottages* |

Hambledon was designed by Samuel Farr circa 1856, for George Gould, a city father who donated the chestnut trees along Bealey Avenue. Today, guests still drive on the carriageway and enter the quiet centrally heated hallway with its timber panelling, sweeping staircase, antique furniture and oriental rugs. Four guest suites, all with ensuite bathrooms, are furnished with collectables and antiques including four-posters and half-tester beds. Full breakfast is served in the Victorian-style dining room, with a special cooked dish each day. Guests can relax on the bay window seat in the private lounge, in the conservatory, or on the wisteria-clad verandah opening to the cottage garden. There are two self-contained heritage cottages on site too.

FACILITIES

- Master Suite: 4-poster king bedroom with sunroom
- Nursery Suite: 1 queen bedroom, 1 twin bedroom & dressing room
- Gertrude's Suite: 1 Victorian king-size half-tester & 1 single bed
- Bishop's Suite: 4-poster king-size bedroom with dressing room & extra single bed
- secluded mature cottage garden
- fax & email available

- crested cotton bed linen, flowers, direct-dial phones, fridge, hair dryers, heating, tea/coffee, TV in all rooms
- complimentary sherry/port, library, guest lounge, wide verandahs & conservatories
- laundry & drycleaning
- 2 self-catering heritage cottages for 2–6 guests
- ample off-street parking

ACTIVITIES AVAILABLE

- 10-min easy walking distance to:
  – Hagley Park & golf course
  – Arts Centre, museum, art galleries
  – Cathedral Square, Town Hall
  – casino, restaurants, theatres
  – city & Merivale shops
  – Botanic Gardens & Mona Vale
  – punting on the Avon
  – walking tours, antique trails
  – Worcester Boulevard trams

- Tranz Alpine day trip
- hot air ballooning
- Antarctic Centre
- gondola; golf
- Dean's Bush
- gardens open to visit
- Ferrymead historic park
- wildlife park & reserve
- QEII pool & centre

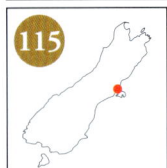

CHRISTCHURCH CITY
Eliza's Manor on Bealey

Hosts Ann Zwimpfer and Harold Williams

82 Bealey Avenue, Christchurch
Freephone 0800 366 859   *Phone* 0-3-366 8584   *Fax* 0-3-366 4946
Email info@themanor.co.nz   *Website* www.themanor.co.nz

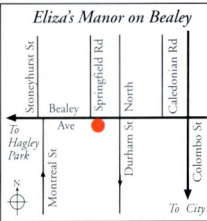

Eliza's Manor on Bealey

DIRECTIONS: From the City, take Colombo St north to Bealey Ave. Turn left & travel to Eliza's Manor on left. From airport, take Memorial Ave to Fendalton Rd. Turn left into Harper Ave & continue into Bealey Ave.

| 8 bdrm | 8 enst | Room rate $175–$265 House rate available | *Includes breakfast* *Private functions extra* |

This Victorian manor house, built in 1861 and carefully restored with antiques and art, now provides eight individually designed guestrooms, each with an ensuite. Original architectural features include the grand entrance hall, ornately carved staircase, and stained glass leadlight windows. The guest lounge incorporates a small guest bar opening to the secluded flagstone courtyard, where gardens complement the fountain, while the established front garden has four notable English trees. Breakfast is served in the dining room or alfresco in the courtyard, depending on the season. Easily accessible, Eliza's Manor on Bealey is within walking distance of the City Centre with its restaurants and cafés, as well as many of the attractions of Christchurch.

FACILITIES

- 8 bedrooms with king, queen & twin bed options
- 8 ensuites, 1 with spa bath, 1 with double French tub
- direct dial phone, tea/coffee, hair dryers, cotton bed linen & electric blankets in all bedrooms
- wedding & function facilities, up to 120 guests catered for
- gas flame fireplaces in hall, dining room & bar

- cooked breakfast served in dining room or courtyard
- guest lounge & bar
- themed evenings & theatre restaurant for function bookings, by arrangement
- complimentary email & fax facilities available
- laundry & dry cleaning, by arrangement, extra
- off-street parking

ACTIVITIES AVAILABLE

- private walled garden & courtyard
- trips, tours & rental cars arranged; assistance with itinerary bookings
- Central City & Hagley Park, within walking distance
- boutique shopping
- railway station & airport
- Botanic Gardens & Mona Vale
- punting on Avon River
- Arts Centre, theatre & cinemas

- restaurants & cafés within walking distance
- Worcester Boulevard trams
- golf course nearby
- museums & art galleries
- Sumner & Brighton beaches, each 20-min drive away
- variety of sightseeing, within 1-hour drive radius
- Mt Hutt ski-field, 1½ hours

The Manor

The Manor

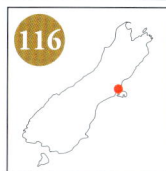

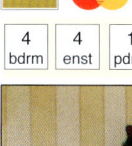

CHRISTCHURCH CITY
Bishops Manor

Host Andrea Richards

14 Bishop Street, St Albans, Christchurch
Phone 0-3-379 7990   *Mobile* 021 453 248   *Fax* 0-3-379 7991
Email info@bishopsmanor.co.nz   *Website* www.bishopsmanor.co.nz

| 4 bdrm | 4 enst | 1 pdrm | **Room rate $240–$370** | *Includes breakfast* | *Dinner extra* |

DIRECTIONS: From City, take Colombo St north to Bealey Ave & turn right. Travel to Bishop St & turn left. Bishops Manor is on the right. From airport turn left into Bealey Ave.

Bishops Manor was built in the 1890s to an England Brothers' design, and now offers four spacious guestrooms upstairs, each with an ensuite including a bath. All bedrooms feature cable television, a phone and refrigerator. Downstairs is the guest lounge and dining room, where a continental breakfast buffet is served, or room service is available if preferred. Dinner, platters, picnic hampers, small wedding and corporate functions can be catered for by prior arrangement. Within walking distance of the City Centre, Bishops Manor is situated on a quiet tree-lined street in a tranquil garden setting. Recently refurbished, it retains the original ornate plaster ceilings and stained glass windows, creating an atmosphere reminiscent of an earlier era.

FACILITIES

- 1 king/twin, 1 king & 2 queen bedrooms, each with ensuite
- 2 dressing rooms
- cotton bed linen; fresh flowers
- bath, bathrobes, hair dryer, demist mirror, toiletries & heated floor in all 4 ensuite bathrooms
- tea/coffee, fridge, cable TV, phone & internet port in all bedrooms
- children welcome

- continental breakfast buffet in dining room, or room service available
- wedding lunches & dinners catered for by arrangement
- beauty salon; powder room
- fax & email available
- guest lounge with artwork, CDs, video
- off-street parking

ACTIVITIES AVAILABLE

- tennis, boating, golf course & fitness track at Hagley Park
- Arts Centre; art galleries
- Court Theatre; Cathedral Square
- gondola; golf courses
- boutique shopping
- Botanic Gardens & Mona Vale
- private gardens open to visit
- Avon River; punting
- Boulevard trams; antiques trail

- restaurants in City Centre & in Merivale Mall
- Christchurch Casino
- hot air ballooning
- Ferrymead historic park
- Lyttelton Harbour
- TranzAlpine day trip
- Antarctic Centre, 20 mins
- airport, 20-min drive
- ski-fields, 1½ hours away

Bishops Manor

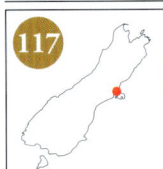

CHRISTCHURCH CITY
Riverview Lodge

Hosts Ernst Wipperfuerth and Sabine Rogge

361 Cambridge Terrace, Christchurch
Phone 0-3-365 2860   *Fax* 0-3-365 2845
Email riverview.lodge@xtra.co.nz   *Website* www.riverview.net.nz

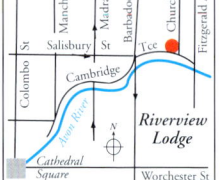

DIRECTIONS: From Cathedral Square, take Colombo St north. Turn right into Salisbury St. Continue into Cambridge Tce. Riverview Lodge on left. From Bealey Ave, turn right into Churchill, then right into Cambridge.

6	5	1
bdrm	enst	prbth

Double $170–$225
Single $100–$160

Includes breakfast for Lodge & Suites
Self-catering in cottages

Set on the banks of the Avon River, this restored Edwardian villa, built in 1903, features the original Queen Anne-style turret, carved kauri and rimu fireplaces and stairs, and stained-glass windows. Next door to Riverview Lodge is an Edwardian townhouse with two self-contained Churchill Suites. Downstairs is a queen bedroom, spacious lounge with French doors opening into a formal courtyard, kitchen and bathroom. Upstairs are two bedrooms, a lounge, kitchen and bathroom. Another four guestrooms and bathrooms are available in the Lodge. For longer stays, there are two historic cottages nearby that are self-contained and have been carefully restored. The 10-minute Avon River walk, past the weeping willows and ducks, takes guests into the City Centre.

FACILITIES

- 1 queen, 1 double/twin, 1 double & 1 single bedroom in house
- 3 ensuites in house & 1 private bathroom for Turret Room
- 2 self-contained Churchill Suites next door: 1 queen downstairs, 1 queen & 1 single upstairs
- flowers, TV, cotton bed linen & hair dryers in all bedrooms
- lounge with open fire, tea/coffee, Sky TV, CD-player & library

- breakfast choice served in turret dining room
- email/fax/phone available; phones in both suites
- balconies open from all double bedrooms
- river views from windows & all verandahs
- German, French, Spanish & Dutch spoken
- off-street parking

ACTIVITIES AVAILABLE

- 2 cottages available nearby
- bicycles available
- kayaks & canoes available for guests' use on river
- golf clubs available
- river walk, 10 mins to City
- punting on Avon River
- Cathedral Square
- Hagley Park
- private gardens to visit

- restaurants, 5-min walk
- Christchurch City shops
- Arts Centre & Botanic Gardens, 20-min river walk
- theatre & concerts
- art galleries
- craft shops
- museum
- Antarctic Centre, 15 mins
- airport, 15-min drive

CHRISTCHURCH CITY
Fitzgerald Cottage

Hosts Danielle DuBois and Christopher Smith

215 Fitzgerald Avenue, Christchurch City
Postal P O Box 36 227, Merivale, Christchurch   *Mobile* 027 434 0015
Email reservations@fleur-de-lys.co.nz   *Website* www.fleur-de-lys.co.nz

2 bdrm	1 prbth

Cottage rate $225 for 2 persons
Extra persons $40 each

Includes continental breakfast provisions
Gourmet provisions extra

DIRECTIONS: From airport, take Memorial Ave. Turn left into Bealey Ave, then right into Fitzgerald Ave. Turn right into Armagh St & u-turn back into Fitzgerald Ave (double carriage way). Cottage on left.

Originally built in 1875, this colonial cottage has been restored to provide self-contained heritage accommodation. As a "Fleur-de-Lys Serviced Cottage of Distinction", Fitzgerald Cottage offers two queen-size bedrooms and a fully equipped kitchen. Guests can self-cater, with breakfast provisions including eggs and sometimes salmon, or gourmet provisions can be supplied by arrangement. Guests enjoy sitting under the fruit tress on the back lawn and even painting in the artist studio. There are shops nearby and the Jade Stadium Conventions Centre and the Town Hall are also within walking distance of Fitzgerald Cottage. The interior design is new, featuring a blend of contemporary and decorative styles and furnishings.

FACILITIES

- one-party bookings only
- 2 queen bedrooms
- 1 private bathroom with bath
- separate toilet
- bathrobes, hair dryer & toiletries
- Sheridan cotton bed linen
- Sky digital TV, DVD & CD-player in guest lounge
- gas fire
- children by arrangement
- breakfast provisions
- gourmet provisions, extra
- fresh flowers
- local phone & guest computer
- self-serve laundry
- artist studio in garden
- passenger transfer by arrangement, extra
- secure off-street parking

ACTIVITIES AVAILABLE

- painting in studio on site
- fruit trees in garden
- shops & restaurants within walking distance
- river walk on Avon nearby
- gym within walking distance
- Convention Centre nearby
- Jade Stadium nearby
- Town Hall nearby
- private gardens to visit
- City Centre
- punting on Avon River
- Central Cathedral & Square, 1km
- Arts Centre, 1.5km
- Botanic Gardens, 2km
- golf course
- casino
- public library
- airport, 8km away

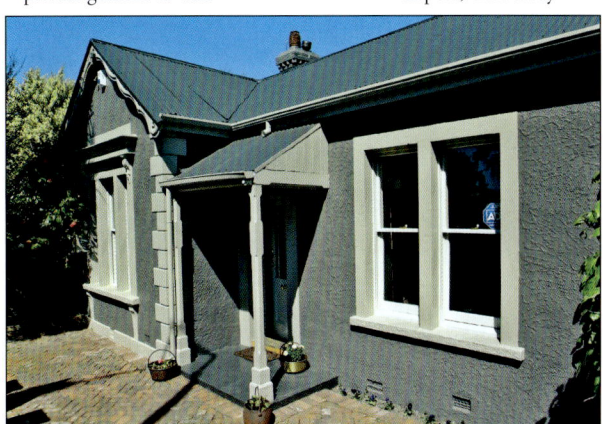

CHRISTCHURCH CITY
The Weston House

Hosts Stephanie and Len May

62 Park Terrace, Christchurch
Phone 0-3-366 0234   *Email* enquiries@westonhouse.co.nz
Fax 0-3-366 5254   *Website* www.westonhouse.co.nz

DIRECTIONS: From the airport, take Memorial Ave. Turn left into Harper Ave. Then turn right into Park Tce. The Weston House is on the left, on the corner of Peterborough St.

| 2 bdrm | 2 enst | 1 pdrm | **Room rate $360–$390** | *Includes breakfast Picnic hampers extra* |

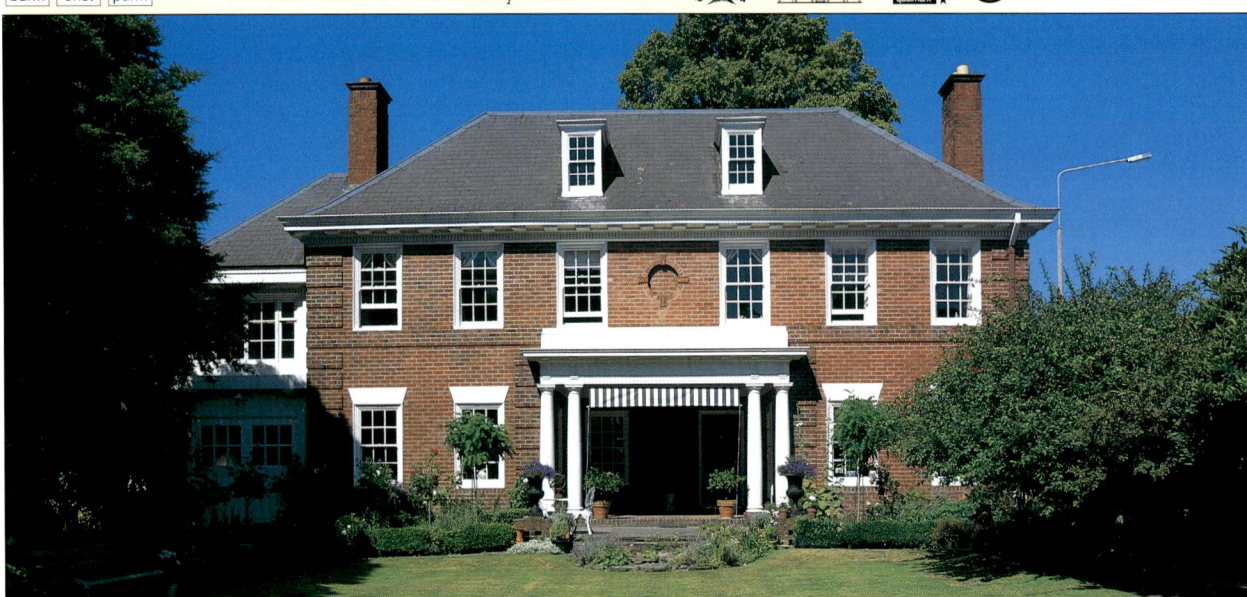

The Weston House was built for Christchurch lawyer, George Weston, from 1923 to 1924 to a neo-Georgian design by architect Cecil Woods. The former servants' quarters have been converted into guest accommodation, comprising an upstairs queen ensuite bedroom and a super-king/twin ensuite bedroom downstairs. Original features include the triple-brick walls with false street window, polished oak floors, and the mature trees in the guest courtyard. Stephanie serves fresh fruit, home-made muesli, bacon and eggs, and whitebait fritters in season, in the breakfast room, and picnic hampers are also available on request. The Weston House is centrally located on a direct route from the airport, yet quiet, opposite the Avon River and North Hagley Park.

FACILITIES

- Peterborough: 1 downstairs super-king/twin bedroom, walk-in wardrobe & ensuite bathroom
- Hagley: 1 upstairs queen bedroom, seating area & ensuite
- toiletries, hair dryers, heated floor, bathrobes in both ensuites
- TV, writing desk, fridge, fresh fruit, home baking & tea/coffee in suites
- complimentary fine NZ wine served each evening before dinner
- continental or traditional English cooked breakfast
- picnic hampers by request
- fresh flowers; central heating
- phone, fax & email
- private guest entrance, staircase & courtyard
- courtesy vehicle on request from airport/railway station
- off-street parking

ACTIVITIES AVAILABLE

- guest courtyard & garden
- croquet lawn on site
- personal guided tours on request
- bus-stop at door; trams
- golf course in Hagley Park
- fitness track in Hagley Park
- licensed restaurants nearby
- punting on the Avon
- casino, 5-min walk
- City Centre, 10-min walk
- Botanic Gardens
- Arts Centre; museum
- art gallery
- gondola
- gardens open to visit
- Sumner Beach, 20 mins
- Lyttelton Harbour, 20-min drive away
- airport, 15-min drive

CHRISTCHURCH CITY
Orari Bed and Breakfast

Host Ashton Owen

42 Gloucester Street, Christchurch City   *Postal* P O Box 1685, Christchurch
Phone 0-3-365 6569   *Email* orari.bb@xtra.co.nz
Fax 0-3-365 2525   *Website* friars.co.nz/hosts/orari.html

DIRECTIONS: From airport, take Memorial Ave into Fendalton Rd. Turn left into Harper Ave, then right into Park Tce. Turn left into Gloucester St. Orari on corner of Montreal St on right.

10 bdrm	8 enst	2 prbth	1 pdrm

Double $160–$200
Single $130–$160

Includes breakfast

Built in 1893 by the renowned England Brothers, Orari was the private townhouse of Annie Macdonald, widow of one of Canterbury's earliest landholders. Restored and refurbished in 1999, retaining the original native kauri construction, Orari now offers 10 guestrooms, each with a bathroom. Each bedroom includes television, phone, and tea or coffee facilities, making it suitable for the entire house to be booked for small conferences or weddings. The living rooms open to verandahs looking out to the garden pool. Orari is located opposite the new Christchurch art gallery, within comfortable walking distance of coffee houses and restaurants, the Arts Centre, Botanic Gardens, Museum, Hagley Park and golf course, and the City Centre.

FACILITIES

- 6 queen, 3 queen/twin & 1 bedroom with 3 singles
- 8 ensuite bathrooms
- 2 private bathrooms with bathrobes & wheelchair access
- hair dryers, heated towel rails & toiletries in all 10 bathrooms
- cotton bed linen
- phone, TV & tea/coffee in all 10 bedrooms
- full cooked breakfast, daily special, in dining room
- complimentary sherry/wine served in sitting room
- fresh flowers
- fax available
- children welcome
- local artwork throughout
- verandahs open to garden
- off-street parking

ACTIVITIES AVAILABLE

- coffee houses & restaurants within walking distance
- central City shopping area
- Christchurch Museum
- Christchurch Convention Centre
- Christchurch Botanic Gardens
- private gardens to visit
- punting on Avon River
- airport, 15-min drive away
- Christchurch Art Gallery, opposite
- Hagley Park
- golf course
- Arts Centre
- casino
- town hall
- public library
- public hospital
- Cathedral Square
- CBD, short walk

CHRISTCHURCH CITY
The Worcester of Christchurch B&B

Hosts Maree Ritchie and Tony Taylor

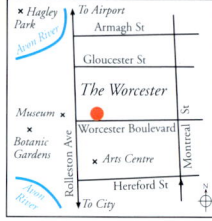

15 Worcester Boulevard, Christchurch
Freephone 0800 365 015   *Phone* 0-3-365 0936   *Fax* 0-3-364 6299
Email info@worcester.co.nz   *Website* www.worcester.co.nz

DIRECTIONS: From airport, take main route to City. Follow Park Tce into Rolleston Ave. Turn left into Worcester Boulevard to The Worcester of Christchurch on left.

| 2 bdrm | 2 enst | Room rate $380 | *Includes breakfast* |

Sited on the inner-city recreated Worcester Boulevard with its restored trams, this 1893 colonial house was originally built for the Chief Constable of Lyttelton. The Worcester of Christchurch is now richly decorated in classical Victorian style, featuring antiques, artworks and leadlight windows. Maree runs her exclusive art business from the house, specialising in major New Zealand works. Upstairs are two super-king guest bedrooms with ensuite bathrooms; one includes a private lounge, and the other a dressing room. A full choice of continental and cooked breakfast is served in the dining room downstairs. The house is complemented by a peaceful garden featuring a gazebo and New Zealand sculpture.

FACILITIES

- 1 super-king/twin bedroom upstairs with lounge & ensuite
- 1 super-king ensuite bedroom upstairs with dressing room
- heated floor ensuites, Les Floralies toiletries, hair dryers & luxurious bath robes
- refrigerators, tea/coffee facilities, ironing board, iron, direct-dial phone, writing desk in bedrooms
- pure cotton bed linen
- full choice of continental & cooked breakfasts served in dining room downstairs
- complimentary in room email/internet access, laptop supplied
- antiques, art & leadlight windows throughout
- baggage elevator
- inner city site

ACTIVITIES AVAILABLE

- personalised hosted tours of Christchurch & surrounding area, wine trails & whale watch tours, by arrangement
- in house art gallery: New Zealand paintings & sculpture for sale
- tourist tram stop opposite
- Court Theatre opposite
- Arts Centre opposite
- Cathedral Square, 5 mins
- cafés & restaurants, 5-min walk
- central city shopping, 5-min walk
- Botanic Gardens, 2-min walk
- Christchurch Casino & Town Hall
- Information Centre
- Christchurch Art Gallery, 3 mins
- Centre of Contemporary Art
- Hagley Park sports: bowls, golf, tennis, boating, croquet, pétanque

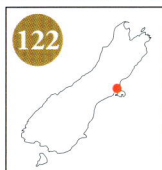

CHRISTCHURCH CITY
West Fitzroy Apartments

Hosts Maree Ritchie and Tony Taylor

Armagh Street, Christchurch   *Postal* 15 Worcester Boulevard, Christchurch
Freephone 0800 365 015   *Phone* 0-3-365 0936   *Fax* 0-3-364 6299
Email info@worcester.co.nz   *Website* www.westfitzroy.co.nz

DIRECTIONS: From airport, take main route to City. Follow Park Tce. Turn left into Armagh St to West Fitzroy on right. Carpark on top level.

4 bdrm	1 enst	2 prbth	**Apartment rate $275 for two persons**	Extra persons $50 each	*Self-catering*
			Multiple-night rates available	*Includes continental breakfast provisions*	

The Worcester at West Fitzroy comprises three self-contained apartments on the historic tram route on Armagh Street. The award-winning West Fitzroy building is centrally located, five minutes' walk from Worcester Boulevard and Cathedral Square. The apartments are designed in contemporary style and complemented with original artworks. Each apartment has a comfortable lounge which opens onto a private full-length tiled balcony with outdoor seating. There is a well equipped kitchen in each apartment which enables self-catering, and continental breakfast provisions are supplied daily. Cafés, restaurants and shops are just a short walk away. There is a guest laundry in each apartment as well as a small gymnasium on site.

FACILITIES

- single-party bookings per apartment
- 1 apartment with 1 king & 1 twin bedroom & 1 ensuite
- 2 apartments, each with 1 super-king/twin bedroom & 1 private bathroom
- apartments serviced daily
- pure cotton bed linen; bathrobes & toiletries
- children welcome, cot available
- continental breakfast provisions
- 1 fully equipped kitchen, lounge & laundry per apartment
- lounges open to tiled balconies with outdoor furniture & smoking area
- TV, stereo & sofa bed in all 3 lounges; TV in each bedroom
- secure carpark
- full security system

ACTIVITIES AVAILABLE

- on-site gymnasium
- personalised hosted tours of Christchurch & surrounding area, wine trails & whale watch tours, by arrangement
- tourist tram stop opposite
- cafés & restaurants, 5-min walk
- central city shopping, 5-min walk
- Cathedral Square, 5-min walk
- Botanic Gardens, walking distance
- Arts Centre close by
- Court Theatre close by
- Christchurch Casino
- Christchurch Art Gallery
- Christchurch Town Hall
- Hagley Park sports
- private gardens to visit
- punting on Avon River
- Christchurch Airport, 20-min drive away

West Fitzroy

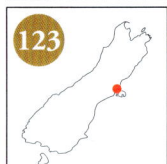

CHRISTCHURCH CITY
Poplars Apartment Hotel

Host Sonia Kennedy   *Phone* 0-3-365 4220

Corner Madras Street and Chester Street East, Christchurch
Postal P O Box 1330, Christchurch   *Fax* 0-3-363 2808
Email info@thepoplars.co.nz   *Website* www.thepoplars.co.nz

39 bdrm	15 enst	22 prbth	1 pdrm

Apartment rate $115–$450

Self-catering
All meals extra

DIRECTIONS: From Cathedral Square, take Colombo St north & turn right into Gloucester St. Turn left into Madras St. Turn left into Chester St East, just before river. Poplars Apartment Hotel on left on corner.

Poplars is a fully serviced hotel comprising self-contained air-conditioned apartments overlooking the Avon River and walks edged with poplar trees. The 20 apartments have been refurbished with attention to detail and provide one or two bedrooms and bathrooms each. Two one-bedroom studios are also offered. On the ground floor there is a spacious Presidential Suite and adjacent is the on-site Oasis Restaurant. Meals are available for guests in the restaurant with special in-house prices, or room service is available. Each apartment includes a fully equipped kitchen for self-catering, if preferred. Guests can enjoy walking or punting along the Avon River that flows beneath Poplars Hotel. Christchurch City Centre is also within walking distance.

FACILITIES

- 3 suites: super-king/twin bedroom & bathroom, 2 with spa baths
- 3 apartments: 1 super-king/twin, 1 queen; 2 bathrooms & spa bath
- 8 apartments: 1 king & 1 twin bedroom; 1 or 2 bathrooms
- 6 apartments: 1 queen & 1 king or double bedroom & 2 ensuites
- 2 studios: 1 super-king/twin bedroom with 1 bathroom each
- room service; children; smokefree
- full kitchen for self-catering in each apartment
- hair dryers, heated towel rails, toiletries, cotton bed linen, TVs, phones & tea/coffee
- lounge with Sky TV, video, DVDs, CDs per apartment
- full laundry per apartment
- air-conditioning & video camera entry in apartments
- on-site secure parking

ACTIVITIES AVAILABLE

- Oasis Restaurant on site
- Avon River walks
- Victoria Square park & shopping area
- Cathedral Square
- Central City shopping. within walking distance
- punting on Avon River
- arts centre
- theatre
- many restaurants, cafés & bars, nearby
- art gallery
- museum
- private gardens to visit
- Botanic Garden
- casino
- Hagley Park
- Antarctic Centre, 30 mins
- Christchurch Airport, 30 mins

CHRISTCHURCH CITY
Cashel Apartments

Host Sonia Kennedy

87 Cashel Street, Christchurch   *Phone* 0-3-365 4220
Postal P O Box 1330, Christchurch   *Fax* 0-3-363 2808
Email cashel.info@thepoplars.co.nz   *Website* www.thepoplars.co.nz

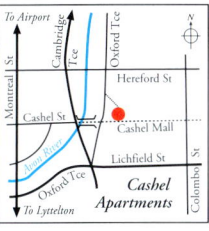

DIRECTIONS: Take Durham St south. Continue into Cambridge Tce. Travel past Bridge of Remembrance to Lichfield St. Turn sharp left into Oxford Tce. Pass Cashel Mall & turn right into Cashel Apartments carpark.

| 8 bdrm | 5 prbth | Apartment rate $165–$350 | *Self-catering* | *No meals available* |

Cashel Apartments are conveniently located in the central city with a boutique shopping mall right on the doorstep. The five self-contained apartments are individually designed, each with one or two bedrooms, a large living area, and French doors opening from the front two onto a balcony overlooking the central city street below. Guest comfort is ensured with air-conditioning and triple-glazing in each apartment, and a fully equipped kitchen is provided for self-catering. All the apartments have direct access to the sunny deck where there is a guest barbecue. Many cafés, restaurants and bars are within minutes' strolling in the heart of the city. The apartments are fully serviced daily and complimentary off-street parking is available for guests.

FACILITIES

- 2 apartments with 1 super-king/twin, 1 queen bedroom & 1 private bathroom in each
- 1 apartment with 2 double bedrooms & 1 private bathroom
- 2 apartments with 1 queen bedroom & 1 bathroom each
- cotton bed linen, phone & hair dryer in all bedrooms
- children welcome; smokefree
- full kitchen for self-catering & laundry in each apartment
- toiletries, heated floors & heated towel rails in all 5 private bathrooms
- air-conditioning, triple glazing & electric skylights
- lounge with digital Sky TV, tea/coffee & CDs per apartment
- video intercom security entry
- on-site parking

ACTIVITIES AVAILABLE

- BBQ on shared sundeck area at rear of all apartments
- 'The Strip' main café & bar area at front door
- Central City boutique shops at front door
- art galleries
- Avon River walks
- punting on Avon River
- theatre
- many restaurants, cafés & bars, within walking distance
- Cathedral Square
- arts centre
- private gardens to visit
- Christchurch Botanic Gardens
- Christchurch Casino
- airport, 30 mins

CASHMERE HILLS, CHRISTCHURCH
Dyers House

Hosts Angela and Barry Hawkins

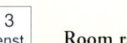

85 Dyers Pass Road, Cashmere, Christchurch
Phone 0-3-337 1675   *Mobile* 021 324 866   *Fax* 0-3-337 1765
Email info@dyershouse.co.nz   *Website* www.dyershouse.co.nz

| 3 bdrm | 3 enst | Room rate $280 | *Includes breakfast* |

DIRECTIONS: From Christchurch City, take main street, Colombo St, south to roundabout. Continue straight ahead into Dyers Pass Rd. Travel uphill to Dyers House on left. (15 mins from City.)

With panoramic views over Christchurch, to the sea beyond, Dyers House is set in the Cashmere Hills in one of the city's oldest hill suburbs. Originally built in 1906, but recently refurbished in keeping with the era, the house has been extensively and thoroughly renovated for accommodation. Dyers House now offers three queen-size ensuite bedrooms downstairs, all opening to a balcony, with the sitting and dining rooms upstairs providing broad vistas over the city. A full breakfast is served to suit guests' tastes at the dining table or in the sunny conservatory. An award-winning café is just two-minutes' walk away and the City Centre is a short drive. Two cats and Joshua, the elderly black labrador dog, complete the family.

FACILITIES

- 3 queen ensuite bedrooms each opening to balcony
- cotton bed linen
- TV, DVD, tea/coffee, phone jacks, iron & ironing board in all bedrooms
- demist mirrors, hair dryers, toiletries, bathrobes, heated floor & towel rails in all bathrooms
- upstairs sitting room with DVDs, library, magazines & sea views

- full breakfast served in dining room with views or sunny conservatory
- TV room with Sky TV
- underfloor heating
- email, fax, phone in office
- complimentary laundry
- closed over Christmas
- courtesy passenger transfer
- off-street parking

ACTIVITIES AVAILABLE

- sightseeing tours arranged
- walking in nearby Victoria Park
- hydropool & fitness centre, 5-min drive away
- art gallery, 15-min drive
- art centre, 15-min drive
- botanic gardens, 15-min drive
- City Centre, 15-min drive
- golf courses
- Ferrymead Historic Park

- café, 2-min walk
- restaurants, 15-min drive
- gardens open to visit
- punting on Avon River
- Sumner beach, 25 mins
- TranzAlpine Express
- Antarctic Centre, 25 mins
- airport, 25-min drive
- Lyttelton, 20 mins
- ski-fields, 1½-hour drive

WEST MELTON, CHRISTCHURCH
Tresillian

Hosts Heather Anderson and Graeme Lindsay   *Mobile* 021 897 283

45 Johnson Road, West Melton, Christchurch   *Phone* 0-3-347 4103
Postal P O Box 6221, Upper Riccarton, Christchurch   *Fax* 0-3-347 4104
Email stay@tresillian.co.nz   *Website* www.tresillian.co.nz

DIRECTIONS: From Christchurch, take SH 73 towards West Coast. Travel about 13km & turn left into Weedons-Ross Rd. Travel 2km & turn left into Johnson Rd. Travel 1.2km to Tresillian on right.

| 3 bdrm | 1 enst | 1 prbth | **Room rate $175–$275** | *Includes breakfast* | *Dinner extra* |

Set in an eight-hectare vineyard, Tresillian offers contemporary accommodation half an hour west of Christchurch City. Purpose-built in 2002, Tresillian was inspired by Frank Lloyd Wright prairie house designs, all three bedrooms opening to verandahs with vineyard views. Breakfast is served in the dining room, guestrooms, or alfresco on the private verandahs, using home-grown produce in season. Dinner is also available by arrangement, accompanied by wine from the cellar. There are restaurants nearby, and the airport is just 20 minutes' drive east. Tresillian offers a peaceful quiet location on part of the original sheep run that was established in 1851. Grousie, the dog, and Gris, the cat, complete the family.

FACILITIES

- 1 super-king/twin ensuite bedroom with private entrance
- 2 queen bedrooms share private bathroom; 1-party booking only
- TV, CD-player, phone, tea/coffee, fridge in all 3 bedrooms, opening to private verandahs
- spa bath, hair dryer, toiletries, demist mirror, heated floor & towel rails in both bathrooms
- cotton bed linen; bathrobes
- breakfast including home-grown eggs & home baking served in dining room, bedrooms, or alfresco on private verandah
- 3-course dinner & wine, by arrangement, $50 pp
- central heating
- email & fax available
- on-site parking
- helicopter access

ACTIVITIES AVAILABLE

- pool table
- pétanque & croquet, on site
- walking or jogging in vineyard
- golf courses nearby
- jet boating at Waimakariri & Rakaia rivers
- aero club, 5km
- motor racing at Ruapuna Park, 7km
- local lavender farm
- TranzAlpine express train
- restaurants, 10–20 mins
- gardens open to visit
- punting on Avon River
- Hagley Park sports
- Antarctic Centre, 20 mins
- International Airport, 20-min drive away
- Christchurch City, ½ hr
- 5 ski-fields within 1½-hour drive

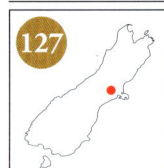

DARFIELD
Meychelle Manor

Hosts Michelle and Brian Walker   *Phone* 0-3-318 1144

3632817 State Highway 73, Darfield, Canterbury   *Freephone* 0800 181 144
Postal P O Box 162, Kirwee, Canterbury   *Mobile* 027 226 0118   *Fax* 0-3-318 1965
Email stay@meychellemanor.co.nz   *Website* www.meychellemanor.co.nz

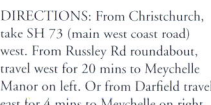

3 bdrm	2 enst	1 prbth	1 pdrm

Double $190–$220
Single $130–$150

Includes breakfast
Children $20–$80 each

DIRECTIONS: From Christchurch, take SH 73 (main west coast road) west. From Russley Rd roundabout, travel west for 20 mins to Meychelle Manor on left. Or from Darfield travel east for 4 mins to Meychelle on right.

Meychelle Manor is set on a small deer and heifer farm, just half an hour from Christchurch airport, and features friendly boer goats, kune kunes, angora goats, ostriches, pheasants and peacocks. Built in 1999, this child-friendly accommodation offers three guestrooms with mountain views over the on-site lake where guests can enjoy rowing and feeding the ducks. There is also a heated indoor swimming pool and golf putting green. A full flexi-time breakfast menu is served downstairs in the dining room to suit guests, and dinner can be delivered to the house from local restaurants. Guests are also welcome to use the kitchen to prepare meals for themselves. Two daughters, Chevonn and Chloe, and Jazz, a small Bichon Frise dog, complete the family.

FACILITIES

- 3 super-king bedrooms, each opening to balcony
- 2 ensuites & 1 private bathroom
- hair dryers, toiletries, heated towel rails, bathrobes
- cotton bed linen; fresh flowers
- central heating; drying room
- babies & children welcome
- complimentary laundry
- breakfast menu
- tea/coffee, baking & bar
- 2 guest lounges with Sky TV, video, DVD, music, books
- pure artesian well water
- complimentary wine & chocolates; telescope
- phone/fax & email in office
- private guest entrance
- closed over Christmas
- on-site parking

ACTIVITIES AVAILABLE

- indoor heated swimming pool & weights gym
- children's play equipment
- on-site pétanque, golf putting green, farm tour, feeding animals & birds, rowboat, & hosted possum shooting with Brian
- 4 golf courses within 20 mins
- TranzAlpine scenic train, 4 mins
- guided hunting & fishing trips
- scenic walks in local hills
- restaurants, 4-min drive; courtesy transport available
- Darfield art gallery, 4 mins
- beauty, health & massage therapy arranged, extra
- sheep shearing demonstration, extra
- jet boating; horse trekking
- Christchurch City & airport, 30-min drive
- courtesy drive to ski shuttle

TAITAPU, CHRISTCHURCH
Chatterley Manor

Host Isabella Hockey

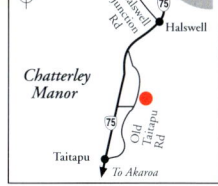

433 Old Taitapu Road, R D 2, Christchurch
Phone 0-3-329 6658   *Mobile* 0274 310 773   *Fax* 0-3-329 6827
Email enquiries@ladychatterley.co.nz   *Website* www.ladychatterley.co.nz

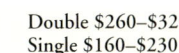

8 bdrm	7 enst

Double $260–$320
Single $160–$230

Includes breakfast
Lunch extra

DIRECTIONS: From Christchurch, take SH 75 south. After Halswell pass 100km sign, then turn left into Old Taitapu Rd. Travel 3.5km to Chatterley Manor on left. From airport, take Halswell Junction Rd to meet SH 75.

Chatterley Manor is a country retreat only 15 minutes' drive from the centre of Christchurch, and less than half an hour from the airport. Chatterley is set in three hectares of landscaped gardens, featuring an island with a small chapel in a lake edged with willows. Guests can choose from a selection of themed rooms – African, Egyptian, Austrian, Mediterranean, Lavender or Lady Chatterley. The larger suites include a mezzanine floor and a lounge area opening directly to the extensive lawns and rose gardens. Country-style breakfast is served, and lunch, picnic baskets, dinner or barbecues are available by request. Children are welcome and guests enjoy the facilities such as the swimming pool, tennis court, sauna, large spa pool and billiards room.

FACILITIES

- 4 queen/twin suites, with ensuites including baths
- family suite with 1 double & 1 twin bedroom, & 1 ensuite
- 1 twin & 1 single, & 1 ensuite
- toiletries, bathrobes, hair dryers
- tea/coffee & CD-player in 5 guest suites
- phone, fax, internet access & email available
- country-style breakfast served
- picnic/lunch, extra
- dinner by request, extra
- guest lounge with open fire
- mezzanine in 4 queen suites
- children of all ages welcome
- complimentary laundry
- courtesy airport transfer
- parking available

ACTIVITIES AVAILABLE

- alfresco barbecue facilities
- guided tours with picnic lunches
- ¾-size billiards table
- sauna & 16-seater spa pool
- swimming pool
- hard-surface tennis court
- extensive gardens & pond
- small chapel on island
- local wineries, 5-min drive
- winery trail
- restaurants, 15-min drive
- horse riding & trekking
- jet boating; fishing
- golf course, 3-min drive
- gardens to visit
- shopping, theatre & casino in Christchurch, 15 mins
- airport, 25 mins
- skiing in winter
- Akaroa, 45-min drive

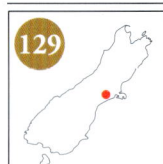
TAITAPU, CHRISTCHURCH
Ballymoney Farmstay and Garden

Host Merrilies Rebbeck

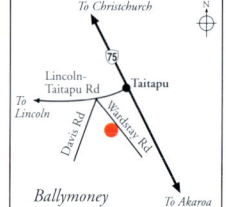

Wardstay Road, Taitapu   *Phone* 0-3-329 6706
Postal Wardstay Road, R D 2, Christchurch   *Fax* 0-3-329 6709
Email info@ballymoney.co.nz   *Website* www.ballymoney.co.nz

| 3 bdrm | 2 enst | 1 prbth | Suite rate $160–$300 | *Includes breakfast* | *Lunch & dinner extra* |
| | | | Farm package: $50 pp extra | *Includes dinner & tour* | |

DIRECTIONS: From Christchurch City, take SH 75 to Taitapu. Turn right towards Lincoln. Travel 2 km then turn into Wardstay Rd. Travel 800 metres to Ballymoney on right.

Ballymoney is a century-old farm cottage with new additions including a conservatory and sitting room opening to the large private garden and pond. The 14-hectare (35-acre) farm is home to many rare breeds of animals and birds such as white peacocks, water fowl, Dorset horn sheep, Dexter cattle, donkeys and Saddleback pigs. The historic part of the farm homestead features native timber, polished floors, open fireplaces, period furniture and original artwork. Named after the family farm in Ireland, Ballymoney offers "slow food" country cuisine prepared from home-grown spray-free produce and local wine with Kiwi/Irish hospitality. The Ballymoney farm package includes breakfast, dinner and a farm tour. The city and airport are easily accessible.

FACILITIES

- Manuka Suite: 1 super-king/twin bedroom with ensuite & private verandah & 1 double bedroom adjoining, with private bathroom & bath
- Kowhai Garden Suite: 1 queen bedroom with extra single bed, ensuite & private courtyard; suite detached from house
- hair dryers, toiletries, heated towel rails & bathrobes
- children welcome
- full breakfast served in country kitchen/conservatory
- Mediterranean BBQ area with Italian pizza oven
- dinner & wine, $40–$50 pp formal, casual or BBQ
- TV, tea/coffee in all bedrooms & fridge in both suites
- 2 sitting rooms with open fires, TV, video & piano in house
- phone, fax & email available

ACTIVITIES AVAILABLE

- farm package includes breakfast, dinner, farm tour & animal feeding
- golden retriever & fox terrier in residence
- pétanque & croquet on site
- courtesy bicycles available
- garden lunches & weddings catered for on site
- garden & chestnut orchard walks, feeding rare animals & birds, & seasonal farm activities on site
- restaurants nearby
- golf course, 5km
- gardens & parks to visit
- horse riding; wine trails
- Lincoln University, 5km
- day trips to Akaroa, 1 hour
- Christchurch City, 20 mins
- airport, 20-min drive
- shuttle bus available from airport & city

Ballymoney

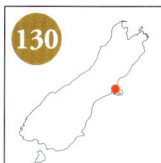
LYTTELTON
Cavendish House

Hosts Jenny and Graham Sorell

10 Ross Terrace, Lyttelton
Phone 0-3-328 9505   *Email* cavendish@clear.net.nz
Fax 0-3-328 9502   *Website* www.cavendish.co.nz

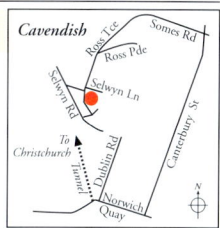

DIRECTIONS: From tunnel, bear left into Norwich Quay towards Lyttelton. Turn left up Canterbury St. At top, take left fork into Somes Rd. Continue past Ross Pde & 50m past Cavendish House sign to gate on left.

2 bdrm	2 enst

Double $160–$200
Single $140–$180

Includes breakfast
Multiple-night rates available

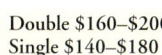

Nestled on Mt Cavendish overlooking the Port of Lyttelton is Cavendish House, built in 1910. This Edwardian villa is set in a terraced garden of perfumed vines, old roses, olive, fig and other fruit trees. Historic features of Cavendish House include the stained glass leadlights, large bay windows, return verandah, and the rare Tasmanian antiques in the Chart Room and former Ballroom. A breakfast selection including free range eggs and fresh garden produce is served in the dining room, or alfresco on the verandah with its Port views to Diamond Harbour and the mountains beyond. Guests can wander down the stepped laneways to the cafés, restaurants and the Port below, then call their hosts to collect them for the homeward journey.

FACILITIES

- Venice Room: 1 super-king/ twin ensuite bedroom with spa bath & writing desk
- Tasman Room: 1 super-king/ twin ensuite bedroom
- cotton bed linen; fresh flowers
- hair dryer, heated towel rails, toiletries & bathrobes
- children by arrangement
- return verandah opening from both lounges

- full breakfast served in former Ballroom or alfresco
- apéritifs, port, teas, coffee, nibbles, writing desk, TV, video & DVD in Chart Room
- French spoken; art collection
- phone, fax & email available
- private guest entrance
- off-street parking
- outdoors cat

ACTIVITIES AVAILABLE

- wedding & honeymoon packages
- BBQ in extensive garden
- watching boats/ships/yachts
- historic Lyttelton buildings
- Diamond Harbour Ferry
- Major Hornbrook Track & other Port Hills walks
- Maritime Museum & Torpedo Boat Museum
- Time-Ball, 15-min walk

- Christchurch City, 15 mins
- restaurants, cafés, bars, shops, 0.5 km downhill in village
- Port, 10-min walk downhill
- Sumner Beach, 10-min drive
- 1½-hr trip on historic steam tug *Lyttelton* on Sundays
- *Black Cat* wildlife tour
- gardens open to visit at Governor's Bay & in City

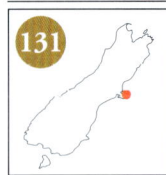

Rowandale Homestead

Hosts Luis and Angela Thacker

Rowandale, Okains Bay, Banks Peninsula
Phone 0-3-304 8615 *Mobile* 027 667 0003 *Fax* 0-3-304 8615
Email rowandalefarm@xtra.co.nz *Website* friars.co.nz/hosts/rowandale.html

DIRECTIONS: From Christchurch, take SH 75 to Hilltop Hotel. Travel down to Duvauchelle, then take 2nd turning left towards Okains Bay. Climb to summit. Continue downhill for 4km to Rowandale on right.

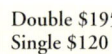

2 bdrm	1 prbth	1 pdrm

Double $195
Single $120

Includes breakfast
Lunch & dinner extra

Located in the countryside surrounded by hills, with views to the sea, Rowandale Homestead offers a peaceful private location to stay, with the fifth-generation owners. Set among established trees, including rowans after which the homestead is named, with large rolling lawns and a formal white garden, the tripled bricked home was built in 1908, using bricks made on site and clay roof tiles. Eight years later, in 1916, the home was finished, to an arts and crafts design by architect Cecil Woods. The spacious rooms feature extensive timber panelling, with antiques throughout and now provide two queen-size guestrooms with private balconies, where guests can sleep in the summer, and a large bath in the shared bathroom, for single parties only.

FACILITIES

- one-party bookings only
- 2 queen bedrooms & balconies
- 1 private bathroom with bath, hair dryer, toiletries, heated towel rails & bathrobes
- cotton bed linen & writing desk
- laundry service, $10
- guest lounge with open fire, tea/coffee, nibbles, bar, Sky TV, video, DVD & CD-player
- full cooked or continental breakfast, room service
- light lunch by request, extra
- dinner with gourmet pizza, cheese board & wine, $25 pp
- espresso coffee & cake
- local wine/beer; fresh flowers
- email, fax & phone available
- courtesy passenger transfer
- on-site parking; heli-landing

ACTIVITIES AVAILABLE

- smoking, fine cigars & nightcaps in billiards room
- BBQ & outdoor baths on site
- large established garden on site
- small conferences, weddings & honeymoons catered for
- in-house music room
- secluded beach nearby
- swimming with dolphins
- Duvauchelle hotel, 10 mins
- restaurants & cafés, 10–20 mins away
- hair/beauty treatments
- local museum; galleries
- fishing days trips
- harbour cruises; wineries
- gardens to visit
- golf course, 15 mins
- Akaroa, 20-min drive
- Christchurch, 1¼ hrs

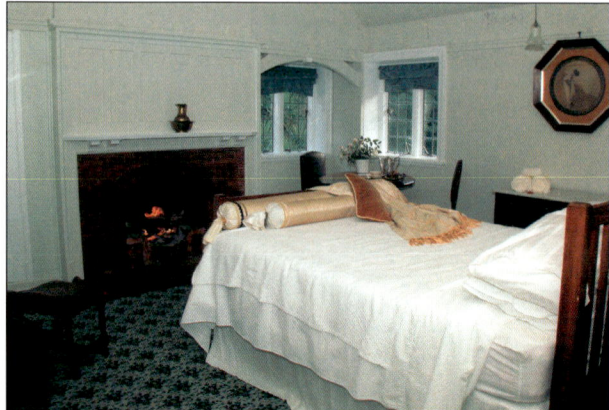

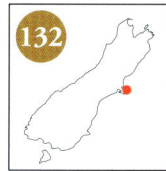

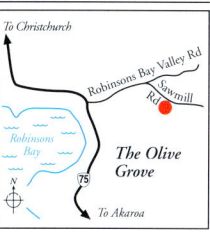

 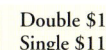

ROBINSONS BAY, BANKS PENINSULA
The Olive Grove

Hosts Alison and Andy Beck

36 Sawmill Road, Robinsons Bay, R D 1, Akaroa, Banks Peninsula
Phone 0-3-304 5190   *Mobile* 021 531 713   *Fax* 0-3-304 5190
Email the_olive_grove@clear.net.nz   *Website* www.theolivegrove.net.nz

4 bdrm	2 enst	1 prbth	Double $160–$220	*Includes breakfast & apéritifs*
			Single $110–$170	*Picnic lunch & dinner extra*

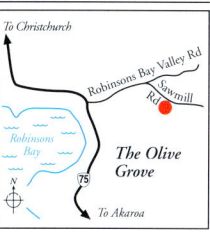

DIRECTIONS. From Christchurch, take SH 75 & travel 1 hr towards Akaroa. At Robinsons Bay, turn left into Robinsons Bay Valley Rd & travel 1km. Turn right into Sawmill Rd. The Olive Grove at end on right.

Olive Grove

Set in a sheltered valley not far from Akaroa, with uninterrupted views of Robinsons Bay, the Olive Grove offers a rural retreat just an hour from Christchurch City. The Olive Grove was planted in 1994 adjacent to a traditional weatherboard 1915 bay villa, restored in 2004 and a second storey added for accommodation. Guests can enjoy the views from the outdoor spa pool, the balcony, their beds and even the baths. A full breakfast is served alfresco if sunny. Picnics are popular in one of the most southerly olive groves in the world, with vistas of sunsets over Akaroa Harbour. Complimentary apéritifs with on-site grown olives are offered, and dinner is served by arrangement. A gentle German short-haired Pointer, Clive, completes the family.

FACILITIES

- 1 super-king & 1 king ensuite bedroom both including baths
- 1 queen & 1 twin bedroom share private bathroom
- cotton bed linen; fresh flowers
- TV in all bedrooms
- hair dryers, toiletries, heated towel rails & bathrobes
- central heating
- email & phone available

- full breakfast indoors or alfresco
- apéritifs & hors d'oeuvres with on-site grown olives
- dinner on request, $40–$60 pp
- guest lounge with open fire, tea/coffee, TV, DVD, CD-player, books & artwork
- friendly German short-haired Pointer dog, Clive, on site
- on-site parking

ACTIVITIES AVAILABLE

- on-site olive oil for sale; olive oil tasting room October–May
- olive grove tours on site
- picnicking in olive grove
- honeymoon packages
- bicycles available
- kayaks for guest use
- pétanque/boules on site
- croquet on site
- walking

- restaurants in Akaroa, 8 mins
- wineries
- harbour cruises
- local gardens open to visit
- swimming with dolphins
- craft shops
- sailing
- cheese factory
- Christchurch City, 70km
- airport, 1 hour

Olive Grove

Olive Grove

387

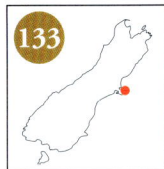

AKAROA, BANKS PENINSULA
Wilderness House

Hosts Liz and Jim Coubrough

42 Rue Grehan, Akaroa, Banks Peninsula
Phone 0-3-304 7517 *Mobile* 021 669 381 *Fax* 0-3-304 7518
Email info@wildernesshouse.co.nz *Website* www.wildernesshouse.co.nz

DIRECTIONS: From Christchurch, take SH 75 & travel 80km to Akaroa. From Rue Lavaud, turn left into Rue Grehan. Travel 200m to Wilderness House on right.

4 bdrm	3 enst	1 prbth	**Double** $220–$240 **Single** $180–$200	*Includes breakfast* *Dinner extra*

This English colonial-designed homestead was built in 1878 in the French-style village of Akaroa on Banks Peninsula. Set in a large traditional garden featuring protected trees, rare camellias, roses and a small private vineyard, Wilderness House provides views of Akaroa Harbour and Grehan Valley. Restored and refurbished in English country style to provide accommodation, this historic house retains many original features. Wilderness House offers four bedrooms, each with its own bathroom, and guests are given a choice of breakfasts served in the dining room, or alfresco on the verandahs or in the garden. A range of restaurants are only a 500-metre walk away in Akaroa village. Two cats named Beethoven and Harry complete the household.

FACILITIES

- 3 queen ensuite bedrooms, 1 including bath
- 1 king/twin bedroom with private bathroom & bath
- cotton bed linen, wool duvets & feather pillows
- fresh flowers, tea/coffee & home baking in bedrooms
- hair dryers, toiletries, heated towel rails & bathrobes
- email, fax & phone available

- full breakfast served
- complimentary glass of house wine with hosts every evening
- dinner by arrangement, $50 pp
- guest lounge with open fire, tea/coffee, TV & writing desk
- guest fridge
- spacious sunny guest verandah
- 2 friendly cats in residence
- off-street parking

ACTIVITIES AVAILABLE

- relaxing in large traditional garden with protected trees, rare camellias & roses on site
- private vineyard on site
- village centre for restaurants, cafés, bars & shops, 500m
- horse riding
- charter fishing trips
- gardens open to visit
- French history museum

- wineries
- harbour cruises
- swimming with dolphins
- tramping & walks
- historic buildings
- boating & diving
- kayaking
- tennis court
- Christchurch, 80km

AKAROA, BANKS PENINSULA
Lavaud House

Hosts Alison and Gavin Porteous

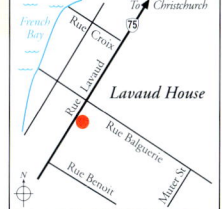

Lavaud House

83 Rue Lavaud, Akaroa   *Phone* 0-3-304 7121
Email lavaudhouse@xtra.co.nz   *Fax* 0-3-304 7125
Mobile 021 442 718   *Website* www.lavaudhouse-akaroa.co.nz

DIRECTIONS: From Christchurch, take SH 75 & travel 80km to Akaroa. Continue along Rue Lavaud to Lavaud House on left. Turn into driveway & park at back.

3 bdrm	2 enst	1 prbth

Room rate $175–$225   *Includes continental breakfast*

Lavaud House

Named after Lieutenant Lavaud who escorted settlers to Akaroa aboard the *Comte de Paris* in 1840, Lavaud House was built in the early 1900s as a doctor's residence. After extensive renovations and refurbishment Lavaud House offers three guestrooms, each with its own bathroom. Upstairs are the Charlotte Rose, Harbour View and French bedrooms with sea vistas, and downstairs is the Woodlands bedroom with a view out to the secluded garden. A full continental breakfast is served in the separate guest dining room with sea views or alfresco on the front lawn overlooking Akaroa Harbour. Guests can stroll along the harbour walk each evening to the nearby restaurants or cafés in Akaroa village for dinner.

FACILITIES

- 1 super-king bedroom & ensuite with bath
- 1 queen bedroom with ensuite
- 1 queen bedroom with private bathroom
- hair dryers & toiletries
- cotton bed linen, feather pillows
- writing desk
- private guest lounge with stereo, Sky TV, gas fire & books
- full continental breakfast in dining room or alfresco
- email & fax available
- garden with tables & chairs
- laundry available
- fresh flowers
- guests' fridge
- expansive sea views
- off-street parking

ACTIVITIES AVAILABLE

- landscaped gardens on site
- walks; scenic drives
- dolphin watching
- boating
- arts & crafts
- winery
- cheese factory & tasting
- adventure tours
- gardens open to visit
- restaurants, cafés, bars & shops, 10-min walk
- golf & mini-golf
- swimming
- lavender farm
- harbour cruises
- fishing
- historic buildings
- beaches & bays
- Christchurch, 80km

Lavaud House

Lavaud House

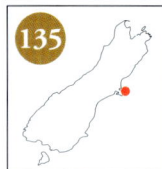

AKAROA, BANKS PENINSULA
Maison de la Mer

Hosts Carol and Bruce Hyland

1 Rue Benoit, Akaroa, Banks Peninsula
Phone 0-3-304 8907   *Mobile* 021 986 221   *Fax* 0-3-304 8917
Email maisondelamer@xtra.co.nz   *Website* www.maisondelamer.co.nz

DIRECTIONS: From Christchurch, take SH 75 & travel 80km to Akaroa. Continue along Rue Lavaud to Maison de la Mer on left, on corner of Rue Benoit.

| 3 bdrm | 3 enst | Room/apartment rate $295 | *Includes breakfast or provisions* |

Maison de la Mer

With uninterrupted sea views from all three guestrooms, as well as the breakfast room and lounge, Maison de la Mer is located in the historic French-style Akaroa village on Banks Peninsula. Set on the waterfront, Maison de la Mer is aptly named "House by the Sea" in French. Originally built in 1910 for a local merchant, this classic two-storey villa has been completely refurbished with antiques, oriental carpets and fine art and is freshened with flowers in every room. A gourmet breakfast selection includes Maison de la Mer's home-made muesli, yoghurt and a platter of seasonal fruits, supplemented with a full menu of cooked dishes. Each bedroom has a mini-bar fridge with wine and beers, port, imported mineral water and home baking.

FACILITIES

- 1 queen bedroom, with double spa bath in ensuite
- 1 queen bedroom with ensuite & private sunroom
- The Boathouse: separate self-contained apartment with 1 queen ensuite bedroom
- fan, fridge mini-bar, TV, DVDs & tea/coffee in each bedroom
- hair dryer, heated towel rails & French toiletries in each ensuite
- full breakfast; or provisions for apartment
- lounge with open fire, TV & writing desk
- guest computer & wireless broadband; fax & phone
- central heating; fresh flowers
- cotton bed linen & bathrobes
- sea views from every room
- off-street parking

ACTIVITIES AVAILABLE

- mountain bikes available
- garden with mature trees & roses, for walking & relaxing
- swimming beach opposite
- seal & penguin colony
- swimming with dolphins
- historic French village
- harbour cruises
- cruises on vintage ketch
- garden tours
- restaurants & cafés nearby
- 4-wheel bike safaris
- horse trekking
- fishing trips
- Banks Peninsula track, 2–4-day tramp
- historic museum
- wineries & golf course
- Christchurch City, 80km
- airport, 1½-hour drive

Maison de la Mer

Maison de la Mer

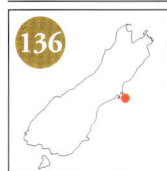

AKAROA, BANKS PENINSULA
Maison des Fleurs

Hosts Margy and Dai Morris

6 Church Street, Akaroa, Banks Peninsula
Phone 0-3-304 7804 *Email* luxury@maisondesfleurs.co.nz
Fax 0-3-304 7804 *Website* www.maisondesfleurs.co.nz

Maison des Fleurs

DIRECTIONS: From Christchurch, take SH 75 to Akaroa. Travel along Rue Lavaud, past the beach into Rue Jolie. Then turn right into Church St. Travel 10m to Maison des Fleurs on left.

1 bdrm | 1 enst

Cottage rate $250–$325

Self-catering

Located just 100 metres from Akaroa Harbour, Maison des Fleurs is a two-storey self-contained cottage, built in 1999. This colonial-style cottage, handcrafted in New Zealand native timbers with natural finishes, is complemented by antique and contemporary furnishings, with a historic open fireplace in the lounge upstairs. The sunny afternoon balcony is a favourite spot for watching sunsets, and the secluded garden courtyard has a swing seat for two. Designed as a romantic retreat, Maison des Fleurs (meaning the House of Flowers) features fresh flowers and extras including aromatherapy oils, chocolates and port.

Maison des Fleurs

FACILITIES

- self-contained cottage
- single-party bookings
- 1 queen bedroom with ensuite
- Pro-natura designed bed (handmade) & cotton bed linen
- king-size spa bath, bidet, demist mirror & heated towel rails
- bathrobes, hair dryer, toiletries, bubble bath & aromatherapy oils
- open fire, CD-player, magazines, guitar & games
- kitchenette for self-catering
- organic teas, coffees, juices, purified water, port & chocolates
- complimentary champagne for 2-night stay
- fresh flowers
- upstairs lounge with antique open fireplace, opens to balcony
- central heating
- romantic retreat
- garden setting

ACTIVITIES AVAILABLE

- swing seat in secluded garden courtyard
- watching sunsets
- historic village walk
- restaurants, cafés & boutique shopping in historic town, 100m walk
- French history museum
- walking; tramping
- local winery
- local cheese factory
- Banks Peninsula track, 2–4 days' tramp
- seal colony tours
- charter fishing trips
- watching & swimming with dolphins
- harbour cruises
- private garden tours
- tennis courts
- golf course
- Christchurch City, 1½ hrs

Maison des Fleurs

Maison des Fleurs

AKAROA, BANKS PENINSULA
Aylmer House

Host Bob Parker

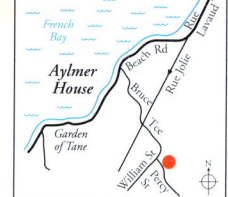

7 Percy Street, Akaroa, Banks Peninsula   *Postal* P O Box 53, Akaroa
Phone 0-3-304 7008   *Mobile* 027 443 4575   *Fax* 0-3-304 7008
Email accommodation@bobparker.co.nz   *Website* friars.co.nz/hosts/aylmer.html

DIRECTIONS: From Christchurch, take SH 75 to Akaroa. Travel along Rue Lavaud & continue into Rue Jolie. Turn left into Bruce Tce & left again into Percy St. Aylmer House 1st on left.

| 2 bdrm | 2 enst | **Room rate $250** | *Includes breakfast* |

Aylmer House is a French colonial home built in 1852 for the first Anglican vicar of Akaroa, the Reverend Aylmer. It has been restored and now offers two king-size ensuite guestrooms, Misty Peaks and Harbour View. Both bedrooms are fully insulated and warm, with heated tiled bathroom, sleigh beds, and with access to a sunny balcony and private guest lounge. Aylmer House is set in a large garden with mature native trees, and a stream boundary complete with historic waterwheel. There is also a swimming pool. Breakfasts are served in the large French country kitchen, and restaurants are within walking distance, in the township of Akaroa. Christchurch City is an hour and a half away.

FACILITIES

- 2 king ensuite bedrooms
- hair dryer, toiletries, bidet, heated floor, heated towel rails & bathrobes in both ensuites
- bath in Misty Peaks ensuite
- cotton bed linen; fresh flowers
- TV, DVD, tea/coffee, CDs & in bedrooms
- guest fridge adjacent to bedrooms

- breakfast with organic muesli, nuts, seasonal fruit, muffins, yoghurt & toast
- open fire, artwork & books, phone & writing desk in lounge
- email, fax & laundry available
- private guest entrance
- off-street parking
- historic architecture

ACTIVITIES AVAILABLE

- swimming pool on site
- walking in large garden with pond, native trees, water wheel & mill
- Akaroa village shops, cafés & restaurants, 5-min walk
- cheese factory
- garden tours

- Within 10–15-min walk:
  – swimming with dolphins in Akaroa Harbour
  – herb gardens to visit
  – hiking trails within the volcanic basin
  – tennis courts
  – fishing; kayaking
  – Maori cultural activities
  – artists' galleries; museum
  – selection of walking tracks
- Banks Peninsula 2–4-day tramp
- Christchurch City, 1½ hours

Aylmer House

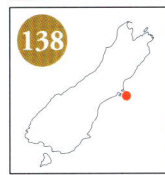

AKAROA, BANKS PENINSULA
Oinako Lodge

Hosts Teresa and Greg Miller

99 Beach Road, Akaroa, Banks Peninsula
Phone 0-3-304 8787   *Email* bookings@oinako.co.nz
Fax 0-3-304 8787   *Website* www.oinako.co.nz

DIRECTIONS: From Christchurch, take SH 75 to Akaroa. From Rue Lavaud continue into Beach Rd. Follow 1-way system into Rue Jolie, turn right into Bruce Tce & left into Beach Rd. Continue to Oinako on left.

6 bdrm	6 enst	Room rate $180–$220	*Includes breakfast*

Originally built in 1865 for an English magistrate, Oinako now provides accommodation in six ensuite guestrooms. Historic features include the spacious entrance hall with open fire and sweeping French staircase, marble fireplaces, and the ornate plaster ceilings and cornices. Carefully furnished, Oinako now incorporates modern amenities and luxurious contemporary touches such as spa baths in four of the ensuite bathrooms. All rooms are of generous proportions and enjoy views of the private tranquil garden setting or Akaroa Harbour beyond. Gourmet breakfasts using fresh, local produce are served in the dining room with its garden outlook. The historic French township of Akaroa with its cafés and restaurants is just a two-minute stroll away.

FACILITIES

- 1 twin, 2 queen & 3 king upstairs bedrooms, all with ensuite bathrooms
- spa bath in 4 ensuites
- hair dryers & toiletries
- quality bed linen, feather pillows, feather or wool duvets & electric blankets on all beds
- balcony overlooking garden with Akaroa Harbour views

- full breakfast served in original dining room
- tea/coffee buffet
- guest fridge
- guest lounge with open fire, books, games & TV
- fresh flowers
- secluded rose garden for reading & relaxing
- off-street parking

ACTIVITIES AVAILABLE

- historic Akaroa township
- swimming & beaches
- art galleries
- Akaroa Museum
- garden visits
- cycling
- peninsula bays tours
- local cheese factory
- wineries

- cafés, restaurants, village shops & main wharf, 2-min stroll away
- harbour cruises & swimming with Hector's dolphins
- kayaking, boating & fishing
- golf course
- heritage trail
- walking & tramping
- Christchurch City, 1½-hour drive

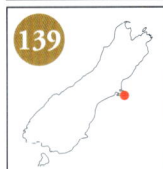
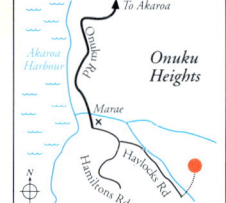

AKAROA, BANKS PENINSULA

Onuku Heights

Host Eckhard Keppler

166 Haylocks Road, R D 1, Akaroa, Banks Peninsula
Email onuku.heights@paradise.net.nz   *Phone* 0-3-304 7112
Website www.onuku-heights.co.nz   *Fax* 0-3-304 7116

DIRECTIONS: From Christchurch, take SH 75 to Akaroa. Travel through village & turn left at bakery into Rue Jolie. Follow signs to Onuku Marae. Continue into Haylocks Rd & travel up to Onuku Heights at end.

| 3 bdrm | 3 enst | Room rate $190–$240 | *Includes breakfast* | *Dinner extra* |

Onuku Heights

Set high overlooking Akaroa Harbour is the historic farm at Onuku Heights. Built in the 1860s, the homestead has been carefully restored and is furnished with antiques and period furniture. With an abundance of birdlife, Onuku Heights is nestled in gardens and orchard, and surrounded by native bush reserves, streams and waterfalls on a 309-hectare working sheep farm. There are two ensuite guestrooms upstairs in the homestead, with a separate ensuite guestroom in a cottage adjacent to the homestead. A full breakfast with home-made bread and jams is served in the downstairs guest lounge or alfresco on the terrace with panoramic sea views. Candlelit dinners by the open fire are available by prior arrangement.

FACILITIES

- 2 king ensuite bedrooms upstairs in homestead
- 1 separate guestroom with king bed & ensuite bathroom
- embroidered bed linen
- hair dryer & toiletries
- fresh flowers
- rose garden with fountain
- private guest entrance
- sunny guest verandah
- cooked or continental breakfast with home baking
- 3-course candlelit dinner by prior arrangement, $40–$60 pp
- private guest lounge with open fire, tea/coffee & sea vistas
- large terrace with sea views
- seats in orchard & garden
- courtesy passenger transfer
- on-site parking

ACTIVITIES AVAILABLE

- heated swimming pool & sauna on site
- 300ha sheep farm on site, farm activities & tours
- walking tracks to 700m altitude with views over harbour & ocean to Alps
- bush walks & waterfall
- pétanque court on site
- pet lambs & hens on site
- wineries
- swimming with dolphins
- kayaking
- horse riding
- Akaroa cafés, restaurants, bars & shops, 5km away
- golf course
- Akaroa Harbour trips
- gardens open to visit
- arts & crafts; museum
- Onuku Marae

Onuku Heights

Onuku Heights

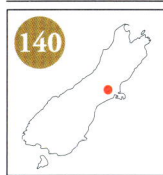

RAKAIA GORGE
Quickenberry

Hosts Christine and Robert Koller   *Phone* 0-3-318 6566   *Fax* 0-3-318 6566

Terrace Downs Golf Resort, The Rowans, Lake Coleridge Road, Rakaia Gorge
Freephone 0800 318 656   *Postal* Terrace Downs, R D 2, Darfield
Email quickenberry@xtra.co.nz   *Website* www.quickenberry.co.nz

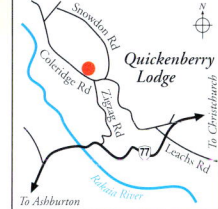

DIRECTIONS: From Christchurch, take SH 73. Turn left at Darfield into SH 77. Travel to Windwhistle & turn right towards Lake Coleridge. Turn left at Terrace Downs then 1st road to right, Quickenberry on right.

4 bdrm	4 enst

Double $300–$400
Single $250

Includes breakfast & dinner

Quickenberry is located in the high country, above the Rakaia Gorge, with rural vistas up the Rakaia River to the surrounding hills and mountains. Purpose built in 2005 to a Swiss design with New Zealand contemporary features, Quickenberry is the Norse mythological name for the rowan berries which abound in the region. Set on Terrace Downs Golf Resort, Quickenberry has a high country garden with New Zealand native plants and tussocks. Accommodation comprises four super-king/twin guestrooms, all with ensuites and balconies, and a spacious guest lounge with exposed beams, open fireplace and sunny courtyard. Dining is a highlight at Quickenberry, with breakfast and dinner served at individual tables in the dining room.

FACILITIES

- 4 super-king/twin ensuite bedrooms opening to balconies
- wheelchair access; fresh flowers
- cotton bed linen, tea/coffee, internet access, DVD & CD-player & phone in bedrooms
- hair dryers, toiletries, demist mirrors, heated floor & heated towel rails; 1 bath
- email, fax & phone available
- pre-dinner drink served
- full cooked & continental breakfast at separate tables
- 4-course dinner included in tariff
- large guest lounge with open fire, music, artwork, library & writing desk, opens to sunny courtyard
- complimentary laundry
- air-conditioning
- on-site parking; helipad

ACTIVITIES AVAILABLE

- garden with native NZ plants
- conferences, weddings & honeymoons catered for
- walks on site
- on-site Terrace Downs golf course available for guest use
- tennis courts nearby
- Rakaia River walkway
- arboretum at Lake Coleridge
- Awa Awa Reserve
- restaurants nearby
- Mt Hutt ski-field
- Castle Hill to view limestone formations
- skiing in winter
- hunting
- mountain-biking
- hot-air ballooning
- jet-boating
- fishing

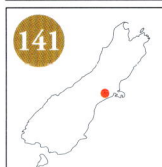

MOUNT HUTT–METHVEN
Green Gables Deer Farm

Hosts Colleen and Roger Mehrtens

185 Waimarama Road, Methven   *Postal* R D 12, Rakaia
Phone 0-3-302 8308   *Email* greengables@xtra.co.nz
Fax 0-3-302 8309   *Website* www.nzfarmstay.com

DIRECTIONS: From Christchurch, take SH 1 to Rakaia. Turn right & travel to Methven. Turn right again into SH 77. Continue into Waimarama Rd, veering left. Travel 4km to Green Gables Farm on left.

| 3 bdrm | 2 enst | 1 prbth | **Double** $140–$180
Single $110–$140 | *Includes breakfast*
Dinner extra |

Green Gables is a working deer farm, where guests can hand-feed Lucy the pet deer and others including the friendly white Royal Danish deer. This centrally located farm is one hour south of Christchurch City and its International Airport. Rural views from every room in the homestead extend to the nearby Mount Hutt ski area. The three guest bedrooms open on to a private verandah, with adjacent parking. Colleen enjoys preparing New Zealand cuisine for guests, and serves meals in the dining room, in front of the log fire in winter. Breakfast with cooked English-style options and dinner featuring the freshest local produce can be arranged, or restaurants are nearby. Green Gables was Supreme Winner in Ashburton's District Tourism Awards.

FACILITIES

- 2 super-king ensuite bedrooms
- 1 super-king/twin bedroom with private bathroom, including bath
- fridges in ensuite rooms
- oil-filled heater, clock-radio, tea/coffee, bathrobes, iron & ironing board in each bedroom
- private entrance, decking & mountain views from all 3 bedrooms
- tea/coffee upon arrival
- full breakfast in dining room
- dinner by request, $50 pp; vegetarians catered for
- dining room with log fire
- open fire, TV & DVD-player in sitting room
- double glazing
- phone, fax & internet jack
- golden labrador, Max
- on-site parking

ACTIVITIES AVAILABLE

- hand-feed pet deer Lucy & her family
- 2 golf courses – Methven & Terrace Downs; golf club & cart hire
- hot air ballooning
- jet boating
- salmon & trout fishing – guides by arrangement
- bush & mountain walks nearby
- licensed restaurants nearby at Mt Hutt/Methven village
- Mt Somers sub-alpine walkway
- private gardens open to visit
- horse riding
- skiing at Mt Hutt – transport from gate (closest accommodation)
- Christchurch International Airport, 1 hour north
- Christchurch City, 1¼ hours

ASHBURTON
Coniston Homestead

Hosts Carolyn and Donald Williamson

30 Methven Highway, R D 6, Ashburton
Phone 0-3-307 8189 *Mobile* 027 435 4705 *Fax* 0-3-307 8179
Email coniston@xtra.co.nz *Website* www.coniston.co.nz

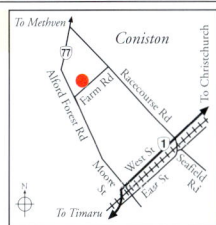

DIRECTIONS: From south end of Ashburton, turn west off SH 1 into Moore St, then continue on Alford Forest Rd (SH 77) for 3km to Coniston on right.

| 4 bdrm | 3 enst | 1 prbth | **Double $180–$220** **Single $140** | *Includes breakfast* *Lunch extra* |

A tree-lined driveway leads to the homestead at Coniston, built in 1918, when the extensive woodland gardens were planted. Recently renovated to provide four guestrooms, Coniston is located on a farm offering sheep, cropping and seed farm tours and activities to guests. The garden attracts birdlife and includes many rare and mature trees, with one planted to commemorate the visit of Queen Elizabeth II in 1981. The rhododendrons, azaleas and camellias feature in the springtime, the blossom reflected in the lake, where guests enjoy rowing. Continental and cooked breakfasts are served in the formal dining room or alfresco on the guest verandahs, looking out into the garden. Dinner is available at Ashburton restaurants nearby.

FACILITIES

- 1 super-king & 1 queen ensuite bedroom with TV & phone; queen room opens to verandah
- 2 twin bedrooms share 1 bathroom with spa bath
- hair dryers, toiletries, heated floors & towel rails, demist mirrors & bathrobes
- fresh flowers
- cotton bed linen
- children over 10 yrs welcome
- full breakfast served
- lunch by request, extra
- phone, fax & email available
- guest kitchenette
- guest lounge with open fire, TV, video, CDs, games, books & writing desk
- laundry available, $5
- on-site parking
- helicopter access

ACTIVITIES AVAILABLE

- 2ha (5-acre) gardens on site
- lake rowing & canal walk, on site
- marquee garden weddings on site; two vintage cars available
- sheep, cropping & seed farm tours & activities on site
- salmon/trout river fishing/guides
- 5 golf courses; horse trekking
- *The Lord of the Rings* sightseeing
- jet boating; hot air ballooning
- Mt Somers subalpine walkway; garden tours
- Lake Hood recreational lake, 10-min drive
- historic plains village & railway museum, 5 mins
- vintage car & farm machinery museum, 5 mins
- art gallery, tennis & indoor swimming, 3-min drive
- Mt Hutt ski-field, 30 mins

GERALDINE
The Crossing Guest Lodge

Manager Patti Epp

124 Woodbury Road, R D 21, Geraldine, South Canterbury
Phone 0-3-693 9689   *Email* srelax@xtra.co.nz
Fax 0-3-693 9789   *Website* friars.co.nz/hosts/crossing.html

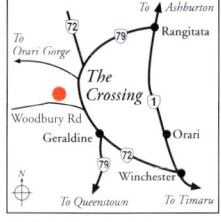

3 bdrm	3 enst	Double $160–$190	*Includes breakfast*	
		Single $140–$170	*Dinner extra*	

DIRECTIONS: Take SH 79 south until 200m past "Welcome" sign. Turn right into Woodbury Rd. Travel 1.5km to The Crossing on right. From Geraldine, take SH 72 north for 3km. Turn left into Woodbury Rd.

The Crossing is an English-style manor house, incorporating a fully licensed restaurant. Named after the original Waihi River crossing on the property, The Crossing was built as a banker's retirement estate in 1908. The lounge still features the panelled dado, open fireplace and grand piano, and with the dining room, opens on to a shady verandah where wisteria frames the expansive garden, rural pastureland and mountains beyond. Upstairs are the three renovated guestrooms, comprising the Sinclair-Thompson Suite with queen bed, bay window sitting area and ensuite, Catherine's Suite with queen and single beds, sitting area and ensuite, and the Sally Barker Suite with double antique and single beds, sitting area and ensuite bathroom.

FACILITIES

- 1 queen, 1 queen/twin & 1 double/twin ensuite bedrooms
- toiletries & hair dryers
- cotton bed linen
- children over 12 years welcome
- board games available
- separate TV lounge
- spacious reading lounges
- dining room with open fire
- peaceful garden for relaxing

- breakfast choice, served in dining room
- à la carte dinner by prior arrangement, extra
- fully licensed in-house restaurant
- guest lounge with open fireplace & grand piano
- bar opens to verandah & established garden
- on-site parking

ACTIVITIES AVAILABLE

- croquet & pétanque on site
- in-ground garden walks
- 14.8ha pasture for strolling
- trekking in Peel Forest & Talbot Forest
- white water rafting at Rangitata
- hunting, guides available
- 18 golf courses, 10-min to 1-hour drive away

- restaurants, 3km south
- salmon & trout fishing, guides available
- vintage car museum
- scenic walks
- private garden visits
- Geraldine, 3km away
- Timaru, 30 mins south
- Christchurch, 1¾ hrs north
- www.thecrossingbnb.co.nz

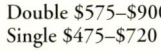

GERALDINE
Four Peaks Lodge

Hosts Ineke and Ashley Pierce

414 Four Peaks Road, R D 21, Geraldine
Phone 0-3-693 8587   *Email* info@fourpeakslodge.co.nz
Fax 0-3-693 8572   *Website* www.fourpeakslodge.co.nz

| 4 bdrm | 4 enst | Double $575–$900 Single $475–$720 | *Includes breakfast, apéritifs & dinner Lunch extra for single-night stays* |

DIRECTIONS: From Geraldine, turn into Woodbury Rd. Travel to Woodbury & turn left into McKeown Rd. Follow signs to Four Peaks Lodge. Or from SH 79, turn into Pleasant Valley Rd & follow signs to Lodge.

Four Peaks

Designed by Heathcote Helmore in 1924, Four Peaks Lodge is a Georgian-style homestead set in formal gardens bounded by woodlands and native bush. Recently renovated, the Lodge offers four ensuite guestrooms upstairs, which include a suite with a private lounge that opens onto a deep balcony overlooking the garden. A chef provides dinner, the meals being served in the formal dining room, or alfresco on the terrace. Guests enjoy the seclusion of Four Peaks with its deer farm and extensive bush and woodland walks where bird-watching is popular. The landscaped gardens can also be viewed from the warmth of a jacuzzi within the gazebo. The Lodge is close to the Inland Scenic Route at Geraldine, en route to Tekapo, Queenstown or Christchurch.

FACILITIES

- 1 queen & 3 super-king/twin ensuite bedrooms upstairs
- hair dryers, toiletries, heated towel rails & demist mirror
- bath, dual basin & double shower in suite with balcony
- cotton bed linen; bathrobes
- open fire & phone in drawing room opening to verandah
- fax & email available; Dutch spoken by hosts
- full breakfast, apéritifs, à la carte dinner & wine served
- light lunch included in tariff for multiple-night stays
- open fire, bar, Sky TV, CDs, games, artwork, books & writing desk in guest lounge, opening to terrace
- central heating; fresh flowers
- complimentary laundry
- on-site parking

ACTIVITIES AVAILABLE

- jacuzzi in formal gardens
- bush, woodland walks & deer farm on site
- golf courses nearby
- gardens open to visit
- high country wilderness tours
- walking & hiking
- native bird-watching
- white water rafting at Rangitata
- kayaking; mountain biking
- trout & salmon fishing
- glass blowing, 5-min drive
- Geraldine township, 10 mins
- vintage car museum, 10 mins
- local chocolate factory & cheese factory to visit, 10 mins
- quality local arts & crafts
- ski-fields & heli-skiing within 1-hour drive away
- Christchurch, 1¾ hrs north

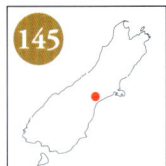

WINCHESTER
Kavanagh House

Hosts Juliearna and Killian Kavanagh

161 State Highway 1, Winchester   *Postal* P O Box 33, Winchester
Phone 0-3-615 6150   *Email* info@kavanaghhouse.co.nz
Fax 0-3-615 9694   *Website* www.kavanaghhouse.co.nz

DIRECTIONS: From Christchurch, take SH 1 south to Winchester. Kavanagh House on right in Winchester. From Timaru, take SH 1 north to Winchester. Kavanagh House on the left in Winchester.

| 3 bdrm | 3 enst | 1 pdrm | Room rate $195–$320 | *Includes breakfast* | *Lunch & dinner extra* |

Kavanagh House is a restored two-storey character home built in neo-Tudor style in 1907 in the rural setting of Winchester. Furnished with flair, Kavanagh House now provides accommodation comprising three ensuite bedrooms, two with private verandahs overlooking the rose garden, pastureland and mountains beyond. Features include the high hand-painted ceilings & carved bannisters. Guests are greeted with a complimentary glass of champagne on arrival and a licensed restaurant serves café-style food during the day and country cuisine in the evening. Gourmet breakfast, including cooked options such as Eggs Benedict and French toast, is served each morning in the café downstairs, and à la carte lunch and dinner are also available.

FACILITIES

- 1 queen & 2 king bedrooms, 2 with verandahs
- 3 ensuite bathrooms with toiletries, bathrobes, 1 spa bath & 2 claw-foot baths
- direct-dial phone, CD-player & fruit platter in bedrooms
- cotton bed linen; fresh flowers
- TV on request
- after 3pm check-in & 12-noon check-out

- gourmet breakfast
- fully licensed in-house restaurant for lunch/dinner
- champagne on arrival
- living room with open fire; central heating
- unsuitable for children under 10 years
- courtesy passenger transfer from Timaru Airport; on-site parking

ACTIVITIES AVAILABLE

- garden walks on site
- salmon & trout fishing; guides available
- trekking in Peel Forest
- golf courses
- white water rafting at Rangitata
- horse riding
- vintage car museum
- private gardens to visit
- hunting

- Winchester, short stroll
- scenic walks & tramping/hiking
- public parks & gardens
- ski-fields, 1-hour drive
- Geraldine, 8km
- Timaru, 30km south
- Lake Tekapo, 96km
- Christchurch, 147km
- Mt Cook, 195km

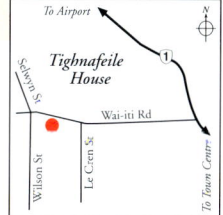

TIMARU
Tighnafeile House

Hosts Bev and Robin Jenkins

62 Wai-iti Road, Timaru   *Postal* P O Box 685, Timaru
Phone 0-3-684 3333   *Mobile* 025 386 272   *Fax* 0-3-684 3328
Email tighnafeile-house@timaru.co.nz   *Website* www.tighnafeile.com

DIRECTIONS: Take SH 1 towards Timaru. On north edge of town, opposite entrance to Caroline Bay, turn right into Wai-iti Rd. Travel 4 blocks to Tighnafeile House on left.

| 4 bdrm | 3 enst | 1 prbth | **Double $340** | **Single $320** | *Includes breakfast* |

Tighnafeile (pronounced "Tine-a-fay-lee") is Gaelic for "House of Welcome". This Dutch Jacobean mansion was designed by Timaru architect Walter Panton and built in 1911 originally for John Matheson, a station owner in the Mackenzie Country, and his wife and six children. After a varied history, the house has been restored and converted for accommodation, now offering two upstairs honeymoon suites, one with four-poster bed, twin bedroom with private bathroom, and single ensuite bedroom. Breakfast is served in the formal dining room downstairs and guests can relax in the private lounge, reading room and balcony, or on the extensive verandah opening to the spacious lawns and landscaped gardens. Caroline Bay is a five-minute walk away.

FACILITIES

- 1 king honeymoon suite
- 1 queen honeymoon suite
- 1 twin bedroom with private bathroom, heated towel rail & bath
- 1 single ensuite bedroom
- cotton bed linen
- TV available for bedrooms
- fresh flowers in bedrooms
- verandah opens to garden
- full breakfast in dining room
- tea/coffee in reading room, balcony overlooking garden
- phone, fax & email available
- TV, video & gas fire in private guest lounge
- laundry available, $5
- children over 12 yrs welcome
- courtesy passenger transfer
- off-street parking

ACTIVITIES AVAILABLE

- gardens & lawn on site
- art gallery, across road
- restaurants & bars nearby
- swimming pool nearby
- Caroline Bay, 5-min walk
- golf course nearby
- tennis stadium
- shopping, 1km
- private gardens open to visit
- Centennial Park, 5-min drive
- Timaru township, 1km
- Timaru Botanic Gardens, 10-min drive
- fishing trips arranged
- sightseeing trips arranged
- winter skiing, 95km
- Lake Tekapo, 105km
- Christchurch, 164km north
- Oamaru, 80km south
- Dunedin, 200km south

TOTARA VALLEY, PLEASANT POINT
Centre Hill Cottage

Host Ian Blakemore   *Mobile* 027 420 1120

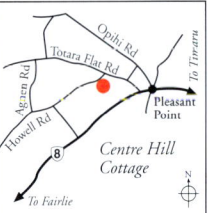

59 Howell Road, Pleasant Point   *Postal* Totara Valley, R D 12, Pleasant Point
Phone 0-3-614 7385   *Email* centre.hill@paradise.net.nz
Fax 0-3-614 7380   *Website* www.centrehillcottage.com

DIRECTIONS: From Timaru, take SH 8 to Pleasant Point. At hotel turn right into Tengawai Rd. Cross bridge, turn left into Totara Flat Rd, then left into Howell Rd. Centre Hill Cottage 1st on left, 5.2km from SH 8 turn-off.

2 bdrm	1 prbth

Cottage rate **$250 for 2 persons**
Extra persons $50 each

Includes continental breakfast provisions
Dinner extra   *Self-catering*

Centre Hill Cottage

Centre Hill Cottage is located on an organic farm where organic produce including meat is available for sampling. The cottage is self-contained with a full kitchen for self-catering. Continental breakfast provisions are supplied, and a chef can provide dinner by prior arrangement. Alternatively, restaurants are just five minutes away at Pleasant Point. Guests are offered two bedrooms, for single-party bookings only, with a large deck opening from the main bedroom and living area. From the outdoor bathtub, guests can enjoy the rural views over farmland to the Southern Alps. Centre Hill is two hours from Christchurch International Airport, 15 minutes from Timaru airport, and one hour from winter ski-fields and Lake Tekapo.

FACILITIES

- single-party bookings
- 1 self-contained cottage
- 1 queen & 1 twin bedroom
- 1 private bathroom & spa bath
- cotton bed linen; phone jack
- bathrobes, hair dryer, toiletries, heated towel rails, demist mirror & heated floor
- outdoor bath
- children welcome
- full kitchen for self-catering
- continental breakfast provisions
- organic venison, beef, lamb & some vegetables available
- chef available for dinner, by prior arrangement only
- tea/coffee, nibbles, TV, CDs, books, artwork & log fire
- laundry available
- on-site parking; garaging

ACTIVITIES AVAILABLE

- BBQ & outdoor bathtub
- swimming pool & tennis court (Oct.–March) on site
- organic farm walks on site
- Pleasant Point restaurants, shops, museum & steam railway, 5-min drive
- lake & river fishing
- Opihi vineyard
- Maori rock drawings
- walks; hiking; trekking
- gardens to visit; photography
- sketching; painting
- artisan gallery; taxidermist
- Timaru airport, 15 mins
- Timaru botanic gardens & beach, 20-min drive
- Lake Tekapo, 1-hour drive
- winter ski-fields, 1-hr drive
- Christchurch City, 2 hours

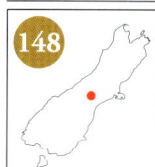
LAKE TEKAPO
Creel House Bed and Breakfast

Hosts Rosemary and Grant Brown

36 Murray Place, Lake Tekapo   *Postal* P O Box 39, Lake Tekapo
Phone 0-3-680 6516   *Email* creelhouse.l.tek@xtra.co.nz
Fax 0-3-680 6659   *Website* friars.co.nz/hosts/creel.html

DIRECTIONS: From Christchurch or Queenstown, take SH 8 to Lake Tekapo. East of church, turn south into Greig Street. At top of hill turn right into Murray Place. Creel House on the left.

3 bdrm	2 prbth	1 enst	**Double $140–$150** **Single $70–$80**	*Includes continental breakfast*

Creel House was named after the angler's fishing basket, Grant's guided fly fishing trips being a highlight for many visitors to Lake Tekapo. Creel House overlooks the lake with alpine views of the Southern Alps beyond. Guests can enjoy the panorama from the expansive balconies and the queen bedroom upstairs. Grant has built Creel House over the past 20 years in Norwegian chalet style, with the family living quarters separate below. Guests have private entrance stairs and a guest lounge featuring raised rimu ceilings and mounted trout. The Browns designed the colour scheme to blend with the Mackenzie Country environment. Rosemary has developed a New Zealand native garden around the house, with many hebes and native grasses.

FACILITIES

- 1 upstairs queen bedroom, with private bathroom & balcony overlooking Lake Tekapo
- 1 twin upstairs ensuite bedroom
- 1 downstairs queen bedroom, with private bathroom & bath
- feather duvets & electric blankets on all beds
- hair dryers & heaters in rooms
- expansive balcony with lake view, opening from lounge
- full continental breakfast with fresh fruit in season, home-made muffins & croissants
- separate guest lounge
- fishing trophies
- private guest entrance
- native garden
- alpine views of alps & lake
- laundry available
- well-behaved children welcome

ACTIVITIES AVAILABLE

- guided fly fishing for brown & rainbow trout with Grant, a member of NZ Professional Fishing Guide Association
- guided salmon excursions
- horse trekking; hunting
- golf course; water skiing
- summer lake swimming
- lakeside & alpine walks
- www.laketekapoflyfishing.co.nz
- scenic flights
- walks up Mt John
- restaurants nearby
- local craft shops
- historic Church of the Good Shepherd
- Mt Cook region
- ski-fields; ice skating
- guided mountaineering
- scenic drives & walks

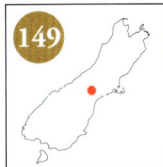

LAKE TEKAPO
Lake Tekapo Grandview

Hosts Leon and Rosemary O'Sullivan

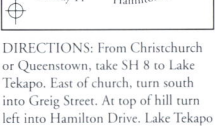

32 Hamilton Drive, Lake Tekapo   *Postal* P O Box 14, Lake Tekapo
Phone 0-3-680 6910   *Mobile* 021 111 3393   *Fax* 0-3-680 6912
Email info@laketekapograndview.co.nz   *Website* www.laketekapograndview.co.nz

DIRECTIONS: From Christchurch or Queenstown, take SH 8 to Lake Tekapo. East of church, turn south into Greig Street. At top of hill turn left into Hamilton Drive. Lake Tekapo Grandview at bottom of hill on right.

| 4 bdrm | 4 enst | 1 pdrm | **Room rate $220–$270** | *Includes breakfast* |

Grandview

Lake Tekapo Grandview was built on an elevated site in 2001 to provide unobstructed lake and alpine views. The interior design complements the surrounding landscape and the four ensuite guestrooms feature hand-embroidered bed linen. Three of the bedrooms open to verandahs with panoramic lake views, and the fourth bedroom has views of the snow-capped mountains. A gourmet breakfast menu is provided and served in the dining room. A hospitality hour is popular with guests before dining at the local restaurants nearby. Lake Tekapo Grandview is set in a newly landscaped garden featuring roses and rocks. Guests enjoy the local golf, boating, fishing, climbing, historic sites and exploring Mount Cook National Park.

FACILITIES

- 2 super-king/twin & 2 king bedrooms, each with ensuite
- cotton bed linen, writing desk, phone, TV & tea/coffee
- spa bath in 2 bathrooms
- hair dryer, toiletries, heated mirror, floor & towel rails
- complimentary laundry
- phone, fax & email available
- fresh flowers
- continental & cooked breakfast menus
- private guest lounge with CD-player, artwork & book exchange
- children welcome
- 1 powder room
- central heating
- private guest entrance
- off-street parking

ACTIVITIES AVAILABLE

- honeymoons & weddings catered for
- newly landscaped garden on site with rocks & roses
- star watching
- scenic walks
- golf courses
- boating; fishing
- climbing; hunting
- salmon farm
- restaurants, walking distance
- historic stone church & collie dog monument at lake edge
- horse trekking
- sightseeing tours
- hydro canals
- scenic flights
- skiing in winter
- Mt Cook National Park
- Timaru, 1¼-hour drive

Grandview

LAKE TEKAPO

Lake Tekapo Lodge

Hosts Lynda and John van Beek   *Mobile* 021 129 9439

24 Aorangi Crescent, Lake Tekapo   *Postal* P O Box 123, Lake Tekapo
Freephone 0800 LAKE TEKAPO   *Phone* 0-3-680 6566   *Fax* 0-3-680 6599
Email lake.tekapo.lodge@xtra.co.nz   *Website* www.laketekapolodge.co.nz

| 4 bdrm | 4 enst | 1 pdrm | Room rate $200–$395 | *Includes breakfast Lunch & dinner extra* |

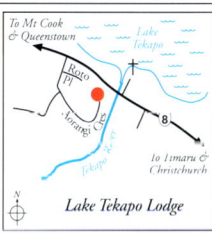

DIRECTIONS: From Christchurch, take SH 1 south to Rangitata. Turn right into SH 79 to Fairlie. Then turn right into SH 8 to Lake Tekapo. Take 2nd turn on left into Aorangi Cres. Lake Tekapo Lodge at end.

Opened in 1998, Lake Tekapo Lodge is built with adobe earth block cladding, with Gothic-style antique church doors from England at the entrance. The dining room and three of the four guest ensuite bedrooms open to the decking with panoramic lake views. The guest lounge also features a star-watching window for star gazing in the clear night sky. The guestrooms are all fire-rated and have underfloor heating, with 100% wool carpets and bed covers ensuring year-round comfort. Meals are served in the dining room beside the open fire, or alfresco on the deck in the sun. The adjacent walkway takes guests directly down to the town amenities. From there it is an easy drive east to Timaru, or west past Lake Pukaki to Mt Cook and Twizel.

FACILITIES

- 2 queen/twin & 2 super-king ensuite fire-rated bedrooms, with phones
- hair dryers, toiletries, heated flooring, heated towel rails, bathrobes & slippers; 1 spa bath
- cotton bed linen; fresh flowers
- 3 bedrooms open to decking
- TV, fridge, tea/coffee, gas fire & star-watch window in guest lounge
- laundry available, $10 per load

- 3-course dinner, $70 pp, BYO, by arrangement
- lunch or picnic hampers, $20 pp, by arrangement
- open fire in dining room
- TV, fax, email available
- private guest entrance
- John speaks Dutch
- courtesy passenger transfer
- off-street parking

ACTIVITIES AVAILABLE

- pétanque, golf putting on lawn
- fishing gear, tennis racquets & mountain bikes available
- spinning demonstrations & lessons, by arrangement
- fishing in rivers & lake; guide available by arrangement
- star watching with guide
- horse treks; shooting
- bird-watching reserve, 10 mins

- 4 restaurants across road
- historic stone church
- sheepdog monument
- golf, 4km; canoeing
- watersports
- walking & hiking tracks
- ice skating & skiing, 30 mins
- scenic flights over Mt Cook, lakes, Fox & Franz Josef glaciers
- Timaru, 1¼-hour drive

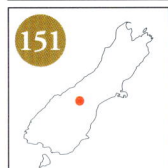

TWIZEL, MT COOK
Matuka Lodge

Hosts Rosalie and Russell Smith

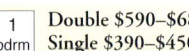

Old Station Road, Twizel   *Postal* P O Box 63, Twizel
Phone 0-3-435 0144   *Email* info@matukalodge.co.nz
Fax 0-3-435 0149   *Website* www.matukalodge.co.nz

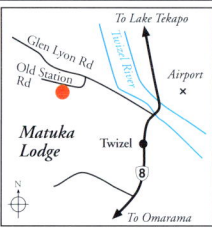

DIRECTIONS: From Lake Tekapo, take SH 8 south towards Twizel. Cross Twizel River, then turn right into Glen Lyon Rd. After 3km, turn left into Old Station Rd. Matuka Lodge is on the left.

3 bdrm	3 enst	1 pdrm	Double $590–$680 Single $390–$450	*Includes breakfast, apéritifs, dinner & wine*

Opened in 2004, Matuka Lodge provides purpose-built contemporary accommodation, in the countryside just north of Twizel. Set on nearly two hectares of tussock land, with uninterrupted views to the Ben Ohau Range, and the Southern Alps beyond, Matuka Lodge is located beside a natural pond, with itinerant trout. Overlooking the pond are the two guest wings, with three bedrooms, spacious ensuites and quality fittings. All meals and wine are included in the tariff. Breakfast and dinner using fresh New Zealand produce, such as salmon and venison, are served in the dining room. Picnic lunches are also available. The lounge opens to the sunroom with decking extending over the pond, and there is a separate den and guest area.

FACILITIES

- 2 super-king/twin bedrooms, each with spa bath in ensuite
- 1 king ensuite bedroom
- dressing room, phone, iron, heat pump/air-conditioner & verandah from each bedroom
- hair dryer, toiletries, heated floors & towel rails in ensuites
- guest lounge with log fire, music, magazines & artwork
- fresh flowers

- cooked & continental breakfast in dining room
- picnic lunch available
- 4-course dinner with wine
- guest area with fridge, tea/coffee, nibbles & computer
- den with Sky TV, videos, DVDs & library
- self-service laundry
- on-site parking; helipad

ACTIVITIES AVAILABLE

- 2ha (4 acres) land with BBQ
- helicopter tours from Lodge to Mt Cook & glaciers
- fishing in rivers, streams or lakes, within 30-min drive
- tours to high country station
- site of climactic battle in *Rings* movie, *Return of the King*
- alpine walks
- Twizel township, 3km south

- tours to black stilt (world's most endangered wading bird) breeding programme
- golf cross; heli-biking
- tramping & hiking
- tours to Aoraki/Mt Cook, 45-min drive
- mountain climbing
- Christchurch, 3 hours north
- Queenstown, 3 hours south

TWIZEL, MT COOK
Aoraki Lodge

Hosts Oksana and Vlad Fomin

32 Mackenzie Drive, Twizel
Phone 0-3-435 0300   *Email* aorakilodge@xtra.co.nz
Fax 0-3-435 0305   *Website* friars.co.nz/hosts/aoraki.html

DIRECTIONS: From Lake Tekapo, take SH 8 to Twizel. Turn right into Ruataniwha Rd. At "T" junction, at service station, turn left into Mackenzie Drive. Travel 100m to Aoraki Lodge on left.

4 bdrm	4 enst	Double $160–$180	*Includes breakfast*
		Single $100	Multiple-night rates available

Aoraki Lodge is located in Twizel, the nearest town to Mount Cook, which is 40 minutes' drive away. The Lodge is also conveniently situated half-way between Christchurch City and Queenstown. Oksana and Vlad operate a tour company, *Rock Wolf*, which provides specialist guided tours including boating day trips, fishing, tramping and weekend family boat trips. Guests enjoy staying several days at Aoraki Lodge to take in the activities of the high country region. The four ensuite guestrooms open to a sunny verandah. A leisurely breakfast, either continental or cooked, includes Oksana's home-made specialities and local produce. A variety of restaurants in the town centre are only a two-minute walk away.

FACILITIES

- 1 queen/twin, 1 double/twin, 1 double & 1 twin bedroom
- 4 ensuite bathrooms with toiletries, heated towel rails, hair dryers & 1 bath
- TV, oil-filled heaters & electric blankets in all 4 bedrooms
- wheelchair access to 2 ensuite bedrooms
- fresh flowers
- smoking outside
- continental/cooked breakfast
- laundry $10
- Sky TV, video, tea/coffee & open fire in guest lounge
- phone, fax & email available
- complimentary laundry
- hosts live off site
- off-street parking
- children welcome

ACTIVITIES AVAILABLE

- guided tours, boat trips, tramping, fishing & weekend family boat trips with hosts
- star gazing
- restaurants in walking distance
- Mt Cook National Park, 40 mins
- alpine walks; tramping
- fishing safaris; hunting
- golf course
- farm tours
- Twizel shops, 2-min walk
- mountain biking
- horse trekking
- mountain climbing
- 4WD safaris
- scenic flights
- winter skiing
- Christchurch, 3 hrs north
- Queenstown, 3 hrs south

Twizel, Mt Cook
Heartland Lodge

Hosts Kerry and Steve Carey   *Phone* 0-3-435 0008

19 North West Arch, Twizel, South Canterbury   *Postal* P O Box 38, Twizel
Freephone 0800 164 666   *Mobile* 021 230 7502   *Fax* 0-3-435 0387
Email heartlandlodge@xtra.co.nz   *Website* www.heartland-lodge.co.nz

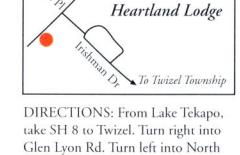

DIRECTIONS: From Lake Tekapo, take SH 8 to Twizel. Turn right into Glen Lyon Rd. Turn left into North West Arch. Travel to Heartland Lodge on left. From Omarama, take SH 8 to Twizel & turn left into Glen Lyon Rd.

| 4 bdrm | 4 enst | 1 pdrm | **Double $200–$250** | **Single $180** | *Includes breakfast* |

Set in a private garden featuring a pond, Heartland Lodge was purpose built to provide four ensuite guestrooms, three with spa baths and one with a therapeutic sauna. Guests are served a full breakfast in the dining room or alfresco in the garden, and restaurants and cafés are nearby in Twizel township. Kerry is of Maori descent and is happy to share her knowledge of Maori history and culture with guests. Steve, a professional fly-fishing guide, is happy to guide guests who wish to go trout fishing. Views of the surrounding mountains inspire the guests to explore the Aoraki/Mt Cook National Park in the region. Guests also enjoy tours of *The Lord of the Rings* sites and the local swimming pool in summer, or skiing in winter.

FACILITIES

- Aoraki, Pukaki, Ben Ohau: 3 super-king/twin ensuite bedrooms with spa baths
- Totara: 1 queen ensuite bedroom with therapeutic private sauna
- toiletries & hair dryers
- complimentary laundry
- lounge with open fire, tea/coffee, nibbles, Sky TV, video, DVD, CD-player & artwork
- powder room
- full cooked or continental breakfast served in dining room or alfresco in garden
- fresh flowers
- email, fax & phone available for guest use
- children welcome
- mountain views
- Maori culture
- on-site parking

ACTIVITIES AVAILABLE

- private garden with pond on site for walking & relaxing
- fly fishing with resident professional guide, Steve
- Maori culture with Kerry
- star gazing from site
- swimming pool
- climbing wall
- Aoraki/Mt Cook National Park
- restaurants, 10-min walk to Twizel township
- *The Lord of the Rings* sightseeing tours
- horse trekking
- kayaking; walking
- mountain climbing
- scenic flights; heli-skiing
- Christchurch, 3 hrs north
- Queenstown, 3 hrs south

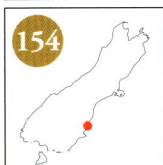

Centrewood Historic Homestead

Hosts Drs Jane and David Loten

Bobby's Head Road, Goodwood, R D 1, Palmerston
Phone 0 3 465 1977 *Email* centrewood@xtra.co.nz
Fax 0-3-465 1977 *Website* www.ccostay.co.nz

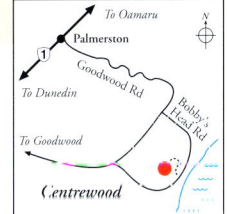

DIRECTIONS: Take SH 1 to Palmerston. Turn east at Warren's Garage into Goodwood Rd. Travel about 10 mins, then turn left into Bobby's Head Rd. Travel 1.5km to Centrewood on right.

| 2 bdrm | 1 prbth | Room rate $200–$400 | *Includes breakfast* | *Dinner extra* | |

Centrewood is a large heritage country homestead set in 20 hectares of farmland and native bush, conveniently situated mid-way between Christchurch and Queenstown. It is adjacent to rugged cliffs, unpopulated sandy beaches, and yellow-eyed penguins and seals. Original features include ornate plaster ceilings, marble fireplaces and spacious rooms. Guests enjoy a separate private wing, containing two bedrooms, bathroom and guest living room with billiards, piano and classical music. Exclusive bookings in the guest wing ensure privacy. Pre-dinner drinks are served in the living room around the open fire, with dinner in the dining room. As Ernest, Lord Rutherford's great-granddaughter, Jane has set up a corner of Rutherford scientific and family memorabilia.

FACILITIES

- single-party bookings only for private guest wing
- 1 king & 1 queen/twin bedroom
- 1 large private bathroom with bath, hair dryer & toiletries
- private guest living room with CD-player, TV, video, billiards table, piano, desk, fridge & tea/coffee
- private guest entrance
- laundry, phone & email

- breakfast – fresh fruit, home-made bread, croissants & cooked option
- lunch, picnic hampers & afternoon tea by arrangement
- dinner – garden-fresh produce & country cuisine, $40–$60 pp
- spacious verandahs
- daffodils, rhododendrons & roses in extensive gardens

ACTIVITIES AVAILABLE

- cliff walk adjacent, to view seals, yellow-eyed penguins, seabirds
- ocean & sandy beach, adjacent to property, in walking distance
- native bird-watching on site
- guided wildlife tours & horse riding by arrangement
- farm activities & tame animals eg horse, goat, calves & cattle
- 2 local golf courses; tennis court on site; bicycles available

- restaurants, 10-min drive
- Rutherford memorabilia
- in-house billiards & piano
- books on natural history & early settlers
- Moeraki Boulders, 20 mins
- Oamaru, 45-min drive north
- Dunedin City, 40 mins south
- Christchurch, 300km north
- Queenstown, 300km west

Centrewood

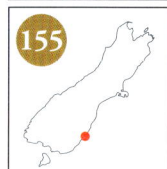

PORT CHALMERS, DUNEDIN
The Ridge Over Blueskin

Hosts Michelle and Mike Turfus

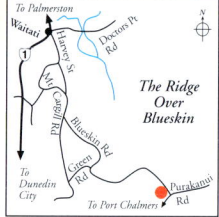

603 Blueskin Road, R D 1, Port Chalmers, Otago
Phone 0-3-482 2126   *Mobile* 027 222 4858   *Fax* 0-3-482 2125
Email relax@theridgeoverblueskin.co.nz   *Website* www.theridgeoverblueskin.co.nz

DIRECTIONS: From Dunedin, take SH 1 north to Waitati. Turn right into Harvey St. Travel 1km & veer right into Mt Cargill Rd. Travel 3.4km & veer left into Blueskin Rd. Travel 3.9km to The Ridge Over Blueskin on right.

| 1 bdrm | 1 prbth | Double $385 Single $330 | *Includes breakfast* *Lunch & dinner extra* |

The Ridge Over Blueskin is a private, secluded replica of an early settler's cottage, built on the sunny ridge of the north face of Mihiwaka. Set 340 metres above sea level, overlooking the Pacific Ocean to the north-east, the cottage also has views to bush-clad hills to the west and the Silver Peak mountain range beyond, with the Kakanui Mountains to the north. Opened in January 2005, the cottage is located on eight hectares (20 acres) surrounded by mature manuka trees and native bush which attracts the birdlife. The Ridge Over Blueskin offers guest privacy, with the hosts' home 40 metres away. A full breakfast is served at the cottage or alfresco on the verandah with panoramic sea views. Dunedin City is just 20 minutes' drive away.

FACILITIES

- 1 private cottage
- 1 king bedroom
- 1 private bathroom with claw-foot bath
- cotton bed linen; bathrobes
- hair dryer & toiletries
- self-serve laundry in cottage
- email, fax & phone available
- honeymoons & special occasions catered for
- full breakfast served in cottage or alfresco
- 4-course dinner, $70 pp
- set menu changed daily; all produce sourced locally
- lounge with gas fire, mini-bar, tea, coffee & microwave
- books, DVD & CD-playcr
- on-site parking; helipad
- hosts in house 40m away

ACTIVITIES AVAILABLE

- in-house naturopath & skincare massage, by arrangement, extra
- individual personalised tours designed by request
- native bush & beach walks
- scenic helicopter sightseeing
- royal albatross colony
- yellow-eyed penguins & seals
- guided trout heli-fishing
- restaurants, 10–25 mins
- heritage architecture
- art galleries, museums
- university; 4WD tours
- Taieri Gorge Railway
- Botanic Gardens
- 13 golf courses
- harbour cruises
- Luxury Chauffeurs (*see pages* 252–3); airport transfer, extra

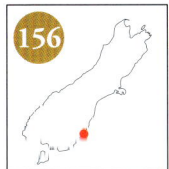

DUNEDIN CITY
Mandeno House

Host Roni Pickett

667 George Street, Dunedin
Phone 0-3-471 9595   *Email* mandeno.house@xtra.co.nz
Fax 0-3-474 5056   *Website* www.mandenohouse.com

DIRECTIONS: From north, take SH 1 into Cumberland St. Turn right into St David St & left into George St Mandeno on right. From south take SH 1 into Gt King St & turn left into Union St, then right into George St.

3 bdrm	3 enst	Double $225	Single $185	*Includes breakfast*

Set in formal green and white gardens, featuring over 100 white roses, Mandeno House has been restored to provide quality accommodation in the heart of Dunedin. Designed by Harry Mandeno in 1936, the architecture of this home is complemented by the interiors, with design elements influenced by Scottish designer Charles Rennie Macintosh. With careful attention to detail, the understated design of Mandeno House provides a sophisticated ambience for guests to relax in. Three ensuite bedrooms are offered upstairs, with a guest lounge and separate dining room downstairs, where a full breakfast is served including fresh fruit in season, home-baked muesli, home-made bread and cooked options, or room service if preferred.

FACILITIES

- 1 twin & 2 queen bedrooms
- 3 ensuites, each with toiletries, hair dryer, demist mirror & bathrobes
- cotton bed linen; fresh flowers
- writing desk, phone & Sky TV in all 3 bedrooms
- guest lounge includes tea/coffee facilities, nibbles, CD-player, games, library & artwork
- extensive music library

- full breakfast served in dining room, or room service available
- supper by request, extra
- central heating
- fax & email available
- fresh flowers
- self-serve laundry
- private guest entrance
- off-street parking

ACTIVITIES AVAILABLE

- BBQ on site
- weddings/honeymoons catered
- tours/dining arranged
- bus passes door
- Dunedin CBD, 5-min easy walk away
- Otago University adjacent
- parks & botanic garden
- private gardens open to visit
- museum

- large variety restaurants, bars cafés & shops in George Street
- steepest street in the world
- wildlife harbour cruises
- Otago Peninsula
- penguin colony
- Larnach Castle & Scottish heritage sites
- Taieri Gorge Railway
- Dunedin airport, 30-min drive

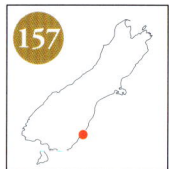

ROSLYN, DUNEDIN
Mahara

Host Rosie Creighton

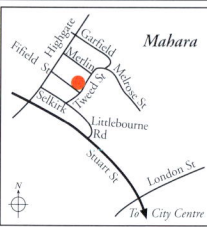

2 Fifield Street, Roslyn, Dunedin
Phone 0-3-467 5811   *Mobile* 021 217 2438   *Fax* 0-3-467 5587
Email reservations@mahara.co.nz   *Website* www.mahara.co.nz

DIRECTIONS: From the Octagon, turn up Stuart St. Turn right into Littlebourne Rd. Turn left into Tweed St. Take 2nd left into Fifield St. Mahara immediately on right, on corner of Tweed & Fifield Streets.

 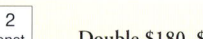

| 2 bdrm | 2 enst | Double $180–$350 | Single $145–$300 | *Includes breakfast* |

Designed by architect E.W. Waldron for retailer Andrew Lee's daughters, Mahara is one of two adjacent Edwardian homes built in 1905. Still retaining its Queen Anne revival features, Mahara now offers two guestrooms upstairs. The carved staircase ascends to a cathedral-size stained-glass window created by R.H. Fraser, and other historic features include the ornate plaster ceilings, carved archways, open fireplaces and bay windows in original sash style with leadlights. Teas, freshly ground coffee, and hot chocolate with marshmallows are available anytime in the drawing room and there is also a billiards room. Annie Lee's Room has antique beds, television area and harbour views, while the Leebank Room has garden views and local artwork.

FACILITIES

- 1 queen ensuite bedroom
- 1 queen/twin with ensuite & claw-foot bath
- cotton bed linen, phone, TV, writing desk, port & mineral water, chocolates, ironing facilities & fresh flowers
- hair dryers, heated towel rails, toiletries, bathrobes & slippers
- photocopier, fax & email
- laundry available, $8

- continental & cooked breakfast in drawing room
- open fire, teas, coffee, hot chocolate, biscuits, books & magazines in drawing room
- children by arrangement; baby's cot available
- central heating
- harbour & city views
- private guest entrance

ACTIVITIES AVAILABLE

- billiards room with full-size table
- landscaped gardens on site with mature trees & rhododendron dell
- Olveston historic home tours
- golf links nearby; beach & bush walks
- royal albatross colony; yellow-eyed penguin adventure tours
- guided heritage tours; NZ's 1st university
- NZ's 1st botanic garden

- Central City restaurants, cafés & shops, 3-min drive
- Moana swimming pool
- Larnach Castle; horse treks
- museums; Carisbrook Oval
- Scottish heritage, Victorian architecture; art galleries
- harbour cruises; wildlife tours
- private gardens open to visit
- Taieri Gorge railway trips

DUNEDIN CITY
Fletcher Lodge

Hosts Keith and Ewa Rozecki-Pollard

276 High Street, Dunedin
Freephone 0800 THELODGE   *Phone* 0 3 477 5552   *Fax* 0 3 474 5551
Email admin@fletcherlodge.co.nz   *Website* www.fletcherlodge.co.nz

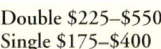

6 bdrm	6 enst	Double $225–$550 Single $175–$400	*Includes breakfast*

DIRECTIONS: Central Dunedin. From The Octagon, travel south along Princes St. Turn right into Rattray St, then left into Broadway. Turn right up High St. Fletcher Lodge is 200m up the hill on the right.

Just minutes' walk from Dunedin town centre, Fletcher Lodge was built in 1923 by Sir James Fletcher, to serve as his private residence while overseeing the construction of the 1926 South Seas Exhibition. Set in secluded mature gardens, this Dutch colonial-style house features decorative brick and plaster work, extensive oak panelling and ornate plaster ceilings, with leadlight and stained-glass windows. The Lodge is richly furnished with antique period furniture. Guests are welcomed in the panelled oak lounge, warmed in winter by a large fireplace and overlooking a sunken garden. The carved staircase with elaborate newel posts leads to the four ensuite guest bedrooms upstairs, with a further two downstairs.

FACILITIES

- 1 super-king, 2 super-king/twin, 1 king & 2 queen bedrooms, all with heated floor ensuites
- quality bed linen; fresh flowers
- direct-dial phone, & flat-screen TV in all 6 bedrooms
- internet access
- guests' coffee/tea facilities
- fax & photocopier available
- laundry service, $20

- full breakfast served in formal dining room, includes fresh orange juice, fresh fruit, cereals, yoghurt, freshly baked croissants, home-made conserves, full cooked option
- complimentary port in oak-panelled guest lounge
- refreshments on arrival
- spa pool, bar & BBQ
- off-street parking

ACTIVITIES AVAILABLE

- tours & dining arranged
- guided heritage tours; Olveston; railway station; Lanarch Castle
- rhododendron festival
- Glenfalloch Woodland Garden
- Royal Albatross Colony
- yellow-eyed penguin tours
- many golf courses
- Speight's brewery tours
- Botanic Gardens

- fine restaurants, within walking distance
- Dunedin City shops, 5-min walk downhill
- international standard museums & art galleries
- Cadbury's tours
- wildlife harbour cruises
- Taieri Gorge Railway
- Carisbrook sports stadium

© Friars' Guide to New Zealand Accommodation for the Discerning Traveller

MORNINGTON, DUNEDIN
Elgin House

Hosts Carolyn and Roger Rennie

31 Elgin Road, Mornington, Dunedin
Freephone 0800 272 940   *Mobile* 027 635 5784   *Phone* 0-3-453 0004
Email inquiry@elginhouse.co.nz   *Website* www.elginhouse.co.nz

DIRECTIONS: From City Centre, turn right up High St. Turn right into Mailer St & continue through Mornington. Turn left into Elgin Rd. Elgin House on left. From south, take Mornington Rd into Elgin Rd.

| 3 bdrm | 1 enst | 2 prbth |

Room rate $250–$295   *Includes breakfast*

Elgin House is a historic Dunedin home built circa 1898, with city and sea views. This three-storey Victorian home now offers guests the Inglenook and Oriel rooms with bay windows and the Garden room opening to the country garden featuring roses. Elgin House retains many original features including the ornate native kauri panelling and stairwells, iron and tiled open fireplaces, and stained glass windows. On arrival, guests are offered tea, coffee, juice and home baking, and can enjoy a complimentary bottle of New Zealand wine in front of a roaring fire or in their rooms prior to visiting a Dunedin restaurant for dinner. A full breakfast is served in the dining room. A small Bichon Frise dog named Sash completes the family.

FACILITIES

- Inglenook: 1 king ensuite bedroom, bay window, window seat & Jetmaster fireplace
- Garden: 1 king bedroom with private bathroom
- Oriel: 1 king bedroom with private bathroom & bay window
- cotton bed linen, TV, tea/coffee, fresh baking, bathrobes & slippers in bedrooms
- toiletries & hair dryers

- full continental or cooked breakfast served
- turn-down service, bottle of wine & port in rooms
- lounge with open fire, video, DVD & CD-player
- laundry service, $25
- email & cordless phone
- fresh flowers
- off-street parking

ACTIVITIES AVAILABLE

- DVDs, music & CDs
- home theatre system
- large cottage garden for reading & relaxing
- bus-stop at doorstep
- Olveston House
- Larnach Castle
- art galleries; museums
- botanic garden
- City Centre, 3-min drive

- restaurants, nearby
- beach walks
- surfing
- golf courses
- albatross & penguin colonies, 30 mins away
- gardens open to visit
- guided heritage tours
- Carisbrook Park
- gateway to Catlins

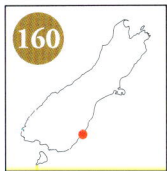

160

CAVERSHAM, DUNEDIN
Lisburn House

Hosts Olivia and Alan Johnston

15 Lisburn Avenue, Caversham, Dunedin
Phone 0 3 455 8888   *Email* stay@lisburnhouse.co.nz
Fax 0 3 455 6788   *Website* friars.co.nz/hosts/lisburnhouse.html

DIRECTIONS: From Queenstown, take 3H 1 into Dunedin. Turn right at 1st lights at Caversham into South Rd. Lisburn Ave is 5th street on left. Lisburn House is on the left.

3 bdrm	1 enst	2 prbth	Double $195–$265 Single $170–$200	*Includes breakfast* **Extra person $70**	*Dinner extra*

Lisburn House was built in 1865 as a townhouse for an Outram farming family. Set in a mature garden, this two-storey Gothic style townhouse still features the original exterior, with decorative polychrome brickwork walls, lattice-work slate roof and stained glass. The interior includes a marble-floor entrance hall with sweeping carved staircase, panelled dining room, tall arched windows, high ceilings, cornices and spindles. Guests enjoy the blend of Irish and Kiwi hospitality, sharing port with Olivia and Alan in front of the oval open fire in the entrance hall, or tiled fireplace in the lounge. Each bedroom has its own style: "Blue", "Rose" and "Victorian" with four-poster beds. Bookings are essential for the in-house boutique à la carte restaurant.

FACILITIES

- 3 queen bedrooms upstairs, 2 with private bathrooms, 1 with bath in ensuite
- 4-poster beds in all 3 bedrooms, with extra single bed in "Rose"
- quality bed linen; fresh flowers
- fresh fruit, chilled mineral water, pot-pourri & towelling bathrobes in all 3 bedrooms
- Historic Places Trust category 1
- children welcome

- à la carte dinner, extra, served in boutique restaurant, in-house, booking essential
- continental & full cooked breakfast choices
- coffee/tea offered on arrival
- open fireplaces in panelled hall, dining & drawing rooms
- laundry available
- off-street parking

ACTIVITIES AVAILABLE

- NZ's 1st Botanic Gardens
- albatross & penguin colonies
- peninsula wildlife tours
- museums & art galleries
- guided heritage tours
- beach & clifftop walks
- historic gold trail train trips
- Carisbrook Sports Park
- restaurants, within walking distance

- Edwardian/Victorian architecture
- St Clair beach; golf courses
- Larnach Castle; Olveston House
- private & public garden visits
- heated fresh- & salt-water pools
- harbour salmon fishing & cruises
- inland guided trout fishing
- City Centre, 5-min drive
- airport, 25-min direct drive
- gateway to Southern Scenic Route

CORSTORPHINE, DUNEDIN
Corstorphine House

Hosts Irina and Nico Francken

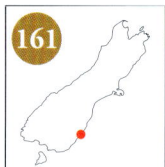

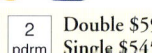

23A Milburn Street, Corstorphine, Dunedin   *Phone* 0-3-487 1000
Postal P O Box 3058, Dunedin   *Fax* 0-3-487 6672
Email info@corstorphine.co.nz   *Website* corstorphine.co.nz

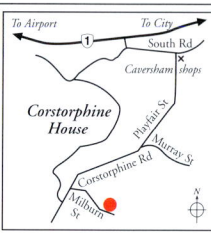

DIRECTIONS: From Dunedin City, take SH 1 south. Take Caversham turn-off, then left into South Rd. Turn right into Playfair St. Continue into Corstorphine Rd. Turn left into Milburn St. Corstorphine House on left.

7 bdrm	7 onct	2 pdrm	Double $595 Single $545	*Includes breakfast Lunch & dinner extra*

Built in 1863 on a hill overlooking Dunedin with views of the harbour and surrounding mountains, Corstorphine House was extended in 1905 by the original family, who lived there for 100 years. This Edwardian mansion has now been fully restored and converted to provide accommodation. Irina, who hails from Russia, and Nico, from the Netherlands, have totally renovated and re-furnished Corstorphine as a luxury private hotel. Seven guestrooms are decorated in individual themes with quality bathroom fittings and great attention to detail. A full breakfast is served in the main dining room or alfresco in the garden or gazebo. À la carte dinner is available in the Conservatory Restaurant, and private dining can be arranged in the house.

FACILITIES

- 1 queen/twin & 6 super-king ensuite bedrooms
- cotton bed linen; fresh flowers
- toiletries, bidets, heated towel rails, heated floor, hair dryers, demist mirrors & bathrobes
- phone, fax & email available
- laundry available
- German, French, Spanish, Russian & Dutch spoken

- full breakfast served in dining room or alfresco
- à la carte lunch & dinner served in Conservatory Restaurant or in private dining room, extra
- fully licensed
- room service
- wheelchair access to 4 rooms
- small conference facilities
- on-site parking

ACTIVITIES AVAILABLE

- formal gardens, organic vegetables, fruits, herbs & nuts, chickens, mature trees & birds, goat, pond & streams on site
- eco-tours on scenic peninsula or Catlins to view albatrosses, penguins & seals – selfdrive, group, boat or private tour
- gardens to visit – botanic, private, public & historic
- sparsely populated beaches with white sand, surf, wildlife & cliffs

- City – art galleries, museums & university, 10-min drive away
- royal albatross colony
- 13 golf courses
- heritage architecture – Olverston House, Larnach Castle & Railway Station
- harbour cruises & fishing
- Taieri Gorge railway & 4WD tours

Above: The Scandanavian bedroom with super-king bed is one of the seven spacious themed guestrooms at Corstorphine House.
Below: A Flowform fountain is featured in the front garden and designed as an aesthetic eco-organ to mimic the heart flow.
Opposite top: Built as an Edwardian mansion, Corstorphine House is set in formal gardens with walks through mature trees.
Opposite bottom left: The spacious ensuite bathroom of the Scandanavian guestroom features a claw foot slipper bath and bidet.
Opposite bottom right: Guests can dine privately in the Russian room, or alternatively in the à la carte Conservatory Restaurant.

© Friars' Guide to New Zealand Accommodation for the Discerning Traveller

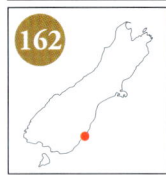

SHIEL HILL, DUNEDIN
Nature Guides Otago / Nisbet Cottage

Hosts Hildegard and Ralf Lübcke

6A Elliffe Place, Shiel Hill, Dunedin   *Postal* P O Box 8058, Dunedin
Phone 0-3-454 5169   *Email* info@natureguidesotago.co.nz
Fax 0-3-454 5369   *Website* www.natureguidesotago.co.nz

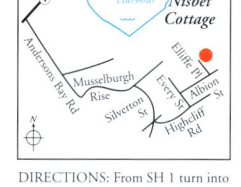

DIRECTIONS: From SH 1 turn into Andersons Bay Rd. Continue into Musselburgh Rise, then Silverton St. Turn left into Highcliff Rd. Turn left again into Every St, right into Albion St, then left into Elliffe Pl to Cottage.

| 2 bdrm | 2 enst | Nature Dunedin package $525–$595 per person   *Includes breakfast*
Nature Dunedin & Catlins package $885–$905 per person |

Guests at Nisbet Cottage enjoy the experience of seeing New Zealand wildlife on Hildegard's nature tours. Her eco-tourism venture *Nature Guides Otago* is designed to give guests first-hand views of penguins, albatrosses and other rarities. Guests stay at Nisbet Cottage, in a quiet area on the hills to Otago Peninsula, in the king-size bedroom or suite. Breakfast is served in the private guest lounge with open fireplace and French doors leading to a spacious semi-circular sundeck overlooking the city and surrounding hills. Guests can choose between a two-night *Nature Dunedin* package, with bed and breakfast, Sunrise Penguin Walk, and full-day guided wildlife tour, or a third night's bed and breakfast with a full-day guided tour to the Catlins.

FACILITIES

- 1 king ensuite bedroom
- 1 king/twin suite
- hair dryer, toiletries & heated towel rails in both ensuites
- TV, phone & coffee/tea in both guest bedrooms
- children by arrangement
- open fireplace in guest lounge
- German spoken
- large sundeck overlooking city

- continental breakfast & cooked on request, served in guest lounge
- computer & email access in 2nd guest lounge area
- courtesy passenger transfer
- regular bus route close by
- off-street parking
- Basil, the fluffy grey cat, an optional extra

ACTIVITIES AVAILABLE

- Nisbet Cottage caters exclusively for guests participating in nature tours
- scenic lookout, easy walk
- restaurants, within walking distance & 5–10-min drive
- Larnach Castle
- Glenfalloch Gardens
- royal albatross colony
- Rhododendron Week, in Oct.

- Nature Dunedin package: 2 nights B&B, Sunrise Penguin Walk (view yellow-eyed penguins) & full-day tour of Dunedin & Otago Peninsula wildlife
- extension tour to 3 nights B&B with full-day tour to Catlins
- *Nature Guides Otago* – Qualmark endorsed visitor activity
- Dunedin City, 8-min drive

MOSGIEL, DUNEDIN
Highland Peaks

Hosts Dr Peter and Di Espie

333 Chain Hills Road, R D 1, Dunedin

Phone 0-3-489 6936   *Mobile* 021 162 9489   *Fax* 0-3-489 6924
Email info@highlandpeaks.com   *Website* www.highlandpeaks.com

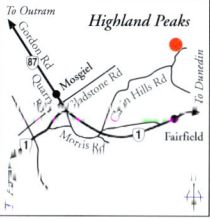

DIRECTIONS: From SH 1 take Mosgiel exit, then turn towards Kinmont into Quarry Rd. Continue left on Morris Rd over motorway. Turn 1st left into Chain Hills Rd. Take left fork to Highland Peaks on left at road end.

| 2 bdrm | 1 enst | 1 prbth | Room rate $195–$295 | *Includes breakfast* | *Dinner extra* |

Completed in 2005, Highland Peaks provides quality accommodation with panoramic mountain and sea views. Located 15 minutes from Dunedin City and the airport, and set in 8.5 hectares (21 acres) of country grounds, guests enjoy the tranquillity, native birdsong and walks. Designed to catch the sun, Highland Peaks features extensive views and energy conservation, the priviate guest wing comprising two comfortable bedrooms and bathrooms. A separate lounge is warmed by a large fire in winter, and dinner is served by arrangement, with quality home cuisine complemented by the wine cellar. Peter guides personalised tours and is well qualified, as an ecologist and former director of the National Trust, to advise about New Zealand's natural heritage.

FACILITIES

- 1 king bedroom with ensuite & dressing room
- 1 super-king/twin bedroom, private bathroom & spa bath
- hair dryer, toiletries, bathrobes, heated towel rails & demist mirror in both bathrooms
- wool/feather duvets, kauri furniture ,TV & phone in both bedrooms
- flowers; guest fridge & safe

- cooked & continental breakfast, served in dining room or alfresco
- dinner by arrangement, extra
- CD-writer, internet, email, fax
- log burner, tea/coffee, video & CD-players & books in guest lounge; wine cellar
- library; private lounge; sundeck & BBQ
- on-site parking

ACTIVITIES AVAILABLE

- cat Jasper, dog Bud, pet sheep, & farm animals on site
- private areas for reading & relaxing on site
- 8.5ha (21 acres) grounds
- mountain bikes; tracks on site
- pétanque/boules on site
- on-site & local nature & beach walks; native birdlife
- royal albatross, penguin, seal & sea lion colonies

- personally guided eco-tours, 4WD tussock grassland & wildflowers in season
- restaurants & cafés, 10 mins
- museums; art galleries
- local golf courses; fishing
- launch trips on Otago Harbour
- scenic Taieri Gorge Railway
- Dunedin heritage architecture

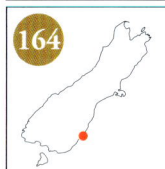

MILTON, SOUTH OTAGO
Garvan Boutique Hotel & Restaurant

Hosts Joanna and Malcolm Lowrey

1097 State Highway 1, Lovells Flat, R D 2, Milton
Phone 0-3-417 8407   *Fax* 0-3-417 8408   *Mobile* 027 442 7826
Email info@garvan.co.nz   *Website* www.garvan.co.nz

DIRECTIONS: 45 mins south of Dunedin. Take SH 1 to Milton. Continue another 10km. Sign on left 500m before Garvan Boutique Hotel. Gate on right of highway.

4 bdrm	2 enst	1 shbth	Room rate $190–$350

*Includes breakfast
Lunch & dinner extra*

Garvan Boutique Hotel was originally built in 1915 as a farm mansion for Peter Boyd. This two-storey Tudor-style home, designed by Edmund Anscombe, features an imposing entrance hall, arched recessed fireplaces, ornately carved pillars, balconies and leadlight windows. French doors open from downstairs rooms to the extensive historic garden, designed by the renowned landscaper Alfred Buxton. Date palms flank the entrance and camellias, spring bulbs, rhododendrons, and old English roses complement the established English trees. Overlooking the garden, the four upstairs bedrooms are furnished in period style, but with today's facilities. Joanna is a professional chef who runs a small restaurant and cooking school in-house.

FACILITIES

- 1 king & 1 queen upstairs bedroom, each with ensuite
- 2 queen upstairs bedrooms share 1 bathroom
- balcony opens from 1 bedroom
- towelling robes, hair dryer, toiletries & heated towel rails in all 3 bathrooms
- conferences, weddings & functions catered for
- phone & fax available

- full breakfast served
- restaurant & licensed bar
- lunch by arrangement
- resident chef
- lounge with open fireplace
- fresh flowers
- 3-ha historic garden with pond, old trees, hazelnut walk, roses
- courtesy passenger transfer
- on-site parking

ACTIVITIES AVAILABLE

- tennis courts on site
- 3-ha garden walks on site
- weddings & other functions, & small conferences
- trout fishing at the Clutha River, 10km away
- 3 golf courses within 10km
- penguins & seals at Kaka Point, 20km away
- private gardens to visit

- gateway to scenic Catlins, 20-min drive
- Milton shops & restaurants, 10km north
- swimming at Kaka Point
- Queenstown/Wanaka turn-off, 3km north
- winter skiing in Queenstown
- en route to Te Anau & Milford
- Dunedin City, 45 mins north

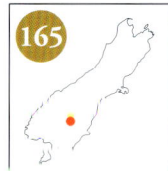

ALEXANDRA, CENTRAL OTAGO
Rocky Range Lodge

Hosts Lisa and Colin Strang   *Mobile* 027 445 0695

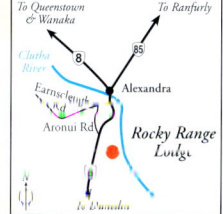

The Half Mile, Alexandra   *Postal* P O Box 323, Alexandra
Freephone 0800 153 293   *Phone* 0 3 448 6150   *Fax* 0 3 448 6150
Email relax@rockyrange.co.nz   *Website* friars.co.nz/hosts/rockyrange.html

DIRECTIONS: From Cromwell, take SH 8 to Alexandra. Continue south, cross Clutha Bridge & travel 1.5km. Rocky Range Lodge on left, up driveway. From Dunedin, take SH 8 towards Alexandra. Lodge on right.

| 4 bdrm | 4 enst | 1 pdrm | Double $400 | Single $325 | *Includes breakfast* |

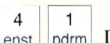

Located on 40 hectares set amid wild thyme and schist rock formations, Rocky Range is a custom-built Lodge on the outskirts of Alexandra. Designed in French Provincial style, Rocky Range offers 360-degree views of Central Otago's rugged beauty. In summer the deep verandahs provide shade, while in winter an open fire in the spacious guest lounge ensures comfort. All four ensuite bedrooms in the Lodge are well appointed, each one planned with individual character. Juliet balconies open from the bedrooms to panoramic views of the surrounding mountain ranges and river valleys. Rocky Range is a private hideaway, where guests can relax, or use the Lodge as a base to explore the myriad activities that the region offers.

FACILITIES

- 1 king, 1 king/twin & 2 queen bedrooms
- 4 ensuite bathrooms
- bathrobes, toiletries, hair dryers & heated towel rails in all 4 ensuite bathrooms
- tea/coffee, TV in bedrooms
- quality cotton bed linen & electric blankets on beds
- private Juliet balconies

- full breakfast served in dining room
- complimentary apéritifs & snacks
- guest lounge with home theatre (TV, DVD, video) & open fire
- double glazing; underfloor heating
- phone, fax & email available
- spacious outdoor patio
- outdoor spa pool set in rocks
- ample private parking on site
- www.rockyrange.co.nz

ACTIVITIES AVAILABLE

- mountain bikes available
- walking on 40-ha site
- Alexandra & Clyde restaurants
- trout fishing; professional guide
- kayaking, guided trips available
- autumn foliage, in April/May; spring blossom festival, in Sept.
- summer stone fruit orchards
- safari excursions with local guide
- eco experience on Lake Dunstan

- wine trail & tasting
- golf course, 5-min drive
- historic gold trail
- Lake Dunstan boat cruises
- scenic & garden tours
- biking & walking Otago Central Rail Trail
- Cromwell, 20-min drive
- Queenstown/Wanaka, 1 hr
- Dunedin, 2-hour drive

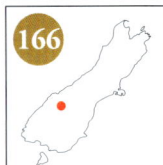

WANAKA
Lime Tree Lodge

Hosts Sally Carwardine and Rebecca Butts

672 Ballantyne Road, R D 2, Wanaka
Phone 0-3-443 7305   *Mobile* 021 529 118   *Fax* 0-3-443 7345
Email revive@limetreelodge.co.nz   *Website* www.limetreelodge.co.nz

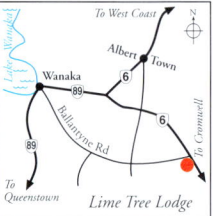

DIRECTIONS: From Wanaka, take SH 6 & travel 6km to Lime Tree Lodge on right, on corner Ballantyne Rd. From Cromwell, take SH 6 towards Wanaka. Lime Tree Lodge on left, on corner of Ballantyne Rd.

| 6 bdrm | 6 enst | 1 pdrm | Room rate $350–$550 |

Includes breakfast & apéritifs
Picnic hampers & dinner extra

Lime Tree Lodge is nestled on four hectares (10 acres) of farmland, featuring uninterupted alpine views. Just six kilometres south of Lake Wanaka, Lime Tree Lodge offers guests two spacious suites and four elegant guestrooms, each with fine linen, ensuite and verandah. An open log fire warms the comfortable, open-plan lounge and dining room, with French doors on to an expansive verandah and barbecue area. Adjacent is the swimming pool which is popular in summer, spa pool and a five-hole pitch and putt golf course. A full breakfast, with buffet and cooked options, is served in the dining room or alfresco in the garden. Restaurants are within an eight-minute drive of Lime Tree Lodge and three ski-fields are 35 to 45 minutes away.

FACILITIES

- 2 super-king/twin ensuite bedrooms
- 1 king/twin & 1 queen bedroom, each with ensuite
- 2 super-king/twin suites & private lounges; 1 with log fire
- hair dryers, fine toiletries, bathrobes & heated tiled floors
- verandah opening from each bedroom to garden
- fresh flowers; cotton bed linen
- traditional cooked or continental breakfast
- 3–4-course dinner, by arrangement, $95 pp
- apéritifs & snacks served
- guest lounge with open fire, tea/coffee, Sky TV, CD/DVD player & library
- internet & business facilities
- ski storage & drying facilities; laundry; parking & helipad

ACTIVITIES AVAILABLE

- spa pool & swimming pool
- barbecue available on site
- 5-hole pitch & putt golf on site
- golf course nearby
- guided fly-fishing for brown & rainbow trout
- rock climbing; canyoning
- day hikes in Mt Aspiring National Park
- mountain biking
- parapenting; tandem skydiving
- snow-boarding, skiing & heli-skiing, June–October
- restaurants, 8-min drive
- Wanaka airport, 5-min drive
- Lake Wanaka, 8-min drive
- wine tasting at local vineyards
- jet boating, kayaking & rafting
- scenic flights to Milford Sound, Mt Aspiring & Mt Cook

Lime Tree Lodge

WANAKA
Cardrona Terrace Estate

Hosts Sharon and Kevin Alderson

84 Morris Road, R D 2, Wanaka
Phone 0-3-443 8020   *Mobile* 021 931 076   *Fax* 0-3-443 1137
Email info@cardronaterrace.com   *Website* www.cardronaterrace.com

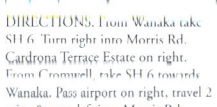

DIRECTIONS. From Wanaka take SH 6. Turn right into Morris Rd. Cardrona Terrace Estate on right. From Cromwell, take SH 6 towards Wanaka. Pass airport on right, travel 2 mins & turn left into Morris Rd.

| 5 bdrm | 5 enst | Room rate $565 – $995 Lodge rate available | *Includes breakfast Lunch & dinner extra* |

Set in 22 hectares of farmland and vineyards, Cardrona Terrace Estate offers panoramic alpine views of Aspiring National Park close to Wanaka. Built in 2004 to reflect the changing colours of the surrounding mountains, the lodge features exposed aggregate exteriors with thermal-mass construction and copper roofing. The five guestrooms are designed to tone in with tribal rugs, complemented with Italian fittings, lighting and tiles. Meals are served in the large dining room downstairs opening to the courtyard, with domesticated farm animals beyond. The cuisine includes seasonal home-grown vegetables and herbs. Guests are welcome to entertain friends at the lodge. Sharon is an artist in residence and will tutor guests by arrangement.

FACILITIES

- 5 super-king/twin ensuite themed bedrooms
- hair dryer, toiletries, heated floor & towel rails in ensuites; 1 with wheelchair access
- cotton bed linen & NZ herbal aromatherapy pillows
- TV, writing desk, phone & tea/coffee in all bedrooms
- conferences, honeymoons & weddings catered
- breakfast menu choices
- seasonal lunch/picnic, extra
- dinner with organic produce, $40-$90 pp, wine available
- fresh flowers; central heating
- laundry available
- basic French spoken by host
- courtesy passenger transfer
- on-site parking; helipad

ACTIVITIES AVAILABLE

- 20ha farm & vineyards on site
- feeding animals, vineyard walks, archery & shooting on site
- mountain bikes; pétanque
- bird watching, celestial star gazing & gym equipment on site
- art instruction with easel, & print making on site
- skiing, June–October
- sailing; mountaineering
- restaurants, 5 mins away, complimentary transport
- fly fishing; fishing; hunting
- rock climbing; golf
- gardens to visit
- vineyards & wine tours
- 'Lord of the Rings' sites
- lake walks; watersports
- flightseeing; airport nearby
- Hawea, 10-min drive

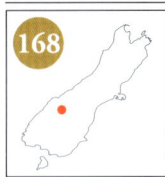

WANAKA
River Run

Hosts Meg Taylor and John Pawson

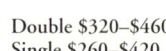

Halliday Road, R D 2, Wanaka
Phone 0-3-443 9049   *Email* adventure@riverrun.co.nz
Fax 03-443 8454   *Website* www.riverrun.co.nz

DIRECTIONS: 5km from Wanaka, on SH 6. Turn left into Halliday Rd. Continue to end of road, to River Run stone entrance. From Cromwell, take SH 6 towards Wanaka. Turn right into Halliday Rd. River Run at end.

| 5 bdrm | 5 enst | Double $320–$460 Single $260–$420 | *Includes breakfast* *Picnic hampers & dinner extra* | |

River Run

Set on an escarpment with sweeping 180-degree views towards the Southern Alps, River Run offers guests a private, relaxed and comfortable retreat from which to explore the region. River Run's 200-hectare (500-acre) property, bordering the Cardrona and Clutha Rivers, provides on-site walks, picnics, fishing, kayaking, jet boating or rafting. Wanaka township is only six minutes away by car, with Mount Aspiring National Park beyond. The lodge is an imaginative composition in recycled materials including kauri doors, bridge and railway timbers, hardwood floors and hand-crafted iron balustrades. A generous breakfast is served with buffet and cooked options. River Run also offers fine cuisine for dinner, with an extensive wine list.

FACILITIES

- 4 king/twin ensuite bedrooms
- 1 queen ensuite bedroom
- cotton bed linen, phone, TV or TV/video in all 5 bedrooms
- 5 spacious ensuites, with power showers, fine toiletries, hair dryers & wrap towels
- deep verandahs
- book, video & CD library
- 2 guest lounges with log fires
- 3-4-course dinner, $90 pp
- fully licensed – local wine list
- picnic hampers available
- buffet & à la carte breakfasts
- evening appetisers served
- high-speed wireless internet
- laundry & drying room
- private outdoor spa pool & entertainment area with alpine views

ACTIVITIES AVAILABLE

- 200ha riverside farmland with walks & picnic spots
- mountain bikes available
- access to fishing, kayaking, rafting, jet boating
- restaurants, 5-min drive
- guided fly-fishing for brown & rainbow trout
- canyoning; paragliding
- heli-hiking; horse trekking
- Lake Wanaka resort, 5-min drive
- wine tasting at local vineyards
- golf course; aircraft museum
- private gardens to visit
- 3 ski-fields, 35–45-min drive
- skiing & heli-skiing, June–Oct.
- scenic flights to Milford Sound, Mt Aspiring & Mt Cook
- walks & day hikes in Mt Aspiring National Park

River Run

DUBLIN BAY, WANAKA
The Stone Cottage

Host Belinda Wilson

Dublin Bay RD 2, Wanaka
Phone 0-3-443 1878   *Email* stonecottage@xtra.co.nz
Fax 0-3-443 1276   *Website* www.stonecottage.co.nz

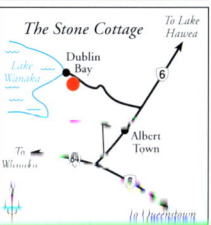

DIRECTIONS: Take SH 6 to or from Wanaka & turn north towards Lake Hawea (& West Coast). Travel 5km then turn left to Dublin Bay. Travel 3km to The Stone Cottage on left. (10-min drive from Wanaka township.)

2 bdrm	2 prbth

Double $250–$270
Single $220

Includes breakfast provisions
Self-catering, or dinner extra

Originally built in 1977 from local schist, and furnished with antique oak furniture, The Stone Cottage at Dublin Bay now features a loft comprising two separate self-contained suites. Dormer windows and private balconies overlook the waters of Lake Wanaka to the Treble Cone ski-field beyond. Each suite has an external staircase providing a private entrance. Both kitchens are well stocked, with fridge, microwave or stove, enabling guests to self-cater, or if preferred, dine with their host, Bindy, downstairs. The Stone Cottage is set in a tranquil lakeside garden featuring spring bulbs and blossom, through to summer roses, followed by dramatic autumn colouring, just 10 minutes' drive from Wanaka township.

FACILITIES

- 1 super-king suite & 1 queen/twin self-contained suite
- electric blankets, bathrobes, heated towel rails, hair dryers & toiletries in both suites
- 2 private guest entrances
- single-party bookings per suite, or 1 party can use inter-connecting door
- phone, fax & email available
- TV, VCR & DVD
- breakfast ingredients & basics provided in both kitchens
- 3-course dinner with wine, pre-dinner drinks & savouries, by arrangement, $65 pp
- complimentary sherry & port
- lake views; fresh flowers
- laundry available, extra
- courtesy passenger transfer
- established garden

ACTIVITIES AVAILABLE

- BBQ on site
- croquet, boules on site
- mountain bikes available
- local walks
- Lake Wanaka, 4-min walk
- fishing guide available
- vineyards; wine-tasting
- private garden visiting
- trout fishing; boating
- restaurants, 10-min drive
- arts & crafts trail
- 18-hole golf course
- horse trekking
- hiking; tramping
- jet boating; scenic flights
- adventure activities
- skiing, from June to Sept.
- 3 ski-fields – Treble Cone, Cardrona & Nordic ski area

Stone Cottage

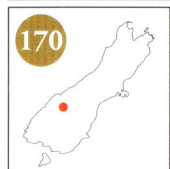

DUBLIN BAY, WANAKA
Dublin Bay Lodge

Hosts Neil Farrin and Emily Wong

Dublin Bay, R D 2, Wanaka
Phone 0-3-443 8833   *Mobile* 021 185 3181   *Fax* 0-3-443 7880
Email info@dublinbaylodge.com   *Website* www.dublinbaylodge.com

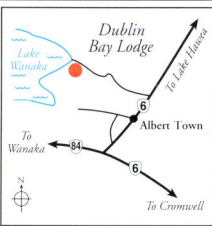

DIRECTIONS: Take SH 6 to or from Wanaka & turn north towards Lake Hawea (& West Coast). Travel 4.1km, then turn left to Dublin Bay. Travel 2.7km to Dublin Bay Lodge on left. (10-min drive from Wanaka.)

1 bdrm	1 enst	Studio rate $250–$295	*Includes continental breakfast provisions*	*Self-catering*

5-bedroom lodge rate $1,200–$1,500   **Photo Adventure day rate $350**

Dublin Bay

Set in a picturesque garden only three minutes' walk from Lake Wanaka, Dublin Bay Lodge was built from New Zealand larch and oregon in 1950 and recently renovated to retain the extensive use of timber and adzed beams. The self-catering studio has panoramic views of the lake and mountains beyond, with trout fishing and kayaking only 200 metres away. The studio features a photographic theme which reflects the main interest of the new host, Neil, an internationally published photographer whose work has appeared in magazines such as *Time* and *Geo*. Neil offers guests to Dublin Bay Lodge a photographic adventure called "Shadowcatcher", individually tailored to each photography enthusiast. Each venture is guided by Neil, through Central Otago.

FACILITIES

- 1 king ensuite studio
- spa bath, hair dryer, toiletries, & heated towel rails in ensuite
- bathrobes
- cotton bed linen
- Sky TV, CD-player, games, books & writing desk in living area
- artwork
- lake & mountain views

- continental breakfast provisions
- microwave, guest fridge, tea/coffee facilities
- central heating
- email, phone & laundry available
- Cantonese/Mandarin spoken by host
- on-site parking

ACTIVITIES AVAILABLE

- full grass tennis court on site
- established grounds with private access to Lake Wanaka
- vineyard tours
- photographic adventures
- trout fishing
- boating
- hiking & tramping
- art & craft tours

- restaurants, 10-min drive
- 18-hole golf course, 10 mins
- scenic flights
- horse trekking
- Transport & Toy Museum
- Fighter Pilots Museum
- 4-wheel motor biking
- 3 international ski-fields
- Wanaka town, 10-min drive

Dublin Bay

Dublin Bay

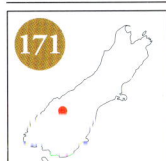
WANAKA
Bluewater Lodge

Hosts Dianne and Doug Purvis

12 Baker Grove, Penrith Park, Wanaka
Phone 0-3-439 4798   Mobile 027 438 8713   Fax 0-3-439 4449
Email stay@bluewater.co.nz   *Website* www.bluewaterwanaka.co.nz

DIRECTIONS: Take SH 84 to Wanaka. Turn right into Lakeside Rd. Continue into Beacon Point Rd At end, turn right into Penrith Park Drive & 1st left into Baker Grove. Bluewater Lodge on right.

3 bdrm	2 enst	1 prbth	Room rate $490–$590	*Includes breakfast*	*Dinner extra*

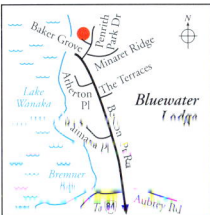

Bluewater Lodge is located right on the lakefront at Wanaka with unobstructed lake and mountain views. Set in landscaped gardens and architecturally designed featuring extensive use of macrocarpa, Bluewater Lodge was opened in 2004 to provide accommodation for six guests. The main upstairs bedroom opens to a private balcony with spa pool, overlooking Lake Wanaka to Treble Cone ski-field beyond. A menu is provided for guests to select a full cooked breakfast, served in the dining room, and three-course dinner with wine is also available indoors or alfresco. There is direct access to a quiet beach and guests enjoy the 20-minute lakeside stroll to Wanaka township with its restaurants, cafés, bars and boutique shopping.

FACILITIES

- Master: 1 king/twin ensuite bedroom, balcony & spa pool
- Peninsula: 1 king ensuite bedroom with wheelchair access
- Twin: 1 twin bedroom with private bathroom & bath
- cotton bed linen, dressing room, TV, phone & fridge in rooms
- hair dryers, twin basins & dual showers, toiletries, bathrobes, heated floor & heated towel rails
- cooked & continental breakfast options served
- 3-course dinner with wine, served, $65 pp
- lounge with tea/coffee, Sky TV, video, DVD, CD-player, nibbles, library & writing desk
- email, fax & phone available
- complimentary laundry; courtesy passenger transfer
- on-site parking & garaging

ACTIVITIES AVAILABLE

- private outdoor spa pool for Master guestroom
- landscaped gardens & grounds for reading & relaxing on site
- barbecue available
- honeymoons catered for
- lakefront & beach walks
- beach in front of Lodge
- swimming & watersports
- 2 ski-fields nearby
- boating & fishing in lake
- restaurants, nearby
- Wanaka township, 20-min walk or 4-min drive
- mountain climbing
- biking
- heli-skiing & para gliding
- trekking
- gardens to visit
- Queenstown, 45 mins

LAKE WANAKA
Atherton House

Hosts Kate and Roy Summers

3 Atherton Place, Wanaka
Phone 0-3-443 8343   *Mobile* 027 228 1982   *Fax* 0-3-443 8343
Email roy.kate@xtra.co.nz   *Website* www.atherton.co.nz

2 bdrm	2 enst	1 pdrm

Double $175–$235
Single $150

Includes breakfast & apéritifs
Dinner extra

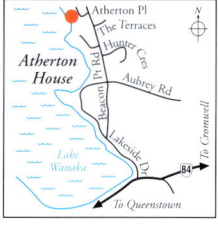

DIRECTIONS: Take SH 6 & SH 84 to Wanaka. Continue on Ardmore St towards lake. Turn right into Lakeside Drive. Turn right into Beacon Pt Rd. Travel 1.5km then turn left into Atherton Pl. Atherton House on left.

Located at the fringe of Wanaka, Atherton House was built on the shore of the lake in 2001. Set in half a hectare of lawns and gardens, surrounded by trees, this contemporary home in classic design enjoys unimpeded views across the lake to the mountains beyond. Furnished with New Zealand and English antiques and featuring contemporary New Zealand art, Atherton House provides two ensuite guestrooms. A full breakfast with home-made bread, jams, preserves and cooked options is served in the dining room or alfresco in the courtyard. Complimentary pre-dinner drinks and hors d'oeuvres are offered, and dinner served with wine is available by arrangement. Guests enjoy the lakefront walk from Atherton House to Wanaka village.

FACILITIES

- 1 king/twin ensuite bedroom
- 1 queen ensuite bedroom
- hair dryer, demist mirror, heated floor & towel rails in both ensuite bathrooms
- cotton bed linen, tea/coffee & fresh flowers
- central heating; guest fridge
- email & fax available
- laundry available
- full cooked & continental breakfast, served in dining room or courtyard
- apéritifs & nibbles
- 3-course dinner with wine, $65 pp, by arrangement
- private guest lounge with open fire, tea/coffee, Sky TV, video, library & writing desk
- guest entrance & verandahs
- on-site parking

ACTIVITIES AVAILABLE

- barbecue available
- lakefront access from site
- nearly 0.5ha (1 acre) lawn, trees & gardens on site
- walks
- vineyards
- wine tasting
- private garden visits
- horse trekking
- hiking
- restaurants, 20-min walk
- Wanaka shops, 3-min drive
- 18-hole golf course
- scenic flights
- fishing guides available
- skiing, June to September
- airport, 10-min drive
- watersports
- Queenstown, 45-min drive

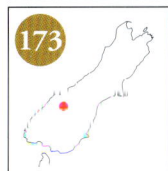

Lake Wanaka
Minaret Lodge

Hosts Fran and Gary Tate

34 Eely Point Road, Wanaka   *Postal* P O Box 352, Wanaka
Phone 0-3-443 1856   *Mobile* 021 644 400   *Fax* 0-3-443 1846
Email relax@minaretlodge.co.nz   *Website* www.minaretlodge.co.nz

DIRECTIONS: From Cromwell or Haast, take SH 6 towards Wanaka. Continue on SH 84 & 89 Ardmore St towards Lake Wanaka. Turn right into Lakeside Drive. Turn right into Eely Pt Rd. Minaret Lodge on right.

5 bdrm	4 enst	1 prbth	Double $395 Single $375	*Includes breakfast* *Dinner extra*

With views of the Minaret Mountains, after which the Lodge is named, Minaret Lodge is set in almost a hectare of spacious grounds with well established trees. The mudbrick construction, with plastered finish, was built in the 1950s for the Ellis family, then in 2001 the guestrooms were added. The three guest chalets all have one or two super-king/twin bedrooms, each with bathroom, tea and coffee-making facilities, fridge with refreshments, and a verandah opening to the garden. One chalet features a special *Lord of the Rings* theme in a guestroom called "Barlimans". Breakfast includes daily specialities and dinner with wine is also available. A short stroll takes guests to the lake, and it is a 10-minute walk to Wanaka's town centre.

FACILITIES

- 2 chalets: 2 super-king/twin ensuite bedrooms in each
- 1 chalet: 1 super-king/twin bedroom, bathroom & lounge with queen-size sofa bed
- tea/coffee, mineral water, TV & phone in all 5 bedrooms
- toiletries, bathrobes, hair dryers, heated floor & towel rails in all 5 bathrooms
- wheelchair access in suite

- traditional cooked or continental breakfast
- 3-course dinner with wine, seasonal menu, $80 pp
- verandah opening from each bedroom to garden
- laundry service available
- email & fax available
- courtesy passenger transfer
- private guest entrance; on-site parking

ACTIVITIES AVAILABLE

- weddings, honeymoons & conferences catered for
- ski storage & drying room
- barbecue available on site
- sauna & spa pool on site
- tennis court on site
- mountain bikes available
- pétanque/boules on site
- pool table on site
- golf course nearby

- many restaurants in Wanaka, 10-min walk
- gymnasium, 5-min drive
- lake activities
- fishing & hiking
- horse trekking
- Fighter Pilots Museum
- scenic flights
- snow boarding & skiing, June to September

LAKE WANAKA
Lakeside Apartments

Hosts The Lakeside Team

9 Lakeside Road, Wanaka   *Postal* P O Box 609, Wanaka
Phone 0-3-443 0188   *Email* info@lakesidewanaka.co.nz
Fax 0-3-443 0189   *Website* www.lakesidewanaka.co.nz

DIRECTIONS: From Cromwell or Haast, take SH 6 towards Wanaka. Continue on SH 84, then into Ardmore St towards Lake Wanaka. Turn right into Lakeside Rd. Lakeside Apartments on immediate right.

| 3 bdrm per apartment | 2 bthrm per apartment | Apartment rate $295–$795 Extra persons $45 each | *Self-catering Breakfast extra* |  |

Lakeside Apartments comprise 21 self-contained apartments each with three bedrooms and two bathrooms, available as one, two, or three-bedroom apartments. Located beside Lake Wanaka, the apartments provide uninterrupted vistas across the lake to the snow-capped mountains beyond. The grounds include a heated swimming pool and spa pool, as well as rock and water features, lawns and extensive landscaping. The architecturally designed apartments feature schist and recycled hardwood beams which blend with steel and glass to give a rustic but contemporary feel. Each apartment includes a full kitchen with quality fittings and a living area that opens to its own spacious lakefront balcony, with cedar shutters ensuring maximum privacy.

FACILITIES

- 5 Superior Apartments on pool & garden level
- 10 Deluxe Apartments on higher level
- 3 Premier Apartments on larger &/or higher level
- 3 Penthouse Apartments, each with spa bath, bidet, BBQ on larger deck, spa pool & seating
- toiletries, bath/spa bath, hair dryers & double basins

- fully equipped kitchen for self-catering per apartment
- all lounges with Sky TV, DVD & CD-player
- underfloor heating in tiled areas & double glazing
- large balconies & laundry facilities in each apartment
- drying room & ski storage
- lock-up garaging
- guest lift to all levels

ACTIVITIES AVAILABLE

- room service from local cafés
- BBQs available
- heated swimming pool on site (for 6-month summer season)
- children's & spa pools on site
- water gardens on site
- extensive decking with loungers & tables on site
- transfer to & from Dunedin & Queenstown airports, extra

- variety of restaurants, short walk away
- aquatic sports
- Wanaka Town Centre, walking distance
- trekking; cycling
- golf course; wineries
- arts & crafts trail
- gardens open to visit
- skiing & heli-skiing

Lakeside Apartments

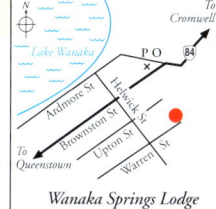

LAKE WANAKA
Wanaka Springs Boutique Lodge

Hosts Lyn and Murray Finn

21 Warren Street, Wanaka   *Postal* P O Box 25, Wanaka
Phone 0-3-443 8421   *Mobile* 027 241 4113   *Fax* 0-3-443 8429
Email relax@wanakasprings.com   *Website* www.wanakasprings.com

Wanaka Springs Lodge

DIRECTIONS: Take SH 6 towards Wanaka & continue on SH 84. Turn left into Brownston St. Take 3rd left into Helwick St, then 2nd left again into Warren St. Wanaka Springs Lodge at end of cul-de-sac on left.

| 8 bdrm | 8 enst | Room rate $295–$330 | *Includes breakfast* |

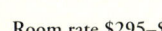

Wanaka Springs was opened in 2000 and reflects traditional Central Otago styles. This in-town retreat is a central base for countless activities and only a three-minute stroll from Wanaka's shops, restaurants and bars. "Wanaka Springs" refers to the natural springs that surface around the Lodge and which form the central water features in the native landscaped gardens. The interior furnishings complement the scenic views of the surrounding mountains and Lake Wanaka. The eight ensuite guestrooms are individually designed, with private deck or courtyard. Guests can enjoy the vistas from the sunny dining room where breakfast is served, relax in the guest lounge with its open log fire, or rejuvenate alfresco in the eight-seater hot tub.

FACILITIES

- 1 twin, 5 queen & 2 super-king/twin bedrooms; wheelchair access to 1 room
- 8 ensuites, each with heated towel rails, hair dryer, heat lamp, toiletries & bathrobes
- imported quality bed linen
- private decks or courtyards
- guest lounge with open log fire & book collection
- laundry service
- special full breakfast
- complimentary afternoon tea, nightcaps & hosted pre-dinner drinks
- Sky TV, DVD & music system
- recycled native timber furniture
- fax & email facilities
- outdoor 8-seater hot tub
- ski gear storage & drying rooms
- off-street parking

ACTIVITIES AVAILABLE

- fishing & hunting – guiding service available
- wine-tasting at local vineyards
- 18-hole golf course
- scenic flights
- garden tours
- jet boating; kayaking; rafting
- sailing; canyoning; paragliding
- mountain biking; 4WD safaris
- horse trekking
- restaurants, cafés, shopping & lake, 5-min stroll
- walks & hikes in Mt Aspiring National Park
- NZ Fighter Pilots & Warbirds Museum
- rock climbing; mountaineering
- heli-hiking
- skiing, heli-skiing, June – Oct; 3 ski areas, 35–45-min drive

WANAKA
Renmore House

Hosts Rosie and Blair Burridge

44 Upton Street, Wanaka
Phone 0-3-443 6566   *Email* rosie@renmore-house.co.nz
Fax 0-3-443 6567   *Website* www.renmore-house.com

DIRECTIONS: Take SH 6 towards Wanaka & continue on SH 84. Turn left into Brownston St. Take 3rd left into Helwick St, then 1st left again into Upton St. Renmore House on corner site on right.

3 bdrm	3 enst	Double $200	Single $150	*Includes breakfast*

Located in the heart of Wanaka, in a quiet cul-de-sac, Renmore House is just 200 metres from lakefront cafés, restaurants, bars and shops, where the long twilight of the south makes it easy to walk to the evening dining venues. Purpose-built in 1999, Renmore House offers three super-king/twin ensuite bedrooms with all guest facilities on the ground floor, separate from the hosts who live upstairs. Landscaped gardens along the banks of the Bullock Creek that runs through the site provide outdoor relaxation for guests. Continental or cooked breakfast is served in the guests' dining area or upstairs with the hosts. Watersports on Lake Wanaka are popular with guests during the summer months, and snow sports are the main attractions in winter.

FACILITIES

- 3 super-king/twin bedrooms
- 3 ensuites with toiletries
- cotton bed linen
- Sky TV in all 3 bedrooms
- guest lounge with tea/coffee, music, games & magazines
- extra single beds available
- fresh flowers
- phone, fax & email available
- central heating throughout
- continental or cooked breakfast served
- laundry available $5
- complimentary tea/coffee
- minibar fridge for guests
- quiet cul-de-sac setting
- children welcome
- hosts live upstairs
- gardens with creek on site
- off-street parking

ACTIVITIES AVAILABLE

- BBQ available in summer
- 200 metres to Wanaka shops
- walking distance to 20 restaurants, cafés & bars
- Lake Wanaka, 3-min walk
- golf
- jet boating
- kayaking; rafting
- windsurfing; water skiing
- tramping & climbing
- fishing & sailing on lake
- mountaineering
- gardens open to visit
- "Warbirds over Wanaka"
- skiing & snowboarding
- heli-skiing; paragliding
- horse riding
- scenic flights over glaciers, Mt Aspiring, Mt Cook & Milford Sound

177

LAKE WANAKA
Te Wanaka Lodge

Hosts Andy and Graeme Oxley

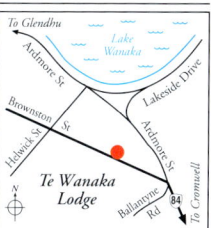

23 Brownston Street, Wanaka
Freephone 0800 WANAKA   *Phone* 0-3-443 9224   *Fax* 0-3-443 9246
Email tewanakalodge@xtra.co.nz   *Website* www.tewanaka.co.nz

  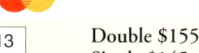

13 bdrm	13 enst

Double $155–$205
Single $145–$195

Includes breakfast

DIRECTIONS: Take SH 6 north of Cromwell towards Wanaka. Continue on SH 84 to Wanaka. At the Caltex service station turn left into Brownston St. Continue 100m to Te Wanaka Lodge on right.

Designed by architects Kurt Lehmann and Walter Heron, Te Wanaka Lodge is a contemporary European-style chalet constructed from New Zealand native timber and corrugated iron. Te Wanaka is an easy walk to the golf course, lake, and township with its restaurants and shops. Decorated with fishing and skiing memorabilia, the lodge has an alpine ambience. On a hot summer's day, guests can relax under the walnut tree or in the private courtyard garden with a cool drink from the house bar. In winter, skiers can enjoy après by the log fire in the guest lounge or a soak in the garden hot tub. Breakfast is served around the huge antique dining table and features a gourmet buffet together with a cooked option that changes daily.

FACILITIES

- 1 king, 8 queen & 3 twin bedrooms, each with ensuite & private balcony
- 1 self-contained garden cottage for up to 3 persons
- bathrobes, hair dryers, heated towel rails, toiletries & mist-free mirrors in all ensuites
- TV lounge, log fire, library lounge, bar lounge, dining room & private courtyard garden

- full gourmet breakfast
- house bar, Sky TV, book, video & CD-library
- gear storage, drying room & guest laundry
- therapeutic massage service
- catering for functions & groups by arrangement
- off-street parking
- fax, internet & business facilities available

ACTIVITIES AVAILABLE

- secluded cedar hot tub on site
- booking service for flights/tours; in-house therapeutic massage
- on-site native & deciduous trees, rhododendrons & roses
- lake-front restaurants, cafés & shopping, 2-min walk
- trout fishing & hunting, guides available by request
- scenic flights over Mt Aspiring, Mt Cook & to Milford Sound

- kayaking; swimming
- horse trekking
- bush walking; golf
- jet boating; sailing
- local crafts
- paragliding
- mountain bike hire
- Lake Wanaka
- skiing & heliskiing in winter

WANAKA
Willowridge House

Hosts Lorraine and Wayne Thorpe

52 Willowridge, Wanaka
Phone 0-3-443 1330   *Email* stay@willowridgehouse.co.nz
Fax 0-3-443 1338   *Website* www.willowridgehouse.co.nz

DIRECTIONS: From Wanaka township, turn left into Ardmore St & travel round lake front. Turn left into Meadowstone Drive. Then take 2nd left into Willowridge. Willowridge House is on left.

4 bdrm	1 enst	1 prbth	**Room rate $245–$370**	*Includes breakfast*	*Lunch & dinner extra*
			Apartment rate $195 for 2 persons	**Extra persons $50 each**	*Self-catering in apartment*

Providing both self-contained and hosted options, Willowridge House is popular year round. Summer watersports in Lake Wanaka are just a 500-metre walk away, and the snow-capped mountains above the lake are attractive on the crisp clear sunny days in winter. Willowridge is designed in three levels with the self-contained apartment opening to the garden. Hosted accommodation on the top level comprises two bedrooms and a bathroom, private lounge and balcony, tea/coffee facilities and fridge. Meals are served on street level in the formal dining room or alfresco on one of the tiled deck areas. Lunch and dinner are provided by request and a barbecue is also available on site. Restaurants are just two kilometres away in the town.

FACILITIES

- two single-party bookings
- 1 self-contained apartment downstairs, with 1 queen & 1 twin bedroom; 1 bathroom
- 2 queen bedrooms upstairs, 1 ensuite; 2 dressing rooms
- extra bedroom available
- hair dryers, toiletries, heated towel rails & demist mirrors
- email facilities available
- fresh flowers; laundry
- full self-catering kitchen in apartment for all meals
- continental breakfast upstairs
- lunch by request, extra
- 3-course dinner extra, BYO
- upstairs meals in formal dining room or alfresco on 2 tiled decks
- wood burner, Sky TV, video, CD-player & piano in upstairs guest lounge
- off-street parking

ACTIVITIES AVAILABLE

- BBQ on site
- 500m walk to lake
- 10-min walk to township
- Wanaka golf course 5 mins
- 6 golf courses within 1 hour
- guided fishing
- swimming in summer
- vineyard, 10-min walk
- scenic flights over glaciers, Mt Cook & Milford Sound
- Wanaka restaurants & shops
- art galleries
- paragliding; heli-skiing
- boating; kayaking; rafting
- jet boating; sailing
- tramping, mountaineering
- Warbirds over Wanaka
- 3 ski-fields, 30-min drive
- Queenstown, 50 mins south

Lake Wanaka
Wanaka Homestead

Hosts Shonagh and Roger North

1 Homestead Close, Wanaka
Phone 0-3-443 5022   *Email* stay@wanakahomestead.co.nz
Fax 0-3-443 5023   *Website* www.wanakahomestead.co.nz

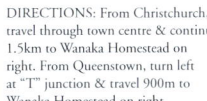

DIRECTIONS: From Christchurch, travel through town centre & continue 1.5km to Wanaka Homestead on right. From Queenstown, turn left at "T" junction & travel 900m to Wanaka Homestead on right.

10 bdrm	7 enst	2 prbth	1 pdrm	Double $245–$299 Single $195–$240 Cottage rate $225–$450	*Includes breakfast & apéritifs* *Self-catering*

Wanaka Homestead

Wanaka Homestead is located 200 metres from Lake Wanaka and provides award-winning environmentally friendly lodge and cottage accommodation. Not far from Wanaka township and overlooking parkland, the purpose-built Homestead lodge has five ensuite bedrooms. Breakfast and evening apéritifs are served by the log fire in the guest lounge, which features recycled timber beams. Alternatively, the two- or three-bedroom cottages offer a self-catering option for couples, groups or families, by providing fully equipped self-contained accommodation. Complimentary facilities for all guests include a broadband Internet Station with wireless internet, guest laundry, outside hot tub and mountain bikes. Guided fly-fishing is a popular activity.

FACILITIES

- 1 California king ensuite bedroom upstairs with double shower & double basins
- 4 super-king/twin ensuite bedrooms, 1 with wheelchair access
- 3-bedroom, 2-bathroom cottage
- 2-bedroom, 2-bathroom cottage with wheelchair access
- children welcome in cottages
- ski storage & drying room

- full breakfast, apéritifs & evening nibbles for lodge guests
- full kitchen in each cottage for self-catering
- bathrobes, hair dryer, toiletries & heated floor in all bathrooms
- open fire in homestead
- TV, VCR, DVD, CDs, books & local artwork
- phones, fax, computer & fast internet access; laundry

ACTIVITIES AVAILABLE

- in-house Fly Fishing Academy
- outside fires, 2 BBQs & hot tub; Jess, a child-friendly collie, on site
- direct park access; 200m to lake
- 18-hole golf course, winery & vineyards, 1km; wine tours
- town centre, 1.5km; art galleries & museum
- skiing, heli-skiing & snow-boarding June – Oct.
- Warbirds over Wanaka air show

- restaurants, cafés & shopping, 15-min walk
- kayaking; white water rafting & sledging; jet boating; canyoning; fly & boat fishing
- 4WD safaris; rock climbing; mountain biking
- walking trails; horse trekking
- tramping & mountaineering
- scenic flights to Milford Sound; skydiving; paragliding

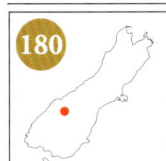

Wanaka
Wanaka Stonehouse Boutique Lodge

Hosts Jaime and Anna Kate Hutter

21 Sargood Drive, Wanaka

Phone 0-3-443 1933   *Email* indulge@wanakastonehouse.co.nz
Fax 0-3-443 1929   *Website* www.wanakastonehouse.co.nz

DIRECTIONS: From Wanaka township, take Ardmore St along lake front into Mt Aspiring Rd. Turn right into Sargood Drive. Wanaka Stonehouse is 300m on left.

4 bdrm	4 enst

Room rate $320–$395   *Includes breakfast*

Wanaka Stonehouse has been refurbished and upgraded and has new hosts. This alpine-style retreat is set in secluded landscaped gardens in Wanaka, close to the lake front, within half an hour of the ski areas. The Lodge is built of local stone with exposed beams and oak panelling creating the ambience of a traditional hunting and fishing lodge. Four spacious ensuite guestrooms are individually designed with contemporary furnishings. Guests enjoy the exclusive use of all Lodge facilities, as the hosts live in a separate cottage on the grounds. Guests can relax in the large open lounge with exposed beams and open fireplace, the private reading room, peaceful garden, and in the conservatory. The spa pool and sauna are also popular with guests.

FACILITIES

- private Lodge; hosts live in separate cottage
- 2 spacious super-king/twin & 2 queen ensuite bedrooms
- bathrobes, wrap towels, heated towel rails, aromatherapy toiletries, hair dryers in ensuites
- TV, phone, tea/coffee, fine bed linen & electric blankets
- laundry service
- complimentary snacks
- full cooked/continental breakfast served in dining room
- NZ wines & beers; guest fridges
- lounge with log fire; reading room; books, games & music system; broadband internet
- spa pool & sauna
- drying room
- gear storage
- courtesy passenger transfer to town; private parking on site

ACTIVITIES AVAILABLE

- itinerary booking service
- short stroll to lakefront, vineyard, shops & restaurants
- private mature gardens on site
- wine tasting at local vineyards
- sauna & spa pool on site
- mountain biking
- golfing
- walking & climbing
- hunting/fishing guides on request
- boating
- sailing
- swimming
- horse trekking
- winter skiing
- heli-skiing
- snowboarding
- scenic flights to Milford Sound, Mt Aspiring, Mt Cook, glaciers & West Coast

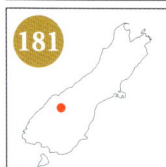

WANAKA
Montebello

Hosts Annette and Brian Costar

14 Sunrise Bay Drive, Wanaka
Phone 0-3-443 5727   *Mobile* 021 942 819   *Fax* 0-3-443 5728
Email montebello@ihug.co.nz   *Website* www.montebello.co.nz

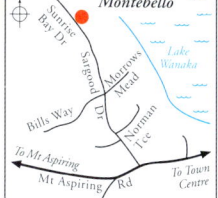

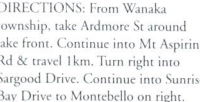

DIRECTIONS: From Wanaka township, take Ardmore St around lake front. Continue into Mt Aspiring Rd & travel 1km. Turn right into Sargood Drive. Continue into Sunrise Bay Drive to Montebello on right.

| 2 bdrm | 2 enst | Room rate $235–$275 | *Includes breakfast* |

Located beside Lake Wanaka, in the park-like grounds of the Sunrise Bay Estate, Montebello, meaning beautiful mountain, features lake and mountain views. Opened in 2005 and built to a contemporary architectural design, Montebello offers two ensuite bedrooms to guests, both with French doors opening to a private patio and the lawns beyond. Guests have full use of the swimming pool and spa pool complex on the Estate, as well as the gymnasium and the tennis court. A full continental breakfast is served in the guest lounge or alfresco on the guest patio. Directly adjacent to Montebello is a well-known vineyard, and Edgewater Resort with its restaurants and bar. Wanaka township is just a 15-minute stroll away along the lake edge.

FACILITIES

- 1 super-king ensuite bedroom
- 1 twin bedroom with king singles & ensuite bathroom
- cotton bed linen
- hair dryer, toiletries, demist mirror, bathrobes, heated floor & towel rails in bathrooms
- internet & fax available
- guest lounge with gas fire, tea/coffee, nibbles, Sky TV, video, DVD, CD-player & library

- full continental breakfast
- barbecue available
- fresh flowers
- separate guest laundry
- drying room
- older children welcome
- friendly cat on site
- courtesy transfer
- separate guest entry; on-site parking

ACTIVITIES AVAILABLE

- swimming & spa pools on site
- gymnasium & tennis court
- stream, river & lake fishing
- skiing, snowboarding & heli-skiing close by
- windsurfing & paragliding
- mountaineering, rock climbing & tramping
- many walking trails
- kayaking, rafting & jet boating

- restaurant & bar adjacent
- Wanaka township, 15-min walk along lakefront
- vineyards & wine-tasting
- scenic flights; golf courses
- horse trekking
- Warbirds over Wanaka
- Fighter Pilots Museum
- mountain biking
- Queenstown, 50 mins

WANAKA
Whare Kea Lodge & Chalet

Host Sheena Denmead

Mount Aspiring Road, Lake Wanaka *Postal* P O Box 115, Wanaka
Phone 0-3-443 1400 *Mobile* 027 243 3253 *Fax* 0-3-443 9200
Email admin@wharekealodge.com *Website* www.wharekealodge.com

DIRECTIONS: Take SH 6 or SH 84 to Wanaka. From town centre, take Ardmore St along lake edge towards Glendhu. Continue into Mt Aspiring Rd. Turn right into driveway to Whare Kea Lodge at end, 7km from township.

| 6 bdrm | 6 enst | 1 pdrm | **Double $1,000–$1,400** **Single $700–$900** | *Includes breakfast & dinner Lunch extra* |

Set on the edge of Lake Wanaka, Whare Kea was designed by John Mayne and built in 1996 in contemporary style featuring timber, steel and glass, to maximise the lake views. The spacious rooms include six ensuite guestrooms. A four-course gourmet table d'hôte dinner and breakfast are served in the large dining room overlooking the lake, with views to the Southern Alps beyond. Whare Kea Lodge is fully licensed, and provides picnic lunches on request. Set on farmland planted with native grasses and trees, Whare Kea is just seven kilometres from Wanaka township. Guests enjoy watersports on the lake during the summer season, and skiing or heli-skiing in winter. There is a fully hosted chalet also available high in the nearby mountains.

FACILITIES

- 6 spacious ensuite guestrooms
- cotton bed linen, dressing room & writing desk in all 6 bedrooms/suites
- double showers, deep baths, hair dryer, heated floor, toiletries & wheelchair access
- phone, fax & email
- guest lounge with open fire, tea/coffee, nibbles, bar, TV, video, library & lake views
- continental or country-style cooked breakfast
- light lunch/picnic, extra
- pre-dinner drinks
- 4-course gourmet table d'hôte dinner served
- central heating
- laundry available
- chalet, 20 mins by helicopter from lodge

ACTIVITIES AVAILABLE

- billiards & table tennis
- walking track on site
- honeymoons & conferences catered for
- barbecue available on site
- helicopter & helipad available on site for scenic flights
- vineyards
- golf
- hiking; fishing
- Wanaka's shops & cafés, 7km
- watersports on Lake Wanaka
- climbing
- garden tours
- bungy jumping; jet boating
- boat trips
- National Parks
- winter skiing & heli-skiing
- Queenstown, 50-min drive south, via the Crown Range

Above: The peaceful setting of Whare Kea Lodge, overlooking Lake Wanaka, features views to the Southern Alps beyond.
Below: A separate fully hosted chalet high in the mountains, 20 minutes by helicopter from Whare Kea, is also available.
Opposite top: Whare Kea's fully licensed dining room and guest lounge feature panoramic lake views and an open fireplace.
Opposite bottom left: Set on farmland planted with native grasses and trees, Whare Kea is just seven kilometres from Wanaka.
Opposite bottom right: Whare Kea offers six spacious guestrooms, with ensuites including deep baths and double showers.

© Friars' Guide to New Zealand Accommodation for the Discerning Traveller

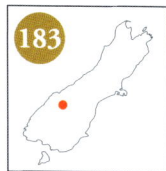

183

WANAKA

Villa South Pacific

Hosts Sue Barltrop and Michael Hughes

155 Stone Street, Wanaka   *Postal* P O Box 614, Wanaka
Freephone 0800 484 437   *Mobile* 021 484 437   *Fax* 0-3-443 9508
Email stay@villasouthpacific.com   *Website* www.villasouthpacific.com

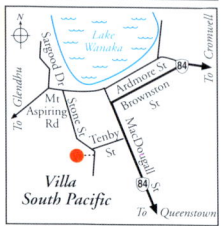

DIRECTIONS: Take SH 84 to Wanaka. Continue into Ardmore St, & travel along lake front. Turn left into MacDougall St, then right into Tenby St. Turn left into Stone St. Villa South Pacific on right, at end of drive.

4 bdrm	3 enst	1 prbth	**Room rate** $995–$1,560 **Villa rate** $1,950–$3,500	*Includes breakfast, dinner & beverages* *Self-catering*	*Chef extra*

Single-party bookings at Villa South Pacific ensure total guest privacy. Designed in Mediterranean style, the Villa includes security gates and is suitable for honeymooners and small parties. Sue has drawn upon her years in Europe to design the indoor/outdoor living spaces, including a verandah bed for summer sleeping. Broad views of Lake Wanaka and the mountains beyond make alfresco dining popular on the verandah, with its wood-fired pizza oven and barbecue. The heated swimming and spa pools overlook the floodlit tennis court. The Villa option allows guests to self-cater in the fully equipped kitchen, or a qualified chef is available by prior arrangement. In addition to the four guest bedrooms there is a studio with a double bed.

FACILITIES

- 2 super-king/twin & 1 twin bedroom & 2 ensuites upstairs
- 1 super-king/twin ensuite bedroom downstairs with spa bath, dressing room, wheelchair access
- cotton bed linen; writing desks
- hair dryer, toiletries, bathrobes, heated floor & towel rails
- laundry, email & fax available
- open fire, wine cellar, Sky TV, video, CDs, books in lounge

- gourmet breakfast
- champagne, cheese, whitebait & fruit platter on arrival
- 3-course dinner served; chef on request, extra
- complimentary wine, beverages & nibbles fridge
- children welcome
- central heating; serviced daily; off-street parking

ACTIVITIES AVAILABLE

- heated swimming pool
- spa pool on site
- tennis court on site
- wood-fired pizza oven on site
- barbecue on site
- golf course, 100 metres away
- 3 ski-fields, 20-min drive
- scenic flights
- Milford Sound, 30-min flight
- town centre, 3-min drive

- restaurants nearby
- Lake Wanaka, within walking distance
- guided fishing
- watersports
- gardens open to visit
- walking; tramping
- climbing; mountaineering
- vineyards
- Queenstown, 50-min drive

Villa South Pacific

Villa South Pacific

184

WANAKA
Mountain Range

Hosts Melanie Laaper and Stuart Pinfold

Heritage Park, Cardrona Valley Road, Wanaka
Postal P O Box 451, Wanaka   *Phone* 0-3-443 7400   *Fax* 0-3-443 7450
Email stay@mountainrange.co.nz   *Website* www.mountainrange.co.nz

| 7 bdrm | 7 enst | Double $225–$280 Single $175–$235 | *Includes breakfast* *Picnic lunch extra* |

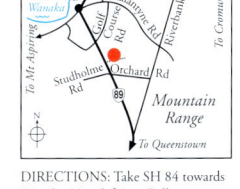

DIRECTIONS: Take SH 84 towards Wanaka. Turn left into Ballantyne Rd, then right into Golf Course Rd. Turn left into SH 89. Travel 500m & turn left into Heritage Park. Mountain Range is 40m on left.

Located in Heritage Park estate, Mountain Range draws its inspiration from the surrounding mountain views. Purpose built in 2002, this ranch-style lodge features local timbers, exposed beams, wooden floors and schist. Mountain Range provides seven guest bedrooms, all with 180-degree mountain views, six opening to private verandahs, and the honeymoon ensuite including a candlelit spa bath. Afternoon tea and evening apéritifs are offered daily. A full breakfast is served in the dining room, or alfresco on the verandah opening onto the landscaped gardens. The private parkland beyond ensures a quiet peaceful stay. Restaurants are situated two kilometres north in Wanaka township, and the lake is within walking distance.

FACILITIES

- 6 super-king/twin ensuite bedrooms
- 1 super-king bedroom with candlelit spa bath in ensuite
- cotton bed linen & direct dial phone in each bedroom
- hair dryers, toiletries, bathrobes, heated towel rails/mirrors/floors
- guest lounge with log fire & entertainment system
- laundry service; fresh flowers
- fresh breakfast with hot option
- complimentary afternoon tea & apéritifs
- fax & email available in office
- drying room for ski storage
- honeymoons, small weddings & corporate retreats catered
- courtesy passenger transfer
- telescope for star-gazing
- on-site parking

ACTIVITIES AVAILABLE

- 8-seater Canadian cedar hot tub in native gardens
- 18-hole golf course
- vineyards; 4WD safaris
- fly fishing tours
- paragliding & skydiving
- walking & hiking
- horse trekking; scenic flights
- Fighter Pilot Museum
- tramping & mountaineering
- restaurants, 2-min walk
- Lake Wanaka & township, 3-min drive
- kayaking; canoeing
- sailing; jet boating
- windsurfing; swimming
- white water rafting
- wake boarding
- skiing & snow boarding
- heli-biking & heli-skiing

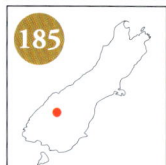

ARROWTOWN
Skyview Magic

Hosts Robina Bodle and Jef Desbecker

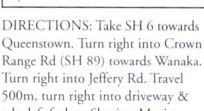

To Arrowtown
To Queenstown
Skyview Magic
Glencoe Rd
To Wanaka
89
Jeffery Rd
6
To Cromwell

DIRECTIONS: Take SH 6 towards Queenstown. Turn right into Crown Range Rd (SH 89) towards Wanaka. Turn right into Jeffery Rd. Travel 500m, turn right into driveway & take left fork to Skyview Magic.

44 Jeffery Road, Crown Terrace, R D 1, Arrowtown
Phone 0-3-442 9405   *Mobile* 027 433 7232   *Fax* 0-3-442 9405
Email info@skyview.co.nz   *Website* www.skyview.co.nz

| 4 bdrm | 3 enst | 1 prbth | Lodge rate $400 for 2 persons
Extra persons $75 each | *Self-catering*
Minimum 2-night stay | *All meals extra* |

Located on 68 hectares (168 acres) on the Crown Range, Skyview is a self-contained lodge built in a unique rustic architectural style with spacious rooms. Totally renovated in 2003, Skyview includes quality fittings and timber feature walls. Providing panoramic mountain views, quiet seclusion and secure privacy, Skyview offers four guestrooms and a spacious lounge which is heated by a wood burner. Living areas open onto a large sundeck and there is a fully equipped kitchen for self-catering. The lodge can sleep up to 12 guests in one-party bookings only, and the hosts live separately, 300 metres away. Guests enjoy the indoor climbing wall, 25-metre solar-heated summer swimming pool, and three kilometres of jogging track around the property.

FACILITIES

- single-party bookings only
- 1 king & 1 queen bedroom upstairs, both with ensuites
- 1 king/twin bedroom downstairs with ensuite
- 1 queen bedroom upstairs with separate access & toilet
- 1 double bed on sundeck with private bathroom, double bath & wheelchair access
- children welcome; laundry
- meals catered by request
- full kitchen for self-catering
- 1 bottle champagne in fridge
- wood burner, Sky TV, DVD, CDs, games, books, phone & writing desk in lounge
- cotton bed linen; hair dryers, toiletries, heated floor
- fax on request; central heating
- garaging; on-site parking

ACTIVITIES AVAILABLE

- outdoor bath; BBQ on sundeck
- indoor solar-heated chlorine-free 25m swimming pool (not available winter); indoor climbing wall; trampoline
- 3km of tracks for walking & mountain biking on 68ha site
- kayaking; wind surfing; canoeing; watersports
- bungy jumping; rafting; sailing; jet boating
- local restaurants, bars, boutique shops & wineries
- 4 golf courses; fishing
- horse trekking; 4WD touring
- hang gliding; parapenting; hot air ballooning
- wilderness tramping & walks; mountain & rock climbing
- alpine & Nordic skiing; snowboarding; heli-skiing & heli-boarding in winter

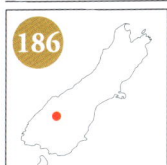

Arrowtown House

Hosts Caroline Hickin and Philip Hickin

10 Caernarvon Street, Arrowtown
Phone 0-3-442 0025   *Email* gold@arrowtownhouse.co.nz
Fax 0-3-442 0051   *Website* www.arrowtownhouse.co.nz

DIRECTIONS: From Queenstown, take SH 6A to Lake Hayes. Turn left and travel to Arrowtown. Continue on Berkshire St to Caernarvon St. Arrowtown House on corner on left.

| 5 bdrm | 5 enst | Double $445 | Single $250 | *Includes breakfast* |

Arrowtown House is located on a tree-lined avenue in Arrowtown's historic precinct. Set in landscaped gardens, featuring a large *Catalpa bignonioides* (Indian bean tree) which flowers in January, rhododendrons in November, and autumn colours, Arrowtown House offers year-round interest for the garden lover. The accommodation is separate from the house, ensuring guest privacy. Each of the guestrooms includes a lounge area, fridge, microwave, phone, fax and modem and its own washer/dryer. The five spacious guestrooms provide mountain and garden views, and three open to verandahs or private courtyard gardens. Brother and sister, Philip and Caroline, serve breakfast at the long kauri dining table in the house, or in the guestrooms.

FACILITIES

- 1 queen, 2 king & 2 super-king/twin spacious ensuite bedrooms
- heated tiled floor, heated towel rails, demist mirror, hair dryer, bathrobes & toiletries in all 5 bathrooms, 2 with double baths
- cotton bed linen; fresh flowers
- phone, fax, modem, writing desk, TV, video, CD-player & seating area in all 5 guestrooms
- guest library; artwork

- breakfast served in house, or continental room service
- washer/dryer, fridge, mineral water, tea/coffee in 5 rooms
- Millbrook Resort/Spa facilities available
- central heating
- wheelchair access
- private guest entrance
- off-street parking

ACTIVITIES AVAILABLE

- relaxing in garden on site
- local historic township, within walking distance
- 5 golf courses; river walks
- mountain biking
- jet boating; fishing
- 4WD excursions
- award-winning museum
- local art-house cinema
- 5 ski-fields, 20–90 mins

- restaurants & cafés, 2-min stroll
- wine bars, wineries & vineyards
- local art tours & galleries
- horse treks; bungy jumping
- gold panning; gardens to visit
- soft adventure tourism options
- Queenstown, 10-min drive
- scenic flights to Milford Sound
- Wanaka, Alexandra, or Cromwell, within 1-hour drive

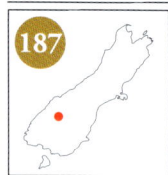

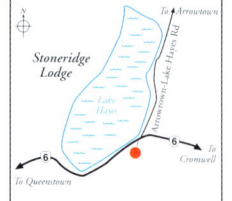

LAKE HAYES, QUEENSTOWN

Stoneridge Lodge

Hosts Suzanne and Wayne Gore

756 State Highway 6, Lake Hayes, R D 1, Queenstown
Phone 0-3-442 1021   *Mobile* 025 843 606   *Fax* 0-3-442 1358
Email enquiries@stoneridge.co.nz   *Website* www.stoneridge.co.nz

| 4 bdrm | 4 enst | Double $525 Single $395 | *Includes breakfast Picnics & dinner extra* |

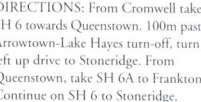

DIRECTIONS: From Cromwell take SH 6 towards Queenstown. 100m past Arrowtown-Lake Hayes turn-off, turn left up drive to Stoneridge. From Queenstown, take SH 6A to Frankton. Continue on SH 6 to Stoneridge.

Purpose-built from stone in 2001, Stoneridge Lodge incorporates recycled church beams and doors as well as bridge beams. This spacious two-storey Lodge is set on a hillside of landscaped gardens which include a number of water features. There are also a private vineyard and wine cellar, adjacent chapel, art gallery, and stone ruins dating back to 1857. All Lodge guestrooms, including the private cottage, overlook the vineyard to Lake Hayes and alpine mountains, extending to Coronet Peak and beyond. The Lodge provides three ensuite bedrooms opening to two private balconies and a verandah. Meals are served in the dining room or alfresco by the pool in the patio. The cottage offers a further ensuite bedroom, hot tub, open fire and kitchenette.

FACILITIES

- 3 queen ensuite bedrooms in main Lodge
- 1 private cottage with 1 queen ensuite bedroom, hot tub, open fireplace, kitchenette & verandah
- cotton bed linen, writing desk, phone, TV, fresh flowers, tea/coffee & courtesy beverage fridge
- hair dryers, toiletries, demist mirrors, bathrobes, heated towel rails & floor; wheelchair access

- full breakfast with espresso & latté coffee
- dinner with wine, $135 pp
- guest lounge with open fire, tea/coffee, Sky TV, video, grand piano, artwork & CDs
- fax & internet/email available
- laundry facilities available
- courtesy passenger transfer
- garaging; wine cellar

ACTIVITIES AVAILABLE

- BBQ; outdoor swimming pool & hot tub on site; mountain bikes available
- wine tasting & cellar, private vineyard & art gallery on site
- historic ruins & authentic wedding chapel; beautician/masseuse by appointment
- hiking up Morven Hill on site
- jet boating; bungy jumping
- horse riding; golf courses

- cafés, restaurants & historic Arrowtown, 5-min drive
- swimming & kayaking, 2 mins
- skiing; heli-skiing
- garden & wine trails; sky diving
- hunting; gondola; gold panning
- fishing excursions; flightseeing
- Milford Sound excursions
- Queenstown, 15-min drive
- 5 ski-fields, 25-min drive away

LAKE HAYES, QUEENSTOWN
The Turret

Hosts Martha and Mark Arrowsmith

Lake Hayes, R D 1, Queenstown
Phone 0-3-442 1107   *Mobile* 021 298 7085   *Fax* 0-3-442 1160
Email theturret@xtra.co.nz   *Website* www.theturret.co.nz

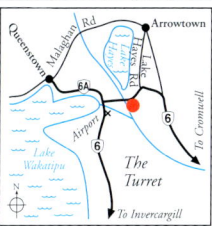

DIRECTIONS: From Queenstown, take SH 6A towards Arrowtown. The Turret on right. From Cromwell take SH 6 towards Queenstown. Travel just past Lake Hayes Rd turn-off to Arrowtown. The Turret on left.

3 bdrm	2 enst	1 prbth	Suite rate for 2 persons $295	Includes continental breakfast
			Room rate for 2 persons $165–$195	Single $135–$195

The Turret is set in an award-winning landscaped garden at Lake Hayes, situated between Arrowtown and Queenstown, with panoramic views across the lake to Coronet Peak. Built in 1990 with a medieval influence, The Turret is named after its central architectural feature – a Queen Anne-style turret. The interior design reflects a Moroccan and French influence. Accommodation comprises three guestrooms, each with its own bathroom and private verandah opening to the garden. An open fire warms the guest lounge, and a continental breakfast is served in the guest dining room, which features lake views. A row boat is available for guest use on the lake. A wide variety of restaurants, cafés and bars are popular in both Queenstown and Arrowtown.

FACILITIES

- 1 upstairs queen suite including claw-foot bath, private living room & balcony
- 1 queen ensuite bedroom & 1 double/twin bedroom with private bathroom, both opening to garden terrace
- hair dryers & toiletries
- cotton bed linen, fresh flowers, tea/coffee facilities & fridge
- lake & mountain views

- continental breakfast served to suit guests' timing
- guest lounge with open fire, tea/coffee, TV & CD-player
- laundry facilities available
- overlooks wildlife sanctuary & walking track
- courtesy passenger transfer
- on-site parking
- email, fax & phone available

ACTIVITIES AVAILABLE

- award-winning landscaped garden on site
- complimentary use of row boat
- golf courses
- fishing
- bungy jumping
- jet boating; rafting
- hot-air ballooning
- vineyards & wineries, 2 mins
- gold panning; museum

- Arrowtown & Queenstown restaurants, cafés, bars & shops
- horse riding; nature walks
- tramping & hiking
- kayaking & jet boating
- historic Arrowtown, 5 mins
- Queenstown, 12 mins
- scenic flights to Milford Sound; parapenting
- 3 main ski-fields nearby

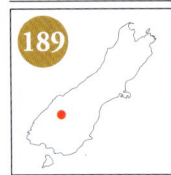

DALEFIELD, QUEENSTOWN
Bellini's of Queenstown

Hosts John Lapsley and Melinda Hayton

578 Speargrass Flat Road, R D 1, Queenstown
Phone 0-3-442 0771   *Email* melindahayton@bellinis.co.nz
Fax 0-3-442 0715   *Website* www.bellinis.co.nz

DIRECTIONS: From Queenstown take SH 6 & turn left into Lake Hayes-Arrowtown Rd. Travel 3km & turn left into Speargrass Flat Rd. Travel 20m & take 1st driveway on left. Bellini's is 1st on right.

3 bdrm	3 enst

Suite rate $395–$565   *Includes breakfast*   *Lunch & dinner extra*

Bellini's is set in large lawns and gardens, surrounded by mountain views. The three suites open to the garden where guests can relax under a willow tree and enjoy alfresco drinks. Bellini's schist and cedar exterior was designed by architect Fred van Brandenburg, with timbered interiors. The lounge ceilings are supported by recycled wooden beams that once braced rural bridges, and the long dining table sits beneath a large iron candelabra which hangs from a high pyramidal ceiling. Bellini's also features a wine cellar, large library, and extensive CD collections in the guest suites which include (of course) Bellini's operas. John and Melinda are happy to help guests choose scenic drives, walks, golfing and fishing venues, as well as restaurants.

FACILITIES

- 1 super-king/twin suite
- 2 queen suites each with own private lounge
- all 3 suites open to garden
- hair dryer, toiletries, heated towel rails, robes in 3 ensuites
- quality bed linen, tea/coffee, fridge, phone, Sky TV, DVD & CD-player in each suite
- fax & email; fresh flowers
- full breakfast menus including salmon caviar & pastries
- lunch, picnic, dinner, or BBQ pack, by arrangement, extra
- children welcome; laundry
- complimentary cocktails & hors d'oeuvres; bar/wine cellar, extra
- original art & sculptures; full Sky TV, DVDs, games, many books & CDs
- on-site parking

ACTIVITIES AVAILABLE

- 1ha (2 acres) garden on site
- artists' galleries & coffee shop, short walk away
- Lake Hayes, with sandy beach & summer swimming, 3 mins
- tennis, gym, beauty & spa facilities available nearby
- 5 golf courses, within 30 mins
- specialist NZ wool & outdoor clothing shops in Arrowtown & Queenstown, 5–20-min drive
- restaurants at historic Arrowtown, 5-min drive
- winery tours & tasting
- heritage gold-mining area
- guided trout fishing
- scenic walks & drives – lakes, mountains & wilderness
- gardens open to visit
- extreme sports; horse treks
- 4 ski-fields, from 15 mins

Above: Both the Garden and the Courtyard suites include a queen bedroom, and a separate lounge room. All suites are spacious, well appointed, and open directly onto lawns and gardens.

Left top: The guests' lounge and library features a schist fireplace, Persian rugs, leather couches, and original artworks. The library area includes books, a stereo, CD player & CDs.

Opposite top: Bellini's backdrop is the snow-capped Remarkables mountain range. This boutique lodge has extensive parkland grounds, with many sheltering trees and colourful flowerbeds.

Opposite bottom left: The three wings of Bellini's are designed and built in different, but coherent, architectural styles.

Opposite bottom right: Alfresco breakfast on the garden terrace is popular at Bellini's. On warm summer evenings, cocktails are served under the canopy of willow trees.

Right centre: Bellini's is surrounded by extensive gardens and has been architecturally designed featuring schist and cedar.

Left bottom: The Mountain suite's spacious garden deck is a private area surrounded by flowers, shrubs and trees.

Below: The Mountain suite is a large studio suite, with a garden deck, and dormer windows, that look out to the Crown Range, home of Coronet Peak and Cardrona ski-fields.

447

DALEFIELD, QUEENSTOWN

White Shadows Country Inn®

Hosts William Bailey and Michael Harris

58 Hunter Road, R D 1, Queenstown
Phone 0-3-442 0871   *Email* info@whiteshadows.co.nz
Fax 0-3-442 0872   *Website* www.whiteshadows.co.nz

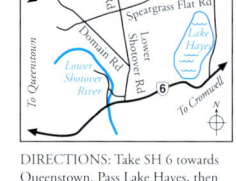

DIRECTIONS: Take SH 6 towards Queenstown. Pass Lake Hayes, then turn right into Lower Shotover Rd. Continue into Hunter Rd & travel 1.5km uphill to White Shadows driveway on the left.

| 2 bdrm | 2 enst | 1 pdrm | **Suite rate $695** **2-night minimum stay** | *Includes breakfast & evening hors d'oeuvres with wine* **Open mid-October to mid-April** |

White Shadows Country Inn was custom-built to the highest of standards with luxury furnishings, traditional and contemporary art and sculpture, and has received a 5-star "Guest & Hosted" Qualmark rating. Separate from the main house is a schist stone cottage with the two guest suites, each including a stone fireplace, lounge area, wood-beamed ceilings, table and chairs. The glass-roofed bathrooms offer views of the overhanging native red beech trees and sky above. Guests also have full use of the ground floor of the main house, where three areas provide relaxation in front of open fires, a grand piano, and window-seat overlooking three cascading garden ponds, with vistas to Coronet Peak.

White Shadows

FACILITIES

- 1 super king/twin & 1 queen suite each with ensuite bathroom
- quality toiletries, hair dryer, bathrobes, heated floor & heated towel rails in each ensuite
- 100% cotton bed linen, goosedown duvets & pillows
- Sky TV, CDs, DVD, alarm clock, phone, fridge with complimentary drinks, tea/coffee, writing desk, seating area & fireplace in suites
- private guest entrances
- lounge in house with open fire & grand piano
- buffet & cooked specialities for breakfast, served in breakfast room or courtyard
- underfloor heating
- guest fax & email available
- fresh flowers
- complimentary guest laundry
- 2 small resident dogs
- courtesy airport transfer

ACTIVITIES AVAILABLE

On site complimentary:

- in-ground spa pool
- 21-speed bicycles
- pétanque/boules; croquet court
- 5.7-ha (14-acre) grounds
- picnicking in summer house

Off site:

- Queenstown, 12-min drive
- Millbrook golf, swimming pool, gym & massage, 5 mins
- airport & helipad, 10-min drive
- bungy jumping; jet boating
- horse riding; vineyard tours
- gardens to visit; trout fishing
- TSS *Earnslaw* steamship cruise
- white water rafting
- parapenting; arts trail
- historic Arrowtown, 10 mins
- tramping; trekking; heliskiing
- Milford Sound day trips

Above: Lying just below the main house and guests' stone cottage is a pergola covered sitting area which, in turn, is on a terrace above the croquet lawn.

Left top: On warm sunny mornings guests can enjoy breakfast on the large stone patio overlooking Coronet Peak, or relax during the day on a chaise longue under an umbrella.

Opposite top: The living room in the main house at White Shadows. The ground floor provides three such areas for guests' relaxation in front of open fires, with views over the garden and ponds to Coronet Peak beyond.

Opposite bottom left: White Shadows Country Inn as seen from Malaghan Road. Adjacent to the main house is the schist stone cottage with the two separate guest suites.

Opposite bottom right: One of the two guest suites in the schist cottage at White Shadows. Each suite includes a stone fireplace, lounge area, wood-beamed ceilings, table and chairs. An ensuite bathroom adjoins each bedroom.

Right centre: Walkways lead down the hill past a waterfall and stream, across a bridge to the largest of the three ponds and an open summer house tucked under a large golden weeping willow tree.

Left bottom: Gourmet breakfasts are served indoors in a double height room surrounded by doors and windows and adjacent to a large open fireplace.

Below: Guests can relax year-round at any time of the day or night in the three-level, tiled spa pool, overlooking green pastures to the snowcapped mountains beyond.

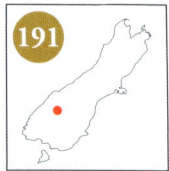

DALEFIELD, QUEENSTOWN
Pear Tree Cottage

Hosts Erina and Terry McLean

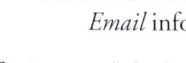

51 Mountain View Road, R D 1, Dalefield, Queenstown
Phone 0-3-442 9340   *Mobile* 027 437 0935   *Fax* 0-3-442 9349
Email info@peartree.co.nz   *Website* www.peartree.co.nz

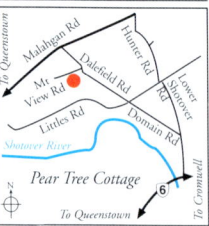

DIRECTIONS: From SH 6, turn north into Lower Shotover Rd, left into Domain Rd & continue into Dalefield Rd. Turn left into Mountain View Rd. Cottage on left. Or from Queenstown, take Gorge Rd (12 mins).

2 bdrm	1 prbth	Cottage rate for 2 persons $240–$350	Includes breakfast
		Extra persons $50–$60 each *Self-catering*	Dinner extra

Set in a secluded valley at the foot of Coronet Peak, this rustic colonial cottage, built circa 1870s, has been lovingly restored to provide guests with every comfort, including central heating. Fully self-contained, this historic rural cottage offers total privacy if desired, or guests are welcome to interact with the hosts who live adjacent. Pear Tree Cottage is one of the earliest European buildings in the district, named after the century-old pear tree in the extensive garden. Hanging baskets from the verandah and flower pots add to the summer colour. The cottage is crammed with Kiwi rural memorabilia and bric-à-brac. Breakfast featuring fresh local produce can be served alfresco in the colourful garden, and dinner can be provided by prior arrangement.

FACILITIES

- exclusive-party bookings only
- 1 queen & 1 double/twin bedroom
- claw-foot bathtub in bathroom
- hair dryer & toiletries
- cotton bed linen & goosedown duvets; bathrobes & slippers
- children welcome on request
- open fireplace, TV, VCR, video & CD-library
- phone, fax & email available

- full breakfast, served in cottage or alfresco in garden
- à la carte dinner with wine, $75 pp
- full kitchen with stocked pantry for self-catering
- guest laundry available
- sunny verandah
- courtesy passenger transfer
- on-site parking

ACTIVITIES AVAILABLE

- back country 4WD tours
- pétanque available
- barbecue available on site
- Coronet Peak ski field
- 3 golf courses, including Millbrook Golf Resort
- arts trail; many walks
- historic Arrowtown & museum
- horse riding/trekking
- helicopter tours arranged

- over 100 restaurants, 12 mins
- fishing arranged
- Shotover jet boating
- white water rafting
- bungy jumping
- garden visits; wineries
- parapenting; sky diving
- *Earnslaw* historic steamship
- Milford & Doubtful Sound day trips arranged

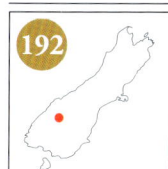

QUEENSTOWN
Kahu Rise Bed and Breakfast

Hosts Angela and Bill Dolan

455 Littles Road, R D 1, Queenstown   *Mobile* 021 104 0009
Freephone 0800 436 111   *Phone* 0-3-441 2077   *Fax* 0-3-441 2078
Email info@kahurise.co.nz   *Website* www.kahurise.co.nz

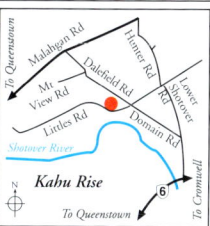

DIRECTIONS: From Queenstown, take SH 6 towards Cromwell. Cross Shotover River & turn left into Lower Shotover Rd. Turn left into Domain Rd & 1st left into Littles Rd. Travel 900m to Kahu Rise on right.

| 2 bdrm | 1 prbth | 1 pdrm | Room rate $190–$220 for 2 persons
Extra persons $50 each | *Includes breakfast*
Dinner extra | |

Opened in 2002, Kahu Rise comprises a cluster of four buildings featuring Colorsteel cladding. With rural views to the mountains, the separate guest wing provides privacy for single-party bookings, the two bedrooms opening to a patio. A full breakfast is served to suit guests' timing in the family kitchen. The living rooms are heated by the central schist fireplace, the house is centrally heated and the hosts live in a separate wing. Children are welcome by arrangement and there is an additional sleepout available for teenagers. Kahu Rise is named after the Australasian harrier that flies over the house most days. Sited between Queenstown and Arrowtown, guests can access all the nearby activities, and the airport is eight minutes' drive away.

FACILITIES

- single-party bookings only
- 1 queen & 1 twin bedroom in guest wing, open to patio & share 1 private bathroom
- hair dryer, toiletries & heated towel rails
- TV, phone jacks, tea/coffee & fridge in both bedrooms
- ensuite sleepout for teenagers
- 1 powder room; fresh flowers
- continental & cooked breakfast served in kitchen
- dinner by request, $45 pp
- home baking & nibbles
- open-plan lounge with wood fire, TV, artwork & books
- heated floor throughout
- children by arrangement
- self-service laundry
- on-site parking

ACTIVITIES AVAILABLE

- expansive lawns & garden from guest wing on site
- 4 golf courses
- wineries
- lake cruises
- ski-fields nearby
- jet boating
- bungy jumping
- garden tours
- Dart River Safaris
- restaurants & galleries
- horse riding/trekking
- tramping/hiking; nature walks
- fly fishing
- Milford & Doubtful Sound day trips
- *Earnslaw* historic steamship
- airport, 8-min drive
- Arrowtown, 10-min drive
- Queenstown, 15-min drive

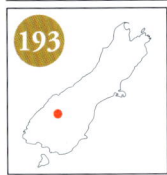

DALEFIELD, QUEENSTOWN
Runnymede Country Manor

Hosts David and Maria Cole

40 Fitzpatrick Road, Dalefield, Queenstown
Phone 0-3-442 5481   *Email* friends@runnymede.co.nz
Website www.runnymede.co.nz

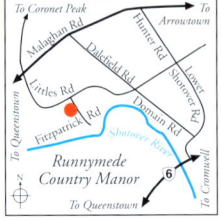

DIRECTIONS: From SH 6, turn right into Lower Shotover Rd, then left into Domain Rd. Turn left again into Littles Rd & travel 2km. Turn left into Fitzpatrick Rd to Runnymede Country Manor, 1st on right.

| 2 bdrm | 1 enst | 1 prbth | Double $350 | Single $300 | *Includes breakfast* |

Runnymede Country Manor is set on a six-hectare (15-acre) estate featuring a large ornamental lake. Its elevated position provides panoramic views of Coronet Peak and the snow-capped Remarkables range. Runnymede offers a guest wing with two bedrooms and bathrooms, as well as a guest sauna. Guests breakfast in the formal dining room on fresh fruit and continental fare or gourmet cooked breakfast with speciality breads, while enjoying the views to Coronet Peak. The Manor opens to a large terrace with 270-degree vistas over the valley to the surrounding mountains. Runnymede is located in the centre of Wakatipu, just 12 minutes from the restaurants and cafés of Queenstown or Arrowtown, the airport and the Coronet Peak ski-field.

FACILITIES

- 1 queen ensuite bedroom
- 1 queen bedroom with private bathroom & spa bath
- cotton bed linen
- hair dryers, toiletries, bathrobes, heated floor & towel rails
- fresh flowers
- formal guest lounge with open fire, Sky TV & CD-player
- grand piano in library

- continental & gourmet cooked breakfasts served in formal dining room
- wine cellar
- central heating
- sauna in guest wing
- pets welcome on request
- guest billiards room
- private guest entrance
- on-site parking

ACTIVITIES AVAILABLE

- 6ha grounds & garden with large ornamental lake on site
- wineries
- walks
- jet boating
- Shotover River
- fishing
- horse trekking
- botanic gardens
- skiing at Coronet Peak, 12 mins

- restaurants, 12 mins
- bungy jumping
- white water rafting
- sky diving
- garden tours
- art galleries
- Arrowtown, 12 mins
- Queenstown, 12 mins
- Queenstown Airport, 12-min drive away

DALEFIELD, QUEENSTOWN
Pinesong Lodge

Hosts Jo Wiseman and Dennis Deavoll

58 Fitzpatrick Road, Dalefield, Queenstown   *Phone* 0-3-442 8483
Postal P O Box 312, Queenstown   *Fax* 0-3-442 5697
Email pinesong@queenstown.co.nz   *Website* www.pinesong.co.nz

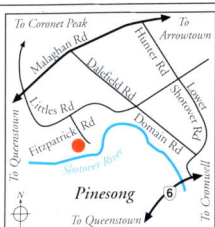

DIRECTIONS: From SH 6, turn right into Lower Shotover Rd, left into Domain Rd & left again into Littles Rd. Turn left into Fitzpatrick Rd. Pinesong on right. Or from Queenstown, take Gorge Rd (15 mins).

   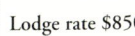 

4 bdrm	4 enst	1 prbth	Lodge rate $850

Self-catering   *No meals available*

This Austrian-style home is nestled in 14 hectares (35 acres) of rolling farmland and is surrounded by mountains, ensuring a quiet, peaceful ambience. Constructed from local stone and cedar, Pinesong offers single-party bookings with three king-size bedrooms in the main house and a separate self-contained chalet. The house includes two ensuite bedrooms upstairs, and another downstairs, as well as a separate spacious spa bathroom. The lounge features an open gas fire and a home theatre. A full kitchen enables self-catering. The Stables Chalet also includes a king-size ensuite bedroom, with an enclosed log burner, lounge and self-catering kitchen. Guests are invited to relax in the large pergola, or stroll the orchard walk to the bathhouse.

FACILITIES

- single-party bookings only
- House: 1 king/twin & 1 king bedroom with balcony upstairs, & 1 king bedroom downstairs
- 3 ensuites & 1 extra bathroom with spa bath in house
- Chalet: 1 king ensuite bedroom
- cotton bed linen
- heated towel rails & toiletries
- children over 14 yrs welcome

- 2 self-catering kitchens
- open gas fire, home theatre, with DVD, Sky TV, 42" plasma TV in house lounge
- underfloor winter heating downstairs in house
- log burner in chalet
- 360° mountain views
- outdoor spa bathhouse
- helicopter access

ACTIVITIES AVAILABLE

- booking assistance with all activities & services
- mountain biking
- 3 ski-fields (within view)
- 4 golf courses nearby
- jet boating; bungy jumping
- whitewater rafting nearby
- wineries & wine trail tours
- arts trail; nature walks
- fishing; sailing; windsurfing

- restaurants/shops, 10–15 mins
- indoor winter ice rink nearby
- historic Arrowtown, 10-min drive
- Queenstown, 15-min drive
- 4WD trips up Skippers Canyon
- TSS *Earnslaw* on Lake Wakatipu
- paragliding; hang gliding
- parachuting; stunt flying
- botanic & private gardens to visit
- Milford & Doubtful Sounds flights

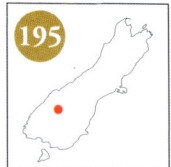

QUEENSTOWN
Remarkables Lodge

Hosts Colleen Ryan and Brian Savage

595 Kingston Road, State Highway 6, Queenstown   *Phone* 0-3-442 2720
Postal P O Box 2144, Queenstown   *Fax* 0-3-442 2730
Email remarkables@xtra.co.nz   *Website* www.remarkables.co.nz

7 bdrm	7 enst	2 pdrm

Room rate $850–$990
Off-season rates available

Includes breakfast & dinner

DIRECTIONS: From Cromwell, take SH 6 towards Queenstown. At Frankton, turn left & follow SH 6 past Remarkables ski-field entrance. Continue 3.4km to Remarkables Lodge on left.

Nestled beneath the Remarkables mountain range, which towers almost 2,500 metres above, Remarkables Lodge offers exclusive accommodation for 14 guests. Formerly the homestead for the historic Remarkables high country station, the Lodge now features mature gardens which open to the lower slopes of the mountains, where easy walks provide panoramic views of Lake Wakatipu. The furnishings of the Lodge have been chosen to reflect the historic character of the property and provide spacious, comfortable seating, a wood fire in the winter, and a pool table and bar with alpine views. Completely refurbished in 2004, there are six upstairs bedrooms and one garden suite. The resident chef serves gourmet cuisine utilising local produce.

FACILITIES

- 3 king & super-king suites
- 1 king garden suite with spa bath
- 3 king/twin ensuite bedrooms
- cotton bed linen; fridge, TV, slippers & bathrobes in rooms
- hair dryers, toiletries & heated towel rails; baths in 5 ensuites
- spacious lounge with open fire
- laundry available
- powder room downstairs
- hot country & continental breakfast menu
- dinner included in tarriff
- licensed bar & snooker room
- shower & toilet in spa area
- phone, fax, email & internet
- ski shuttle bus connections & airport transfers
- on-site parking; helipad
- ski storage & drying room

ACTIVITIES AVAILABLE

- hydrotherapy spa; sauna
- solar-heated swimming pool
- sun lounge opening to pool
- mature gardens on site
- mountain walks; tennis court
- wine tasting & local wineries
- 3 golf courses, 10–20-min drive
- heli-hiking from lodge & heli-glacier hiking
- lake cruises
- Milford & Doubtful Sounds day trips
- trout & salmon fly fishing
- alpine & cross country skiing; heli-skiing
- jet boating
- white water rafting
- paragliding
- guided tramping

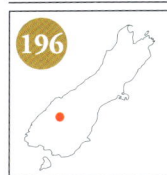

QUEENSTOWN
Pencarrow

Hosts Kari and Bill Moers

678 Frankton Road, Queenstown
Phone 0-3-442 8938   *Fax* 0-3-442 8974
Email info@pencarrow.net   *Website* www.pencarrow.net

4 bdrm   4 enst   **Suite rate $450**   *Includes breakfast*

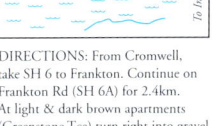

DIRECTIONS: From Cromwell, take SH 6 to Frankton. Continue on Frankton Rd (SH 6A) for 2.4km. At light & dark brown apartments (Greenstone Tce) turn right into gravel drive uphill to Pencarrow at top.

Located on a hillside overlooking Lake Wakatipu to the Remarkables beyond, Pencarrow provides views from every room. Named after New Zealand's first lighthouse, Pencarrow is set in extensive gardens of almost two hectares, with space for guests to relax on the local schist flagstone and timber decks and around the outdoor fireplace. Each of the four spacious guest suites includes a private sitting room and jet spa bath in the ensuite. Guests can play billiards on the full-size historic English snooker table and socialise around the open fireplace in the New River Lounge and Bar. A country breakfast is served in the dining room with its antique fireplace. Guests enjoy sharing their day's adventures over a complimentary drink in the evening.

FACILITIES

- 2 king suites upstairs
- 2 king suites with extra queen sofa bed downstairs
- writing desk, phone, Sky TV, video & tea/coffee facilities
- jet spa bath, double basin, hair dryer, bathrobes, heated floor & towel rails in all bathrooms
- guest lounge with open fire, nibbles, mineral water, bar, CD-player, artwork & library

- full cooked country breakfast with specials each day
- wine cellar with local & international wines for sale
- videos & fax available
- fresh flowers
- laundry service, $30 per load
- children over 12 yrs welcome
- honeymoons catered for
- on-site parking

ACTIVITIES AVAILABLE

- outdoor spa pool on site
- ski drying facilities on site
- snooker table & darts
- in-house exercise machine
- table tennis oudoors
- almost 2ha garden & grounds
- golf clubs & gold-mining pans available for guest use
- walks & hiking
- historic Arrowtown

- numerous restaurants nearby
- wineries; botanic gardens
- golf courses; arts trail
- hot air ballooning; gondola
- fishing; white water rafting
- horse riding; jet boating
- skiing, cross-country skiing & heli-skiing; sky diving
- parapenting & hang gliding
- Milford Sound day trips

Pencarrow

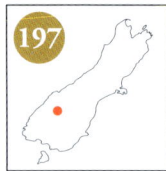

2 bdrm	2 enst

QUEENSTOWN
Twin Peaks

Hosts Margaret and Derek Bulman

661 Frankton Road, Queenstown
Phone 0-3-441 8442   *Mobile* 021 685 520   *Fax* 0-3-441 8575
Email bulman@twinpeaks.co.nz   *Website* www.twinpeaks.co.nz

Double $300   Single $275   *Includes breakfast*

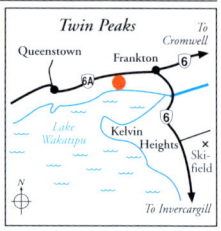

DIRECTIONS: Take SH 6A out of Queenstown. Travel 3km & turn right into Twin Peaks driveway. From Cromwell, take SH 6 towards Queenstown. Continue 2.4km on SH 6A past Frankton to Twin Peaks on left.

Built on the waterfront of the Frankton Arm of Lake Wakatipu, Twin Peaks provides panoramic lake and mountain views. This architecturally designed contemporary home offers two ensuite guestrooms with quality fittings such as the massage shower and marble vanity tops. Both bedrooms include tea and coffee-making facilites, television, fresh flowers and bathrobes. The house is elevated on rock, with schist walls and courtyard garden and is north-facing to catch the all-day sun. Continental or cooked breakfast is served in the dining room at Twin Peaks, with views over the lake to the snowcapped Remarkables. The township of Queenstown is only five minutes' drive away for restaurants, cafés, bars and boutique shopping.

FACILITIES

- 2 queen ensuite bedrooms
- bathrobes, hair dryers, toiletries, heated floor, heated towel rails, demist mirrors, massage shower rose & marble vanity tops in both ensuite bathrooms
- cotton bed linen
- fresh flowers, tea/coffee facilities & TV in both bedrooms
- phone, fax & email available
- complimentary laundry

- continental or cooked breakfast, in dining room
- complimentary drinks & nibbles
- guest lounge with open fire, TV, video & music
- central heating
- 220° lakefront views
- private guest entrance
- off-street parking

ACTIVITIES AVAILABLE

- bookings arranged for activities
- mountain bikes available
- walking track to Queenstown
- 4 golf courses, including Millbrook
- TSS *Earnslaw* Steamboat Cruise
- white water rafting
- bungy jumping
- gardens open to visit
- 2 ski-fields within 20-min drive

- Queenstown shops & restaurants, 5-min drive
- jet boating
- parapenting
- wineries
- fishing
- wilderness hikes
- 5-min drive to airport for scenic flights, eg to Milford Sound

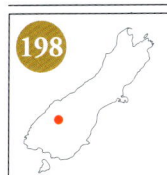

QUEENSTOWN
Amokura Lodge

Host Jenny Mason

351 Frankton Road, Queenstown
Phone 0-3-441 1175   *Mobile* 027 417 3161   *Fax* 0-3-441 1173
Email enquiries@amokuralodge.co.nz   *Website* www.amokuralodge.co.nz

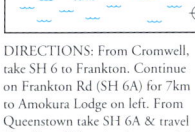

DIRECTIONS: From Cromwell, take SH 6 to Frankton. Continue on Frankton Rd (SH 6A) for 7km to Amokura Lodge on left. From Queenstown take SH 6A & travel 2km from PO to Amokura on right.

4 bdrm	1 enst	1 prbth	2 pdrm

Guest-wing rate $300–$400   *Includes continental breakfast & apéritifs*
Apartment rate $1000   *Self-catering in apartment*   *Brunch & dinner extra*

Overlooking Lake Wakatipu, Amokura Lodge was built in 2003 to provide contemporary accommodation with classically styled interiors. This three-storey home offers a separate guest wing on the middle floor, and a self-contained apartment on the lower floor, both with lake views. There is a home theatre in the guest lounge upstairs, and continental breakfast is served either in the apartment, the upstairs dining room, or alfresco on the terrace. Lunch is available on request, and complimentary pre-dinner wine and cheese are offered, followed by dinner by arrangement. A full kitchen enables apartment guests to self-cater and a barbecue is available in the grassed courtyard. Queenstown restaurants are just a 20-minute lakeside walk away.

FACILITIES

- 1 self-contained apartment: 2 super-king/twin bedrooms; 1 bathroom & powder room
- 1 guest wing: 1 super-king/twin & 1 twin bedroom; 1 bathroom & powder room
- hair dryers, toiletries, heated towel rails, demist mirrors, heated floors & bathrobes
- cotton bed linen; fresh flowers
- children welcome

- continental breakfast; pre-dinner wine & cheese
- brunch & dinner, extra
- gas fire, Sky TV/video/DVD/CD, artwork, games, books & writing desk in 2 guest lounges
- large sundecks from all levels
- central heating; laundry, email, phone & fax available
- courtesy passenger transfer; off-street parking & garaging

ACTIVITIES AVAILABLE

- home theatre system
- BBQ; cat on site
- direct access to woodland/lake shore walk to Queenstown, 20-min walk or 10-min bike ride
- scenic & recreational reserves adjacent
- Central Otago wine trails (from door)
- 4 golf courses; skiing
- wilderness hikes

- restaurants, 5 min-drive
- bungy jumping; horse treks
- scenic flights; parachuting
- Lake Wakatipu activities from beach access:
  – fishing charters
  – water-skiing
  – jet skiing
  – other watersports
  – picnicking
  – sailing to town

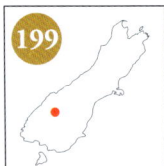

Queenstown
Mountvista Boutique Hotel

Host Murray Inwood

4 Sydney Street, Queenstown
Phone 0-3-442 8832   *Email* stay@mountvista.com
Fax 0-3-442 4233   *Website* www.mountvista.com

DIRECTIONS: Take SH 6A into
Queenstown. Frankton Rd continues
into Stanley St. Then turn left into
Sydney St. Mountvista Boutique
Hotel on right.

| 14 bdrm | 14 enst | 1 pdrm | **Double $550–$595** **Single $450–$520** | *Includes breakfast, apéritifs & hors d'oeuvres* |

Mountvista offers boutique accommodation in the heart of Queenstown. Guests enjoy the friendly atmosphere of this Qualmark five-star European-style boutique hotel, where a gentle three-minute stroll takes them to the waterfront and the town centre's international-class restaurants, shops and galleries. The nine bedrooms and five suites are spacious, with attention to detail, including the natural possum fur or mohair throws that add a touch of luxury. The spacious guest lounge features an open fire, popular for après ski and sharing the day's experiences over a complimentary local wine and gourmet canapés. The in-house Finnish sauna is welcome after the adventure activities of Queenstown such as paragliding and jet boating.

FACILITIES

- 14 super-king/twin ensuite guestrooms, all with luxury bedding, writing desk, ISD phone, Sky TV, fast ISDL internet access, teas/coffee & fridge with mini-bar
- hair dryer, bathrobes, toiletries, heated towel rails & floor in all bathrooms; baths in 12
- 8 bedrooms with balconies/patios; wheelchair access in 2 rooms
- children 12 years & over welcome
- gourmet cooked breakfast; pre-dinner canapés & Central Otago wine tasting
- large guest lounge with open fire, tea/coffee, CD & DVD-player, kitchenette, & library
- laundry service, extra
- ski storage & drying room
- private guest entrance
- off-street parking

ACTIVITIES AVAILABLE

- guest sauna downstairs, adjacent to guest lounge
- honeymoons catered for
- walking tracks
- established Queenstown Gardens, walking distance
- horse trekking
- bungy jumping
- luge & gondola
- jet boating
- Queenstown restaurants, cafés, bars & shopping, 2-min walk away
- lakeside twilight dining
- tandem & single parachuting
- paragliding
- scenic flights
- Lake Wakatipu trips
- skiing in winter
- historic Arrowtown, 15 mins

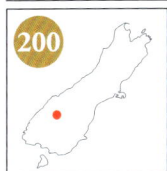

Queenstown
Balmoral Lodge

Hosts Cis and Les Walker

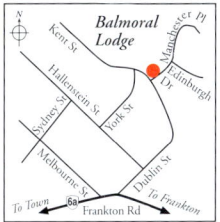

24 York Street, Queenstown   *Postal* P O Box 1463, Queenstown
Phone 0-3-442 7209   *Email* balmoral.lodge@xtra.co.nz
Fax 0-3-442 6499   *Website* www.zqnbalmoral.co.nz

DIRECTIONS: From Cromwell, take SH 6A towards Queenstown. As Frankton Rd approaches township, turn right into Dublin St. At "Give Way" sign, Balmoral Lodge on right.

| 5 bdrm | 5 enst | Room rate $225–$395 | *Includes breakfast* |

Balmoral Lodge is situated on Queenstown Hill, just 800 metres from the township. The Lodge features panoramic views of the lake, mountains and township from every room. Flowers picked from the rose garden freshen each room. The upstairs honeymoon suite includes a double spa bath and the downstairs family suite opens to the lawn and rose gardens. Guests also enjoy relaxing with complimentary drinks on the sundecks opening from the guest lounge, and the pool room is popular. A full hearty breakfast is served each morning in the dining room, with its picture postcard window overlooking the lake. Balmoral Lodge was designed for guest comfort in 1999 and furnished with antiques. Two friendly cats are in residence.

FACILITIES

- Honeymoon Suite: 1 king/twin ensuite bedroom & double spa bath
- 1 queen & 1 king ensuite bedroom upstairs; spa bath in king
- Downstairs Suite: 1 queen & 1 twin bedroom, with 2 ensuites
- cotton bed linen, phone jack, TV, tea/coffee & fridge in bedrooms
- hair dryers & toiletries
- phone, fax & email; laundry available
- full hearty breakfast served in dining room
- guest lounge with tea/coffee, Sky TV, video, music, opens to sundecks
- fresh flowers in all rooms
- children welcome
- 2 cats on site
- private guest entrance
- off-street parking

ACTIVITIES AVAILABLE

- pool room on site
- relaxing in rose garden on site
- luggage storage while guests on walking tracks
- guest activities booked
- boutique shopping, 800m
- walking tracks; tramping
- horse trekking
- fly fishing; jet boating
- gardens open to visit
- restaurants, 800-metre walk
- tandem & single parachuting
- gondola; Fly by Wire
- scenic flights
- bungy jumping
- Lake Wakatipu trips
- kayaking; rafting
- skiing & heliskiing
- Queenstown Gardens

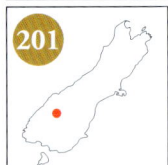

QUEENSTOWN
Queenstown House
A SMALL HOTEL

Host Louise Kiely

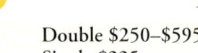

69 Hallenstein Street, Queenstown
Phone 0-3-442 9043   *Email* queenstown.house@xtra.co.nz
Fax 0-3-442 8755   *Website* www.queenstownhouse.co.nz

15 bdrm	15 enst

Double $250–$595
Single $225

Includes breakfast & apéritifs
Dinner extra

DIRECTIONS: 300 metres from Queenstown P O. Take Ballarat St north to "T" junction. Turn left into Hallenstein St. Queenstown House is on the right, on the corner of Malaghan St.

Queenstown House is a Bed and Breakfast Hotel with panoramic views overlooking Queenstown Bay. The town centre is just a 200-metre walk away. The 15 ensuite guestrooms all feature lake or alpine views and are individually styled. The new suites and studios feature private lake view decks, some with fireside sitting rooms, kitchenettes and laundry. All guestrooms include fresh flowers from the garden. The hosts, knowledgeable about Queenstown, can assist guests to maximise their time or to relax. A gourmet breakfast menu is offered in the lakeview dining room or by room service. Guests are invited to a pre-dinner get-together in the fireside sitting room or alfresco, to sample New Zealand cheeses and seasonal treats while sharing experiences.

FACILITIES

- 8 king & 3 queen bedrooms with ensuites
- 2 king suites, 2 studios
- crisp white linen, fluffy duvets, plump pillows
- TV, coffee/tea in bedrooms
- toiletries & hair dryer in each ensuite bathroom
- fireside sitting room
- private lake viewing decks
- breakfast in dining room, or room service available
- dinner by prior arrangement
- pre-dinner social hour
- wireless internet, email, fax & phone available
- guest laundry or valet service
- luggage & car storage
- separate guest entrance
- off-street parking

ACTIVITIES AVAILABLE

- daily excursions planned & arranged by staff
- small weddings & family holidays catered for
- small conference venue
- golf arranged
- 4-min stroll to town for Queenstown shopping
- Queenstown Gardens with tennis & bowling clubs
- restaurants, cafés & bars, 5-min walk
- local & longer walks
- winter ski-fields, transport from door
- landscape painting opportunities
- private gardens to visit
- fishing tours
- winery tours

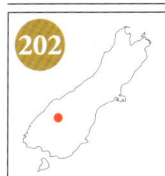

202

| 1, 2, 3 or 4 bdrm | 1, 2, 3 or 4 enst |

Apartment rate $225–$2,500

QUEENSTOWN
The Glebe

Host Anne Henley

2 Beetham Street, Queenstown   *Phone* 0-3-441 0310
Freephone 0800 484 345   *Fax* 0-3-441 0309
Email stay@theglebe.co.nz   *Website* www.theglebe.co.nz

Continental breakfast extra
Self-catering

The Glebe

DIRECTIONS: Take SH 6A into Queenstown. Frankton Rd continues into Stanley St. Travel to Beetham St. The Glebe on right-hand corner.

The Glebe offers 38 spacious apartments, each containing a fully equipped kitchen, balcony, and a choice of one to four bedrooms, with spa baths in 11 of the ensuites. The 632-square metre penthouse apartment (6,800 square feet) has wide lake views, four ensuite bedrooms, its own gymnasium, sauna, spa pool and home theatre system. Located between two churches, The Glebe features two landscaped courtyards, and its name refers to the church-land where abundant natural produce was raised. Now set in the heart of Queenstown, a wide variety of restaurants are within walking distance, and a continental breakfast can be delivered to the apartments. The Glebe overlooks Lake Wakatipu, with views to Cecil and Walter Peaks.

FACILITIES

- 38 self-contained apartments
- 2 1-bedroom, 15 2-bedroom 18 3-bedroom & 3 4-bedroom apartments, including penthouse
- 1–4 ensuites per apartment, with hair dryers, toiletries, heated floor, demist mirrors & double basins
- phone, TV, writing desk & tea/coffee in all apartments
- 1 communal guest lounge with open fireplace; fresh flowers

- continental breakfast in apartments, $12 pp
- full kitchen for self-catering per apartment
- balcony, spa bath, double shower, Sky TV, video, CD-player & artwork in most apartments
- email & fax available
- children welcome
- garaging

ACTIVITIES AVAILABLE

- BBQ available
- boules/pétanque on site
- in-house gymnasium
- walking, hiking & trekking
- native bird-watching
- white water rafting
- fly fishing; hunting
- private gardens to visit
- Queenstown Botanic Gardens

- many restaurants & cafés within walking distance
- golf courses; lake cruises
- steamboat trips on lake
- flightseeing; heliskiing
- bungy jumping
- hot air ballooning
- vineyards & wine tastings
- Queenstown airport, 10-min drive

The Glebe

The Glebe

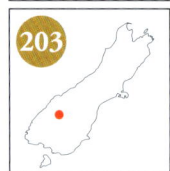

ARTHURS POINT, QUEENSTOWN
Shotover Lodge

Hosts Jeanette and Steve Brough

61 Atley Road, Arthurs Point, R D 1, Queenstown
Phone 0-3-441 8037   *Email* luxury@shotoverlodge.com
Fax 0-3-441 8058   *Website* www.shotoverlodge.com

| 5 bdrm | 5 enst | Double $478 | *Includes breakfast* |
| Single $433 | *Dinner extra* |

DIRECTIONS: From Queenstown, take Gorge Rd towards Coronet Peak. Cross historic stone bridge & travel 500m. Turn right into Atley Rd. Take right fork to Shotover Lodge on left.

Shotover Lodge

Steve and Jeanette are past winners of a New Zealand Tourism Award. Guests enjoy the tranquil rural location of Shotover Lodge (*see above right*), which is still only five minutes' drive to Queenstown. The atmosphere is that of an elegant country house on the clifftop above the Shotover River dramatically below. The design of the Lodge as a collection of buildings enhances privacy. Spacious suites, each with a private balcony or coutyard, are detached from the main Lodge where cuisine is a top priority. The Shotover Jet, horse riding, white water rafting and restaurants are within walking distance. Hiking and mountain biking trails lead directly from the Lodge, which is close to Coronet Peak ski resort. Flights to Milford Sound are popular.

FACILITIES

- 5 suites – king/queen or twin beds, each with ensuite
- hair dryers, bathrobes, heated towel rails & toiletries in ensuites
- private balcony or courtyard opens from all rooms
- quality cotton bed linen & electric blankets on all beds
- tea/coffee, fridge with NZ wines, mineral water & juices, TV, direct-dial phone & fresh flowers

- contemporary dining, extra; espresso coffee
- complimentary pre-dinner drinks & hors d'oeuvres
- guest lounge with log fire
- bar & wine cellar
- snooker room & library
- reservations service/advice
- wedding planning service
- drying room

ACTIVITIES AVAILABLE

- jacuzzi with mountain views; massage/beauty treatments
- helipad, 2-min drive away
- 18-hole golf course, 10-min drive
- walk to Shotover Jet, white-water rafting, horse riding & hiking trails
- scenic flights to Milford Sound
- art & crafts trail near lodge
- day spa, 10-min drive
- ski resort entrance, 2-min drive

- 4 restaurants, short walk
- fly fishing, guides available
- spin-fishing & trolling, boat available
- Lake Wakatipu excursions
- wine tasting & vineyards
- museums; mountain biking
- tours to Skippers Canyon
- special interest tours; Shotover Safaris

Shotover Lodge

ARTHURS POINT, QUEENSTOWN
The Canyons Country Lodge

Hosts Sally and Andy Hemingway

13 Watties Track, Arthurs Point, Queenstown   *Postal* P O Box 1772, Queenstown
Phone 0-3-442 6108   *Mobile* 027 254 7717   *Fax* 0-3-442 6208
Email info@thecanyonslodge.com   *Website* www.thecanyonslodge.com

5 bdrm	4 enst	1 prbth

Room rate $495–$1,400   *Includes breakfast & apéritifs*

DIRECTIONS: Take SH 6A to Queenstown. Turn right from Stanley St into Shotover St & left into Gorge Rd. Travel towards Arthurs Pt for 4 mins. Turn right into Watties Track to The Canyons Lodge, 2nd on left.

Set on a two-hectare estate, The Canyons Country Lodge was purpose built in 2004 overlooking the Shotover River and Coronet Peak ski-field. With views of the Shotover Canyon and Coronet Peak from every room, guests can enjoy the serene setting, yet still be within five minutes' access of Queenstown centre. The Canyons Lodge offers guests four spacious bedrooms each with a claw-foot slipper bath in its own Italian tiled bathroom, and there is a spa pool on site for guest use. Sally, a London qualified chef, provides a tasty breakfast menu including freshly made pastries and pancakes, and serves canapés with a bottle of local wine each evening. Andy is a river guide and happy to assist guests with hunting, fishing and tramping activities.

FACILITIES

- 1 king & 3 queen ensuite bedrooms open to balconies
- 1 twin bedroom
- cotton bed linen, TV, writing desk, tea/coffee & fridge in 4 bedrooms
- claw-foot slipper bath, hair dryer & toiletries in all 4 bathrooms
- fresh flowers; central heating
- wireless internet, email, fax & phone available for guest use

- full cooked or continental breakfast served in dining room or alfresco; room service available
- guest lounge with log fire, tea/coffee, nibbles, Sky TV, video, DVD & CD-player
- German spoken by hosts
- complimentary laundry
- courtesy passenger transfer
- on-site parking; helipad

ACTIVITIES AVAILABLE

- spa pool on site
- large lawn & garden area
- weddings & honeymoons catered for on site
- adventure activities
- walking; tramping
- bungy jumping
- horse trekking
- wine tours
- vineyards

- many restaurants, bars & cafés, nearby
- scenic flights
- ski-fields in winter
- trout fishing; hunting
- jet boating
- golf courses
- gardens open to visit
- Queenstown centre, 5 mins
- Arrowtown, 10-min drive

Queenstown
The Dairy

Host Elspeth Zemla

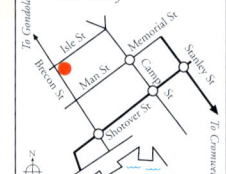

Corner of Isle and Brecon, Queenstown *Postal* P O Box 773, Queenstown
Freephone 0800 333 393 Phone 0-3-442 5164 Fax 0-3-442 5166
Email info@thedairy.co.nz *Website* www.thedairy.co.nz

DIRECTIONS: Take SH 6A to Queenstown. Continue along Stanley St. Turn left into Memorial St, then continue into Man St. Turn right into Brecon St to The Dairy, Private Luxury Hotel on right, on corner of Isle St.

| 13 bdrm | 13 enst | 1 pdrm | **Room rate $290–$385** | *Includes breakfast* |

Dairy Guesthouse

The Dairy, Private Luxury Hotel takes its name from the original 1920s corner store or dairy, where breakfasts are now served. Built around the dairy, the Private Hotel now offers 13 spacious bedrooms, mostly super-king/twin size. The Dairy was recently refurbished with new beds, quality linen, Italian fittings in the bathrooms, and soft furnishings. There are two private balconies and most guestrooms have vistas of The Remarkables ranges. There are also views of Lake Wakatipu, Coronet Peak and Queenstown township. The host, Elspeth, welcomes guests with her home-baked afternoon teas. The Dairy is located centrally, within walking distance of the bars and restaurants in Queenstown.

FACILITIES

- 13 ensuite bedrooms
- bath included in 7 ensuites
- phone, internet, Sky TV, tea/coffee & views from all bedrooms
- hair dryers, bathrobes & full-length mirrors in each bedroom
- large guest lounge with open fire
- underfloor heating
- cooked breakfast served
- 6-seater hydrotherapy spa pool
- laundry service arranged
- private library
- guest internet access
- phone available
- ski storage
- off-street parking
- passenger transfer arranged

ACTIVITIES AVAILABLE

- mountain bike for guest use
- gondola to Skyline restaurant, adjacent
- many restaurants, cafés, bars & shops within walking distance
- *Earnslaw* steamer on Lake Wakatipu
- local wineries & vineyard tours
- alpine winter sports
- Milford Sound day trips
- Queenstown Botanic Gardens
- Dart River jet boats
- walks; fishing
- helicopter flights
- bungy jumping
- garden tours
- sightseeing
- eco-tourism
- golf courses
- winter skiing

QUEENSTOWN
Brown's Boutique Hotel

Hosts Nigel and Bridget Brown

26 Isle Street, Queenstown
Phone 0-3-441 2050   *Mobile* 025 222 0681   *Fax* 0-3-441 2060
Email stay@brownshotel.co.nz   *Website* www.brownshotel.co.nz

DIRECTIONS: Take SH 6A to Queenstown. Continue along Stanley St. Turn left into Man St, then right into Brecon St. Turn left into Isle St. Brown's Boutique Hotel is on left.

| 10 bdrm | 10 enst | 1 pdrm | Double $260 | Single $240 | *Includes breakfast* |

Designed by architect Maurice Orr along traditional European lines, with thick solid walls, this intimate Hotel is sited in the older part of Queenstown above the bay, just a three-minute walk from the centre of town. Brown's Boutique Hotel offers 10 king-size ensuite guestrooms, eight of which include baths, and all rooms have television, phone, and tea and coffee making facilities. The upstairs rooms open to Juliet balconies with views of The Remarkables mountain range and Queenstown Bay, and the downstairs rooms open to a paved walled courtyard with outdoor fireplace. A breakfast buffet and daily cooked option are offered in the dining room downstairs or alfresco in the courtyard, and the adjoining guest lounge features an open fire.

FACILITIES

- 10 super-king/twin ensuite bedrooms, 8 with baths
- cotton bed linen, phone, TV & tea/coffee in each bedroom
- hair dryer, bathrobes, toiletries
- sunny, private Juliet balcony from each bedroom
- guest lounge with open fire, tea/coffee, TV, video, CD-player, artwork & library
- wheelchair access
- continental breakfast & daily hot option served in dining room
- powder room
- central heating
- email & fax available
- laundry service available
- downstairs living areas open to walled courtyard
- off-street parking

ACTIVITIES AVAILABLE

- European-style courtyard with outside fireplace on site
- gondola, 1-min walk
- downtown Queenstown shops, 3-min walk downhill
- jet boating
- rafting
- bungy jumping
- horse riding
- garden tours
- large variety of Queenstown bars, cafés & restaurants
- lake cruises
- kayaking
- Botanic Gardens
- historic Arrowtown, 15 mins
- mountain walks
- Remarkables, 45-min drive
- Coronet Peak winter skiing, 20-min drive away

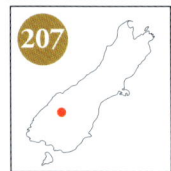

SUNSHINE BAY, QUEENSTOWN
Evergreen Lodge

Hosts Murray and Lettitia Acklin

28 Evergreen Place, Sunshine Bay, Queenstown   *Phone* 0-3-442 6636
Postal P O Box 2053, Wakatipu, Queenstown   *Fax* 0-3-442 6637
Email reservations@evergreenlodge.co.nz   *Website* www.evergreenlodge.co.nz

DIRECTIONS: Take Lake Esplanade to Fernhill roundabout. Continue on Glenorchy Rd for another 2km. Turn right into Fernhill Rd. Take 1st left into Arawata Tce, then left again into Evergreen Pl. Turn left to Lodge drive.

4 bdrm	4 enst	Double $395–$435	Single $325	*Includes breakfast*

Evergreen Lodge

Unobstructed views of Lake Wakatipu feature from every window of the guestrooms, dining and living rooms at Evergreen Lodge. Guests enjoy privacy in the spacious rooms designed to capture the lake and mountain vistas, with the hosts in a separate wing. Locally crafted oak and swamp kauri furniture features in the four ensuite guest bedrooms where breakfast can be served. Guests enjoy using the in-house gym, sauna and solarium. Outside, the Lodge's guest courtyard and garden attract native birdlife. Complimentary apéritifs are offered each evening, before guests go out to dine. Queenstown's many restaurants and cafés are only a short drive along the lakefront.

FACILITIES

- 2 super-king/twin bedrooms each with ensuite bathroom
- 2 king ensuite bedrooms
- 4 ensuite bathrooms include baths, hair dryers, heated towel rails, toiletries & bathrobes
- cotton bed linen & electric blankets on all beds
- TV, video, CD-player, phone, fridge & tea/coffee in rooms
- nightstore & convection heating

- gourmet breakfast menu served in dining room
- apéritifs & finger-food
- open fire & CDs in lounge
- double glazing
- ski drying room
- guest laundry
- fax & email available
- off-street parking
- courtesy passenger transfer

ACTIVITIES AVAILABLE

- in-house gym,
- in-house sauna & solarium
- relaxing in guest courtyard
- reading in library
- playing chess or backgammon in living room by open log fire
- native birdwatching
- beautician/masseuse arranged
- *Earnslaw* steamer on Lake Wakatipu

- restaurants, cafés & bars, 3km
- guided walks
- fly fishing, guide available
- private garden tours
- golf
- kayaking
- bungy jumping
- lake cruises
- winter skiing
- day flights to Milford Sound

Evergreen Lodge

Evergreen Lodge

TE ANAU, FIORDLAND
Takaro Peace Resort

Host Joel Sutton

914 Takaro Road, Te Anau   *Postal* P O Box 225, Te Anau
Phone 0-3-249 1166   *Email* contact@takarolodge.com
Fax 0-3-249 1189   *Website* www.takarolodge.com

DIRECTIONS: From Queenstown/Dunedin, take SH 94 towards Te Anau. 5km before Te Anau, turn right into Kakapo Rd. Travel 15km, then turn left into Takaro Rd. Travel 6.4km to Takaro Peace Resort gate & driveway.

10 bdrm	10 enst	1 pdrm

Suite rate $1,055–$1,660

Includes breakfast & dinner Lunch extra

Set on the edge of a native beech forest in Fiordland, now known for its scenery in *The Lord of the Rings,* Takaro Peace Resort is designed for relaxing, unwinding and recovering from the stresses of daily life. Takaro provides five turf-roofed chalets, themed to the Chinese Elements by a Feng Shui consultant to encourage total relaxation and peaceful sleep. The restaurant offers gourmet dining using produce from the organic gardens, home-made breads, Takaro dairy products and wine. Located on a 1,000-hectare estate, with trout fishing in the Upukerora River, Takaro features an Energy Clinic glass spa with steam room, sauna, fitness centre and large indoor heated ozone-purified swimming pool, and specialises in rejuvenating multi-hands energy massages.

FACILITIES

- 5 chalets, all with 2 suites including 1 king or 2 queen ensuite bedrooms in each
- hair dryer, toiletries, heated towel rails, demist mirror, bathrobes, spa bath or massage shower in all 10 ensuites
- balcony, tea/coffee, nibbles, bar, suround-sound home theatre TV, DVD, CDs, writing desk, 3 phones & high-speed internet access in all 10 suites

- breakfast & dinner served in dining room or suite
- courtesy concierge service
- children welcome; car valet
- fresh flowers; central heating
- aquariums in 2 suites; open fires in 8 suites
- German, French, Croatian, Chinese, Slovenian spoken
- wedding planner available

ACTIVITIES AVAILABLE

- heated swimming & spa pools; steam sauna & fitness centre
- spa treatments; 2–10-hands therapeutic massage
- small conferences, weddings & honeymoons catered
- helipad & airstrip on site
- 1,000ha grounds with BBQ, surrounded by hills & forest for trekking, mountain biking & horse riding

- native bird-watching & fishing on site
- hiking in Fiordland National Park; Milford, Doubtful Sound, Routeburn & Kepler tracks
- golfing in Te Anau
- scenic flights
- glow-worm caves
- Te Anau township, 30km
- Queenstown, 175km north

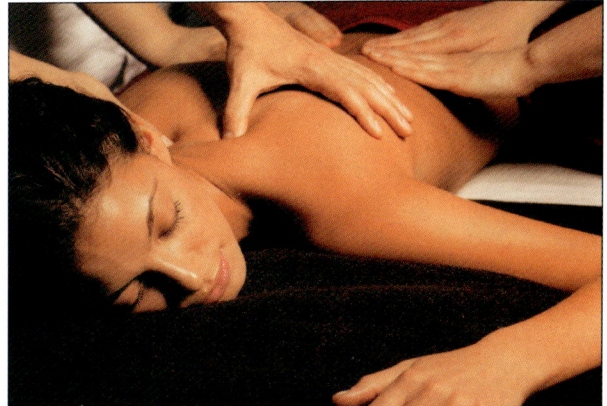

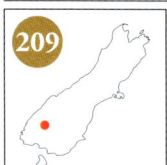

TE ANAU, FIORDLAND
Mt Prospect High Country Homestead

Hosts Joan and Ross Cockburn

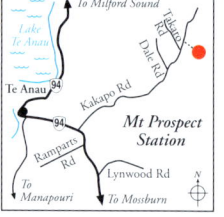

1338 Kakapo Road, Te Anau   *Postal* Mt Prospect Station, R D 2, Te Anau
Phone 0-3-249 7082   *Email* prospect@fiordland.net.nz
Fax 0-3-249 7085   *Website* friars.co.nz/hosts/prospect.html

   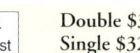

DIRECTIONS: From Queenstown or Dunedin, take SH 94 towards Te Anau. 5km before Te Anau, turn right into Kakapo Rd. Travel 16km, then turn right into Mt Prospect Station.

4 bdrm	4 enst	Double $385 Single $325	*Includes breakfast & farm tour* **Multiple-night rates available**	*Lunch & dinner platter extra*

Mt Prospect

Mt Prospect Station portrays a whole farm experience on a working sheep station of 3,400 hectares (8,500 acres). A guided activity programme with working dogs, sheep and cattle is included in the package. Originally built in 1971, this large country homestead was extensively altered and refurbished to provide guest comfort in 2000. The high-country station has been in the Cockburn family since 1913, and scenic drives are always popular up Mt Prospect on the property to view the Te Anau Basin to Lakes Te Anau and Manapouri beyond, from a height of 1,000 metres. In addition guests have superb views of the Murchison Mountains and Mt Luxmore from the homestead and expansive garden. Guests enjoy dining at a nearby country restaurant.

FACILITIES

- private guest wing & entrance
- 4 king ensuite bedrooms
- heated towel rails & hair dryers
- French doors open to private patios from each bedroom
- complimentary laundry
- internet, email & fax available
- children welcome; peaceful secluded setting
- check-in from 4pm
- full breakfast in dining room
- light lunch $15 pp, by request
- light gourmet dinner platter with wine, $35 pp
- vegetarians catered for
- TV, piano & music in lounge
- rural views
- expansive country garden
- passenger transfers to/from Te Anau, $15 pp each way

ACTIVITIES AVAILABLE

- guided activity programme on Simmental stud cattle farm
- seasonal activities with merino sheep, cattle & working dogs
- drive 1,000m up Mt Prospect on site, for scenic views of Fiordland
- farm & bush walks
- on-site trout fishing in Whitestone River, guide by arrangement
- fishing in Lakes Te Anau & Manapouri
- local country restaurant, 10-min drive
- Lake Te Anau & Te Anau township, 21km
- Milford & Doubtful Sounds day trips
- Milford, Routeburn & Kepler tramping tracks
- Fiordland National Heritage Park; flightseeing
- Queenstown, 170km north

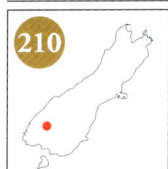

LAKE TE ANAU, FIORDLAND
Te Anau Lodge

Host Nikola Trevor

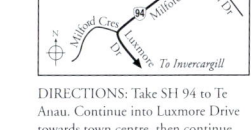

52 Howden Street, Te Anau
Phone 0-3-249 7477   *Mobile* 021 064 9354   *Fax* 0-3-249 7487
Email info@teanaulodge.co.nz   *Website* www.teanaulodge.com

DIRECTIONS: Take SH 94 to Te Anau. Continue into Luxmore Drive towards town centre, then continue into Milford Rd. Take 2nd left into Howden St. Travel to Te Anau Lodge at end on right.

| 8 bdrm | 7 enst | 1 prbth | Double $180–$250 | Single $150–$220 | *Includes breakfast* |

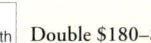

Te Anau

Built in 1936 as a convent, the Lodge was re-located to Te Anau and set on 2.7 hectares of parkland with panoramic lake and mountain views. Situated on the northern edge of Te Anau township, the Lodge enjoys a tranquil location, yet is only five to 10 minutes' walk from the town centre. Carefully restored, with contemporary facilities in the eight guestrooms, the interiors still include the original oak panelling with rimu battening and polished timber floors. Leisurely breakfasts are served in the former chapel, with its stained glass feature windows, and there is always tea, coffee and cake in the library. Guests are invited for apéritifs in the evening. Wandering through the gardens, watching the sunsets, and star gazing are popular guest pursuits.

FACILITIES

- 2 super-king/twin & 1 queen ensuite bedroom upstairs, 2 with spa baths, 1 with private lounge
- 1 super-king/twin bedroom & king single, private bathroom
- 4 queen ensuite bedrooms downstairs, 1 wheelchair access
- 1 guide's room with ensuite
- hair dryers, toiletries, heated towel rails & demist mirrors
- central heating

- full breakfast served in chapel or alfresco in courtyard
- open fire, tea/coffee, nibbles, bar, TV, DVD, video, CDs, books, games & computer in guest library upstairs
- refreshments & apéritifs
- phone, fax & wireless internet
- laundry & luggage storage
- on-site parking
- children welcome

ACTIVITIES AVAILABLE

- 2.3ha landscaped gardens
- access to Lake Te Anau
- sunsets & bird-watching
- BBQ; star-gazing on site
- farm tours; kayaking
- scenic plane
- glow-worm caves
- trout fishing & hunting, guides available
- Te Anau township nearby

- restaurants & bars, 2-min drive or 5–10-min walk
- 300km walking tracks in Fiordland National Park
- heli-flights
- Milford, Routeburn, Kepler & Hollyford hiking tracks
- Doubtful Sound day trips
- Lake Manapouri, 30 mins
- Queenstown, 2 hours north

Te Anau

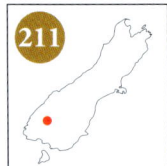

LAKE TE ANAU, FIORDLAND
Fiordland Lodge

Hosts Robynne and Ron Peacock

472 Te Anau-Milford Highway, Te Anau   *Postal* P O Box 196, Te Anau
Phone 0-3-249 7832   *Email* info@fiordlandlodge.co.nz
Fax 0-3-249 7449   *Website* www.fiordlandlodge.co.nz

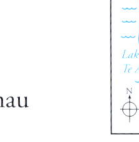

DIRECTIONS: Take SH 94 to Te Anau. Continue 4.72km north towards Milford Sound. Turn right into driveway at number 472 & travel uphill to Fiordland Lodge & Log Cabins on left.

14 bdrm	10 enst	2 prbth	Lodge room rate $460–$980	*Includes breakfast & dinner for Lodge*
			Log Cabin rate $240–$360 for 2 persons	*Includes breakfast for Cabins*

Fiordland Lodge

Fiordland Lodge and Log Cabins are located at Lake Te Anau in a rural setting ensuring peace and quiet, en route to Milford Sound. With panoramic lake views and mountain backdrops, the Lodge is constructed from Oregon logs and local riverstone, and features a spacious lounge with open log fire and soaring ceilings. The Lodge provides 10 ensuite guestrooms, each opening to a balcony, and the two Log Cabins are also available for single parties. Table d'hôte menus of New Zealand cuisine created by the in-house chef are served in the Lodge. Weddings, functions, corporate retreats and small conferences can be catered. Resident guide, Ron Peacock, offers fishing, walking and bird-watching tours in the adjacent Fiordland National Park.

FACILITIES

- 10 super-king/twin ensuite bedrooms in Lodge, each with writing desk, phone, TV, bathrobes & balcony
- spa bath & private lounge in executive suite in Lodge
- 2 log cabins each with 1 queen bedroom, twin/triple mezzanine, 1 bathroom & lounge
- hair dryers & toiletries
- heated floors/mirrors in ensuites
- full breakfast served in Lodge dining room with lake views
- 3-course table d'hôte dinner in Lodge tariff; licensed
- wheelchair access to Lodge
- children welcome
- fax & email available
- small conferences & weddings
- on-site parking
- helipad

ACTIVITIES AVAILABLE

- library in Lodge
- guided fly-tying on site
- Lake Te Anau, across road
- guided fishing trips
- brown & rainbow trout fishing
- nature walks & bird-watching
- glow-worm caves
- kayaking; horse trekking
- Milford, Routeburn, Kepler & Hollyford Tracks
- Fiordland National Park
- golf course
- scenic flights & cruises
- hunting
- Te Anau township, 5 mins
- Milford & Doubtful Sound scenic tours
- Milford Sound, 2-hr drive
- Queenstown, 2 hours north
- Invercargill City, 160km

Fiordland Lodge

Fiordland Lodge

LAKE MANAPOURI
About Time B&B

Hosts Liz and Steve Futter

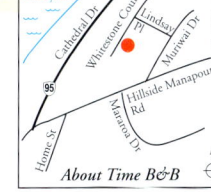

2 Whitestone Court, Lake Manapouri   *Postal* P O Box 18, Manapouri
Phone 0-3-249 6962   *Mobile* 021 678 472   *Fax* 0-3-249 6954
Email stay@abouttimemanapouri.co.nz   *Website* www.abouttimemanapouri.co.nz

| 2 bdrm | 2 enst | **Room rate $210** | *Includes breakfast* | *Dinner extra* |

DIRECTIONS: Take SH 94 towards Te Anau. Turn left into Hillside Manapouri Rd. Turn right into Muriwai Drive & left into Lindsay Place. Turn left again into Whitestone Court. About Time B&B on left.

Located in a quiet cul-de-sac overlooking Lake Manapouri to the snow-capped mountains beyond, About Time B&B was architecturally designed in 2003 to maximise the lake views from every room. Offering two upstairs bedrooms, each with an ensuite including a bath, this contemporary home provides hosted accommodation just 15 minutes south of Lake Te Anau. About Time incorporates central heating and double glazing for warmth in the winter months. Guests enjoy panoramic lake views over a full breakfast, served in the dining area or alfresco on the terrace. Guests are welcome to share the evening meal and complimentary wine with the hosts, by arrangement. Boat cruises to Doubtful and Milford Sounds are popular.

FACILITIES

- 1 super-king/twin & 1 king bedrooms upstairs
- 2 ensuite bathrooms, each including a bath
- toiletries, hair dryer & demist mirror in both bathrooms
- writing desk in both bedrooms
- lake views from all rooms
- double-glazing
- central heating
- full cooked & continental breakfast served in dining room or alfresco on terrace
- family dinner with wine, $30 pp by arrangement
- Sky TV, DVD, video & CD-player in lounge
- Scottish terrier dog on site
- email, fax & phone available
- off-street parking

ACTIVITIES AVAILABLE

- spa pool on site
- Lake Manapouri, 400 metres
- Lake Te Anau, 15-min drive
- tours & boat cruises to Doubtful & Milford Sounds
- swimming in summer
- kayaking
- jet boating
- fishing
- scenic flights
- restaurants, 15 mins
- golf
- walking tracks
- gardens to visit
- hiking
- Fiordland National Park
- skiing in winter, 1½ hrs
- Invercargill, 1¾ hrs south
- Queenstown, 2-hour drive north

213

LAKE MANAPOURI, FIORDLAND
Murrells' Grand View House

Hosts Jack and Klaske Murrell

7 Murrell Avenue, Manapouri   *Phone* 0-3-249 6642
Postal P O Box 7, Manapouri 9660   *Fax* 0-3-249 6966
Email murrell@xtra.co.nz   *Website* www.murrells.co.nz

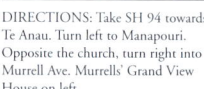

DIRECTIONS: Take SH 94 towards Te Anau. Turn left to Manapouri. Opposite the church, turn right into Murrell Ave. Murrells' Grand View House on left.

| 3 bdrm | 3 enst | Double $260–$280 | Single $260 | *Includes breakfast* |

Built as an accommodation house by Jack's grandparents in 1889, this colonial guesthouse continues to be restored by Jack and Klaske. The nineteenth-century ambience is enhanced by the original oil paintings in the guest library and the historic photographs of the area. Jack is New Zealand's longest operating host, having lived in Murrells' Grand View House since 1934, with Klaske joining him in 1987. Named because of its uninterrupted vistas of Lake Manapouri and the mountains beyond, Murrells' offers three ensuite bedrooms, all with views. Complimentary refreshments are offered on guests' arrival, alfresco on the lawn overlooking the lake, or by the fire in the guest sitting room. Full breakfasts are served in the dining room.

FACILITIES

- 1 king/twin & 2 queen ensuite bedrooms
- bathrobes, hair dryers, heated towel rails in ensuites
- tea/coffee in bedrooms
- mountain & lake views
- fresh flowers
- phone & fax available
- unsuitable for children
- laundry, $10 per load
- complimentary refreshments on guests' arrival
- full breakfast served in dining room
- open fire in guest lounge
- historic artwork
- Jack speaks basic German & Spanish
- on-site parking
- helipad

ACTIVITIES AVAILABLE

- reading in library by fire
- relaxing on verandah in sun
- feeding pet deer on site
- swimming in Lake Manapouri, 2-min walk
- kayak & canoe hire
- lake & sea kayaking
- fishing, guides available
- scenic flights by helicopter or fixed-wing
- gateway to Doubtful Sound, reservations essential
- Milford Sound day trips
- Fiordland National Park walking tracks
- day trips on Kepler track & Circle track
- Lake Te Anau, 20km
- Invercargill, 160km south
- Queenstown, 180km north

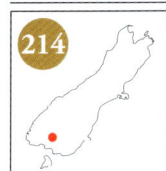

BALFOUR, GORE
Brentleigh Homestead

Hosts Brian and Mary Dillon *Mobile* 0274 578 186

1032 Riversdale-Ardlussa Road, Balfour *Postal* Ardlussa, R D 6, Gore
Freephone 0800 202 018 *Phone* 0-3-201 6166 *Fax* 0-3-201 6168
Email bdillon@esi.co.nz *Website* www.brentleigh.co.nz

DIRECTIONS: From Gore, take SH 94 towards Balfour. Travel 33km, then turn right into Riversdale-Ardlussa Rd. Travel 10.32km to Brentleigh Homestead on right.

3 bdrm	2 enst	1 prbth

Double $265–$325
Single $180–$250

Includes breakfast, cocktail hour, dinner & farm tour
Lunch extra

Brentleigh Homestead is located on a 376-hectare (929-acre) mixed farm 30 minutes from Gore. The farm includes 250 hectares of cereal crops such as wheat, barley, oats and peas, and grazing for sheep, dairy heifers, cattle and deer, and diversified into growing paeonies as well. The Mataura River runs through the farm and is famous for its brown trout fishing. There are a further 10 rivers nearby and fishing guides can be arranged. Set in a large country garden with 1,000 paeonies flowering through November and December, Brentleigh Homestead was built in 1950 in the typical brick and rough cast of the era, with verandahs added in 2000. Country kitchen cuisine is provided with varied menus served in the dining room or alfresco on the patio.

FACILITIES

- 2 detached queen/twin ensuite bedrooms with tea/coffee facilities & verandah
- 1 queen/twin bedroom upstairs, with private bathroom, spa bath & robes
- hair dryer, heated towel rails & toiletries in bathrooms
- cotton bed linen & mineral water in bedrooms
- complimentary laundry
- light/full cooked breakfast
- light lunch, $12 pp
- 2–3-course country kitchen dinner with wine
- guest lounge with open fire, tea/coffee, Sky TV, video & library
- sunroom for reading & TV
- email, fax & phone
- on-site parking

ACTIVITIES AVAILABLE

- farm tour on site
- large country garden with 1,000 paeonies on site
- Jack Russell dog, Jac, on site
- barbecue available
- fishing on site, in Mataura River
- 9-hole golf courses, 3 courses within 20-min drive
- garden tours
- hiking; winter skiing
- Balfour village, 5-min drive
- trout fishing, guides arranged
- vintage aircraft at Mandeville
- Te Anau, 1-hour drive west
- Invercargill, 1-hr drive south
- The Catlins, 1 hr south-east
- Queenstown, 1½ hrs north
- Dunedin, 2½ hrs north-east
- Milford Sound, 3 hrs north

© Friars' Guide to New Zealand Accommodation for the Discerning Traveller

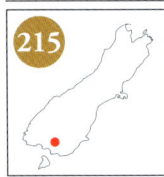

WINTON, SOUTHLAND
The Lodge at Tikana

Hosts Donna-Maree Day and Dave Lawrence

374 Livingstone Road, Browns, R D 1, Winton
Phone 0-3-236 4117   *Email* info@tikana.co.nz
Fax 0-3-236 4117   *Website* www.tikana.co.nz

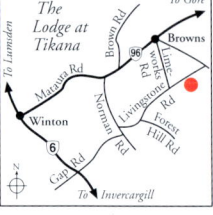

DIRECTIONS: Take SH 6 to Winton. Turn east to Mataura. Travel 8km to Browns. Turn right into Limeworks Rd. Travel 1.4km to "T" junction. Turn left into Livingstone Rd. The Lodge is 1st house on right.

2 bdrm	1 enst

Double $1,400
Single $1,015

Includes breakfast, dinner & drinks
Extra person $600

Located on a working deer farm in rural Southland, the Lodge at Tikana provides private accommodation separate from the hosts' residence. Built with straw-bale construction, the Lodge features contemporary interiors with inlaid-timber flooring. The dual-level Lodge is set in a private garden with sundeck overlooking the valley to the rolling hills beyond. The main bedroom and spacious ensuite bathroom are on the mezzanine floor. The living area downstairs includes a surround-sound home theatre, wine cellar, built-in espresso machine and deli nibbles. Meals are served at the Lodge according to guests' tastes, featuring local seasonal produce such as venison, lamb, blue cod, oysters and whitebait.

FACILITIES

- single-party bookings
- 1 super-king ensuite bedroom
- 1 double bedroom downstairs
- double bath, double basin, hair dryer, toiletries, bidet & demist mirror in ensuite upstairs
- Egyptian cotton bed linen; bathrobes; possum throw
- fresh flowers; artwork
- underfloor heating throughout

- full breakfast or brunch served
- gourmet dinner with wine
- kitchenette; antipasto platter
- wine cellar, classic NZ wines
- phone, internet access & desk in Snug
- open fire, home theatre system, Sky TV, DVDs, CDs
- laundry, wash & fold service
- on-site parking; helipad

ACTIVITIES AVAILABLE

- wapiti deer stud, thoroughbred horses & farm walks on site
- lawn tennis court on site
- outdoor spa pool on site
- eco-tourism/wilderness trips
- heritage/arts day trips
- scenic flightseeing by floatplane
- guided fly fishing, deer hunting & skeet shooting
- day spa available on site

- wilderness jet boating on Wairaurahiri River
- Manderville vintage aircraft restoration museum
- Tiger Moth flights
- Fiordland day trips
- Stewart Island day trips
- Winton 9.5km north-west
- Invercargill, 30 mins south
- Queenstown, 1½ hours north

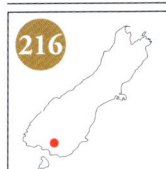

216

The Oaks Lodge

Hosts Lynn and John Frew

453 Norman Road, R D 1, Winton
Phone 0-3-236 0646 *Mobile* 025 362 270 *Fax* 0-3-236 9664
Email theoaks@woosh.co.nz *Website* friars.co.nz/hosts/theoaks.html

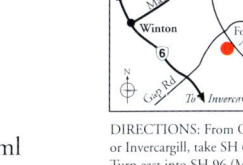

DIRECTIONS: From Queenstown or Invercargill, take SH 6 to Winton. Turn east into SH 96 (Mataura Rd) & travel about 5km. Turn right into Norman Rd, & travel 3km to The Oaks Lodge on right.

| 3 bdrm | 1 prbth | Room rate $280 | *Includes breakfast* | *Lunch extra* |

In a rural setting with views over rolling countryside to the Hokonui Hills, The Oaks Lodge is surrounded by two hectares (five acres) of landscaped gardens. Built in 1995, the Lodge has an upper floor for the exclusive use of guests, with two queen bedrooms and an extra bedroom for children. There are three separate lounges, one upstairs and two down, and breakfast is served in the dining room, with French doors opening to the patio. Guests are invited to share pre-dinner drinks and nibbles with the hosts, and restaurants are nearby. A light lunch is available by arrangement. The Oaks Lodge is set on a 10-hectare deer farm, with a walking track through native podocarp forest to a bush reserve nearby. Fly-fishing is also popular with guests.

FACILITIES

- private-party bookings only
- upstairs guest floor includes 2 queen bedrooms, bathroom, 1 children's room & lounge
- bath, hair dryer, toiletries & demist mirror; separate toilet
- cotton bed linen; bathrobes
- children by arrangement
- fax & email; fresh flowers
- self-service laundry
- continental or cooked breakfast served in dining room
- light lunch, extra
- apéritifs & hors d'oeuvres with hosts in lounge
- open fire, TV, CD-player, artwork & books in 3 lounges
- phone, tea/coffee & nibbles in upstairs lounge
- on-site parking; helicopter access

ACTIVITIES AVAILABLE

- 2ha landscaped garden walks
- lawn tennis
- 10ha deer farm on site
- Forest Hill Reserve walking track, 5-min drive
- river fishing; guide available
- sea fishing & diving charters
- high country farm tours
- gardens open to visit
- Winton, 5-min drive west
- restaurants within 5-min drive
- 18-hole golf course, 5-min drive away
- Southern Scenic Route, 20 mins away
- Tiger Moth flights, 45 mins
- Invercargill, 30 mins south
- Stewart Island, 20-min flight or 1 hour by ferry
- Queenstown or Te Anau, 1½-hour drive

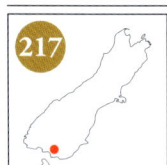

217

Tudor Park Country Stay and Garden

Hosts Joyce and John Robins

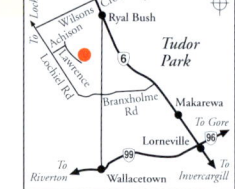

21 Lawrence Road, Ryal Bush, R D 6, Invercargill
Phone 0-3-221 7150   *Mobile* 025 310 031   *Fax* 0-3-221 7150
Email tudorparksouth@hotmail.com   *Website* www.tudorpark.co.nz

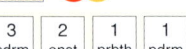

| 3 bdrm | 2 enst | 1 prbth | 1 pdrm |

Double $130–$180
Single $100–$140

Includes breakfast
Lunch & dinner extra

DIRECTIONS: From Invercargill, take SH 6 north for 6km. Turn left into Branxholme/Makarewa Rd. Travel 7km & turn right into Achison Rd. Travel 1km & turn right again at "T" junction. Tudor Park 1st on left.

Set in almost two hectares (four acres) of tranquil gardens, Tudor Park is only 15 minutes north of Invercargill City, near the Southern Scenic route. The gardens, featuring two ponds and over 300 old roses, were assessed as a Garden of Significance by the Royal New Zealand Institute of Horticulture. This neo-Tudor home has three upstairs bedrooms with garden views, one has a private bathroom with double bath, and the other two have ensuites. Breakfast is served in the dining room downstairs and includes juices, fresh fruit compote, yoghurt, cereals, home-made bread and muffins. Cooked breakfast is also available. Lunch is offered alfresco in the garden in summer, and dinner is available by arrangement, with special diets accommodated.

FACILITIES

- 1 king/twin ensuite bedroom
- 2 double bedrooms, both with bathrooms, 1 with double bath
- hair dryer, bathrobes & toiletries
- cotton bed linen
- fresh flowers in rooms
- supervised children welcome
- lounge with tea/coffee, TV, video, books & artwork
- powder room downstairs
- continental & cooked breakfast served in dining room downstairs
- lunch or picnic, $15 pp
- 3-course dinner with wine, $40–$60 pp
- email, fax & phone available
- laundry available, $5
- off-street parking
- courtesy passenger transfer

ACTIVITIES AVAILABLE

- 2ha garden walks on site
- viewing horses, dogs, sheep & calves on site
- beef & dairy farm visits
- bush walks
- bird-watching
- private garden visits
- golf nearby
- art gallery featuring NZ art
- museum with NZ tuatara
- restaurants nearby
- fishing nearby
- beaches nearby
- largest old roses planting in NZ
- aluminium smelter
- Winton or Invercargill, 15 mins
- Stewart Island, 20-min flight or 1-hour ferry trip
- Southern Scenic route
- Queenstown or Te Anau, 2 hrs

Tudor Park

Tudor Park

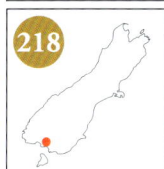

218

RIVERTON, SOUTHLAND
Nautical Haven

Hosts Gail and Tommy White

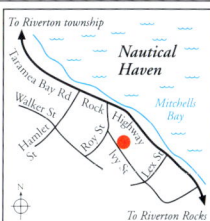

9 Ivy Street, Riverton   *Postal* 5 George Street, Riverton, Southland
Phone 0-3-234 8/55   *Mobile* 021 159 2758   *Fax* 0-3-234 8755
Email gail.w@ihug.co.nz   *Website* www.harbourviewhouse.biz

| 3 bdrm | 1 prbth |

House rate $250 for 2 persons
Extra persons $100 each

Self-catering
Includes breakfast

DIRECTIONS: From Riverton township take Richard St towards Riverton Rocks. Turn right into Roy St, travel 40m, then turn left into Ivy St. Nautical Haven on left. (Approx. 3km from township.)

Located on the southern coast of New Zealand, Nautical Haven is a fully self-contained house providing single-party bookings for up to six guests. With panoramic views over Foveaux Strait, Nautical Haven has two queen bedrooms opening through French doors to a large deck overlooking the ocean. Originally built circa 1920, Nautical Haven was carefully restored in 2001 to provide self-contained accommodation featuring a nautical theme. There is a fully equipped kitchen for self-catering, and a full breakfast is included in the tarriff. A restaurant is within walking distance, and Riverton township is three minutes' drive away. Nautical Haven is mid way on the southern scenic route.

FACILITIES

- private-party bookings only
- 2 queen bedrooms, both with French doors opening to deck & wide ocean views
- 1 twin bedroom
- 1 bathroom with spa bath, hair dryer, toiletries & demist mirror
- bathrobes; cotton bed linen
- marine theme in house & garden
- 180-degree ocean views
- full breakfast included in tarriff
- full kitchen for self-catering
- open fire, TV, CD-player, video, games & books in lounge, opening to deck
- honeymooners welcome
- self-serve laundry
- garaging
- courtesy restaurant transfer

ACTIVITIES AVAILABLE

- BBQ on site
- safe swimming beach, 4 mins
- ocean & river watersports
- paua shell factory;
- art centre
- Maori craft studio
- craft shops
- horse trekking, 4km
- scenic walks
- bowling club, 5 mins
- restaurants & cafés, 500m
- heated swimming pool, 5-min drive
- fishing trips; wind surfing
- 9-hole golf course, 5 mins
- heritage trail
- restored working flax mill
- vintage machinery, 6km
- Invercargill, 42-min drive
- Te Anau, 1¾ hour drive

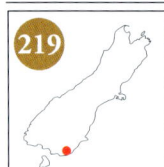

THE CATLINS
Catlins Farmstay

Hosts June and Murray Stratford

174 Progress Valley Road, South Catlins   *Phone* 0-3-246 8843
Postal R D 1, Tokanui, Southland   *Email* catlinsfarmstay@xtra.co.nz
Fax 0-3-246 8844   *Website* www.catlinsfarmstay.co.nz

DIRECTIONS: From Balclutha, take coastal route south. Travel 95km & turn left into Progress Valley Rd. Travel 2km to Catlins Farmstay on right. From Invercargill, take inland route, or coastal route via Curio Bay.

| 3 bdrm | 3 enst | Double $180–$250 Single $130 | *Includes breakfast* Extra persons $50 each | *Dinner extra* | |

Refurbished in 2002, Catlins Farmstay provides hosted accommodation on a genuine working farm. Murray first established the 392-hectare farm (nearly 1,000 acres) in 1966 and has since developed it to run 2,500 sheep, 500 deer and 150 cattle with three sheep dogs. June is locally born and bred and specialises in cooking home-grown meals which she serves in the dining room. Located in the heart of the Catlins, the homestead provides garden views to the surrounding rural forest. Guests enjoy on-site brown trout fishing, walking the hills with coastal views, and seasonal farm activities. A 10-minute drive takes guests to the petrified fossil forest at Curio Bay, where dolphins and yellow-eyed penguins can sometimes be seen.

FACILITIES

- 1 king self-contained suite with writing desk, TV, tea/coffee, kitchenette & sofa bed
- 1 queen & 1 queen/twin bedroom, each with ensuite
- hair dryer & toiletries; heated mirror & floor in 2 bathrooms
- lounge with TV & open fire; piano in dining room
- fresh flowers; central heating
- bedrooms open to gardens

- cooked & continental breakfast in dining room
- dinner with wine & local produce, $50 pp
- vegetarians catered for
- email, fax & phone, laundry & BBQ available
- children welcome
- on-site parking
- helicopter landing available

ACTIVITIES AVAILABLE

- large garden on site
- seasonal farm activities on site
- tennis court on site
- trout fishing on site
- heritage trail
- Niagara Falls, 2km
- yellow-eyed penguins
- seals & sea lions
- museum, 6km away

- café, 2km drive away
- Hector's dolphins, 10 mins
- petrified fossil forest at Curio Bay, 10-min drive
- McLean & Purakaunui Falls, 20-min drive away
- Cathedral Caves, 25 mins
- Mataura fishing, 30 mins
- Waipapa lighthouse, 30 mins
- Nugget Point, 1½-hour drive

Catlins Farmstay

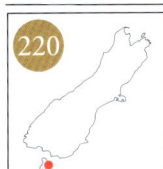

STEWART ISLAND
Sails Ashore

Hosts Iris and Peter Tait

11 View Street, Stewart Island   *Phone* 0-3-219 1151
Postal P O Box 66, Stewart Island   *Fax* 0-3-219 1151
Email tait@taliskercharter.co.nz   *Website* www.taliskercharter.co.nz

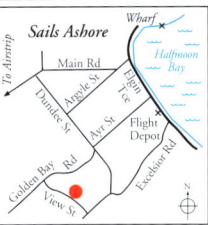

DIRECTIONS: From Bluff, take Foveaux Express catamaran (1hr), or from Invercargill airport take Stewart Island Flights plane (20 mins). Hosts meet guests at wharf or flight depot, with courtesy car to Sails Ashore.

| 2 bdrm | 2 enst | Suite rate $350 | *Includes breakfast* | *Dinner extra* | |

Sails Ashore

Sails Ashore provides accommodation on remote Stewart Island, with only 400 residents, and home to New Zealand's 14th and newest National Park. To complement their successful charter yacht, Talisker, Iris and Peter offer accommodation in two suites at Sails Ashore. Overlooking Halfmoon Bay, Sails Ashore has easy access to walks and guided tours of the native forest. The bird sanctuary on nearby Ulva Island provides unique opportunities to view native birdlife close at hand, and walk through untouched native bush. Guests enjoy fishing the abundant blue cod, and cruising around inlets and off-shore islands. There are good restaurants within minutes of Sails Ashore, and the mainland is a half-hour flight away, or one hour by sea.

FACILITIES

- 2 king/twin suites
- hair dryer, toiletries, heated towel rails & demist mirror in 2 ensuites; wheelchair access
- writing desk, phone, fridge & tea/coffee in both suites
- fresh flowers; central heating
- balcony with sea views
- nibbles, TV, video, DVD, CD-player, games, artwork, books & writing desk in lounge
- breakfast served in guest room or conservatory
- lunch by arrangement, extra – local seafood a speciality
- à la carte dinner by prior arrangement, extra
- sunroom; extensive library of natural history & DVDs
- email, fax & complimentary laundry; children welcome
- courtesy passenger transfer

ACTIVITIES AVAILABLE

- 2 border terriers on site; mature garden with exotics & natives
- in-house natural history library, local books, videos & photographs
- hosts are Department of Conservation concessioned guides
- *Talisker*, 17m charter yacht
  – sea trips for up to 6 guests
  – 3 double centrally heated cabins
  – raised saloon for all-weather observations
- restaurants nearby
- kayaking & fishing trips, extra
- township centre & main wharf, 5-min walk
- Ulva Island bird sanctuary, 15 mins by boat
- viewing undisturbed birds & marine mammals
- guided diving

Sails Ashore

Sails Ashore

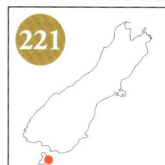

STEWART ISLAND
Stewart Island Lodge

Hosts Margaret and Doug Wright

14 Nichol Road, Stewart Island   *Phone* 0-3-219 1085
Postal P O Box 5, Halfmoon Bay, Stewart Island   *Fax* 0-3-219 1085
Email silodge@xtra.co.nz   *Website* www.StewartIslandLodge.co.nz

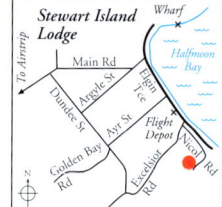

DIRECTIONS: From Invercargill, either take the *Foveaux Express* catamaran to Stewart Island – 1 hour. Or take Stewart Island Flights – 20 mins flying time. Hosts meet all guests, with courtesy car to Lodge.

5 bdrm	5 enst

Double $600   **Single $300**   *Includes continental breakfast & dinner*

Stewart Island Lodge

Stewart Island Lodge is the southernmost lodge in New Zealand. Separated from the South Island by 24 kilometres of the Foveaux Strait, Stewart Island is reached either by catamaran or air. Surrounded by off-shore islets, the island is 750 square kilometres, with extensive walking tracks through temperate podocarp rainforest, rich with native ferns and orchids. Because of its isolation, Stewart Island boasts the largest accessible population of native birds, many of them endangered species, and it is the only place in the world where the brown kiwi can be viewed in its natural habitat. Boat charters are available for cruising, fishing, diving and sightseeing. The licensed Lodge provides gourmet meals with an abundance of seafood and unimpeded ocean views.

FACILITIES

- 5 king/twin bedrooms, each with ensuite, private patio & ocean views
- baths, hair dryers & toiletries
- tea/coffee, home baking, fresh fruit & flowers in bedrooms
- central heating
- laundry available
- private guest lounge with open fire, tea/coffee, TV & video

- continental breakfast
- packed or served lunch, extra
- 3-course dinner, with local seafood & home-grown veges
- complimentary cocktail hour
- liquor licence
- email, fax & phone available
- weddings, honeymoons & conferences catered for
- courtesy passenger transfer

ACTIVITIES AVAILABLE

- garden walks on site
- bird-watching on site
- 6-hole golf course
- museum & craft shops
- 230km bush walking tracks
- viewing brown kiwi
- penguin & albatross watching
- endangered NZ native birds
- seals & dolphins in season

- guided nature tours
- sandy beaches
- historical sites
- sightseeing
- skin diving
- 1-hour bus tours
- boat charters & fishing
- offshore islets
- South Island, 1 hour by sea or 20 mins by air

Stewart Island Lodge

Stewart Island Lodge

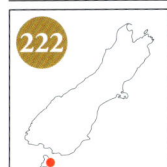

STEWART ISLAND
Port of Call

Hosts Philippa Fraser-Wilson and Ian Wilson

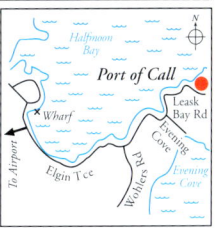

Leask Bay Road, Stewart Island   *Postal* P O Box 143, Stewart Island
Phone 0-3-219 1394   *Mobile* 027 244 4722   *Fax* 0-3-219 1394
Email info@portofcall.co.nz   *Website* www.portofcall.co.nz

   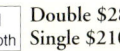

DIRECTIONS: From Bluff, take Foveaux Express catamaran (1hr), or from Invercargill airport take Stewart Island Flights plane (20 mins flying). Hosts meet guests at wharf or airport, with courtesy car to Port of Call.

| 2 bdrm | 1 enst | 1 prbth | **Double $285** **Single $210** |

Includes breakfast
Lunch & dinner extra

Self-catering in Studio

Ian and Philippa own and operate eco-tourism businesses on Stewart Island, offering guests a customised trip, tailored from their experience as a sixth generation Island family. Port of Call is surrounded by 20 hectares of tracked native bush stretching from coast to coast, which attracts the birdlife. On site are several historic buildings and farm animals. The 1997 homestead provides one guestroom with ocean views, a guest lounge, deck and courtyard area. Nearby is the secluded self-contained Studio. Its bedroom opens to the lounge which steps down into the kitchen. Alfresco dining is popular on the decking overlooking the sea.

FACILITIES

- 1 super-king/twin bedroom & private bathroom in house
- Studio: 1 queen/twin ensuite bedroom, full kitchen, lounge area, decking with BBQ
- fresh fruit, flowers, baking, tea/coffee, mineral water & decking opening from rooms
- hair dryer, toiletries, bathrobes & heated towel rails
- central heating
- phone, fax & laundry
- continental breakfast
- lunch & dinner by arrangement, extra
- private guest lounge in house with open fire, tea/coffee, TV, video, artwork, CD-player & library
- private guest entrances
- courtesy passenger transfer; helipad

ACTIVITIES AVAILABLE

- honeymoons & weddings catered for
- pétanque/boules on site
- 20ha (50 acres) native bush with cottage garden on site
- hosted island eco tours
- bush walks on site
- row boat available
- water taxi run by hosts, Qualmark endorsed
- Ulva Island bird sanctuary, 10 mins by boat
- early 1830s Harrold's Bay Stone House on site, 5-min walk
- coastal track, hiking
- Acker's Pt Lighthouse walk
- fishing, scenic & pelagic trips
- scenic flights
- guided kiwi spotting by night
- kayaking trips
- southernmost golf course in the world

ACCOMMODATION INDEX

ACCOMMODATION INDEX

ACCOMMODATION INDEX

HOSTS INDEX

HOSTS INDEX

HOSTS INDEX

© Friars' Guide to New Zealand Accommodation for the Discerning Traveller

HOSTS INDEX